WILD PLACES

of Southern Africa

Tim O'Hagan

Illustrations by Annalé O'Hagan

To
The children of Appletown
Running through the rivers of the windfall light

ISBN 1 86812 798 2

First edition 1996
Second edition 1999
2 4 6 8 10 9 7 5 3 1

Published by
Southern Book Publishers (Pty) Ltd
(A member of the Struik New Holland Publishing Group)
PO Box 5563, Rivonia 2128

While the author and publisher have endeavoured to verify all facts, they will not be held responsible for any inconvenience that may result from possible inaccuracies in this book.

Cover design by Micha McKerr
Maps by CartoCom, Pretoria
Set in Garamond and Neue Helvetica by Positive Proof cc
Reproduction by Positive Proof cc
Printed and bound by Creda Communications (Pty) Ltd, Cape Town

Never until the mankind making
Bird beast and flower
Fathering and all humbling darkness
Tells with silence the last light breaking
And the still hour
Is come of the sea tumbling in harness

Dylan Thomas

CONTENTS

ACKNOWLEDGEMENTS

This book would not have been possible without the generous support of the national parks boards of South Africa, Zambia, Zimbabwe, Botswana, Namibia, Malawi, Swaziland and Mozambique, and the tourism authorities of these countries, particularly the South African Tourism Board.

I would like to thank Trevor Dearlove and Elmarie Booysen of the National Parks Board of South Africa for their information, photographs and invaluable advice on South Africa's national parks and animals.

A special thanks, too, to Dr George Hughes, Roger de la Harpe and Alexandra Miles of the KwaZulu-Natal Nature Conservation Services for the detailed information on their parks.

Also a special thanks to Wilderness Safaris, particularly Tim Brown for the detailed information and photographs of their exceptional lodges; Mike O'Sullivan and Louis Gerke of Afro Ventures; Darren Raw of Big Game Parks of Swaziland; Natalie Abratt of the Conservation Corporation; Karen Litson of Shamwari Game Reserve; Sarah Rattray of Gametrackers; and Alexa McNaughton of Penduka Safaris for their generous assistance. My thanks also go to the lodge owners and managers who generously accommodated me and showed me around. I am particularly indebted to Johan de Beer of Namushasha and Auob lodges, Namibia; Bou Raath and Warwick Fraser of Marlin Lodge, Mozambique; Roger Hooper of Vilanculos Beach Lodge and John Law of Barra Lodge.

To Dee-Jean Bezuidenhout, of Dee-Jean Travel Promotions, who helped with logistics and friendly support, thanks Dee, your help was invaluable. My thanks also go to that master brewer, raconteur and friend, Chris Prophet, and to Gavin Stigling, for the time they spent writing and wrestling crocodiles.

Thanks, too, to Victoria Nash of Landela Safaris, Zimbabwe; Jurie and Pippa Moolman of Djuma Bush Lodge; Nicky Brown of Tuli Safari Lodge; Liz Manke of Hartley's Safaris; Shona Caulfield of Exeter Safaris; Jane Henderson; Zimbabwe Sun Hotels and the scores of bush camp owners and rangers from the Okavango through to Zambia who contributed to the material in this book.

I would also like to thank Suzanne, Anya and Caitlin, who came along on the trip and collected the berries; and Annalé, who chased the hyenas away (and did the superb illustrations).

Finally, a special word of thanks to Reneé Ferreira, Louise Grantham and Kate Rogan of Southern Book Publishers who had the foresight and patience to take the best part of Africa to the rest of the world.

INTRODUCTION

The subcontinent of Southern Africa is an amphitheatre of extraordinary beauty. Crafted over millennia by wind, water, sun, sand and rock it has survived the predations of man to become one of the world's greatest natural sanctuaries of birds, animals, trees and plants.

Wild Places of Southern Africa is a book designed to take travellers and nature lovers to the heart of the subcontinent's most alluring havens of the wild — places where the spirit of nature is free, where animals roam in habitats undisturbed by man.

Eight countries south of the Kunene River are featured in this book: South Africa, Swaziland, Namibia, Botswana, Zimbabwe, Zambia, Malawi and Mozambique, and from them the author has selected the most scenically attractive wildlife destinations. All the major national parks of these countries have been featured, in addition to more than 180 lodges, wilderness areas, private game reserves and remote camping sites.

Whether you're looking for five-star luxury in an island lodge off the coast of Mozambique, a rustic bush camp in the Kruger National Park or Hwange Game Reserve, or a place to pitch your tent in the Makgadikgadi Pans, you will find it in this book.

Concise directions will lead you to hippos snorting in the channels of Zambia's South Luangwa National Park, southern right whales cruising along the South African coastline, or wild dogs outrunning wildebeest in the Okavango Delta.

Section One — On Safari in Southern Africa — tells you the range of safari options available, where to see animals, when to view them, what to take with you, gamewatching tips, how to travel, who to travel with, cost, how to photograph wildlife and going it alone.

Section Two details the wild places, carefully describing their wildlife, natural attractions, accommodation options and accessibility. Special 'at a glance' boxes with each main entry show you how to get there, when to go, what to take with you, climatic conditions, special precautions and amenities, and road conditions.

Highlighting the entries are special boxes on animal behaviour, so you'll be able to learn more about the animals you see. Many of the entries are complemented by superb illustrations, colour photographs by leading wildlife photographers and detailed maps.

Finally, Section Three — Safari Tours in Southern Africa, lists the most popular safari packages available, the major tour operators in Southern Africa and how to contact them.

Whether you're new to Southern Africa or a seasoned traveller, this book offers you an unforgettable itinerary into Africa's most exciting wildlife destinations.

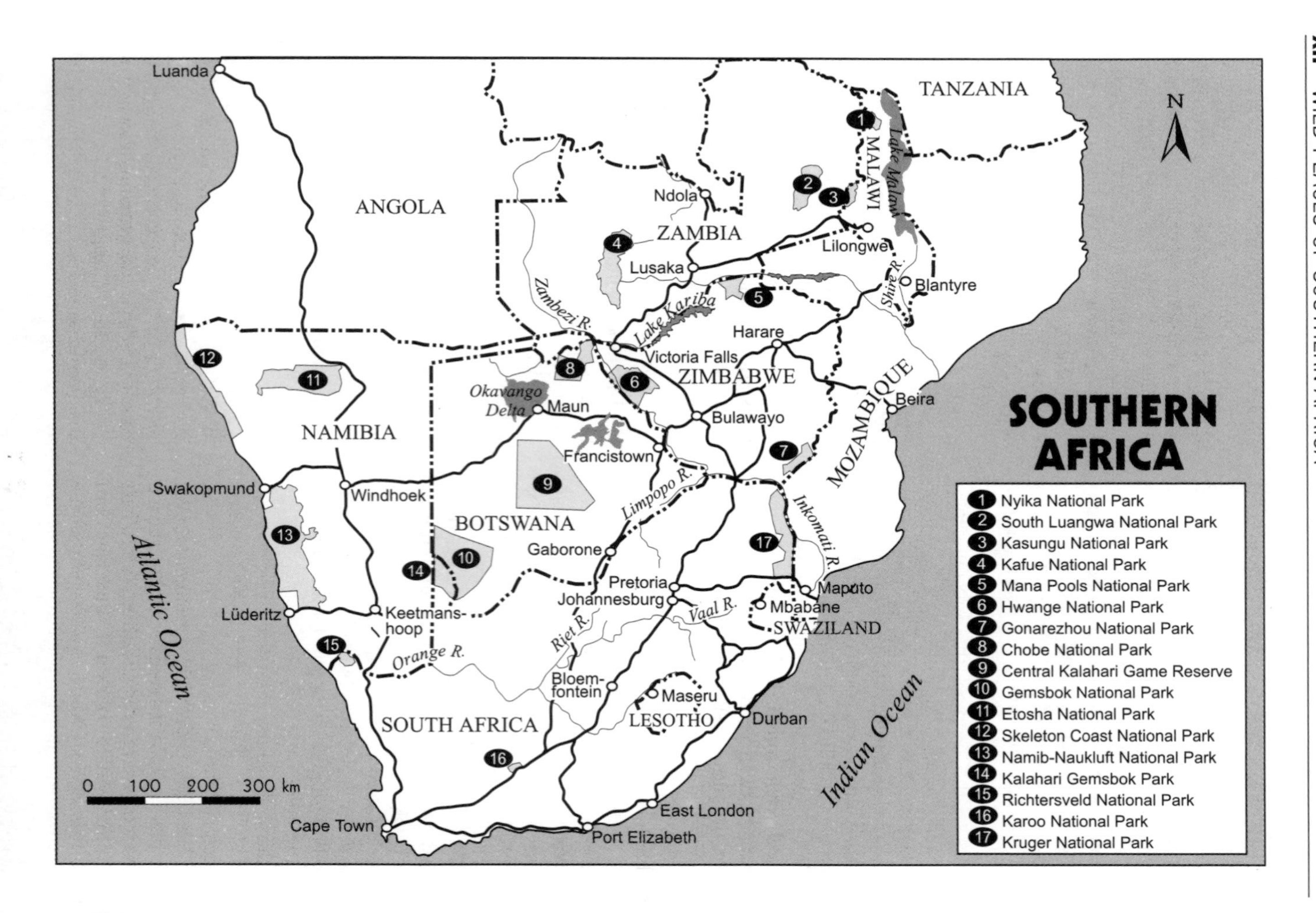
SOUTHERN AFRICA
1 Nyika National Park
2 South Luangwa National Park
3 Kasungu National Park
4 Kafue National Park
5 Mana Pools National Park
6 Hwange National Park
7 Gonarezhou National Park
8 Chobe National Park
9 Central Kalahari Game Reserve
10 Gemsbok National Park
11 Etosha National Park
12 Skeleton Coast National Park
13 Namib-Naukluft National Park
14 Kalahari Gemsbok Park
15 Richtersveld National Park
16 Karoo National Park
17 Kruger National Park
N
TANZANIA
MALAWI
Lake Malawi
Lilongwe
Blantyre
Shire R.
MOZAMBIQUE
Beira
Maputo
Inkomati R.
ZAMBIA
Ndola
Lusaka
Lake Kariba
ZIMBABWE
Harare
Bulawayo
Victoria Falls
Zambezi R.
ANGOLA
Luanda
NAMIBIA
Windhoek
Swakopmund
Lüderitz
Keetmans-
hoop
BOTSWANA
Maun
Okavango Delta
Francistown
Gaborone
Limpopo R.
SOUTH AFRICA
Pretoria
Johannesburg
Vaal R.
Riet R.
Orange R.
Bloem-
fontein
Mbabane
SWAZILAND
Maseru
LESOTHO
Durban
East London
Port Elizabeth
Cape Town
Indian Ocean
Atlantic Ocean
0 100 200 300 km

ON SAFARI IN SOUTHERN AFRICA

The spine-chilling roar of a lion in the night; the unseen rustling of bushes outside your tent; the eerie shriek of a spotted hyena drifting across the savannah; the haunting duet of ground hornbills around your camp. These are the sounds of Africa — the primal voices of the dark continent, and destination's end for safari-lovers seeking the heart of the wild places of Southern Africa.

Safari, the Swahili word for journey, suggests the ultimate adventure. It is an African word conjuring up images of wild Africa: untamed bushveld, singing grasslands and acacia trees; giraffes silhouetted against the setting sun; sundowners around the campfire; stories of savagery and survival. Most of all, it kindles the spirit of adventure in the hearts of travellers.

Whether you're new to travelling in Southern Africa, or a seasoned wildlife expert who wants to see the best game-viewing regions on the continent in relaxed comfort, hundreds of safari packages are available, covering all the countries south of the Kunene River.

For sheer variety, these packages are unbeatable. They offer some of the best game-viewing in the world, from the plains and bushveld animals of South Africa's Kruger National Park and Timbavati Game Reserve, to the water-loving animals of the Okavango Swamps.

Types of safari

Each country has different safari packages, geared to the tastes of travellers, their level of fitness and their time available. These range from overland, 20-day four-wheel-drive journeys across rugged and inhospitable countryside, to three-day, fly-in wilderness trips to private game reserves.

For more adventurous gamewatchers there are customised balloon safaris, canoe safaris, horseback safaris and even white-water rafting safaris down the Zambezi River (see p. 294). Some regard a houseboat safari across Lake Kariba as one of the best gamewatching options in Southern Africa.

Many safaris are graded according to the ruggedness, distance covered and physical discomforts such as heat and dust.

Grade one safaris are the easiest for leisure-minded people; grade five are the most rugged, and usually involve long days of travelling, hiking and canoeing.

The grade five safaris — sometimes called participation safaris — require travellers to help pitch tents, strike camp and assist with the small everyday chores required on safari in the wilds.

Wilderness Safaris, one of Southern Africa's leading tour operators, grades its packages with paw ratings, ranging from five-paw safaris (selectively pampered) to three-paw safaris (partly self-sufficient).

Afro Ventures grades its luxury safaris one and two, while the more rugged safaris are graded three, four and five.

Overland safaris

Southern Africa's ultimate safari is the overland adventure that takes travellers across bush, desert or delta in customised four-wheel-drive vehicles. These safaris are led by professional guides and trackers, who bring travellers face to face with the big game of Africa, and the chance to rough it in tented camps, or in sleeping bags under the night sky.

This is the safari of life-and-death tales around a crackling fire, of lions grunting in the bush around your camp, or of dark shapes moving across the skyline at night.

The more sophisticated overland trips accommodate travellers in luxury lodges or hotels along the way, and include the services of a travelling cook and hostess.

Air travel, or travel by boat, canoe or mokoro (dugout), such as at Kariba or in the Okavango Delta, may occupy some of the travelling time on overland safaris.

Afro Ventures specialise in overland tented and lodge safaris in Zimbabwe, Botswana, Namibia and South Africa, and offer more than 200 scheduled safaris departing from Maun and Kasane (Botswana), Windhoek and Swakopmund (Namibia), Johannesburg (South Africa) and Victoria Falls (Zimbabwe).

Another major overland safari company is Karibu Safari, which has been operating in Botswana, Zimbabwe and South Africa for 10 years (see 'Safari Tours in Southern Africa', p. 351).

Which Way Adventures offers a 46-day overland adventure from Cape Town to Kenya, taking in Namibia, Zimbabwe, Zambia, Malawi, Tanzania and Kenya. This must rate as one of the most exciting safaris in Africa, and is restricted to travellers between the ages of 16 and 65.

The journey requires flexibility, open-mindedness and enthusiasm, and asks travellers to pitch in with the chores of the safari for the experience of a lifetime. This safari is for the more budget-conscious who want to see Africa from the door of their tents, and not from the lofty comfort of a luxury safari lodge. For more details contact PO Box 2806, Durbanville 7551, tel (021) 975-2189.

Fly-in safaris

These safaris take guests by air to private landing strips in remote areas, and then ferry them to luxury lodges or private bush camps. Chartered flights operate from all of Southern Africa's major cities: Johannesburg, Durban, Cape Town, Windhoek, Gaborone, Maun, Victoria Falls, Lilongwe, Harare, Lusaka and Blantyre.

Fly-in safaris offer personalised game-viewing trips from the safari home base and limit long stretches of overland travelling. They specialise in a high standard of cuisine, accommodation and service.

Walking safaris

Hundreds of walking trails crisscross the game reserves and national parks of Southern Africa, from leaf-strewn, fern-clad paths through rainforests, to scorching tracks across semi-desert, and game paths through parkland and bushveld.

Two very comprehensive guides on the market are Willie and Sandra Olivier's *Hiking Trails of Southern Africa* (Southern Book Publishers) and Jaynee Levy's *Walks and Trails of Southern Africa* (Struik).

Most of the game reserves and national parks offer walking trails through wild country inhabited by lions, leopards, rhinos, elephants, buffaloes and other large and small mammals.

Among the most streamlined and adventurous are those of South Africa's KwaZulu-Natal Nature Conservation Services, which pioneered the concept of wilderness trails in the 1960s.

The Umfolozi–Hluhluwe Game Reserve and Itala Game Reserve offer a variety of overnight wilderness trails, during which trailists sleep in the bush at night and walk by day. The trails are limited to eight people (minimum age 14), and you may book up to nine months ahead.

When booking a wilderness trail, ask if accommodation and catering are provided. If not, you'll have to take a tent, backpack, cooking and eating utensils, your own food, sleeping bag (with blanket), high-density foam mattress, hiking boots, and a basic first-aid kit.

For full details of hiking and trail options on the subcontinent, contact the Hiking Federation of Southern Africa, PO Box 1420, Randburg 2125, tel (011) 886-6524.

Elephant-back safaris

Ker and Downey, an upmarket international touring company, offers unique elephant-back safaris in Botswana. The safaris leave from Abu's Camp, an idyllic retreat in the Okavango Delta, under the personal supervision of Randall Moore, a conservationist who has played an important part in returning circus elephants to the wild.

Abu, Kathy and Bennie form the nucleus of Randall's 10 safari elephants and provide excellent game-viewing from their backs.

Ker and Downey fly guests in to Abu's Camp from Maun, which has connecting flights to Gaborone, Johannesburg, Harare and Lusaka.

The elephant-back safaris may be combined with a photographic safari to Ker and Downey's lovely camps in Botswana — Machaba, Pom Pom or Shinde Island. For more details Contact Ker and Downey, PO Box 40, Maun, tel (09267) 211; or contact Air North West, PO Box 412, Lonehill 2062, tel (011) 465-1185.

Canoeing safaris

Shearwater Adventures, a Zimbabwean safari company, lures adventurers to the waters of the Zambezi River and Lake Kariba with a variety of canoe safaris, ranging from the three-day Gorge Safari from Kariba to Chirundu, to the 10-day Zambezi Long Classic, which covers the length of Lake Kariba.

The three-night Mana Canoe Trail — which takes in one of the richest wildlife areas in Zimbabwe — is recommended.

Canoe trailists are backed up by a four-wheel-drive support crew who lay on comfortable campsites and excellent meals on the river bank.

In spite of crocodiles and hippos along the way, Shearwater claims its safety record is without equal. For details write to Shearwater Adventures, PO Box 3961, Harare or tel (09263-4) 75-7831.

Houseboat safaris

Lake Kariba and Lake Malawi are the main venues for spectacular houseboat trips. Call of Africa Safaris has a wide selection of houseboats and also runs white-water rafting trips and safaris to Matusadona and Mana Pools national parks.

The *Catalina,* one of Kariba's most luxurious cruisers, plies the length of the lake, providing guests with stunning views of wildlife on the shore and magical sunsets. The *Catalina* has four double *en suite* bedrooms, a diningroom, bar and lounge, and an open sundeck and plunge pool. (Contact Tsankaruka Fishing and Wildlife, PO Box 9099, Hillside, Bulawayo or tel (09263-9) 4-4005.)

You may charter a complete houseboat from Kariba Ferries, based in Harare. For details tel (09263-4) 6-5476, or contact the South African agents at (011) 789-2440.

Other recommended Kariba houseboat safaris are run by Hungwe Tours and Safaris, PO Box 5438, Harare, tel (09263-4) 73-3087; Mcheni Safaris (over 50 boats) which also runs canoeing, river-rafting and fishing safaris; and Kilimanjaro Marine (contact Kariba Houseboating Safaris, tel (011) 918-1289).

Balloon safaris

More than 2 000 people a year take to the air in balloons above the wild places of Southern Africa on an aerial safari that provides excellent views of game in unobtrusive silence.

Airtrack Adventures, which has the largest fleet of hot-air balloons in Southern Africa, is the only balloon company allowed to fly over South Africa's national parks. The company can accommodate between four and 60 passengers a day and uses the best pilots available. For details tel (011) 957-2322.

Another balloon company, Bill Harrop's Original Balloon Safaris, offers select packages where guests stay at country lodges before taking to the air on their balloon safaris. For further information and reservations tel (011) 705-3201.

Birding safaris

A number of select safari operators lead bird safaris through the subcontinent. Afro Ventures has 11-day accommodated and 14-day camping safaris conducted by senior birding guide Dominic Chadbon.

These trips explore the rich diversity of birdlife in places such as the Okavango Delta, the Chobe National Park and the Kalahari Desert (see 'Safari Tours in Southern Africa', p. 351).

Karibu Safari offer a 12-day birdwatching safari to the Okavango, Botswana and Victoria Falls with South Africa's Professor Gordon Maclean, author of *Roberts' Birds of Southern Africa.*

Horse safaris

Many of the subcontinent's national parks, game reserves and private lodges provide gamewatching trails on horseback. The parks include the Mountain Zebra National Park, Royal Natal Park, Golden Gate Highlands National Park, Giant's Castle Game Reserve (South Africa); the Matobo Hills National Park (Zimbabwe); and Mlilwane Game Reserve (Swaziland). Jabulisa Lodge also lays on horseback trails through a 22 000-ha private reserve near Hwange National Park.

Equus Trails, a South African-based company, offers exclusive trails on horseback from a private bush camp on the Waterberg Plateau, just three hours' drive from Johannesburg. As you ride through a 22 000-ha reserve you can see elephants, white rhinos, giraffes, buffaloes and a variety of antelope from the saddle. The bush camp accommodates 12 guests. Write to Equus Trails, 36, 12th Avenue, Parktown North 2193 or tel (011) 788-3923.

White-water safaris

Frontiers White-Water Rafting offers one of the world's most breathtaking white-water rides through the boiling rapids below the Victoria Falls' Batonka Gorge.

Duration of the trips ranges from a couple of hours to eight days.

If this ride isn't enough to get your adrenalin going, you may try a bungee jump from the Victoria Falls Bridge (tel (011) 444-0540 or (09263-4) 73-2948) or a flight in a microlight above the Zambezi River (contact Tongabezi Camp, Private Bag 31, Livingstone, tel (09260-3) 32-3235).

Tailormade safaris

Most reputable safari groups will organise safaris to suit individual requirements, ranging from groups of six upwards. After discussion with a consultant, you can design your own itinerary, and leave the organisation to the operator.

Where to stay

During the past 20 years there has been an explosion of bush camps, safari lodges, chalets, cottages, houses and hotels, built to cater to the ever-increasing number of visitors to Southern Africa's wild places.

Depending on your tastes and level of desired comfort, you can choose between staying in the pampered luxury of a five-star safari lodge or roughing it in a sleeping bag under the stars.

The lodges

Most of the safari lodges are located either next to or within a game reserve or national park. These lodges are upmarket and expensive, but the cost is worth it.

Shangaan-style thatched cottages, with ethnic African furnishings; A-frame chalets perched in the branches of trees; cottages built of local stone, nestling under canopies of indigenous forest giants — these are some of the options available.

Most of the lodges offer *en suite* bathrooms or showers, electricity or solar-powered lighting.

The lodge will probably also have a terrace bar, game-viewing platform, swimming pool and its own private waterhole.

A focal point of the safari lodges is the boma or lapa — an outdoor dining area encircled by dry bushes or the branches of thorn trees — and a main dining room and residents' lounge.

The lodge usually offers the services of a general manager, professional hostesses, game rangers and trackers who'll escort you on daily game drives through the bush and give you an invaluable insight in the ways of the wild.

Bush camps

A few lodges serve as bases for wilderness foot safaris during which trailists overnight in basic bush camps. These consist mostly of between six and 12 solar-powered, Meru-style tents set on a concrete foundation and furnished with comfortable beds, a dressing table and shower, and protected by mosquito netting.

Other bush camps consist only of a clearing where travellers may pitch their tents, or a shelter protected by a rock overhang or rock wall.

Overland safari camps

If you're doing an overland safari with a company such as Karibu Safari, you will be accommodated in comfortable two-person tents, equipped with groundsheet, large aerating windows, a thick foam mattress and a comfortable chair. The tents are well insulated, mosquito-proof and spacious, and a portable bush shower is provided.

Some companies also lay on a large marquee tent to provide shade in the dry season and shelter when it rains.

On safari

Safari vehicles

Safari vehicles used for long, cross-country hauls through the bush or desert are extremely tough and durable, and are tailored to make game-viewing easy and comfortable. These vehicles — which include all-terrain Toyota Safari Wagons and Mercedes Benz vans — accommodate between six and 16 people.

Afro Ventures and Penduka Safaris use specially modified four-wheel-drive safari vehicles, which seat up to 10 passengers in comfort, and are equipped with long-range fuel and water tanks, roof-racks and sunroofs for game-viewing.

They are also equipped with either pop-up or fold-out game-viewing hatches, observation roof rack, large easy-to-open sliding windows and a ladder for stepping onto or off the roof.

Karibu Safari also supply cooking equipment, water containers, first-aid kit and field guides on mammals and birds.

Luggage is restricted to about 12 kg.

Other vehicles favoured by tour operators in the game reserves are spacious nine- or ten-seater minibuses or roof-modified four-wheel-drive Land Rovers.

Meals

Most overland safari vehicles are equipped with freezers, refrigerators and iceboxes, which keep food and drink fresh under the hottest conditions. Luxury safari operators take along their own cook who prepares and serves all meals to travellers. Bush cuisine is usually of a high standard, and wine or beer is served with evening meals. Most of the meals are prepared on an open wood fire beneath the stars, although lodge visitors may expect a more formal setting and cuisine.

Cost

The cost of different safari packages varies considerably, and obviously the standard of accommodation on safari is a major factor. Check out the costs carefully, and be sure that the operator you choose is licensed, and that your guides are qualified.

Tips for travellers

Here are some vital tips to observe while you're on safari in Southern Africa:

- **Wash your hands regularly**
- **Don't drink river or tap water**
- **Don't use ice made from local water**
- **Only drink water that has been boiled for at least 15 minutes.**

What to take

Whether you're going on an organised package safari or doing it on your own, you should take a strong torch or flashlight, wide-angle binoculars, a space blanket (optional), a compass, spare batteries for torches, recorders and cameras, a money belt, and a mammal and bird checklist.

If you are going alone, take a comprehensive map. Study the map carefully, and plan your trip meticulously. Travellers have been known to die of thirst at the roadside after losing their way in the Kalahari, Namibia, Zimbabwe and Zambia.

Field guides and books

Southern Book Publishers have produced a series of visitors' guides to the countries of Southern Africa, including Botswana, Zimbabwe, Namibia, Swaziland, Malawi and Zambia. These provide an excellent overview of each country with vital information on getting around, accommodation, where to go, what to do and general information on history, climate, population and details of the economy.

Also recommended is Sandra and Willie Olivier's book, *A Guide to Namibian Game Parks* and Peter Joyce's book, *Guide to Southern African Safari Lodges* (Struik).

Good field guides, one each for birds and mammals is essential. Consider Chris and Tilde Stuart's *The Mammals of Southern Africa* (Struik), *The Safari Companion* by Richard D Estes (Russell Friedman Books), or *A field guide to the Tracks and Signs of Southern and East African Wildlife* (Southern Book Publishers).

Highly recommended among the bird books are *Newman's Birds of Southern*

Africa by Ken Newman (Southern Book Publishers) and *Roberts' Birds of Southern Africa* by Gordon Lindsay Maclean (Trustees of the John Voelcker Bird Book Fund).

What to wear

Be sure to pack clothes appropriate to the season: in summer you can wear light, khaki-coloured clothing (two pairs of shorts and two pairs of longs; and two short-sleeved khaki shirts) For winter pack in long-sleeved khaki shirts and longs, an anorak or down jacket and a warm jersey. Also include a widebrimmed safari hat; training shoes or hard-soled walking boots (depending on terrain).

Going it alone

Have four-wheel-drive, will travel? The subcontinent and its wild open spaces are yours for the taking. From an overland adventure across the calcrete seas of the Makgadikgadi Pans to the dusty sand tracks of Khaudum Game Park, the options for choosing your own routes are many.

The major wild destinations of Southern Africa are covered comprehensively in this book, and phone numbers are supplied of game wardens, tour operators, national parks, wildlife bodies and game rangers who will help you plan your own safari.

Getting around

Air travel

International airlines service South Africa, Botswana, Namibia, Malawi, Zimbabwe, Zambia, Swaziland and Mozambique, and any registered travel agency in these countries will furnish schedules of international and domestic flights which link visitors with safari destinations throughout the subcontinent.

South Africa's major airports are Johannesburg International Airport in Gauteng, Cape Town International Airport in the Western Cape, Durban International Airport on the KwaZulu-Natal coast and Port Elizabeth International Airport in the Eastern Cape.

Namibia's main airport is Eros Airport at Windhoek, while Botswana is serviced by Sir Seretse Khama International Airport, 16 km from Gaborone.

Zimbabwe has international airports at Harare and Victoria Falls, and these service dozens of charter flights to private game reserves and lodges throughout the country. Zambia's Lusaka International Airport, some 25 km from the city, is a concourse for flights from South Africa, Britain, Kenya, Namibia, Zimbabwe, Angola, Mozambique and others.

Swaziland's main airport is Matsapha Airport just outside Manzini, which links up with most of Southern Africa's other major airports, while Malawi is served by Kamuzu International Airport, 23 km from Lilongwe. Mozambique's main airport is Mavalane International Airport on the outskirts of Maputo. Mozambique's national airline (LAM) flies daily between Johannesburg and Maputo.

Most of the upmarket bush lodges, from the Okavango Swamps to Mpumalanga, have their own airstrips — usually within a few kilometres of the safari camp. These service the hundreds of single engined (six-seater) or twin-engined (10-seater) charters that bring visitors in on fly-in packages. These are the main form of transport to the Okavango Delta, where roads are nonexistent in many places.

In Botswana, Namibia, Malawi, Zimbabwe and Zambia the usual mode of transport is customised Land Rovers, while in South Africa spacious minibuses are used.

On the road

Road conditions vary from tarred highways to dusty tracks, rivers of thick sand in the Kalahari, and soft, clayey soils such as those found in the Makgadikgadi and Etosha pans after the rains. In fact, the condition of roads in some parts of the Kalahari is so bad that tour operators, such as Penduka Safaris, use specially designed four-wheel-drive vehicles for their overland safaris.

Check in advance whether the park or game reserve you intend visiting is navigable by two-wheel-drive vehicle, and whether the roads are closed at certain times of the year because of flooding (as in the Mana Pools National Park).

The danger of getting bogged down on the pans or in the sandy wastes of Botswana and Namibia is very real. Keep your vehicle on the tracks at the fringes of the pans and don't venture off them.

Be sure to check road conditions with the Automobile Association of the country concerned before your trip (see below), and if your vehicle breaks down in a remote area, stay with it until help arrives.

If you're travelling in northern or western Namibia or Botswana take extra petrol along as a precaution.

Vehicle hire

Four-wheel-drive vehicles or saloon cars may be hired from international vehicle-hire firms such as Avis, Hertz and Imperial, in the major towns and cities. By arrangement you may pick up the vehicle in the town where you start your safari, and leave it where you end it.

For any enquiries about travel or car hire in Southern Africa contact the following: *South Africa:* Automobile Association of South Africa, AA House, 66 De Korte Street, Braamfontein 2001, tel (011) 403-5700 or 080010101; or AA House, 40 Sir Lowry Road, Cape Town 8001, tel 080010101; *Namibia:* Automobile Association of Namibia, PO Box 61, Windhoek 9000, tel (09264-61) 22-4201; *Zimbabwe:* Automobile Association of Zimbabwe, Ground Floor, Fanum House, Samora Machel Ave, Harare, tel (09263-4) 70-7021; *Botswana:* Department of Wild-life and National Parks, PO Box 131, Gaborone, tel (09267) 37-1405; *Swaziland:* Avis Car Hire, Matsapha Airport, tel (09268) 8-4928; or Hertz/Imperial, Matsapha Airport, tel (09268) 8-4393 or Mbabane (09268) 4-1384; *Zambia:* Tour Operators Association of Zambia, PO Box 30263, Lusaka, tel (09260-1) 22-4248; *Malawi:* Avis Car Hire, Blantyre, tel (09265) 62-4533 or Lilongwe (09265) 76-0290.

Where to see animals

With the recent explosion of safari lodges, bush hotels, wilderness camps and organised safaris in Southern Africa, there are literally hundreds of places which provide easy access to the subcontinent's populations of game.

The national parks of South Africa, Botswana, Zimbabwe, Namibia, Zambia, Swaziland and Malawi attract the lion's share of visitors, because they are home to the broadest range of species. The very number of the national parks is breathtaking — 17 in South Africa, 11 in Zimbabwe, eight in Botswana and 19 in Zambia — and most of them (with the exception of Zambia) have facilities geared to bringing visitors as close to the game as possible.

Each country has a national park or game reserve that's usually head-and-shoulders above the rest: in South Africa it's the Kruger National Park (home to 273 species of mammal and 718 bird species); in Zimbabwe, Hwange National Park is easily the most visited; in Namibia it's the Etosha National Park; in Botswana the Moremi Game Reserve and the Okavango Swamps are the star attractions; in Zambia visitors converge on the South Luangwa

National Park; and in Malawi Kasungu is often the first choice for visitors.

However, a smaller proportion of gamewatchers, seeking remoteness and a greater degree of privacy (or luxury), head for private game reserves and the safari lodges, many of which have traversing rights over larger reserves. Some even rival the larger national parks in variety of mammal and bird species, and often have the added advantage of personal gamewatching trips overland or on water.

In South Africa alone there are more than 300 wildlife sanctuaries, ranging from national and provincial parks to exclusive private game reserves and marine reserves. A large number of these are covered in this book.

The Big Five

Serious gamewatchers always want to see the Big Five (elephant, lion, leopard, rhino and buffalo), and many private lodges and game reserves use these as their draw-card. Some reserves, such as Mala Mala Game Reserve in South Africa's Mpumalanga province, specialise in making sure visitors see the Big Five. Mala Mala's Big Five Club offers membership to those who've seen these prized animals, and boasts that 76 per cent of all visitors belong to this club.

Other upmarket private game reserves in South Africa where you may see the Big Five are Timbavati, Manyeleti, Kapama, Shamwari, Londolozi, Mbili, Sabi Sabi and Sabi Sand. In Zimbabwe you'll certainly see the Big Five at Hwange National Park, Matusadona or Mana Pools, and in Botswana the Okavango Delta and Chobe Game Reserve will yield similar sightings.

Many lodges in Botswana, Namibia, Zimbabwe and Zambia run escorted game drives for sightings of the Big Five.

Other animals

While the Big Five easily attract most visitors' attention, the wealth of other mammals is enough to make a visit to most Southern African reserves a rewarding experience. Apart from the Big Five, most reserves in South Africa's Mpumalanga province — and in Namibia, Zimbabwe, Zambia and Botswana — are populated by plains antelope, wildebeest, buffaloes, giraffes, zebras, hyenas, hippos, cheetahs (and a variety of smaller cats), warthogs, water monitors, crocodiles, mongooses, baboons and vervet monkeys. There are a few 'special' species you may be lucky to see in one or two reserves only: such as wild dog, roan and sable antelope, Defassa waterbuck, Cookson's hartebeest, the tiny suni or the relatively rare puku, oribi or sitatunga.

Dedicated nature lovers will also be on the lookout for the smaller animals — from jackals, genets, rock rabbits, springhares and mongooses to lizards and snakes, dune and dung beetles.

Habitats

The types of animal to be seen depend mainly on habitat and environmental influences. So obviously the herbivores such as wildebeest, zebra and the antelope species will be found largely among the savannah plains and parkland where grass is abundant.

Water-loving antelope such as red lechwe, sitatunga and waterbuck inhabit such places as the Okavango Delta, the shoreline of Lake Kariba and the floodplains of Zimbabwe's Mana Pools; while bushbuck, bushpigs, vervet monkeys and genets are usually found in dense coastal or rainforests.

Desert-adapted creatures, including brown hyenas, gemsbok, bateared foxes, meerkat, ground squirrels, Namaqua sandgrouse and tenebrionid beetles, will be found in the Kalahari or in parts of the Namib Desert.

Some species of course, such as elephant and lion, springbok, spotted hyena and blackbacked jackal, live successfully in a variety of habitats, from dense bushveld to sparsely grassed plains. There is even a community of desert elephants on Namibia's desolate Skeleton Coast.

Because all animals are part of the food chain, the presence of many animals in a particular area will depend on others living in the same environment. For instance, one reason why Zimbabwe's Matobo National Park has one of the highest populations of black eagles in the world is that it is home to a huge number of dassies (hyraxes) which form the black eagles' staple diet.

Similarly, leopards are often found in rocky hillside environments because baboons, which they eat with relish, live there too.

In general, where you get large numbers of plains animals, from springbok, impala and other antelope species, to Burchell's zebra and wildebeest, you'll find a retinue of carnivores: lions, leopards, spotted hyenas, and blackbacked and sidestriped jackals. White and black rhinos are animals of the bushveld and Kalahari, but, because of game-relocation operations in recent years, you'll also find them on Namibia's Waterberg Plateau and in the volcanic parkland of the Pilanesberg National Park.

When to see animals

Typically, the best time of the year to see game in Southern Africa is during the dry season (the winter months, April–October), when the grass is short and the absence of rain brings animals to waterholes or natural springs in large numbers. This is particularly true of the northern, northeastern and western parks such as Kruger National Park, Timbavati Game Reserve, Etosha National Park, the Okavango Delta, Khaudum Game Park, and most of Zambia's, Zimbabwe's and Botswana's national parks (including Chobe National Park).

Bear in mind, however, that the summer rains that fill the vast salt pans of the Makgadikgadi in Botswana and Etosha in Namibia bring with them hordes of migratory waterbird, that turn these typically dry areas into a birdwatcher's paradise between December and April.

Daily game-viewing

Early morning and late afternoon are the best times to see most of the large mammals, and safari operators generally run their gamewatching trips at these times.

Animals which are mostly seen in the early morning include rhinos, lions, leopards and giraffes.

Lions are very active in the early morning, and this is when you may see a pride at a kill or moving around with their young. As the day wears on, the animals usually retire to the shade of a tree or bush and may spend the best part of the day sleeping, only to emerge in the late afternoon or evening.

Spotted hyenas, too, are very active in the morning, and are often seen scavenging at a lion kill. They rest in shade in the heat of the day and start leaving their dens towards twilight.

Some other carnivores, such as wild dogs and jackals, and some browsers, such as giraffe, may be seen throughout the day. Cheetahs often hunt in the middle of the day while other cats, such as leopards and servals, are resting. Just about the only time you're likely to see a leopard is early morning, or at night, flitting across the road.

Elephants like to move towards water in the early morning and late afternoon, and rest up during the heat of the day.

Antelope of the forest, such as Damara dik diks and bushbuck, are best seen in the early morning, but other plains antelope, including springbok, impala and kudu, as well as zebras, congregate at waterholes in the heat of the day.

Game-viewing at night

Most safari lodges and private game reserves, and some of the bush camps in the Kruger National Park, offer spotlight-assisted game-viewing drives at night.

This is when the large carnivores — except wild dogs and cheetahs — do their hunting, and if you're lucky you may stumble upon a lion kill. You'll also have a chance to spot mammals seldom seen during the day, such as porcupines, aardvarks, pangolins, whitetailed genets, some species of mongoose, caracal, African wild cats, bushbabies and ever nomadic brown hyenas.

Some national parks and many lodges and game reserves illuminate campside waterholes with solar-powered floodlights, enabling visitors to watch game right through the night.

The waterhole at Okuakuejo Camp in Namibia's Etosha National Park has one of the finest floodlit waterholes in Africa, where lion kills are common. The gamewatching is so good here, in fact, that visitors once had the opportunity of watching a lion bring down a kudu within the camp itself!

Climate

The extreme ranges of climate are also important when considering a visit to the subcontinent's wild places. It gets so hot in parts of South Africa, Botswana, Namibia, Zimbabwe and Zambia in midsummer that an overland safari, for instance, could turn into an exercise in survival.

October in Zimbabwe and Zambia is known as 'suicide month' because it gets so stiflingly hot that it is said to drive some people to the brink of self-destruction. Although the rains start falling then, some lodges close down between November and March because of the heat.

In South Africa's Kalahari Gemsbok Park the management offers guests a 25 per cent discount off usual rates because of the scorching summer temperatures from November to February.

The cooler months, from March through to September, are mostly preferred for gamewatching trips. During this time the days are mostly mild to warm, although the nights are extremely cold.

Bear in mind that Southern Africa is particularly dry: the average annual rainfall varies between 502 mm and 200 mm in parts of South Africa, against a world mean of 857 mm. In the Kalahari several months often pass without one cloud appearing in the sky.

The rainfall is more generous in the north, with 700 to 1 200 mm recorded annually in Zambia and Mozambique.

Gamewatching tips

Game-viewing in the national parks and private game reserves is concentrated mostly around natural or man-made waterholes, springs and salt licks. Some of these waterholes are set right within or near a safari camp, along a gamewatching route chosen by your ranger or along the roadside.

Whatever your form of transport you will inevitably encounter a variety of animals. While professional rangers or trackers usually head an overland safari, there are some vital rules to observe, especially if you're on foot. These will improve your chances of getting good photographs and avoid potentially dangerous situations with large mammals.

Always move as quietly as possible through the bush. Approach large mammals such as rhinos (especially black rhinos) and buffaloes (particularly males) with caution, and have your eye on a possible escape route — such as a tree or rocks nearby.

Elephants are less likely to charge, but be sure not to corner or crowd a female and her calf. If you come across a group crossing or 'camping' on a road, keep a respectful distance, turn off the car's engine and wait until they move off.

You can get very close to lions in a vehicle, but don't open your door or get out for a photograph. Avoid cornering lion cubs.

A young man was savaged and killed in a KwaZulu-Natal lion park some years ago when he got out of his vehicle and moved towards a pride.

The best advice is to be patient, whether you're in your car overlooking a waterhole or at a hide — the animals will arrive. Similarly, if you're at the edge of a river looking at a pod of hippos, one of them is bound to provide you with that gaping yawn, so have your camera set or your tripod mounted.

Trackers often advise their charges to scan the bush and the ground not just for the larger game, but also for the smaller, but no less interesting species. You'll probably get as much enjoyment watching the antics of a family of banded mongooses or suricates as you will watching a lion crunching the bones of a zebra.

Photography

A 35-mm single-reflex camera with telephoto lenses is probably your best bet on safari in Southern Africa. The camera should ideally have a bayonet mount for quick switching of lenses, a 50- to 55-mm lens which usually comes with a 35-mm camera, and a 300-mm lens (or a 400-mm lens if you're photographing birds). Add to these a 135- to 200-mm telephoto lens, a zoom lens (85–200 mm) and a sturdy camera case to protect your equipment while you're bumping through the bush, and you'll be more or less assured of getting some good shots.

The speed of various films ranges from 25 ASA to 1 000 ASA. In Southern Africa's sunny conditions it's unlikely that you'll ever need to use a film as high as 1 000 ASA. But do use a relatively high-speed film for early-morning and late afternoon photography in poor light (Ektachrome or Kodachrome 200), and a slower film (Kodachrome 64) for better light conditions. Remember that the slower the film, the better the resolution of the print or transparency, and the faster the film the grainier the end result.

To eliminate camera shake — one of the most common faults of amateur photographers — set the speed of your camera to 1/500th of a second or faster.

If you're photographing from your car, turn off the engine first, and rest your long lens on a shock absorber, such as a length of rubber.

Health risks and requirements

Visitors to Southern Africa must be inoculated against yellow fever and have a valid International Certificate of Vaccination. Malaria is present in some parts of the subcontinent, so you should take a course of antimalaria tablets before your trip. Bilharzia and rabies are other, more remote, health risks while on safari.

More common problems experienced on safari are sunburn, dehydration, heat exhaustion, tick-bite fever and water-borne excremental diseases, which mostly can be avoided by boiling your water when you're in the wild.

Common dangers

Wild animals, especially the larger carnivores, hippos and sometimes buffaloes, rhinos and elephants, pose some degree of risk if you're on an overland safari in Southern Africa. There are recorded cases of tourists being killed by lions in Etosha, of a young woman trampled to death by a buffalo in Mana Pools National Park, of people on foot safaris — and cars — being charged by elephants or rhinos.

However, if you obey the rules of the bush, keep a safe distance from animals, back off slowly if you disturb a large animal, and travel in the company of an experienced scout or ranger, you will be quite safe.

Don't sleep under the stars in the company of predators. Hyenas and lions have been known to pull people out of their sleeping bags at night. One couple sleeping in Namibia's Khaudum Game Park were run over by a pack of wild dogs pursuing a duiker.

Don't ever leave food — especially meat and fruit — lying around your camp, in your car or outside your tent. Monkeys and baboons can ruin a camping trip by persistent raids on food that has not been stowed away. Jackals and dassies, too, can be very persistent in stealing scraps from your camp floor.

On foot safaris wear strong, high-ankled hiking boots as protection against snakes. At night sleep in a tent sealed against invasion by mosquitoes, scorpions, ants or ticks.

Illness and injury

Most safari operators offer some form of emergency insurance against illness or injury while on safari. Speak to your travel agent or tour organiser about medical facilities before you leave for your trip.

First-aid kit

If you're going on a private safari or long hike, particularly in Namibia, Botswana, Zimbabwe, Zambia or Swaziland, a proper first-aid kit is essential.

Include in your kit: Sterile compresses, cottonwool and gauze roll dressings, bandages, disinfectants (Savlon, mercurochrome and Betadine ointment), broad-spectrum antibiotics (Bactrin or Septrin), anti-amoebic dysentery tablets (e.g. Flagyl), anti-diarrhoeal medication (e.g. Imodium), antihistamines (e.g. Piriton), oral rehydration sachets, insect repellent (e.g. Tabard), sunscreen, sunburn lotion and lip balm. Speak to your doctor about taking snake-bite serum along.

Travel checklist

If you're arriving from another country be sure to have your passport, visa, immunisation certificates, international drivers' licence, traveller's cheques, travel insurance and credit cards. In Mozambique be sure to have your car's registration papers if you're driving into the country.

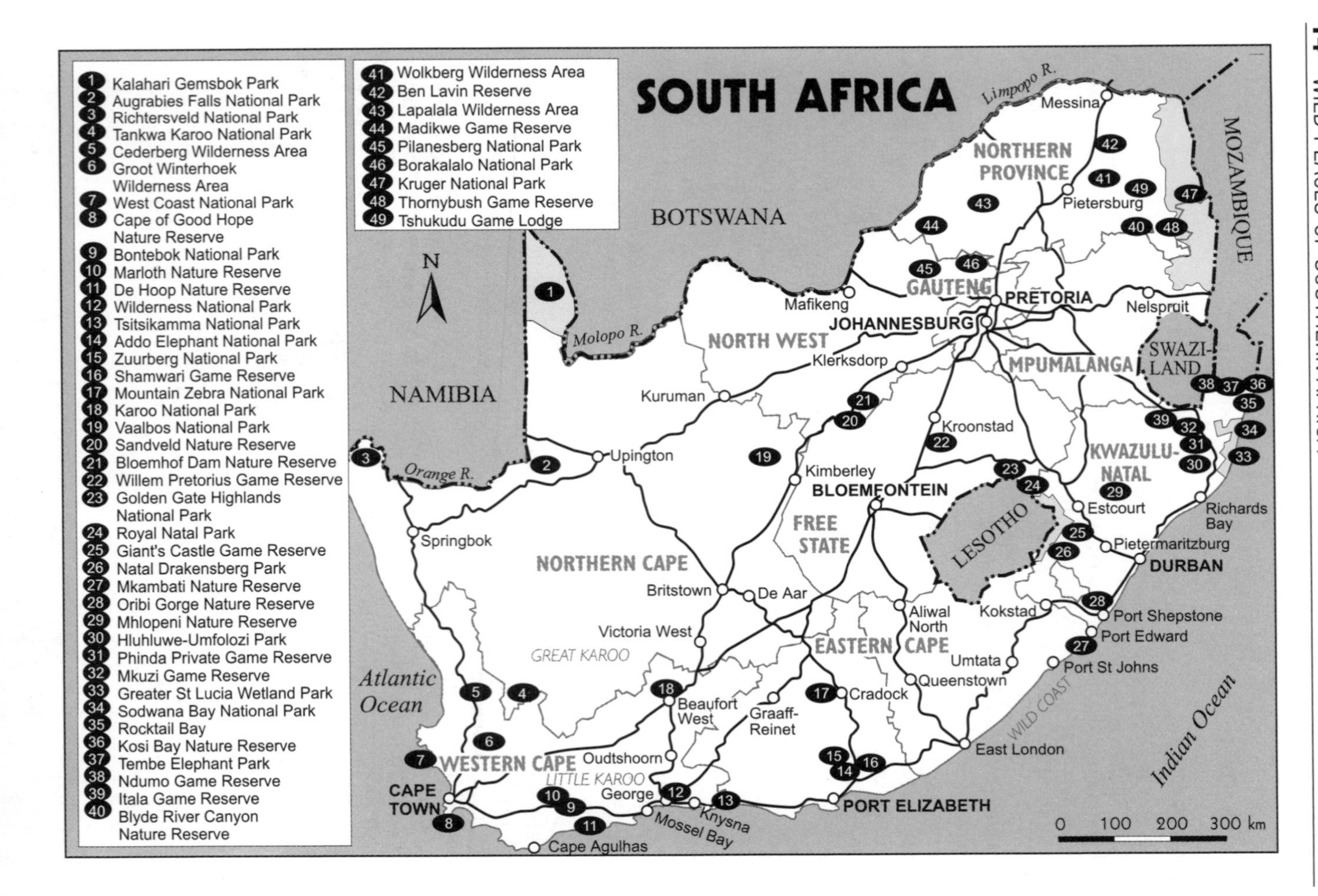
SOUTH AFRICA
1 Kalahari Gemsbok Park
2 Augrabies Falls National Park
3 Richtersveld National Park
4 Tankwa Karoo National Park
5 Cederberg Wilderness Area
6 Groot Winterhoek Wilderness Area
7 West Coast National Park
8 Cape of Good Hope Nature Reserve
9 Bontebok National Park
10 Marloth Nature Reserve
11 De Hoop Nature Reserve
12 Wilderness National Park
13 Tsitsikamma National Park
14 Addo Elephant National Park
15 Zuurberg National Park
16 Shamwari Game Reserve
17 Mountain Zebra National Park
18 Karoo National Park
19 Vaalbos National Park
20 Sandveld Nature Reserve
21 Bloemhof Dam Nature Reserve
22 Willem Pretorius Game Reserve
23 Golden Gate Highlands National Park
24 Royal Natal Park
25 Giant's Castle Game Reserve
26 Natal Drakensberg Park
27 Mkambati Nature Reserve
28 Oribi Gorge Nature Reserve
29 Mhlopeni Nature Reserve
30 Hluhluwe-Umfolozi Park
31 Phinda Private Game Reserve
32 Mkuzi Game Reserve
33 Greater St Lucia Wetland Park
34 Sodwana Bay National Park
35 Rocktail Bay
36 Kosi Bay Nature Reserve
37 Tembe Elephant Park
38 Ndumo Game Reserve
39 Itala Game Reserve
40 Blyde River Canyon Nature Reserve
41 Wolkberg Wilderness Area
42 Ben Lavin Reserve
43 Lapalala Wilderness Area
44 Madikwe Game Reserve
45 Pilanesberg National Park
46 Borakalalo National Park
47 Kruger National Park
48 Thornybush Game Reserve
49 Tshukudu Game Lodge
N
MOZAMBIQUE
BOTSWANA
NAMIBIA
SWAZI-LAND
LESOTHO
Indian Ocean
Atlantic Ocean
Limpopo R.
Molopo R.
Orange R.
NORTHERN PROVINCE
GAUTENG
MPUMALANGA
KWAZULU-NATAL
NORTH WEST
FREE STATE
NORTHERN CAPE
EASTERN CAPE
WESTERN CAPE
GREAT KAROO
LITTLE KAROO
WILD COAST
Messina
Pietersburg
Nelspruit
PRETORIA
JOHANNESBURG
Mafikeng
Klerksdorp
Kroonstad
Richards Bay
Pietermaritzburg
DURBAN
Estcourt
Port Shepstone
Port Edward
Port St Johns
Kokstad
Umtata
East London
Queenstown
Aliwal North
BLOEMFONTEIN
Kimberley
Cradock
Graaff-Reinet
PORT ELIZABETH
De Aar
Britstown
Victoria West
Beaufort West
Kuruman
Upington
Springbok
Oudtshoorn
George
Knysna
Mossel Bay
Cape Agulhas
CAPE TOWN
0 100 200 300 km

SOUTH AFRICA

Enormous changes have swept through South Africa since the country won its democracy in the 1994 general elections. Not the least of these is a massive increase in tourism from around the world. The Rainbow Nation, once regarded as the polecat of the world, is now seen as one of its most attractive holiday destinations.

More significantly, its national parks, game reserves and beautiful lodges are being targeted by discerning gamewatchers as the best in Africa.

South Africa is a huge country. Covering 1 223 410 km^2, it is larger than France, Italy, Belgium, Holland and western Germany combined.

Lying at the southern tip of Africa between the Atlantic and Indian oceans, the country has an amazing variety of attractions: dazzling beaches, towering rainforests, tranquil lake districts, mountain giants, dense bushveld and sweeping savannah plains alive with animals and birds.

Combine these with first-world cities such as Cape Town, Johannesburg and Durban, the diversity of languages, customs, colours and creeds of its nearly 40 million people, and you have a cultural melting pot of fascinating proportions. South Africa is, indeed, a world in one country.

The land

South Africa's interior consists of a sprawling, semicircular plateau, ranging in height from 900 m in the Kalahari to some 3 km in the Mont-Aux-Sources region of the Drakensberg. Surrounding the plateau is a coastal fringe which extends from Alexander Bay on the west coast to Kosi Bay in the east and which ranges from dry desert to subtropical forest.

Because of the huge differences in climate the plateau consists of a number of highly divergent vegetation zones, from the bushveld and dry woodlands of Mpumalanga (formerly Eastern Transvaal) and the Northern Province to the flat scrubland of the Karoo, and the ochre dunelands of the Kalahari.

Wildlife

More than 290 species of terrestrial mammals and more than 800 species of bird live in and around the game sanctuaries of South Africa.

For professional or amateur gamewatchers the opportunities have little equal on earth: on any day in any major game reserve or national park you can put a tick on your animal checklist next to lions, elephants, black and white rhinos, giraffes, hippos, crocodiles, buffaloes, cheetahs, leopards and a large variety of antelopes.

If you're observant you'll also see monkeys, baboons, rock rabbits, mongooses, jackals, genets, civets, caracals, African wild cats, servals, bateared foxes, pangolins and porcupines.

The wild places

The national parks of South Africa and the public and private game reserves cover roughly eight million hectares of the country's total area. There are 17 national parks and one national lake area, all under the control of the National Parks Board. Eleven of these can accommodate overnight visitors. A further 620 smaller reserves and private lodges cater to a huge influx of local and foreign tourists.

Mpumalanga and Northern Province are the prime places to see animals in South Africa. Extending eastwards to the Lebombo Mountains on the Mozambique border, the area embraces more than a third of the country's game-viewing territory, including the Kruger National Park and dozens of private game reserves and lodges. Recently, many of the fences which separated the Kruger National Park from these private reserves have come down, allowing Kruger's animals into them.

Another prime game-viewing region is northern KwaZulu-Natal, where wildlife populations flourish in reserves administered by KwaZulu-Natal Nature Conservation Services. There are 74 sanctuaries totalling 627 240 ha in KwaZulu-Natal. There are 23 rest camps and 31 camping sites in these reserves, accommodating about 12 500 people.

Kruger National Park

One of the top 10 national parks in the world, Kruger is the showpiece in Southern Africa's theatre of the wild. Extending some 350 km from north to south, and 60 km from east to west, the park hosts the largest diversity of animals and plants on the continent.

It was proclaimed by President Paul Kruger in 1898 as a government game reserve, and today covers about two million hectares of bushveld.

The park is home to 130 species of land mammals, 512 species of bird, 114 reptile species and 33 amphibian species — statistics which make it one of the world's greatest animal and birdwatching paradises.

The numbers of individual species in Kruger are staggering: 8 100 elephants, 120 000 impala and 2 000 lions are just some of the figures that attract visitors.

The park is one of the country's major tourist destinations, pulling in some 750 000 visitors a year.

Kalahari Gemsbok National Park

This park lies in the northwestern part of South Africa, right across the subcontinent from the Kruger National Park, on the border of Botswana and Namibia. Unlike Kruger, it is dusty and dry and receives only a paltry amount of the rain that falls on the Mpumalanga Lowveld in summer.

Covering nearly a million hectares, the park has many of the mammals found in the Kruger National Park, but instead of the thick, lush bushveld of Kruger, it is characterised by the ochre sand-dunes of the Kalahari, fossil river beds and grassland adapted to semi-desert conditions.

In spite of its remoteness, the park still offers excellent accommodation in air-conditioned chalets and huts, and even has a swimming pool and fine restaurant at its main camp, Twee Rivieren.

If you're driving there, be prepared for a long haul — it's 904 km from Johannesburg.

The other national parks

South Africa's enormous diversity of vegetation and habitats guarantees that each of the national parks has a unique character, ranging from the beautiful sandstone formations of the Golden Gate National Park in the valley of the Little Caledon River, to the splendour of the Orange River tumbling over the Augrabies Falls in the Augrabies Falls National Park.

Along the southern Cape coast, on a beautiful coastal terrace between mountain and sea, lies the country's first marine national park, the Tsitsikamma Coastal National Park, a tranquil refuge on the edge of a rainforest. Here you may take underwater snorkelling trails, walk through the forest, or simply laze on the little golden beach.

Two other coastal retreats are the West Coast National Park, home of a stunning variety of seabirds, and the Wilderness National Park at the foot of the Outeniqua Mountains, a seaside paradise of lagoons, lakes, forests, fynbos and golden beaches.

Apart from elephants, the Addo Elephant National Park near Port Elizabeth in the Eastern Cape supports a wealth of other game: Cape buffaloes, black rhinos, kudu, various antelope species and more than 180 species of bird.

The Bontebok National Park, near the Western Cape town of Swellendam, is known as the park that rescued the bontebok from extinction. Here, in a floral paradise of more than 470 species, you may overnight on the banks of the Breede River and enjoy the sounds of the wilderness.

Another park dedicated to the saving of a species is the Mountain Zebra National Park — a reserve within driving distance of Port Elizabeth — which was established in 1937 to rescue the mountain zebra from extinction.

The Golden Gate Highlands National Park mentioned above is the Free State's only national park, and offers superior drives and game walks through sandstone canyons, grasslands and wooded valleys, home to a variety of mammals and 140 species of bird.

The Richtersveld National Park is an adventurers' paradise — a mountainous semi-desert between the Orange River in the north and east and the Atlantic Ocean in the west.

This park lures hikers, overnight campers, four-wheel-drive safari operators and canoeists who challenge the Orange River as it winds down to the sea.

KwaZulu-Natal reserves

The most popular — and oldest — of the reserves is the Hluhluwe-Umfolozi reserve, combined in recent years to form one 96 000-ha park. This is lion, leopard, rhino and elephant country, and also a superb birdwatching area, lying just about 60 km from the blue expanse of the Indian Ocean.

Further inland is the beautiful Itala Game Reserve, where guests may view some 80 mammal species and stay in superb bush-lodge accommodation.

Other sought-after destinations north of Durban are the Greater St Lucia Wetland Park, a tranquil wilderness of water, swamps, forest and vleis. This park is also home to a stunning variety of birdlife, and offers visitors tidy campsites at the edge of the sea, lodge accommodation on the fringes of lakes and extensive walks through a wilderness of crocodiles and hippos, pelicans and flamingoes.

Other wild places of KwaZulu-Natal featured in this book are Ndumu Game Reserve and Tembe Elephant Park on the Mozambique border; Sodwana Bay; the lovely chalet resort of Rocktail Bay, and the mountain reserves of the Drakensberg, notably the Giant's Castle Game Reserve and the Royal Natal Park.

Private game reserves

South Africa hosts some of the most luxurious and scenically attractive private game lodges in the world, most of them in the Mpumalanga Lowveld and KwaZulu-

Natal. Conspicuous among these are Londolozi Game Reserve, Mala Mala, Tanda Tula, Ngala Game Reserve, Makalali Private Game Reserve, Singita Game Reserve, Kapama Game Reserve and Motswari Private Game Reserve in Mpumalanga, Shamwari Game Reserve in the Eastern Cape and Phinda Resource Reserve in KwaZulu-Natal. Another popular getaway destination is Madikwe Game Reserve in the Northwest Province, near South Africa's border with Botswana.

Where to stay

Accommodation in the national parks' public rest camps is of a very high standard, and you may choose between cottage or chalet-type accommodation, guesthouses, tented camps and even tree camps. In private reserves and lodges the standard of accommodation, food and facilities is among the best in the world, and these are discussed in detail in the individual entries. Alternatively, contact the National Parks Board at PO Box 787, Pretoria 0001, tel (012) 343-1991; or PO Box 7400, Roggebaai 8012 (Cape Town), tel (021) 22-2810.

Climate

Much of South Africa is hot, arid and dry. The northern and western parts, in particular, regularly experience temperatures higher than 40 °C in summer, while daytime winter temperatures in the major game-viewing areas fluctuate from the low teens to the mid-twenties.

Bear in mind that while winter days may be mild to warm, temperatures often plummet to below freezing at night.

The average annual rainfall is just 502 mm, against a world mean of 857 mm, and it's so dry in the northwestern part of the Northern Cape and the Kalahari that you may not see a cloud for months.

When to go

Northern Province, Mpumalanga and KwaZulu-Natal For gamewatchers the dry season between May and September is the best time to visit these regions. This is the time animals congregate at waterholes in greater numbers, and they are easy to see from the roadside, because the vegetation is sparse.

It is advisable to visit the Kalahari Gemsbok, Richtersveld and Augrabies Falls national parks in winter because summers tend to be scorchingly hot.

Eastern Province This region, which includes the Addo Elephant National Park and Shamwari Game Reserve, is a transition zone between summer and winter rainfall, and is suitable for game-viewing throughout the year.

Western Cape Summer (October–March) would be the time to visit these parts of the country, because winters are cold, wet and miserable.

How to get there

At least 44 international airlines (including Air Botswana, Air Malawi, Air Namibia, Air Zimbabwe, Royal Swazi National Airways and Zambian Airways) fly in and out of South Africa's three international airports (Johannesburg, Durban and Cape Town) regularly.

There are also direct, well-surfaced road links through various border posts from neighbouring Namibia, Zimbabwe, Botswana and Swaziland.

Getting around

By air The international airports and six other major airports service commercial operators who fly into the national parks and game reserves throughout Southern Africa.

Johannesburg is by far the busiest airport, with regular flights to Nelspruit, Skukuza and the private lodges and game reserves of Botswana, Namibia, Zimbabwe, Zambia and the Mpumalanga Lowveld. Most travel agents will provide details of the charter flights and fly-in safaris available.

By road South Africa maintains an excellent network of highways and tarred roads throughout the country. Along these you can easily reach all the national parks and most of the private game reserves and lodges by car, minibus or luxury bus.

The main highways are the N1 (Cape Town–Johannesburg–Zimbabwe), the N2, (Cape Town, George, Port Elizabeth, East London, Durban and Swaziland); the N3 (Durban–Johannesburg), the N4 (Pretoria–southern Kruger National Park), and the N7 (Cape Town–Namibia).

Car-rental companies (Budget, Avis and Imperial) operate in most major towns and cities, at the nine major airports and in the bigger game parks and nature reserves (there is a car-hire facility in Skukuza, the Kruger National Park's main camp).

For more details on car hire tel Avis Rent a Car at 0800-10-1111 or (011) 974-2571, or Budget Rent a Car at 0800-01-6622 or (011) 392-3907, or see 'On Safari in Southern Africa', p. 8.

Drivers must possess an international driver's licence, and have at least five years' driving experience.

Tour operators run regular scheduled trips to the national parks and game reserves from all the major cities. The mode of transport varies from six-seater minibuses to large luxury buses. A list of tour operators and packages is featured on p. 362 under 'Safari Operators in Southern Africa'.

If you want to organise your own trip, contact Intercape, (tel (011) 33-5231), Greyhound Citiliner (tel (011) 838-3037), or Translux (tel (011) 774-3333).

Railways South Africa operates two of the world's most luxurious train services: Rovos Rail and the Blue Train. Rovos Rail runs adventurous steam safaris between Pretoria and the Kruger National Park, Pretoria and Cape Town, and between Cape Town, Pretoria and Dar es Salaam (tel (012) 323-6052). The Blue Train, which operates between Cape Town and Pretoria, Johannesburg, Pretoria and the Victoria Falls and Pretoria and Nelspruit, is highly recommended (tel (011) 773-5878/9).

Entry requirements

Most foreigners must have a passport to enter the country, but holiday-makers from the European Union, the United States, Canada, Australia, New Zealand, Singapore, Switzerland, Austria, Japan, the Republic of Ireland, Namibia, Brazil and Botswana do not need a visa.

Health precautions

Some reserves in the north and in KwaZulu-Natal are malaria areas, so take precautions before you visit. Bilharzia is another health risk in some reserves (ask your travel agent).

If you're arriving from a yellow-fever zone, you will need a valid international yellow fever vaccination certificate.

Travel information

Contact the Tourist Rendezvous Travel Centre, Sammy Marks Complex, corner of Prinsloo and Vermeulen streets, Pretoria 0002, tel (012) 308-8909; or Capetour Pinnacle Building, PO Box 1403, Cape 8000, tel (021) 426-4267/8. Alternatively, contact Tourism Johannesburg, suite 4608 46th Floor, Johannesburg 2001, tel (011) 331-2041.

ADDO ELEPHANT NATIONAL PARK

There's little more African than the acrid scent of elephants, which drifts up to your chalet porch as the sun sets over the Addo Elephant National Park, between the Zuurberg and the fertile Sundays River Valley in the Eastern Cape.

And there's nothing more relaxing than having a sundowner in close company with 15 large pachyderms gathered around a floodlit waterhole virtually at your feet.

You sit there hypnotised, as a weaving tapestry of trunks moves among these graceful, grey sages of the bush. What makes it more special is the fact that these elephants are part of a breed that was nearly exterminated by a hunter hired to kill their ancestors in 1919.

The hunter — the last of the legendary great hunters — was Major P J Pretorius. He was commissioned by the Administrator of the Cape Province to rid the area of elephants. Major Pretorius shot 120 elephants, but 11 survived by fleeing to the sanctuary of a near-impenetrable tangle of trees and creepers known as Harvey Bush. The shooting of the elephants was greeted with outrage by some conservationists, and resulted in the formation of the Addo Elephant National Park in 1931.

Today there are more than 284 elephants in this 100 000-ha park and, together with a variety of large and small mammals, they have made Addo a special and accessible place to visit (the park is just 72 km north of Port Elizabeth).

Other species that survived persecution by humankind include the Eastern Cape's last remaining herd of disease-free Cape buffalo; and a breeding group of the very scarce East African species of black rhino. Today there are 30 of these rhinos at Addo, and their numbers are increasing annually.

Antelope abound in the park: among them eland, kudu, red hartebeest, common duiker and grysbok. At night, spotlight-assisted game drives introduce guests to blackbacked jackals, caracals, mongooses, porcupines, bushpigs or aardvark. Less conspicuous among the inhabitants is the flightless dung beetle, found almost exclusively at Addo.

About 250 species of bird, including ostriches, hawks, finches and francolins,

Charge of the angry elephant

The elephant's large size, its menacing posture and its flapping ears deter most predators threatening it or its youngsters.

But if the pachyderm's body language fails to stop a lion or other predator, it will unfurl its ears, shake its head, hold its tusks parallel to the ground and charge the hostile carnivore, coming to a halt metres from the intruder. In fact, in 90 per cent of cases the elephant will stop short of its victim — a fact that the San (Bushmen) of the Kalahari knew only too well, and enabled them to stand their ground unharmed in the path of a charging elephant.

Elephants can run at up to 40 km/h, but are incapable of jumping over tiny obstacles.

They move about silently on the tips of their toes and cushioned feet and, when coming to a halt, often pick up one leg to rest it. Elephants can swim and sometimes use their trunks as snorkels.

flourish in the diverse valley-bushveld vegetation of spekboom, guarri, sneezewood, acacia, and various succulents and bushes.

Since the park has grown from a tiny retreat in the bush to an excellent game-watching area, equipped with all the modern conveniences. Today, following the incorporation of the Zuurberg National Park, it has become a favoured destination for nature-lovers throughout the world.

Game drives and trails There's no shortage of outdoor activities at Addo. Two attractive walking trails have been laid out in the park. The shorter one is within the fenced-off rest camp, but the four-hour Spekboom Trail explores a 400-ha botanical reserve within the park, fenced off from elephant and rhino to protect the natural vegetation. The trail takes in a secluded hide, where you can

Addo Elephant National Park at a glance

Locality:	In the Sundays River Valley of the Eastern Cape Province, 72 km north of Port Elizabeth.
Climate:	Warm to hot summers, mild to cold winters, with 450 mm of rainfall throughout the year.
Number of camps:	One.
Game drives:	Day and night drives are available.
Hides and waterholes:	One of two walking trails includes a hide overlooking a waterhole where elephant and rhino come down to drink. The rest camp overlooks a waterhole.
Trails:	Two walking trails.
Other attractions:	Swimming pool.
Amenities:	Á la carte restaurant, post office, curio shop.
Accommodation:	Two luxury six-bed family cottages; six two-bed chalets with shower and toilet, electric stove, fridge, cutlery and crockery; 24 air-conditioned, serviced chalets, fully equipped with bathroom and kitchen. Two of these are adapted to serve paraplegics. There is also a caravan park and campsite, with electric power points for caravans.
Booking address:	National Parks Board, PO Box 787, Pretoria 0001, tel (012) 343-1991; or PO Box 7400, Roggebaai 8012, tel (021) 22-2810.
When to go:	Throughout the year.
What to take with you:	Warm clothing in winter; torch, binoculars, camera.
How to get there:	National air links serve Port Elizabeth daily. By road, drive east from Port Elizabeth along the N2 to the Swartkops River. Take the exit ramp on to the R335 and drive to Addo (29 km). Continue via Coerney and follow signboards to the park.
Nearest doctor:	Sunlands, 16 km away.
Nearest petrol:	Available in the park between 07:00 and 18:00. Nearest garage and medical services Addo, 15 km away.
Open:	07:00–19:00 throughout the year.
Special precautions:	Be patient if elephants cross in front of you. Retreat quietly and slowly if an elephant shows any signs of aggression.

watch the animals come down to do their ablutions at a waterhole.

Day and night drives in open 4x4s are also available on request.

Where to stay The rest camp has 59 air-conditioned, serviced chalets, with two single beds and a couch-cum-double bed, a bathroom, lounge and fully equipped kitchen. Each chalet overlooks the main waterhole.

There are also two luxury air-conditioned, serviced, six-bed family cottages, and six two-bed chalets sharing a communal kitchen. Bedding is provided.

You could also have the unique experience of sitting in the à la carte licensed restaurant under the raised trunk and sweeping tusks of an elephant bull known as Hapoor, which went on the rampage in 1968, broke out of the reserve, and was reluctantly shot by park officials who had no other alternative.

Hapoor enjoyed a 24-year reign as the dominant bull in the park, and reached the peak of his power after fighting — and killing — a junior challenger called Bellevue. Hapoor also killed a cow called Ouma, but paid dearly for his deed when Ouma's son, Lanky, drove him out of the herd.

For less formal accommodation there's a camping and caravan park, which has access to a communal kitchen, a shop and petrol pump. A maximum of six people is allowed per caravan site.

You may visit Addo Elephant National Park just for the day, or stay a week or more, but be sure to book ahead (see 'At a glance' box for details). No firearms or pets are allowed in the reserve, and be sure not to feed the elephants.

Augrabies Falls National Park

Approached from the south, the Augrabies Falls announces itself with the drone of distant thunder, rising from the desolate, lunar landscape of the northwestern Northern Cape. As you near the mighty cleft of the Augrabies Gorge, the sound thickens and roars like some angry river god. You step back and watch in awe as a seething cauldron of white water cascades 56 m over the ancient granite crest into the boiling pot below.

Tip for travellers

An unwelcome inhabitant of Augrabies Falls National Park is the black fly, which annoys visitors by crawling into the ears and nose. The best way to keep these pests at bay is to swat them away with a leafy branch.

There the dazzling waters of the mighty Orange River, flanked by precipitous walls of 3 000-million-year-old granite, gather momentum again and move forward on their journey to the sea.

This is the heart of the Augrabies Falls National Park, a place the Khoikhoi (Hottentot) pastoralists called 'Aukoerebis' — the place of great noise. The first European to see the falls was a Swede, Hendrik Jakob Wikar, who arrived there in 1799, and gave the falls their present name.

Without the Orange River and its mighty falls, the 28 000-ha Augrabies National Park may well have resembled some distant desert outpost, its endlessly flat skyline punctuated by prehistoric-looking kokerboom and desert bushes. But the river has brought life and sustenance to the area, and the park should be on your itinerary of wild places.

Wildlife The banks of the Orange here are lined by ribbons of lush, green vegetation. This contrasts sharply with the dull euphorbia-like shrubs, blackthorn and grasses that squeeze life out of cracks in the gneissic domes flanking the river. This vegetation and the abundant waters of the Orange support a rich and varied community of mammals and reptiles.

There are no less than 51 mammal species, the more obvious of which are black rhinos, eland, baboons, monkeys and small antelope, such as klipspringer, which congregate in the shade of camelthorn, white karee, wild olive and Karoo boerbean.

Less conspicuous, but no less important, are the 13 species of predator, among which leopards, wild cats, genets and mongooses are seen at night. Another very common mammal is the dassie, which shares the smooth rock surfaces with toad grasshoppers.

In the confines of the camp a frequent visitor is the ground squirrel, which emerges from its burrow only when the sun shines, and uses its bushy tail as an umbrella to shield its body from the sun.

But the animals which are most closely associated with Augrabies are the reptiles, represented by no less than 24 species of gecko, lizard, skink, agama and leguaan. The most abundant reptile is the Cape flat rock lizard — the male being the most conspicuous with its deep blue forequarters and bright orange tail.

Sad-eyed lady of the lowlands

The dainty, feminine little antelope known as steenbok do not possess the defensive mechanisms of the larger buck species – lethal horns, long fur and brute strength. So they rely on their speed and agility to avoid being caught by predators such as lions, leopards, cheetahs, hyenas and wild dogs.

Because of the tremendous amount of energy these sad-eyed antelope use in their sudden dash for cover, they produce huge amounts of heat very quickly. For this reason their fur is very thin, enabling them to dissipate the heat immediately.

Steenbok are browsers which excavate roots and bulbs with their pointed hooves. In the Kalahari you'll see them just after sunrise, browsing among the bushes or tugging at succulent plants, grasses and the leaves of camelthorn and shepherd trees.

You'll find steenbok in open country, where there's some cover. In arid regions they tend to stick to the vicinity of low-lying, dry river beds.

Steenbok are often confused with similar-sized duiker or oribi. However, distinguishing features are a white patch above the large eyes, reddish brown back and sides, and white undersides and insides of legs.

In addition there are 19 snake species, 17 species of rodent, two tortoise species and 12 fish species, including smallmouth yellowfish, mudfish, exotic carp and barbel.

Birdlife The lush banks of the Orange attract 183 species of bird, from martial and black eagles to palewinged starlings and rosyfaced lovebirds. A pair of black eagles rearing a chick is known to consume between 250 and 300 dassies a year.

The falls In times of flood, 405 million litres of water a minute hurtle over the main falls — one of the six great waterfalls of the world — and 18 secondary cataracts. The second largest of these is Bridal Veil Falls, which joins the main fall in heavy floods.

The gorge itself is 18 km long, and the river drops a further 35 m along this course in a series of spectacular rapids. You may witness the full majesty of the gorge and the falls from Ararat Rock, just over 2 km

Augrabies Falls National Park at a glance

Location:	Far north of the Northern Cape Province (894 km from Cape Town) on South Africa's border with Namibia.
Climate:	Very hot summer days; warm winter days (average 25 °C); cold winter nights; average rainfall 107 mm per annum.
Number of camps:	One.
Game drives:	30-km network of game drives. Gariep Three-in-One Adventure.
Trails:	Three-day Klipspringer Hiking Trail; Spiespunt (one hour), Maalgate (one-and-a-half hours) or Maanrots (one hour).
Viewsites:	Arrow Point, Ararat, Echo Corner.
Other attractions:	Extraordinary granitic formations; photography; birdwatching.
Amenities:	Restaurant; petrol; firewood delivered to chalets; shop with groceries, meat, fresh bread, liquor, ice.
Accommodation:	59 three- and- four-bed, air-conditioned chalets (with bathroom, kitchenette and braai area); camping area.
Booking address:	National Parks Board, PO Box 787, Pretoria 0001, tel (012) 343-1991; National Parks Board, PO Box 7400, Roggebaai 8012, tel (021) 22-2810; the Park Warden, Augrabies Falls National Park, Private Bag X1, Augrabies 8874, tel (054) 451-0050.
When to go:	Between October and January, when the falls are at their best.
What to take with you:	Hikers — sleeping bags and trail food. Rest camp visitors — warm clothing (in winter), cameras, binoculars, walking shoes.
How to get there:	By road from Johannesburg (915 km); Cape Town (894 km); Durban (1 458 km).
Nearest doctor:	At Kakamas, 40 km away.
Nearest garage:	At Kakamas, 40 km away.
Open:	1 September: – 31 March: 06:30–19:00; 1 April–31 August: 07:00–18:30.
Special precautions:	Extremely hot (up to 46 °C in summer). Do not scale protective barrier fences near the falls. Beware of slippery rocks. No pets allowed in park. Take antimalaria precautions before you go.

west of the rest camp. There you will understand why 19th-century explorer George Thompson described this sight as 'a combination of beauty and grandeur, such as I never before witnessed'.

Author Lawrence Green described Augrabies as mile after mile of gigantic rockfaces, washed and polished by the floods of centuries, naked, slippery, steep and deadly.

'Deadly' is an apt description of the falls — no less than 20 people have lost their lives since the park was proclaimed in 1966, most of them by falling from the slippery rocks on which even the geckos seem insecure. So when you do venture towards the various lookout points, don't even think about scaling the protective, chest-high fence, as some have done with tragic results in the past.

Where to stay There's a rustic, cool charm to the shaded National Park rest camp, where you can hire three- and four-bed, air-conditioned chalets with bathroom, kitchenette and braai area (cooking utensils, a two-plate cooker, fridge, towels and soap are provided). There are three swimming pools, one for every 20 chalets which are a short stroll from a large à la carte restaurant. Nearby is an information centre and a quaint museum displaying the gemstones, rocks, fauna and flora of the area. There's also a lovely caravan park and camping site under shady trees, with easy access to the swimming pools, ablution block and braai sites.

Trails and drives The three-day Klipspringer Hiking Trail takes you from the rest camp along the southern bank of the Orange through the Augrabies Falls Gorge and back again. You overnight in stone huts (Fish Eagle Hut and Mountain Hut) with bunks, toilets and braai facilities, and have the opportunity to swim in pools along the river. Take your own food, sleeping bags, swimming costume and cooking equipment. Then relax under the stars, and enjoy the surroundings as the San and Khoikhoi did, while they fished from the river's banks for the giant barbel that inhabit the river courses, or feasted on the roots, berries and beans that grow there.

For shorter rambles, try the Spiespunt (one hour), Maalgate (one-and-a-half hours) or Maanrots (one hour) trails. A particularly good vantage site is Arrow Point near the camp.

Ben Lavin Nature Reserve

Just four-and-a-half hours along the road north of Johannesburg, in one of the finest sweetveld grazing areas in the Northern Province, lies the 2 500-ha Ben Lavin Nature Reserve, a relaxed and friendly slice of bush country where you can mingle with a large variety of wild animals and birds.

The reserve was donated to the Wildlife Society of Southern Africa by conservationist Molly Lavin after the death of her husband, Ben, in the early 1970s. And because it is administered by the Wildlife Society, it's one of the few game reserves in the country that offers very reasonable rates and a high standard of accommodation.

It lies in the shadow of the Soutpansberg Mountains, 12 km southeast of Louis Trichardt, a transition zone between the sandveld of the arid northwestern region of the Northern Province and the lusher Mpumalanga Lowveld.

Wildlife Among the more than 50 mammal species, you'll find Burchell's zebras, giraffe, hartebeest, wildebeest, tsessebe, kudu, impala, waterbuck, duiker, steenbok, bushbuck, nyala, reedbuck and blackbacked jackals. There are also more than 230 species of bird, among which are birds of prey such as Wahlberg's eagle, and smaller species, such as crimson-breasted shrikes and Heuglin's robin.

Game drives and trails Visitors to Ben Lavin may choose between driving along a network of some 45 km of game-viewing roads or hiking any of the four game trails (4 to 8 km) to encounter most of the game at close quarters.

These popular circular trails, well within the capabilities of anyone who's moderately fit are the Tshumanini Springs Trail (5 km) which starts from Zebra Dam in the reserve's northern sector, the Tabajwane Trail (8 km) noted for its panoramic vistas of the Soutpansberg Mountains, the Waterbuck Trail (3 km) and the Fountain Trail (4 km) along the banks of the Doring River. Trailists are limited to groups of six at any one time, and maps are available at the reserve's entrance.

Because no dangerous predators are found in the reserve, it is perfectly safe to choose your own hiking path through the bush. However, be sure to take enough water and check yourself for ticks afterwards as they tend to thrive in this area.

Tips for travellers

- **A map is available at the curio shop or the entrance gate.**
- **You may leave or enter the reserve outside the normal hours (06:00–19:00) at a fee of R5 per vehicle.**
- **Birdwatching opportunities are excellent here, so bring along a good field guide.**

There are three game-viewing hides, one of which is within an easy walk of the rest camp. Various short game trails radiate from the camp and lead to waterholes where game-viewing and birdwatching are excellent. Experienced field staff regularly conduct birding walks through the bush.

Night drives in an open 4x4, using a spotlight, are offered for viewing the various nocturnal species.

For a novel way of exploring the bush, you can hire a mountain bike from the curio shop.

Where to stay There are three camps. The shaded main rest camp, which lies snugly in the shade of riverine bushes and trees on the banks of the dry Doring River, offers four fully equipped, thatched lodges, two huts and two tents. The huts and lodges have crockery, cutlery, linen and towels, and overhead fans and a fridge. Each hut has five beds, a handbasin and toilet.

The thatched lodges (three beds and five beds) are fully equipped, with hot and cold showers and toilets. All the huts and lodges have their own braai facilities.

The tents, pitched on a concrete floor under a thatched roof, also have a fridge and braai facility, and access to communal ablution facilities.

There's also a secluded, self-catering bush camp nestling in riverine woodland 4 km from the main camp, in the north-eastern part of the reserve. The camp has two rustic, thatched huts, a kitchen and ablution facilities, with hot water and an outdoor boma.

Twenty people may be accommodated here. Beds, mattresses, crockery, cutlery, firewood, chairs and a deep freeze are supplied, but guests must bring their own provisions and linen.

There's also a luxury tent camp with *en suite* bathrooms and kitchens overlooking the Doring River floodplain. The unique Sekelbosskerm conference centre has restaurant and bar facilities. Other amenities include a swimming pool and shop offering basic groceries and toiletries, ice-cream, cold drinks, sweets, venison and a wide variety of souvenirs and environmental literature.

Ben Lavin Nature Reserve at a glance

Locality:	Northern Province, 12 km southeast of Louis Trichardt.
Climate:	Summers warm to hot with thundershowers; winters mild to cool, but cold at night.
Number of camps:	Three.
Game drives and trails:	45 km of game-viewing roads; four hiking trails (4 km to 8 km). You may choose your own path through the bush.
Hides and waterholes:	Three hides and waterholes.
Other attractions:	Mountain bike trails (bikes available at the shop); guided birding trails.
Amenities:	Curio shop and office. Groceries, venison, ice-cream, braai wood and maps are available at the shop.
Accommodation:	The main camp offers huts, lodges, tents and campsites. The bush camp offers two rustic huts and the luxury tented camp has *en suite* bathrooms and kitchens.
Booking address:	Ben Lavin Nature Reserve, PO Box 782, Louis Trichardt 0920, tel (015) 516-4534.
When to go:	Throughout the year, but winter is best for game-viewing.
What to take with you:	Binoculars, hiking boots, camera, your own provisions and (only in the bush camp) linen.
How to get there:	The reserve lies 400 km north of Johannesburg. Drive north from Pretoria on the Great North Road to Louis Trichardt. Approximately 8 km before Louis Trichardt turn right on to a tarred road signposted Fort Edward, and drive 5 km before turning left at the main entrance gate.
Nearest doctor:	Louis Trichardt, 15 km away.
Nearest petrol:	Louis Trichardt, 15 km away.
Open:	06:00–19:00 throughout the year.
Special precautions:	None.

BONTEBOK NATIONAL PARK

Just south of Swellendam the languid waters of the Breede River float past a green terrace of aloes, grass and riverine bush. Here in the lee of distant mountains and tumbling hills, a small rest camp flanks the river in the corner of the Bontebok National Park.

In this tranquil region of coastal fynbos and renosterveld, not much more than 200 years ago, elephants, lions, leopards, rhinos and large herds of plains animals wandered around the countryside, largely unhampered by humankind. Soon, however, hunters came with guns blazing and, apart from the lions, leopards and elephants, the bontebok became prime targets.

The rest camp at the waterside is a peaceful place to reflect on the folly of these men, whose greed for the bontebok's piebald hide brought the animal to the brink of extinction last century. Thanks to the intervention of some farmers in the area, who tried to protect the bontebok on their lands from about 1864, the species was momentarily spared. But by 1921 there were just 121 bontebok left in the world — 20 of them in this part of the country.

In 1931 the National Parks Board stepped in and established a national park near Bredasdorp, pledging to rescue the species from extinction. Later (in 1960) the park was relocated to its present site and the numbers of bontebok have risen sharply, enabling the authorities to stock other parks. The total world population is now about 3 000.

Today the Bontebok National Park is acclaimed as one of Southern Africa's finest examples of the power of nature conservation. And for those who love the quiet country air of the southwestern area of the Western Cape, and the sights and sounds of its animals and birds, this is an ideal venue.

It doesn't boast the variety of species of the larger, more remote reserves, but among the 36 mammal species you will see bontebok, Cape mountain zebras, red hartebeest, Cape grysbok, common and grey duikers and steenbok.

The large carnivores are long gone, but if you're lucky you may spot nocturnal species such as aardwolf, caracals, African wild cats and spotted genets. Bateared foxes are sometimes seen snuffling and digging for insects, and you may catch a glimpse of a Cape clawless otter (with young, if you're lucky) scampering into the riverine bush.

Tip for travellers

If you're overnighting at the park, fresh provisions may be bought at Swellendam, 6 km away.

Birdlife Although world attention has focused on the park because of its bontebok, the variety and abundance of its birds are enough to make the park a very special place.

The four main habitat zones attract 192 species of bird. Particularly notable is the colourful array of fynbos-related species such as malachite, orangebreasted and lesser doublecollared sunbirds. Other species include the crimsontailed swee waxbill, a variety of pipits (plainbacked, longbilled and Richard's), and cisticolas. The fruit-bearing shrubs of the park's riverine thicket zone attract Cape bulbuls, Cape robins and southern boubous.

Also prominent among the bird population are the nine species of raptors, such as the martial eagle, redbreasted sparrowhawk and the blackshouldered kite.

Game drives and trails From the reception area in the north, there are 25 km of game-viewing roads that form two loops around the park. And if you don't spot a lot of game, consider stopping your car to walk around and examine some of the magnificent flora in the reserve. There are 470 plant species here, including a variety of proteas, leucadendrons and leucospermums (pincushions). Keep a lookout for such specials as the impressive king protea, *Leucospermum conocarpodendron* and the fairly common *Leucospermum cordifolium*, with its bold, orange-coloured blooms. Included among the heaths and ericas is *Erica versicolour.*

Two trails lead into the park from the rest camp. The Aloe Hill Trail ascends the slopes near the water's edge, and the elevation affords fine views of the clusters of flame-red *Aloe ferox*, and a large part of the reserve stretching northwards to distant mountains. The 2-km Acacia Walk, also near the Breede, takes you through riverside yellowwood, white milkwood, sweet thorn, acacia and Cape beech trees.

Where to stay Whether you're camping or staying in one of the caravans, you'll find the rest camp at Bontebok National Park cosy and comfortable. The camp is situated on a riverside terrace under canopies of acacia and other trees. You may swim or fish in the river (angling licence available at office).

Six-berth caravans, equipped with gas stove, refrigerator, crockery, cutlery and cooking utensils, are available for hire. Each caravan has a side tent and its own braai site. Caravanners and campers have access to an ablution block.

Other attractions The Bontebok National Park is within easy driving range of the wine routes of Swellendam, Robertson and Montagu. Swellendam, one of South Africa's oldest towns, is a living museum of historical Cape Dutch buildings.

Just outside the town is the beautiful Marloth Reserve — starting point of the six-day Swellendam Hiking Trail. Permits to enter the reserve are obtainable from the Swellendam State Forest Station. For further details and booking, tel (021) 402-3043.

Montagu is worth a visit for its hot springs, while the Breede River is a favourite venue for canoeists.

Bontebok National Park at a glance

Locality:	6 km south of Swellendam; 224 km east of Cape Town.
Climate:	Temperate, with cool to cold rainy winters and hot, dry summers. Temperatures range from 40 °C in summer to 2 °C in winter.
Number of camps:	One.
Game drives:	25 km of game-viewing roads.
Trails:	Two: The Aloe Hill Trail (2 km) and the Acacia Walk (2 km).
Other attractions:	Swimming, angling, historical buildings in Swellendam, wine routes of Robertson and Montagu.
Amenities:	Shop supplying curios, sweets, essential groceries, soft drinks and charcoal; information office.
Accommodation:	Four cabins (connected to caravans); 25 caravan/camping sites.
Booking address:	National Parks Board, PO Box 787, Pretoria 0001, tel (012) 343-1991; National Parks Board, PO Box 7400, Roggebaai 8012, tel (021) 22-2810.
When to go:	Throughout the year, but summer is preferred.
What to take with you:	Your own braai grid, firewood, angling equipment, bathing towels, swimming costume, walking shoes, torch, camera.
How to get there:	Take the N2 from Cape Town to Swellendam. The park lies just east of Swellendam.
Nearest doctor:	Swellendam, 6 km away.
Nearest petrol:	In the park.
Open:	1 October–30 April: 08:00–19:00; 1 May–30 September: 08:00–18:00.
Special precautions:	While hiking, keep a lookout for puffadders, especially in spring and summer.

Borakalalo National Park

Elephant and hippo footprints form large, circular craters in the mud, a short way from your safari tent on the banks of the lazy Moretele River in the Borakalalo National Park. And as evening falls they are joined by the less conspicuous spoor of an impressive variety of smaller animals — warthog, kudu, waterbuck, nyala and impala.

Borakalalo ('the place where people relax'), was established on 1 April 1984, and the wildness of its 14 000 ha of rolling sandveld, vleis, kloofs, riverine bush and koppies is a remarkable monument to the efforts of the former Bophuthatswana National Parks Board, which transformed it from an overused recreational area into the peaceful sanctuary it is today.

Borakalalo's recovery began with the restocking of animals that occurred naturally in the area, before they were almost annihilated by hunters.

Less than two hours' drive from Johannesburg, and about an hour's drive from Sun City in the south, Borakalalo is an ideal retreat for the work-weary individual seeking true relaxation in the wild. The eastern half of the reserve is a wilderness area and is closed to the public.

Wildlife If you're a dedicated gamewatcher, Borakalalo hosts most of the larger mammals seen in its sister reserve, the Pilanesberg National Park — all in all 3 727 animals, representing more than 35 species of mammal. And, although there are no lions or cheetahs, the numbers of other species are impressive: 300 zebras, 73 giraffes, 114 gemsbok, 283 black wildebeest and 34 white rhinos.

You may also see leopards, brown hyena, aardwolf, roan antelope, hartebeest, eland, tsessebe and mountain reedbuck.

Birdlife There is an impressive variety of birds (more than 300 species), prominent among which are the waterbirds drawn to the Moretele River and Klipvoor Dam, one of the finest inland fishing resorts in Southern Africa.

Ballerinas of the wild

Impala are the graceful high-jumpers of the Southern African wild. Fleet-footed and sleek, they glide in sure-footed, synchronised leaps over the bush and thorny scrub of their home environment, classically adapted to flee rather than fight.

In fact, it is not only their spectacular leaping ability that enables impala to escape the jaws of marauding predators: nature has given them a set of very distinctive black bands on their rumps. These bands, set against the pale hindquarters of an airborne, fleeing impala, serve as a highly visible directional guide to other fleeing members of the herd, keeping the group together when they're on the run.

Even amateur gamewatchers cannot confuse the identity of these athletic antelope with their rufous coats and pure white undersides, soaring to heights of 3 m and covering distances of up to 12 m at a time.

Impala are survivors not only by virtue of their great jumping prowess: their vulnerability to a number of predators has led them to form an alliance with monkeys and baboons, which sound the alarm if they spot a predator from their treetop perches. The impala, in turn may pick up the danger first, and send the primates scurrying to cover.

Herons, fish eagles, great crested grebes, kingfishers, storks (yellowbilled and marabou) and African finfoots are among the more common. Sefudi Dam in the south is a particularly good birdwatching spot.

Inland, among the bush and scattered woodland, you'll see the colourful crimsonbreasted shrike, the redcrested korhaan and many other species.

Walks and trails A beautiful picnic area in the savannah woodland south of Klipvoor Dam is the starting point for several trails that include a climb up Pitjane Koppie and an amble along the Moretele River. The trails vary from 1 km to 4 km.

Game drives Some 100 km of gravel roads, accessing Moretele, Pitjane and Phuduphudu campsites, offer excellent game-viewing opportunities. The drives bypass the scenic Mogoshane Hills, and track the western perimeter of the Klipvoor Dam and the Moretele River as it winds through the western part of the reserve.

Summer (in the early morning and late afternoon) is the best time for viewing game. Less obvious species to watch out for are Cape clawless otter, Cape fox, seven species of mongoose, caracal, genet, baboon and vervet monkey.

Where to stay There are three rest camps in the park.

MORETELE CAMP This camp, beautifully situated in the shade on the banks of the Moretele River, offers accommodation in 10 fully furnished safari tents (two beds and a stretcher in each) and 10 campsites for visitors with their own tents or caravans. Facilities here include ablution blocks (with washing-up facilities, hot showers and flush toilets) and a braai area. Bring your own food, cooking and eating utensils, firewood or charcoal.

Borakalalo National Park at a glance

Locality:	60 km north of Brits.
Number of camps:	Three.
Game drives:	60 km of autotrails on gravel.
Trails:	Variety of self-guided trails.
Other attractions:	Angling in Klipvoor Dam.
Amenities:	Shop at entrance gate supplying basic provisions.
Accommodation:	**Moretele Camp** offers 10 furnished safari tents and 10 camping sites; **Phuduphudu Camp** has four safari tents; **Pitjane Campsite** has 20 camping sites.
Booking address:	Golden Leopard Resorts, PO Box 6651, Rustenburg 0300, tel (014) 555-6135.
When to go:	Summertime (October–March) is the best for game-viewing.
What to take with you:	Food and general provisions, torch, binoculars, camera, charcoal.
How to get there:	From Brits drive north on the R511 towards Thabazimbi. After 60 km turn right at the 'Leeupoort' signpost, drive 6 km, then turn right at the 'Klipvoordam' signpost. Follow the Borakalalo signposts to the reserve.
Nearest doctor:	Brits.
Open:	September–March: 05:00–19:00; April–August: 06:00–18:30.
Special precautions:	Take care on game trails — there are white rhinos in the park.

Tips for travellers

- The shop at the gate supplies fishing equipment, tinned food, other provisions, cold drinks, beer and curios.
- Borakalalo welcomes day visitors.

The camp is close to some ideal game drives and walks, including a tranquil ramble along the banks of the Moretele River.

PHUDUPHUDU CAMP You could almost pass by this camp without noticing it, so well is it concealed in the thick savannah woodland surrounding the Moretele River. Look closer and you'll see four safari-style tents, with access to a modest swimming pool, outdoor boma and a reed-walled structure enclosing flush toilets and hot-water showers. There's also an attractive rock-walled lounge/diningroom and patio, and a fully equipped kitchen. Cooking utensils and bedding are provided, but you must bring your own food and do your own cooking. Each tent has two beds and a stretcher.

PITJANE CAMPSITE Lying along the north shore of the Klipvoor Dam, at the base of Pitjane Koppie, this campsite accommodates 20 camp tents, each with its own braai area. Bring your own tents and provisions (including firewood, available at the gate shop). The camp is not as cosy or private as Phuduphudu, and because it is frequented mainly by weekend anglers, seeking the rich harvest of kurper, carp, barbel, makriel and yellowfish in the dam, it has less of the wildlife appeal of the other camps. But it does offer the prospect of fish (kurper, tilapia or catfish) sizzling on the braai, or the chance to go on a controlled canoe trail. Boating and swimming are not allowed in the dam, and fishing licences (available at the gate) are required. Bring your own fishing tackle. For your ablutions, Pitjane has a reed-walled enclosure with flush toilets and hot-water showers.

CEDERBERG WILDERNESS AREA

Silver streams winding through secret valleys, waterfalls cascading over fern-clad rocks, mysterious caves buried in the mountains, crystalline pools that invite exploration. Such is the magic and the radiance of the Cederberg Wilderness Area, one of the truly wild places of Southern Africa.

Extending from the Middelberg Pass at Citrusdal to just north of the Pakhuis Pass near Clanwilliam, about 220 km north of Cape Town, the Cederberg covers 71 000 ha of mountainous terrain — an extension of the Cape Fold Mountains.

Many visitors are struck by the sheer, desolate beauty of the Cederberg's lonely mountain peaks; the phantomlike presence of trees gnarled by age; the silent aura of timelessness; and the corridors of flowers that fringe the many rivers. But perhaps the greatest attraction of the Cederberg is the bizarre formations of its rocks. Over the centuries, wind and rain have sculpted extraordinary shapes out of the sandstone, and today these stand as hallowed landmarks, attracting mountaineers, hikers, photographers and nature-lovers, who trek kilometres to marvel at their majesty.

The classic rock formations include a fantastic 30-m cleft called the Wolfberg Cracks, a 20-m-high pillar of rock known as the Maltese Cross, and the Wolfberg Arch, whose oxide-tinged flanks reflect a rare radiance in the mountain sun.

Each of these formations is accessible via a day walk from one of the farms in the area. In keeping with the tradition of wilderness areas in Southern Africa, the length of your hike depends entirely on when you want to stop. But be sure to take along a forestry map (available at Algeria Forest Station) and a compass before you set out.

The flora Another major attraction for nature-lovers is the serene beauty of the indigenous fynbos which covers the mountains and valleys. The Cederberg mountains were named after the Clanwilliam cedar, which grows only in this region, and which teeters on the brink of extinction — thanks to its wanton destruction by early settlers, who used it for furniture and telephone poles, among other things. Today the Department of Nature Conservation has set aside some 5 000 ha as a cedar sanctuary and hundreds of these trees are being propagated by seed here.

Heaths, ericas and proteas abound in the wilderness area; among the more treasured botanical delights is the pure-white snow protea which flourishes above the snowline in its sole habitat on earth.

More commonly seen species of fynbos are laurel proteas, blazing red rocket pincushions, silky conebush, sand olive and yellow daisies.

Another interesting protea species is the waboom, or 'wagon tree', so named by the pioneering Voortrekkers for its thick, tough branches which were used to make wheels for their wagons.

Down in the gorges and ravines huge yellowwood trees tower above other local species — red and white els, hard-pear and

The stealthy hunter of the heathlands

The African wild cat stalks with a cheetah-like gait through the grass- and heathlands of the Cederberg in search of its favourite prey: rats or mice. Suddenly it halts, crouches down on quivering hindfeet, then pounces upon a multimammate mouse nibbling unawares on an insect.

Sharp canines sink into the rodent's neck, instantly wedging the vertebrae apart and severing the spinal cord. The cat holds grimly on to the neck of its victim for a full minute, keeping a cautious watch behind it for signs of other predators. Then, securing a better hold on the mouse's neck, the cat walks towards its lair, the limp body of its victim swinging between its front legs.

The lair is a deep recess on the near-vertical face of a rocky krantz, and only the wild cat can gain access to it, springing along narrow ledges with its dextrous padded feet.

Seen for the first time, the African wild cat could be confused with a domesticated tabby cat, but its tail is shorter and its legs are proportionally longer. The backs of the ears are a reddish brown, while the tabby's are grey.

Wild cats are known to interbreed with domestic cats in some rural parts of Southern Africa, and are sometimes reared as domestic pets after being picked up in the wild.

In his book *The Mammals of the Southern African Subregion* the late Reay Smithers reports that the offspring of wild cats cross-bred with domestic cats do not carry the tell-tale reddish marking at the backs of the ears by which pure-bred African wild cats can be identified immediately.

Tip for travellers

Day walkers and overnight hikers require permits to enter the Cederberg Wilderness Area. Reservations may be made four months in advance. Because of the area's popularity and the limit on numbers, it is advisable to book as early as possible.

Cape beech. Higher up, flowering red disas flank the streams and plateaus.

Wildlife You are unlikely to see great numbers of animals in the Cederberg, but keep an eye open for baboons, dassies and such smaller antelope species as steenbok, grysbok, grey rhebuck and klipspringer. Although caracal, wild cat and leopard prey on Cape hares and other small mammals, hunting is usually nocturnal, so you're unlikely to see them. If you have a spoor guide with you, watch out for the tracks of porcupines, Cape clawless otters, honey badgers, grey mongooses, striped polecats and Cape foxes.

Tributaries of the Olifants River, which flow through the wilderness area, are home to eight of South Africa's indigenous fish species, including Clanwilliam yellowfish, Clanwilliam redfin minnow and the fiery redfin minnow.

A word of warning: the 16 species of snake found here include the potentially

Cederberg Wilderness Area at a glance

Locality: Western Cape, about 200 km north of Cape Town.

Climate: Summers are warm (up to 40 °C) and dry, with prevailing southeasterly winds; winters cold and wet. Most of the rain falls between May and September, and it often snows on the higher ground.

Number of camps: Two.

Trails: Choose your own trail for a wilderness adventure unequalled in South Africa.

Other attractions: San rock art, photography.

Amenities: None, except for natural swimming pools.

Accommodation: **Algeria** has 46 camping and caravan sites and two bungalows; **Kliphuis** in the north has camping and caravan sites.

Booking address: Department of Nature Conservation, Private Bag X1, Citrusdal 7340, tel (02331) 7-0783.

When to go: Recommended times to visit the Cederberg are spring, summer and autumn.

What to take with you: Camping gear, cooking utensils, food, sleeping bags, tents and water (in summer).

How to get there: Drive north from Citrusdal along the N7 for 21 km. Turn right and follow the road signposted Algeria, for about 10 km.

Nearest doctor: Citrusdal, 31 km away.

Nearest petrol: Citrusdal.

Open: 24 hours a day.

Special precautions: When hiking through the Cederberg wear thick, strong hiking boots, and be alert to the presence of snakes — particularly puffadders in spring and summer. Hikers should take a basic first-aid kit for treatment of bites, stings and scratches.

lethal berg adder and the puffadder, and the black spitting cobra.

Birdlife Of the 100 bird species in the Cederberg, 81 are fynbos dwellers. The vibrant colours of orangebreasted, redbreasted and malachite sunbirds blend with the more gentle colours of flowering proteas in winter and spring. The variety of raptors include black eagles, jackal buzzards and rock kestrels.

Getting around The centre of the Cederberg, and chief departure point for hikers, is the Algeria Forest Station, a charming, reclusive camping site fringed by trees at the edge of a river, and dominated by the mountain sentinels of Protea Peak, Vensterberg, Algeria Peak and Uitkyk Peak (for access, see the 'At a glance' box). Travel in the Cederberg is on foot only, but guides or donkeys may be hired to help you get around. Hikers may choose any route they like and wander at will, overnighting in the mountain hut or cave of their choice.

A number of scenically spectacular trails radiate from Algeria, the most popular of which is the two-day hike to the delightful Crystal Pool and back. On the way, hikers may stop over at the scenic waterfall at Helsekloof, just above Algeria, sleep over at Crystal Pool, or put sleeping bags down at the hut nearby. Physical fitness is essential for this hike, which takes you up some rugged and physically demanding terrain.

Other popular hikes include the one-day hike from Sanddrif to the Wolfberg Cracks and Arch; the hike to the Maltese Cross; and (for those who have a head for heights) the summit of Sneeuberg — at 2 027 m, the highest peak in the Cederberg.

From the top there are breathtaking views of the Cederberg, extending as far as Table Mountain 150 km away.

In the northern Cederberg a superb hike is the triangular, three-day trail which begins and ends at Kliphuis Campsite on the Pakhuis Pass. You may overnight at Heuningvlei stable, or at a cave near Dwarsrivier blockhouse.

Two shorter (two and three hours), but equally attractive, hikes are at Nuwerust in the southeastern part of the Cederberg. The accommodation at Nuwerust is basic, and hikers must take their own sleeping bag and provisions.

For conservation and hiking purposes, the Cederberg has been subdivided into three distinct blocks of 24 000 ha each, with each block allocated a maximum of 50 people per day (each group is limited to a maximum of 12 and a minimum of two people per day).

Permits for hiking in the Cederberg are available from the Nature Conservator's office at Algeria.

Rock art Among the earliest known inhabitants of the Cederberg were San (Bushman) hunter-gatherers and Khoikhoi (Hottentot) pastoralists. The former left a rich legacy of rock paintings on the rocky overhangs and in the sandstone caves reflecting wildlife that inhabited the area. The paintings date back between 300 and 6 000 years.

Bushmanskloof Wilderness Reserve

This beautiful reserve, 270 km north of Cape Town in the foothills of the Cederberg, is home to the world's largest natural gallery of San rock art dating back around 6 000 years. Some 125 well-preserved sites lie among the granite peaks and kloofs of the reserve, declared a World Heritage Site for its contribution to nature conservation.

The reserve consists of plains, kloofs, waterfalls and prehistoric rock formations and is home to five different botanical communities.

Visitors are accommodated in 10 elegant thatched lodges that overlook rolling lawns and gardens on the banks of the Boontjies River.

All the lodges have designer *en suite* bathrooms, underfloor heating to combat the cold Cape winters, air-conditioning and mini bar fridges. Buffet-style lunches and three-course dinners are served in the diningroom or around the campfire.

The Homestead has a lounge, bar, diningroom, library, billiard room and sauna, and a natural rock swimming pool.

Game drives take visitors among roving populations of gemsbok, eland, red hartebeest, black wildebeest, rhebok and springbok and chacma baboons, while predators include aardwolf and bat-eared foxes. Another attraction is the profusion of wild flowers which bloom between August and October.

Those looking for a bit of physical exertion will find some excellent mountain climbing, mountain biking and abseiling. Afterwards you can cool off in the numerous rocky pools and waterfalls so characteristic of the region.

For booking details write to Bushmanskloof Wilderness Reserve, PO Box 53405, Kenilworth 7945, tel (021) 797-0990.

De Hoop Nature Reserve

At the southern tip of the African continent, between the rolling wheatlands of the southern Cape and the shimmering waters of the Indian Ocean, lies one of the most diverse of nature's secret sanctuaries — De Hoop Nature Reserve.

Covering an area of 36 000 ha, with a marine reserve extending 5 km out to sea, the reserve includes a huge, landlocked vlei, limestone hills, massive sand-dunes and the Potberg mountain range.

Wildlife This isn't elephant, lion or hippo country, and you won't find Land Rovers crashing through the bush in search of game. But you will certainly come close to touching the very pulse of nature in the extraordinary wealth of the reserve's plants and flowers, the huge population of waterbirds that thrive on its wetlands, and the wealth of smaller mammals that inhabit the reserve.

But for those who love the sea, the real thrill of De Hoop is the sight of the southern right whales that cruise in the marine reserve between Skipskop and Cape Infanta in the north.

To stand upon the ivory dunes at Koppie Alleen, the southwesterly wind blowing in your face, and to watch these beautiful leviathans heave their massive frames out of the water in an eruption of salt and spray, is truly one of the most unforgettable wildlife experiences in Africa, if not the world.

The marine reserve of De Hoop is one of the world's premier calving grounds for southern right whales, and the time to see them in their greatest numbers is between July and November each year, after their migration to our shores from sub-Antarctic waters.

For those who have sampled tranquil evenings at the fireside on the edge of the vlei, watched the ghostly shadows of unknown animals flitting beneath the broad canvas of stars outside their rondavel, or heard the chilling shriek of black oystercatchers skimming along the shore, De Hoop is a very special place.

The 16-km-long vlei is at the heart of the reserve, and is an oasis for a large percentage of the 260 bird species found here. They include greater flamingoes, Cape shovellers, yellowbilled ducks, redbilled and Cape teals, Egyptian geese and South African shelducks. Other waterbirds you're likely to see from your rondavel or campsite are grey herons, egrets, coots and cormorants, as well as two resident pairs of African fish eagles. Near Windhoek, at the northern end of the vlei, a large cave serves as home to five species of insectivorous bats. It has been estimated that these bats consume more than 410 kg of moths and mosquitoes every night!

Inland, away from the vlei, sugarbirds and sunbirds feed off the nectar-rich blooms of proteas and ericas; while up on the rockfaces of the Potberg range there are 15 breeding pairs of the endangered Cape vulture — the only regular breeding colony of the species in the winter rainfall region of South Africa.

Down at the coast — just a few minutes' drive from your bungalow or camping site — you may stand on the shifting dunes of Koppie Alleen and see dolphins frolicking in the turquoise waters that have eroded the sandstone buttresses into weird and wonderful shapes. Hollows have been scoured into the sandstone ledges, and

De Hoop Nature Reserve at a glance

Locality:	Southern Cape, near Bredasdorp.
Climate:	Mediterranean, with mild winters and warm summers. Annual rainfall is 380 mm (August being the wettest month). The prevailing winds in summer are southeasterly and southwesterly.
Number of camps:	One.
Game drives:	There are various game drives around the reserve, and one leading down to the sea at Koppie Alleen.
Trails:	Vlei Trail (10 km); Potberg Trail (10 km); Klipspringer Trail (5 km); Whale Trail (five days). Mountain Bike Trail (three days).
Other attractions:	Birdwatching, coastal walks, exploring the flora, snorkelling, watching the whales.
Amenities:	Firewood supplied. No restaurant or shop. Nearest shop is 15 km away.
Accommodation:	Four-bed rondavels (stove, fridge, ablution facilities). Bring bedding, kitchen utensils and food. Camping sites.
Booking address:	The Manager, De Hoop Nature Reserve, Private Bag X16, Bredasdorp 7280, tel (028) 542-1126.
When to go:	Between July and December when the whales are there.
What to take with you:	Bedding, kitchen utensils, food, binoculars, diving mask and snorkel.
How to get there:	From Caledon take the R316 to Bredasdorp; then switch to the R319. The signpost to De Hoop is about 9 km further on.
Nearest doctor:	At Bredasdorp, 50 km away.
Nearest petrol:	At Ouplaas, 15 km away.
Open:	Between 07:00–18:00 daily (report to the office before 16:00 on the day of arrival). Nominal fee payable per person and per vehicle.
Special precautions:	When hiking, be on the lookout for snakes, particularly puffadders in October and November. Take great care when swimming in the sea.

these harbour a magical world of marine animals — sea anemones, starfish, mussels, limpets and hermit crabs. In the deeper pools you'll find alikreukel and sea urchins, red rock crabs and octopuses. On the beach, damara terns and curlew sandpipers scurry along the sand; while seagulls, albatrosses and cormorants form flying convoys above the sea.

Take your swimming costume, and a diving mask and snorkel along — there are plenty of tidal pools for you to explore. Remember, however, that parts of this coastline can be very dangerous, so be careful when you're in the water.

At the core of De Hoop's success as a natural sanctuary is the abundance of fynbos — a distinctive type of vegetation that includes proteas, ericas, heaths, and bulb- and reedlike plants — which supports a variety of birds, insects and mammals, of which there are 86 species at De Hoop. These include caracals, Cape foxes, yellow mongooses, baboons, Cape mountain zebras, eland, bontebok, grey rhebok, steenbok and duiker.

De Hoop also hosts a teeming community of reptiles ranging from puffadders, Cape cobras and tree-snakes to less poisonous varieties such as whip snakes, herald snakes and skaapstekers.

Where to stay There are four-bed rondavels, with stove, fridge and electricity and ablution facilities. Bring your own bedding, kitchen utensils and food. There are also sites for camping.

Trails De Hoop is a hiker's paradise, and there is no shortage of options: The 10-km Vlei Trail provides unlimited bird-watching opportunities; the circular 10-km Potberg Trail takes you to the summit of Potberg Mountain; and the Klipspringer Trail (5 km) leads to a small cave where you may see a Cape vulture. Highly recommended is the five-day Whale Trail, along the coast towards Cape Infanta.

A more recent addition to De Hoop's attractions is the Mountain Bike Trail in the eastern part of the reserve. This three-day trail takes you over rugged terrain to Cupidoskraal (11 km), an overnight hut from which you can launch day trips to the coast along demarcated jeep tracks. There's accommodation for 12 people at Cupidoskraal, as well as a gas stove, indoor fireplace, lighting and pots and pans. Bring your own bedding and eating utensils along.

There are five main bike trails, some more arduous than others. They are: the Vaalkrans Route, the Lekkerwater Route, the Hamerkop Route, the Stilgat Route and the Noetzie Route, all of which provide stunning sea views.

Between July and December you'll also see southern right whales basking offshore.

GIANT'S CASTLE GAME RESERVE

The great basalt wall of the Drakensberg erupts from the undulating hillsides of KwaZulu-Natal like a fearsome giant, trespassing in some gentle paradise. Serrated peaks more than 3 km high pierce the clouds above a wilderness of plateaus, rolling grasslands and valleys incised by icy streams.

Here in the Giant's Castle Game Reserve the Drakensberg reveals itself as a 35-km-long wall of rock, dominated in the southwest by Giant's Castle itself, a 3 314-m mass of basalt that towers above the rest.

The brooding presence of this peak inspired fear in the African communities that lived in the valleys below. They believed that Giant's Castle's vicious thunderstorms and unrelenting barrages of lightning were signs of the mountain's anger. So they called it *iNtabayaikonjwa* — 'the mountain at which one must not point'.

Today Giant's Castle is a breathtaking beacon that draws visitors from all over the world to the beautiful game reserve at its feet, and to the extraordinary array of walks and trails that explore some of the finest mountain scenery in Africa. Apart from its natural splendour, this part of the Drakensberg (Dragon's Mountain) range holds one of the richest stores of San art on the continent.

Giant's Castle Game Reserve covered just 7 000 ha when it was proclaimed in 1903, but additions of land over the years, including the Injasuti area, have brought the total area to 34 600 ha.

The reserve is situated in western KwaZulu-Natal, just 63 km west of Mooi River, at the headwaters of the Bushman's and Little Tugela rivers. It is bordered in the west by Lesotho, and ranges in height from 1 300 m to 3 280 m.

From the air, the reserve reveals itself in three distinct levels, ranging through the forested valleys and gorges of the Lower Berg, the undulating grasslands of the Middle Berg; and the icy upper reaches of the High Berg, where only the hardiest heaths and shrubs can survive.

The valleys and gorges are fringed with luxuriant forests of yellowwood and ironwood, white stinkwood and Cape chestnut which, in turn, attract a teeming population of riverine birds.

The grasslands are peppered with dense stands of fynbos and proteas, among which are *Protea dracomontana, P. roupelliae* and *P. caffra*, with its attractive, goblet-shaped flower heads.

Wildlife The most commonly seen mammals are the 10 species of antelope: eland (about 600), blesbok, reedbuck, mountain reedbuck (300), grey rhebok (more than 400), red hartebeest (21), grey duiker, oribi, bushbuck and klipspringer. Hikers, however, are also likely to see baboons (in troops of up to 30), rock dassies, blackbacked jackals and any one of the three mongoose species. Less conspicuous are the nocturnal cats — servals, African wild cats and caracals.

Hikers should take heed that reptiles in the reserve include the highly venomous puffadder and berg adder, as well as the yellowbellied house snake and the spotted skaapsteker.

Birdlife There are about 174 species of bird at Giant's Castle, the most prized of which is the bearded vulture, or lammergeier, whose home range in Southern Africa is exclusive to the mountainous

Tips for travellers

- **Thunderstorms in this part of the Drakensberg are sudden and violent. Be prepared for a sudden change in weather conditions. If you're overnighting at one of the mountain huts, be prepared for extreme cold in winter.**
- **Detailed maps of the reserve, and of available walks, can be obtained at the superintendent's office at Giant's Castle Camp.**
- **Vehicles may only travel on the access road to the camps. Other travel in the park is by foot or on horseback.**
- **Angling is allowed. Enquire at the camp superintendent's office.**
- **Before embarking on a walk, sign the camp's walks register or the mountain rescue register.**

regions of KwaZulu-Natal and Lesotho. You may see these graceful birds soaring on the thermals above the main camp, or watch them feeding at the Vulture Restaurant, established by the KwaZulu-Natal Nature Conservation Services near Bamboo Hollow, east of the camp. On Saturday and Sunday mornings between May and September, bones are laid out and the vultures come down to feast.

There's also an abundance of black eagles, Cape vultures, martial, longcrested and crowned eagles, peregrine and lanner falcons, yellowbilled and blackshouldered kites and three species of harrier.

The grasslands support grass warblers, francolins, quails and longclaws, while in the forests you may spot one of five species of owl, woodpecker or robin.

Feasting off the nectar of proteas which grace the steep slopes are a procession of multicoloured sunbirds, and the less conspicuous sugarbird. Along the rivers you'll see the beautiful malachite kingfisher eyeing the waterways for a tasty morsel, or the longtailed widow.

The immediate vicinity of the hutted camp provides ideal birdwatching opportunities, especially in spring and summer, when dozens of species start nesting among the undergrowth and trees.

Where to stay There are two main hutted camps: Giant's Castle Camp (Main Camp) in the south, and Injasuti Camp on the northern border of the reserve. Giant's Castle Camp offers accommodation consisting of four self-contained cottages with kitchens, 13 bungalows (four four-bed, one three-bed and eight two-bed) with bathrooms, and Giant's Castle Lodge. Accommodating seven people at a time, this is probably the most luxurious of all the KwaZulu-Natal Nature Conservation Services lodges. The bungalows access a communal kitchen.

INJASUTI CAMP The imposing turrets of Cathkin Peak, Monk's Cowl and Champagne Castle tower above this lovely camp lying between the Injasuti (Little Tugela) and Cowl-Fork rivers.

Lethal reptile of the grasslands

Hikers in the Giant's Castle Game Reserve, and throughout South Africa, should be wary of puffadders which frequent this reserve — they are one of the most venomous kinds of snake on the continent. And what makes them even more dangerous is their habit of lying dead still.

If a puffadder happens to be lying on a footpath or mountain track, hikers have a fair chance of stepping on it and getting a series of retaliatory strikes.

When a puffadder bites, its long fangs inject lethal cytotoxic venom into its victim, causing huge tissue destruction and bleeding, which results in death if medical help is not sought and received immediately. Death is often caused by shock resulting from loss of blood.

The colour of the snake ranges from light brown to black, with chevrons across the tail and back. Individuals from the Cape and KwaZulu-Natal have brighter markings — usually orange, yellow or black.

A protection against this and other snakes in Southern Africa's wildlife sanctuaries is a pair of thick hiking boots.

The camp offers 17 six-bedded cabins with two bedrooms, and two eight-bedded cabins, each with their own braai area. Visitors cook their own food, but a cleaning service is available.

Injasuti also has a campsite with access to an ablution block and braai facilities.

There's also an open campsite at Hillside, which offers trail riders an attractive overnight stop in beautiful surroundings. Here campers may revel in the majestic vistas of the wilderness in the northern part of Giant's Castle Game Reserve.

MOUNTAIN HUTS Visitors walking the longer trails that radiate from Giant's Castle Camp may overnight at any one of the four mountain huts. Giant's Hut, at the base of Giant's Castle Peak, is an easy 10-km walk from the rest camp, and accommodates eight people; Bannerman's Hut, about 8,5 km from the main camp, also accommodates eight people; Meander Hut, just 5 km from the rest camp, has a beautiful view overlooking Meander Valley. Centenary Hut is on the 2 200 m contour level. Mountain huts must be booked in advance through the KwaZulu-Natal Nature Conservation Services (see *Booking address*, 'At a glance' box).

Rich legacy of the San The Giant's Castle area used to be the exclusive domain of the San, known anthropologically as hunter-gatherers. For centuries they occupied the caves and crevices of Giant's Castle's mountain ramparts in summer, vacating these in winter to hunt eland and other antelope in the valleys.

The scattered San community here is believed to have numbered no more than a few hundred. The arrival of Nguni and European settlers in the 19th century seriously threatened the livelihood of the San, and eventually they had to flee.

However, they left behind a rich legacy — more than 50 known sites and 5 000 individual examples of San rock art. The best places to view these paintings are at Main Caves, where there are 546 individual paintings, and at Battle Cave in the Injasuti Valley, north of the reserve (750 paintings).

Other artefacts include metal and stone arrowheads, and bone fragments of animals and the San themselves.

Main Caves Site Museum A former San shelter 2 km southwest of the rest camp has been converted into a fascinating museum exhibiting lifelike San models, artefacts of tools and weapons, an open hearth and clothes worn by the San.

Walks and trails From *Main Camp* there are at least 20 lovely day walks, ranging from 3 km to 26 km. Among them are the walks to:

- Col. Durnford's Camp, the Main Caves and the Bushman Museum (3,2 km; 2 hours). The Main Caves open on the hour every hour between 09:00 and 15:00 every day, including Sundays and public holidays.
- Main Caves Forest (5 km; 2 hours). This route passes through a beautiful forest, bypassing San paintings and clear, deep pools. Take your bathing costume along.
- Bergview Walk (5 km; 2 hours). This ramble offers some of the best views of the Drakensberg at Giant's Castle.
- Giant's Pass and Giant's Castle (19 km; 8 hours). A fairly tough climb takes you to the edge of the escarpment for breathtaking views of the reserve.
- Langalibalele Pass (26 km; 8 hours). An historically fascinating walk, which takes hikers past the graves of British soldiers and local tribesmen who were killed during an engagement at the top of the pass in the Langalibalele Rebellion of 1873.

Injasuti Camp is the starting point for 10 demarcated walks, including a guided trail to Battle Cave and the Injasuti Valley, where San rock art adorns the walls of the caves. For more details of these and other walks, ask the camp superintendent for the booklet on the Giant's Castle Game Reserve.

Hikers may overnight in the Lower Injasuti, Junction or Fergie's caves, but must reserve a cave when the booking is made.

Horse trails Half-day, guided rides, departing from the Hillside section of the reserve, are available on a daily basis, depending on the weather. Longer, two- to five-day pony trails through the spectacular scenery of the northern part of the Drakensberg are also available. To book, contact the KwaZulu-Natal Nature Conservation Services headquarters in Pietermaritzburg (see *Booking address,* 'At a glance' box).

Fishing The rivers and streams of the KwaZulu-Natal Drakensberg teem with brown and rainbow trout, and the Giant's Castle area, particularly the Injasuti River, is no exception. Fishing permits are obtainable from the camp superintendent, and are renewable on a daily basis.

Giant's Castle Game Reserve at a glance

Locality: Western KwaZulu-Natal on the Lesotho border.

Climate: Summers mild to cool at night. Winters very cold with frost, and snow at the higher altitudes. About 1 100 mm of rain falls a year, mostly in the form of thunderstorms between September and April.

Number of camps: Two camps, one campsite.

Game drives: There are no game drives.

Trails: Dozens of walking and horse-riding trails are available.

Other attractions: Photography, magnificent scenic vistas.

Accommodation: **Main Camp:** four cottages, 13 bungalows (four four-bed, one three-bed and eight two-bed) with bathrooms, and a lodge; **Injasuti:** 17 six-bedded cabins, and two eight-bed cabins. Campsites at Injasuti and Hillside.

Booking address: KwaZulu-Natal Nature Conservation Services, PO Box 13069, Cascades 3202, tel (0331) 845-1000.

When to go: September to March, when birdlife is at its best.

What to take with you: Hikers should take a contour map of the area, basic first-aid kit, good hiking boots, anorak, hat, torch, whistle, waterbottle, basic provisions (nuts, raisins, chocolates, biltong).

How to get there: Injasuti: from the north, turn off at the Central Berg Resorts interchange, travel into Estcourt and take the Ntabamhlope Road (at the intersection of Connor and Lorne streets). Follow the signs to Giant's Castle. From the south enter Mooi River village at the toll plaza, from where the road to the reserve is clearly signposted.

Nearest doctor: Mooi River or Estcourt (69 km and 63 km).

Nearest petrol: At the main entrance gate.

Open: 1 October–31 March: 05:00–19:00; 1 April–30 September: 06:00–18:00.

Special precautions: Hikers should be on the lookout for snakes.

Golden Gate Highlands National Park

The towering sandstone buttress of Golden Gate forms a radiant beacon in the valley of the Little Caledon River, a land of bizarre sandstone sentinels that mark the Free State's only national park — a spectacular retreat for hiking, birdwatching, game drives and horseback riding.

Lying between the Rooiberge and the Maluti Mountains, and bordered by the Caledon River in the south, the Golden Gate Highlands National Park covers 11 630 ha of rolling mountain landscapes, dominated by the gold and copper cliffs of Clarens sandstone.

This is an enigmatic countryside, whose eroded vaults of mud- and siltstone have yielded fossils of mammal-like reptiles that stalked the land 200 million years ago.

Very much later prehistoric people inhabited the area, and were followed by bands of San. Stone-Age implements and beautiful galleries of rock art, inscribed on the walls of caves in the area, testify to the presence of humans long before Europeans arrived in Southern Africa. The rock paintings also show that huge populations of game roamed the valley of the Little Caledon several hundred years ago.

James Chapman, a traveller here in 1849, wrote of hundreds of thousands of blesbok, black wildebeest, springbok and zebras passing by in front of his wagon.

The days of the vast game populations were numbered, however: white hunters colonising the area in the 19th century shot out so much game that this part of the Free State came to be known as 'Riemland' — the land of thongs — a reference to the enormous number of hides and skins stripped from the carcasses of slaughtered animals. During 1871 alone, a total of 311 000 wildebeest hides were shipped to Durban, and in 1866 a Kroonstad firm exported 152 000 blesbok hides.

One of the early settlers in the area was J N R van Reenen who, seeing the flaming sandstone buttress in the setting sun, christened it Golden Gate.

The name stuck, and in 1963 it became the official title of the Free State's first national park, whose area has nearly trebled since then.

Visitors entering the park encounter a sylvan setting of French poplars and weeping willows flanking the Little Caledon River. In autumn the golden hues of the sandstone ramparts are accentuated by the burnished leaves of the poplars, often found near dense stands of ouhout, the most common tree in the park. In summer veld flowers — watsonias, fire lilies, arum lilies and red-hot pokers — bring an explosion of colour to the countryside, which supports more than 50 species of grass.

Wildlife Of the hundreds of thousands of black wildebeest that roamed the Free State's grasslands before the advent of Europeans, just 660 survived by the end of the 19th century. Today, the descendants of these imperilled survivors find perfect sanctuary at Golden Gate. These, and Southern Africa's largest antelope, the eland, graze along the slopes of the valleys, in the company of mountain reedbuck, blesbok, springbok, grey rhebok, oribi, buffaloes and Burchell's zebras. If you're following one of the many hiking trails (see overleaf) you are likely to encounter chacma

Tip for travellers

The nearest regional office of the Automobile Association of South Africa (Head Office in Johannesburg: tel (011) 799-1000) will supply road maps and details of road conditions in the area.

baboons, mongooses, dassies and, if you're lucky, a Cape clawless otter. Less often seen are the wild cats, blackbacked jackals, genets and porcupines.

The large dassie population ensures that black eagles, which soar majestically above the sandstone turrets, are quite abundant here, and they share the thermals with bearded vultures (lammergeiers), pallid and black harriers and the rare Cape vulture.

The park's 140 species of bird also include purple herons, blackshouldered kites, rock kestrels, lesser kestrels, Swainson's and greywing francolins, Klaas's cuckoo, giant and malachite kingfishers, red bishops and golden bishops.

Vulture restaurants and hide Unique sightings of seldom-seen raptors are possible at a new bird hide opened in the mountains at Golden Gate in 1993. The hide complements five different vulture restaurants where raptors are fed, and visitors may see as many as 150 birds feeding at a time.

Game drives There are two game-viewing drives, which take you into the mountains, offering panoramic views of the highlands, the Maluti Mountains and the Drakensberg. Guided tours are laid on during holidays (booking at Brandwag reception office), and environmental education courses (one to five days) can be organised through the Pretoria booking office.

Trails The 30-km Rhebok Hiking Trail is a lovely two-day hike that meanders across mountain streams and grassy kloofs to the park's highest mountain tops. The first day's hike is about seven hours, and ends at the overnight stop, Oudehoutskloof Hut, where there are beds for a maximum of 18 hikers. There's a small kitchen with a gas stove but no bathroom facilities. Hikers must take their own sleeping bags, food, cooking and eating utensils and, in summer, a bathing costume.

The second day of the trail takes hikers to the top of Generaalskop, at 2 757 m the highest point in the park. The walk back to Glen Reenen Rest Camp is about two hours.

Booking for the trail may be done through the National Parks Board (see 'At a glance' box).

A variety of other trails, ranging from one to five hours, radiates outwards from the Brandwag and Glen Reenen rest camps. Of these the Wodehouse Kop Trail from Glen Reenen is fairly strenuous, and hikers should report their departure and return times at the Glen Reenen shop. Other trails from Glen Reenen take hikers to the sandstone formation of Mushroom Rocks, and through a ravine known as Echo Ravine. Other interesting walking trails are the 20-minute ramble from the Gladstone administrative centre in the west to a cave with some excellent San paintings, and a two-and-a-half-hour hike to Cathedral Cave.

Horseback trails Several options are available for horseback trails from the stables at the Gladstone administrative centre, of which the longest trail is two days. The most popular, however, is the Rhebokspruit Trail, which leaves daily at 14:00.

Where to stay There are two rest camps in the park: Brandwag, the main camp, and Glen Reenen.

BRANDWAG REST CAMP This complex offers single and double rooms with double beds, *en suite* shower or bathroom. There are also four-bed chalets, comprising a livingroom with two single beds, a balcony room with one double bed, kitchenette and *en suite* bathroom. The rooms and chalets are equipped with TVs and telephones. Other amenities here are a restaurant serving three meals daily, a ladies' bar, a curio shop, and such recreational facilities as snooker, tennis, table tennis, bowling and horse riding.

GLEN REENEN REST CAMP This tree-lined camp offers three- and four-bed bungalows with a loft, kitchen and *en suite* shower and toilet.

There's also an attractive camping and caravan site. A rock pool behind the shop at Glen Reenen is a refreshing place to cool off after a hike or pony ride.

Wilgenhof Youth Hostel accommodates 80 youngsters in four dormitories.

Golden Gate Highlands National Park at a glance

Locality:	Northeastern Free State, 360 km south of Johannesburg and 300 km northeast of Bloemfontein.
Climate:	Summer: warm to cool with rain; winter: cold to very cold with occasional snow. Rainfall: 800 mm per annum.
Number of camps:	Two.
Game drives:	Two game-viewing drives.
Trails:	30-km Rhebok Hiking Trail. Several one- to five-hour trails from Glen Reenen Camp.
Other attractions:	Vulture hides, swimming pool, birdwatching, tennis, bowls, horse riding.
Amenities:	Postal agency and shop at Glen Reenen Rest Camp (groceries, perishables, firewood and liquor); there's a licenced restaurant, coffee shop and ladies' bar, and a laundromat and dryer at Brandwag Rest Camp.
Accommodation:	**Brandwag Rest Camp:** four-bed chalets and single and double rooms; **Glen Reenen Rest Camp:** Four- and three-bed bungalows, and caravan and camping sites.
Booking address:	National Parks Board, PO Box 787, Pretoria 0001, tel (012) 343-1991; National Parks Board, PO Box 7400, Roggebaai 8012, tel (021) 22-2810; the Park Warden, Golden Gate Highlands National Park, Private Bag X3, Clarens 9797, tel (058) 255-0012.
When to go:	Throughout the year, but spring and autumn are exceptional for their colours.
What to take with you:	Rucksack, warm clothes, binoculars, raincoat, walking shoes, bathing costume, camera.
How to get there:	From Harrismith take the N5. Just before Bethlehem turn on to the R711 to Clarens.
Nearest doctor:	At Clarens, 20 km away.
Nearest petrol:	Available at Glen Reenen Rest Camp.
Open:	There is no gate to the park. Reception hours: Brandwag Rest Camp 07:00–20:00; Glen Reenen Rest Camp–Monday to Thursday 07:00–17:00 (summer) and 07:30–15:00 (winter); Friday and Saturday 07:00–18:00 (summer) and 07:30–17:00 (winter); Sunday 08:00–16:00 (summer) and 08:00–15:00 (winter). Visitors arriving after hours will find a note on the office door directing them to their room or chalet.
Special precautions:	While hiking, keep a low profile in the presence of wildebeest and baboons.

Greater St Lucia Wetland Park

Fringed by languid coral seas, a golden ribbon of sand sweeps northwards along the KwaZulu-Natal north coast, forming gentle bays and terraces of rock wedged between land and sea. On the eastern side of this coastal terrace, sand-dunes cloaked by stunted forests of green form a massive barrier of sand between the sea and the interior.

If you stand on top of these dunes — the highest of their kind in the world — and gaze northwards, a huge expanse of water unfolds before you, stretching endlessly towards the distant horizon. This is Lake St Lucia, the largest estuarine body of water in Southern Africa. The lake starts in the southwest as a 20-km tidal channel connected to the sea, and then opens out into a much wider body of water, some 40 km long.

Around this shallow, shimmering lake, a complex of vleis, pans, swamp forests and grasslands weave textures of green, brown, silver and gold.

This is the heart of the Greater St Lucia Wetland Park, a 275 000-ha wilderness that is the third largest wildlife sanctuary in Southern Africa, and for those who love the coast, one of the most popular.

The park, which extends roughly from Sodwana Bay (see separate entry, p. 134) and the Lower Mkuze Road in the north to Mapelane in the south, is a natural jigsaw puzzle of many pieces, and represents no less than five separate ecosystems. These include the lake; a marine conservation area extending 5 km out to sea; a wilderness area known as Mfabeni and Tewati (formerly the Eastern Shores); the reed and papyrus wetland of the Mkuze swamps in the north, and the Western Shores, a fossil shoreline more than 25 000 years old that abounds with the fossils of its earlier marine life.

This vast wilderness of water, swamps, forest, vleis and grassland was once inhabited by Iron-Age people. But the arrival of the Portuguese in the 16th century, and the incursions made by white explorers and hunters in the 19th century, had devastating effects on the wildlife populations of the area. During the first 70 years of the 19th century white hunters shot elephants *en masse* for their tusks, and wreaked havoc among populations of buffalo, black rhino and hippo.

At one stage it seemed that damage to the wildlife was irreversible. But in 1897 conservationists stepped in, and the whole lake, its islands and Mapelane became the first game reserve to be proclaimed in Africa.

Since then, bit by bit, the Greater St Lucia Wetland Park has emerged as a consolidation of separate areas: Sodwana Bay National Park was established in 1950; the Tewate Wilderness Area was transferred to the Natal Parks Board in 1987; St Lucia Marine Reserve was proclaimed in 1979, and the Maputaland Marine Reserve proclaimed in 1986.

Today the Greater St Lucia Wetland Park represents the very best of the conservation efforts of man. And although much of the area is inaccessible to visitors, the KwaZulu-Natal Nature Conservation Services has offered the public access to many of its finer treasures.

Wildlife The Greater St Lucia Wetland Park is the meeting place of tropical and temperate forms of animal and plant life, and therefore guarantees a uniqueness and richness of fauna seldom matched by other sanctuaries in Southern Africa.

For one, it has the greatest variety of amphibians in South Africa — some 36 species, including an abundance of crocodiles and hippos, and hinged terrapins and water monitor lizards in lesser numbers.

There are more than 420 species of bird, inhabiting forest, shoreline, the estuaries, lake and marshlands. The islands of Lake St Lucia are important breeding grounds for white pelicans, greyheaded gulls, spoonbills, Caspian terns and red-winged pratincoles, while the beaches will reveal their quota of black oystercatchers, sandpipers, cormorants and plovers.

One reason for the abundance of birds is the extraordinary variety of trees. More than 140 species of tree are found in the western shores forests alone. Here, among the canopies of marula, kei-apple, tamboti and Natal mahogany, you may see anything from hadeda ibis to Knysna lourie.

The variety of marine mammals is impressive: humpback, minke, southern right and sperm whales cruise the depths in the company of six species of dolphin, among them bottlenosed, Fraser's and spotted dolphins, and three species of marine turtle.

Land mammals are abundant, too, ranging from such wetland species as Cape clawless otter and water mongoose, to buffalo, black rhino, brown hyena, leopard, nyala and waterbuck. Among the reptiles are pythons and gaboon adders.

Last but not least are the smaller life forms: the fiddler crabs that scuttle along the sand between the tortuous network of roots in the mangrove forests; mudskippers that climb trees, frogs that create weird symphonies of sound along the lakeshore and its surrounding swamps; and the teeming world of marine creatures — vertebrate and invertebrate — inhabiting the intertidal zones and the deeper waters beneath the coral reefs.

Hiking trails The Greater St Lucia Wetland Park is truly a hiker's paradise, with dozens of trails, ranging from 1-km,

Compassionate crocodiles

One of the Greater St Lucia Wetland Park's more fearsome and fascinating residents is the Nile crocodile. While most other amphibians and reptiles are indifferent parents, the crocodile cares for its offspring extraordinarily well.

The female digs a nest on a sandbank above the highwater mark and deposits her clutch of eggs — numbering between 40 and 50 — and allows them to incubate for about three months.

When the eggs start hatching and the youngsters crawl out, they start yelping for their mother. She approaches, picks them up and admits them into the back of her mouth — known as the gular pouch. She then slides into the water and releases them gently.

If some of the eggs don't hatch, the male is known to pick up individual eggs and roll them between his teeth to crack them, so that the hatchling can escape.

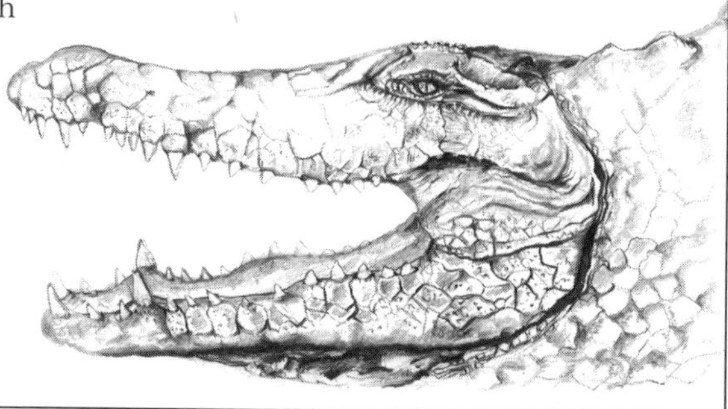

20-minute strolls around base camps to sojourns lasting several days.

One of the more adventurous trails is the three-day Lake St Lucia Wilderness Trail, which starts and ends at the base camp at Mission Rocks, 35 km north of St Lucia.

The trail leads through the beautiful hinterland of the Indian Ocean coastline and reaches the western shores of Lake Bhangazi, where trailists spend the first and last nights of the trail. The second and third nights are spent at Swate Camp on the eastern shores of Lake St Lucia, giving hikers the chance to see hippos, crocodiles and the abundant birdlife.

All equipment and catering is provided and carried by pack donkeys, leaving hikers free to walk unencumbered. The trail is available between April and September and advance booking is essential.

Other trails are the Umvube Trail at Cape Vidal, Dugandlovu and Mpophomeni trails at False Bay Park, the Mziki and Lake trails in the Eastern Shores State Forest and Nature Reserve, the Isikhova and Umkhumbe nature trails at Charter's Creek and the Umkhiwane Trail at Fanie's Island. For further details of these trails, see under the individual entries below.

Tips for travellers

- Chance encounters with hippos are possible. If you stumble upon one, stand perfectly still, then move back quietly.
- Travellers in the Greater St Lucia Wetland Park Complex are asked not to feed the monkeys, and to keep food in tents or bungalows securely stowed.
- The speed limit throughout the park is 40 km/h.
- It is dangerous to paddle or swim in the St Lucia Estuary because of sharks and crocodiles.

Where to stay First-time visitors to the park may be a bit confused by the geographic fragmentation of the region, but essentially there are six areas that have specific attractions for nature-lovers. They are:

MAPELANE NATURE RESERVE Lying just across the estuary from St Lucia Village, on the southern bank of the mouth of the Umfolozi River, Mapelane is a delightfully remote hideaway offering beautiful walks through the forests and bush, excellent skiboat and surf fishing, and magnificent opportunities to see many of its 200 species of bird. Access to Mapelane is via a narrow, sandy road, unsuitable for vehicles with a low clearance, but once you've got there, you'll find a lovely, small bay and perfect tranquillity. New trails are being developed here.

Mapelane offers 10 self-catering log cabins within the dune forest, and 45 campsites. There is no fuel, and the nearest shop is 50 km away.

ST LUCIA ESTUARY The village of St Lucia Estuary lies on the eastern bank of the channel that joins the main body of the St Lucia Estuary to the Indian Ocean. Three attractive campsites — Sugarloaf (92 sites), Iphiva (79 sites), and Eden Park (20 sites) — offer campers access to a swimming pool, shops, a hotel, banks, a library and an airstrip.

Major attractions here are deep-sea fishing trips (arranged through the St Lucia Skiboat Club), coastal fishing, crayfishing, swimming in the sea and boating in the estuary.

The *Santa Lucia*, an 80-seater launch with observation deck and bar, offers three bird- and hippo-viewing cruises across the estuary every day. The cruises last two hours and catering may be organised on request.

Highlights of a visit to the Crocodile Centre are the feeding sessions (once a week on Saturdays at 15:00) where you may see Nile crocodiles, longsnouted crocodiles and dwarf crocodiles displaying the bone-crunching power of their amazing jaws.

ST LUCIA GAME PARK Proclaimed in 1895, this small park near the Crocodile Centre has some of the densest concentrations of common reedbuck in the world, as well as larger mammal species such as blue wildebeest, Burchell's zebra, impala, sidestriped jackal and waterbuck.

A variety of self-guided trails (brochure available), meander through the dune forests, Umdoni parkland and marshes, including a 2-km walk from the Crocodile Centre which takes you down to the bank of the estuary.

Another attractive self-guided walk is the 1,5-km Gwalagwala Trail, which starts and ends at Eden Park and leads through coastal forest on the edge of the estuary.

CAPE VIDAL This attractive resort, whose main camp lies between Lake Bhangazi and the Indian Ocean, some 32 km north of the village of St Lucia, is known as the last outpost of the dedicated camper. Its remoteness, ambience of gentle forest and sea, and quality accommodation make it a favourite among visitors sampling the natural sanctuaries along the KwaZulu-Natal coast.

Accommodation is in 30 five- and eight-bed Swiss-style log cabins, with a further 50 campsites in the dune forest. The fully equipped log cabins have two bedrooms, a bathroom and shower, as well as a kitchenette.

All visitors have to bring is their own food and drink (there are no provisions at Cape Vidal). Further south there are five fishing cabins (from eight to 20 beds each), ideal for small fishing groups.

For accommodation on the wild side, Bhangazi Bush Camp, on the western shores of Lake Bhangazi, offers four two-bed units, as well as a kitchen and a lounge. The whole camp has to be booked at one time. Bookings for this camp and the fishing cabins must be made three months in advance through the KwaZulu-Natal Nature Conservation Services (see *Booking address*, 'At a glance' box).

The major attractions here are hiking (the Mvubu Trail leads from the camp through a forest to the shores of Lake Bhangazi), deep-sea fishing, scuba-diving and snorkelling. The 3-km self-guided Imboma Trail leads through the wetlands south of Lake Bhangazi.

FALSE BAY PARK Abundant game, fishing, boating, birdwatching, hiking and photography bring visitors back time and again to this lovely park flanking the western extremity of Lake St Lucia. The 3 200 ha of woodland, sand forest and grassland support 280 bird species and a variety of animals, including hippos, crocodiles, spotted hyenas, bushpigs, zebras, nyala, bushbuck, warthogs, impalas, reedbuck, red duiker and such water-loving antelope species as suni and waterbuck. You can see many of these on the park's two trails: the self-guided 16-km Dugandlovu Trail (about six hours), which gives backpackers access to the Dugandlovu Rustic Camp; and the Mpophomeni ('Waterfall') Trail — a pleasant 7 to 10-km walk suitable for individuals or families.

Along the lake's shoreline are 36 enchanting campsites, some south of Lister's Point and the rest on the north side.

The Dugandlovu Rustic Camp occupies a scenic position on the banks of the Hluhluwe River and its floodplain, and accommodates guests in four four-bed huts. Lighting is supplied by paraffin lamps, and there are bucket-showers and flush toilets as well as drinking water and firewood. Two small gas cookers and open braai places are available for cooking.

Visitors to False Bay Park must bring their own food and sleeping bags. Cooking and eating utensils are provided at the camp.

Ticks can be a problem, so check your clothing carefully after a hike.

Greater St Lucia Wetland Park at a glance

Locality:	Northern KwaZulu-Natal coast, between St Lucia Estuary and Sodwana Bay.
Climate:	Subtropical climate with hot summers (peaking January–March) and mild winters. Most rain falls in summer.
Number of camps:	Camping facilities at Mapelane, St Lucia Estuary, False Bay Park, Fanie's Island, Charter's Creek, Cape Vidal.
Trails:	A large variety of trails, including the St Lucia Wilderness Trail, a three-day excursion which starts and ends at Mission Rocks.
Other attractions:	Boating, angling, birdwatching, photography.
Amenities:	Swimming pool, shop at St Lucia Estuary.
Accommodation:	**Mapelane:** 10 self-catering log cabins and 45 campsites; **St Lucia Estuary:** three campsites, hotels; **Cape Vidal:** 30 log cabins, 50 campsites, 5 fishing cabins; **Charter's Creek:** cottage, huts; **Fanie's Island:** cottage, huts, campsite.
Booking address:	KwaZulu-Natal Nature Conservation Services, PO Box 13069, Cascades 3202, tel. (0331) 845-1000 (from nine months in advance). Campsite bookings to be made through the Officer-in-Charge: Mapelane: Private Bag St Lucia, 3936, tel (035) 590-1407; St Lucia Estuary: Private Bag, St Lucia, 3936, tel (035) 590-1340; Mfabeni and Cape Vidal: Private Bag, St Lucia 3936, tel (035) 590-9012.
When to go:	Throughout the year.
What to take with you:	Sturdy hiking boots, torch, binoculars, camera. Light clothes in summer.
How to get there:	Mapelane: turn off opposite the Kwambonambi turnoff on the Empangeni-Mtubatuba road, and drive 50 km. St Lucia Estuary: turn off the N2 at Mtubatuba, north of Empangeni, and drive east for 25 km. Cape Vidal: drive 35 km north of St Lucia Estuary on the gravel road through Eastern Shores. False Bay Park: take the turn-off to Hluhluwe on the N2. The park is 14 km east of the railway station. Fanie's Island: turn off to the camp 20 km north of Mtubatuba, then drive 12 km before turning left. The camp is 14 km further on.
Nearest doctor:	St Lucia Estuary village.
Nearest petrol:	St Lucia Estuary village.
Open:	Mapelane: 08:00–09:30, 11:00–12:30, 14:00–16:30; St Lucia Estuary: 08:00–12:30 and 14:00–16:30; Cape Vidal: 05:00–21:00 (summer) 06:00–21:00 (winter); False Bay Park: 08:00–12:30 and 14:00–16:30. Fanie's Island: 08:00–12:30 and 14:00–16:30.
Special precautions:	Antimalaria precautions should be taken before a visit to this area.

CHARTER'S CREEK AND FANIE'S ISLAND
Towards the southern end of Lake St Lucia are two delightful KwaZulu-Natal Nature Conservation Services camps, Charter's Creek and Fanie's Island, both of which are sought-after for their tranquil settings.

Perched on the western shore of Lake St Lucia, to the south of Fanie's Island, Charter's Creek is an excellent birdwatching and boating area. Visitors have ample opportunity to view local bird species along the 7-km Isikhova (Owl) Trail, which meanders through coastal forest, across streams and around glades of powder-puff trees.

Another lovely ramble is the Umkhumbe Trail (5 km), which traverses coastal forest of white stinkwood, wild banana and wild plum trees and the lake shore before returning to the camp. *Umkhumbe* is the Zulu word for red duiker which, together with bushbuck, abound in the area.

There is one boat to hire.

Accommodation consists of one seven-bed cottage, 10 four-bedded huts, four three-bedded huts and one two-bedded hut. Communal kitchen and ablution facilities are supplied, but you must bring your own provisions.

Fanie's Island is also a mecca for avid birdwatchers and fishermen, offering 12 two-bed rest huts, one seven-bed cottage and 20 shaded campsites near the water's edge. All the rest huts are fully equipped, but bring your own provisions. Two central kitchens and an ablution block serve the needs of visitors. You may bring your own boat or hire one (bring your own motor).

The Umkhiwane Trail is an attractive 5-km jaunt leading through coastal forest and parkland, where you may see grey duiker, monkeys, hippo, bushbuck, reedbuck or red duiker. Birds common in the area include trumpeter hornbills, purple-crested louries and Narina trogons.

Groot Winterhoek Wilderness Area

The rumble of cascading water filters through the cool spring air as you walk across the valleys of the Groot Winterhoek range. All around, jagged sentinels of sandstone tower above the rolling grassland and fynbos, rich with the colours of spring. Nearing the course of the river that tumbles southwards to the sea, the grass thickens, reeds and sphagnum moss appear and, suddenly, you're in a little corner of Eden. A silver waterfall empties into a still, dark pool. Sunbirds and sugarbirds flit from bush to bush, the air is crisp and clean, and the deep blue of the sky holds the promise of summer.

This is the heart of the Groot Winterhoek Wilderness Area, a 30 000-ha refuge for nature-lovers, where you can walk kilometres through rocky valleys rich with proteas, ericas and heaths.

Just two-and-a-half hours north of Cape Town, the Groot Winterhoek has several major attractions, not the least of which is that you can lay your sleeping bag down anywhere off the beaten track and sleep under the stars.

The wilderness area is a 40-minute drive from Porterville in the Western Cape, along a route that is as scenic as it is precipitous. You ascend the Dasklip Pass north of Porterville, and at the summit there's a lookout point (and launching pad for hang-gliders), which gives you panoramic views of the Olifants River valley below you. You bypass a signposted turn-off to the Beaverlac Nature Reserve, and continue for another 10 km to the forester's office, from which several footpaths radiate. All you have to do is park your car, and start walking.

Wildlife Most of the mammals in the Winterhoekberge are very shy and elusive. But if you scan the countryside with binoculars you may see, between the rocks and pockets of king proteas and mountain roses, such animals as baboons, dassies, one of nine leopards in the area, klipspringer and grysbok, or chance upon the remains of a Cape hare, recently killed by a caracal.

Birdlife Among the birds you're likely to see on your Groot Winterhoek adventure are Cape sugarbirds, sunbirds, Victorin's warblers, ground woodpeckers, and such birds of prey as blackshouldered kites, majestic black eagles, jackal buzzards, peregrine falcons and rock kestrels. The black eagles prey primarily on dassies which are found here in abundance.

Where to stay Although there are three basic huts (without any amenities) which are suitable as shelters for hikers, you can sleep anywhere you want to. Look for cosy night-time camping spots along one of the rivers.

Walks and trails About 90 km of footpaths meander over the rugged landscape, dominated by the Groot Winterhoek Peak (2 077 m). Hikers may wander off the established tracks, but should have a reliable compass and a map.

The favourite route is that which takes you to Die Hel, where the thundering waters of the Vier-en-Twintig River plunge into a deep ravine. There are two ways to get to Die Hel: a semi-circular route via the Klein Kliphuis River, and a direct route which flanks the Vier-en-Twintig River.

The direct route is popular with weekend hikers, because there's a pleasant overnight stop among granite boulders under the stars, just 1 km from the starting point. This means you can arrive late on Friday, walk to your camping spot and pitch your tent within 20 minutes of arriving.

There's plenty of fresh drinking water in the tributaries of the Vier-en-Twintig River, as they cascade through red disa-covered kloofs and valleys. And you can stop and strip at innumerable pools, plunge in and enjoy nature at its tranquil best. All the time, you're surrounded by an amphitheatre of sandstone rocks and cliffs, some sculpted by the wind over aeons into grotesque and bizarre shapes.

Up among the kloofs and cliffs are hidden caves — once the home of San hunters who sheltered here. These caves, and others on the farms Driebos and Eselfontein, on top of the Dasklip Pass, contain magnificent specimens of San art.

Die Hel The walk to Die Hel takes two days, and the ravine comes as some surprise when the steps start descending precipitously towards a deep pool of clean, black water far below. Here the thundering deluge of the Vier-en-Twintig Rivier plummets into the gorge, sending a white sheet of spray soaring skywards. Halfway down the ravine is a huge San cave overlooking the pool, where you may refresh yourself before continuing to the pool. Take care as you go down: the going is steep.

Tips for travellers

- **A maximum of 24 people, in groups of up to 12, are allowed in the wilderness area at any one time, so it's essential to book several months in advance (see 'At a glance' box). Only 12 people a day may hike to Die Hel.**
- **Fires are prohibited, so take your own gas stove. Be scrupulous about cleaning up at your chosen overnight camping site; take refuse bags along.**

Groot Winterhoek Wilderness Area at a glance

Location:	Western Cape, just north of Porterville.
Climate:	Summers are usually warm and dry; winters can be extremely cold with snow. There may be mist or rain at any time of the year, although 80 per cent of the rain falls between April and September.
Number of camps:	Any number of natural camping places.
Trails:	90 km of footpaths include two major return routes: the two-day trail to Die Hel; and the circular route through Groot Kliphuis, with optional extension to Perdevlei.
Other attractions:	Birdwatching, exploring the mountains and caves, studying the flora, swimming in the pools.
Amenities:	None supplied.
Accommodation:	Three huts near each other at De Tronk; caves; open countryside.
Booking address:	The Forester, Groot Winterhoek Wilderness Area, PO Box 26, Porterville 6810, tel (022) 931-2900.
When to go:	Spring and summer are the best times to go, since the winters are extremely wet and cold (sometimes with snow).
What to take with you:	All the necessities for camping outdoors for three or more days. In particular food, water, sleeping bag, binoculars, camera, compass and map. Swimming costume, light clothing in summer.
How to get there:	Drive north from Cape Town on the N7 to Piketberg. Turn right on the R44 for Porterville. From Porterville drive north along the R365 for 3 km. Turn right at the signpost marked Cardouw. Ascend Dasklip Pass. After the summit drive 4 km, then fork right and drive another 8 km to the parking area.
Nearest doctor:	At Porterville, 45 minutes away.
Nearest petrol:	At Porterville, 45 minutes away.
Open:	You may arrive at any time, provided permits have been granted and the group has been paid for.
Special precautions:	When hiking, keep a lookout for snakes, especially puffadders in October and November.

HLUHLUWE-UMFOLOZI PARK

The Hluhluwe-Umfolozi Park, covering 96 000 ha, is one of the largest game parks in Southern Africa. It comprises three reserves: Hluhluwe and Umfolozi — two of South Africa's oldest reserves — and the linking Corridor Reserve. The park is the showpiece of the KwaZulu-Natal Nature Conservation Services and is world-renowned for its population of white and black rhino.

Hluhluwe Game Reserve

In the long shadows of a summer afternoon the treetop game-viewing platform at Muntulu Bush Camp commands a perfect view across the emerald humpbacked hills and valleys of Hluhluwe.

Below, in the afterglow of a scorching day, the Hluhluwe River meanders gently southwards, easing through dense riverine thickets towards a wild horizon, until it is lost in the gathering gloom.

Summer evenings at Hluhluwe have their own special magic. It's a time for sundowners and serenity as guests relax on the Rest Camp's observation deck, and watch as a procession of animals filters through the groves of Ntombothi bushes on the opposite bank, to drink at the river's edge.

This is Hluhluwe at its pristine best — one of Africa's oldest game reserves, offering all the creature comforts you need, in the isolation of bushveld with its huge variety of animals. No less than 84 mammal species have been recorded here, including 36 elephants, 70 black (or hooklipped) rhinos, 390 white rhinos, 70 lions, 630 buffaloes, 500 Burchell's zebras and some 2 700 nyala. There are also warthogs, waterbuck, grey duiker, red duiker, some 120 blue wildebeest, hippos and crocodiles.

A staggering 425 species of bird live in the tangled bushveld, grasslands and misty riverine forest flanking the beautiful Hluhluwe River.

What makes this variety particularly awesome is the fact that just 50 years ago, more than 70 000 game animals were shot in Zululand because they were thought to be spreading the tsetse-fly-borne disease, nagana. Thanks to careful conservation measures by the KwaZulu-Natal Nature Conservation Services, the game populations have been brought back from the brink of extinction to thrive here once again.

Driving through the park for the first time, you're struck by the gentleness of the countryside — slow-flowing rivers course through deep valleys and circle rounded hills covered by forests which give way to open grassland and hilly crests.

Tip for travellers

Petrol is available at the camp during office hours. No pets are allowed in the reserve. Bush camp guests must check in at Hilltop Camp before 16:00. The speed limit in the reserve is 40 km/h.

Where to stay On one of these outcrops is Hluhluwe's Hilltop Camp. Originally built in 1933, KwaZulu-Natal's oldest hutted camp was upgraded in 1992 to provide 20 attractive, self-catering, thatched chalets overlooking the tumbling valleys of the lowlands. The chalets each have their own kitchen and bathroom, and are decorated with grass mats and cane furniture to create an ethnic feel.

There are also seven two-bedded and 22 four-bedded self-contained chalets and 20 two-bedded chalets which are not self-contained. These are next to a new, licenced restaurant, which serves breakfast, lunch and dinner.

Mtwazi Lodge at Hilltop offers three *en suite* bedrooms and an *en suite* annex, also with three bedrooms. The lodge has its own private garden, too.

Equally appealing, but perhaps more rustic, are the tree-top units of the Muntulu Bush Lodge, perched on a krantz overlooking the Hluhluwe River. There are four fully equipped, two-bed thatched units with shower, washbasin and toilet. Sliding doors in each unit open on to a wooden verandah which provides panoramic views of the lush valleys below. The units are connected by a boardwalk, which leads to a communal lounge and dining area with an adjoining game-viewing platform.

At Muntulu guests are assigned a personal cook, who will light a fire and braai meat for them.

Munyanweni is another bush lodge with four *en suite* bedrooms overlooking the Hluhluwe River.

Game drives There are 90 km of game-viewing drives at Hluhluwe, including the

Northern and Southern autotrails, both of which are 43 km long, and take about three hours to complete. Various hides, picnic spots and viewing points are marked on the map, and visitors may get out of their cars at certain places at their own risk. Two booklets describing the trail carry maps, and are given to guests booking in.

Walks Bush walks in the company of a game guard are a top priority at Hluhluwe, and offer you the chance to meet giraffes, buffaloes, rhinos, antelope and maybe even lions at close quarters. There's a self-guided trail from Hilltop Camp through the Mbhombe Forest; and a walk from Muntulu Bush Camp that takes you across the Hluhluwe River.

Birds to look out for are emeraldspotted doves, ground hornbills, brown snake eagles, bee-eaters, brownhooded kingfishers and blackbellied korhaans.

Umfolozi Game Reserve is featured as a separate entry on p. 153.

Giants of the savannah seas

Gamewatchers at Hluhluwe are often surprised by the nimbleness of giraffes moving through the bush. This fleetness of foot earned them the Arabic name *Xirapha*, which means 'one who walks swiftly'. Later the ancients called it *Camelopardis*, because it had the stature of a camel and the spots of a leopard.

None of the old descriptions, however, mention the giraffe's other magnificent physical features — long, prehensile tongue, extraordinary neck and regal eyes.

The 40-cm-long tongue extends into the upper reaches of a favoured tree, curls around a branch and neatly pulls it down to the animal's mouth. The branch is then stripped of leaves, berries or fruit.

In Southern Africa, giraffes enjoy several species of acacia tree, chewing and swallowing the leaves and spiky thorns with relish.

The huge, condescending eyes, lined with long, gracious eyelashes, are not just cosmetic. They have extraordinarily good vision and, mounted so conveniently on top of their neck-turrets, have a sweeping view of the bush for kilometres.

It is not uncommon for a small group of giraffes to position themselves side-to-side and back-to-back, so that they have a 360° view of the veld around them. And although a giraffe may not hear stalks of long grass being flattened by an approaching lion, the chances are it will see the lion in good time to make a getaway.

Hluhluwe Game Reserve at a glance

Locality:	Hluhluwe is in KwaZulu-Natal, 280 km (three-and-a-half hours' drive) north of Durban on the N2.
Climate:	The winters are mild to warm, the summers hot and wet (Hilltop Camp records 978 mm of rain a year).
Number of camps:	Three.
Game drives:	There are 90 km of game drives. Places to see game are Gunjaneni Gate, Zincakeni Dam (elephants), Magangeni Lookout Point (buffaloes, rhinos).
Hides and waterholes:	Several hides, dams and waterholes are found around the reserve.
Trails:	Various three-hour walking trails are available, accompanied by a game guard. The Mbhombe Forest Trail is a 30-minute ramble near Hilltop Camp. Two autotrails are the Northern and Southern autotrails (maps and booklet available at the main camp).
Other attractions:	Birdwatching, photography.
Amenities:	A shop equipped with basic provisions, restaurant.
Accommodation:	Chalets, duplexes and simplexes at **Hilltop** can accommodate 710 people. **Muntulu** and **Munyanweni Bush Lodges** each have four thatched units accommodating 24 people. **Mtwazi Lodge** has three *en suite* bedrooms and an *en suite* annex with three bedrooms.
Booking address:	KwaZulu-Natal Nature Conservation Services, PO Box 13069, Cascades 3202, tel (0331) 845-1000.
When to go:	May to September, when game congregates at rivers and dams.
What to take:	Hiking boots, binoculars, sunhat, torch. Visitors to Muntulu must take own food and drink; self-catering visitors at Hilltop may prepare their own food or dine in the restaurant.
How to get there:	Drive north from Durban on the N2. 50 km past Mtubatuba turn left for the Memorial Gate entrance. To reach Gunjaneni Gate, turn left on to the R618 just past Mtubatuba at the signpost reading Nongoma/Umfolozi Game Reserve.
Nearest doctor:	Hluhluwe Village, 30 km away.
Nearest petrol:	Hilltop Camp.
Open:	1 October–31 March: 05:00–19:00; 1 April–30 September: 06:00–18:00.
Special precautions:	Take antimalaria precautions before you enter the reserve. Exercise caution on game walks. Wear hiking boots. Don't bathe in rivers and dams: there may be crocodiles or bilharzia.

Itala Game Reserve

The turrets of bungalows rise like anthills through the canopy of lush bush at Itala Game Reserve's Ntshondwe Camp. From the hide nearby you look down on the shimmering waters of a natural lake as a convention of animals drifts down to drink.

True to the tradition of the KwaZulu-Natal Nature Conservation Services, no comfort has been overlooked as you revel in nature at its best: the restaurant adjoining your hide offers excellent cuisine; sundowners are on call at any time of the day; if the heat's getting to you, there's a sparkling pool set attractively among large boulders around the corner.

Ntshondwe, Itala's main camp, nestles among boulders on the slopes of the Ngoje plateau, and offers spectacular views of the reserve. There is accommodation for 200 people here in 39 two- to six-bed chalets. Each chalet is fully equipped and serviced, with a lounge-diningroom, bathroom, toilet and kitchenette. The restaurant has its own take-away facility and bar, as well as a small shop offering basic provisions.

A separate three-bed luxury lodge, built in a saddle on Ntshondwe cliff, has its own swimming pool and its own attendant cook.

Proclaimed in 1972, Itala Game Reserve has grown to become one of KwaZulu-Natal's most accommodating sanctuaries. Covering 29 653 ha, it offers an abundance of animal and birdlife, thriving in three distinctly separate vegetation zones in a landscape of rolling hills and valleys.

Wildlife More than 80 species of mammal, and close to 100 species of amphibian and reptile occupy the lowveld, grassveld and mountain sourveld of Itala. Among the more conspicuous mammals you're likely to encounter on walks or drives through the bush are elephants, giraffes, cheetahs, white rhinos, black rhinos, eland, waterbuck, kudu, blue wildebeest, red hartebeest, zebras, impala, klipspringer and warthogs.

Animals considered rare or endangered include greater bushbabies, leopards, honeybadgers, brown hyenas, pangolins, tsessebe, goliath herons, bald ibis, bat hawks, martial eagles, brownheaded parrots and Cape eagle owls.

Birdlife Itala is a natural paradise for birders, with more than 320 bird species ranging from raptors such as black eagles, African hawk eagles, Wahlberg's eagles, fish eagles, brown snake eagles, blackbreasted snake eagles and southern banded snake eagles to several species of francolin (including Shelley's), nightjars, doves, swifts, plovers, dikkops, woodpeckers, parrots, louries and larks. Three honeyguide species live here, including the sharpbilled honeyguide, as well as the yellowspotted nicator and black cuckooshrike.

Game drives and trails The self-driven Ngubhu Loop Autotrail (30 km) has 24 demarcated stops at points of interest, and takes about three hours to complete. The park authorities supply a handsome booklet with full details of what you may expect to see on the Ngubhu Autotrail.

Tsessebe and rhino usually inhabit the grasslands in the vicinity of the airfield. The tall grasslands at the northern part of the Ngubhu loop road usually attract blue wildebeest, eland, white rhino, red hartebeest and warthogs.

Ranger-led day walks (usually early morning or late afternoon) are available at Itala, and are included in the accommodation tariff.

Also on offer are eight bushveld trails (maximum eight per trail) led by a game guard, during which trailists sleep in tents. The trails run from March to October, and can be booked through the KwaZulu-Natal Nature Conservation Services (see *Booking*

Tips for travellers

- **Do not gather firewood around the picnic area or campsites at Itala. Charcoal is on sale at Ntshondwe Camp, and firewood is available at Tochgevonden Gate. You may bring your own wood.**
- **No pets are allowed in the reserve.**

address, 'At a glance' box). All camping gear is supplied on these trails, but you must bring your own food and drink.

Where to stay There are three campsites with basic facilities for up to 20 people, including a cold-water shower, flush toilet and communal lounge, diningroom and kitchen. No caravans are allowed, however, and campers must bring all their own food, drink and equipment.

Apart from Ntshondwe Camp, Itala has three very attractive bush camps — Thalu, Mbizo and Mhlangeni, all equipped with gas stoves and fridges, cutlery, crockery, linen and cooking utensils. The reed-, thatch- and tar-pole units can house four, eight or ten people respectively, and each unit has been built to ensure complete privacy. Because of the absence of crocodiles and bilharzia, swimming is allowed at Mbizo and Thalu camps.

Itala Game Reserve at a glance

Locality:	Northern KwaZulu-Natal, northeast of Vryheid.
Climate:	Summers hot and humid with rain; winters cool to warm.
Number of camps:	Four.
Game drives:	Ngubhu Autotrail (three hours).
Hides and waterholes:	One bird hide at waterhole near Ntshondwe Camp.
Trails:	Ranger-led, short walking trails; weekend wilderness trails.
Other attractions:	Swimming pool, birdwatching, swimming in the rivers.
Amenities:	Restaurant, take-away facility, bar.
Accommodation:	**Ntshondwe** has 39 two- to six-bed chalets (*en suite* bathroom and lounge). Three bush camps: **Mhlangeni** has five two-bed units; **Mbizo** has two four-bed units; **Thalu** has one unit accommodating four people. Three campsites for 20 people. Cold-water shower, flush toilet and communal lounge, diningroom and kitchen.
Booking address:	KwaZulu-Natal Nature Conservation Services, PO Box 13069, Cascades 3202, tel (0331) 845-1000. For camping, contact the Officer-in-Charge, Itala Game Reserve, PO Box 42, Louwsburg 3150, tel (0388) 7-5239. Ntshondwe Camp reception, tel (0388) 7-5105.
When to go:	The winter months (April through to September) when the vegetation is not too dense.
What to take with you:	Food, drink, torches, binoculars, camera, hiking boots.
How to get there:	From Durban travel via Eshowe and Melmoth to Vryheid. From there take the tarred road to Louwsburg, via Hlobane. Itala lies very near to Louwsburg. From Northern Province, Gauteng and Mpumalanga, travel via Piet Retief and Paulpietersburg to Vryheid. From Pietermaritzburg travel via Ladysmith, Wasbank, Dundee and Vryheid.
Nearest doctor:	Vryheid.
Nearest petrol:	Available at the entrance gate.
Open:	1 October–31 March: 05:00–19:00; 1 April–30 September: 06:00–18:00.
Special precautions:	Take antimalaria precautions before going to Itala.

Mhlangeni Bush Camp, tucked among trees on top of a granite koppie, is probably the most attractive of the three bush camps. Fringed by aloes, euphorbias and cussonias, the camp has panoramic views over the surrounding bushveld, including the Ncence Stream. From the comfort of a large observation deck you can sip sundowners and gaze across the bushveld below, where white rhinos, bushbuck, waterbuck, giraffes and eland congregate in substantial numbers. Mhlangeni is one of the very few places where you can watch game while you take a shower in your bungalow.

Mbizo Bush Camp — on the banks of the Mbizo River — has two eight-bed, fully equipped bungalows (two bedrooms each), with an open diningroom and kitchen. Most meals are cooked in the open under the stars by camp staff. Right in front of the lodges is a natural swimming pool which has formed in the riverbed.

A magnificent open braai area perched above a sparkling pool is an attractive feature of Thalu, a small bush camp (maximum four people) with two bedrooms situated on either side of a central lounge/ diningroom area. A hot/cold shower and flush toilet are provided.

Kalahari Gemsbok Park

Deep in the dunes of the Kalahari, the crimson edges of the setting sun sink beneath the western horizon. From the east, chariots of darkness race across the desert floor, rousing the primal spirit of the hunt among creatures of the night.

Under the umbrella of a camelthorn tree, eight lions and lionesses rise like grey ghosts from their daytime torpor.

You watch this ritual silently from your car, careful not to break the silence that falls with such serene swiftness in the Kalahari. And you realise suddenly that here, in the vast expanse of the Kalahari Gemsbok Park, you're as close to nature as you're ever likely to get.

Wedged between Namibia and Botswana, the park is the largest nature conservation area in Southern Africa (nearly a million hectares), and together with the adjacent Gemsbok National Park, covers a total area of 3,6 million hectares.

To reach it, you have to travel a long, dusty way (358 km north of Upington) from the major cities. If you're driving from Johannesburg or Cape Town, give yourself plenty of time for the journey, so you can stretch your legs on the way, or picnic under a roadside camelthorn tree.

Wildlife Winding through the park are the dusty beds of two ancient rivers, the Auob and the Nossob, and these are populated by huge herds of springbok and wildebeest, lured by the rich grasses born in the silt of previous floods.

Smaller groups of gemsbok, red hartebeest and eland also trample the dry beds of these two rivers, while the carnivores — lions, cheetahs, leopards, wild dogs, blackbacked jackals, caracals and brown and spotted hyenas — roam the grassland and thorny scrub between the dunes.

The scenery is typical Kalahari — sanddunes, tinged red by iron oxide, form gentle hillocks between the expanse of short and tall Bushman grass, and the camelthorn, African blackwood, wild pomegranate and raisin bushes that cover them. If you scan the surrounding countryside carefully, you may see a leopard draped across the branches of a tree, a family of bateared foxes trotting along the dry beds, or a lion perched on a sand-dune.

Where to stay There are three rest camps — Twee Rivieren, Mata Mata and Nossob. Twee Rivieren is the largest, and easily the most comfortable, with fully equipped, air-conditioned three-, four- and six-bed chalets catering for up to 96 people. The thatched chalets are clean and airy. The camp has its own restaurant, an attractive swimming pool, and a shop stocked with groceries, eggs, bread, liquor and frozen meat. There's also a lapa (walled enclosure), where you can braai under the star-studded sky and listen to the sounds of Africa. You can also book a hire-car at Twee Rivieren, but do so well in advance.

Mata Mata accommodates 21 people in three-bed huts and six-bed cottages; while Nossob, 179 km northwest of Twee Rivieren, has room for 32 people. Nossob also has an information centre that tells you about the plant- and animal life in the park.

All three camps have landing strips for light aircraft, campsites with ablution facilities, open braai areas and petrol and diesel pumps.

Graceful prancers of the plains

Less than 100 years ago huge herds of springbok, numbering between 100 000 and more than a million, trampled across the great plains of the Kalahari, sending plumes of golden dust kilometres into the sky.

Farmers — and the San — watched in awe as the moving mass advanced across the fossil river beds of the Auob and Nossob, trampling to death anything in its path — cattle, sheep or smaller game. Individual springbok that stopped along the way suffered the same fate.

One column was estimated at more than 210 km long and stretched across a front of more than 20 km.

Today, relics of the great herds can still be seen in the fossil riverbed of the Auob in the Kalahari Gemsbok Park, but, sadly, their numbers are greatly diminished — owing to the encroachment of farmland, and the carnage caused by hunters and poachers during the past 100 years.

Nevertheless, these graceful antelope of Southern Africa, with their majestic lyrate horns and graceful pronking leaps through the air, are a special sight for gamewatchers in this part of the world.

Game-viewing drives As you leave Twee Rivieren, the two main game-viewing roads closely track the course of the Auob (to Mata Mata) and Nossob (to Union's End) in a northwesterly and northeasterly direction respectively. If you stop your car anywhere along the way, you're certain to see any one of the larger mammals, or smaller animals such as steenbok, duiker, bateared foxes and porcupines.

Generally, you'll probably see more game between Twee Rivieren and Mata Mata (133 km), than on any of the other roads. The Auob riverbed between these points is one of the best places in the world to watch cheetahs hunting (there are about 50 in the park); and your chances of seeing lions on the northern part of the route, between Kamqua and Mata Mata, are excellent. Waterholes worth visiting along this drive are Houmoed (wildebeest), Rooibrak (raptors), Dalkeith (cheetahs) and Craig Kockhart (leopards).

Keep a pair of binoculars at your side — birdlife is prolific (215 species) and includes yellowbilled hornbills, secretarybirds, kori bustards, marabou storks, bateleurs and martial eagles.

The road from Twee Rivieren to Union's End is peppered with waterholes: Leeudril (15 km from Twee Rivieren) and Rooiputs (24 km from Twee Rivieren) are good places to see herds of springbok and flocks of sandgrouse coming down to drink in the morning.

Further north, between Rooiputs and Kikkij, watch out for a pack of resident spotted hyenas (there are 60 spotted hyenas and 120 brown hyenas in the reserve). The next waterhole is Melkvlei (49 km from Twee Rivieren), where there is a picnic site and toilets.

If you're looking for lions along this route, stop at Chileka, Kaspersdraai or Cubitje Quap. Dikbaardskolk tends to attract snakes.

A feature of the park are the huge 'thatched' nests that occupy the branches of camelthorn trees. These are the 'sectional title' apartments of the sociable weavers.

A warning to first-time visitors: summers are extremely hot here, with temperatures frequently in the high 40s. Those who can take the midsummer heat — from November to February — qualify for a 25 per cent discount off the fee.

Kalahari Gemsbok Park at a glance

Locality:	Northwestern corner of South Africa, between Namibia and Botswana.
Climate:	Very hot summer days; warm winter days (average 25 °C); cold winter nights.
Number of camps:	Three.
Game drives:	The two main ones follow the course of the Auob and the Nossob river beds.
Waterholes:	Numerous waterholes scattered through the park include Houmoed (wildebeest), Rooibrak (raptors), Dalkeith (cheetahs), Craig Kockhart (leopards).
Other attractions:	Swimming pool, picnic spots.
Amenities:	Restaurant; petrol; shop with groceries, meat, fresh bread, liquor, ice.
Accommodation:	Three-, four- and six-bed, air-conditioned chalets (with bathroom, kitchenette and braai area); four-bed huts (with shower, toilet and kitchen).
Booking address:	National Parks Board, PO Box 787, Pretoria 0001, tel (012) 343-1991; National Parks Board, PO Box 7400, Roggebaai 8012, tel (021) 22-2810; the Park Warden, Kalahari Gemsbok Park, tel (054) 561-0021.
When to go:	The best months for game-viewing are February to May.
What to take with you:	Water and extra provisions in the event of a breakdown; binoculars, camera, sunhat.
How to get there:	The park lies 358 km northwest of Upington, and may be reached by road from Johannesburg (904 km), Cape Town and Durban.
Nearest doctor:	At Upington, 358 km away.
Nearest garage:	At Upington, 358 km away.
Open:	January and February 06:00–19:30; March 06:30–19:00; April 07:00–18:30; May 07:00–18:00; June and July 07:30–18:00; August 07:00–18:30; September 06:30–18:00; October 06:00–19:00; November and December 05:30–19:30.
Special precautions:	Extremely hot (high 40s in summer). No pets allowed. Don't get out of your car except at designated picnic spots. Take antimalaria tablets before your visit.

Karoo National Park

The ghost of the Red Bed dinosaur, *Massospondylus*, stalks the plains between the koppies of the Karoo National Park. And on moonlit nights, when the black clouds skim silently over the tops of the thatched bungalows, you wonder how it must have been when the shadows of giant pterodactyls sent smaller animals fleeing in terror.

For here, in the middle of the Karoo, there's an aura of prehistory that is quite overwhelming. If you stand upon the summit of the Nuweveld Mountains, and look east across the Karoo's endless sheet of shrubs and sand, you will see the natural vault that contains one of the world's greatest treasure chests of fossils, dating back some 250 million years.

These are the bones of fearsome mammal-like reptiles that stalked the swamplands in the dawn of time; creatures such as *Rubidgea*, a fierce, flesh-eating mammal, and *Bradysaurus*, an armour-plated monster with a massive head, and claws protruding from each ungainly leg.

Today, in the Karoo National Park, you can walk in the footsteps of these mammal-like reptiles, whose 50-million-year dynasty ended abruptly and violently when great volcanic eruptions spilled lava across the interior about 190 million years ago. Fossil legacies of these momentous events are on view along the park's Fossil Trail.

The Karoo National Park covers an area of 32 792 ha, and is clearly signposted just 3 km south of Beaufort West. If you're dri-

The flying phantom of the bush

Game rangers and naturalists know the kudu as the 'phantom of the bush' because of its habit of freezing in the face of danger. Indeed, motionless in thick bush, the cinnamon or fawn-grey body melts imperceptibly into the changing light and shade of the foliage, and to the untrained eye it becomes almost indistinguishable from its surroundings.

Once you see it, the kudu is a magnificent creature — the male's large, spiralled horns rise elegantly above the white chevron between its eyes; the robust flanks are painted with narrow, white vertical stripes; and the large rounded ears cock forward toward any telltale sound of danger.

If its presence is betrayed, the kudu runs for cover, its tail curled upward to reveal the white hair on its underparts. This gesture serves as a warning signal to other members of the herd and a visual indication of its direction of escape. In flight, the male points its nose forward, laying its long horns against its shoulders to avoid making contact with low, overhanging branches.

ving from Cape Town (500 km away) to Johannesburg (1 000 km away) on the N2, it's an ideal point to spend the night and relish the cool, clean plateau air.

The haunting landscape of the park was proclaimed in 1979 as a sanctuary for future generations of animals and visitors, when farming needs made serious inroads into the Karoo's natural vegetation.

Wildlife There are no less than 66 reptile species in the park, including 37 species of gecko. On summer evenings, between sunset and darkness, the Karoo stillness is broken by the chants of barking geckos and the choral symphonies of eight species of frog. Bird species number 170, among which are bateleurs and black eagles, jackal buzzards, saddlebilled storks and crowned hornbills.

The 48 mammal species in the park include the Cape mountain zebra — brought back from the brink of extinction in the Mountain Zebra National Park (see p. 101) — and plains animals such as gemsbok, red hartebeest, springbok and black wildebeest.

These are complemented by a variety of other antelope, among them kudu, duiker, steenbok, grey rhebok and klipspringer. Pride of the low-lying ground, however, is the bateared fox which, with its huge, sensitive ears, scans the surface for subterranean termites. The Karoo is an excellent feeding ground for this likeable little fox — termites comprise 56 per cent of the insects in the park.

Where to stay Karoo Rest Camp nestles in the tranquil foothills of the Nuweveld Mountains, and offers comfortable accommodation in six- and three-bed thatched chalets, all fully equipped, self-contained, air-conditioned and serviced. Just in front of the camp is a sparkling swimming pool.

The beautiful caravan park nearby is an oasis of greenery in a landscape as rugged as it is arid. There are communal cooking and ablution facilities here, and electric power points.

Amenities include a swimming pool, shop, restaurant, information centre and the Ou Schuur environmental centre at Stolshoek, 1 km from the rest camp.

Mountain View Rest Camp, on the upper plateau of the Nuweveld Mountains, is highly recommended if you want to taste the fresh mountain air and have sweeping views of the surrounding countryside. The rondavels here are equipped with beds, mattresses and an ablution block, but you must bring your own food, light, bedding and towels.

Game drives and trails The Springbok Trail (36 km) is a circular, three-day hike (maximum 12 people) from the Main Rest Camp to the Mountain View Hut on the summit of the Nuweveld Mountain range (1 890 m).

On the way you may see one or more of the 20 breeding pairs of black eagles that prey upon the nearly 28 000 dassies inhabiting the dolerite krantzes. The concentration of these eagles is one of the densest in the world, and is attributed to the abundance of their natural and favoured food. The trail is closed from 1 November to the end of February.

A number of one-day trails are also available, including the attractive, 11-km Fonteintjieskloof Nature Trail, about 4 km from the caravan park, and the Potlekkertjie Children's Walk.

The Fossil Trail (adapted for the blind and disabled) gives you the chance to walk in the footsteps of the dinosaurs, and to see live samples of fossils representing the evolutionary period which spans 250 million years.

More than 60 Karoo plants (each numbered and cross-referenced in a brochure), with such names as bloubos, dikvoet and kruisbessie, are the highlights of the 0,8-km Bossie Trail near the park's restaurant.

The 4x4 trail This is the first trail of its kind among the national parks of Southern Africa, and opens up a new dimension in seeing the more inaccessible parts of the Karoo Park. The trail was designed to have minimal impact on the environment, and offers visitors the chance to experience nature in the raw. A ranger will introduce you to the delicate ecosystems encountered during the trail, and give you a better understanding of how animals and plants interact in their continual battle for survival. The trail is 80 km long, with one overnight stop at a hut on the Afsaal plains.

Other game drives include a drive to the middle plateau on the Klipspringer Mountain Pass and a shorter, circular drive (about 12 km) to Lammertjiesleegte, northeast of the rest camp.

Karoo National Park at a glance

Location:	South of Beaufort West, just off the N2 between Cape Town and Johannesburg.
Climate:	The plains are hot in summer, but it is quite cool in the Nuweveld Mountains. Winters are cold, with occasional snow on the mountains. Annual rainfall 260 mm.
Number of camps:	Two.
Game drives:	Karoo 4x4 Trail (80 km), and two other drives.
Hiking trails:	Springbok Trail (36 km), Fossil Trail (0,4 km), Bossie Trail (0,8 km), Fonteintjieskloof Trail (11 km).
Other attractions:	Birdwatching, examining fossils, exploring the flora, swimming.
Amenities:	Licensed restaurant with à la carte menu, swimming pool, shop, information centre. Firewood supplied.
Accommodation:	**Karoo Rest Camp** offers Cape-Dutch-style cottages (six-bed) and chalets (three-bed), fully equipped, with air-conditioning, cooking utensils, crockery, cutlery, bedding, towels and soap. **Mountain View Rest Camp** offers beds and mattresses only in the huts which accommodate 25 people.
Booking address:	National Parks Board, PO Box 787, Pretoria 0001, tel (012) 343-1991; or the National Parks Board, PO Box 7400, Roggebaai 8012, tel (021) 22-2810.
When to go:	Throughout the year, but cooler in winter.
What to take with you:	Hikers should take warm clothing, map, rucksack, sleeping bag, binoculars and camping necessities, such as a gas stove, food and cutlery.
How to get there:	There's a signpost to the park 3 km south of Beaufort West on the N2.
Nearest doctor:	At Beaufort West, 3 km away.
Nearest petrol:	At Beaufort West, 3 km away.
Open:	From 05:00–22:00 daily. Reception: 07:30–20:00.
Special precautions:	When hiking, keep an eye open for snakes and scorpions.

Kosi Bay Nature Reserve

The Kosi Bay Nature Reserve is a wild, wetland paradise in the far northeastern corner of KwaZulu-Natal, known as Maputaland, just south of the Mozambique border. Covering 11 000 ha, the reserve extends 30 km along the eastern seaboard and is prominent for a forest-fringed peninsula of sand that protects a massive inland estuary.

The heartbeat of the entire reserve is the waters of the Indian Ocean which flow through this estuary and spill over into four interconnecting lakes.

This tide of warm water enters Lake Makhawulani from the sea through a massive estuary of translucent water, bearing a teeming, ever-changing community of marine creatures, ranging from huge reef fish to microscopic organisms. The water then spills into Lake Mpungwini and Lake Nhlange, bringing life and nourishment to the mangrove swamps and magnificent forests of swamp and sycamore fig trees, wild orchids and raffia palms that surround the shores.

Nhlange ('the place of reeds') which is by far the biggest lake, stretches southwards for 8 km, and is 5 km wide and 50 m deep.

South of Nhlange is Lake Amanzimnyama ('black waters'), whose palm-fringed banks are the resting places of crocodiles and hippos. Lakes Makhawulani and Mpungwini are renowned for their crystal-clear waters, while lakes Nhlange and Amanzimnyama have a tannin-coloured appearance.

The landscapes of Kosi Bay are an amazing contrast of shapes and forms, and range from tangled bush and towering, creeper-clad trees to open savannah and some of the highest forested sand-dunes in the world. Around the wetlands the tidal surge is ever-present as lethargic streams of tepid water curl around the roots of swamp fig trees and giant sycamore figs.

Wildlife Around this fantastic water-world more than 300 species of bird have found a home: among the raffia palms you'll find palmnut vultures and Pel's fishing owls; in the forests the calls of trumpeter hornbills and goldenrumped tinker barbets reverberate across the canopies of the high trees, while all along the lake shore you'll see African fish eagles, herons, kingfishers and flufftails.

Duiker and bushbuck roam the forests in the company of vervet and samango monkeys and red squirrels, while hippos and crocodiles frequent the lakeshore areas. Along the coastline, leatherback and loggerhead turtles come ashore to lay their eggs.

Marine life Kosi Bay is internationally renowned for its wealth of marine life. The limpid waters of the inland channel and reef teem with fish, while further out superb coral reefs and their associated wealth of colourful marine creatures are an irresistible attraction to snorkellers and scuba-divers.

Tips for travellers

- Bathing is banned in the lakes because of crocodiles and hippos. There is bilharzia in Lake Amanzimnyama.
- Divers should keep a wary eye open for sharks, scorpionfish and stonefish.
- The Kosi Bay Trail is physically demanding. Make sure you're in good condition before trying it.
- Firewood is available from the camp superintendent.
- Reservations may be made up to six months in advance.

Anglers land good catches of bream, sea pike, spotted grunter and queenfish in the lakes. Shore fishing is allowed from the campsite only, but you may bring your own boat and fish in the lakes.

Where to stay Kosi Bay Rest Camp lies along the banks of Lake Nhlange, and offers three thatched lodges (two-, five- and six-bed). Trained cooks and maids are allocated to each lodge, but guests must bring their own food and drinks. In addition there are 15 attractive campsites among the trees, with access to hot- and cold-water showers. Caravans are not recommended due, in part, to the poor state of the roads at times.

Walks and trails There are various guided walks around the lake system and other places of interest. Reservations for overnight hikes to Lake Amanzimnyama may be made through central reservations (see *Booking address*, 'At a glance' box).

Kosi Bay Hiking Trail This 34-km trail, known also as the Amanzimnyama Trail, lasts four days and skirts the flanks and perimeter of all four of Kosi Bay's lakes. The trail starts and ends at Nhlange Base Camp on the western shore of Lake Nhlange, the haunt of giant and pied kingfishers and wood owls.

After spending the night in two large, thatched huts, hikers head northwards to

Monkeying around on the ground

The grizzled grey coat and the small, clownish black face and sparkling eyes of the vervet monkey chattering away in the trees is a familiar sight at Kosi Bay.

Black hands, toes and tail-tip constantly on the move, the vervet seems to have an insatiable appetite. But its habit of popping seeds, fruit and other tidbits into its mouth is deceptive. The food is not being swallowed or chewed, to be regurgitated later — it is being stored away in expandable cheek pouches, in the manner of squirrels.

These expandable cheek pouches are part of nature's plan to help the species survive. Because vervets are extremely vulnerable to carnivores on the ground, they have little time to eat while they forage. So they scamper about quickly, popping food into their pouches, then make for the safety of the trees to enjoy their meal at leisure.

The monkeys live in closely knit troops of 15 to 20, but lack the power and combined strength of baboon troops. Individually, they weigh in at only 5 kg and are 50 cm high on their haunches. But their opportunistic nature often helps them outwit the enemy.

Mshwayisa Camp on the eastern shores of Lake Makhawulani, and then on to the tented camp at Bhanga Nek, which is just 30 m from the edge of the Indian Ocean.

Here the KwaZulu-Natal Bureau of Natural Resources and the KwaZulu-Natal Nature Conservation Services monitor the movements of loggerhead and leatherback turtles which come ashore to lay their eggs before returning to the sea. In February you may see the hatchlings being surveyed at night.

From Bhanga Nek the trail heads to its southernmost point at Sihadla Camp, south of Lake Amanzimnyama, and bypasses large groves of giant raffia palms where you may spot the rare palmnut vulture.

At Sihadla, hikers may relax in the shade of their thatched huts which encircle a central braai area. The next day the trail crosses the Sihadla River on a raffia palm pont, then heads north for the final 10-km leg through swamp forests to Nhlange Camp.

Shorter hikes, led by game scouts, enable you to explore the dune and swamp forests, the mangrove swamps and marshes and the surrounding bush country.

At Lake Makhawulani, the local Tembe villagers build wooden fish traps known as 'kraals' which channel fish such as spotted grunter, mullet, kingfish and barracuda into smaller enclosures where they are speared.

Kosi Bay Nature Reserve at a glance

Locality: Northeastern KwaZulu-Natal, near the Mozambique border; six hours' drive from Durban.

Climate: Summers are warm to hot with thunderstorms; winters mild to warm.

Number of camps: One permanent camp; four overnight camps on the Kosi Bay Hiking Trail.

Trails: 34-km Kosi Bay Hiking Trail; numerous escorted day walks offered from Main Camp.

Other attractions: Angling, birdwatching.

Accommodation: **Kosi Bay Rest Camp** offers three thatched lodges (two-, five- and six-bed), and 15 campsites. There are four overnight huts and tents on the **Kosi Bay Hiking Trail**.

Booking address: KwaZulu-Natal Nature Conservation Services, PO Box 13069, Cascades 3202, tel (0331) 845-1000, or telephone the reserve at tel (035) 0234/5/6.

When to go: Throughout the year.

What to take with you: For the trail: food, water, sleeping bag, hiking boots, basic toiletries, hat, torch, swimming costume, mask and snorkel, camera, eating utensils.

How to get there: From Durban drive north on the N2 past Empangeni and Jozini, heading for Kwangwanase. The route between Kwangwanase and the reserve is clearly signposted.

Nearest petrol: Kwangwanase, 13 km from the reserve.

Open: 06:00–18:00 throughout the year.

Special precautions: The reserve falls within a malaria zone, and you should therefore take anti-malaria precautions before you set off. Swimming is not recommended because of bilharzia and crocodiles.

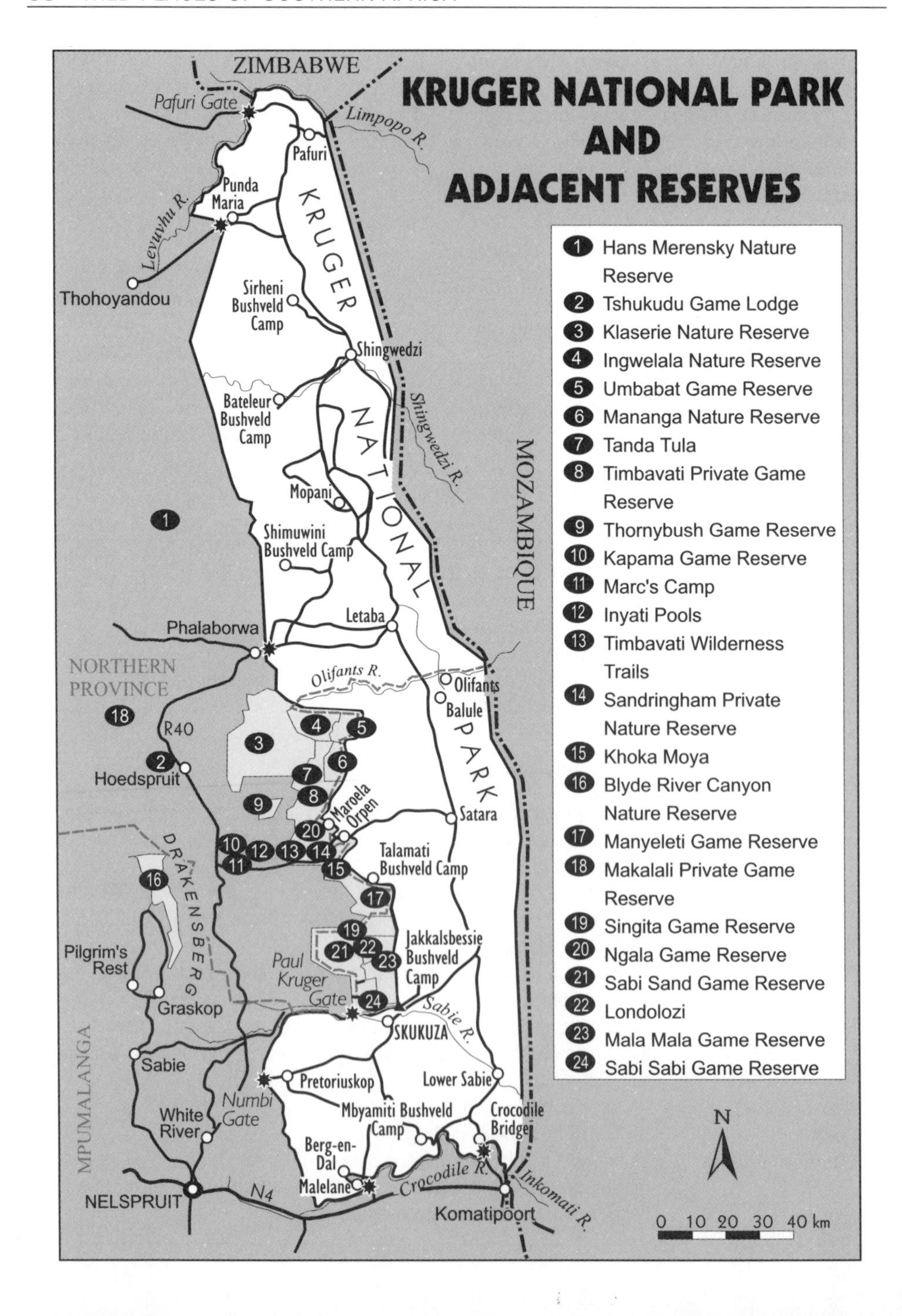
KRUGER NATIONAL PARK
AND
ADJACENT RESERVES
1 Hans Merensky Nature Reserve
2 Tshukudu Game Lodge
3 Klaserie Nature Reserve
4 Ingwelala Nature Reserve
5 Umbabat Game Reserve
6 Mananga Nature Reserve
7 Tanda Tula
8 Timbavati Private Game Reserve
9 Thornybush Game Reserve
10 Kapama Game Reserve
11 Marc's Camp
12 Inyati Pools
13 Timbavati Wilderness Trails
14 Sandringham Private Nature Reserve
15 Khoka Moya
16 Blyde River Canyon Nature Reserve
17 Manyeleti Game Reserve
18 Makalali Private Game Reserve
19 Singita Game Reserve
20 Ngala Game Reserve
21 Sabi Sand Game Reserve
22 Londolozi
23 Mala Mala Game Reserve
24 Sabi Sabi Game Reserve
ZIMBABWE
Pafuri Gate
Limpopo R.
Pafuri
Punda Maria
Levuvhu R.
Thohoyandou
KRUGER NATIONAL PARK
Sirheni Bushveld Camp
Shingwedzi
Shingwedzi R.
Bateleur Bushveld Camp
MOZAMBIQUE
Mopani
Shimuwini Bushveld Camp
Letaba
Phalaborwa
NORTHERN PROVINCE
Olifants R.
Olifants
Balule
R40
Hoedspruit
Maroela
Orpen
Satara
DRAKENSBERG
Talamati Bushveld Camp
Jakkalsbessie Bushveld Camp
Pilgrim's Rest
Paul Kruger Gate
Graskop
Sabie R.
SKUKUZA
MPUMALANGA
Sabie
Pretoriuskop
Lower Sabie
Numbi Gate
White River
Mbyamiti Bushveld Camp
Crocodile Bridge
Berg-en-Dal
Malelane
Crocodile R.
Inkomati R.
NELSPRUIT
N4
Komatipoort
N
0 10 20 30 40 km

KRUGER NATIONAL PARK

Roughly the size of Wales, or the American state of Massachusetts, the Kruger National Park is Africa's oldest, and one of the world's greatest, wildlife sanctuaries.

Covering nearly two million hectares, the park stretches 350 km from north to south and 60 km from east to west — a massive playground of bush, grassland and thornveld, bordered in the east by Mozambique and in the west by the private game parks of Mpumalanga.

There is no reserve in Southern Africa with more animal species, and there are few places on earth that can match its huge network of magical rest camps — 25 in all — attracting more than 700 000 visitors every year.

The park has become the major wildlife destination for tourists visiting Southern Africa since its establishment in 1898, and it's easy to see why: no less than 147 species of mammal, including the Big Five, congregate with some 507 species of bird, 114 reptile and 34 amphibian species. There are also 336 species of tree and 49 different kinds of fish.

The array of mammals includes most of the cats of Africa in breathtaking numbers: 2 000 lions stalk the grasslands in the company of 1 000 leopards and 200 cheetahs. Smaller cats — African wild cats, servals, caracals — are also abundant but rather elusive.

But the real pride of Kruger is its elephants. About 7 630 pachyderms saunter along well-worn paths through the bush, stopping occasionally to 'camp' in the middle of one of Kruger's many roads, or to bathe in the muddy shallows of a waterhole. In their midst you may see any number of Kruger's 100 000 impala, 30 000 zebras, 21 880 buffaloes or several thousand giraffe.

Less often seen are the wild dogs, which number just under 400, roan antelope, tsessebe and black rhinos. But armed with a good pair of binoculars, a will to travel and patience, most visitors will spot a large cross-section of Kruger's animals and birds.

Getting there Kruger's main camp, Skukuza, is about 500 km from Johannesburg, an easy eight-hour drive. Tour operators, safari companies and travel agents will organise fly-drive packages to suit individual tastes (see 'Safari Operators in Southern Africa', p. 362). Another option is a coach tour, of which there is a large variety available, departing from Cape Town, Johannesburg or Durban.

The only airline running regular flights to Skukuza is SA Express, but Airlink and Metavia run regular flights to Phalaborwa and Nelspruit.

There are eight access gates to Kruger, and the roads in the park are either tarred or well gravelled.

Visitors must be aware that the park and camp gates close between 17:30 and 18:00 every day, so it is important to reach the gates well before this time (see 'At a glance' box for gate hours). The travelling times between the park's gates and the respective camps vary from a few minutes to four-and-a-half hours.

Facilities There's an excellent range of facilities for visitors to the main camps, including swimming pools, licenced restaurants, shops and conference venues. At Skukuza alone there are two restaurants, a bank, library, doctor and AA emergency service for vehicles.

Driving in the park Several options are available for seeing the Kruger National

Park, the most popular of which is to hire a car in the park (at the main camp, Skukuza) if you don't have your own.

Wilderness trails Seven wilderness trails transverse the Kruger Park — Bushman, Metsi-Metsi, Napi, Nyalaland, Olifants, Sweni and Wolhuter. Each one has been carefully designed to lead visitors through large, unspoilt areas in the company of armed trail rangers.

The overnight sites along these trails have been selected for their rustic and scenic beauty and proximity to large numbers of animals. Some lie on the edge of waterholes, others along the banks of muddy rivers, while there are more in remote valleys far from traditional roads.

The two-day, three-night hikes are broken by tranquil overnight interludes at a bush camp along the way, where hikers retire to sleep in four two-bed huts, after sundowners and supper around the fireside in an enclosed boma. Groups are limited to eight, and advance booking is essential. For details see *Booking address*, 'At a glance' box.

Athletes of the wild

Cheetahs are reputed to be the fastest mammals on earth, achieving speeds of up to 112 km/h. But what about the other animals?

In a 100-m dash across the savannah the cheetah would win hands down, with the springbok running a close second at 96 km/h.

Interestingly, third place would be a tie between a wildebeest, an ostrich and a lion (80 km/h).

Following at 64 km/h would be the spotted hyena and zebra, leaving buffaloes (56 km/h) and wild dogs (48 km/h) in a trail of dust.

Think an elephant (40 km/h) is slow? Consider that it would tie with a white rhino and run close behind a giraffe and warthog (48 km/h).

Here is the full result of a 100-m dash in the bush: 1. Cheetah (112 km/h), 2. Springbok (96 km/h), 3. Lion, ostrich, wildebeest (80 km/h), 4. Zebra, spotted hyena (64 km/h), 5. Buffalo (56 km/h), 6. Giraffe, warthog, wild dog (48 km/h), 7. Elephant, white rhino (40 km/h).

Where to stay Before your visit you must decide which camp suits your needs. Kruger's camps include ordinary Rest Camps (14), Private Camps (5), Bushveld Camps (6) and sponsored accommodation (about 100 units). Within these there's a huge array of accommodation options, ranging from elaborate, sumptuously furnished guest-houses to family cottages, chalets, huts, rondavels and tents.

The following entries describe many of the sought-after **rest camps** in the park, detailing their location, natural attractions and facilities.

BALULE On the southern bank of the Olifants River, 87 km from Phalaborwa Gate.

This rest camp is geared for those who want to be in the midst of nature without all of the creature comforts. There's no electricity, shop or restaurant, but the accommodation is comfortable. Guests are accommodated in six rustic three-bed huts, and on 15 sites for tents and caravans, with access to a communal kitchen, scullery and coal stoves.

BERG-EN-DAL On the banks of the Matjulu Spruit, 12 km from Malelane Gate.

This camp, one of the larger ones in the park, has been christened the Rhino Camp because of the many white rhinos in the vicinity. The clean, clinkered facebrick chalets are set among indigenous riverine vegetation, with each chalet leading on to a grassy garden.

The camp overlooks the Matjulu Dam, which provides excellent game- and bird-watching opportunities. Apart from crocodiles, visitors regularly see kudu, bushbuck and waterbuck come down to the water to drink. Bird species include whitefronted bee-eaters, fish eagles, common waxbills and greater blue-eared starlings.

The Rhino Walk leads you along a paved walkway that flanks the Matjulu River, and offers a braille trail for the blind.

A major attraction at Berg-en-Dal are night game-viewing drives, which must be booked in advance.

Accommodation consists of 68 three-bed chalets and 23 six-bed family chalets, with kitchen and *en suite* bathrooms; two sponsored houses, Rhino and Le Roux, available when not occupied by their sponsors; 70 camping and caravan sites, with ablution blocks and kitchens.

Facilities: Air-conditioned restaurant, well-stocked store, cafeteria, fast-food take-away and open-air theatre (where wildlife films are screened).

Things that go bump in the night

Jan van der Merwe, manager of the restaurant at the Lower Sabie rest camp in the Kruger National Park, had an encounter with a hippo he would rather forget.

He was driving back from Skukuza along the banks of the Sabie River at night with his three-year-old son George when there was an incredible crash from the left.

The car was knocked off its wheels and Mr van der Merwe and his son were sent flying out of the open door. The two tumbled down the banks of the Sabie River and came to rest near the water's edge. Mr van der Merwe was unconscious, but his son was uninjured.

It turned out a hippo was crossing the road to get to the river when it collided side on with the car, knocking it over.

Unknown to little George, a pride of lions was padding along the river bank nearby. The toddler cried as he tried to climb the bank. A little later an official in a patrol car saw the damaged car and stopped to investigate. He heard little George crying for help. Seeing the lions nearby, the official chased them off, then helped the youngster and his dad to safety.

Mr van der Merwe was rushed to hospital with a broken jaw, fractured and cracked ribs and cuts on the face, chest and hands — and a new-found respect for hippos.

CROCODILE BRIDGE Southeastern corner of the park, 13 km from Komatipoort.

This small camp near the bank of the Crocodile River serves as the southerly entrance gate to the park, and is often used as a one- or two-night stop before venturing further into the park. Some 5 km from camp, visitors may leave their cars and walk to the river to watch hippos basking in the pools. Elephants and rhinos are regularly seen in the vicinity.

Two- and three-bed huts, with fully equipped kitchens and *en suite* shower and toilet provide comfortable accommodation. There are also eight two-bed chalets on stilts.

Facilities: First-aid centre, petrol, shop, braaiing facilities, laundromat, public telephone.

LETABA On the southern bank of the Letaba River, 50 km from the Phalaborwa Gate.

The terraces of this beautiful camp overlook a sweeping bend in the Letaba River, where generous branches of sycamore fig and other riverine trees shade elephants, waterbuck, zebras and buffaloes which come down to the river to drink.

In and around the camp, large appleleaf, umbrella thorn and mopane trees, alive with vervet monkeys, shade a large variety of cottages, huts and four-bed tents. Around these, the terraced lawns are coloured by a profusion of flowering plants.

Letaba lies at the confluence of three major game drives: to Shingwedzi in the north, and to Satara and Olifants to the south, so gamewatching safaris from this camp have a lot of animals to offer.

A particularly scenic drive is that to the Olifants Rest Camp along the Letaba River. Visitors should include the Engelhardt and Mingerhout dams on their itinerary — both attract elephants, roan antelope, eland, impala and Sharpe's grysbok.

The Letaba camp is medium-sized with six-bed cottages, an assortment of two-, three- and four-bed huts, and two sponsored guest-houses, Fish Eagle House and Melville House, next to the camp. The six-bed cottages have *en suite* bathrooms and a fully equipped kitchen with gas stove and oven.

Some of the huts don't have cooking utensils and provide communal ablution facilities, so state your preference when booking.

Facilities: AA emergency service and workshop, petrol and diesel, restaurant, self-service and take-aways at the cafeteria, a shop, information centre and braai sites. Communal kitchens have cooking facilities, but no cooking utensils.

LOWER SABIE Southern Kruger, 35 km north of Crocodile Bridge.

The lush, riverine vegetation and bushveld surrounding the Sabie River are occupied by large numbers of lions, attracted to the area by grazing herds of wildebeest, zebras and impala.

Lower Sabie Rest Camp is an ideal base for several game drives, including the rewarding drive along the south bank of the Sabie River. A small dam just 1 km from the camp is home to crocodiles and hippos, and attracts large numbers of birds.

The camp is a popular family retreat, with sweeping lawns and shade trees, and offers scenic views of the Sabie River below. Several five-bed cottages, and three guesthouses (Keartland House, Steenbok Cottage and Moffat Cottage) complement one-, two- and three-bed huts, some with shower and toilet, others with baths. Some of the huts do not provide cooking utensils, crockery and cutlery, and share an ablution block.

Facilities: Petrol and diesel, electricity, first aid centre, restaurant, self-service and take-aways at the cafeteria, laundromat and irons, shop, braai sites. Communal kitchens have cooking facilities, but no cooking utensils.

MAROELA Southwestern Kruger, 4 km from Orpen Gate.

This is a small but attractive camping area on the banks of the Timbavati River. There's no electricity, and visitors must first report to the reception office at Orpen Gate.

MOPANI Central Kruger, 74 km north-east of Phalaborwa Gate.

Rough stone, local wood and thatch have been used to build the cottages and huts of this beautiful rustic camp on the eastern bank of the Pioneer Dam.

Accommodation includes six-bed cottages with fully equipped kitchen and two bathrooms, and various huts with fully equipped kitchens, sleeping porches and bathrooms or shower *en suite.* Two of the huts have been adapted to cater for handicapped people. There's also a guest-house (Xanatseni House) which caters for eight people.

Facilities: Petrol and diesel, electricity, shop, information centre, restaurant and ladies' bar, swimming pool, self-service and take-aways at the cafeteria, laundromat and irons, shop, braai sites.

OLIFANTS Central Kruger, 82 km from Phalaborwa Gate.

Built in 1960, this lovely camp lies on the northern bank of the Olifants River, near its confluence with the Letaba River. A scenic drive follows the course of the two rivers which are flanked by sycamore figs, tree euphorbias, jackalberry and fever trees — shady venues for elephants, kudu, impala and zebras. Two-, three- and four-bed thatched huts, with *en suite* shower and toilets, overlook the river and distant escarpment in one of the most beautiful settings in the park.

New to the camp are the superbly located Lebombo and Nshawu sponsored guest-houses, which are available to visitors when not being used by their sponsors.

Visitors may stroll to a shaded observation platform on the cliff line and watch as a variety of antelope, buffalo, elephant and hippo emerge from the densely wooded plains to congregate at the river's edge.

The thick vegetation in and around the camp includes a profusion of aloes, flame creepers and knobbly fig, whose large clusters of fruit attract a variety of birds. Among them are the whitebellied and marico sunbirds, bateleurs, Wahlberg's and African hawk eagles and yellowbilled kites.

Morning and evening game drives are available at Olifants, but must be booked at the camp's office in advance.

Facilities: Petrol, diesel, restaurant, cafeteria with take-aways, shop, laundromat and irons, communal kitchen and braai sites. There are no camping facilities.

ORPEN Western boundary of central Kruger.

This small gate camp is an ideal starting point for a tour of the park, and offers visitors immediate access to a variety of game at a waterhole just outside the camp. Another prime game-viewing spot is Rabelais Dam, 7 km from the rest camp.

Acacias, marula and bushwillow trees and an indigenous rock garden provide a cool and scenic setting for the two- and three-bed huts and the three family cottages.

Cooking utensils, crockery and cutlery are not provided in the huts, and only some have fridges. The family cottages, however, are fully equipped, with bathrooms, showers, kitchen (with stove and fridge), and cooking utensils. There is electricity in the family cottages and two of the huts.

Facilities: Petrol and diesel, shop, first-aid centre, communal kitchen with cooking facilities and sink.

PRETORIUSKOP Southwestern Kruger, 9 km from Numbi Gate.

Lying in the lee of Shabeni Hill, Pretoriuskop is the oldest and third largest of Kruger's camps. Fringed in summer by the lush foliage of marula, kiaat and sicklebush trees, it serves as a restful and scenic base for excursions through granite-studded hills into rhino, sable and zebra country.

The drive to Skukuza, 51 km to the northeast, is one of the park's finest. Alternatively, take the Hippo Pool and Doispane roads for exquisite views of the Sabie River.

Historical points of interest are the Voortrekker Road, birthplace of the legendary Jock of the Bushveld, and the Albasini Ruins near the camp.

The large variety of accommodation includes two-, three-, four- and five-bed huts or cottages, with varying degrees of facilities. Among the sponsored accommodation available is Pierre Joubert House (eight people) and the Doherty Bryant Boma (nine people).

Facilities: Petrol and diesel, cafeteria with take-aways, pool, shop, first-aid centre, laundromat, film shows on wildlife themes, electricity and restaurant.

PUNDA MARIA Northern Kruger, 10 km from Punda Maria Gate.

Situated in what is referred to as 'the botanical garden' of the Kruger Park — the Sandveld — Punda Maria is one of the most tranquil and remote camps in the park. No less than 83 species of shrub and tree are found in and around the camp.

It lies among the vast mopane plains of the north, a region inhabited by elephants and plains animals such as the rare tsessebe and sable antelope, eland, impala, buffalo and large herds of zebra.

Two rows of whitewashed chalets, consisting of 18 two-bed units and four three-bed units, stand unobtrusively on a hillock adjoining a pleasant campsite. Nearby are two four-bed cottages. All the units are air-conditioned, some have bathrooms, some have showers. The three- and four-bed units have a fully equipped kitchen.

There are three attractive game drives from Punda Maria, among them the popular 28-km Mahonie Loop, which encircles the camp and may yield sightings of wild dogs, hyenas or leopards among the myrtle bushwillow and pod mahoganies so typical of the region. Another drive takes you from Punda through the mopane woodlands to the Luvuvhu River at Pafuri, a birder's paradise, where tropical boubous, yellowbellied sunbirds and Narina trogons are part of the vast community of birds.

SATARA Central Kruger, 48 km from Orpen Gate.

Set among the rich knobthorn veld of southern Kruger, Satara, the second-largest camp in the park, is ideally located for those who want to watch lions. The big cats prey on the ample numbers of antelope that seek the rich grasses of these plains, and compete with wild dogs, blackbacked jackals and spotted hyenas for their kills. Rare antelope inhabiting the area include sable, eland and nyala, and you will most certainly see black and white rhino.

The camp may not have the great views of Sabie, Orpen or Letaba, but its own rustic charm is enhanced by the jackalberry, knobthorn and marula trees, flowers and birds, such as yellowbilled hornbills, glossy blue-eared starlings and Natal francolins, which occupy the camp.

The drive to Orpen gate 48 km to the west is a rewarding excursion for game-watchers, but take time to branch off right to the Timbavati picnic spot after 18 km, and follow the course of the Timbavati River for views of crocodiles, hippos and other game.

Two and three-bed huts complement three large guest-houses (Rudy Frankel House, Stanley House and Wells House) and nine six-bed cottages. There are also two-bed huts, some with facilities for handicapped people. The huts have showers, toilets, refrigerator and verandah, but no cooking utensils, crockery or cutlery.

Facilities: AA emergency service for vehicles, petrol and diesel, cafeteria with take-aways, shop, first-aid centre, laundromat and irons, regular film shows on wildlife themes, electricity, restaurant, communal kitchens with sinks and cooking facilities, but no cooking utensils, crockery or cutlery.

SHINGWEDZI Northeastern Kruger, 70 km from Punda Maria Gate.

Situated in the mopane country of the north, Shingwedzi is a charming, friendly camp of square bungalows interspersed with mopane trees and brilliant pink impala lilies. The camp is set in typical elephant country, where more than 900 leopards stalk the long grass in search of prey such as impala, nyala and duiker. The Shingwedzi River heads south of the camp, its ample waters hosting crocodiles and hippos, and its lush, riverine forests attracting waterbuck and reedbuck.

These animals may be viewed on a game drive along the river to the Tshange observation point and the Kanniedood Dam and Crocodile Pool.

Two-, three- and five-bed huts with shower, toilet and refrigerators (some with stoves) offer guests comfortable accommodation. More luxurious is the four-bed cottage and single guest-house (Rentmeester House), which takes up to seven visitors.

Facilities: Petrol and diesel, cafeteria with take-aways, shop, first-aid centre, swimming pool, laundromat and irons, film shows on wildlife themes, electricity, restaurant, communal kitchens with sinks and cooking facilities (but no cooking utensils, crockery or cutlery) and braai facilities.

SKUKUZA Southwestern Kruger, 12 km from Paul Kruger Gate.

The word Skukuza means 'he who sweeps clean' and it was the name given to the park's first warden, James Stevenson-Hamilton, for the unremitting war he waged against poachers in the park's early days.

The camp is the administrative and operational headquarters of the park, and has more facilities than any other rest camp. The most impressive of these is one of the largest thatched structures in the southern hemisphere which houses a restaurant, shop and various offices.

There are various historical sites within the camp, including the Selati Rail Museum, a bell tower, old pontoon bridge and the Campbell Hut Museum.

There are several guest-houses here accommodating between four and nine people each, as well as two- and three-bed huts, luxury caravans, cottages and furnished tents under shade nets capable of accommodating about 600 people.

In spite of Skukuza's modern ambience, the countryside around the camp is well populated by game of all sorts, and the Stevenson-Hamilton Memorial Information Centre in the camp will supply full details of routes to take and which animals you may expect to see.

Facilities: Doctor, AA emergency service for vehicles, petrol and diesel, post office and public telephone, bank, information centre, courier services, library, cafeteria with take-aways, shop, first-aid centre, laundromat and irons, nursery for indigenous plants, film shows on wildlife themes, electricity, restaurant and Selati Train Restaurant, communal kitchens with sinks and cooking facilities (but no cooking utensils, crockery or cutlery).

The entries listed next are the **bushveld camps** in the park, with their locations, natural attractions and facilities.

BATELEUR They call it the smallest, oldest and friendliest camp in Kruger, and it lies on the bank of the Mashokwe Spruit, 40 km southwest of Shingwedzi Rest Camp.

A pack of wild dogs, spotted hyenas or lions could be part of your roadside reception committee on the way to Bateleur.

Seven thatched family cottages nestle in the shade of leadwood, mopane and apple-leaf trees, providing generous nesting and feeding quarters for a rich variety of birds.

A hide sheltered by a giant jackalberry overlooks the Mashokwe Spruit and a nearby waterhole where, inevitably, you'll see elephants, buffaloes, leopards and lions.

A private road network includes stops at two dams, Rooibosrant and Silvervis, frequented by dozens of large and small mammals. Among the birds you'll see here are greater honeyguides, freckled nightjars, brownheaded parrots and giant eagle owls.

Attractions at Bateleur include day and night drives, and there's such an abundance of game that you would do well to take a field guide or two.

Facilities: Petrol and provisions available at Shingwedzi Rest Camp; braai sites, conference facilities. Units serviced; beds, towels and soap provided. Wood, ice available at office.

MBYAMITI Location: Southern Kruger, on the bank of the Mbyamiti River, 40 km from Malelane Gate.

This bushveld camp is appropriately named — Mbyamiti means 'place of many trees' — because it lies in a region generously covered by marula, bushwillow, buffalo, knobthorn, sausage and jackalberry trees. The rich vegetation attracts all manner of game, and the drives along the 22-km stretch of road restricted to camp residents will invariably yield sightings of leopards, giraffes, kudu, impala and duiker. Other recommended drives are the one north to Mpondo Dam (noted for its prolific birdlife), or the one southeast to Crocodile Bridge.

Ranger-led game drives from Mbyamiti also bring guests into close contact with such bird species as giant eagle owls and whitefaced owls, Wahlberg's eagles, scarletchested sunbirds and brownhooded kingfishers.

The camp itself offers a choice of 15 family cottages accommodating a maximum of 70 guests. An interesting feature of the camp is a short trail that leads past a hide through indigenous, labelled trees.

Facilities: No petrol or provisions, but petrol is available at Lower Sabie, Berg-en-Dal and Crocodile Bridge. Electricity is solar powered; fridges without freezing compartments (communal freezer is available), braai facilities, open parking.

TALAMATI Central Kruger, about 30 km southeast of Orpen Gate.

Flowering blood lilies bring splashes of colour to the countryside around this smallish camp after early summer rains. The camp lies on the banks of the N'waswitsontso River in central Kruger, which is renowned for its variety of cats, including the very rare king cheetah.

Talamati offers 15 thatched cottages, fringed by leadwood and russet bushwillow trees. All the cottages have *en suite* bathrooms, with an open-plan livingroom-kitchen and a separate braai area.

Along the river's banks, jackalberries and sycamore fig trees offer refuge to baboons and a variety of birds. Two waterholes near the camp attract so many mammals in the dry season that you may see as much game as you could hope for (including lions and breeding herds of elephants), without going on a game drive.

The game drive to Mondzweni Dam produces sightings of wildebeest, herds of impala and zebras and, if you're lucky, white rhinos and cheetahs.

Facilities: Refrigerators, braai sites, solar panels provide electricity for lights and fans, nearest shop at Orpen Rest Camp (30 km). Towels, bedding and soap are provided.

SHIMUWINI Upper reaches of Shimuwini Dam, 50 km from Phalaborwa Gate.

The tree-lined banks of the Letaba River make a perfect setting for this camp, which offers excellent birdwatching opportunities.

There are 15 family cottages, comprising nine five-bed units, five four-bed units and one six-bed unit. Some of the cottages have baths, some showers, and all are equipped with cooking facilities, fridges, crockery and cutlery. The camp accommodates up to 71 visitors.

Facilities: Nearest shops at Letaba and Mopani rest camps; electricity supplied by solar units; braai facilities; communal freezer. Units are serviced; towels and bedding provided.

SIRHENI Bank of Sirheni Dam, 54 km from Punda Maria Rest Camp.

Beautifully situated for gamewatching purposes, Sirheni has 15 family cottages, consisting of 10 six-bed cottages (with open verandah), and five four-bed cottages. Most of the units have bathrooms or showers, gas stove, fridge, cooking utensils, crockery and cutlery.

Facilities: Electricity for lights and fans supplied by solar panels, braai facilities, communal freezer, serviced units, with bedding, towels and soap; nearest shop at Shingwedzi Rest Camp.

Tips for travellers

- **When travelling in the park it is important to remember that the opening and closing times of camp gates change from month to month (see 'At a glance' box). The gate times at Olifants Camp, for instance, change nine times a year. Gate times are usually recorded on wooden 'clock owls' at the entrance to the camps.**
- **The National Parks Board gives preference to bookings made 13 months in advance. Such reservations are confirmed 11 to 12 months in advance.**

JAKKALSBESSIE On the banks of the Sabie River, 7 km from Skukuza Rest Camp.

The easy access to Skukuza makes Jakkalsbessie popular among those who want a true bush experience close to their creature comforts.

The camp has eight family cottages accommodating 32 guests in two four-bed cottages with open verandah and six four-bed cottages with living/diningroom. Some of the units have baths, others have showers. All the units have a stove (some don't have an oven), fridge, cooking and eating utensils.

Facilities: Electricity, braai facilities, serviced units with bedding, towels and soap; nearest shop at Skukuza Rest Camp.

In addition to the public and bushveld camps, there are five **private camps** in Kruger, each of which has to be booked completely by one group at a time. The camps are totally private in that they are not open to other tourists in the park, and they do not have a resident rest camp manager.

MALELANE Southern Kruger, 3 km from Malelane Gate.

Accommodation: 18 people in two three-bed and three four-bed huts, with air-conditioning, shower, toilet and washbasin.

Facilities; Electricity, ablution block, communal kitchen, braai facilities; nearest shop at Berg-en-Dal Rest Camp (9 km).

JOCK OF THE BUSHVELD Southern Kruger, 40 km from Berg-en-Dal Rest Camp on the Skukuza Road.

Accommodation: Three family huts.

Facilities: Communal lounge/diningroom, open both sides, communal kitchen, solar-powered lighting, braai facilities; nearest shops at Berg-en-Dal, Skukuza.

NWANETSI Southwestern Kruger, 27 km from Satara.

Accommodation: 16 people in two two-bed huts and four three-bed huts (shower, toilet, washbasin in each hut).

Facilities: Communal diningroom/lounge with bar, communal kitchen, gas lamps (no electricity), braai facilities; nearest shop at Satara Rest Camp.

ROODEWAL Central Kruger, 40 km from Olifants Rest Camp.

This delightful camp, nestling under a riverine canopy of knobthorn, nyala berry and armed horn thorn on the banks of the Timbavati River is exceptional for its architect-designed, thatched chalets, lovely lawns and lush surroundings.

Thanks to a perennial spring, game is always abundant and visitors can expect to see leopards, elephants, lions and a wide variety of antelope — even when the river's dry.

Accommodation: 19 people in one family cottage (four beds) and three huts (each with five single beds, shower, toilet, washbasin and fridge).

Facilities: Observation platform over Timbavati waterhole, separate diningroom and kitchen (stove, fridge, freezer, cooking and eating utensils), braai facilities, solar-powered lights; nearest shop at Olifants Rest Camp (40 km).

BOULDERS Central Kruger, 50 km north of Letaba Rest Camp.

Accommodation: Camps on stilts accommodating 12 people in thatched units connected by boardwalk accessing lounge/diningroom, bar, kitchen (oven, fridge, freezer), cooking and eating utensils. Open patio overlooks waterhole, 100 m away.

Facilities: Solar-powered lights and fans, braai facilities; nearest shop at Letaba Rest Camp.

Kruger National Park at a glance

Locality:	Mpumalanga Lowveld/Northern Province on the western border of Mozambique.
Climate:	Subtropical, with hot, wet summers. Rain falls between October and March (from 700 mm in the south to 400 mm in the north). Winters sunny and warm with ideal game-viewing.
Number of camps:	There are 25 rest camps in the park, comprising 14 public camps, six bushveld camps and five private camps.
Game drives:	There are 2 600 km of tarred and gravel roads throughout the park.
Hides and waterholes:	Check with your camp warden about hides and waterholes near your camp.
Trails:	Seven: Bushman, Metsi-Metsi, Napi, Nyalaland, Olifants, Sweni and Wolhuter.
Other attractions:	Photography, birdwatching.
Amenities:	See under Facilities in individual entries.
Accommodation:	Ranges from fully furnished guest-houses to family cottages, chalets, huts, rondavels and tents. There are caravan and camping sites at Balule, Berg-en-Dal, Crocodile Bridge, Letaba, Maroela, Lower Sabie, Pretoriuskop, Punda Maria, Satara, Shingwedzi and Skukuza.
Booking address:	National Parks Board, PO Box 787, Pretoria 0001, tel (012) 343-1991; or National Parks Board, PO Box 7400, Roggebaai 8012, tel (021) 22-2810.
When to go:	Summer, with its attendant rain, is the best time to visit the park; but winter, with less water, is also good.
What to take with you:	Check your camp brochure to see what facilities are available in your camp. These vary considerably throughout the park. Take along sunglasses, light clothing in summer, warm gear in winter; camera, binoculars, field guide and get a good map from the rest camp shop.
How to get there:	Eight entrance gates service the park: Pafuri and Punda Maria in the north, Phalaborwa and Orpen in the central region; and Paul Kruger, Numbi, Malelane and Crocodile Bridge in the south. To access the southern part from Johannesburg take the N4 to Nelspruit, through to Komatipoort and Crocodile Bridge; for the central part take the N1 north from Johannesburg, branching off east on the R71 to get to Phalaborwa via Tzaneen; for northern Kruger (Punda Maria Gate) branch off the N1 on to the R524 at Louis Trichardt.
Nearest doctor:	There is a doctor's consulting room and dispensary in Skukuza Rest Camp.
Nearest petrol:	Available at most entrance gates, with the exception of Malelane, Paul Kruger, Numbi, Phalaborwa, Pafuri and Punda Maria. Also at all the camps with the exception of the bushveld camps, private camps, Balule and Maroela.
Open:	January–February: 05:30–18:30; March: 05:00–18:00; April: 06:00–17:30; 1 May–31 August: 06:30–17:30; September: 06:00–18:00; October: 05:30–18:00; 1 November–31 December: 05:30–18:30.
Special precautions:	Take antimalaria precautions before you visit the park.

Lapalala Wilderness Area

Lapalala is one of the largest singly-owned private reserves in South Africa, covering 35 350 ha of pristine wilderness in the Waterberg Mountains of the northwestern part of the Northern Province.

It forms the heart of a much larger sanctuary — the 80 000-ha Waterberg Nature Conservancy, a jigsaw puzzle of private reserves run by nine different landowners that offers travellers a variety of attractions, including big game, horse trails, San paintings and rustic accommodation in beautiful surroundings.

Lapalala lies about 100 km northeast of Marakele National Park which promises to become one of the great parks of Africa.

The reserve offers you the freedom to explore the bush in peace and tranquillity, kilometres away from the nearest human habitation. Here eroded buttresses of sandstone soar above the placid waters of the Lephalala and Blocklands rivers as they wind 53 km through the reserve, cascading over rapids and emptying out into huge, deep pools fringed by waterlilies.

These rivers form the idyllic setting for six fully equipped hutted bush camps, each situated kilometres apart from the next one, in an atmosphere of privacy and peace.

After checking in at the reserve's reception area, and being settled in the camp of your choice, you are on your own. Lapalala is for walking, and no driving is allowed. There's plenty to see and do: you can venture out on game-viewing expeditions, explore the krantzes and their galleries of San art, or swim in the clear, bilharzia-free waters of the rivers.

Just a three-hour drive or 55 minutes by air from Johannesburg, the Lapalala Wilderness sprawls across a large plateau 1 100 m above sea level, inviting guests to revel in its fresh mountain air and panoramic views.

Wildlife Although Lapalala boasts a huge diversity of other animals, much of its attention is focused on restoring Africa's dwindling populations of black rhinos (down from 65 000 in the sixties, to less than 2 500 in the mid-nineties).

In 1990 Lapalala became the first private reserve in South Africa to obtain black rhinos (a founder group of five black rhinos were bought from the KwaZulu-Natal Nature Conservation Services for R22 million). Two years later five more rhinos were bought and were released into a special 10 000-ha game-fenced section of the wilderness area. Today, this breeding nucleus of rhinos is a major attraction for visitors.

One of Lapalala's most eminent residents is Bwana Tshiwana (Mr Orphan), the first black rhino born in the reserve, and later abandoned by its mother in 1992.

Fifty-nine other mammal species have found sanctuary in the Lapalala Wilderness Area. The larger mammals include hippos, black and white rhinos, blue wildebeest, giraffes, red hartebeest, eland, Burchell's zebras, leopards, cheetahs, kudu, impala, duiker, brown hyenas, roan and sable antelope, aardvark and aardwolf, while the smaller residents include bateared foxes, African wild cats, caracals, chacma baboons, pangolins, monkeys and various species of mongoose. Reptiles abound here, and include African rock pythons, leopard tortoises, hingeback tortoises, Egyptian and Mozambique spitting cobras, black mambas, puffadders, eastern tiger snakes, southern stiletto snakes, yellow-bellied sand snakes and common egg-eaters.

Birdlife Among the 270 bird species there is an impressive list of raptors, such as black eagles, martial eagles, brown snake eagles, Ayres' eagles and booted eagles. Others include buzzards, goshawks, falcons, kites and three species of vulture (whitebacked, lappetfaced and Cape). There are nine species of kingfisher, various honeyguides, owls, cuckoos and hornbills.

Where to stay Kolobe Lodge is an idyllic mountain retreat with unsurpassed views of virgin bushveld that pampers 16 guests in four thatched, fully equipped rondavels, each with *en suite* bathroom. Evening meals around a fire are served in a boma under the canopy of a giant fig tree.

Kolobe opened in 1990 and its many attractions include a swimming pool, tennis court and a superb bar (the Explorer's Bar), where conversations mingle with the romantic sounds of the wilderness around you. Talks on natural history are offered to give guests a deeper insight into the ways of the wild.

For accommodation of a different kind, try one of Lapalala's six bush camps: Tambuti, at the confluence of the Lephalala and Blocklands rivers, has eight beds; Marula and Lepotedi, both on the Lephalala River, have six; Umdoni and Manadu have four beds each, and Mukwa two. No staff are in attendance, and the accommodation is rustic and comfortable. There are showers and an inside toilet. Bedding, crockery and cutlery, fridges, gas rings and paraffin lamps are provided, as well as a rustic boma for fireside meals.

Rhino Camp, a rustic eight-bed tented camp on the banks of the Kgogong River, is run by Clive Walker Safaris, and features an open-plan diningroom and lounge under thatch, not far from a cosy boma/braai area.

Another tented camp is Mogonono, which is used exclusively as a base for Clive Walker Trails and Safaris (to organise a safari contact the booking address in the 'At a glance' box).

Game trails and drives Four-wheel-drive excursions and walking trails are organised from Kolobe Lodge in the company of an experienced ranger-guide. The Lapalala River Trail is a three-day guided trail along the Lephalala River.

Other attractions There are nine sites along the Kgogong and Lephalala rivers featuring Late Stone-Age San paintings. In addition, the wilderness area is peppered with Iron-Age sites which date between AD 1500 and 1800. Two sites between Ndrobo and Tambuti bear remains of pottery shards and stone-walled buildings, while another fascinating stone-walled site still exists on Malora Hill.

The wilderness area is also the site of the Lapalala Wilderness School, a centre established on the farm Moerdyk, for the environmental education of teachers and scholars. The main camp here is Rapula House, a 36-bed, stone-and-thatch building. Two smaller camps, Molepe and Mosetse, accommodate up to 32 students who learn about ecology, mammal and bird identification and soil erosion.

Touchstone Game Ranch

Flanking the Lapalala Wilderness Area along the eastern banks of the Lephalala River is the 18 000-ha Touchstone Game Ranch, a conservancy populated by elephants, white rhinos, buffaloes, leopards, black impala and warthogs.

The reserve is just a three-hour drive northwest of Johannesburg and is developing fast into one of the country's more sought-after private sanctuaries.

Apart from its wildlife, Touchstone is popular for its San rock art and the fact that the reserve is malaria-free.

Where to stay Visitors have a choice of excellent accommodation in any of the following:

Millstone Lodge is an attractive thatched complex comprising four double, *en suite* rooms, with the services of a ranger and cooking staff. Game trails are available on foot or in a 4x4.

Flagstone Lodge consists of thatched cottages with *en suite* bathrooms and accommodates up to ten guests. The lodge is fully catered with optional game drives.

Flintstone Camp sleeps six guests in double tents with *en suite* bathrooms. Escorted game drives are available.

Rock Lodge is a rustic, 12-bedded rock cabin with a swimming pool. Game drives are available on request.

Trails The Fig Tree and Milkwood hiking trails give you the chance to explore the diversity of wildlife in the Waterberg. The Fig Tree trail is serviced by wood cabins accommodating 12 people. The Milkwood Trail has a 12-bed tented camp which serves as a base for exploring Touchstone Game Ranch.

For booking details contact Touchstone Game Ranch, PO Box 57, Marken 0605, tel (014) 765-0230.

Lapalala Wilderness Area at a glance

Locality:	Waterberg Mountains of the northwestern Northern Province, north of Vaalwater and northwest of Melkrivier (300 km from Johannesburg).
Climate:	Summers are warm to hot, with thunderstorms; winter days are mild and sunny, but the nights can be cold.
Game drives:	Bush drives on the back of an open Land Rover are offered at Kolobe Lodge. There are no game drives from the bush camps.
Trails:	Various walking trails are offered. For details contact Lapalala Wilderness Area (see booking address below).
Other attractions:	Rock art, Iron-Age sites.
Amenities:	Diningroom and bar at Kolobe Lodge.
Accommodation:	Four rondavels at **Kolobe Lodge**. Eight bush camps: **Tambuti, Marula, Lepotedi, Umdoni, Manadu, Mukwa, Rhino Camp** and **Mogonono. Touchstone Game Ranch:** Millstone Lodge, double *en suite* rooms; Flagstone Lodge, thatched cottages; Flintstone Camp, three double tents; Rock Lodge, 12-bed rock cabin.
Booking address:	Lapalala Wilderness, PO Box 645, Bedfordview 2008, tel (011) 453-7645.
When to go:	All year round.
What to take with you:	Hiking boots or tough shoes, torch, charcoal, camera, film, binoculars, hat. Guests staying in the bush camps must take their own provisions.
How to get there:	Drive north on the N1 from Johannesburg and take the Nylstroom/Vaalwater turn-off. From Vaalwater take the Melkrivier road. After 40 km turn right at Melkrivier School and follow the signposts to the reception area.
Nearest petrol:	Vaalwater.

Marakele National Park

The Tswana name Marakele means 'place of sanctuary', and you couldn't find a better one than this secluded reserve in the heart of the Waterberg Mountains, 250 km north of Johannesburg. It lies in the transitional zone between the arid western and the wetter eastern parts of South Africa and therefore serves as home to an abundance of mammal and bird species common to both regions.

Lions, elephants and rhino are some of the large mammals inhabiting the reserve which boasts the largest population of breeding pairs of Cape vultures in the world — 800 individuals. The park has beautiful landscapes of mountains, hills and valleys, and is home to towering yellowwoods and cedar trees. You'll also find giant cycads and tree ferns.

A rustic six-tent safari camp on the banks of the Matlabas River accommodates 24 people. The tents have private bathrooms, fully equipped kitchens with refrigerator/freezers and stoves. There are also braai facilities.

Access to the park is via Thabazimbi and is restricted to four-wheel-drive vehicles only. Office hours are 08:00–17:00 (1 May to 31 August) and 08:00–18:00 (1 September to 30 April).

For more details contact the park at (01477) 37-1745.

Kudu Canyon

This attractive 200-ha game ranch flanking the Hans Strydom Dam Nature Reserve, between Vaalwater and Ellisras, entices visitors with more than 50 mammal species, including rhino, leopard, buffalo and bontebok and more than 300 species of bird.

There are four lodges and one tented bush camp: Loerie Lodge accommodates six people in one double room with toilet and basin and two bedrooms sharing a bathroom. There's also a separate toilet and shower. Kingfisher Lodge accommodates six in one *en suite* bedroom and another bedroom and upstairs loft with two single beds sharing a bathroom. Hornbill Lodge accommodates two in one *en suite* double room. Bush Shrike Lodge is an attractive double *en suite* bedroom on stilts with beautiful views. The tented bush camp sleeps 12 people in six tents and has a fully equipped kitchen, showers and toilets. Guests must bring their own sleeping bag, pillow and towels.

All lodges and the tented camp are serviced and have their own swimming pool and braai facilities and all lodges are fully equipped with kitchen utensils, gas stove, fridge, crockery, bath towels, swimming towels and linen.

Attractions at Kudu Canyon include nature trails, boat trips on the dam where you can see crocodiles, fishing and birdwatching.

For more details contact Kudu Canyon at PO Box 39904, Bramley 2018, tel (011) 608-2149.

Londolozi Game Reserve

A wooden balcony, supported 20 m above the ground by the branches of an ancient jackalberry tree, provides a scenic view across the mellow-coloured sunset. Below, impala kebabs sizzle on a boma braai, sending the aroma of grilled meat wafting into the starry sky above the untamed bush.

This is Londolozi Game Reserve, described by experienced gamewatchers as the most beautiful camp in Africa.

Home of the Londolozi leopards, refuge of the rich and famous, sanctuary to an extraordinary array of animals and birds — including the Big Five — Londolozi offers probably the best you'll find in any game reserve anywhere in Africa — at a price, of course.

Hidden by a canopy of thick bushveld country alongside the western boundary of the Kruger National Park, Londolozi won the Asata Award for excellent service three years in a row.

Its philosophy is based on three precepts: care of the land, care of animals and care of people. It is uniquely luxurious — a perfect marriage of the wild outdoors with the convenience of pampered accommodation. Finally, it is private, with immediate access to a variety of game, large and small. Lastly, but by no means least, Londolozi is exceptionally beautiful.

Londolozi, which means 'protector of all living things', started assuming its present shape when conservationist brothers John and Dave Varty took it over in the early 1970s. Then it consisted of only four primitive rondavels, a bush shower and an ablution block. The Varty brothers removed alien vegetation which was threatening to cripple the indigenous growth, restored some of the dwindling populations of game, such as cheetah and elephant, and offered bush trails and safaris.

Wildlife In 1979 leopards started making an appearance in the reserve, and it soon became the most popular sanctuary for leopards in the country. Today it is world famous for its leopard sightings, and a number of books have been produced on the famed leopards of Londolozi. But, apart from these magnificent cats, Londolozi has a huge abundance of game, ranging from elephants, lions, rhinos, hippos and buffaloes, to nyala, bushbuck, wild dogs, white rhino, spotted hyenas, waterbuck and warthogs. In addition, the herds of wildebeest and zebras, so prolific in the area earlier this century, are returning. These, and a variety of smaller mammals, make game-watching trips just minutes away from the camps a highly memorable experience.

Birdlife More than 200 species of bird inhabit the sycamore figs, sausage, Natal mahogany and jackalberry trees around the camps. Fish eagles, blackheaded herons, kori bustards, cuckoo hawks, blackeyed bulbuls and giant eagle owls are just some of the birds you're likely to see.

Where to stay Covering an area of some 14 000 ha of pristine bushveld, Londolozi offers guests a choice of three totally different camps.

MAIN CAMP The camp accommodates 24 people, and lies discreetly camouflaged by red ivory and jackalberry trees in thick bush overlooking the beautiful Sand River.

There are eight double chalets here, each with its own teak verandah and private plunge pool, an elevated private balcony and an *en suite* bathroom with splendid views of the river.

A short way from Main Camp are two exclusive Granite Suites, built on boulders overlooking the tranquil rock pools of the Sand River.

A major attraction of Main Camp is the magnificent dining verandah which offers buffet lunches and English breakfasts.

Evening meals are served in the boma, the central attraction of which is a charming bar, set under flowering bougainvilleas, and overlooking the crystalline cascade of the Sand River over granite rocks far below. There's also a delightful swimming pool and a curio shop.

▲ 1

1 Elephants near the cosy Addo Elephant National Park Rest Camp in South Africa's Eastern Cape province.
2 An Addo elephant browses among a floral carpet in the Addo Elephant National Park.
3 A quiver tree typical of the area around the Augrabies Falls National Park. The San used the bark as quivers for their arrows.

▲ 2

3 ▼

4 A caracal – also known as a lynx – prepares to feast on prey it has just killed in the Bontebok National Park.
5 The bontebok of the Bontebok National Park near Swellendam teetered on the brink of extinction a few years ago.
6 The Bontebok National Park lies in a tranquil region of fynbos and renosterveld just south of Swellendam.

▲4

▲5

6▼

▲ 7 8 ▼

▲ 9 10 ▼

7 Towering sandstone buttresses welcome visitors to Golden Gate Highlands National Park.

8 Awesome mountainscapes such as these leave indelible memories for visitors to Giant's Castle Game Reserve.

9 The Indian Ocean thunders into a cove along De Hoop Nature Reserve's enigmatic shoreline.

10 De Hoop Nature Reserve's beautiful coastal trail affords hikers superb views of southern right whales.

▲ 11

12 ▼

▲ 13

14 ▼

11 Thatched, self-contained cottages in Giant's Castle Game Reserve are on a par with the best in the world.
12 Charter's Creek, in the Greater St Lucia Wetland Park, is a paradise for birdwatchers and boating enthusiasts.
13 Giant's Castle Camp looks across to the snow-covered basalt walls of the Drakensberg.
14 Thatched rondavels catch the rays of the early morning sun at Charter's Creek.

▲ 15

16 ▼

▼ 17

15 Trees form stark silhouettes along the shoreline at Rocky Point in False Bay Park on the western fringes of Lake St Lucia.
16 A cottage at Fanie's Island, another tranquil retreat in the Greater St Lucia Wetland Park.
17 A modern, elegantly furnished cottage at Fanie's Island.

18 ▼ ▲ 19

▲ 20 21 ▼

18 The day ends at Fanie's Island in a celebration of colours, bringing stillness to the lake shore.
19 The recently upgraded Hilltop Camp in Hluhluwe Game Reserve overlooks undulating valleys and grasslands.
20 White rhinos graze in the lush grasslands of Hluhluwe, one of Africa's oldest game reserves.
21 The ochre-walled, thatched chalets of Hluhluwe's Hilltop Camp are furnished with ethnic cane furniture.

▲ 22

▲ 23

▲ 25

▼ 24

22 A family of cheetah rest in the shade of an acacia tree in the Kalahari.
23 The sands of the Kalahari, tinged ochre by iron oxides, form a canvas of rich textures and shapes in the Kalahari Gemsbok National Park.
24 Rain brings an explosion of growth and colour to the Kalahari Gemsbok National Park.
25 The haunting landscape of the Karoo National Park is a legacy of great volcanic eruptions which occurred nearly 200 million years ago.

▲ 26

▲ 27

26 The rest camp in the Karoo National Park lies on one of the world's richest vaults of ancient fossils.
27 Duiker such as this one relish the rich grasses of the Karoo National Park.
28 One of Kruger's 2 000 lions yawns before settling down to a full-day nap.

▼ 28

▲ 29

▲ 30

▲ 31

▲ 32

29 Gamewatchers stop at the river's edge on one of the Kruger National Park's wilderness trails.

30 A Kruger National Park wildebeest performs its ablutions.

31 A ranger scans a valley of acacia and mopane trees on a Kruger National Park wilderness trail.

32 Boulders Private Camp in central Kruger offers attractive thatched units on stilts.

▲ 33

▲ 34

35 ▼

33 The green terraces of Letaba Camp in the Kruger National Park overlook a bend in the Letaba River.
34 A protective elephant cow guides her tiny calf between her legs in the Kruger National Park.
35 Shimuwini Bushveld Camp is a birdwatchers' paradise in western Kruger National Park.

▲ 36

36 A redbilled hornbill scans the ground for a potential meal in the Kruger National Park.
37 Draped over a dead branch, a leopard slumbers between kills in the Kruger National Park.
38 The ground hornbill's duet is one of the more common sounds heard towards evening in the Kruger National Park.

▲ 37

▲ 38

▲ 39

40 ▼

▼ 41

▼ 42

39 These rustic and comfortable chalets accommodate overnight hikers on the Olifants Wilderness Trail in the Kruger National Park.
40 There are more than 21 000 buffaloes in the Kruger National Park. Trailists give these bad-tempered mammals a wide berth.
41 The Tree Camp boma at Londolozi Game Reserve, which some gamewatchers regard as the best camp in Africa.
42 Madikwe River Lodge, one of South Africa's newest game reserves, offers 16 thatched chalets on the banks of the Marico River.

▲ 43

44 ▼

43 Ethnic chalets at Makalali Private Game Reserve – one of Southern Africa's newest wild places.
44 Quaint African architecture complements excellent local cuisine in the outdoor dining area at Makalali.
45 Mkuzi Safari Camp, tucked away in the bush, is tailor-made for gamewatchers who seek tranquillity.

▲ 45

46 ▼

▲ 47

▲ 48

49 ▼

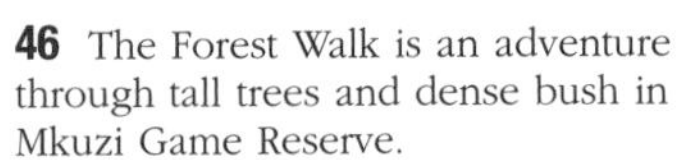

46 The Forest Walk is an adventure through tall trees and dense bush in Mkuzi Game Reserve.
47 Trailists pause on the edge of Ensumo Pan at sunset during a walk in Mkuzi Game Reserve.
48 The Cape mountain zebra has been rescued from extinction by reserves such as the Mountain Zebra National Park in the Karoo.
49 An elevated wooden deck overlooks Banzi Pan in Ndumo Game Reserve.

▲ 50

51 ▼

▼ 54

▲ 52

▲ 53

50 Guests on a game drive in Ndumo Game Reserve along KwaZulu-Natal's northern border with Mozambique.
51 Perched among the trees at Ndumo Wilderness Camp are these luxury tents with private views.
52 The main lounge and leisure area of Ngala Game Reserve.
53 Dinner at Ngala Game Reserve is a romantic affair under a star-studded sky.
54 Guests at Phinda Resource Reserve can enjoy leisurely cruises along the Mzinene River.

▲ 55

56 ▼

57 ▼

55 The Richtersveld, a barren mountainland bisected by the Orange River, is a paradise for seekers of solitude.
56 The bare soil of the Richtersveld is dotted with brightly coloured flowers in spring.
57 Visitors to Rocktail Bay Lodge relax at the poolside in the warm summer sun of the Maputaland coast.

Gatherings in the boma are memorable occasions with excellent cuisine, a real African atmosphere, and pampered attention from the hosts.

TREE CAMP This spectacular camp, whose central dining complex has been built in the branches of a ebony tree 25 m above the ground, is regarded as one of the finest in Southern Africa. The luxurious chalets blend in with the riverine habitat, and offer privacy and an eagle's-eye view of the surrounding countryside. Each chalet has its own cascading plunge pool and a cosy covered deck in the treetops. The chalets are elegantly furnished with soft silks and Zanzibarian lamps and have spacious *en suite* bathrooms and an outdoor shower.

Tree Camp, which accommodates eight people, offers the services of a private hostess and game ranger.

Londolozi Game Reserve at a glance

Locality:	Mpumalanga, on the western border of the Kruger National Park.
Climate:	Summers hot with thundershowers; winters mild to cold and dry.
Number of camps:	Three.
Game drives:	Day and night drives are led by professional rangers.
Trails:	Armed Shangaan rangers conduct bush walks on request.
Other attractions:	Photography, relaxing at the poolside.
Amenities:	Swimming pool in each camp, and curio shop.
Accommodation:	**Main Camp**, eight double chalets (24 people), with private balcony and *en suite* bathroom; **Tree Camp**, six luxury chalets (8 people), with *en suite* shower, bath and toilet facilities; **Bush Camp**, eight rock chalets, with *en suite* bathrooms and outdoor showers.
Booking address:	Londolozi Game Reserve, The Conservation Corporation, Private Bag X27, Benmore 2010, tel (011) 784-6832.
When to go:	Throughout the year, but game-viewing is better in winter.
What to take with you:	Cool, light clothing in summer; warm clothing (including anorak) in winter. Binoculars, camera, field guide, bathing costume, walking boots, sunhat, dark glasses.
How to get there:	From Johannesburg drive east on the N12, which links up with the N4 at Witbank. Continue on the N4 to Nelspruit, then take the R40 to Hazyview via White River (at either of these towns telephone your camp to inform them of your estimated time of arrival). From Hazyview take the R536 towards the Paul Kruger Gate and Skukuza for 36 km. Turn left on to gravel 1 km past the Lisbon Store and follow the signs to Londolozi. There are daily commercial flights from Johannesburg to Skukuza. The Conservation Corporation will meet you there and transfer you to your lodge.
Nearest doctor:	Sabie, an hour's drive away.
Nearest petrol:	Sabie, an hour's drive away.
Open:	Visitors must check in at 12:00 and vacate their lodges by 11:00.
Special precautions:	Antimalaria precautions are essential for visitors to Londolozi.

The camp's swimming pool, set among natural rock formations, has a waterfall which cascades over the edge of a ravine.

BUSH CAMP At the luxury Bush Camp there are eight secluded rock chalets with *en suite* bathrooms and outdoor showers, built discreetly into the dense riverine vegetation. From the spacious rooms are panoramic views of hippos, elephants and antelope which wander about below.

The elevated swimming pool shimmers under the shading branches of 100-year-old jackalberry trees.

Game trails and walks Dawn game-viewing drives are available by Land Rover, accompanied by an armed ranger and tracker. You're likely to see any of the animals mentioned above as well as cheetah and crocodiles.

After the morning drive, gamewatchers tuck into a sumptuous breakfast. Optional nature walks are led by an armed Shangaan tracker. A popular destination is a hippo pool nearby.

Towards sunset, fortified by sundowners, guests set off again in search of Africa's big game and nocturnal hunters. The evening ends with a meal around a log fire under the stars, where visitors recount their day's experiences.

If you'd like to sample the delights of Londolozi, bear in mind that in the high season (summer), when it caters mainly for overseas visitors, Londolozi is expensive. More economical winter 'specials' are available.

Madikwe Game Reserve

One of the newest — and the fourth-largest — game sanctuary in South Africa, Madikwe Game Reserve offers guests a superb wildlife experience in the scorching Kalahari sandveld and acacia bushveld of the Northwest Province.

Just 7 km south of the Botswana border near Gaborone, and a three-and-a-half hour drive north of Johannesburg, Madikwe covers 75 000 ha — a pristine sanctuary, with comfortable accommodation and an abundance of wildlife.

Its gates opened in October 1994, after the largest game relocation programme in the country. The programme, known as Operation Phoenix, brought 8 500 animals into Madikwe from as far afield as Zimbabwe's Gonarezhou National Park, the Kruger National Park and Namibia's Etosha National Park.

Wildlife The 10 000 animals at Madikwe today comprise 27 mammal species — including the Big Five — lion, leopard, elephant, rhino and buffalo. The 260 elephants are the second largest population on a private reserve in South Africa, and the variety of other animals is impressive.

There are wild dogs, lions, spotted hyenas, brown hyenas, black and white rhinos, buffaloes, cheetahs and leopards, as well as antelope and many of the smaller mammals found in the large South African reserves.

Birdlife Some 230 species of bird thrive here, including secretarybirds, korhaans, Namaqua sandgrouse, yellowbilled hornbills and a variety of raptors.

Where to stay Various private concessionaries run private lodges within the park. Among these are Tau Game Lodge and Madikwe River Lodge.

TAU GAME LODGE This lodge, with its 30 ethnically decorated two-bed chalets and family suites overlooking a waterhole blends naturally into the surrounding bushveld. The *en suite* luxury chalets were built from natural materials and are ideal for individuals seeking a quiet refuge or for conference groups. To book contact Tau Game Lodge, PO Box 51, Nietverdiend 2874, tel (0140) 67-2030.

MADIKWE RIVER LODGE This lodge offers luxury accommodation in 16 thatched chalets on the banks of the Marico River. The units are tastefully — and colourfully — furnished with cosy beds, ethnic mats and artwork, tiled floors and mosquito-netting. Each two-bed chalet has an *en suite* bathroom, lounge and wooden viewing deck overlooking the Marico.

Children sharing with their parents are accommodated on sleeper couches, and cots are also available. Babysitters are provided at no extra charge.

The thatched central entertainment/dining area has a magnificent viewing deck, a swimming pool and open-plan bar, lounge and diningroom.

Game drives and trails Dawn and dusk drives are offered daily in customised vehicles. Walking trails are available as well. Special game drives can be organised for children.

Madikwe Game Reserve at a glance

Locality:	In North-West Province near the South African/Botswana border, just south of Gaborone.
Climate:	Hot summer days and warm nights; winters mild to warm, but nights cold.
Number of camps:	None.
Game drives:	Dawn and dusk drives; special children's game drives.
Hides and waterholes:	Several waterholes.
Trails:	Walking trails on request.
Amenities:	Swimming pool, open-air boma.
Accommodation:	**Madikwe River Lodge:** 16 thatched two-bed chalets, with sleeper couches for children. **Tau Game Lodge:** 30 rustic two-bed chalets and family suites.
Booking address:	Madikwe River Lodge, PO Box 17, Derdepoort 2876, South Africa, tel (0147) 78-0891. Tau Game Lodge, PO Box 51, Nietverdiend 2874, tel (0140) 67-2030.
When to go:	Throughout the year.
What to take with you:	Camera, binoculars, field guides, sturdy walking boots, light clothing.
How to get there:	From the centre of Zeerust follow the signs to Gaborone on the R505. About 85 km north of Zeerust a sign on the left side of the road marks the entrance to the reserve. Turn right here and follow the signs to Madikwe River Lodge — about 35 km. The drive to the gate takes about three-and-a-half hours; from the gate it is another hour's drive to the lodge.
Nearest doctor:	At Derdepoort, 7 km away. The reserve is also serviced by medical rescue.
Nearest petrol:	Derdepoort.
Open:	08:00 to 19:00 daily throughout the year.
Special precautions:	There is no malaria at Madikwe. As in any Southern African reserve, you should be vigilant on game walks.

Makalali Private Game Reserve

Ragged roofs of thatch rise primitively through the branches of jackalberry trees in the untamed bushveld and mopane woodlands on the western border of the Kruger National Park.

Not far away lions pad through the rich, green foliage of summer, and elephants crash through groves of acacia and wild fig.

The setting is so wild and the structures so African that first-time visitors may well imagine they've stumbled across the village of some undiscovered tribe.

But as you get closer, the breathtaking ethnic architecture of the thatched units, a sparkling swimming pool and the scent of sizzling impala kebabs dispels the notion.

This is Makalali Private Game Reserve — one of the newest and most exciting of Africa's wild frontiers. Some 485 km by road from Johannesburg, Makalali is a 30 000-acre reserve along the banks of the Makhutswi River.

It was opened to the public in April 1996 and lies just north of Singita, Ngala and Londolozi lodges on the western border of the Kruger National Park.

The rugged terrain includes rocky hillocks and lush, riverine vegetation which

Makalali Private Game Reserve at a glance

Locality:	On the western border of the Kruger National Park.
Climate:	Summers hot with thundershowers; winters mild to cold and dry.
Number of camps:	Four.
Game drives:	Morning and evening game drives.
Trails:	River hikes, koppie trails with armed rangers.
Other attractions:	Photography, pan-African cuisine, golf, visits to Kruger National Park.
Amenities:	Swimming pool at each camp and curio shop.
Accommodation:	Six luxury two-bed chalets with *en suite* bathrooms and elevated viewing deck.
Booking address:	Makalali Private Game Reserve, The Forum, 15th Floor, cnr Maude and 5th streets, Sandton 2146, tel (011) 883-5786; Singita Game Reserve, PO Box 650881, Benmore 2010, tel (011) 234-0990.
When to go:	Throughout the year, but game-viewing is better in winter.
What to take with you:	Cool, light clothing in summer; warm clothing and anorak in winter. Hiking/walking shoes, binoculars, camera, field guides, bathing costume, sunhat, dark glasses.
How to get there:	Daily flights from Johannesburg International Airport to Hoedspruit (SA Express) or Phalaborwa (SA Airlink). By road: Travel east from Pretoria on the N4 for 240 km to Belfast. From Belfast follow the R540 to Lydenburg and then the R36 through the J G Strijdom Tunnel. After 10 km turn left on to the Tzaneen Road (R36), travel another 10 km and turn right into the sandy Gravelotte Road. Makalali is 9 km further on, and it is a further 7 km to your camp.
Nearest doctor:	Hospital at Hoedspruit, 70 km away.
Nearest petrol:	Manoutsa, 25 km away.
Open:	Visitors must check in at midday and vacate chalets by 10:00.
Special precautions:	Antimalaria precautions are essential.

then tapers off into a mix of mopane woodland and bushveld, backdropped by the spectacular Drakensberg.

Wildlife Makalali shares many of the large and small mammals found in the Kruger National Park, including lions, leopards, elephants and white rhinos. Other 'favourites' are cheetahs, spotted hyenas, hippos, giraffes and crocodiles.

There's a variety of antelope such as waterbuck, kudu, impala, nyala, eland and bushbuck.

Birdlife This is raptor country, and commonly seen among the reserve's 213 bird species are Cape, whitebacked and lappetfaced vultures, lesser spotted eagles, Wahlberg's eagle, African hawk eagles, longcrested eagles, martial eagles and crowned eagles.

Other birds common to the bushveld include ground hornbills, secretarybirds and saddlebilled storks.

Where to stay Four secluded, 12-bed camps nestle on the shady banks of the Makhutswi River. Each luxury camp consists of six thatched, tastefully furnished double chalets, each with hand-carved doors and individually forged latches. Inside, African sculptures, rough patterned plaster walls and balustrades hewn from trees knocked down by elephants create a distinctly 'African' ambience.

The guest rooms are painted in ethnic colours and adorned with bright fabrics and artefacts. Each room has an *en suite* bathroom and elevated viewing deck, which doubles as a covered outdoor sleeping area.

A shaded, elevated timber deck over the river serves as a romantic lunchtime venue, while dinner is served around the fire in the open-air boma.

Makalali also boasts a group entertainment, conference and dining area comprising a luxurious, 60-seat thatched main building adjoining an open kitchen and entertainment area, which are illuminated at night by flaming torches for a special African ambience.

Game drives and trails Morning and evening game drives are available, and there is particular emphasis on interactive wilderness activities, such as walking, birding and night-sky viewing with experts.

The hikes follow the river's banks, and head up to some of the attractive koppies (hillocks) in the area, which serve as excellent vantage points (remember to bring your binoculars along).

Other attractions These include river rafting on the Olifants River, day trips to the Kruger National Park and Drakensberg Escarpment, golf at the Hans Merensky Golf Course and visits to a cultural village and a cheetah breeding centre.

SINGITA GAME RESERVE

This beautiful reserve next to the Kruger National Park has the distinction of hosting not only the Big Five, but the 'Little Five' as well — the rhino beetle, elephant shrew, buffalo weaver, antlion and leopard tortoise.

So whether you're looking for large mammals from the back seat of a Land Rover, or walking through the bush looking for smaller wildlife, you won't leave disappointed. Singita has an abundance of game that includes nocturnal species such as lion, leopard, hyena, blackbacked jackal and owls.

Singita means 'the miracle' in Shangaan, and the lodge lives up to its name, with superb accommodation by way of two attractive lodges, Ebony and Boulders.

Ebony Lodge's nine luxurious double suites on the banks of the Sand River have an ethnic African ambience, with air-conditioning, a double-sided fireplace, cosy lounge area, bathroom and indoor and outdoor showers, a private swimming pool and secluded game-viewing deck.

Boulders Lodge is situated downstream of the Sand River and has nine sumptuously furnished air-conditioned double suites, with bathroom and private indoor or open-air showers. Like Ebony, the suites have a double-sided fireplace, exclusive living area, private swimming pool and leisure deck overlooking the river.

Day and night game drives in an open Land Rover are available for guests and passengers are limited to six per drive.

Singita has its own private airstrip, or you can fly into nearby Skukuza from Johannesburg on SA Express. For enquiries and reservations write to Singita Game Reserve, PO Box 650881, Benmore 2010, or tel (011) 234-0990.

Mala Mala Game Reserve

Regarded by the well heeled and the well travelled as one of the top sanctuaries in the world, Mala Mala Game Reserve lives up to its reputation with an extraordinary wealth of wild animals.

It is one of the largest private big game sanctuaries in South Africa, covering some 18 000 ha of land, including a 33-km common boundary with the Kruger National Park. In this pristine wilderness of the Mpumalanga Lowveld, there's plenty of room for an abundance of wildlife: more than 200 species, from plains animals and predators of the thick bush, to burrowers, tree-climbers and amphibians, Mala Mala has just about everything.

Wildlife The variety of wildlife, coupled with the high standards of Mala Mala's rangers and trackers, ensures that most visitors will see more game than they bargained for. A ranger is assigned to each group of six visitors during their stay. In fact, 76 per cent of all the people who have ever visited Mala Mala belong to the reserve's Big Five Club. Membership is conferred on those who have seen lions, leopards, rhinos, elephants and buffaloes in one visit.

Moonlit night-drives in a Land Rover will reveal prides of lions stalking through the grass, or a leopard dragging an impala up a tree. On the way, you may also see spotted hyenas, blackbacked jackals and a variety of smaller mammals.

During the day you may see elephants, hippos, buffaloes, white rhinos or any number of antelope. But the real prize at Mala Mala is the sighting of a pack of wild dogs in pursuit of a zebra or antelope; or the curls of dust that signal a cheetah streaking through the bush.

Game drives and trails The rangers and game guides at Mala Mala are among the reserve's greatest assets. They're highly professional, experienced and dedicated. A ranger is assigned to each visitor during his or her stay, and sets out to provide the best game-viewing trips available. He also helps guests with local information on the animals and their habitats. Daytime safaris in open Land Rovers include the services of a tracker, and two-way radio contact with other vehicles. Night-time spotlight safaris take visitors to the four corners of the reserve. Walking safaris may be arranged on request.

Where to stay Three magnificent camps, each with its own distinctive character, bring visitors back to Mala Mala time and again.

MALA MALA MAIN CAMP This discreet assembly of thatched, ochre-walled rondavels, set on well-manicured, terraced lawns on the banks of the Sand River, has few peers among the safari lodges of the world.

The bushveld atmosphere, charm and simple luxury of its accommodation — the whole camp is furnished with rattan furniture — is tailormade for travellers who like to be pampered.

Each rondavel, set in the shade of indigenous trees, is tastefully furnished with extra-large twin beds decorated with animal prints, and offers the full range of modern conveniences: telephone, air-conditioning, insect-proof screens and bathrooms.

Breakfast and lunch are served in a spacious, air-conditioned diningroom, while guests traditionally dine outside in a circular, reed-walled boma, with tables arranged around a crackling fire.

In the Buffalo Lounge nearby, the mounted head of a huge Cape buffalo, with its magnificent sweep of horns, gazes solemnly over the elegant sets of rattan chairs and cushions, while the walls are adorned with skins of lions, antelope and zebras.

The lounge leads out to an elevated verandah where you may sip cocktails at sunset and watch the animals come down to drink at the Sand River. In the cosy bar inside, the mounted heads of impala, buffalo, sable and steenbok peer over guests having drinks at the bar.

In the southern corner of the camp is the luxury Sable Suite — a 16-person thatched chalet overlooking a lovely swimming pool. The 'Sable' has its own diningroom, lounge, bar, boma and viewing deck. It may be reserved by one party or individually, according to visitors' needs.

HARRY'S CAMP This camp in the southern part of Mala Mala Game Reserve offers Ndebele-style cottages (seven air-conditioned double-roomed units) accommodating no more than 14 people at any one time.

The cottages, shaded by trees, overlook a swimming pool and green lawns that sweep down to the river's edge.

Dinner is served in the reed-walled boma outside (venison is a speciality). A window here overlooks the spotlit Sand River, so that diners may watch game coming down to the river to drink.

A large verandah and a reed-ceilinged bar with floor-to-ceiling windows, offer excellent game-viewing opportunities. There's also a spacious lounge equipped with a blazing log fire for cold winter nights.

KIRKMAN'S KAMP Just 20 guests are accommodated in the green corrugated-iron-roofed cottages at Kirkman's Kamp, which, from its elevated location in the southern part of Mala Mala Game Reserve, offers spectacular views of the bushveld.

The camp, named after one of South Africa's eminent former conservationists, W Harry Kirkman, is built on a property known as Toulon, which borders the Kruger National Park on two sides.

The original homestead, built in the 1920s, has been restored, and offers a large lounge and diningroom furnished in 1920s style, and adorned with period photographs and memorabilia, and another lounge known as the Parlour, where you may sit in front of a blazing log fire and swop gamewatching stories under the steely gaze of a mounted buffalo head.

The semi-detatched cottages each have a private verandah and *en suite* bathroom, featuring ball-and-claw-footed baths.

As with the other camps, day and night game drives are on the daily menu of things to do, as well as walking trails on request. A reed-walled boma invites guests to savour delicious local dishes.

Next to Kirkman's Camp are Kirkman's Cottages — four comfortable units with access to their own diningroom and lapa.

Safari shops at all the camps sell curios, film and safari outfits.

Mala Mala Game Reserve at a glance

Locality:	Just north of Skukuza, flanking the western boundary of the Kruger National Park.
Climate:	Summers hot with thundershowers; winters mild to cold and dry.
Number of camps:	Three.
Game drives:	Day and night drives are led by professional rangers.
Trails:	Walking trails arranged on request.
Amenities:	Safari shops (all camps), swimming pool.
Accommodation:	**Main Camp:** tastefully decorated, thatched, ochre-walled rondavels, as well as the Sable Suite (16-person entertainment unit); **Harry's Camp:** 12 Ndebele-style double-roomed cottages; **Kirkman's Kamp:** 14 green, corrugated-iron roofed cottages; **Kirkman's Cottages:** four residential units with own boma, diningroom and kitchen.
Booking address:	Mala Mala Game Reserve, PO Box 2575, Randburg 2125, tel (011) 789-2677.
When to go:	Throughout the year, but game-viewing is better in winter.
What to take with you:	Light clothes in summer; warm clothes in winter; sunscreen, camera, binoculars, field guides.
How to get there:	Take the N4 from Johannesburg to Nelspruit. From Nelspruit take the R40 to Hazyview via White River (at either of these towns telephone your camp to inform them of your estimated time of arrival). From Hazyview take the R536 to Paul Kruger Gate/Skukuza. After 37,5 km turn left, and follow the Mala Mala, Kirkman's Kamp or Harry's signs to the respective camps.
Nearest doctor:	Skukuza, 25 km away.
Nearest petrol:	In the reserve.
Open:	All year round.
Special precautions:	Since this is a malaria area, antimalaria precautions should be taken.

Manyeleti Game Reserve

Beautiful and remote, the 23 000-ha Manyeleti Game Reserve lies on the western border of the Kruger National Park, just five hours' drive from Johannesburg. The name is the Shangaan word for 'place of the stars', and there's no better place to view them than from the heart of Manyeleti's untamed bushveld.

The reserve's rolling grasslands, peppered with koppies, knobthorn and marula trees, lie north of the Sabi Sand Game Reserve and south of the Timbavati Game Reserve.

Wildlife Run by the Gazankulu Department of Nature Conservation, the reserve is home to a large variety of mammals (including the Big Five) and birds. Apart from the Big Five, there is an abundance of antelope — especially impala — as well as vervet monkeys, baboons, warthogs, hippos, giraffes, wildebeest and waterbuck.

Birds Among the diverse population of birds you can see here are pied kingfishers, fierynecked nightjars, threestreaked tchagras and green pigeons. Larger birds such as water dikkops, pearlspotted owls, bateleurs and snake eagles are also frequently seen.

Where to stay There's a comfortable public camp and two excellent private camps at Manyeleti — Honeyguide and Khoka Moya — the latter more luxurious than the former. The public camp is run by the Gazankulu Parks authorities and offers basic rondavels (self-catering), with access to a swimming pool, restaurant, bar, shop and post office.

HONEYGUIDE TENTED SAFARI CAMP

'Out of Africa' is the theme at this beautiful camp, which operates in a private concession of more than 7 000 ha and has traversing rights over all of Manyeleti. The camp's not cheap, but neither are the service and the standard of personal attention.

Among the various mod-cons you'll find here are solar-powered electricity, hot and cold running water and flush toilets. There's also an attractive diningroom, the main feature of which is a table made of railway sleepers, that serves superb cuisine (roast leg of venison is a speciality). Other attractions are a cosy bar and swimming pool.

Twelve East African tents, with safari-style furnishings and *en suite* bathroom facilities, accommodate a maximum of 24 people. Each carpeted tent is equipped with inner-spring mattresses, and leads on to an outdoor deck overlooking the dry river bed.

Just 100 m away from the camp a hide overlooks a waterhole.

HONEYGUIDE GAME DRIVES AND TRAILS

The camp operates two excellent walking safaris, as well as drives in open 4x4 vehicles, accompanied by professional rangers.

The four-day safari starts at Honeyguide Camp, where a guide and tracker give a short orientation talk before leading trailists across the savannah to the Outpost Bush Camp, which is set among a grove of tamboti trees on the edge of a small river. After sundowners supper is cooked on an open fire, and later guests retire to comfortable, twin-bedded tents.

The second day is devoted to exploration of the vicinity of the Outpost Camp, including Vulture Pan, before guests return for another night at the bush camp.

On day three trailists trek to the northern wilderness area of Manyeleti, and have brunch in the Mohwareng Hills, which command spectacular views of the bushveld and Drakensberg escarpment. Later the group walks back to Honeyguide and prepares for an evening game drive, followed by a sumptuous fireside meal in the camp's boma.

The fourth day combines a game drive with a walk which enables trailists to apply their newly acquired game-tracking skills. The trail ends with a farewell brunch at Honeyguide Camp.

Tip for travellers

Half of the accommodation fee must be paid within one month of making the booking, before you arrive at the game reserve.

In addition, weekend trails departing on a Friday or Saturday are also offered at Honeyguide.

For booking and enquiries, contact Lodges of Manyeleti, PO Box 781959, Sandton 2146, tel (011) 341-0282.

KHOKA MOYA GAME LODGE Translated from Shangaan Khoka Moya means 'capture the spirit' — a reference to the rustic wildness of this private camp of the same name that lies 8 km from Orpen Gate on the border of the Kruger National Park.

Manyeleti Game Reserve at a glance

Locality:	Northern Province, on the western border of the Kruger National Park.
Climate:	Hot summers (up to 40 °C) with thundershowers; mild winter days (20 °C), cold nights.
Number of camps:	Three.
Game drives and safaris:	Safariplan provides three fly-in safaris a week and two vehicle tours per week. Self-drive packages may also be organised. For details tel Safariplan at (011) 886-1810.
Hides and waterholes:	Honeyguide has an attractive hide 100 m from the camp.
Trails:	Honeyguide: Four-day and weekend trails; Khoka Moya: four- to five-day wildlife safaris and shorter bush hikes.
Other attractions:	Photography, birdwatching.
Amenities:	Swimming pool, restaurant, bar, shop and post office.
Accommodation:	The public camp offers self-catering rondavels, with access to a swimming pool, restaurant; **Honeyguide Tented Safari Camp** has 12 twin-bedded East African tents; **Khoka Moya:** 10 twin-bedded timber and thatch huts; **Skybeds bush camp:** four twin-bedded huts under thatch.
Booking address:	The Manager, Manyeleti Game Reserve, PO Manyeleti 1362, tel (01311) 6-5733. Honeyguide Camp, PO Box 781959, Sandton 2146, tel (011) 341-0282 or (011) 880-3912. Khoka Moya Game Lodge, Country Escapes, PO Box 11068, Hatfield 0028, tel (012) 362-1375, 080 111 4448, or (015) 793-1729.
When to go:	Throughout the year, but game-viewing is better in the winter months (April–August).
What to take with you:	Light clothes in summer; warmer gear in winter. Sturdy hiking boots, torch, camera, lots of film.
How to get there:	From Pretoria take the N4 to Belfast, then the R540 to Dullstroom and on to Lydenburg and Ohrigstad. Continue towards Hoedspruit, past the Abel Erasmus Pass and J G Strijdom Tunnel. After the Blyde River turn right towards Orpen. Continue past the Klaserie turn-off to Orpen Gate signpost. Turn left and continue 36 km to the Manyeleti Game Reserve. Air charters fly regularly to Manyeleti from Johannesburg International Airport and Pretoria's Wonderboom Airport.
Nearest doctor:	70 km away, at Hoedspruit.
Nearest petrol:	Within the reserve and at Orpen Gate.
Open:	06:00–17:00 throughout the year.
Special precautions:	Take antimalaria precautions before you go.

The camp consists of 10 bandas — two-bedded timber and thatch huts on stilts. Each banda has *en suite* shower and toilet facilities, and leads on to an open verandah. Reed blinds in the huts can be peeled back to reveal star-studded skies at night. The huts overlook a tranquil garden, with a swimming pool and hammocks slung between the trees.

At night the aroma of roast venison rises from the attractive reed-walled boma, main venue for fireside suppers under the stars.

The pride of Khoka Moya, however, is Skybeds — an intimate bush camp enclosed by a reed boma. Four twin-bedded reed huts mounted on stilts and linked by a boardwalk offer superb accommodation overlooking a waterhole.

Khoka Moya Wildlife Encounters offers daily game drives and walking trails, ranging from short rambles through the bush for groups of up to eight people, to two-, four- and five-day wildlife safaris.

Mhlopeni Nature Reserve

High above the soaring cliffs and krantzes of northern KwaZulu-Natal, a black eagle hurtles through the air, taking in tow a huge, squealing dassie (rock hyrax).

Far below, a stream winds through a wild and beautiful river valley, covered by a patchwork of aloes, euphorbias and acacia bushland. This is the heart of Mhlopeni Nature Reserve, one of the lesser-known of Southern Africa's wild sanctuaries. Here, after a day's walking, you can sit around the campfire under the stars, and listen to the murmur of the river and the gathering sounds of nocturnal animals moving about in the dark. In the mornings, the new day comes alive with the sound of myriad birds calling from the trees.

Mhlopeni — the Zulu name for the small, white stones found in the river valley and stream — is set in the dramatic, craggy thornveld of northern KwaZulu-Natal, and offers nature-lovers a pristine wilderness, inhabited by a diverse and interesting population of animals and birds.

The reserve came into being in 1978, when a group of businessmen bought the 808 ha around the Mhlopeni stream. Their intention was to create a natural sanctuary for animals and birds, and to establish a centre for environmental education. In 1992 the reserve was extended to 1 325 ha with the purchase of land flanking the old reserve, thereby increasing its stock of game and scenic delights.

Wildlife The krantzes and ravines of Mhlopeni serve as sanctuary for leopards, chacma baboons, mountain reedbuck, klipspringer and caracal; while among the grassy plains, dense bush and rolling hills you'll find zebras, blesbok, impala, bushbuck, common reedbuck, duiker, klipspringer, oribi and bushpig. Other species include aardwolves, honey badgers, blackbacked jackals, aardvarks, four species of mongoose, thicktailed bushbabies, fourtoed elephant shrews and dassies.

Birdlife The diverse vegetation of Mhlopeni attracts 208 species of bird, ranging from spotted eagle owls, blackshouldered kites and helmeted guineafowl to smaller species such as scarletchested sunbirds and Cape canaries.

Apart from the black eagles that feast on the teeming community of dassies, martial eagles, crowned eagles, brown snake eagles, falcons and buzzards cruise the thermals above the high ground.

In the valley a variety of waterbirds compete for the rich pickings of the stream and riverine vegetation: kingfishers, hamerkops, marabou, black and white storks, Egyptian geese, ibises and egrets. In the trees and among the bushes you'll see such diverse species as trumpeter and ground hornbill, woodpecker, francolin, lourie and seven species of dove.

Where to stay There are three bush camps on the southern bank of the Mhlopeni stream, surrounded by acacia bushland, and not far from the site of an Iron-Age village. From here you can follow self-guided trails into the surrounding countryside, which features a huge variety of plants and trees: there are weeping boerbeans, large-leaved rock figs, six species of acacia, river euphorbias and bush willows, tamboti and sneezewood trees, and, peppering the cliffs and

Tips for travellers

- **The bush camp huts are each equipped with basic cutlery and crockery, and offer access to separate ablutions (flush toilet and shower), but you must bring along your own bedding and provisions.**
- **The road leading to the reserve is not in good condition, and 4x4 vehicles are recommended during the rainy season (September–April).**

Mhlopeni Nature Reserve at a glance

Locality:	KwaZulu-Natal Midlands between Greytown and Muden (170 km from Durban).
Climate:	Summer rainfall, fluctuating between 380 mm and 1 400 mm. Winters are mild, while summers may be very hot — up to 43 °C.
Trails:	Several footpaths and trails bisect the countryside, including the attractive Chairman's Trail along the Mhlopeni stream.
Other attractions:	Birdwatching, examining artefacts, swimming in rock pools.
Amenities:	The village of Muden 12 km away has a shop, post office and bottle store.
Accommodation:	There are three bush camps, each equipped with basic cutlery and crockery, and access to separate ablutions (flush toilet and shower). Bring along your own bedding and provisions.
Booking address:	The Warden, Mhlopeni Reserve, PO Box 386, Greytown 3250, tel (03346) 722, (031) 83-9655.
When to go:	Any time of the year (the going is heavy in the wet season, September–April).
What to take with you:	For the rustic camps, your own bedding and provisions. If camping, take all own requirements. Binoculars, camera.
How to get there:	The turn-off to Mhlopeni is 3 km from Muden, on the Greytown-Muden Road, about 90 km east of Pietermaritzburg (170 km from Durban).
Nearest doctor:	Muden, 12 km away.
Nearest petrol:	Muden, 12 km away.
Open:	24 hours a day.
Special precautions:	None.

krantzes, are aloes and wild olives, rock alders and camphor trees.

Walks and trails The walking trails take you across the river, ascending the high, rocky cliffs to a height of over 1 200 m. Apart from the nature trails, you can cool off in the pools below the Mhlopeni waterfall, or take a rocky slide down a natural water-chute.

Artefacts For those with an interest in history, there are a number of important Early, Middle and Later Stone-Age sites at Mhlopeni, indicating a once-thriving population of San hunter-gatherers and later Nguni communities. Some of the artefacts date back to AD 550, and include potsherds, shell beads (made from giant snails), ostrich shells, iron smeltings, slag and associated clay artefacts.

Mkuzi Game Reserve

The haunting call of a fish eagle echoes across the reed-fringed waters of Nhlonhlela Pan. From the observation deck of the bush camp above the pan, visitors soak in a scene of rare tranquillity. Fever trees hang silently over the water, their branches reflected perfectly on the blue-green canvas of water; African jacanas stride across the lily-pads; and pied kingfishers sit sentinel in the trees, waiting to pounce on unwary fish.

As the first rays of dawn filter through the leaves of tamboti and knobthorn, and strike the thatched turrets of the bungalows at Nhlonhlela Bush Camp, guests start preparing for a guided game walk deep into the heart of one of Africa's loveliest game reserves.

Serene, rustic and uncompromisingly wild, Mkuzi Game Reserve was established in 1912 and covers 36 000 ha of savannah bushveld between the Mkuze and Umsunduze rivers — an idyllic haven for a large variety of mammals, birds and reptiles. The recent extension of the reserve to include the Enxwala Wilderness Area in the southeast has boosted animal populations and game-viewing opportunities tremendously.

Here the ever-changing landscape ranges from open grasslands to thick, almost impenetrable forests; from dry and ancient sand-dunes to pans covered in waterlilies. On the edges of the pans aloes bloom in great sprays of scarlet, their blooms merging with the ochre cliffs behind them.

Once covered by the sea, this area is a natural museum of marine fossils, such as mussels and crustaceans, and petrified trees that stand as unique monuments to an age long gone.

The weather can be moody — ranging from seasons of drought to tropical storms wreaking havoc on the land.

Wildlife In spite of its tempestuous nature, the weather has not affected the game populations at Mkuzi: more than 10 000 impala and 7 000 nyala browse among the black monkeythorn and shepherd's trees that flourish here. In addition, there are some 3 500 warthogs, more than 120 white rhinos, 70 black rhinos and over 1 000 blue wildebeest, occurring near the southernmost part of their range.

Other species you're sure to see are giraffe, hippo, kudu, bushbuck, grey duiker, klipspringer, eland, zebra, mountain and common reedbuck, steenbok, bushpig and red duiker.

Carnivores that stalk the long grass at night include leopards, spotted hyenas, cheetahs, servals and sidestriped and blackbacked jackals. Porcupines, suni, pangolins and antbears are more rarely seen. In the vicinity of the camps, keep a lookout for largespotted genets and any one of the five species of mongoose.

Birdlife The fact that several pans are included in the reserve complex means that there's an abundance of waterbirds, as well as hundreds of savannah species. More than 410 species flourish here — a particularly rich avian population in the Southern African context. They include such varieties as hamerkops, whitebacked vultures, pied kingfishers, Egyptian geese, crested guineafowls, whitebrowed scrub robins, gorgeous bush shrikes, orange-breasted bush shrikes and emeraldspotted doves.

Where to stay At Mkuzi you can choose to stay at the main camp (Mantuma Hutted Camp), two bush camps or a campsite at the Emshopi entrance gate. Mantuma Hutted Camp offers six comfortable three-bed huts, five five-bed bungalows, four three-bed bungalows and two self-contained cottages, each with seven beds and

Dangerous bite of the baboon

Visitors to Southern African parks and game reserves are warned not to lure baboons to their car windows with morsels of food. Chacma baboons are known to capture and kill young antelope such as nyala, impala and klipspringer, and tear the flesh from their carcasses. There have also been cases where they have injured humans.

An honorary ranger at the Kruger National Park saw a large male chacma emerge from a troop of about 35 baboons and charge an impala ewe. The baboon grabbed the ewe's hindquarters and started biting great chunks out of the stricken animal's body.

It was joined by another younger male, and the two ate the impala alive. Thirty minutes later the older male put the animal out of its misery by crushing its skull with its teeth.

Old, bad-tempered baboons have been known to attack and seriously injure human beings, and rogue baboons have been put down after attacking visitors to the Cape of Good Hope Nature Reserve near Cape Town.

The baboon's ability to kill is clearly obvious from the structure of the jaw: the long, dog-like muzzle supports upper canines that are sharper and longer than those of a lion; long rows of molar teeth enable it to grind grasses, seeds, roots, bulbs, mushrooms, wild fruits, pods and shoots to a pulp.

a fridge. It also has a small safari camp. An experienced cook will prepare your meals here.

The Safari Camp — part of the Mantuma Camp — has 10 two-bed tents with *en suite* showers, basins and toilets. The tents are provided with electricity, a fridge, crockery and linen, but visitors must provide their own food.

The units are serviced once a day, but visitors must do their own cooking and washing up.

Tips for travellers

- **The best game-viewing times are between 09:00 and 12:00. Be sure to bring your own food and drink.**
- **Visitors may follow established walking trails, or leave their cars at designated picnic spots, but they do so at their own risk. There are crocodiles in the Mkuze River and in some of the pans, and a woman has been killed here by a white rhino, so be careful.**

THE BUSH CAMPS Nhlonhlela Bush Lodge, positioned on the upper edge of the 3-km Nhlonhlela Pan, has four two-bed bungalows, each connected by a boardwalk to a reed-walled, open-sided dining area, where you can listen to the dawn chorus of birds, and watch the first stirrings of life in the reserve. The huts are self-contained, with bedding and linen, and are equipped with a shower, toilet and washbasin. Nhlonhlela is open throughout the year.

Umkumbi Bush Camp, used as a normal bush camp from October to March, consists of four two-bed safari tents, each equipped with a fridge, wardrobe, *en suite* shower, washbasin and toilet. Nearby, overlooking a natural pan, is a thatched wood-and-reed lounge, dining-room and bar.

At Umkumbi and Nhlonhlela you will have a cook at your service, and a game guard to escort you on game walks.

Game trails and drives An 84-km network of game-viewing roads bisects Mkuzi Reserve, with excellent picnic spots

Nyala knee-deep in trouble

In the searing heat of a midsummer's day, the Bube Waterhole at Mkuzi Game Reserve had been reduced to a slushy quagmire.

From out of the treeline a thirsty young nyala wandered down for a drink. Gamewatchers in the nearby Masinga Hide watched in astonishment as the nyala walked into the water, then started sinking into the mud. There it struggled belly-deep for half an hour.

Then three warthogs emerged from the surrounding bush and cautiously approached the struggling animal.

To those watching it seemed as if the warthogs were trying to help the nyala by nuzzling, pushing and breathing on it, to save it from suffocation.

While the warthogs bumped and shoved the antelope, an adult nyala arrived and sniffed the trapped animal. Soon the onlookers were joined by a troop of baboons.

As the minutes ticked by, it seemed the nyala would certainly suffocate. Then a ranger arrived, waded into the mud and rescued the animal.

at Ensumo Pan, Nxwala, Ediza and alongside the reception area in the main camp. The recommended route to follow is the Mkuzi Autotrail (41 km), which takes about three hours to complete (brochure available at the office). The best game-viewing areas are on the Loop Road, at Ensumo Pan and near the airstrip.

Four game-viewing hides have been built next to the Kubube, Kumasinga, Kwamalibala and Kumahlala pans. Here you park your car nearby and enter the hides through reed-enclosed tunnels. The best time to see game is during winter when the natural waterholes dry up and the animals congregate at these man-made pans in good numbers. There is also an observation platform at Ensumo Pan.

For many the highlight of a visit to Mkuzi is the 8-km Nhlonhlela Trail (three hours). This ranger-led trail departs from the Mantuma Hutted Camp each morning, and leads to a lookout point above the Nhlonhlela Pan.

Another popular walk is the Fig Forest Walk (3 km), a self-guided trail which crosses a suspension bridge over the Mkuze River and leads through enchanting forests of sycamore fig and fever trees. Here you'll hear the sounds of trumpeter hornbills, goldenrumped tinker barbets and purplecrested louries.

Be sure to take a camera and a good pair of binoculars along.

Mkuzi Game Reserve at a glance

Locality:	Northeastern KwaZulu-Natal, about 335 km from Durban.
Climate:	Summers are hot and humid with rain (sometimes subtropical storms); winters cool to warm.
Number of camps:	Four.
Game drives:	84 km of game-viewing roads, including the 41-km Mkuzi Autotrail.
Hides and waterholes:	Four hides: Kumahlala, Kwamalibala, Kumasinga, Kubube; Ensumo observation platform.
Trails:	Nhlonhlela Trail (8 km), Mkuzi Fig Forest Walk (3 km). Shorter walks accompanied by game guard.
Other attractions:	Birdwatching, photography.
Amenities:	Curios, books, charcoal and cold drinks are available at the camp shop, but you must bring your own food and other basic provisions.
Accommodation:	Two hutted camps, a safari camp, two bush camps and a campsite.
Booking address:	KwaZulu-Natal Nature Conservation Services, PO Box 13069, Cascades 3202, tel (0331) 845-1000.
When to go:	Game-viewing is at its best in the dry season, between June and October.
What to take with you:	Food, drink, torch, warm clothes (in winter), sunhat, sturdy hiking boots.
How to get there:	Drive north from Durban on the N2. About 40 km north of Hluhluwe turn right and drive 16 km on the gravel road.
Nearest doctor:	Mkuze Village.
Nearest petrol:	At the reserve's entrance gate.
Open:	08:00–12:30, 14:00–16:30 daily. Sundays: 08:00–12:30, 14:00–16:00.
Special precautions:	Antimalaria precautions must be taken before your trip.

MOUNTAIN ZEBRA NATIONAL PARK

This bracing and beautiful mountain wilderness, interspersed with the gentle valleys and grassy plains of the Little Karoo, has been described as one of South Africa's most scenic national parks. It is also the setting for one of the miracles of conservation — the rescue from extinction of one of the world's most endangered species, the Cape mountain zebra.

When the park was proclaimed in 1937, there were just six of these animals left in the area — one mare and five stallions. Under the care and protection of the National Parks Board of South Africa, this handful of tiny orange-muzzled zebras grew to 25 in 1964, and there are 130 in the park today.

Since the park's establishment, a significant number of zebras have been given to other reserves, and the park itself has expanded to 6 536 ha.

Lying across a plateau just 25 km southwest of Cradock, the Mountain Zebra National Park is typical of the Eastern Cape's Karoo country, with a colourful variety of such local plant species as Karoo aster, globe karoo and koggelmandervoetkaroo. Here the aloe- and bush-covered mountains roll down to valleys where acacia, wild olive, white stinkwood and kiepersol trees spring up between the short-tufted grasslands. Among the plains, rocky hillocks known as 'koppies' rise up, their sides flecked with broken rocks and other volcanic debris.

Wildlife The mountain zebra shares its habitat on the northern slopes of the Bankberg with 56 other mammal species, including eland, springbok, black wildebeest, red hartebeest, blesbok, reedbuck and klipspringer. Many of these may be seen on the Rooiplaat plateau.

Tip for travellers

If you're walking the Mountain Zebra Trail, take along at least six litres of water, because water isn't always available along the way.

Graceful gliders of the mountains

Just about every mountainous area — including the Mountain Zebra National Park — that is populated by dassies will have a few nesting black eagles in the high areas. For these big birds have an insatiable appetite for dassies and other smaller mammals.

Black eagles are found in the Pilanesberg National Park, in Namibia's Skeleton Coast National Park and in the Lapalala Wilderness Area. You'll also see them soaring on the thermals in the Cederberg Mountains and across the granite turrets of the Groot Winterhoek Wilderness Area. Down at the coast you may see them above Table Mountain or on the mountain slopes of Hout Bay.

In Zimbabwe's Matobo hills dassies account for 98 per cent of a black eagle's diet — and a breeding pair will routinely drag 200 of these squealing mammals from the ground each year to feed their young.

These eagles live in huge stick nests on the cliff faces, which they line with grass and green leaves in preparation for the nesting season.

Less visible mammals are nocturnal predators such as blackbacked jackal, aardwolf, caracal, Cape fox and four species of mongoose, among them water mongoose and the Cape grey mongoose.

There are more than 200 bird species, including the rare booted eagle, the black eagle and the martial eagle. You may also see Cape eagle owls, blue cranes and pale chanting goshawks.

Twenty-two species of snake have been recorded in the park.

Where to stay The park offers 18 two-bedroom (four-bed) chalets and an attractive caravan and camping area (20 sites), set on lawns among shady trees. The chalets have a bathroom, livingroom and fully equipped kitchen, while ablution and braai facilities are available for those staying in the camping site.

Nature-lovers seeking to experience the accommodation and charm of yesteryear may stay in a restored Victorian farmhouse — the Doornhoek Guest Cottage,

Mountain Zebra National Park at a glance

Locality:	Eastern Cape midlands, 25 km from Cradock.
Climate:	Summers warm to hot (temperatures in the 40s); winters mild with very cold nights. Average rainfall 392 mm, most of which falls in summer. Snow falls on the mountains in winter.
Number of camps:	One.
Game drives:	37 km of good gravel roads.
Trails:	Three-day, circular Mountain Zebra Hiking Trail (25,6 km). There are several other shorter trails, ranging from 15 minutes to several hours.
Other attractions:	Horse riding, exploring, San paintings.
Amenities:	Shop, restaurant, swimming pool.
Accommodation:	18 two-bedroom (four-bed) chalets; three-bedroom Victorian guest-house; 20 caravan and camping sites.
Booking address:	National Parks Board, PO Box 787, Pretoria 0001, tel (012) 343-1991; or PO Box 7400, Roggebaai 8012, tel (021) 22-2810. For trail details contact the Warden, Mountain Zebra National Park, PO Box X66, Cradock 5880; tel (048) 881-2486.
When to go:	All year round.
What to take with you:	Hikers should take their own sleeping bag, space blanket, eating utensils and food; torch, camera, warm clothes in winter, walking shoes, binoculars and bathing costume.
How to get there:	Some 6 km north of Cradock turn off the R32, and head west on the Graaff-Reinet road. After 5 km turn left at the signpost indicating the park about 12 km away.
Nearest doctor:	Cradock, 25 km away.
Nearest petrol:	In the park.
Open:	1 October–30 April: 07:00–19:00; 1 May–30 September: 07:00–18:00.
Special precautions:	Make sure you are protected against the heat in summer and that you have plenty of water.

which nestles in a secluded valley overlooking Doornhoek Dam.

The cottage, which has been declared a national monument, was originally built in 1836 and was used in the filming of Olive Schreiner's *Story of an African Farm.* With its exquisite yellowwood ceilings and floors of Oregon pine, Doornhoek offers an elegant and comfortable Victorian livingroom, three bedrooms (two with double beds) with *en suite* bathrooms and a fully equipped kitchen.

Other facilities in the park include a shop stocked with non-perishable groceries, film, fresh meat, bread, firewood, liquor and curios. There is also a swimming pool, a fully licensed à la carte restaurant offering sumptuous cuisine and horseriding stables.

Game drives and trails There are some 37 km of good gravel roads providing rewarding viewing of the various animals and birds, but the way to see the real beauty of the park is on foot.

The longest and most arduous of the park's trails is the Mountain Zebra Trail — a three-day, 25-km circular hiking trail, starting and ending at the park's office. Hikers (in groups of up to 12) overnight in two rustic stone huts: the Olien Hut and the Karee Hut. Facilities are basic: there are bunk beds, chemical toilets and showers when water is available.

The walk is a fairly tough one, ascending the slopes of the Grootkloof on the first day, and then climbing up the Bankberg to 1 885 m on the second day. The last day is a gentler walk which takes you along the Wilgerboom River and past the Doornhoek Dam.

There is an optional shorter route — a circular day walk which takes you through a forest, and ends back at the park's office.

There are several other shorter trails ranging from 15 minutes to several hours.

Ndumo Game Reserve

An early morning mist hovers like a grey ghost above the sleepy waters of Nyamithi Pan. A pair of African jacanas, strutting gingerly along the lily-pads, take to the air as a crocodile cruises by, sending ripples drifting to the reed-fringed banks.

High above, a pair of fish eagles soar gracefully with the thermals, their white and rufous underparts reflected in the first light of day.

Dawn at Ndumo — with its profound stillness, and the stirring of its myriad creatures — has a magic of its own, one that brings visitors back to the reserve time and again.

The reserve lies along KwaZulu-Natal's northern border with Mozambique, about 470 km from Durban. Its pulse beats to the rhythm of the Pongola River, whose seasonal floodwaters spill over into a network of pans. Nyamithi (6 km long), with its delicate fringes of fever trees, is the largest of these, followed by Banzi Pan (4 km), a crucible for multicoloured water lilies and other wetland flowers. Smaller pans, such as Sabatana and Bakabaka, rise and recede according to the whims of the great Pongola. As the dry season approaches the level of the pans recedes, exposing large beds of aquatic vegetation which, in turn, attract thousands of insects and birds.

Wildlife Animals are plentiful at Ndumo, and include about 5 700 nyala (the hunter F C Selous collected specimens of nyala here for the London Zoo), white and black rhinos, a herd of about 80 buffaloes, giraffes, Burchell's zebras, impala, nyala, bushbuck, bushpigs, grey and red duiker and reedbuck. Nocturnal species such as pangolin, aardwolf and aardvark search the dry ground for food at night, while hippos and crocodiles are commonly seen near the water's edge by day.

Birdlife The festival of birds is undoubtedly the major attraction at Ndumo, and it provides birdwatching opportunities unrivalled anywhere else in South Africa. More than 420 species — almost as many as are found in the Kruger National Park, which is 190 times Ndumo's size, choose this 10 117-ha reserve as their home — thanks largely to the diversity of the vegetation here.

Apart from the network of forest-fringed pans, there's an abundance of lush, subtropical bush, huge fever and fig trees, and stretches of sandveld nourishing such indigenous trees as marula, velvet bushwillow, silverleaf and black monkeythorn acacia.

The cosmopolitan community of waterbirds includes such species as pelicans, hamerkops, black herons, pygmy geese, water dikkops and fishing owls, while other birds of the forests include gorgeous bush shrikes, green coucals, pinkthroated twinspots and African broadbills.

The pans are teeming with fish: barbel and bream, tilapia and tigerfish, and these are an important source of food for the crocodiles, and some of the predatory birds.

Where to stay Two very different camps offer visitors to Ndumo scenic views in beautiful surroundings. The Ndumo Wilderness Camp, on the edge of Banzi Pan, is mounted on wooden platforms under a canopy of giant fig trees in an area not usually open to the public. This camp, a joint venture between Wilderness Safaris, the KwaZulu-Natal Nature Conservation Services and the local community, offers eight tented rooms with *en suite* bathrooms and access to a separate bar/dining area. The entire camp is linked to a tree canopy walkway several metres above the ground.

Ndumo's Main Camp, which nestles beneath huge marula trees on a hill in the southern corner of the reserve, has seven three-bed bungalows, each equipped with a gas-powered fridge, linen, bedding, cutlery and crockery. There is also a communal kitchen (with a chef) and ablution facilities. Electricity is available from 05:00 to 22:00.

Main Camp is positioned some 64 m above the Pongola River floodplain, and overlooks the river on its east side. To the left of the camp the terrain falls away to the Nyamithi Pan and the Usutu River beyond it. The views are spectacular. In the distance you may see Mozambique and the distant Lebombo Mountains.

Visitors to Ndumo should take their own provisions. A supermarket near the entrance gate offers most basic provisions as well as petrol and diesel. There's also a caravan park and campsite near the reserve's entrance.

Game drives and bush walks Canopied Land Rover tours are offered around the pans twice daily. A self-guided autotrail

Tips for travellers

- No swimming is allowed in the pans or the river.
- The speed limit in the reserve is 40 km/h.
- Do not get out of your vehicle unless you are accompanied by a game guard or ranger.

takes you from Main Camp past the southern end of Nyamithi Pan, and then follows a loop in the central part of the reserve. Directions and a map of this trail are available in the reserve.

There are several nature walks through the forests and bush. Keep a lookout for venomous species of snake in the area, particularly Mozambique spitting cobras, Egyptian cobras and puffadders.

Ndumo Game Reserve at a glance

Locality:	Northern KwaZulu-Natal, 470 km from Durban.
Climate:	Subtropical, with dry winters and hot, moderately wet summers.
Number of camps:	Two.
Game drives:	Ranger-led drives twice daily. Ndumo Autotrail.
Hides and waterholes:	Birdwatching at Nyamithi and Banzi pans is excellent.
Trails:	Day walks are arranged on request.
Amenities:	No provisions of any kind can be bought in the reserve.
Accommodation:	Ndumo's **Main Camp** has seven three-bed bungalows, equipped with gas-powered fridge, linen, bedding, cutlery and crockery. Communal kitchen (with a chef) and ablution facilities are available. Electricity is available from 05:00 to 22:00. Ndumo **Wilderness Camp** offers eight tented rooms with *en suite* bathrooms, and access to bar and restaurant.
Booking address:	KwaZulu-Natal Nature Conservation Services, PO Box 13069, Cascades, tel (0331) 845-1000.
When to go:	The summer months are best for birdwatching (particularly September when many migratory birds arrive), but it can get very hot.
What to take with you:	Your own food and drink. Binoculars, camera.
How to get there:	Drive north from Durban on the N2. About 10 km north of Mkuze Village take the Jozini exit. Drive 66 km to the T-junction, then follow the signs to Ndumo Village and the reserve, 14 km further on.
Nearest petrol:	At Jozini, Ingwavuma and a roadside store 2 km from the entrance to the reserve.
Open:	Sunrise to sunset all year round. Visitors must report to the camp superintendent before 16:00.
Special precautions:	This is a malaria area, so take precautions prior to departure. When hiking, watch out for snakes.

Ngala Game Reserve

Ngala Game Reserve, the only private game reserve to be incorporated in the Kruger National Park, lies on the doorstep of immense populations of game that roam the plains, mopane woodland and bush of the Timbavati River Valley. There's so much game, in fact, that in the long, warm evenings of the bushveld summer, animals are often seen wandering around the thatched chalets at Ngala Lodge, *en route* to a waterhole that lies right in the middle of the camp.

The waterhole at Ngala is actually an extension of the swimming pool, so that you can lounge in your deckchair soaking up the summer sun as elephants come down to drink a few metres away.

This is just one of the extraordinary attractions of the Ngala Lodge, which was totally transformed by a R4-million facelift in 1992.

The change came after private enterprise and the National Parks Board took over joint administration of the lodge, and acquired an extra 14 000 ha of land to establish the Ngala Game Reserve.

Today it is owned and run by the Conservation Corporation, and ranks among Southern Africa's most luxurious game lodges, offering five-star comfort and cuisine in one of the subcontinent's most densely populated game areas.

Wildlife Ngala is the Shangaan word for 'lion', and there's no shortage of these cats here — few visitors to Ngala depart without at least one sighting of lions lazing on the sandy bed of the Timbavati River, or stalking antelope in the long grass.

A major attraction, too, is the huge, breeding herds of elephants which thunder through the dense mopane forests around Ngala, often lumbering about in the shade of jackalberry, bushwillow and buffalo-thorn trees that cloak the camp.

Tip for travellers

Ngala is close to four more of Southern Africa's most talked-about private lodges: Thornybush, to the southwest, and Tanda Tula, Mbali and Motswari to the north (see Timbavati Game Reserve, p. 142). Your Mpumalanga safari could include one or more of these lodges. Ask your hosts about visiting Ngala's two sister reserves: Londolozi to the south, and the lovely Phinda Private Game Reserve in KwaZulu-Natal.

Most of Africa's game animals are found here, and a walk or game drive in the camp's vicinity may reveal giraffes, the elusive leopard, cheetahs, large herds of buffaloes, white rhinos, spotted hyenas and blackbacked jackals. Uncommon species include wild dogs, pangolins, aardvarks, porcupines, caracals, civets, lesser bushbabies and spotted genets. Among antelope species found here are common duiker, steenbok, impala, bushbuck, waterbuck and kudu.

Birdlife More than 350 species of bird find sanctuary at Ngala. If you're lucky you may catch a glimpse of giant eagle owls, martial and bateleur eagles; or any of the smaller species of woodland bird such as paradise flycatchers.

Where to stay The spirit of old Africa has truly been captured with sumptuous decor at Ngala Lodge. Twenty luxurious thatched bush chalets, spaced well apart to ensure complete privacy, nestle in the shade of indigenous trees festooned with beautiful orchids. A short distance away there's a sparkling swimming pool, fringed by such flowering shrubs as impala lily. The ice-blue waters of the pool spill over into a natural rock pool that serves as a watering spot for animals.

You may eat dinner inside the spacious lounge, diningroom and bar complex, with its high thatched roof, green slate floors and bushveld artefacts. Or you may choose to dine by candlelight in The Courtyard, on a terrace of slate under the stars, and drink fine wine from crystal glasses.

Lying in the shade of bushwillow and buffalo-thorn in an isolated corner of the camp is Ngala's Safari Suite, probably one of the most luxurious suites of its kind in Southern Africa.

There's an ambience of Edwardian bushveld luxury as you stroll into the livingroom, with its open thatch and tar-pole roof, exquisite furnishings (including a painting of wildebeest above the fireplace) and large adjoining sundeck, which you access through French doors.

The bedroom, also with its own fireplace and sundeck, has an *en suite* bathroom, with a white 1920s bathtub and a twin shower overlooking a waterhole and the canopy of surrounding trees. The Safari Suite also has its own swimming pool, private Land Rover and exclusive gamewatching expeditions.

Game drives and trails An experienced team of rangers, assisted by Shangaan trackers, conduct game drives and walks through the open plains, woodlands and bush surrounding the Timbavati River. At sunrise, coffee and rusks are served in the lounge, followed by a game drive. You'll visit waterholes where you can watch the animals and birds at their early morning ablutions. The late afternoon game drive is often accompanied by light refreshments along the way.

Keep a lookout for a pride of lions and their cubs lying on the sandy bed of the Timbavati River, or follow the spoor of leopard along the muddy fringes and through the long grass.

Spotlight-assisted night drives invariably lead to leopards and lions, and, if you're lucky, serval, bushbabies, porcu-

Cub killers and cannibals

Juvenile male lions leave the pride when they are two to three years old to form a tightly knit bachelor group with other young males. They wander around for about a year and then form their own pride — either by overthrowing the males of an established pride, or by joining a group of females without males. It is quite common for these young males to kill all the cubs in the pride so that the females come into breeding condition soon, and the males can mate and produce their own offspring.

A study of the social behaviour of 150 lions by American zoologist George Schaller confirmed that lions can be ruthless killers of their own kind.

While observing a pride of 14 lions, Schaller saw a neighbouring pride surprise a group of sleeping cubs while their mother was hunting. The intruders knocked the cubs around, then killed them.

One was savagely devoured; another was carried off in the mouth of its killer; the third cub was left dead on the ground.

When the mother returned from her hunt, Schaller saw her nonchalantly sniff at her cub's corpse, then eat it.

pines and caracals. Afterwards you can recount your experiences around a campfire, where you'll be serenaded by the haunting calls of owls and nightjars.

Another option for those with an adventurous spirit is to overnight at Mashaba's Rest, a sleep-out boma at the fringe of a waterhole where you'll be disturbed only by the trumpet of an elephant or the roar of a lion. The next morning you'll witness the brillance of sunrise in the African bush.

Ngala Game Reserve at a glance

Locality:	In the northwestern corner of the Kruger National Park, 515 km from Johannesburg.
Climate:	Hot summers with thunderstorms (nights average 20 °C); winter days mild to warm, but cold at night.
Number of camps:	One.
Game drives:	Variety of drives in vicinity of the Timbavati River.
Hides and waterholes:	The camp itself has a fine waterhole, and the one at Mashaba's Rest is highly recommended.
Trails:	Various walking trails are organised by the rangers.
Other attractions:	Sundowners in the bush.
Amenities:	Swimming pool, licensed restaurant and bar.
Accommodation:	20 luxurious thatched, air-conditioned bush chalets; the Safari Suite.
Booking address:	The Conservation Corporation, Private Bag X27, Benmore 2010, tel (011) 784-6832.
When to go:	All year round.
What to take with you:	Light, khaki clothing and a sunhat in summer; warm clothing in winter.
How to get there:	Comair operates daily flights to Skukuza from Johannesburg, from which your hosts will pick you up and transfer you to Ngala. From Johannesburg take the N4 to Belfast, then head north on the R540 for Lydenburg. From Lydenburg continue north on the R36 past Ohrigstad and through the Abel Erasmus Pass. After passing through the J G Strijdom Tunnel, follow the signposts to Hoedspruit. There turn right on to the R40 for 7 km and then left on to the Argyl Road. After 31 km turn right at the sign marked Ngala.
Nearest doctor:	Hoedspruit.
Nearest petrol:	Hoedspruit.
Open:	24 hours a day.
Special precautions:	Take a course of antimalaria tablets before you enter Ngala Game Reserve.

Phinda Private Game Reserve

It's sunset on the languorous waters of the Mzinene River. The *Zulu Belle* glides downstream, past sleeping crocodiles and hippos on the river banks. Goliath herons, kingfishers and pygmy geese prepare to nest for the night, while jacanas stalk the waterlily pads searching for supper.

As you sip sundowners on the upper deck, a wilderness of sycamore fig and fever trees, interspersed with rolling bushland and ilala palm veld, slips by — an ever-changing pageant of natural wonders.

This is the heart of the Phinda Game Reserve, a 17 000-ha sanctuary in Maputaland, between Mkuzi Game Reserve and the Greater St Lucia Wetland Park. Just a few hours' drive north of Durban, Phinda is a major drawcard for tourists because, apart from its own extraordinary array of attractions, it offers visitors adventures beyond its own physical boundaries.

It also lies in an area which represents the junction of bird species migrating north and other tropical species migrating south, so that there's a huge array of birds (the wetlands of Maputaland support 430 species), and a variety of different habitats.

The opening of Phinda Reserve in 1991 was a major event on the wildlife calendar of Southern Africa, for it revealed to the public the full extent of its game-restocking programme — the biggest ever launched on private land in Southern Africa.

Wildlife The reserve's ethnic name, Phinda Izilwane, means 'return of the wildlife', and it aptly describes what the reserve is all about. In addition to accommodating lions, elephants, rhinos, giraffes and hippos, Phinda is a natural sanctuary for a huge variety of mammals, reptiles and birds, including the largest private herd of nyala in the world.

Birdlife Waterbirds are the major attraction for birdwatchers, and feature a variety of kingfishers, including malachite kingfishers, squacco and purple herons, pelicans, fish eagles, woollynecked storks, crested guineafowl and eagle owls.

Where to stay The architecture of Phinda's four breathtaking luxury lodges is quite unique among the bush camps and game lodges of the subcontinent. And although they cater unashamedly to just about any whim you can think of, they have been built to blend into the bush as inconspicuously as possible.

FOREST LODGE There's a distinctly oriental feel to the 16 exquisite glass-walled suites at Forest Lodge. Raised on stilts above the forest floor, the suites were built around the growing trees, and the twisted trunks of orangewood and torchwood were given right of way, rearing through the wooden platforms to bring shade and serenity to the occupants.

Here the residents become one with the living forest, sharing the sights and songs of tree birds such as Narina trogons and purplecrested louries. Below, secretive suni, red duiker and nyala browse among the bushes of the forest floor. Each suite has a sunny bathroom, and is fully equipped with telephone, bar fridge, airconditioning and ceiling fan.

Nearby a central diningroom, lounge and sparkling pool look out of the forest on to an open, grassy vlei. Many evenings are spent around the fire in the Forest Boma, where you may be served indigenous ilala palm wine, and the very best cuisine.

VLEI LODGE Sumptuous suites of thatch, teak and glass have been built at the edge of a forest, overlooking Phinda's unique and colourful wetland system. Each suite, which is built on stilts, has a large double bedroom with spacious *en suite* bathroom, private plunge pool and outdoor deck, ideal for birdwatching or game spotting. The lodge also boasts South Africa's first silent safari vehicle which enables visitors to ride into the midst of game without them hearing a thing.

MOUNTAIN LODGE overlooks the stunning panorama of the Ubombo Mountains merging in the distance with the coastal plains of Lake St Lucia. The ethnically furnished, split-level suites, with private lounge and *en suite* bathrooms open up to a private deck overlooking the reserve.

ROCK LODGE This attractive lodge in the south of the reserve consists of six suites built of roughly hewn stone and adobe walls with ochre wooden roofs suspended over the edge of a rocky cliff. Each suite has its own private lounge, deck and plunge pool and an outdoor shower for bush bathing.

There's a main lounge and bar which open out on to shady verandahs with panoramic views. A sparkling pool area, elevated above the surrounding countryside, enables you to relax in the sun while nyala or rhinos graze on the slopes below.

Lunch is usually served in the diningroom or adjoining patio, while drinks and dinner are served in an open-air boma, where Zulu fireside tales bring a romantic end to a spectacular day.

Game drives and trails When visitors arrive at Nyala or Forest Lodge a ranger discusses adventure options available.

Phinda Private Game Reserve at a glance

Locality:	Maputaland, between the Greater St Lucia Wetland Park and Mkuzi Game Reserve.
Climate:	Winters are mild to warm; summers are humid and hot with thundershowers. Average daytime temperatures range from 20 °C to 35 °C.
Number of camps:	Two.
Game drives:	Morning and evening drives offered daily.
Trails:	Daily walks led by Zulu trackers.
Other attractions:	Excursions to Mkuzi Game Reserve, Lake Sibaya, Lake St Lucia and Maputaland beaches. Game fishing, flying safaris.
Amenities:	Executive conference room accommodating 72 people and a curio shop.
Accommodation:	Four luxury lodges: **Forest Lodge, Vlei Lodge, Mountain Lodge** and **Rock Lodge**.
Booking address:	Central Reservations, The Conservation Corporation, Private Bag X27, Benmore 2010, tel (011) 784-6832.
When to go:	All year round.
What to take with you:	Light clothing in summer, jersey or anorak in winter; camera, binoculars, hat, snorkelling gear, sturdy walking shoes.
How to get there:	Drive north from Durban on the N2 to Hluhluwe Village. Just past Hluhluwe take the Ngewni/Sodwana Bay offramp, cross back over the N2 and turn left at the stop sign. Drive 4 km, cross the railway line and turn right for Sodwana/Phinda. Phinda Nyala gate is 8 km further on.
Nearest doctor:	Hluhluwe, 30 km away.
Nearest petrol:	Hluhluwe, 30 km away.
Open:	24 hours a day.
Special precautions:	Take antimalaria precautions before you go to the reserve.

Early morning and evening game drives take guests through the reserve's seven different ecosystems, and usually include either a bush breakfast or a refreshment stop in the bush at sunset, before the drive continues after dark.

A spotlight on the vehicle reveals various nocturnal creatures — lions, leopards, porcupines, eagle owls, bushbabies, spotted genets or whitetailed mongooses. The day drive may include a stop at Thabo Nkosi Hill ('the meeting place of the king'), followed by a walk to its summit from which there are spectacular views of the reserve and Nyala Lodge below.

The drive continues past groves of ilala palms, grasslands and open pans and a rare sand forest (home of suni and red squirrel). Keep an eye open for elephants, Burchell's zebras, giraffes and blue wildebeest.

The day ends with dinner under the shade of a huge camelthorn tree, or at a table for two under the stars.

Other options offered at Phinda are a sunrise or sunset cruise on the *Zulu Belle* down the Mzinene River, which forms the southern boundary of the reserve. Guests may also hire a canoe to explore the waterways at leisure.

Maputaland adventures Phinda Private Game Reserve is within an easy drive of some excellent scenic and wildlife attractions, all of which are offered to guests as extra adventure packages during their stay. These include:

- Birdwatching excursions to Ensumo Pan in Mkuzi Game Reserve
- Flights over breathtaking Lake Sibaya, one of the largest freshwater lakes in Southern Africa, and across the St Lucia Wetland Complex, a jigsaw puzzle of different vegetation types
- Trails through forests of fever and fig trees
- Excursions to the pristine beaches of Maputaland, just 10 minutes away by light aircraft
- Scuba-diving and snorkelling off the coral reefs of the Maputaland coast, where more than 1 200 species of tropical fish have been identified
- Game-fishing expeditions in the Indian Ocean, where the big prizes are tropical fighters such as barracuda, blue and black marlin, sailfish, dorado and tunny
- Angling on Lake Sibaya
- Picnicking on Lake St Lucia's Nibela Peninsula.

Pilanesberg National Park

The Pilanesberg National Park is undoubtedly one of Southern Africa's favourite reserves. Abundant game, an excellent choice of accommodation, and remote, supremely beautiful surroundings make Pilanesberg a nature-lover's and game-watcher's paradise.

Lying on the eroded remains of a 1 200-million-year-old extinct volcanic crater — one of only three in the world — Pilanesberg is the fourth largest national park south of the Limpopo. Proclaimed in 1979, the park covers 550 km^2 (55 000 ha) of broad, green plains, scattered hills and densely wooded ravines conjuring up images of ancient Africa.

Here among the singing grasslands and granite outcrops you'll find more than 100 species of the great trees of Africa, from the generous-canopied marula and river bushwillow to the less leafy sweet-thorn and black monkeythorn, which dominate the thickets.

For many, part of the park's attraction is that it is just two hours' drive away from Johannesburg, and just a few minutes' drive away from the roulette wheels, slot machines and gaming tables of Sun City, and its companion hotel/holiday complex, the Lost City (23 km away). But the real drawcard at Pilanesberg is its extraordinary population of animals.

Wildlife The concentric boundaries of Pilanesberg National Park are home to more than 8 000 animals — including 35 species of large mammal. With the recent introduction of three prides of lions (20) from the Etosha National Park, the park is now one of the privileged reserves hosting the Big Five.

The most recent game census showed that there are 74 elephants, more than 2 000 impala and warthogs, 353 buffaloes and 1 800 Burchell's zebras.

In addition, there are black and white rhinos (the third largest population of white rhinos in the world), 16 species of antelope, 25 hippos, giraffes, cheetahs, leopards and hyenas.

A major reason for Pilanesberg's diversity of animals is that it lies in the transition zone between the arid Kalahari in the west and the humid Lowveld of the North-West Province. Typical Kalahari species, such as gemsbok, honey badger, aardwolf and brown hyena, are therefore able to coexist with animals more common in the eastern, higher rainfall regions, such as bushbuck, waterbuck and hippopotamus.

Another important reason is that in the early 1980s the park was on the receiving end of 'Operation Genesis', the largest game relocation operation ever undertaken, when 6 000 animals were released on the rugged green plains.

Elephants came from Addo National Park, red hartebeest from Namibia and 17 rhinos were donated by the National Parks Board.

Among Pilanesberg's reptiles and amphibians are 35 species of snake and 27 different lizards. The venomous snakes include Mozambique spitting cobras, vine snakes, tree-snakes, black mambas and puffadders. Less venomous varieties are green watersnakes, African pythons and common egg-eaters.

Birdlife The seven different habitats at Pilanesberg attract a rich and diverse population of birds (more than 300 species), among them brilliantly coloured malachite kingfishers, pied and brownhooded kingfishers, crimsonbreasted shrikes, lilacbreasted rollers, crested barbets and fish eagles. The granite outcrops, thickets and fringes of the waterways are home to such species as arrowmarked babbler, goldenbreasted bunting, black eagle, Cape vulture and kurrichane thrush.

Game drives and trails An excellent 200-km network of roads includes a number of hides and vantage points for watching the animals and birds.

Visitors may use their own vehicles for game-viewing, or join one of the organised drives on which a ranger will take you to selected spots and point out game on the way. Game-viewing drives leave the camps in the early morning and late afternoon, but visitors may elect to join a night drive.

Other options for seeing game are on foot (nature walks must be booked in advance) or by hot-air balloon. A special geological autotrail (booklet supplied) gives you a first-hand introduction to the forces that shaped this land. Twelve sites of interest, including volcanic debris, have been mapped. Visitors may also see an abandoned fluorite mine, Moepo.

Pilanesberg National Park is one of the few parks that will lay on champagne breakfasts, bush barbecues and other forms of entertainment for business groups or private parties. The venue is usually a boma in the bush, and the cuisine is generally of a very high standard.

Where to stay If you're looking for a 'wild' holiday in the bush, without the trappings of a five-star hotel, look no further than the Pilanesberg Safari Camps. You'll stay in a comfortable East African safari tent deep in the bush, where the stillness is interrupted only by the sounds of birds and animals. Your needs will be attended to by a ranger and hostess.

MANKWE BUSH CAMP This rustic, self-catering camp overlooks Mankwe Dam, and is ideal for watching the animals that rely on it for water throughout the year. Ten thatched log cabins (sleeping four each) and 10 safari tents (three each) nestle among the bushes of the savannah woodland.

There's no electricity here, but gas and paraffin are provided. A reed-walled ablution block encloses flush toilets and hot-water showers under the stars. Bring your own food and drink, and cooking and eating utensils.

MANYANE CAMP This camp is one of the finest chalet and caravan camps in the southern hemisphere. There are 60 self-contained chalets (two- to six-bed), safari tents under shade, and 100 electrified caravan stands, all offering access to swimming pools, picnic areas and an à la carte restaurant (fully licensed). Each chalet has its own garden furniture and braai place where you can relax with a drink outside before your meal. Four communal ablution blocks are equipped with hot and cold water. Major attractions at Manyane

Fearless clown of the veld

The comical-looking warthog, described once as an 'incarnation of hideous dreams' and a 'disgrace to nature' is, in spite of its appearance, a responsible, loyal parent, and a fearless defender of its young. An adult boar won't hesitate to use its sharp tusks and thickset, powerful neck to rout a threatening predator. Cheetahs and even leopards stalking juvenile warthogs have been put to flight by the headlong rush of an adult brandishing its razor-sharp incisors. There is one record of two warthog boars chasing off a pack of 16 wild dogs in Kenya.

The warthog's peculiar-looking face has been fashioned to enable it to keep its place successfully in the community of animals. The unattractive, flattened snout acts like a spade in digging and rooting out the berries, seeds and plants it eats with such relish; the 'warts' — a pair of thick outgrowths of skin beneath each eye — protect the warthog's eyes when it is grubbing for food, and also exaggerate the size of its head, giving adults a more aggressive appearance. Hard protective calluses protect the warthog's knees when it goes down on its forelegs to dig for food.

are the Manyane Bird Sanctuary, with a walk-in aviary housing 60 species of bird, and the Goldfields Education Centre. There's also a trampoline, jungle-gym, swings and slide for children.

METSWEDI SAFARI CAMP This secluded camp, tucked away in a wild corner of the park, has seven safari tents, with access to two ablution blocks, and a thatched lounge and diningroom which overlooks

Pilanesberg National Park at a glance

Locality:	North-West Province of South Africa.
Climate:	Summer days hot to very hot (summer mean 36 °C), evenings mild to cool; winter days mild to warm; cold in the evenings. Summer rain in the form of thunderstorms (620 mm per annum).
Number of camps:	Four.
Game drives:	There is a 200-km network of roads offering autotrails or escorted drives by professional rangers.
Hides and waterholes:	Hides, waterholes and picnic spots are scattered throughout the park, including one at Metswedi Safari Camp.
Trails:	An 8-km self-guided trail has been marked out in the Extensive Education Zone; and the geological autotrail (mapped).
Amenities:	Restaurant, swimming pool, trampoline, jungle-gym, swings and slide for children at Manyane Camp.
Accommodation:	Safari camps: **Mankwe Bush Camp:** 10 thatched four-bed log cabins, 10 three-bed safari tents; **Manyane Camp:** 60 chalets (two- to six-bed), safari tents, 100 caravan stands; **Metswedi Safari Camp:** seven safari tents; **Kololo Camp:** four safari tents. Luxury accommodation at **Kwa Maritane Lodge, Tshukudu Lodge** and **Bakubung Lodge.**
Booking address:	Mankwe Bush Camp, Manyane Camp, Metswedi Camp and Kololo Camp: Contact Central Reservations, Golden Leopard Resorts, PO Box 6651, Rustenburg 0300, tel (014) 555-6135/9. Kwa Maritane Lodge, Bakubung Lodge and Tshukudu Lodge, write to: Stocks and Stocks, PO Box 39, Sun City 0316, or tel (014) 552-1860/1 (Kwa Maritane) and (014) 552-1868/9 (Bakubung and Tshukudu).
When to go:	Throughout the year.
What to take with you:	Bathing costume, light clothing in summer, walking shoes, camera and binoculars, guide book (birds and mammals).
How to get there:	Drive north to Rustenburg from Johannesburg and Pretoria. From Rustenburg drive north on the R510 towards Thabazimbi. After 60 km turn left towards the park and Manyane Gate.
Nearest doctor:	Sun City or Rustenburg.
Nearest petrol:	At Manyane Camp Gate.
Open:	September–March: 05:00–20:00; April–August: 05:30–19:00.
Special precautions:	If you're staying at Mankwe Camp, be alert to 'foraging' expeditions by vervet monkeys and baboons. Keep all food stowed, and don't feed the animals.

a waterhole. Here you can enjoy scrumptious meals after a sundowner or two around a nearby campfire. There's a hostess to attend to your needs, and a ranger to show you the game.

KOLOLO CAMP The four East African safari tents standing on a hill at Kololo Camp overlook the lush plains and rocky valleys of the Pilanesberg. In the evening, when the sun sinks over the horizon, a primeval chill descends on the camp, and there's comfort in the thought that dinosaurs no longer stalk this land.

Bedding is provided, but bring your own provisions, and prepare yourself for quiet contemplation — each tent is placed well away from the next one to ensure your privacy.

BOSELE CAMP This camp offers attractive log cabins with bunk beds, and accommodation for up to 180 people, but there's little of the privacy you'll find in the bush camps.

KWA MARITANE, TSHUKUDU AND BAKUBUNG LODGES Visitors who want luxurious accommodation need look no further than the luxury hotel and timeshare resorts of Kwa Maritane Lodge, Tshukudu Lodge and Bakubung Lodge. Kwa Maritane is exceptional for the hide in front of the main hotel restaurant, which you reach through a long underground tunnel.

The six luxury chalets and three cabins of Tshukudu, set among indigenous trees on a koppie in the southwestern section of Pilanesberg National Park, provide sweeping views of the volcanic plains and the variety of animals that graze on the lush grasses there.

Tshukudu means 'rhinoceros' in Setswana, and chances are good you'll see them come down to the waterhole in front of the koppie.

Other attractions at Tshukudu include a cosy restaurant called The Nest, which serves English breakfasts and typically African cuisine, a swimming pool and a braai area.

Nearby Bakubung Lodge, like its sister lodge Tshukudu, offers comfortable chalet accommodation and day and night game drives to the more interesting parts of the Pilanesberg.

RICHTERSVELD NATIONAL PARK

Brooding mountains scarred by bone-dry gorges rise eerily from the quartzite plains of northern Namaqualand. Here and there, incredibly defying the dreadful heat, human-looking trees raise their limbs to the sky — ghostly silhouettes in a land of lunar shapes.

Impossibly hot and strangely barren, the Richtersveld could be mistaken for a halfway house on the road to hell — its landscape christened with such titles as Gorgon's Head, Devil's Tooth, Skeleton Gorge and Helskloof. Reinforcing the desolation along the Orange River are abandoned diamond mines, sand-blasted memorials to the vain hopes of prospectors.

For lovers of comfort and coolness, this is no place to be. But for the adventurous, seeking a taste of untamed wilderness, the Richtersveld has charms beyond the imagination of ordinary people.

The adventure lies in 162 445 ha of rugged mountain desert, proclaimed in August 1991 to protect the world's richest variety of succulents and a diverse community of animals. This landscape of pure desolation and tranquillity is known as Richtersveld National Park.

Here you may roll out your sleeping bag beneath the stars, and listen to the sunset bark of baboons or the howl of black-backed jackals, or feel the coolness of the Atlantic fog as it creeps inland overnight.

The park's northern boundary lies in the loop of the Orange River as it meanders from Vioolsdrif to the sea near Alexander Bay. In spite of its proximity to water (the Atlantic is just kilometres away), the park is one of the driest parts of South Africa. It is the country's only true desert, receiving an average annual rainfall of between five and 200 millimetres.

More than 50 per cent of the plants here are endemic to the region, and owe their survival to cool banks of fog (known by the Nama as 'Malmokkie'), which roll inland from the Atlantic during the night.

Tips for travellers

- Entry permits for day visits and overnight camping must be obtained at Sendelingsdrif.
- There is no fuel inside the park — the nearest fuel is available at Alexander Bay.
- The roads in the park are mostly narrow farm tracks, many of them following the course of river beds or tracking the sides of steep mountains. For this reason only 4x4s are recommended for use in the park. Abnormally wide vehicles aren't allowed in the park.
- Visitors have to be completely self-sufficient, and must remove all the refuse they generate in the park.
- Don't take part in organised hikes unless you are fit.
- When leaving the park, try and travel home through the southern Richtersveld, through the towns of Kuboes, Lekkersing and Eksteenfontein to join the tar road between Port Nolloth and Steinkopf.

A fascinating example is the endangered 'halfmens' (half-human tree) — one of the rarest xerophytes in the world.

Nama legend has it that these strange trees with human-like branches are the living remnants of their ancestors who were driven south across the Orange River by the San from the north. As the Nama fled, they stopped to look back at their beloved homeland with great sadness in their hearts. God took pity on them, and turned them into 'halfmens' — a form of life that was half plant, half human.

Today the feathery tops of the halfmens trees turn towards the north — giving credence to the Nama legend. The quiver tree and the maiden's quiver tree, whose bark was used to hold the arrows of the San, are other important species that flourish in the Richtersveld National Park.

Much of the Richtersveld National Park consists of sandy plains, peppered here and there with succulent ground cover. Inland a backbone of black mountains reaches its summit at Kodas Peak — at 984 m, it is one of the highest in the Richtersveld.

For travellers, the sandy tracks, sheer cliffs and interminable outcrops of rock create undreamed-of challenges, as well as vistas of vast plains, such as Springbokvlakte, reaching to distant horizons.

Wildlife In spite of its aridity, the Richtersveld National Park supports no less than 55 mammal species, 51 species of reptile, seven amphibian and 14 fish species. Semi-desert-adapted antelope such as klipspringers, steenbok, grey rhebok and duiker are seen in the park, as well as Hartmann's mountain zebras, baboons, leopards and caracals.

Birdlife The birdlife is plentiful, with 194 species, especially along the river courses and in the scrubland.

Where to stay The five-bedroomed Arieb Guest Cottage accommodates 10 people, with two bathrooms as well as a lounge, diningroom and kitchen. Bedding, soap and towels are provided and the kitchen is fully equipped.

Camping spots (without toilets, hot or cold water or shelters) have been set aside at Potjiespram (3), De Hoop (8), Richtersberg (3), Kokerboomkloof (3) and De Koei (3). Here you may pitch your tent, walk around freely taking in the pristine beauty of the surroundings, and relax at the riverside or in the shade of a halfmens or quiver tree. If you intend staying overnight, try to take a stretcher with you, because scorpions scuttle across the rocky ground at night. Remember, too, that firewood may not be collected, and all refuse must be taken away after your stay.

Another point to consider is the fact that in terms of a contract entered into between the National Parks Board and the Nama community, they are allowed to live and graze livestock in the area. The park authorities ask visitors to respect their rights and privacy, and not to photograph them.

Trails Three demarcated trails are available to visitors from 1 April to 30 September. They are the Vensterval Trail (4 days, 3 nights), the Lelieshoek-Oemsberg Trail (3 days, 2 nights) and the Kodaspiek Trail (2 days, 1 night).

Tours into the Richtersveld Organised tours of the Richtersveld are offered by a company in Springbok called the Richtersveld Challenge. The tours include: Guided vehicle safaris of five days or

Doing the foxtrot before supper

As rivulets of heat shimmer above the scorched plains of the Richtersveld, an animal about the size of a domestic dog trots along the horizon. Here and there he stops, puts his ears to the ground, digs furiously then trots off again.

The bateared fox is looking for supper again. The animal is something of an oddity, with a black, lone-ranger mask and huge ears completely disproportionate to his body. He puts his ears to the ground to listen for the subterranean insects and grubs on which he feeds. They amplify the slightest sound so that he can pinpoint his quarry exactly.

Although this fox is partial to termites, it will also devour mice, lizards, scorpions and small birds. The large jaw muscles and impressive dental armoury of 50 teeth enable it to enjoy a hasty meal — just in case there are other predators around.

Brown hyenas, jackals and large birds of prey such as martial eagles, are a constant threat to these little animals.

In the presence of the enemy, the bateared fox will warn its companions by arching its back and tail. The others may rush to its aid and 'pronk' in much the same way as a springbok does, and then release a barrage of high-pitched barks.

longer, covering about 800 km; a combined vehicle and walking safari lasting five days, which covers 800 km (4x4) and 45 km (hike); and an excursion that includes a ride down the Orange River on an inflatable dinghy, a vehicle tour and a hike.

All equipment is supplied by the organisers (except for sleeping bag, clothing for all weather conditions, sunscreen lotion, toiletries and liquor). Hikers should bring their own hiking equipment, and be fit.

Tours leave from and return to Springbok (554 km from Cape Town). Groups are restricted to 12 people, but a minimum of eight is acceptable. For details contact the Richtersveld Challenge, PO Box 142, Springbok, Namaqualand 8240, tel (0251) 2-1905.

Richtersveld National Park at a glance

Locality:	Far northwestern Northern Cape, on South Africa's border with Namibia.
Climate:	One of the driest areas in South Africa, rainfall ranges from 5 mm to 125 mm per annum. Summer temperatures may exceed 50 °C. Generally cool at night.
Number of campsites:	Five.
Game drives:	There are hundreds of kilometres of sandy tracks crisscrossing the park. A map is available at the park's headquarters at Sendelingsdrif. The Richtersveld Challenge (tel (0251) 2-1905) offers guided tours and hikes through the Richtersveld, and trips down the Orange River.
Trails:	The National Parks Board is developing walking trails within the park, and full details are available from the warden (see booking address below).
Other attractions:	Swimming in the Orange River.
Amenities:	There are no shops in the park. The nearest shops are at Alexander Bay, Kuboes, Lekkersing and Eksteenfontein.
Accommodation:	Arieb Guest Cottage (5 bedrooms). Chalets and camping sites at Brandkaros, 20 km upriver from Alexander Bay. Campsites at Potjiespram, De Hoop, Richtersberg, Kokerboomkloof and De Koei.
Booking address:	The Warden, Richtersveld National Park, PO Box 406, Alexander Bay 8290, tel (0256) 831-1506.
When to go:	The winter months (April–September) when it is cooler.
What to take with you:	All you need to accommodate yourself during your stay. Food, plenty of water, firewood; cooking and eating utensils, including gas stove; warm and cool clothing; toiletries and refuse bags.
How to get there:	From Springbok take the N7 towards Steinkopf, then continue westwards towards Port Nolloth. From Port Nolloth head northwards to Alexander Bay. From Alexander Bay follow the signposts for 93 km to Sendelingsdrif, the park's headquarters.
Nearest doctor:	Alexander Bay.
Nearest petrol:	Alexander Bay and Lekkersing.
Open:	08:00–16:00 daily.
Special precautions:	Take precautions against dehydration and heat exhaustion. If you must sleep on the ground, watch out for scorpions. Exercise caution when swimming in the Orange River. The river has claimed many lives.

Rocktail Bay Lodge

The tinkling call of a fierynecked nightjar mingles with the drone of surf crashing on the shore. You lie in the comfort of your reed-panelled treehouse, listening to the gathering chorus of birds: the piet-my-vrou chatter of the redchested cuckoo, the lilting call of the rattling cisticola, and the whistling symphony of puffbacks, calling from the tops of the trees. Suddenly you hear the rustling of leaves.

Beneath the canopy of red and white milkwoods that surround your rustic quarters, vervet monkeys leap from branch to branch, briefly halting the serenade of birdsong.

In this brief silence, you realise how lucky you are to share the luxury of such tranquillity at one of Southern Africa's most secluded seaside lodges: Rocktail Bay.

Named after a ship that was wrecked there, Rocktail Bay lies just inside, and about halfway up, the Maputaland Coastal Forest Reserve that runs from Sodwana Bay in the south to Kosi Bay, near the border of Mozambique.

The lodge and its chalets on stilts nestle among the fringe of trees just behind the first row of sand-dunes. The beach is a five-minute stroll from your chalet — along a boardwalk shaded by avenues of milkwood and jackalberry.

The chalets were built by the KwaZulu-Natal Bureau of Natural Resources in 1991, and were designed to be as ecologically 'friendly' as possible. That's why the power supply is solar, and gas is used for cooking.

There aren't many spots along the coastline that are as secluded as this one. Here you can walk for kilometres along the bronzed, sloping beaches, alone in the company of surf, spray and deep blue sky.

During your stay, you'll be pampered by your hosts (the staff ratio is 26 staff to 20 guests), and because some of them are naturalists and marine specialists, they'll leave no question unanswered.

Wildlife Although Rocktail Bay is by no means big-game country, the owners of the lodge are proud of their own 'Big Five' — the leatherback and loggerhead turtles, Buiton's skink, lionfish, and Zululand cycad. The leatherback and the smaller loggerhead turtle have chosen this remote

Bushpigs tusk out their territory

Bushpigs, such as those found in the forests around Rocktail Bay, have a fascinating way of marking their home turf — they slash or 'tusk' the lower bark of trees with their razor-sharp canines.

Some naturalists believe the slashing takes place when the animal rubs its facial scent glands against the tree to mark its territory. Most of the marked trees are found on the fringes of the bushpigs' feeding areas. A bushpig's territory may extend up to 4 km or more, and is always crisscrossed by clearly marked paths.

Along the coastal fringe of northern KwaZulu-Natal, bushpigs have helped establish new forests by eating the fruits of trees in other parts and depositing the pods or seeds in their faeces at their chosen latrine sites.

The bushpig's constant grovelling for food beneath the soil wears away its teeth. By the age of eight, they're so worn down that it cannot defend itself against youngsters trying to dominate the sounder.

stretch of coast as their breeding ground, and today it is regarded as the most important in the world.

Each summer these giant creatures haul themselves from the surf and slog up the sloping sands to excavate nests and lay their eggs. Two months later hundreds of tiny turtles hatch out and begin their perilous scramble to the shelter of the waves.

The Buiton's skinks of Black Rock are the only ones of their kind in the world. You may see them, or the turtles trundling back to the sea from the high ground, on the 6-km beach walk to Black Rock. Keep your eye on the sea, too, and you may catch a glimpse of a humpback whale or dolphin. It's a scenically beautiful walk to Black Rock, and the shoreline abuts coastal and dune forest, vleis and open grass plains. If the distance is too much for you, the lodge's staff will do the round-trip with you in a 4x4, or bring you back if you choose to walk there.

Apart from vervet monkeys, the animals of the coastal forest include common reedbuck, bushpigs, red duiker, common duiker, largespotted genets, dwarf mongooses, banded mongooses, water mongooses, thicktailed galagos, samango monkeys and the lovely red squirrel.

Gaboon adders are among the rarer snakes here, but you'll also find vine snakes, black file snakes, green mambas and spotted bush snakes. Other reptiles include variable and striped skinks, and Zululand dwarf chameleons.

But the real attraction of the area's forest canopies are the birds — which include emerald cuckoos, pinkthroated longclaws, paradise flycatchers, grey waxbills, little bee-eaters, Knysna and purple-crested louries, Rudd's apalis and brown-hooded kingfishers.

Birds of prey include blackbreasted snake eagles, yellowbilled kites, African fish eagles, African goshawks and gymnogenes, while waders and terns frequent the shoreline.

Marine life For those who love exploring the sea's submarine treasures, Rocktail Bay offers the very best in snorkelling and diving (you can borrow flippers and snorkel from the lodge).

If you want to browse around in quite shallow water, then snorkel along the shelf that runs out to the breaker zone on the south side of the bay.

As you head out into deeper water, you'll find an extraordinary variety of sea life: shoals of speckled snapper, lionfish, rays and skates pass by beneath you. Then the bigger fish come into view: giant kingfish, king mackerel, queenfish and even sharks, such as the blacktip reef shark.

Not surprisingly, Rocktail Bay is an angler's and spearfisherman's paradise, and there are few who come away empty-handed. Species you may expect to catch include barracuda, blacktail, springer, shad, stumpnose and bonefish. Rods, reels and bait are supplied by the lodge, and there are facilities for freezing your catch.

Where to stay Ten thatched A-frame chalets, mounted on stilts beneath the forest canopy, offer two- or three-bed accommodation for a maximum of 20 people. A short boardwalk leads to a cosy thatched diningroom and bar-lounge. You may dine inside or under the giant mahogany trees.

Day drives Rocktail Bay Lodge serves as an ideal springboard for visiting some of the reserves and marine resorts nearby. You can choose between Sodwana Bay (just an hour's drive away), where you can arrange a deep-sea fishing charter or diving expedition to one of the coral reefs; Ndumo Game Reserve (96 km), where Wilderness Safaris has a luxury safari camp; Kosi Mouth (62 km); Kosi Bay camping area (44 km), where snorkelling and boat trips are available; the Tembe Elephant Park (65 km) or Lake Sibaya.

Rocktail Bay Lodge at a glance

Locality:	Northern KwaZulu-Natal coast.
Climate:	Summers humid and hot with thunderstorms; winters mild to warm.
Number of camps:	One.
Game drives:	Day drives available to Sodwana Bay, Ndumo Game Reserve, Tembe Elephant Park, Lake Sibaya.
Trails:	Variety of beach walks, including 6-km walk to Black Rock.
Other attractions:	Swimming, birdwatching, snorkelling, angling, walking, relaxing.
Amenities:	Outside bar area, filtered swimming pool, curio shop.
Accommodation:	Ten two- and three-bed chalets (20 people), with diningroom and bar-lounge.
Booking address:	Wilderness Safaris, PO Box 78573, Sandton 2146, tel (011) 883-0747.
When to go:	Throughout the year.
What to take with you:	Torch, binoculars, camera, fishing rod and reel, mask, snorkel, flippers.
How to get there:	If you have a 4x4 you can drive right up to the lodge. Access is via the road from Manzengwenyana. If you don't have a 4x4, park your car at Manzengwenyana, and arrange to be picked up by a Wilderness Safari 4x4 vehicle. You can reach Manzengwenyana from Durban by branching right off the N2 just north of Mkuze, and driving through Jozini. From Johannesburg take the route via Jozini and Sihangwane. You will be given detailed directions and a map showing you how to get there when you book. A small airfield 12 km from the lodge is available for fly-in visitors. Transfers are organised by the lodge.
Nearest doctor:	Manguzi.
Nearest petrol:	Jozini.
Open:	Sunrise to sunset all year round.
Special precautions:	Take antimalaria precautions before you visit Rocktail Bay.

ROYAL NATAL PARK

The full majesty of Southern Africa's Drakensberg reveals itself in this spectacular national park, a wilderness of rivers, ravines, peaks, pinnacles and rocky giants, created 200 million years ago by fantastic volcanic eruptions beneath the earth's crust.

Dominating the entire park is a brooding arc of volcanic basalt, 500 m high and 5 km long, known as the Amphitheatre, which affords mountaineers and hikers the most panoramic views of the 350-km-long Drakensberg range on the subcontinent.

Flanked in the southeast by the pedestal of the Eastern Buttress, and in the west by Beacon Buttress and the fang-shaped Sentinel, the Amphitheatre forms the precipitous edge of a misty plateau, known as Mont-Aux-Sources (mountain of springs). The summit of Mont-Aux-Sources was scaled for the first time by two French missionaries in 1836, who then named it for its profusion of springs (eight rivers have their source here). One of them is the mighty Tugela River, whose breathtaking journey over the rim of the Amphitheatre makes it the world's second-highest waterfall.

The Tugela and numerous other rivers and streams tumble down the folds of the park's emerald mountains into liana-draped ravines of yellowwood, white stinkwood and wild chestnut. Higher up, grasslands dotted with crimson-flowered *Protea caffra* and *Protea roupelliae* merge with other fynbos species — heaths, ericas and a profusion of other veld flowers.

Wildlife Obviously, the scenic beauty of Royal Natal is the major drawcard, but an added bonus is the chance to see some of the mammals or birds which inhabit the park. Such species as grey duiker, klipspringer, bushbuck and mountain reedbuck may be seen early in the morning, while baboons, rock dassies, blackbacked jackals, hares and otters are spotted any time during the day.

Less-often seen species include such nocturnal animals as genets, servals and caracals, as well as water mongooses and Cape grey mongooses. Of the snakes found in the park the one to watch out for is the puffadder, a reptile capable of inflicting a fatal bite.

Tip for travellers

Picking or plucking flowering plants in the park exposes them to fatal attacks by bacteria and fungi. Visitors are therefore asked to leave the plants alone.

Birdlife More than 184 species of bird find sanctuary in the park. Among them, birds of prey are common: they include bearded vultures, black eagles, a variety of falcons, kestrels, kites and vultures — including the Cape vulture. Other smaller species include Ayres' cisticolas, tawny-flanked prinias, fierynecked nightjars and arrowmarked babblers.

Where to stay Amid the lushness and tranquillity of Royal Natal's undulating mountains lies one of the most scenically beautiful camps in Southern Africa — the Tendele Hutted Camp.

Here guests have a choice of 13 three- and five-bed bungalows, each with a view of the Amphitheatre, 13 three- and five-bed chalets, and two self-contained six-bed cottages. In addition, the luxurious Tendele Lodge accommodates six people in three snug bedrooms, with bathrooms *en suite*. The lodge has its own kitchen, spacious lounge with fireplace and an outdoor braai area. Meals in the cottages, bungalows and lodge are prepared by a cook, but the chalet accommodation is self-catering. Guests must bring their own food and drink.

There are two attractive open campgrounds: Mahai and Rugged Glen. Mahai Campground, set in lovely treed surroundings, has facilities for up to 400 campers and caravanners, with access to a central ablution block (with hot and cold water) and a safe, central playground for children.

Rugged Glen Campground to the east has campsites for 45 people (and hot and cold running water). Campers may book six months in advance, and must supply all their own provisions and tents.

The Royal Natal Park Hotel offers comfortable accommodation, modern facilities and a swimming pool (see *Booking address*, 'At a glance' box).

San paintings The San are believed to have lived among these mountain peaks from as early as the 15th century, but towards the end of the 19th century they were hunted down ruthlessly.

Today evidence of their moving artwork remains in caves and shelters around the park. Four of these sites can be easily visited. They are: Cannibal Caves near Surprise Ridge in the northern part of the park; beneath a rock on Devil's Hoek path near Tendele Hutted Camp; beneath another rock close to the foot of the Mudslide; and in the Sigubudu Caves west of the Rugged Glen Campsite.

Getting around Various options are available for exploring the park.

ON FOOT Twenty-five beautiful walks and trails radiate from the Royal Natal Park Hotel, the main campsite, Tendele camp and Rugged Glen. These KwaZulu-Natal Nature Conservation Services routes afford visitors the best possible exposure to the panoramic vistas of the Amphitheatre and the surrounding mountains and peaks.

The Visitors' Centre supplies an excellent brochure and map listing all the walks, and showing the various contour lines, mountains, peaks, valleys and rivers.

Among the most popular and picturesque of these are: The 7-km Gorge Walk (from Tendele Camp), The Lion (from the Gorge car park) and Surprise Ridge and Cannibal Cave (from the hotel area). For a more ambitious trail, consider the Mont-Aux-Sources Walk, a two-day trip (45 km, 17 hours) to the summit of the Amphitheatre, where walkers overnight (take a tent along with you). If you spend a second night on the Amphitheatre, you will have enough time to visit the summit of Mont-Aux-Sources (3 282 m).

Park authorities are concerned that in spite of clear guidelines and the warnings contained in the brochure, fatalities still occur — mainly as a result of walkers deviating from established routes and taking unnecessary risks. Some simple guidelines to walking in Royal Natal are:

- In summer leave early when it's cooler, so you may get back before thunderstorms set in during the afternoons.
- Be aware of sudden changes in the weather. Swirling mists often set in, reducing visibility to nil. If this is the case, stay where you are — don't try to walk back.
- Before you set out on a trail, always let someone at your camp know where you're going, and when you expect to return. Hikers intending to go higher than the 2 300-m contour or to the summit of Mont-Aux-Sources, must sign the mountain register at the office.

BY CAR You can drive to the Sentinel car park, and then tackle the two-hour walk to the summit of the Amphitheatre. Don't consider this walk if you suffer from vertigo — it involves a near-vertical ascent with the help of chain ladders. Also bear in mind that to reach the car park at the base of the Sentinel, you'll have to drive 130 km out of the Royal Natal into the Free State, and back via the Witsieshoek Mountain Resort to the car park. The Visitors' Centre will give you full directions.

Tips for travellers

- **Visitors may picnic and light fires in designated fireplaces – but not in the hills away from these areas.**
- **Motorists are asked to observe the 40km/h speed limit and to watch out for horse-riders, dassies and children.**

BY HORSE Rugged Glen Campsite offers some delightful trails on horseback.

BY HELICOPTER Flights over the Drakensberg are offered by Drakair from Cathedral Peak Hotel, an hour away from Royal Natal. Contact the hotel at tel (036) 488-1888.

Trout fishing Visitors may catch trout in the rivers during the open season (1 September–31 May). Licences are available at the Visitors' Centre.

Freshwater fishing is permitted throughout the year in the Royal Natal and Rugged Glen dams.

Royal Natal Park at a glance

Locality:	The northern Drakensberg of KwaZulu-Natal, on the border of Lesotho and the Free State.
Climate:	Summers warm to hot; winters cool with frost in June and July. The average rainfall is between 1 040 mm and 1 290 mm, and comes mainly in the form of summer thunderstorms.
Number of camps:	Three.
Trails:	25 popular trails offer unlimited scenic delights.
Other attractions:	Swimming in the rivers and streams is popular.
Amenities:	Two well-stocked souvenir and gift shops. Small store near hotel stocked with basic provisions.
Accommodation:	Tendele Hutted Camp: 13 three- and five-bed bungalows, 13 three- and five-bed chalets, two six-bed cottages and one luxury lodge (accommodating six). Campsites at Mahai and Rugged Glen.
Booking address:	**Tendele Hutted Camp:** KwaZulu-Natal Nature Conservation Services, PO Box 13069, Cascades 3202, tel (0331) 845-1000. **Mahai** or **Rugged Glen campgrounds:** The Officer-in-Charge, Royal Natal, Private Bag X1669, Bergville 3350, tel (036) 438-6303. **Royal Natal Park Hotel:** Private Bag X1673, Bergville 3350, tel (036) 438-6200. **Hlalanathi Berg Resort** (chalets and camping sites), Private Bag X1621, Bergville 3350, tel (036) 438-6308.
When to go:	Throughout the year, but summer is preferred by most.
What to take with you:	Campers must be fully equipped with own provisions and tents. Visitors to Tendele must bring own food and drink.
How to get there:	From the north: Just south of Ladysmith turn off for Bergville. The park is 53 km from Bergville on the Bergville-Harrismith road. From the south turn off the N3 at the Winterton/Berg Resorts turn-off, passing through Winterton and Bergville. Turn left at the Drakensberg North signpost and drive 16 km to the park entrance. From the northeast and south travel via Bergville, which is 45 km from the park.
Nearest doctor:	Bergville, but first-aid treatment is available at the warden's office.
Nearest petrol:	The Royal Natal Park Hotel has two petrol pumps at the turn-off to Tendele Camp.
Open:	1 October–31 March: 05:00–19:00; 1 April–30 September: 06:00–18:00.
Special precautions:	Watch out for sudden changes in the weather and for bush fires.

Sabi Sabi Private Game Reserve

This game reserve, set among the acacia bushveld, open grass plains and combretum and riverine forest of the Mpumalanga Lowveld, has an astonishing variety of game that wanders free in exceptionally wild surroundings.

It is bordered in the south by the Sabie River, which separates it from the Kruger National Park, while to the north are the luxury, internationally renowned reserves of Londolozi (see p. 83) and Mala Mala (see p. 90).

Like its peers, Sabi Sabi offers first-class lodge accommodation, excellent cuisine and the best professional rangers and trackers, whose services are available around the clock.

The reserve is situated within one of southern Africa's oldest reserves, the Sabi Sand Game Reserve, and one of its main assets is the fact that it lies in the middle of traditional migration routes of animals from the Kruger National Park.

Wildlife Because there are no fences to impede the movement of animals, guests are rewarded with excellent sightings of most of the animals found in the Kruger National Park, including the Big Five. Other residents include cheetahs, wild dogs, spotted hyenas, giraffes, zebras, crocodiles, hippos and a large variety of antelope. At night you may see spotted hyenas, genets, scrub hares, bushbabies and an assortment of mongooses.

Birdlife Birdwatchers have more than 350 species of bird to identify, including the rare African finfoot, the lesser black-winged plover and the Narina trogon. In addition there are owls, vultures, pigeons, parrots, woodpeckers, hornbills, weavers and a variety of other birds.

Warthogs vs wild dogs

Warthogs are known to be aggressive scavengers, and the following incident in Sabi Sabi Private Game Reserve underscores this.

A wild dog singlehandedly brought down an impala ewe and was tearing chunks of flesh from it when two warthog boars trotted up. One boar managed to avoid the defensive charge of the wild dog, ran in, tore out the impala's rumen, and devoured it.

The wild dog then chased the boars away. A short while later, another group of four warthogs arrived, put the wild dog to flight and proceeded to feed off the impala's carcass.

The feast didn't last for long, however. The wild dog returned with two other males from its pack, chased off the warthogs and finished off the carcass while one of the dogs kept guard, trotting in a circle around the impala.

Where to stay Apart from the abundance of wildlife, Sabi Sabi has an excellent reputation for the high standard of its accommodation and service. There are three very attractive, unfenced bush lodges: River Lodge, Bush Lodge and Selati Lodge. All three lodges have swimming pools, while Bush and River lodges are air-conditioned, have overhead fans, flyscreens and *en suite* bathrooms with shower.

The blast of a kudu horn and the thumping of African drums summon visitors to meals, which include sumptuous buffet breakfasts and lunches served in the diningroom or Safari Lounge of each lodge. Dinners are served under the stars in reed-enclosed, open-air bomas.

Bush Lodge offers real rustic charm with its 22 twin-bedded thatched chalets and five luxury suites, set in dense bush overlooking a waterhole.

River Lodge has 20 delightful twin-bedded thatched chalets and two luxury suites, nestling in the shade of jackalberry trees, as well as the super-luxury Mandleve Suite which is situated on the banks of the Sabie River.

Here smaller mammals such as vervet monkeys, warthogs, bushbuck and any number of birds are part of the passing parade outside your window, while hippo snort and grunt in the river nearby.

Selati Lodge lies on the banks of the Msuthlu River (between the Sabie and Sand rivers) in the northern part of Sabi Sabi Game Reserve. There's a turn-of-the-century style and decor to the eight *en suite* thatched chalets here. Six of the chalets are standard and there is one honeymoon suite and one presidential suite. The African ambience is enhanced by the use of gas geysers for hot water, and paraffin lamps and lanterns instead of electric lights.

Home-cooked cuisine is served on open verandahs overlooking the river bed, while dinner is enjoyed in an open-air boma. There's also a cosy, fully licensed bar.

Tips for travellers

- There are no fences around Sabi Sabi, so you should not walk around the camps at night. Apart from encountering various harmless mammals which may wander into the camp after dark, you could also encounter lion or a hippo. If you have to walk around at night, try to arrange a local escort.
- Don't leave the camp unaccompanied on foot during the day.
- Swimming in the rivers or dams is dangerous.

Game drives and trails All the lodges offer regular day and night game drives in open Land Rovers, driven by professional rangers and led by experienced Shangaan trackers. Numerous walking trails in the reserve take in some attractive hides, including one known as Warthog Wallow.

Other attractions The owners of Sabi Sabi offer an attractive package which they describe as 'a taste of African safari and a pinch of colonial luxury'. The package consists of two days at Sabi Sabi followed by two days in an 'Out of Africa' setting at Blue Mountain Lodge, which lies hidden in the forests near Hazyview in Mpumalanga.

Getting there There are regular scheduled flights from Johannesburg to Skukuza near the Kruger National Park, where reserve staff will meet you in open Land Rovers and transport you to your quarters at Sabi Sabi.

For a completely different experience, you can fly to Skukuza in a 1930, 15-seater Junkers JU52. The Junkers, known affectionately as the *Tante Ju*, cruises at a speed of just 127 km/h, and enables passengers to roll down their windows and watch the Lowveld and all its animals passing by below. For more information contact Historic Flights, PO Box 2969, Parklands 2121, tel (011) 486-0874.

Sabi Sabi Private Game Reserve at a glance

Locality:	500 km east of Johannesburg; 800 km northeast of Durban.
Climate:	Hot summers with thundershowers; dry, mild to cold winters.
Number of camps:	Three.
Game drives:	Variety of day and night game drives.
Hides and waterholes:	Warthog Wallow is one of the many popular hides.
Trails:	Several escorted trails are available to lovely hides.
Other attractions:	Star-gazing, eating out in open-air boma.
Amenities:	Fully licensed bar at Selati; three swimming pools; curio shop (the Bundu Shop).
Accommodation:	Three lodges: **Bush Lodge**, 22 thatched chalets, five luxury suites; **River Lodge**, 20 thatched chalets and two luxury suites, and the super-luxury Mandleve Suite; **Selati Lodge**, eight thatched chalets.
Booking address:	PO Box 52665, Saxonwold 2132, tel (011) 483-3939.
When to go:	Throughout the year, but game-viewing is better in winter.
What to take with you:	Summer: light, informal clothing; winter: warm clothing; walking shoes; swimming costume; binoculars, camera.
How to get there:	Drive from Johannesburg via Nelspruit and Hazyview. Take the R536 from Hazyview, and after about 40 minutes turn left (1 km past Lisbon Store) for Sabi Sand's Kingston Gate 8 km further on. Daily scheduled flights from Johannesburg to Skukuza in the Kruger National Park. You can also fly from Durban to Nelspruit and drive (two hours) to the reserve from there. Fly-in safari packages available on request. Daily minibus departures from Johannesburg.
Nearest doctor:	Skukuza.
Nearest petrol:	There is petrol at Sabi Sabi and Hazyview.
Open:	24 hours a day.
Special precautions:	Antimalaria precautions should be taken before your visit.

SABI SAND GAME RESERVE

Together with Timbavati Game Reserve and Klaserie Private Nature Reserve, Sabi Sand is one of the world's largest private game reserves, covering about 60 000 ha of bushveld between Skukuza and Manyeleti Game Reserve in the north.

The reserve hosts some of the world's best game lodges and bush camps and, although not cheap, it is to be highly recommended as a prime game-viewing area, with top-class rangers and trackers. One of the reasons for its huge diversity of game is that in recent years the fence separating Sabi Sand from the Kruger National Park in the east has come down, giving Kruger's massive game populations free range into Sabi Sand's territory.

The larger and more prestigious game reserves within Sabi Sand, such as Mala Mala, Londolozi and Sabi Sabi Game Reserve are featured comprehensively as separate entries in this book.

However, there are other smaller lodges and camps within Sabi Sand that may not be as large or opulent as the others, but they're certainly no less attractive as wildlife destinations, and in many ways are preferred for their remoteness, rustic ambience and pristine surroundings.

Many connoisseurs of Africa's wild places make a point of including one of Sabi Sand's Exeter Game Lodges on their itinerary, for their abundance of game, high standard of accommodation and excellent personal service. The three lodges, situated 200 m apart in the southern section of Sabi Sand, are run by Exeter Safaris and personally supervised by owners Gail Rattray Fisher and Leon Steyn. They are Exeter Camp (fully catered), Hunter's Safari Lodge and Leadwood Lodge (both self-catering). The lodges are fully equipped to provide guests access to the Big Five (lion, elephant, buffalo, rhino and leopard) as well as giraffes, cheetahs, wild dogs and a variety of antelope. More than 200 species of bird may be seen on game drives from any of the lodges and include blackheaded oriole, scarletchested sunbird, chinspot batis, greenbacked heron and Burchell's coucal. Three other lodges, Djuma Bush Lodge, Chitwa Chitwa Game Lodge and Notten's Bush Camp, offer equally good accommodation and excellent game-viewing.

Exeter Camp Small and luxurious, this camp nestles on the banks of the Sand River under a canopy of shady trees. Accommodation is in 12 beautifully designed thatched chalets — each with *en suite* bathroom, air-conditioning and mosquito nets.

Breakfast and lunch are served under an open-sided thatched complex on the banks of the Sand River; dinner, usually a bush braai, is served in a reed-walled boma.

For those in search of a larger slice of luxury, there's also a magnificent Safari Suite, with its own lounge and patio.

Afternoons may be spent on game drives, bush walks or just lazing around the sparkling swimming pool.

Hunter's Safari Lodge This colonial-style lodge, with its exquisite, ethnic furnishings, accommodates eight guests in four luxury, air-conditioned bedrooms (with mosquito netting). The lodge's interior is spacious, with four bathrooms, two lounges (with a thatched bar) and a large, fully equipped kitchen.

Although the lodge is self-catering, it is fully equipped and has a four-man staff at the disposal of guests. A cook may be supplied if required.

Leadwood Lodge Some of the finest game-viewing in the world is available at this beautiful lodge, with its five spacious double bungalows fringed by indigenous trees on the edge of the Sand River. Although the lodge is self-catering, each bungalow has a fully equipped modern kitchen and a three-man staff, including a cook, available to assist visitors.

The bungalows are superbly furnished, with twin *en suite* bathrooms and a private *en suite* bush shower. Large sliding doors lead out on to a cool verandah overlooking the river.

The swimming pool, flanked by a sweeping canopy of thatch on poles, also commands views of the river, so that bathers can watch game from within the pool.

Highlights of a visit to Leadwood Lodge include game walks along the river in search of hippos and crocodiles, and an attractive boma, venue for venison bush braais at night.

For further details and information of the Exeter Lodges, contact Exeter Safaris, PO Box 988, Umhlanga Rocks 4320, tel (031) 562-8112 or PO Box 2060, Nelspruit 1200, tel (013) 741-3180.

Djuma Bush Lodge The word Djuma means 'roar of the lion' — and that's what you can expect to hear at this scenically lovely lodge in the Sabi Sand Game Reserve. Djuma covers some 9 000 ha, and no fences separate it from the Kruger National Park on its eastern border, so gamewatchers will be rewarded with a huge variety of animals on their doorstep. Not just the Big Five, but also all the plains mammals of the bushveld may be sighted on game drives with the help of Tsonga rangers and trackers. There are also more than 300 species of bird.

The lodge, which caters for a maximum of 10 people, is a unique wood-and-thatch structure, with magnificent views of the African savannah from its upper deck.

Each of the six chalets is a comfortably furnished three-sided thatched pyramid, with *en suite* bathroom and hot water.

A double-storey dining and recreation area with a bar offers guests convivial surroundings in which to relax after cooling off in the pool.

A special attraction is the personal involvement of owner-biologist Jurie Moolman and his wife, Pippa, who start your day with a game drive just after 05:00, followed by a hearty breakfast. Jurie also leads bush walks, and is an informed and reliable guide to the ecology of the area.

Night-drives are available on request and introduce visitors to nocturnal predators and other mammals.

In and around the camp you may expect to see several small mammals, including baboons, cavorting around a waterhole, spotted hyenas and their cubs, tsessebe and a buffalo called 'Ou Staatmaker' — one of the lodge's esteemed guests.

Access to the lodge is by air and road (special charters are arranged from Johannesburg to Djuma and back, at reasonable prices).

For further information and details write to PO Box 338, Hluvakani 1363, tel (013) 735-5118.

Ulusaba Game Reserve This beautiful sanctuary occupies 8 000 ha in the heart of the Sabi Sand Reserve, a region of tumbling hills and rolling green bushveld. Like other reserves in the area, Ulusaba is not enfenced, so large populations of game, including the Big Five, wander freely across its boundaries.

The two lodges at Ulusaba, Rock Lodge and Safari Lodge, are architectural masterpieces of a distinctly different kind. Rock Lodge is a complex of eight chalets and two suites — the two-bed Bateleur Suite and the four-bed Martial Eagle Suite — which have been built against a granite cliff overlooking the grasslands below. Huge boulders frame the rooms and the diningroom is carved into the rockface of the mountain.

Safari Lodge offers 10 twin-bedded chalets built under huge trees on elevated platforms above the Mabrak River. The lodge has a delightful boma where guests congregate around a crackling fire and listen to the sounds of the reserve's resident lions roaring in the dark. Dinner is served in the boma, while drinks are available at the well-stocked bar.

Rock Lodge has its own diningroom and bar, and a sparkling pool where you can cool off after a game drive. The lodge opened in the early 1990s and has proved popular among visitors looking for luxury in wild surroundings.

To get there from Johannesburg, take the N2 to Witbank, and then take the N4 to Middelburg and Nelspruit. From there take the R40 to Hazyview and then turn on to the R536 for the Paul Kruger Gate of the Kruger National Park. After 36 km turn left at the Ulusaba signpost and follow the signs until you reach the reserve within the Sabi Sand Gate.

Chitwa Chitwa Game Lodge You'll see just about any of Southern Africa's land mammals, from lesser bushbabies to elephants, at this upmarket lodge in the northern part of Sabi Sand.

And if the rigours of a dusty game drive are not for you, you may relax with cocktails at the thatched bar, shoot pool or play darts in superb bushveld surroundings.

Day and night game drives follow lions, leopards, buffaloes, impala, kudu and many other species, and the owners will offer you drinks around the fireside as a prelude to a night drive, assisted by a halogen spotlight.

There are two superb lodges at Chitwa Chitwa — Safari Lodge, which accommodates 10 guests in spacious, air-conditioned rondavels, and Game Lodge, which has six rondavels with great views overlooking the surrounding bush and a waterhole.

There's a sparkling swimming pool, cosy bar and a boma where guests can dine around a crackling fire and listen to the sounds of the wild.

An African wild cat's dying embrace

Few stories about animal families in the wild are as poignant as that involving a female African wild cat and her kittens.

A farmer walking through open scrubland in the Eastern Cape saw an African wild cat about to pounce on an unseen quarry. Regarding the cat as vermin, he picked up his rifle and shot the animal. Badly wounded, the cat ran towards a rocky cliff, where it pulled itself up to a half-concealed lair.

The farmer followed to finish the cat off, but put his rifle down when he saw three kittens within, running up to suckle their mother.

On reaching the little ones, she immediately lay down, exhausted. Except for her panting, she was very quiet for some time. Then she lifted her head and tried to wash her babies. She took one in her arms and licked it all over.

This done, she took the baby's neck in her mouth and killed it with one sharp bite. Then she took the second kitten, washed it, and killed it in the same way. The third died after the same ritual washing.

The drama was not over. The mother then gathered the three limp bodies to her side and tried to cuddle them, protecting them against further threat from this menacing intruder.

As the farmer neared the cats, the mother spat at him in defiance. As she did so, there was a rush of frothy blood from her mouth. A bullet had punctured her lung, with devastating effect. Her legs kicked violently, scattering her dead kittens. Death spasms shook the cat's whole body as it tensed, shivered and then relaxed.

For more information contact the lodge at Chitwa Chitwa, PO Box 784052, Sandton 2146, tel (011) 883-1354 or (013) 735-5357.

Notten's Bush Camp Gilly and Bambi Notten offer guests personal attention in a relaxed and informal atmosphere at this small bush camp, just 8 km inside the gate of the Sabi Sand Game Reserve.

Five cosy chalets with double beds accommodate 10 people. There's a swimming pool, a waterhole in front of the chalets and a delightful family atmosphere about the camp.

Game drives and bush walks are arranged according to guests' needs, and they bring gamewatchers into close contact with a large variety of birds and game.

There is no electricity — lighting is supplied by paraffin lamps. Guests must bring their own drinks as the camp is not licensed. For further information and details write to Notten's Bush Camp, PO Box 622, Hazyview 1242, tel (013) 735-5105.

Sabi Sand Game Reserve at a glance

Locality:	Northeastern Mpumalanga between Manyeleti Game Reserve in the north and Kruger National Park in the east.
Climate:	Summers hot with thundershowers; winters mild to cold and dry.
Game drives:	All the private bush lodges and camps offer game drives daily.
Hides and waterholes:	Individual lodges have their own waterholes.
Trails:	Bush walks held daily at most of the camps.
Other attractions:	Swimming, star-gazing.
Amenities:	Some camps cater, others are self-catering. Most have a swimming pool.
Accommodation:	Ranges from tented bush camps to exquisitely furnished chalets and bungalows.
Booking address:	**Exeter Lodges:** PO Box 998, Umhlanga Rocks 4320, tel (031) 562-8112; **Djuma Bush Lodge:** PO Box 338, Hluvakani 1363, tel (013) 735-5118; **Chitwa Chitwa Game Lodge:** PO Box 784052, Sandton 2146, tel (011) 883-1354; **Notten's Bush Camp:** PO Box 622, Hazyview 1242, tel (013) 735-5105.
When to go:	Throughout the year, but game-viewing is better in winter.
What to take with you:	Light clothes in summer; warm clothes in winter; hiking boots, torch, sunscreen, camera, binoculars, field guides.
How to get there:	Exeter Lodges and Notten's Bush Camp: From Johannesburg take the N4 to Nelspruit; then take the R40 to Hazyview via White River (at either of these towns telephone your camp to inform them of your estimated time of arrival). From Hazyview take the R536 to Paul Kruger Gate/Skukuza. After 37 km follow the signs to the Sabi Sand Game Reserve Gate and the camps in question. Djuma Bush Lodge and Chitwa Chitwa: From Nelspruit take the R40 to Acornhoek where you turn right for Hluvakani (27 km), then follow the signs to Gowrie Gate and the respective lodges.
Nearest doctor:	An emergency helicopter service to Nelspruit is available to most of the lodges in Sabi Sand.
Open:	Twenty-four hours a day, all year round.
Special precautions:	Take antimalaria precautions before your trip.

Shamwari Game Reserve

Hippo cows grunt and splash with their calves in the Bushman's River just below your boma as you sample a sunset cuisine that is as fresh as the chill evening air at Shamwari Game Reserve in the Eastern Cape.

'Shamwari' — the Shona word for friend — is the most southern private reserve in Africa, a game-ranch complex covering 10 000 ha of countryside teeming with animals. More important, it is one of the few reserves in South Africa hosting the Big Five (lions, elephants, rhinos, hippos and buffaloes) a mere hour's drive from a major city (Port Elizabeth).

The reserve is relatively new, but it has been launched with such dedication to the principle of conserving wildlife that in time it will become one of South Africa's most popular game lodges.

Wildlife Shamwari lies in the pristine valley bushveld between Port Elizabeth and Grahamstown. Because the area receives both summer and winter rain, seven different ecosystems flourish here — providing animals with a generous choice of habitats.

It's such a rich vegetational region that, just over 100 years ago, large herds of elephants, lions, leopards, rhinos and buffaloes roamed free. Then the hunters came, and the animal populations were ruthlessly cut down; some survived, scrambling for the safety of the thick bush now comprising the Addo Elephant National Park.

The rolling hills of the Eastern Cape, emptied of their game, never really recovered from the hunter's bullet — until Adrian Gardiner, an ex-Zimbabwean and Port Elizabeth entrepreneur, decided to bring the animals back to the Eastern Cape.

Hippos were brought in from Pafuri in the Kruger National Park; elephants came from Kruger and from East London; white and black rhinos (the largest privately owned group in Africa) were brought in from the Hluhluwe-Umfolozi complex. Other animals settled at Shamwari include white blesbok, black springbok, zebras, giraffes, eland, nyala, black wildebeest, hyenas and leopards.

Add to this nocturnal species such as aardvark, aardwolf, caracal and genet, and you have a very comprehensive list of mammal species.

The reintroduction of animals has been so successful that Shamwari now has a greater number of antelope than any other private sanctuary in South Africa.

Birdlife The reserve is also home to more than 200 species of bird, including Cape and spottedback weavers, southern boubous, honeyguides, neddickies, fiscal flycatchers, spotted dikkops, crowned eagles and gymnogenes.

Apart from the game, its rangers are an integral part of Shamwari — being among the most experienced in the country.

Where to stay What makes Shamwari an exceptional bushveld retreat is the luxury and comfort of its accommodation. You'll find safari ranches under thatch, and fully restored settler homes with gabled rooftops, pillared verandahs and period furniture.

The lodges and mansions offer all the home comforts, with sumptuous meals served around the campfire or in the pampered interior of your rooms.

Long Lee Manor, an Edwardian mansion built in 1920 — beautifully restored to its former glory — accommodates up to 23 people in stylish comfort. Sumptuous sofas, animal skins on the floor, trophies on the walls and four-poster beds are special features in this manor, which offers period, *en suite* double bedrooms.

Nearby, a riverside boma overlooks the Hippo Pool in the Bushman's River.

Shamwari Lodge, at the northern end of the reserve, nestles snugly in the rolling canopy of bush that is often frequented by big game. The lodge offers five double *en suite* bedrooms, a pool, gymnasium and steam bath.

In addition, there are two self-contained, lovingly restored Settler homes, Highfield and Carningly, resplendent with yellowwood and sneezewood fittings, and fully equipped with electricity and television. The homes, originally built in 1860, accommodate six people each and are exquisitely comfortable.

Bushman's River Lodge is a large four-bedroom house which accommodates eight and offers the services of a qualified game ranger and hostess.

Game drives and walking trails Early morning and late afternoon game drives through the wilderness take place daily in a specially equipped game-viewing vehicle. Ranger-led night-drives, using a mounted spotlight, are also available. Or you can walk along superb hiking trails in the company of an armed ranger.

The walks will take you through a landscape of aloe- and thornbush-covered hills, which slide into the narrow gorges of

Shamwari Game Reserve at a glance

Locality: Eastern Cape Province, 72 km northeast of Port Elizabeth.
Climate: Winters cool to cold and wet; summers hot.
Game drives: Morning, late afternoon and night drives.
Trails: Variety of trails through the reserve.
Other attractions: Day drives to Addo Elephant National Park, the 1820 Settler towns of Grahamstown, Bathurst and Salem.
Amenities: Swimming pool, gymnasium, tennis courts, steam bath.
Accommodation: **Shamwari Lodge** (six double *en suite* bedrooms); **Long Lee Manor**, an Edwardian mansion with double *en suite* bedrooms; **Highfield** and **Carningly** are two self-contained settler homes; **Bushman's River Lodge** accommodates eight people.
Booking address: Shamwari Game Reserve, PO Box 32017, Summerstrand 6014, tel (042) 203-1111.
When to go: Throughout the year.
What to take with you: Camera, binoculars, walking shoes, light clothes in summer.
How to get there: Three railway carriages are available for guests on the Algoa Express from Johannesburg, to Paterson siding near Shamwari. By road head northeast along the N2 from Port Elizabeth. Branch off on the R32 for Paterson and the Addo Elephant National Park. At Paterson turn right. Travel a few kilometres then bear left for Sidbury. This road passes through the reserve.
Nearest doctor: Paterson, 10 km away, or Alicedale.
Nearest petrol: Paterson.
Open: Sunrise to sunset throughout the year.
Special precautions: There are no real hazards at Shamwari, but obviously care should be exercised while walking through the bush in the company of lions, elephants and rhinos.

the Bushman's River as it winds and twists towards the coast. This is the heart of the country once penetrated by the 1820 Settlers and their descendants, some of whom built wattle-and-daub huts before they were replaced with more sturdy structures. The region is dry, and dominated by grassy plateaus and stands of spekboom — a favourite food for elephants.

A unique rhino-tracking project has been established at Shamwari, in conjunction with the National Parks Board and the University of Port Elizabeth. A microchip-sized transmitter has been implanted in the horns of some rhinos so that they can be followed by researchers equipped with directional radio-frequency antennas.

Algoa Express In keeping with their attention to the needs of their guests, Shamwari has laid on three special railway carriages for bringing visitors to the reserve in style.

You can reserve a seat on the Elephant Carriage of the Algoa Express in Johannesburg, and the coach will be delivered to the Boesmanspoort siding, overlooking Long Lee Manor.

On the way, you'll be wined and dined in sumptuous surroundings.

Sodwana Bay National Park

Coral reefs washed by waters of crystalline blue, magical walks through coastal dune forests, chalets resting on the edge of a sleepy lake — such are the attractions of this beautiful seaside park in far northern KwaZulu-Natal.

Lying within the boundaries of the Greater St Lucia Wetland Park, Sodwana Bay National Park covers 1 300 ha of coastal dune forest, bordered by the St Lucia Marine Reserve in the east.

About 25 ha of coastal forest protect a string of tent and caravan sites, carefully positioned to ensure privacy.

The reserve's coastline is a major breeding ground for loggerhead and leatherback turtles, which come ashore in summer. The marine section harbours an enormous variety of fish, including marlin, sailfish and tuna. Apart from these prized gamefish, anglers may also land king mackerel, yellowtail, queenfish, dorado, kingfish and garrick.

Down at Jesser Point a rocky ridge runs seaward, creating a sheltered bay to the north — a mecca for powerboats, diving enthusiasts and game fishermen who flock there in summer.

Sodwana Bay is regarded by many as one of the finest diving spots in Southern Africa, and perhaps the finest marlin fishing region in the world.

Tips for travellers

- No pets are allowed in the park.
- Permits are required to take vehicles on to the beach.
- Air compressors may not be used at campsites.

Where to stay There's no shortage of accommodation at Sodwana Bay. Before you book you may consider the following options:

KWAZULU-NATAL NATURE CONSERVATION SERVICES MAIN CAMP This camp has 20 fully equipped five- and 10-bed chalets, as well as a number of open campsites. Thirty-three luxury campsites, with water and electricity, are available at the Gwalagwala Campground.

Visitors must bring their own tents, caravans and camping equipment.

Because of Sodwana Bay's popularity it is advisable to book well in advance (bookings will be accepted up to nine months ahead). To reserve a campsite, contact the Camp Manager, Sodwana Bay National Park, Private Bag 310, Mbazwana 3974, tel (035) 571-0051.

SODWANA BAY LODGE This hideaway on 35 ha overlooking Lake Shabiza opened in December 1989 and boasts the longest system of boardwalks in Southern Africa. Three kilometres of walkways, erected above the ground to protect the fragile plant life and to allow for proper drainage, link lakeside chalets and timeshare units to beautiful forest glades, the lakeshore and a unique thatched pub known as the Crowned Eagle, which nestles on stilts beneath the trees.

The lodge offers 20 two-bed cottages, with access to a restaurant, pool and patio terrace. There are also 40 private cottages and fully equipped timeshare units.

These six- and eight-bed units, tastefully furnished with wall hangings, grass mats and various ethnic fabrics, are ideal for fairly large families. They offer two bedrooms, one with *en suite* bathroom, and two loft rooms upstairs for children. Electricity and hot and cold running water are supplied.

The lounge and master bedroom lead on to a spacious verandah under reeds. Supper may be served on the restaurant terrace or around the fire in the boma nearby.

Among the lodge's major drawcards are its facilities for novice and experienced divers, including an internationally standardised dive pool — one of two in the country, two professional diving instructors, and lecture facilities to help novices qualify for deep-sea dives. There's a dive and tackle shop where you may rent any diving equipment you may need (including underwater cameras).

There's also a 6,6-m Acecat fishing and diving boat available to take guests sea-

Huberta's incredible journey

If ever a hippo deserved a place in the *Guinness Book of Records* it was Huberta, a two-ton vagrant cow that walked more than 1 600 km from Lake St Lucia in KwaZulu-Natal down to the Keiskamma River on the Eastern Cape coast. Huberta's incredible journey, which took three years to complete, started in November 1928 and included memorable stopovers at Durban, Port St Johns and East London.

Pondos on the Wild Coast revered her as the incarnation of a legendary diviner and paid homage to her as she trundled through the rolling Transkei landscape.

In Port St Johns she foraged in the gardens of local inhabitants, and became the first hippo to wallow in the waters of the Umzimvubu for more than 100 years. When she reached East London, she fell asleep on a railway line and was gently nudged out of the way by a friendly engine-driver.

Wherever she went, Huberta was feted as a hero. Motorists stopped for her and pedestrians watched wide-eyed as she lurched on ...

Tragically, Huberta's wanderings came to an end while she was bathing in the Keiskamma River. Hunters shot her — unaware that she had became a legend in her own lifetime.

Sodwana Bay National Park at a glance

Locality:	Northern KwaZulu-Natal, within the Greater St Lucia Wetland Park.
Climate:	Subtropical climate with hot, humid summers and mild winters. Thundershowers in summer.
Number of camps:	One main chalet and tented Nature Conservation Services camp (with 600 stands accommodating up to 4 000 people); three privately run tented camps; one luxury lodge and timeshare units.
Game drives:	Sodwana Bay Lodge offers various game drives to Lake Sibaya and to Umfolozi-Hluhluwe and Mkuzi game reserves.
Trails:	Nature Conservation Services camp: Two self-guided trails — the Ngoboseleni Trail (5 km) and the Jesser Point Trail (1,5 km). Turtle tours take place every day from mid-December through to mid-January, weather permitting (booking at main office at 15:00 on day of tour).
Other attractions:	Curio shop, game- and spearfishing, scuba-diving, swimming, bird-watching.
Amenities:	Nature Conservation Services Camp: supermarket; boat and caravan storage; fuel, firewood, freezing facilities.
Accommodation:	**KwaZulu-Natal Nature Conservation Services Camp:** 10 five-bed chalets and 10 eight-bed chalets, campsites; **Sodwana Bay Lodge:** 20 two-bed cottages; fully equipped six- and eight-bed timeshare units; **Sodwana tented camp:** 45 two-bed tents (self-catering).
Booking address:	For chalets in the NCS camp, contact the KwaZulu-Natal Nature Conservation Services, PO Box 13069, Cascades 3202, tel: (0331) 845-1000; for campsites contact The Camp Manager, Sodwana Bay National Park, PO Box 310, Mbazwana 3974, tel (035) 571-0051.
When to go:	December and January for turtle tours; winter months for a more tranquil holiday.
What to take with you:	Visitors to the Nature Conservation Services camp must bring their own tents, caravans and camping equipment.
How to get there:	From Durban take the N2 northwards to Hluhluwe. Some 10 km north of Hluhluwe Village take the Sodwana Bay/Ngweni turn-off, and drive 60 km to Mbazwana, along the lower Mkuze Road. Continue past Mbazwana, passing Sodwana Bay Lodge on the left, until you reach the park's entrance 6 km past the lodge. Follow the signposts to Mgoboseleni River Bridge and turn right just beyond the bridge. The park's headquarters are situated 2 km further on.
Nearest doctor:	At Hluhluwe, 102 km away by road. Primary emergency care room (Medical Rescue International) at reception office.
Nearest petrol:	In the park.
Open:	Throughout the year from 08:00–12:15 and 14:00–16:45. Dive shop hours: 08:00–12:30 and 14:00–17:00.
Special precautions:	Take precautions against malaria before, during and after your visit.

wards along the coral reefs that flank this coastline, either to catch marlin or other billfish, or to explore the crystalline depths.

Sodwana Bay Lodge also offers nature walks and driving trails to beautiful surrounding areas such as Hluhluwe and Umfolozi game reserves, Lake Sibaya, Kosi Bay and Mabibi.

To book contact the lodge at PO Box 5478, Durban 4000, tel (031) 304-5977.

SODWANA TENTED CAMP Sodwana Lodge Charters runs a self-catering tented camp deep in the dune forests of the Sodwana Bay National Park. The camp is not far from the KwaZulu-Natal Nature Conservation Services' camping area. Here 45 two-bed tents are scattered over some distance among the groves of the forest, guaranteeing privacy for campers.

All the tents have access to a central cooking, dining and living area — a sisal and wooden structure, which is raised off the ground, close to an open braai area where staff prepare the fires every night. There's an ablution block nearby.

Game drives and trails Four-wheel-drive vehicles may drive (with a permit) 25 km north and south of Jesser Point for angling excursions, beach walks or just to explore the rock pools. Such beach drives are confined to the area below the high-water mark, to protect the fragile dune vegetation.

The beaches can get crowded, so for a quieter option try a walk through the coastal forest and hinterland — a tranquil home to an interesting variety of animals and birds.

Two easy self-guided trails — the Ngoboseleni Trail (5 km) and the Jesser Point Trail (1,5 km) — are available from the Nature Conservation Services camp, and take trailists through beautiful groves of Natal strelitzia and wild silver-oak.

These forests are alive with the sound of birdsong, and keen birdwatchers may

The elephant's amazing cooling system

Although the elephant's large ears are custom built to trap more sound waves than smaller ears, these delicate appendages have two other very important functions: they signal the animal's emotional state, and also cool it down.

The cooling effect is achieved by a rich supply of blood vessels transporting blood through the ears (where the skin is only about 1–2 mm thick) at a rate of 5–12 litres a minute, cooling it down in much the same way as a radiator cools the water of a motor vehicle. The elephant also cools itself by flapping its ears vigorously on hot days.

The elephant's trunk is a feat of extraordinary engineering — powered by tens of thousands of muscles, it has a variety of uses, from caressing its mates to reinforce social bonds to feeling the air for the presence of other animals.

It can detect another animal from 200 m away in this way.

The trunk also has such powers of expansion and contraction that it can grasp an object as small as a needle or as large as a tree trunk.

On average, elephants draw up to 17,5 litres of water into their trunks at a time, and drink about 80 litres every 24 hours. However, an adult bull is capable of drinking up to 322 litres of water at once.

see coucals, trumpeter hornbills, Knysna and purplecrested louries, Woodwards' batis, Rudd's apalis and fish eagles along the way.

Observant walkers may also catch a glimpse of such animals of the coastal dune forest as reedbuck, bushpig, aardwolf, suni, vervet and samango monkeys, Tsonga red squirrels and banded and water mongooses.

In December and January daily tours to the turtle breeding grounds are offered.

TEMBE ELEPHANT PARK

Dense sand forests, grassland, swamps and pans are the setting for this 30 000-ha park on KwaZulu-Natal's border with Mozambique. It is one of the wilder and more remote of the wild places of Southern Africa, and would be a tranquil place to end a tour of KwaZulu-Natal's excellent game parks.

The park lies between Ndumo Game Reserve in the west and Kosi Bay Nature Reserve in the east, and can be reached easily from either of these sanctuaries.

The landscape incorporates a large variety of trees in open and closed woodland, the forest canopy ranging from some 20 m in height down to three or four metres. The forests taper off to palm-veld and sandy plain peppered with sicklebush, black monkey orange and, in the wetter parts, by ilala and wild date palm.

The reserve is home to about 100 elephants — survivors of the great herds that once occupied the marshlands and forests of Mozambique before humankind brought settlement and war to the region.

Up until 1980 they were the only free-ranging herd in South Africa — apart from the Knysna elephants — and migrated frequently between Mozambique and Maputaland's Mosi Swamp/Sihangwane Forest area. Shortly afterwards, in 1983, the park was proclaimed, and the area was protected by an electric fence.

From then on the elephant numbers have increased steadily, and the park's gates were opened to the public on 9 September 1991.

The reserve lies in a tropical/subtropical transition zone, and the maximum capacity of the dry sand- and shrubveld vegetation here is 120 elephants.

Tips for travellers

- You may only enter the park in a 4x4 vehicle.
- No pets are allowed in the park.
- The speed limit throughout the park is 40 km/h.
- No walking outside the camp area or in the reserve.

Wildlife Apart from the elephants, animals you're likely to see include white rhinos, leopards, giraffes, blue wildebeest, hippos, waterbuck, suni, impala, eland, nyala, kudu, bushpigs, reedbuck, duiker, vervet monkeys and bushveld gerbils. Among the mongooses are the banded, Selous, slender and whitetailed species.

You may also be lucky enough to catch a glimpse of largespotted genets, bushbabies and warthogs.

Tembe is the natural home of the Nile crocodile, but smaller reptiles such as the water monitor lizard, the rock monitor lizard, Jones's girdled lizard and tree agama, are also found here. Snakes include the Natal rock python, Egyptian cobra, puffadder and green mamba.

Birdlife Many species reach the southern limit of their distribution in Tembe, so there's no shortage of birdlife — more than 300 species. These include Narina trogon, blackcrowned night heron, Woodwards' batis, Rudd's apalis, redwinged pratincole and pinkthroated twinspot. There is also a variety of raptors, including bateleurs, martial and southern banded snake eagles.

Where to stay Tembe Safari Camp has luxury two-bed Chobe-style tents accommodating a maximum of eight people. There's access to a communal kitchen with a gas stove, freezer and fridge, as well as a delightful swimming pool.

Hot and cold water showers are available, but there's no electricity. Each tent has a bedside table, a small cupboard and lanterns. A chef and a camp attendant are

Tembe Elephant Park at a glance

Locality:	On the Mozambique border with northern KwaZulu-Natal, between Kosi Bay Nature Reserve and Ndumo Game Reserve.
Climate:	Subtropical, with dry winters and hot, moderately wet summers. It can get very humid in summer.
Hides and waterholes:	A beautiful hide overlooks a pan in the Mosi Swamp.
Number of camps:	One.
Game drives:	A trail guide will escort visitors on drives through the park.
Trails:	No walking is allowed outside the camp area or in the reserve, but there are some lovely walking trails at Ndumo Game Reserve nearby (see separate entry p. 103)
Other attractions:	Trips to Ndumo Game Reserve, which is just 6 km away, Kosi Bay Nature Reserve and Lake Sibaya.
Amenities:	There's a shop at Kwangwanase outside the park.
Accommodation:	Tembe Safari Camp has four two-bed tents; communal kitchen (gas stove, freezer and fridge). Hot- and cold-water showers.
Booking address:	KwaZulu-Natal Nature Conservation Services, PO Box 13069, Cascades 3202, tel (0331) 845-1000 or Tembe Safaris, PO Box 6085, Durban 4000, tel (031) 202-9090.
When to go:	Summer is best for birdwatching, but winter is cooler and less uncomfortable.
What to take with you:	Take your own food and drink, torch, firewood, camera, field guides, and light clothing.
How to get there:	Tembe is a four hour drive from Durban. Take the N2 north to Jozini. Follow the signposts from Jozini until you arrive at the entrance gates 72 km away. You can also fly into Tembe from Durban's Virginia Airport, tel: Tembe Safaris (031) 202-9090.
Nearest doctor:	Jozini.
Nearest petrol:	At Kwangwanase outside the park and at a roadside store 2 km from the entrance to Ndumo Game Reserve.
Open:	08:00–12:00; 14:00–16:00.
Special precautions:	Take antimalaria precautions before you go to the reserve.

available to cook for you. Meals are served outside around the braai area or in the dining tent, which is equipped with tables and chairs.

Apart from people staying at Tembe, only one group of day visitors is allowed into the park at a time. Each group, and their 4x4, are escorted through the park by a guide. A fascinating stop along the way is the animal hide which overlooks the Mosi Swamp. Be sure to bring a braai pack — the guide has a skottelbraai and water bottle for a picnic.

Other attractions Regular excursions are offered to Ndumo Game Reserve and the coastline between Kosi Bay and Ponte de Oro to see leatherback turtles.

Snorkelling and scuba-diving trips on the Maputaland coast are a major drawcard.Other trips are available to Lake Sibaya and the coastal forests.

Thornybush Game Reserve

This magnificent reserve just 30 km from the Orpen Gate of Kruger National Park covers 11 500 ha of undulating bushveld west of Timbavati Game Reserve.

Although Thornybush is one of South Africa's oldest reserves, the recent addition of various new lodges and the acquisition of more land enables it to compete with the best lodges in Southern Africa for its diversity of accommodation, spectacular scenery and abundance of mammals and birds.

Wildlife Elephants are a major attraction at Thornybush and they can often be seen padding along the Mowana River which flanks the lodges. Visitors can also expect to have close encounters with rhino on game walks through the bush. Other daytime sightings include zebras, blue wildebeest, eland, waterbuck, bushbuck, giraffes, common duiker, kudu, impala and steenbok. At night you might chance upon leopards, spotted genets or porcupines.

Where to stay The reserve boasts five exclusive lodges, all of which have swimming pools and offer unique dawn and dusk safaris with qualified rangers and trackers. The lodges are Main Lodge and its satellite lodges — Serondella, n'Kaya, Chapungu and Jackalberry.

MAIN LODGE offers thatched, *en suite* air-conditioned suites for a maximum of 40 people overlooking the seasonal Mowana River. Each suite has an outdoor shower and private deck and overlooks undulating savannah bushveld and a waterhole.

SERONDELLA Suspended wooden walkways lead from luxurious suites along the Mowana River to hides tucked among the treetops — perfect vantage points for watching big game and birds coming down to the two adjoining waterholes for a drink.

N'KAYA This small, cosy lodge accommodates eight people in generous double suites with private lounges and *en suite* facilities overlooking n'Kaya Pan, the camp's own waterhole.

CHAPUNGU This colonial-style lodge accommodates a maximum of 10 guests in luxury suites which offer home comforts and superb African cuisine. An elevated deck overlooking a waterhole affords excellent game-viewing opportunities. Diners have a choice of eating around the fire in the boma or taking a table in the well-appointed diningroom.

JACKALBERRY This rustic camp, which also accommodates 10 people, offers breathtaking views of the Drakensberg and is a favourite destination for bird-watchers from all over Southern Africa. A colourful array of more than 250 species of bird and abundant game inhabit the bush around the lodge. A crackling camp-fire and mouthwatering meals draw visitors to the boma at night to revel in the sounds of Africa.

Game drives and trails Rangers lead two game drives a day (morning and evening), as well as bush walks. The latter range from the one-hour Khehla Walk to the four-hour M'fana Walk — with tracking tips and wildlife orientation courtesy of the ranger.

Breakfast or a romantic dinner under the stars may be served in the bush during a game drive.

Special night trips include visits to bush shelters, where guests share sundowners and fireside yarns before rolling out their sleeping bags under the stars.

Thornybush Game Lodge at a glance

Locality:	30 km northwest of the Kruger National Park's Orpen Gate.
Climate:	Summers are hot with thunderstorms, winters mild to cool with no rain.
Number of camps:	One main camp.
Game drives:	Morning and evening drives daily.
Hides and waterholes:	A beautiful bird hide overlooks Black Dam.
Trails:	Khehla Walk (1 hour); M'fana Walk (4 hours).
Other attractions:	Visit to the Cheetah Research Station at Kapama Game Reserve, some 20 km away.
Amenities:	Swimming pool, fully licensed bar.
Accommodation:	The reserve has five lodges: **Main Lodge**, **Serondella**, **n'Kaya**, **Chapungu** and **Jackalberry**. **Kwa-Mbili Lodge** has three African-style safari tents, swimming pool and pub.
Booking address:	Thornybush Game Lodge, PO Box 798, Northlands 2116, tel (011) 883-7918 or write to the lodge at PO Box 169, Hoedspruit 1380, tel (015) 793-1976. Kwa-Mbili Lodge, PO Box 1188, Hoedspruit 1380, tel (015) 793-2773.
When to go:	The best time for game-viewing is winter when the vegetation thins out, but summer is great for poolside tanning and night-time game-viewing drives.
What to take with you:	Light clothing in summer; anorak, jersey in winter.
How to get there:	Drive north (or east) from Johannesburg via Lydenburg and Hoedspruit. There are scheduled flights from Johannesburg to Phalaborwa or Hoedspruit, with transfers to the lodge. Private air charters are also available to Thornybush's private airstrip.
Nearest doctor:	Hoedspruit Airforce Base, about 10 km from the lodge.
Nearest petrol:	Petrol and diesel are available at the lodge.
Open:	Twenty-four hours a day, but office hours are from 07:00 to 19:00.
Special precautions:	Antimalaria precautions should be taken before your visit.

Other attractions Guests at Thornybush can opt for a day visit to the Kruger National Park or the bird-rich Klaserie Dam area with one of the rangers, or take a helicopter ride to the Drakensberg for lunch. Other attractions include a scenic drive to the forests of Mariepskop on the slopes of the Drakensberg or a visit to the Moholoholo Wildlife Rehabilitation Centre, where injured and orphaned wild animals are cared for.

One of the main attractions at Thornybush is a visit to the Research and Breeding Centre for Endangered Species at Hoedspruit, where guests may watch these animals being fed in their enclosures.

Kwa-Mbili Game Lodge This lodge lies within the Thornybush Game Reserve and has the distinction of being one of the very few private reserves where you can view the Big Five from a bicycle saddle. You may hire mountain bikes here, and cycle through the reserve in the company of an armed escort.

Wildlife is plentiful and, includes the Big Five, zebras, wildebeest, impala and cheetahs, as well as a host of smaller mammals.

The lodge is small and offers 10 guests a choice of chalets decorated with ethnic African furniture or cosy, African-style safari tents, and comfortable, mosquito-protected beds.

The camp has an African theme, portrayed in Ndebele prints on the walls, carved figurines of wild animals, hides and woven mats on the floors.

The boma outside — rich with the aromas of roast impala or other cooked game — opens up to an attractive garden, swimming pool and a pub called The Midden.

Timbavati Game Reserve

Flanking the western section of the Kruger National Park, Timbavati Game Reserve covers 68 000 ha of some of the finest game-viewing country in Southern Africa. It was created by combining some 30 different farms into one huge private wilderness sanctuary, modelled on the Kruger National Park. The farmers pooled their resources, outlawed any form of trophy hunting and imported a wide variety of animals, including white rhinos and sable antelope, to supplement the resident game populations.

Recently the fences separating Timbavati from the Kruger Park have come down, enabling a free flow of most of the species you may expect to see in the Kruger National Park.

The one major difference between the two game sanctuaries, however, is that Timbavati's lodges and game ranches are geared to safari-style luxury, pampering its guests with top-rate accommodation, excellent cuisine and round-the-clock game drives and bush trails.

The private reserves and lodges within the Timbavati rate among the country's best. From the gamewatcher's point of view, the most notable among these are the Big Five of the Timbavati: Tanda Tula, Motswari and Mbali, Ngala Game Lodge and Thornybush Nature Reserve (the last two are covered as separate entries on pp. 105 and 140 respectively).

Other smaller, but no less important, wildlife hideaways in the Timbavati Game Reserve are: Kambaku Private Nature Reserve (previously known as Cheetah Trails), Timbavati Wilderness Trails, Tshukudu Game Lodge, Umlani Bushcamp, and Sandringham Private Nature Reserve (see entry on p. 150).

Tanda Tula Bush Camp This tented camp — Tanda Tula means 'to love the quiet' — is a haven of peace and tranquillity right among the big-game populations of Mpumalanga. Covering about 7 000 ha of bushveld in the Timbavati, Tanda Tula is ideal for small groups looking to be pampered by excellent cuisine and service in a pristine environment.

The camp is quite new, having opened up in late 1994 after its relocation from an old site 8 km away, and among its many attractions are:

- A thatched, open-sided lounge, dining area and bar overlooking a waterhole on one side, and leading on to a grassed terrace and swimming pool.
- Eight luxury safari tents, neatly appointed with *en suite* bathrooms (toilets and showers).
- Game drives, led by professional game rangers accompanied by trackers in open, custom-built safari vehicles. The game drives are offered twice daily. The morning drive includes a breakfast or brunch in the bush, while the afternoon drives include sundowners and game-viewing into the evening.
- Meals are enjoyed around the fireside in the boma outside.

Another place to stay at Tanda Tula is Hlahlane ('green trees'), a new thatched lodge accommodating eight people. The lodge has two main bedrooms with bath, outside shower and verandah, and an open-plan kitchen, dining and livingroom. Tanda Tula's facilities may be used by prior arrangement.

For further information and booking contact Tanda Tula at PO Box 32, Constantia 7848, tel (021) 794-6500.

Warning bay of the jackal

Blackbacked jackals are regarded by many as cowardly scavengers that circle the perimeters of lion kills and then dash in to snatch a piece of the spoils.

Back at the den, however, the youngsters show a different, lesser-known side to the jackal character — one that very often involves considerable danger.

Left at home by their parents to 'babysit' a newborn litter of pups, the older brothers and sisters of the new cubs carefully guard the entrance to the den.

If a predator such as a spotted hyena approaches, one of the babysitters issues a sharp warning — raised hackles, and a furious growl or warning bark that sends the youngsters tumbling into the safety of the den.

Babysitting duties don't end there. If a predator such as a hyena is undeterred by the warning, the jackal may lunge at it with snapping jaws. Its lightning reflexes enable it to rush the hyena, inflict a bite to the hindquarters and dart away, before the hapless animal knows what's hit it.

Kambaku Private Nature Reserve Previously called Cheetah Trails, this reserve covers some 4 000 ha of prime game-viewing bushveld in a belt of mopane woodland that stretches halfway up the subcontinent.

Taken over and upgraded in 1993, Kambaku is a popular haunt for herds of elephants and lions, but also includes an abundance of impala, wildebeest and zebras. Predators here include cheetahs, lions, spotted hyenas, leopards, African wild cats, spotted genets and civets.

Twice-daily game-viewing drives are provided in open 4x4s, and bush walks are led by experienced rangers and Shangaan trackers.

Dinner is usually served in an open-air boma and includes such specialities as crumbed warthog and venison.

A comfortable lounge and bar lead on to a verandah from which guests may see a colourful pageant of indigenous birds.

The boma and pool area overlook a small waterhole and marula trees on the perimeter of the camp. Shangaan dancing and singing keep visitors entertained in the evenings.

Sixteen guests can be accommodated in pole-and-reed thatched chalets with *en suite* bathrooms.

Highlight of a stay at Kambaku is a night out at Khankhanka (Shangaan for 'cheetah') Bush Camp, which offers a reed-covered sleeping area, ablution facilities, a braai area and a verandah. Guests may sit back with their sundowners and listen to the sounds of the wild as supper is prepared by the ranger and tracker.

Trips to the Kruger National Park and other scenic parts of Mpumalanga may be arranged on request.

For further information contact Bushveld Breakaways, PO Box 926, White River 1200, tel (01311) 5-1998, or contact the lodge at PO Box 1117, Hoedspruit 1380, tel (015) 793-2250.

Umlani Bush Camp Situated in the northern Timbavati near the eastern border of Klaserie Nature Reserve, Umlani accommodates guests in six rustic reed-and-thatch rondavels, with doors made of roll-down grass mats.

Here hammocks have been strung out beneath the jackalberry trees in front of the camp, for lazy siestas on sunny afternoons, or as vantage points across the Nharalumi River (the river only flows during the rainy season in summer).

There's a superb bird- and game-viewing hide upstream (where you may spend the night in your sleeping bag if you wish), and game drives are available.

A donkey boiler provides hot water at Umlani, and the light is gas-powered.

For further information write to PO Box 26350, Arcadia 0083, or tel (012) 329-3765.

King's Camp Sumptuous lodge accommodation and the chance to get close to big game are the main drawcards of this delightful camp. The camp has access to about 100 km^2 within the Timbavati Game Reserve, and has made use of its exposure to an abundance of game by building some excellent hides. Elephant, lion, leopard, rhino and buffalo regularly visit the waterholes and visitors can expect to get some great photographs.

Pride of the reserve is its lodge consisting of eight double *en suite* thatched bungalows and three suites with outside showers, air-conditioning and mini-bar. The lodge accommodates a maximum of 22 guests.

There's a lounge-bar, swimming pool and a viewing deck overlooking a waterhole at the main camp. South African cuisine is served in the boma or at a braai in the bush under the stars.

Other facilities include a curio shop, and laundry and conference facilities. Professional game rangers take guests on private safaris and birdwatching trips. Those who wish to sleep out in the bush will be accommodated.

To get to King's Camp from Johannesburg turn left off the N4 at Belfast and follow the signposts for Lydenburg, Orighstad and Hoedspruit. In Hoedspruit, turn right onto the R40. Eight kilometres from Hoedspruit, turn left at the Timbavati sign to the Timbavati control gate. From there turn right at the Kings Camp signboard.

The lodge has a private, tarred runway and you can fly in from Eastgate. To contact King's Camp write to PO Box 427, Nelspruit 1200, or tel (015) 793-3633.

Timbavati Wilderness Trails This rustic 4 000-ha reserve on the farm Birmingham in the southernmost section of the Timbavati offers safari-style accommodation in wood-panelled, two-bed cabins on stilts, next to the Timbavati River.

From your cabin — or from the two bomas which open out onto the Timbavati River — you will see a passing parade of mammals, including giraffes, Burchell's zebras, waterbuck, impala, and smaller mammals such as mongooses, civets, genets and porcupines. The two-, three- and four-day trails are delightful excursions into the heart of the bushveld.

Several hundred bird species inhabit the area, including the brownheaded parrot and secretarybird.

The absence of electricity, and the long-drop toilets may not be the last word in luxury, but they contribute to the rustic ambience of the reserve. And the steaming venison stews served on earthenware plates in the boma will bring you back for more.

For more information and bookings, write to PO Box 70137, Overport 4067, or tel (031) 207-1565.

Motswari Private Game Reserve Unbridled luxury in the midst of big-game country is the major drawcard at this private reserve which covers 14 000 ha of mopane veld in the northern part of the Timbavati. The reserve has two lovely camps: Motswari ('to keep and conserve'), and M'Bali ('the blossom'), and both are small and intimate.

Motswari is the more luxurious of the two camps, offering beautifully appointed thatched bungalows with *en suite* bathrooms on the banks of the Sohebele River. A central bar and verandah complex offers guests communal relaxation before dinner is served in the open boma.

M'Bali, geared for the more adventurous gamewatcher, nestles in a breathtaking setting on the banks of the Sharalumi River. East African habitents under thatch are set against the river bank, with *en suite* facilities below and a verandah overlooking the river and plains beyond.

Both Motswari and M'Bali offer game drives, escorted hikes through the bush and game-viewing from hides at various waterholes.

For more information, write to PO Box 67865, Bryanston 2021, tel (011) 463-1990.

Several very attractive game lodges and smaller reserves lie within an hour's drive west of the Timbavati Game Reserve in the Hoedspruit-Klaserie area. They include: Tshukudu Game Lodge (p. 148), Matumi Game Lodge (p. 148), Moholoholo Forest Camp, Marc's Camp, Nyati Pools, Kapama Game Reserve and Mohlabetsi Safari Lodge.

Kapama Game Reserve One of the larger and very popular private reserves,

Kapama covers 13 000 ha of big-game country southwest of Hoedspruit, about 30 km from the Kruger National Park's Orpen Gate.

Its indigenous game includes the Big Five and most of the larger mammals found in the Kruger National Park.

The reserve is also the home of the world-renowned Hoedspruit Research and Breeding Centre for Endangered Species, a project involving propagation of, and essential research into, endangered species. Conducted tours introduce visitors to more than 60 cheetahs, including tame ones, the rarely seen king cheetah, wild dogs, young white rhinos and other endangered animals. The centre is open Monday to Saturday from 08:00 to 14:00, and also on Sundays during school holidays. Another attraction is the Hoedspruit Safari Park, which has braai and ablution facilities for day visitors.

Kapama's Buffalo Camp has six luxury East African-style safari tents, built on wooden platforms on stilts above a dry river bed to preserve the bushveld vegetation below. Each tent has its own private bathroom with hot-water shower and flush toilet and is superbly located for those who wish to experience the sights and sounds of the bush in rustic surroundings. Buffalo Camp has its own homely thatched bar-cum-lounge.

Dinners are usually served in the diningroom or in the boma around a crackling fire.

Another option for those who like exquisite African furnishings and uninhibited creature comforts is the Kapama Guest House, which offers four double bedrooms (eight people), a bar, lounge, diningroom, outside boma, swimming pool and a host and hostess, if requested.

Game drives are offered twice daily, and guided bush walks are available on request. Highlight of the night game drive is dinner in the Elephant Inn Boma in the bush. After dinner adventurous guests may opt to stay in the Lion's Den, a three-storey house constructed of wood, with a spacious balcony for enjoying meals outside. A top-floor lounge serves as an observation post for the variety of game wandering through the bush. Guests must bring their own food and drinks if they wish to breakfast the next morning.

For luxury, service and stunning bushveld surroundings, Kapama rates

Fearless fighter of the wild

The bushbuck ram is one of the most courageous fighters of the Southern African wild. Cornered by a predator, or even poachers' dogs, it will charge, ramming its long, slightly spiralled horns into the enemy.

Wild dogs, leopards and even humans have been killed by a bushbuck turning the tables on them.

A bushbuck will defend its territory against a trespassing ram to the death. If an intruder threatens him, the bristles on his back and neck will rise with uncontained fury. Then he may back off, lower his head and horns, and charge.

Head-on-head collisions are sometimes followed by bouts of horn sparring, each fighter looking for an opening into which he can thrust his deadly horns.

In spite of its courage, however, a bushbuck will flee through the bush if there is a chance of escape, or swim across a river. One bushbuck, driven by floods from its territory, swam three kilometres to safety without stopping.

highly on the list of Southern Africa's wild places. But be sure to take a camera and binoculars along.

For further information contact Kapama Game Reserve, PO Box 912031, Silverton 0127, tel (012) 804-4840.

Marc's Camp This camp along the Klaserie River is small compared to most other private camps in the Timbavati area, but for a group looking for cosy and private comfort in the bush it's ideal.

Four lovely tree-houses, made of thatch, reeds and timber, nestle in the riverine forest, some of them in the branches of old jackalberry trees — ideal vantage points for watching the abundant birdlife and forest mammals such as bushpig, bushbuck and other antelope.

The thatched lapa, with its viewing platform mounted on stilts over water, is a wonderful place to relax in the sun and watch the animals come down to drink. Animals you might see include giraffes, wildebeest, impala, mongooses, serval, ostriches and spotted genets.

The central reception area at Marc's Camp is fronted by a shady garden and a swimming pool and accommodates a bar and lounge. The camp is set on 200 ha and the owners have traversing rights over 500 ha of land on an adjacent farm.

For further information and bookings contact Marc's Camp, PO Box 3043, Cresta 2118, tel (011) 476-8842.

Moholoholo Forest Camp This lovely camp nestles among rain forest and acacia woodland on the slopes of Moholoholo ('the Great One'), or Mariepskop, one of the highest peaks of the Mpumalanga Drakensberg.

Because of its elevated position, there are stunning views of the Drakensberg's tumbling mountains and valleys on one side, and of the sweeping savannah plains of the bushveld towards Kruger National Park in the east.

Seven rustic thatched chalets on stilts accommodate 14 people under a canopy of indigenous trees. Each chalet has *en suite* facilities and ceiling fans in the bedrooms.

A large, open verandah overlooks the forest and a waterhole where you may see baboons, kudu, impala, tsessebe, giraffe, eland, waterbuck, vervet and samango monkeys, bushbuck and red and grey duiker. At night the sounds of bushpigs and leopards can be heard within the surrounding forest.

More than 300 species of bird, including some 34 raptor species, inhabit the bush, mountains and trees.

Moholoholo is special for its Wildlife Rehabilitation Centre, where injured and orphaned animals are cared for before being released back into the wild. Here visitors may come into close contact with such species as zebra, crowned eagle, owl, serval, antbear, duiker and many other animals.

Game- and birdwatching trails are undertaken on foot during the day, although you really have to go no further than the local waterhole to see a large selection of animals and birds.

Night drives are held in an open vehicle and are ideal for seeing the nocturnal animals around Moholoholo.

The camp is also well positioned for day drives to the Kruger National Park (60 km to Orpen Gate), the Blyde River Canyon, Pilgrim's Rest, Bourke's Luck Potholes, Graskop and Sabie, a 230-km round trip which includes some stunning waterfalls.

Other destinations reached easily from Moholoholo are the Cheetah Breeding Project (16 km), Blyde River Dam and the Echo Caves (50 km).

The concept of Moholoholo was based on the environment and nature, and for this reason the camp does not have a swimming pool, television, radio, shop, liquor licence or telephone. However, there is a shop supplying essential provisions and a petrol station at Kampersrus nearby.

Meals are served buffet-style in the reed-walled boma, and range from a light breakfast to a hearty brunch and a braai for supper.

For further information and bookings contact Moholoholo at PO Box 1476, Hoedspruit 1380, tel (015) 795-5236.

Tshukudu Game Lodge Situated just to the west of the Klaserie Nature Reserve, Tshukudu covers some 5 000 ha of game country, with a further 3 500 ha of traversing rights on the banks of the Blyde and Olifants rivers.

This lodge has a facility for orphaned animals and guests mingle freely with some of its adopted 'children' — two elephants, a lion, a warthog and a wildebeest.

Fourteen thatched bungalows (one- and two-bedroomed), with *en suite* bathrooms lead on to a terrace with a sparkling pool. More rustic self-catering lodges are available at Bush Camp in a more remote section of the reserve.

With its beautiful sycamore forests and proximity to water, Tshukudu is a birdwatcher's paradise; there's no shortage of game either, and species include cheetah, white rhino, crocodile, hippo and a variety of antelope.

For further information and bookings write to PO Box 289, Hoedspruit 1380, tel (015) 793-2476.

Mohlabetsi Safari Lodge Lying just north of Tshukudu, in the Balule Nature Reserve, Mohlabetsi ('place of sweet water') is a private 1 068-ha game reserve offering six twin-bedded rondavels with *en suite* bathrooms set in lovely garden surroundings in Main Camp.

Guests also have the option of staying at the rustic Bush Lodge. The lodge has five two-bedded thatched rooms which overlook the Mohlabetsi River. There is also a lovely swimming pool. If you like, you can hire the entire lodge for a reasonable price, but you must cater for yourself.

The atmosphere is homely, and although the lodge is not in the same league as the larger, more expensive game lodges, it nevertheless offers comfortable accommodation, guided walks and some good game-viewing.

Daily game drives and walks are available at reasonable prices and among the animals you may see are leopards, wildebeest, nyala and red hartebeest. Lowveld birds are abundant here — among them Shelley's francolin and brown snake eagles.

For further information and bookings write to PO Box 662, Hoedspruit 1380, tel (015) 793-2166.

Matumi Game Lodge This lodge at the foot of the Mpumalanga Drakensberg is a holiday game farm for the whole family — a place where you can pat a tame impala ewe on the head and watch her offspring graze among the chalets all day.

Just 46 km from the Kruger National Park's Orpen Gate, Matumi offers 12 cosy four-bed and two six-bed thatched chalets with private bathrooms, air-conditioning and access to a lovely 20-m swimming pool. There is also a bush camp with 10 tents connected by a maze of boardwalks.

Regular outings are provided to a nearby rehabilitation centre for injured animals, and to a lion resettlement scheme, where you can get almost to within touching distance of the king of beasts.

Matumi has an outdoor boma, and a superb restaurant where guests may feast on venison or other bushveld specialities. Above the restaurant is a 16-m-high observation post, with panoramic views of the surrounding countryside.

Other activities at Matumi include swimming or angling in the Klaserie River, taking a walk along the 8-km Giraffe Hike, game-viewing and sleeping outdoors in the lapa. For families and singles it's an ideal destination, and very reasonably priced.

Package tours to the Blyde River Canyon, the Kruger National Park, Swadini Reptile Park and the Cheetah Breeding Project, are also available.

For further information contact Matumi Game Lodge at PO Box 1483, Hoedspruit 1380, tel (015) 793-1518.

Sandringham Private Nature Reserve Covering 5 000 ha of pristine wilderness between the Timbavati and Kruger National Park, Sandringham is a delight-

Timbavati Game Reserve at a glance

Locality:	500 km (5 hours' drive) north of Johannesburg on the western boundary of the Kruger National Park.
Climate:	Hot summers with thunderstorms; mild to cold winters without rain.
Number of camps:	There are literally dozens of camps, ranging from tented safari camps to exclusive bush lodges.
Game drives:	Most of the game lodges offer game drives at least twice daily.
Hides and waterholes:	Waterholes and hides abound around the private lodges; many have been constructed within the camps themselves.
Trails:	Bush trails on foot are offered by all the lodges and camps. Timbavati Wilderness Trails offers two-, three- and four-day trails through the bush.
Other attractions:	Excursions into the nearby Kruger National Park or the Blyde River Canyon.
Amenities:	Swimming pools and licensed restaurants are a feature of many, but not all, of the luxury lodges.
Accommodation:	Ranges from sumptuous safari suites and tastefully furnished chalets and bungalows to rustic tented accommodation.
Booking address:	See individual entries.
When to go:	All year round, but winter is better for game-viewing.
What to take with you:	In summer cool, lightweight clothing, bathing costume; winter: warm clothing, hiking shoes, hat, torch, sunglasses, binoculars, camera.
How to get there:	Most of the Timbavati area's lodges are easily accessible from Phalaborwa, Hoedspruit or Klaserie.
Nearest doctor:	There's a doctor at Hoedspruit Air Force base and at Skukuza in the Kruger National Park.
Nearest petrol:	Many of the lodges provide their own petrol and diesel, but Hoedspruit is close to most of them if they don't.
Open:	Most of the lodges are open around the clock throughout the year.
Special precautions:	Take antimalaria precautions before you visit the Lowveld; try and secure a mosquito net if one is not provided,

fully rustic camp which offers four *en suite* stone-and-thatch chalets accommodating eight people. The small camp is just off the main access road to Orpen Gate, and within easy reach of Kruger and the Blyde River Canyon.

Among its features are a fine restaurant under thatch, a sparkling swimming pool, a river lapa for breakfast and watching game and a boma for dinner under the stars.

Animals which roam freely between the hardekool, sandvaalbos and jackalberry trees include lions, buffaloes, leopards, giraffes and blue wildebeest.

Guests can choose between bush trails on foot or game drives in the comfort of an open Land Rover.

For more information and bookings contact Sandringham Private Nature Reserve, PO Box 1214, Hoedspruit 1380, tel (015) 793-2449.

Nyati Pools For a holiday with a difference, a group of eight can hire the campsite at Nyati Pools for next to nothing and explore the abundance of animals and birds of the Lowveld in lovely bushveld surroundings.

Among the attractions here are a Botswana-style tented camp in the Mozambanga River Valley which has a lovely boma overlooking a waterhole, a great restaurant called Jungle Jack's (after owner Jack Mudd) and game walks to view the resident wildlife — mainly buffaloes, giraffes and zebras as well as smaller mammals and abundant birdlife.

Nyati Pools is small (just 250 ha) but it is homely and personal and likely to bring you back for more.

For more details contact the owners at PO Box 664, Hoedspruit 1380, tel/fax (015) 283-1676.

Tsitsikamma Coastal National Park

Nestling against the fringes of an emerald forest along South Africa's Garden Route is a narrow coastal terrace that shears off into the deep blue canvas of the Indian Ocean.

A sprinkling of log cabins tucked into a corner of this coastal garden peer out across the sea and its impossibly empty horizons. Here and there a dassie sniffs the air, then scurries for the cover of the bush. In the sea, bottlenose dolphins carouse and skid through gathering swells.

This is Storms River Rest Camp, heart of the Tsitsikamma National Park, an 80-km strip of paradise extending from Nature's Valley in the west to the Groot River in the east, and which embraces the sea for a distance of 5 km. The park also includes De Vasselot Nature Reserve surrounding Nature's Valley, and a 24 500-ha area inland, known as Soetkraal.

Although the coastal section of the park is just 6 km from the N2 connecting Port Elizabeth and Cape Town, it is one of the most sought-after coastal refuges on the subcontinent of Africa. The reasons, once you get there, are obvious.

It offers peace, tranquillity and comfortable accommodation in extraordinarily beautiful surroundings, as well as access to the sea, mountains and coastal trails which radiate from it.

Tips for travellers

- **No pets, boats, roller skates or skiboards are allowed in the park.**
- **Scuba-divers who wish to explore the marine trails must possess a third-class SAUU or equivalent diving certificate.**

Wildlife The forests, mountains and coastal fringe teem with birds: 220 bird species, including such notables as Narina trogon, bluemantled and paradise flycatcher, sombre bulbul, rameron pigeon, forest buzzard, chorister robin, forest canary and Knysna lourie find sanctuary under the forest canopy.

Along the coast there are 40 species of seabird, ranging from whitebreasted cormorant and Cape gannet to black oystercatcher and kelp gull.

Animals of the kloofs and rocky regions include leopards and chacma baboons, while in the forests you may be lucky to see bushpigs, blue duiker, otters, vervet monkeys, honey badgers and caracals.

Marine life Tsitsikamma is a Khoikhoi word meaning 'the place of clear waters', and it refers to the crystalline waters that wash these gentle shores. For lovers of the sea — and marine life — there is probably no better place along the Garden Route to explore its submarine life. For beginners, numerous deep rock pools (one the length of a football field) harbour a dazzling array of local marine species. The most popular of these is Goudgate, near the start of the Otter Trail, where you can expect to see anything from sea anemones and sea urchins to butterflyfish, blaasop and rockcod.

Experienced snorkellers, swimmers and scuba-divers may follow more ambitious marine trails, which radiate from the small beach in front of the restaurant. Here you may expect to see such larger reef fish as galjoen, blacktail, red steenbras and musselcracker, as well as hammerhead, raggedtooth and blacktip sharks.

Where to stay Fringed by white milkwood trees on the terraces of Storms River Camp are 31 fully equipped timber cabins, each with an exquisite view of mountain and sea. Further to the west are 17 oceanettes, (in an A-frame complex overlooking the sea). In addition there are 70 spacious caravan and 30 camping sites,

Tsitsikamma's furry sun-seekers

Dassies love the sun. As the sun rises across the sea in the Tsitsikamma National Park, you may see them outside your tent or bungalow, peeping bleary-eyed from their rocky lairs, or scurrying across the grass towards a sunbathing rock.

This habit is not a sign of laziness. Their inability to regulate their body temperature according to the air temperature means that in cold weather they need as much sun as possible. Similarly, in very hot weather they retire to the coolness of their rocky chambers.

This closely knit group of brown, badger-like sunbathers gets its alternate name 'dassie' from the Dutch for badger 'dasje'.

They have one of the most streamlined — and effective — security systems in the wild. The success of this system depends on a vigilant 'female sentry', appointed to keep a special watch for lurking predators while the dassie group feeds.

A single, piercing cry of alarm, uttered through the sentry's half-open lips will immediately 'freeze' the feeding group. If the sentry follows her alarm by bounding off to her rocky lair with a shrill scream, the rest of the group will follow suit, dispersing in all directions.

with access to laundry facilities. The De Vasselot Camp Site at Nature's Valley offers 45 camping and caravan sites shaded by coastal forest.

Whether you stay in a cabin, oceanette, tent or caravan, you're always within five minutes of a swimming pool, smaller rock pools, a bronze, sandy beach (with excellent, safe swimming) next to the main restaurant, angling spots and forest walks.

The walking trails The deep, mysterious forests of the Tsitsikamma are a rambler's dream. And there's no better place to explore them than at Tsitsikamma National Park. Here 12 trails take you into

Tsitsikamma Coastal National Park at a glance

Locality:	On the Garden Route, 180 km west of Port Elizabeth.
Climate:	Temperate, with mild to cold winters and warm summers. Rainfall 1 200 mm per annum (May and October are the wettest months; June and July the driest).
Number of camps:	Two.
Drives:	Day drives from the park include Nature's Valley, the Bloukrans Pass and Groot River Pass.
Trails:	There are 12 trails. The major ones are: Storms River–Loerie (one hour), Blue Duiker (two-and-a-half hours), Otter (four days) Waterfall (three hours); De Vasselot–Tsitsikamma (five days), Kalanderkloof (two-and-a-half hours), Groot River (two hours), Salt River Route (five-and-a-half hours), Salt River Mouth Route (two-and-a-half hours).
Other attractions:	Birdwatching, snorkelling, swimming, angling, exploring the forests.
Amenities:	À la carte licensed restaurant and shop, laundromat and dryer.
Accommodation:	Three types of two-bedroom beach cabins, all with bathroom; one- and two-bedroom oceanettes, each with bathroom. Caravan and camping sites, with power available.
Booking address:	The National Parks Board, PO Box 787, Pretoria 0001, tel (012) 343-1991; or National Parks Board, PO Box 7400, Roggebaai 8012, tel (021) 22-2810. For more details contact the Park Warden, PO Storms River 6308, tel (042) 541-1607.
When to go:	Midsummer, between November and February.
What to take with you:	Binoculars, goggles, snorkel and flippers, a fishing rod and some firm hiking boots.
How to get there:	Travelling from Port Elizabeth on the N2, cross the Paul Sauer Bridge over the Storms River and turn left 9 km later, following the signposts to the park's entrance.
Nearest doctor:	At Kareedouw (55 km). Daily clinics at the Tsitsikamma Forest Inn, tel (042) 3-3601.
Nearest petrol:	Petrol and diesel at Storms River Bridge.
Open:	Daily from 5:30 to 21:30.
Special precautions:	Although the sea is quite safe, always exercise caution in the water, particularly during the spring tides.

an enchanting world of tangled bush, dominated by forest giants such as the Outeniqua yellowwood, bastard ironwood and stinkwood. At the coast, gnarled canopy trees such as candlewood and white milkwood provide cover for orchids, creepers, indigenous ferns and flowers.

The principal trail at Tsitsikamma is the Otter Trail (48 km), regarded as Southern Africa's finest coastal walk. The trail leads west from Storms River Mouth to Nature's Valley, crossing a landscape of lonely beaches, rocky shores, tumbling mountains bisected by rivers and ravines, and gentle plateaus covered by leucadendrons, ericas and proteas.

Timber huts, equipped with bunks, mattresses, firewood and water, are perched on stunning vantage points overlooking forest and sea along the way. After a hard day's slog, you can peel off your shoes and socks, dip your feet into a mountain stream, and absorb the views of thundering surf on this rocky shore.

Longer (64 km), and certainly more rigorous, is the five-day Tsitsikamma Hiking Trail from Kalander at Nature's Valley to Storms River Mouth.

To walk either of these trails, you'll need to book at least a year in advance (see 'At a glance' box), and make sure that you are fit, because both trails are physically demanding.

Other trails leaving from the main rest camp are:

- The Loerie Trail (1 km), which meanders through the forest fringing the camp. The trail owes its name to the attractive bird that lives off the fruits of the forest canopy.
- The Mouth Trail, an easy 1-km ramble along a boardwalk to the mouth of the Storms River. Here you may cross the 80-m suspension bridge, and scale the heights on the other side of the Storms River for exquisite views of the ocean, rest camp and mouth below you. The trail bypasses a Strandloper Cave, where there's an archaeological display of seashells, bones and other artefacts dating back several centuries.
- The Blue Duiker Trail (4 km), named after the dainty, rare antelope that has all but disappeared from Southern Africa. You may not see a blue duiker here, but keep a lookout for bushbuck.
- The De Vasselot section of the park at Nature's Valley offers seven scenic trails, and it would be worth your while to spend a few days at the De Vasselot Campsite just outside Nature's Valley.
- Particularly recommended are: the Kalanderkloof Trail (6 km) which takes you through forest to a superior vantage point, and then back through a precipitous gorge; and the Salt River Mouth Route (3 km), a circular trail that leaves the cafe in Nature's Valley and tracks the course of the river.

Umfolozi Game Reserve

As you creep low through the tangled bush of Umfolozi Game Reserve your ranger stops suddenly, quietly signalling you to get down. You freeze in your tracks. Dead ahead, less than 50 m away, four white rhinos graze in the dappled shade of a knobthorn tree.

Although your heart's racing and the adrenalin is surging through your veins, there's a breathless sense of wonder at being so close to these mighty land mammals, once described as the ugly prima donnas of the bushveld.

You're on one of Umfolozi's bush trails

— a ranger-led adventure that takes you through a community of animals that few other game sanctuaries in the world can match for numbers and diversity.

No fewer than 1 600 white rhinos and about 300 black rhinos flourish in this game reserve — an amazing phenomenon if you consider that these lumbering giants of the savannah faced extinction in the 1920s (in 1922 there were just 20 rhinos left in Umfolozi).

In the 1960s the Natal Parks Board launched a massive campaign to save them — one that has been so successful that Umfolozi and Hluhluwe together have sent 3 500 rhinos to other reserves in Southern Africa.

Wildlife Rhinos aren't the only attraction here: more than 40 lions pad through the acacia savannah thornveld, in the company of a huge variety of animals. Among those you're likely to see on bush walks or autotrails include elephants, giraffes, blue wildebeest, leopards, cheetahs, impala, reedbuck, kudu, buffaloes, red and grey duiker, nyala, steenbok, spotted hyenas, baboons, blackbacked jackals and zebras.

Among the 300 species of bird are the marabou stork, Wahlberg's eagle, blackbellied korhaan, trumpeter hornbill, Shelley's francolin, crested barbet, little bee-eater, whitebacked vulture and bateleur.

Umfolozi (47 753 ha) lies among rolling hills between the Black and White Mfolozi Rivers in central Zululand, and, together with Hluhluwe Game Reserve, shares a common destiny. Both reserves were proclaimed in 1897, which makes them the oldest game reserves in Africa. Recently the two reserves were linked together by a strip of land known as the Corridor, qualifying them jointly as the largest park — the Hluhluwe-Umfolozi Park (96 000 ha) — in South Africa (see also Hluhluwe Game Reserve, p. 53).

Where to stay Umfolozi has two hutted camps, Mpila and Masinda; two bush camps, Sontuli and Nselweni — these may be booked independently or used as overnight stops on wilderness walking

Rhinos back from the brink

Black rhino are an endangered species, their numbers dwindling in Africa from about 65 000 in 1970 to about 3 000 today, of which 1 050 are in South Africa and Namibia.

The animal has now become extinct in 12 African countries, and only six countries have populations exceeding 100. The last sole surviving black rhino which occurred naturally in the Kruger National Park was last seen in 1936.

Today the black rhino's survival in Southern Africa is largely due to the efforts of the KwaZulu-Natal Nature Conservation Services and reserves such as Umfolozi, with its 300 black rhino, where they have been able to propagate free of poaching.

trails. They are both on the banks of the Black Mfolozi River. There is one trails camp, Mndindini. Mpila and Masinda have electricity at night only, and hot and cold water. Bedding, cutlery and crockery are supplied, and cooks are available for all accommodation, except chalets. Bring all your own food, since food is unavailable in the reserve. Film and can be bought at small curio shops in the reserve.

MPILA CAMP Beautifully located on the hummock of a hill, Mpila offers 12 attractive four-bed bungalows, with separate kitchen and ablution facilities, two seven-bed, self-contained cottages, and six five-bed chalets. Here you can sit on the grassy terraces, braai under the stars, and listen to the sounds of wild Africa around you.

MASINDA CAMP This camp offers six four-bed huts and one seven-bed lodge.

NSELWENI BUSH CAMP Nselweni has four fully equipped thatched huts (two beds each), and an observation platform

Umfolozi Game Reserve at a glance

Locality: Northeastern KwaZulu-Natal, 260 km from Durban.

Climate: Summers hot and humid (average daytime temperature 32 °C) with rain; winters cool to warm.

Number of camps: Five.

Game drives: Umfolozi Autotrail (61 km).

Hides and waterholes: Mpapha Hide.

Trails: Wilderness trails, day self-guided walks (Emoyeni, Mpila Hill and Masinda); ranger-led walks.

Other attractions: Birdwatching, visiting Iron-Age sites.

Amenities: Curio shops provide film and camera accessories, but no food.

Accommodation: Hutted camps: **Mpila** and **Masinda** offer a variety of accommodation in huts, cottages, chalets and the luxury **Masinda Lodge**. Bush camps: **Sontuli** and **Nselweni**, built of poles, reed and thatch. **Mdindini Trails Camp** available as a bush camp from December to February.

Booking address: KwaZulu-Natal Nature Conservation Services, PO Box 13069, Cascades 3202, tel (0331) 845-1000.

When to go: Winter — May through September — when the vegetation is not too dense.

What to take with you: Binoculars, camera, torch, strong hiking boots, your own food (including perishables).

How to get there: The clearly signposted turn-off is on the N2, 3 km north of the Mtubatuba turn-off (some 260 km from Durban and 300 km from Piet Retief).

Nearest doctor: Hluhluwe Village.

Nearest petrol: In the reserve.

Open: 1 October–31 March: 05:00–19:00; 1 April–30 September: 06:00–18:00.

Special precautions: Take antimalaria precautions before you go to the reserve. Be alert to a possible charge by white or black rhino while walking in the reserve, and heed the advice of your game ranger.

built on stilts among a canopy of trees overlooking the river. During your stay here you will be assigned a game guard and a cook. This is a very attractive, remote camp, and gives you immediate access to all manner of wildlife (including black rhinos, buffaloes and lions). Keep an eye open for troops of baboons in the vicinity of the river.

SONTULI BUSH CAMP This camp also has four fully equipped huts with two beds each. Ranger-led walks are available on request.

MDINDINI TRAILS CAMP This camp lies on the banks of the White Mfolozi River, and may be booked as a normal bush camp from December to February. From March to November, however, it is used as a stopover point for wilderness trails.

Game walks and wilderness trails It is important to distinguish between the walks and wilderness trails at Umfolozi. The walks include two morning or afternoon excursions into the bush with a game guard. These will take you to the top of Mpila Enkulu, Mpila Omncane and Masinda Omncane hills for superb views of the surrounding countryside. Other walks are the three self-guided rambles near the respective camps: Emoyeni, Mpila Hill and Masinda.

Wilderness trails were pioneered by the Natal Parks Board in the early 1960s, and offer the ultimate wildlife experience — a few days and nights in the bush, sleeping under the stars in the company of lions, rhinos, elephants, hyenas and the rest of the game that roams the Umfolozi Reserve.

The trails are limited to eight people (minimum age 14), and may be booked up to nine months in advance.

For the wilderness trail you'll need a backpack, sleeping bag (with blanket), high-density foam mattress, hiking boots, and a basic first-aid kit. Catering is organised by the KwaZulu-Natal Nature Conservation Services.

Although gamewatching is the major attraction of the wilderness trails, keep a lookout for any one of several Iron-Age sites at Umfolozi. Some still bear the remains of smelting furnaces, slag, shards of pottery and old grinding stones.

Be sure to take along a good field guide to the birds of Southern Africa.

Game drives The 61-km Umfolozi Autotrail encompasses a major part of the reserve and offers superb game-viewing opportunities, particularly at the thatched Mpapha Hide between 09:00 and 12:00. Other recommended stops are the three major picnic sites at Umbondwe, Mpila and the Sontuli Loop.

Special three-hour night-drives in an open safari vehicle (accompanied by an armed ranger) are also provided, and usually take in the Sontuli loop and other private roads.

WEST COAST NATIONAL PARK

Just 100 km north of Cape Town, the turquoise waters of the Atlantic Ocean roll eastwards through two headlands into Saldanha Bay, a massive expanse of water that funnels southeastwards into a beautiful lagoon.

Some 16 km long and in places 4 km wide, this lagoon, known appropriately as Langebaan ('long path'), is the heart of the West Coast National Park — one of Southern Africa's most important wetland areas.

From the air, the 26 000-ha park appears to be dominated by the vast lagoon, whose eastern shores merge with a peninsula, punctuated by gentle hills and low-lying strandveld. In winter the seaward side of this peninsula is lashed by northwestern Atlantic gales; in summer its golden coastline, known as Sixteen Mile Beach, is a place of perfect tranquillity — a natural sanctuary where hikers may stand and watch southern right whales cruising offshore.

Lying between Langebaan and the fishing village of Yzerfontein to the south, the West Coast National Park was proclaimed in 1985 to protect the sensitive wetland area along the western seaboard of South Africa. Apart from the lagoon, it also incorporates the beautiful Postberg Nature Reserve on the western peninsula, the tiny hamlet of Churchhaven, the islands of Malgas and Jutten at the entrance to Saldanha Bay, and Marcus and Schaapen islands closer to the lagoon.

Wildlife In summer the islands of the West Coast National Park serve as landing strips and nesting sites for some 750 000 seabirds. Local species such as cormorant, gannet and jackass penguin are joined by a literal invasion of about 100 000 Arctic birds. Curlew sandpipers form the bulk of these, and they are joined by sanderlings, knots, whimbrels, godwits and green-

West Coast National Park at a glance

Locality:	West Coast of South Africa, between Yzerfontein and Langebaan.
Climate:	Summers hot and dry, with southeasterly winds; winters cold and wet.
Game drives:	Postberg offers scenic drives through the wild flower area.
Trails:	Two-day Postberg Hiking Trail (24 km); two-day Strandveld Educational Trail (30 km); Sandveld Trails (outside park), 16,5 km and 8 km.
Other attractions:	Power-boating, yachting, wind-surfing, diving.
Amenities:	Information centre.
Accommodation:	**Geelbek Homestead** accommodates up to 30 hikers; overnight huts available on Sandveld trails.
Booking address:	The Park Warden, West Coast National Park, PO Box 25, Langebaan 7357, tel (022) 772-2144.
When to go:	In the flower season, between late July and September, or during summer.
What to take with you:	Warm clothing in winter, camera, hiking boots, bathing costume, binoculars, guide book to seabirds.
How to get there:	The park: Drive north from Cape Town on the R27, turning left at the Langebaan sign. Follow signposts to Langebaan. Postberg: Drive north from Cape Town on the R27 for about 90 km, turning left at the West Coast National Park sign.
Nearest doctor:	Langebaan.
Nearest petrol:	Langebaan.
Open:	There is an entrance gate to the park, and the park is open throughout the year. Postberg Nature Reserve is open between 09:00 and 17:00 during the flower season (August–September).
Special precautions:	Take adequate sun protection when hiking in summer.

shanks. The islands also host the largest colony of kelp gulls in Southern Africa.

It has been estimated that the salty water of this wilderness is home to some 60 million bacteria per cubic metre. Algae, molluscs, crustaceans and other organisms thrive in such abundance that they provide easy pickings for the avian communities, which consume about 150 tons a year.

There are 255 different bird species in the park, and the area supports more waterbirds than any other wetland in Southern Africa.

For details of boat trips to Malgas Island and the lagoon, contact the Park Warden (see *Booking address,* 'At a glance' box).

Postberg This beautiful reserve on the western shores of Langebaan Lagoon attracts large numbers of day visitors eager to view the wildflowers that carpet the countryside in spring.

It is home to various large mammals, including eland, bontebok, Cape mountain zebra, red hartebeest, springbok, gemsbok, blue wildebeest and kudu, as well as a diverse community of birds.

There are three picnic sites with ablution facilities. Advance booking is not available for day visitors, so it is advisable to get there early. An overnight trail is available (see hiking trails below).

South of Postberg are the tiny lagoonside hamlets of Stofbergsfontein, Churchhaven and Schrywershoek (named after Ensign Isaq Schrijver, a 17th-century explorer employed by the Dutch East India Company). This is a particularly scenic part of the Western Cape.

Where to stay The former Langebaan Lodge has been demolished, however new accommodation facilities are being established.

Geelbek Homestead, a national monument restored to its 1860 glory, is the alternative place to stay, but you have to be part of a hiking group on the Strandveld Educational Trail (see below), to sample its tasty West Coast cuisine, enjoy the bar service, and overnight in its comfortable double bunks.

Hiking trails For breathtaking views of the West Coast's springtime floral extravaganza, the two-day Postberg Hiking Trail can't be beaten. The circular 24-km trail is available only in August and September. It tracks a beautiful part of the coastline (Sixteen Mile Beach), past Kreeftebaai and Plankiesbaai, and offers elevated views of southern right whales that cruise along these shores in spring. Hikers should take their own tent and braai grid. For booking and enquiries, contact the Park Warden, West Coast National Park (see *Booking address*, 'At a glance' box).

The Strandveld Educational Trail is a 30-km hike which includes three nights at Geelbek Homestead. The hike consists of two loops — 14,4 km and 16 km — which traverse strandveld, granite outcrops, dunes and seashore, before returning to Geelbek.

Two lovely trails (16,5 km and 8 km), known as the Sandveld Trails, are available just beyond the park's boundaries in the south. They start at the farm Blombos, and here hikers may book two bungalows. There's another overnight shelter known as 'Witpan se Hut' further along the trail. Take your own sleeping bag, food and gas stove. To book, tel Mrs Wightman (021) 24-2755; 14 Higgo Crescent, Higgovale, Cape Town 8001.

Other attractions Boating in Langebaan Lagoon and Saldanha Bay is a major attraction for visitors to the area. The park offers trips from Langebaan Lodge, across the lagoon from Postberg. Further details are available at the information desk at the Park Warden's office.

A less obvious attraction of the park is its huge store of fossils — some of the richest deposits in the world. Palaeontologists have discovered fossils representing some 200 species of vertebrate and invertebrate that lived here five million years ago.

Wolkberg Wilderness Area

Huge armadas of cumulonimbus clouds march across the serrated peaks of the Wolkberg Wilderness Area in summer, rumbling out a warning of wicked storms and imminent rain.

In the forested valleys and ravines below, the tremble of the wind in the marula trees and rolling grasslands sends animals and birds scurrying for shelter.

The deluge comes with jagged streaks of lightning and drenching rain, sending cascades of water plummeting down the quartzite slopes of the Devil's Knuckles and other mountains. The Mohlapitse, Mawedzi and Shobwe rivers, and their tributaries, fattened by the rain, tumble south- and eastwards, spilling over rainbowed waterfalls, and dive through lush, subtropical forests.

In the pristine silence after the storm, wreaths of mist rise from the valley floor to encircle the pinnacles and peaks in seas of silver. This is the Wolkberg Wilderness Area at its most beautiful, an Eden of magic and mystery, described by author Harry Klein as the 'Valley of the Silver Mists'. It was here that English writer John Buchan, inspired by the legendary beauty of the area, wrote *Prester John*. Today the Wolkberg inspires dedicated nature lovers and hikers seeking the ultimate escape from civilisation.

The Wolkberg Wilderness Area covers 22 000 ha of rolling mountains, singing grasslands, subtropical forest and deeply incised gorges between the northern Drakensberg and the eastern rim of the Strydpoort Mountains, southwest of Tzaneen. It was proclaimed in 1977 as one of South Africa's seven official wilderness areas.

Its huge success as a sanctuary for animals and birds is due in part to the magnificent diversity of its habitats which includes a 500-ha tropical forest, the 'Wonderwoud', known to regular hikers as the Lost Forest. Here the dense canopies of yellowwood, wild teak, marula, kiaat, beech and bushwillow provide refuge and food for a variety of birds and animals.

A forest of an entirely different nature is that in Cycad Valley at the western part of the Wolkberg Wilderness Area, where 4 000 Modjadji cycads — the largest of the Southern African cycads — cling to the

Tips for hikers

- **Before entering the Wolkberg Wilderness Area, you should be reasonably fit.**
- **Discuss your proposed route or routes with the forestry officer at the Serala Forestry Station, where an information booklet and detailed map are available. He will advise hikers which options are the best for their particular experience.**
- **You should not attempt certain climbs, particularly the C-grade route over the Devil's Knuckles, unless you are a reasonably experienced climber.**
- **Spend at least three or four days in the Wolkberg Wilderness Area to properly explore its marvels.**

hillsides. These huge cycads — some grow up to 13 m in height — were named after the legendary Mujaji or Rain Queen of the Lobedu people. Elsewhere in the reserve the mountain forests mingle with stands of Transvaal mountain sugarbush, everlastings, aloes and curry bushes, whose explosion of blooms bring a carpet of yellow to the mountain slopes

Towering above the lush landscape of undulating hills, ravines and waterfalls are the turrets of Serala Peak (2 050 m) and Krugerkop in the east, a rocky buttress which earned its name for its likeness to Paul Kruger, one-time president of the Zuid-Afrikaansche Republiek.

Wildlife Although the animals of the Wolkberg Wilderness Area are shy, sharp-eyed hikers may spot antelope such as reedbuck, bushbuck, klipspringer, grey rhebok and duiker, darting through the bush. Less seldom seen are the leopards which prowl the rocky high ground, or such felines as wild cats, caracals and civets. Other carnivores include spotted hyenas, blackbacked jackals and honey badgers. The smaller mammals are also well represented, and you may see Cape clawless otters, porcupines, genets or such primates as lesser bushbabies, samango monkeys and chacma baboons.

Wolkberg Wilderness Area at a glance

Locality:	Southwest of Tzaneen where the Strydpoort Mountains meet the Drakensberg.
Climate:	Winters mild to cold (9 °C–20 °C); summers warm to hot (24 °C–35 °C). Rain falls between November and February (500 mm in the southwest to 1 350 mm in the northeast).
Number of camps:	One.
Game drives:	No vehicles permitted within the reserve.
Trails:	Wide choice of paths and jeep tracks.
Other attractions:	Scenic splendours, Iron-Age sites.
Amenities:	None.
Accommodation:	Take your own tent.
Booking address:	The Officer-in-Charge, Wolkberg Wilderness Area, Private Bag X102, Haenertsburg 0730, tel (015) 276-1303.
When to go:	March to May (but be prepared for cold weather into May).
What to take with you:	Warm clothing all year (include thermal underwear, gloves and anorak in winter; choice of light clothing in summer), waterproofing for your pack, your own tent, camp stove and all provisions, sun hat.
How to get there:	From Tzaneen head southwest along the R528 to Haenertsburg. Southwest of the town take the gravel road for 14 km to where the road forks. Bear left here, and again at the intersection 6 km on. From here it is 25 km to the Serala Forestry Station (ignore two turn-offs to the right).
Special precautions:	When hiking be sure of your day's destination, and arrive in time to pitch your tent before dark. Don't attempt the hike unless you are fit. Watch out for snakes and ticks.

Hikers should be aware that snakes are also common and include the African python, and such venomous species as black mambas, green mambas, puff-adders and berg adders.

Birdlife No less than 157 bird species, including the rare bat hawk, are found in the area. More common species include hamerkop, goliath heron, forktailed drongo, blackfronted bush shrike, secretary-bird, black and martial eagle, forest buzzard, blackshouldered kite, lanner falcon and crested guineafowl.

The watercourses in the valleys attract riverine species such as brownhooded kingfisher, moorhen, Egyptian goose and yellowbilled duck, while you may see blackeyed bulbuls, lilacbreasted rollers, speckled mousebirds and swee waxbills among the savannah and grasslands.

Where to stay In spite of its natural beauty, the Wolkberg Wilderness Area is not for those who seek the comforts of hearth and home. There is a small campsite (with showers and toilets) at the Serala Forestry Station — the only point of entry — but there is no accommodation within the Wolkberg Wilderness Area, and there are no ablution facilities. Hikers have to take their own sleeping bags, tents and camp stoves, and be totally self-sufficient.

Hiking A popular and scenic route to follow is the jeep track that leads from the Serala Forestry Station down to the Mohlapitse River, and which runs along part of the Klipdraai River. Beautiful waterfalls, bizarrely shaped potholes and riverine birds are among the attractions here. If you continue along this track, you'll eventually turn north along the Mogwatse River to Mampa's Kloof, from where a network of paths leads to Thabina Waterfall, Wonderwoud, Krugerkop and Serala Peak.

Another shorter but more arduous option is to follow the Mohlapitse River upstream, cross the rocky turrets of the Devil's Knuckles and then descend into the Wonderwoud before continuing to Serala Peak.

History Early Stone-Age artefacts suggest that the area was inhabited as far back as the fourth century AD. Remains of dry stone walls suggest Sotho people occupied the area more recently.

Tips for travellers

- **There are no route markers in this area and the going can get tough. Travel in groups of four or more (a maximum of 10 people are allowed on overnight trails).**
- **Take a detailed map of the area (available at the forestry station) and a compass.**
- **Although there is a basic entry fee, the costs of hiking the Wolkberg Wilderness Area are minimal. Book well in advance.**

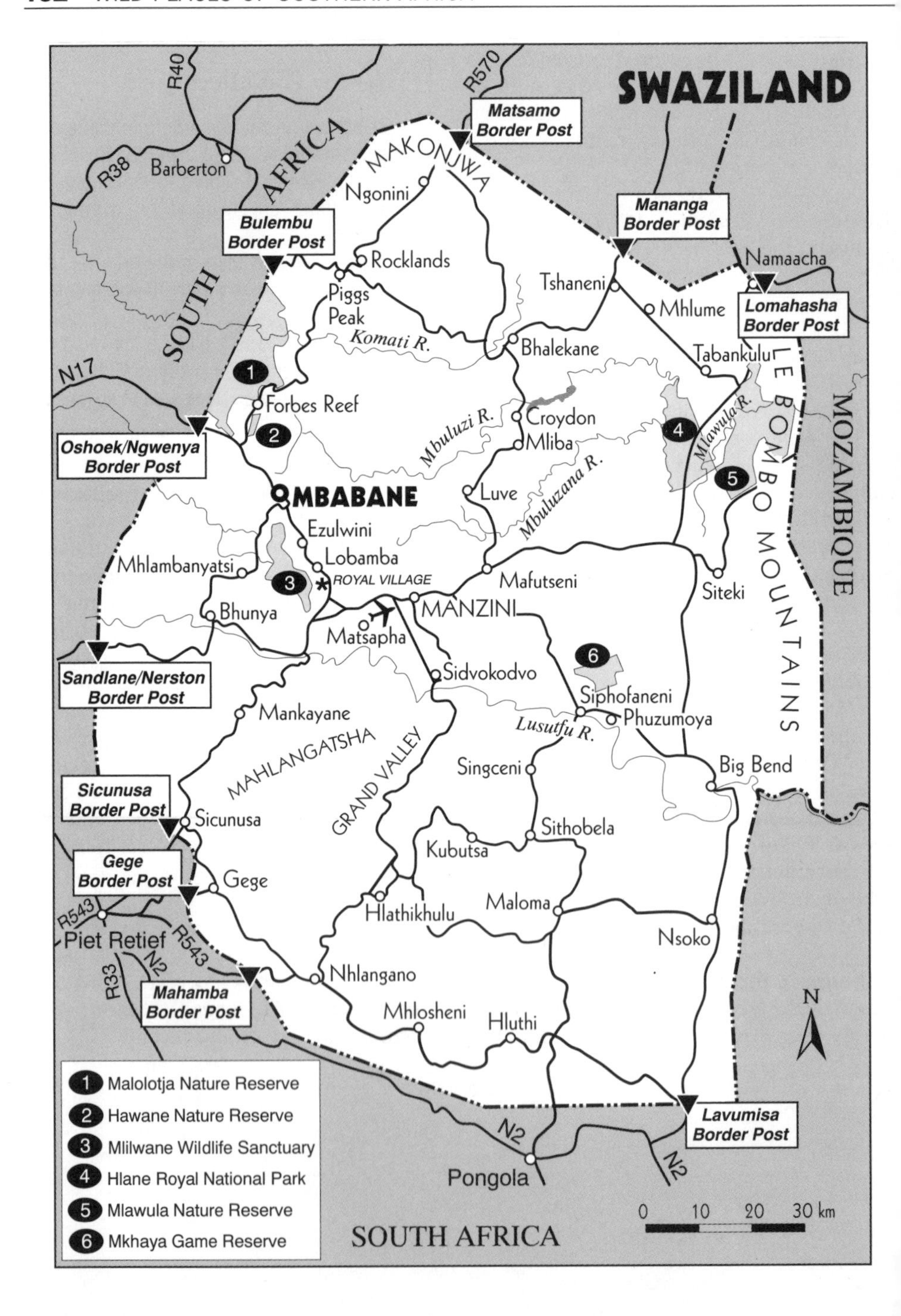
SWAZILAND
SOUTH AFRICA
MOZAMBIQUE
SOUTH AFRICA
MAKONJWA
LEBOMBO MOUNTAINS
MAHLANGATSHA
GRAND VALLEY
MBABANE
MANZINI
Matsamo Border Post
Bulembu Border Post
Mananga Border Post
Lomahasha Border Post
Oshoek/Ngwenya Border Post
Sandlane/Nerston Border Post
Sicunusa Border Post
Gege Border Post
Mahamba Border Post
Lavumisa Border Post
R40
R570
R38
N17
R543
R33
N2
Barberton
Ngonini
Rocklands
Piggs Peak
Komati R.
Tshaneni
Mhlume
Namaacha
Tabankulu
Bhalekane
Forbes Reef
Mbuluzi R.
Croydon
Mliba
Luve
Mbuluzana R.
Mlawula R.
Ezulwini
Lobamba
ROYAL VILLAGE
Mhlambanyatsi
Bhunya
Matsapha
Mafutseni
Siteki
Sidvokodvo
Siphofaneni
Phuzumoya
Lusutfu R.
Mankayane
Singceni
Big Bend
Sicunusa
Sithobela
Kubutsa
Gege
Hlathikhulu
Maloma
Piet Retief
Nsoko
Nhlangano
Mhlosheni
Hluthi
Pongola
N
0 10 20 30 km
1 Malolotja Nature Reserve
2 Hawane Nature Reserve
3 Mlilwane Wildlife Sanctuary
4 Hlane Royal National Park
5 Mlawula Nature Reserve
6 Mkhaya Game Reserve

SWAZILAND

Occupying some 17 364 km^2 — roughly the size of Wales — Swaziland is a small, friendly kingdom landlocked in the north, south and west by South Africa, and in the east by Mozambique.

Scenically the most exciting part of Swaziland is the western region, home of the Malolotja wilderness area and such lofty mountains as Piggs Peak and Mount Emlembe, the country's highest point.

Here, on a plateau some 1 200 m high, numerous rivers have their source, hurtling past San caves and Iron-Age mining sites to cascade as majestic waterfalls into rolling mountain valleys and mysterious forests. Among these are the beautiful Malolotja Falls, the highest in Swaziland, the Phophonyane Falls north of Piggs Peak and the Magonigoni Falls to the east.

Swathes of wildflowers, including proteas, cover the slopes of this plateau which gently descends eastwards through the middleveld to the eastern lowveld, a region of thorn trees and grassland, and home to two of Swaziland's premier wildlife sanctuaries — Hlane and Mkhaya. These reserves are host to forest giants such as 1 000-year-old leadwood trees, marulas, wild fig and red ivory trees.

Eastern Swaziland is watered by innumerable rivers and streams, among them the Usutu, Komati, Mlumati, Mbuluzi, Usushwana and Mkhondo — plunging eastwards towards Mozambique and the sea.

On the country's border with Mozambique the land rises sharply to meet the north-south axis of the Lebombo Mountains.

Wildlife

Viewed historically, it's amazing that there's any wildlife in Swaziland at all today. Wholesale slaughter of the country's once-huge wildlife community by European farmers and hunters in the first half of the century nearly destroyed the delicate fabric of wildlife. Hundreds of thousands of wildebeest were slaughtered — many by machine guns — in the 1930s, predators were shot for trophies, and poachers killed for money until the 1960s.

It was only through the intervention of the late King Sobhuza II and game conservationist Ted Reilly that the wildlife was saved.

Today the country's carefully protected reserves host most of the large mammals seen in Southern Africa's other big reserves. Among these are elephants, lions, rhinos, buffaloes, giraffes, jackals, leopards, roan and sable antelope, tsessebe, waterbuck, kudu and nyala.

Reptiles are fairly common — among them pythons, cobras, mambas and adders — while the watercourses are populated by water monitors and crocodiles.

Birds

Swaziland boasts more than 470 species of bird, including one of the rarest species on the subcontinent — the blue swallow. In the forests of Malolotja you'll find Knysna louries, Cape batis, green twinspots and cuckooshrikes, while typical grassland species — ground woodpecker, secretarybird and whitebellied korhaan — inhabit the middle- and lowveld.

The wild places

Five major sanctuaries preserve Swaziland's rich wildlife heritage — Mlilwane Wildlife Sanctuary, Malolotja Nature Reserve, Hlane Royal National Park and Mlawula Nature Reserve.

Mlilwane Wildlife Sanctuary About halfway between Mbabane and Manzini, this rustic sanctuary was the original family farm of Ted Reilly in the Ezulwini Valley.

Today it serves as a tranquil retreat with thatched wooden huts and traditional grass beehive huts overlooking a hippo pool. There's also an attractive restaurant, called the Hippo Haunt, overlooking the pool.

It's an ideal family reserve, with tame animals wandering among the rondavels.

Malolotja Nature Reserve Some hikers rate this wilderness area among the most scenic in Southern Africa. It's a land of lofty peaks, sweeping river valleys, deep green forests, waterfalls — including Swaziland's highest, the 97-m Malolotja Falls — and panoramic views over the South African border near Ngwenya. Visitors may view game by car or on foot along the variety of trails criss-crossing the mountains and valleys.

Hlane Royal National Park This is Swaziland's largest conservation area, which is being held in trust for the nation by King Mswati III. It is a must for any visitor to the kingdom. Elephants, white rhinos, wildebeest, zebra and numerous other mammals, including lions — introduced in 1994 — live here.

Self-catering thatched huts and camping facilities are available.

Mkhaya Game Reserve One of the most affordable game lodges in Southern Africa, Mkhaya is situated in the central lowveld, not far from Siphofaneni. The reserve covers 6 200 ha and is dedicated mainly to the protection of endangered species. Its delightful Stone Camp, friendly staff and rewarding game drives into groups of elephants, buffaloes, white rhinos and various antelope species, make a visit memorable. Guided game drives, walks and waterhole stake-outs are part of the Mkhaya experience.

Mlawula Nature Reserve Extending from the lowveld to the barrier of the Lebombo Mountains, Mlawula covers some 18 000 ha and incorporates Nzindza National Park. Game found here includes wildebeest, impala, zebra, duiker, samango monkeys and Sharpe's grysbok. Mlawula's Sipisi Campground accommodates caravans and tents on the banks of the usually dry Sipusu Stream. There's an ablution block with hot and cold baths, showers and washing-up facilities.

Where to stay

International-standard hotels — some with casinos and swimming pools — are to be found in the major towns, among them the Swazi Inn in Mbabane, the Legogo Sun, the Royal Swazi Sun and the Ezulwini Sun in the Ezulwini Valley and the New George Hotel in Manzini.

Most of the reserves have comfortable accommodation in thatched chalets or offer suitable camping facilities.

Climate

Like South Africa, Swaziland gets plenty of sun throughout the year. The highveld has a temperate climate, with summer temperatures in the low 20s, and winter temperatures some 10 degrees lower. The lowveld, however, can get very hot — up to 40 °C in summer — and enjoys mild to warm winters.

Swaziland is a summer rainfall area, most of the rain (1 000–2 000 mm) falling in the western highveld. Further east towards the lowveld, annual rainfall drops to 500–900 mm.

When to go

As in most Southern African reserves, the best game-viewing months are in winter (May–August), when the vegetation is less dense, and animals are more easily spotted. Birdwatching, however, is best in summer (November–April) when the migratory species are home.

How to get there

By air There are regular flights from Johannesburg, New York, London, Rome, Paris, Frankfurt, Hamburg, Rio de Janeiro, Sydney, Perth, Hong Kong, Lisbon, Brussels, Amsterdam and a host of other European cities to Swaziland. Royal Swazi Air operates services to Nairobi, Dar es Salaam, Lusaka, Harare, Maputo, Johannesburg, Cape Town, Maseru and Entebbe. For further details contact Royal Swazi Airways, PO Box 939, Manzini, tel (09268) 4-3386 or (011) 616-7323.

By road There are five main border posts into Swaziland, the main one being Oshoek–Ngwenya, 22 km west of Mbabane on the South African border. From Johannesburg take the N4 past Middelburg, turn right to Carolina and carry on to the Oshoek–Ngwenya border post (Johannesburg to Ngwenya is 351 km — a four- to five-hour drive).

During peak holiday season you can try the border post at Nerston–Sandlane. From Durban, travel along the North Coast Road via Mtubatuba, Hluhluwe and Mkusi to Golela–Lavumisa, for the main road to Big Bend.

By coach For coach tours to Swaziland from other neighbouring countries, contact Umhlanga Tours, PO Box 2197, Mbabane, tel (09268) 4-6416.

Entry requirements

Foreign visitors to Swaziland must have a valid passport. Some countries are exempt from visa requirements. All visas are issued by the Chief Immigration Officer, Mbabane.

Getting around

By air Scan Air Charter, based at Matsapha Airport at Manzini, offers trips to towns and villages throughout Swaziland and its neighbouring countries in five- or nine-seater aircraft. For details contact Scan Air Charter Ltd, Matsapha Airport, PO Box 1231, Manzini, tel (09268) 8-4474.

By road All the major routes into Swaziland are tarred. A good network of well-signposted, tarred and untarred roads covers Swaziland, giving ready access to game reserves and other wildlife sanctuaries. A massive dual carriageway between Mbabane and Manzini is currently under construction, and the roads between

Mbabane and Mhlambanyatsi, and Siteki and Big Bend are also tarred.

The major car-hire companies are Avis and Hertz (Imperial Car Rental) both of which have offices in Manzini and Matsapha International Airport. Manzini: Avis, tel (09268) 8-6350; Hertz, tel (09268) 8-4393; Matsapha: Avis, tel (09268) 8-6222; Hertz, tel (09268) 8-4393.

Tour operators

Probably the easiest, most comfortable way of seeing Swaziland (and some neighbouring territories) is on a package tour. Highly recommended are Big Game Parks of Swaziland tours, which give you personal attention and expertise on trips to Mkhaya, Hlane and Mlilwane game reserves, as well as trips to neighbouring countries (contact Big Game Parks of Swaziland, PO Box 234, Mbabane, tel (09268) 4-4541). Another major tour operator in Swaziland is Umhlanga Tours, whose packages range from half-day outings from Mbabane to three-day adventure tours incorporating the major reserves.

The tours are personal — in Land Rovers or minibuses — and include, among others, South Africa's Kruger National Park, Hawana Park and the big game reserves of Swaziland (for more details write to PO Box 2197, Mbabane, or tel (09268) 4-6416).

Tip for travellers

Travelling in Swaziland is pleasant and the road surfaces are good. Petrol hours are generally 07:00 to 18:00, although some service stations (particularly in the Ezulwini Valley) are open 24 hours a day.

Health precautions

Visitors from yellow fever or cholera regions must possess valid inoculation certificates. Malaria is endemic in certain parts and a course of antimalarial medication should be taken before your visit. Also be aware of the presence of bilharzia in some dams.

Travel information

Contact Big Game Parks of Swaziland, PO Box 234, Mbabane, tel (09268) 4-4541) or Umhlanga Tours and Safaris, PO Box 2197, Mbabane, tel (09268) 4-6416.

Hlane Royal National Park

Covering some 30 000 ha in northeastern Swaziland on the western border of the Lebombo Mountains, Hlane National Park is the largest conservation area in the kingdom. It also flanks the site of the annual *Butimba* — a week-long royal hunt led by the monarch, after which slaughtered game is presented to him.

'Hlane' means wilderness — and that's what it is — a vast expanse of acacia and broadleaf savannah plains, peppered with bushveld of knobthorn, stunted thickets and dry riverine forests.

Looking down on the wilderness today from the peaks of the Lebombo Mountains in the east, the landscape stretches out in a tapestry of undulating greens and yellows, intersected by the Black Mbuluzi and Mbuluzana rivers.

It is difficult to imagine that amid the pristine beauty and seemingly timeless tranquillity of this lowland paradise animals died in their thousands in poachers' snares; or that game rangers risked their lives trying to prevent the wholesale destruction of game.

Between 1950 and 1960, during the laying of the railroad to Maputo, poaching started in earnest and Hlane's once teeming herds were either drastically reduced or eliminated altogether.

Sensing total destruction, the owner of the Mlilwane Wildlife Sanctuary, Terence Reilly, prevailed on King Sobhuza to intervene, and was appointed official custodian of the park before it was proclaimed in 1967 — a position he holds to this day.

Reilly became known to poachers as 'Msholo' — 'he who sleeps in the bush and appears in unexpected places' — because of the dramatic impact he and his rangers had in stopping poaching altogether.

In a few short years the rangers of Hlane found more animal snares than there were wild ungulates in Swaziland.

Aided by a game restocking programme, which included white rhino and warthog from Mlilwane Wildlife Sanctuary, Hlane's wildlife recovered rapidly. In fact, the recovery was so quick that within a decade Hlane boasted the highest concentration of wildebeest per square kilometre in Africa, including the Serengeti.

Then, on 9 February 1994, came the climax to Hlane's game restocking programme — three young lions, symbol of the Swazi monarch and emblem of the Hlane Royal National Park, returned to King Mswati's kingdom. They had been sent in to Hlane, drugged, from the Kruger National Park, to serve as the nucleus for the propagation of lions in Swaziland.

Wildlife Apart from lions, visitors will see a large variety of mammals and birds (the variety of birds of prey is the largest in the kingdom, and includes the most southerly nesting colony of marabou storks).

Slaughter of the rhinos

Early Dutch settlers called the white rhino the 'wyd' rhino — a reference to its broad mouth. Later, British settlers, misunderstanding the meaning of the word 'wyd', interpreted it as 'white' — hence the name white rhino.

One of Africa's rarest animals, the white rhino once roamed the subcontinent in great numbers, but in the 1850s, after Europeans arrived in Southern Africa, the animal was in grave danger of becoming extinct. Trophy hunters and traders in rhino horn perceived these animals as one of the great prizes of the hunt, and they were mercilessly killed in their thousands.

The slaughter didn't end there. As recently as 1992, white rhinos were massacred at bomas in Hlane by sprays of AK47 bullets, and poachers have targeted this animal throughout Swaziland.

More recently, rangers have been empowered by law to track down poachers, and they are now armed with R5 automatic rifles and LM5 repeaters to defend themselves against indiscriminate firing by poachers.

Stately congregations of elephant gather around the waterholes together with giraffe, waterbuck, kudu, nyala and wildebeest. White rhinos, dehorned for their own safety, are regularly seen in the vicinity of Ndlovu Camp. Smaller mammals include warthogs, mongooses, black-backed jackals and porcupines, while the rivers and their banks teem with hippos and crocodiles.

Game drives and walking trails There are about 100 km of game-viewing roads throughout the park (maps are available at the gate), but heavy rain renders some of these impassable. Enquire about the condition of the roads at Ndlovu Gate before you leave. You may drive yourself, or ask for a ranger to escort you at a nominal fee.

Escorted walking trails through the bush are available daily.

Where to stay Bhubesi or 'Lion' Camp, on the banks of the Mbuluzana River, was opened in April 1991 by King Mswati III. Here the three Hlane stone cottages nestle among riverine bush and hardwood trees, affording a scenic and private retreat for nature-lovers. Each four-bedded cottage has a bathroom, lounge and natural air-

Hlane Royal National Park at a glance

Locality:	Northeastern Swaziland near the Mozambique border.
Climate:	Hot summers (November–March) with peak temperatures in the 40s. Winters (May–August) warm but cool at night. Average annual rainfall 600 mm throughout the year.
Number of camps:	Two.
Game drives:	100 km of game-viewing roads. Self-guided or escorted game drives available.
Hides and waterholes:	Mahlindza Waterhole and Ndlovu Camp Waterhole, plus numerous wallows during the summer months. Hides are being constructed at the moment.
Trails:	A variety of ranger-led walking trails is available.
Amenities:	No shop or restaurant. Nearest shopping centre 10 km from Ndlovu Gate.
Accommodation:	**Bhubesi Camp:** three fully furnished two-bedded self-contained cottages; **Ndlovu Camp:** one three-bedded fully furnished rondavel, as well as one family rondavel with two double bedrooms and a loft with four single beds. Large caravan and camping site available.
Booking address:	Central Reservations, PO Box 234, Mbabane, tel (09268) 4-4541 or 6-1591 after hours. All visits must be booked in advance.
When to go:	Winter is best for game-viewing.
What to take with you:	Warm clothes in winter, walking shoes, torch, hat, camera and binoculars.
How to get there:	Hlane is just 67 km from Manzini on the road to Maputo and the Kruger National Park.
Nearest doctor:	10 km away at Lusoti Village, Simunye.
Nearest petrol:	10 km away at Lusoti Village, Simunye.
Open:	Sunrise to sunset.
Special precautions:	Take antimalaria precautions during the summer months.

conditioning, as well as electricity, stove and fridge. Crockery and cutlery are supplied, as are bedding and towels. Each cottage has its own verandah with an open fireplace and superb view across the river. Footpaths for strollers lead down to the river.

Ndlovu Camp, 18 km from Bhubesi, rests on the edge of a waterhole and offers one three-bed rondavel, and a family rondavel with two double bedrooms downstairs and a loft with four single beds. Both huts are fully furnished and have access to a central ablution block. Paraffin lamps and candles provide lighting, and there's a gas fridge in each hut.

The huts are suitably stocked with bedding, towels, cutlery, crockery, glasses and cooking utensils. A large caravan and camping site is available.

Malolotja Nature Reserve

Hikers who have ventured deep into the heart of Malolotja Nature Reserve get starry-eyed and breathless when they try to describe its hidden treasures. For this pristine mountain wilderness is ranked among the most scenically beautiful places of Southern Africa.

Here soaring peaks surge skywards above a cloak of undulating, flower-covered mountains whose folds conceal kloofs, ravines and gorges, fringed with rich, riverine forests. The valleys and gorges were eroded in the dawn of time by scores of rivers and their tributaries racing down the enigmatic mountains of Malolotja.

In their rampant journey to the low ground such rivers as the Malolotja, Nkomati and Yingayingeeni have laced this mountain wilderness with ribbons of white water cascading down 27 different waterfalls.

For visitors to Malolotja the waterfalls and their magical pools, surrounded in some places by amphitheatres of rock, tree ferns and secret forest glades, represent the very tabernacles of contentment — the closest man can come to true tranquillity in the wild.

Malolotja Nature Reserve itself is relatively close to civilisation — just 15 km from the Oshoek–Ngwenya border post between Swaziland and South Africa, and 35 km north of Mbabane, the country's capital. It covers 18 000 ha of Afro-montane forest, riverine scrub, bushveld and short grassveld.

The highveld terrain ascends two of Swaziland's highest places: Ngwenya Peak (1 829 m) in the south, and Silotfwane Peak (1 680 m) in the west.

Sometimes shrouded in morning mists, at other times sweltering in the summer sun, this landscape is garlanded by a profusion of wildflowers and plants throughout the year. No less than 1 000 plant species — cycad (including the woolly cycad and Kaapsehoop cycad), aloe, protea, red-hot poker, orchid, amarylid, disa and Barberton daisy — bring extravagant colour combinations to the mountain slopes and grasslands which lie between 615 m and 800 m above sea level.

The reserve was named after Swaziland's highest waterfall, the Malolotja Falls, which plummet 90 m into the Nkomati River gorge.

Wildlife There are some 56 species of mammal which roam the hills and valleys. These include leopard, black wildebeest, zebra, red hartebeest, blesbok, black-backed jackal, caracal, serval, honey badger, warthog, bushpig, baboon, vervet monkey, aardwolf, klipspringer, common duiker and impala. Among the endangered, less-seen species at Malolotja are mountain rhebok, grey rhebok and oribi.

Birds More than 280 bird species inhabit the Malolotja wilderness. The valleys are alive with the songs of bee-eaters, cukooshrikes, hornbills, louries and flycatchers, while in the higher areas you'll see Stanley's bustards, buffstreaked chats, ground woodpeckers, blue cranes and nesting colonies of rare blue swallows. Breeding colonies of bald ibises occupy the cliffs above the Malolotja River, while the protea-covered hillsides are a magnet for sunbirds and Gurney's sugarbirds. Other rarer species include African finfoot, broadtailed warbler and blackrumped and Kurrichane buttonquail.

Trails and drives A 200-km network of self-guided trails ranging from short rambles lasting an hour or two, to seven-day hikes, venture deep into the stunning mountain wilderness.

Six day-walks, ranging from two to three-and-a-half hours, may also be undertaken by day visitors or overnight guests. They are:

- The Malolotja Falls Walk, which leads to the point where Swaziland's highest falls cascade into a pool in a forest setting. Along the way you may see a nesting colony of bald ibis;
- The Malolotja Vlei Walk — a botanical excursion revealing displays of flowering orchids, amarylids and lilies in a setting of upland grasslands and swamp;
- Two Upper Majolomba Walks, which take you to the Silotfwane Viewpoint and the Majolomba Gorge;
- The Nkomati Viewpoint Trail, which provides panoramic views of the Nkomati River and pine plantations fringing Piggs Peak; and
- The Gold Mine Walks, which begin and radiate from the car park.

Tips for hikers

- **Some people have experienced problems with the water at Malolotja. If you are sensitive to 'foreign' water, take your own along, or use water-purifying tablets.**
- **When walking, do not feed the baboons and give them right of way if they cross in front of you.**

There are some important points to consider before setting out on a hike. It's very easy to get lost in the reserve if you don't have a detailed map. The trails are not established paths, but rather rough routes following game paths through the bush. Although they are marked with cairns, some are ill defined, particularly towards the south, so you must study your proposed route carefully and discuss it with an official at the tourist office before your departure.

The trails are physically demanding, with very steep climbs, so trailists should be fit, particularly on long hikes.

There are about 25 km of roads open to visitors in the reserve. Guests are free to stop at any point and follow a route of their choice, but must remember that some of these roads are impassable during the rainy season.

Where to stay For backpackers 17 campsites (with no facilities) are scattered throughout the reserve, each one connected to the trail network and accommodating a maximum of 10 people each. Some campsites cater for only one tent, so be sure to plan your overnight stops in accordance with the number in your hiking group.

Some of these campsites lie in spectacular surroundings, among them Lower Mahulungwane (or Camp 12), a riverside stop flanked by a forest and an amphitheatre of rock. Other scenic sites are Upper Mahulungwane campsite and Maphandakazi (Camp 7), which also lies in a forest on the edge of a river.

Main Camp, near the main entrance of the reserve, offers 15 camping sites (some suitable for caravans), five furnished log cabins (each with double beds accommodating six) and an A-frame hut for three. The cabins have a kitchen with stove and fridge, separate bathroom and toilet and lounge with fireplace. The camping sites are served by a communal ablution block, and firewood may be bought at the office. Guests must bring their own provisions and towels.

Other attractions For those with an interest in geology, Malolotja is a living museum of some of the world's oldest

Malolotja Nature Reserve at a glance

Locality:	Northwestern Swaziland, 15 km from Oshoek–Ngwenya border post.
Climate:	Summers warm to hot; winters cold. Average annual rainfall 1 525 mm, mostly in the form of summer thunderstorms.
Number of campsites:	17 campsites for backpackers, some with room for only one tent. Maximum 10 people per site. Main Camp has 15 campsites (some for caravans).
Trails:	200 km, from easy walks to strenuous ascents.
Other attractions:	Stone-Age sites; identifying flowers and plants.
Amenities:	Shop at entrance. One map per party is allocated in the reserve. There are also brochures, fauna and flora checklists and a hiking guide available at the reserve.
Accommodation:	17 campsites (with no facilities) for backpackers; five furnished log cabins (six people each); one A-frame hut (three people); communal ablution block with hot and cold water.
Booking address:	The Warden, Malolotja Nature Reserve, PO Box 1797, Mbabane, tel (09268) 4-3060; or Malolotja Nature Reserve, PO Box 100, Lobamba, tel (09268) 416-1151 or 416-1178.
When to go:	Throughout the year.
What to take with you:	Backpackers must take gas lamp and stove, own provisions (including water), sleeping bag, tent, cutlery and cooking utensils, warm clothing in winter (including anorak), binoculars, camera, compass.
How to get there:	From Swaziland's Oshoek–Ngwenya border post follow the main road to Mbabane for 7 km, then turn left to Forbes Reef and Piggs Peak. The entrance to Malolotja is 8 km further on, along this road.
Nearest doctor:	Mbabane, 35 km away.
Nearest petrol:	Mbabane, 35 km away.
Open:	Summer 06:30–18:30; winter 07:00–18:00.
Special precautions:	Take antimalaria precautions before you leave and during your hike.

fossils — blue-green algae dating back 3,5 billion years are found in the sedimentary rocks which are among the oldest in the world.

In the south, near Ngwenya, is one of the oldest mining sites in the world, Lion Cavern Mine, where Stone-Age miners tapped the rich deposits of haematite-chert ironstones 41 000 ago. They used the ironstones to make their tools, an abundance of which were found on the northeastern side of the mine — a terraced pit containing deep pools of water.

Anglers may catch trout in the dam and river (angling licences are available at the reserve), and if that's not enough, visitors may consider a walk to the Barberton Cycad Forest or the Komati River Valley.

Mkhaya Game Reserve

Bone-jarring thuds reverberate through your body as the open Land Rover bumps through the bush of Mkhaya Game Reserve. You hang on grimly, and duck as the branches of acacia trees and sicklebushes swing towards you with their needle-sharp spikes seeking soft skin. The vehicle dips down into a donga, hurtles up the other side, surmounts the crest, and brings you face-to-face with two tons of raw menace. The black rhino right in front of you snorts, shakes its head and veers off at a canter into the undergrowth.

This is the heart of Mkhaya Game Reserve, an unforgettable bushveld paradise in eastern Swaziland, where you can get so close to the large mammals that you can literally touch them. More importantly, however, Mkhaya is one of Africa's great refuges for endangered species, a sanctuary where you are more likely to see black rhino than anywhere else in the world.

The reserve is the brainchild of world-renowned conservationist Ted Reilly, who started it in 1979 as a sanctuary for pure-bred Nguni cattle, threatened with extinction because of crossbreeding. The programme was so successful that Reilly, backed by the Swaziland Monarchy, the South African World Wildlife Foundation and other foreign bodies, decided to develop Mkhaya into a fully-fledged game sanctuary.

His associations with Mlilwane Wildlife Sanctuary (formerly the Reilly family's farm) and the Hlane National Park, which he also runs, virtually guaranteed Mkhaya's success.

Wildlife Today Mkhaya teems with a cosmopolitan wildlife community: from elephants which lumber through the bush to white rhinos basking in mud wallows. The variety of mammals is endless — buffaloes, giraffes, roan and sable antelope, tsessebe, waterbuck, kudu, nyala, reedbuck, zebras, wildebeest, red and grey duiker, steenbok, warthogs, impala and ostriches soak in the luxury of undisturbed wilderness, while crocodiles and hippos bask on the sand banks and in the waterholes.

Less conspicuous are Mkhaya's hyenas, jackals, leopards, pythons and the smaller mammals, such as mongooses. But the most important mammals at Mkhaya are the six black rhinos, Africa's second most endangered land mammal.

Birdlife There are more than 100 species of bird, including such raptors as booted, crowned, tawny and martial eagles, bateleurs, and whiteheaded, lappetfaced, whitebacked, southern hooded and Cape vultures. Swaziland's national bird, the purplecrested lourie, crested guineafowl, Narina trogons and pink-throated twinspots are common visitors to Stone Camp. You'll also see African jacanas, goshawks, parrots, francolins, egrets and hornbills in and around the camps.

Getting around The Mkhaya brochure tells you that here you will find 'real bush, real thorns and really bad roads'. The roads are so bad, in fact, that rangers meet you on the main road outside the reserve and escort you to the rangers' base where you swop your car for a ranger-driven Land Rover for the duration of your visit. There are no regrets, however — the 4x4-drives up sandy riverbeds, dongas and through thick pockets of bush are exhilarating and exciting.

Where to stay A cool summerhouse, 10 safari tents, a stone cottage and a central eating area fringed by giant leadwoods, sausage trees and sycamore figs entice visitors to stay at Stone Camp on the banks of the dry and sandy Little Crocodile River.

The large canvas tents here each sleep a family of three or four, and are furnished with single or double beds, chests and washstands. The tents are spaced well apart to ensure maximum privacy under the trees. The hot-and-cold-water showers and toilets are open to the bush, so that you can revel in the sights and sounds of nature while you shower.

Accommodation of a more luxurious nature is available at the exclusive Nkonjane Cottage. The name Nkonjane (Swallow's Nest) comes from the cottage's dolerite rocks, which resemble the mud encasing of swallows' nests. The outer walls are just one metre high, giving the occupants full exposure to the bush beyond.

Swazi hostesses prepare all your meals on an open fire, and the aromatic flavours of traditional dishes waft through the camp from bubbling black pots as night descends on the camp. Dishes include impala, warthog and wildebeest steaks, braaied on the coals.

As evening settles over Stone Camp, you can sit outside your tent or cottage and listen to the sounds of bushbabies, nightjars and owls in the trees above you. In the distance you may hear the whinny of a zebra, the shriek of hyenas or the baying call of the blackbacked jackal.

Game trails and drives Day and night drives, transporting up to eight people, are offered in open Land Rovers. The day drives, starting at 10:00 and ending at 16:00, include a mouth-watering venison lunch.

Heart of the giraffe

One of the finest examples of nature's gifts to her children is the amazing circulatory system of the giraffe.

The massive heart, weighing up to 11 kg, is the greatest pump in the wild, capable of pumping blood three metres up the long neck into the giraffe's brain.

To prevent the blood flooding the brain, or evacuating it when the animal stoops to drink, nature has given it a highly efficient multiple transmission system, located at the base of the brain.

This system, known as *rete mirabile*, controls the animal's blood pressure by regulating the expansion of the small arteries, thereby allowing normal oxygenation of the brain.

Bush walks are very popular and bring hikers into contact not only with the larger animals, but also the smaller creatures of the ground: antlions, rhino beetles, leopard tortoises, buffalo weavers and elephant shrews.

Special attractions Apart from the night drives, one of the treats at Mkhaya is the Sibhaca dance routines staged by the rangers and staff. This is real African cabaret, providing a colourful and fascinating end to a day in the bush.

Another attraction is white-water rafting down the Great Usutu River as it forces its way through the Bulungu Gorge near Mkhaya. One-day trips in tough, eight-man inflatable rafts are available during summer, with smaller two-man 'croc rafts' used in the drier winter period.

These not only offer the ride of a lifetime, but also the chance to see basking crocodiles, beautiful waterfalls and stunning natural scenery. Equipment is provided, and the only requirement to take part is the spirit of adventure. Trips in winter include the chance to try your hand at abseiling, using mountaineering gear right alongside the Bulunga Falls.

No experience is required for these activities but general age limits are 16 and 65, although these can be adjusted at the expedition leader's discretion. Minors need parental approval.

Mkhaya Game Reserve at a glance

Locality: Eastern Swaziland, 90 minutes' drive from Mbabane.
Climate: Summers hot, with temperatures in the high 40s. Winters: warm days, cold nights.
Number of camps: One.
Game drives: Day and night ranger-driven jaunts available. Night drives with spotlights.
Hides and waterholes: There are a variety of waterholes where you may stop and view game.
Trails: Walking trails are led by Swazi rangers.
Other attractions: White-water rafting on the Great Usutu River, and abseiling.
Accommodation: **Stone Camp** accommodates 34 people in five standard and five luxury safari tents, as well as a stone cottage. Each tent sleeps three or four, and has access to hot and cold water showers and toilets. The luxury suites offer *en suite* facilities. **Nkonjane Cottage** is more luxurious and open to the bush.
Booking address: Mbabane Central Reservations Office, Mkhaya Nature Reserve, PO Box 234, Mbabane, tel (09268) 4-4541 or 6-1591 after hours. All visits must be booked in advance.
When to go: All year round.
What to take with you: Warm clothes in winter; light bush clothes in summer. Binoculars, torch and camera.
How to get there: Drive east from Manzini, past Siphofaneni to Phuzumoya. After you cross the bridge at Phuzumoya, turn left on to a dirt road, and stop at the shop signposted Mkhaya. A ranger will meet you there and escort you into the reserve.
Open: Rangers meet visitors outside the entrance at 10:00 and 16:00 daily.
Special precautions: Take antimalaria precautions before visiting Mkhaya.

Mlilwane Wildlife Sanctuary

Mlilwane, the oldest and most-visited park in the kingdom of Swaziland, lies between the Ezulwini and the Malkerns Valley in what locals call the Valley of Heaven — a scenic and tranquil retreat backdropped by the forest-fringed, cobalt humps of the Swazi escarpment.

For the wildlife populations of Swaziland, Mlilwane ('little fire') is indeed a piece of heaven, for without it and the amazing conservation efforts of the country's Reilly family, the game in Swaziland would probably have disappeared altogether. They turned their 460-ha family farm into a sanctuary for the country's beleaguered animals.

For it was here, in the lush bushveld beneath the granite peaks of Nyonyane ('place of the small bird') and Sheba's Breasts that the remnants of the decimated animal communities found shelter, survival and renewal in an intensive game-relocation programme undertaken by the Reillys. It was fitting that this rescue programme took place not far from Lobamba, site of Swaziland's Royal Kraal and traditional heart of the kingdom.

In the old days, when the San lived among the caves of the escarpment, the valley and plains teemed with herds of plains mammals, converging from the lowveld and highveld.

During the 1930s and 1940s vast columns of wildebeest, impala and zebras, stretching from one horizon to the other, were observed from vantage points on the Lebombo and Malindza mountains.

Game was so abundant, in fact, that local cattle farmers viewed some species as a scourge. During the 1930s great migrations of wildebeest moving down from the Komati flats were halted by any means possible. One hunting group mounted a Vickers machine gun on the back of a pick-up truck and fired indiscriminately into the migrating herds.

Waterholes were poisoned with cyanide by some farmers, while others just ran animals down with their vehicles.

The hunter's bullet and the poacher's snare aggravated the situation. In the late 1930s the last tsessebe was killed, and in 1961 the last roan antelope was found dead in a snare.

Today Mlilwane, the proud mother of conservation, is a favourite destination for lovers of wildlife in Southern Africa, attracting guests from all over the world.

Wildlife Officially opened on 12 July 1974, Mlilwane has grown tenfold since then to cover 4 650 ha. Today it is home to 40 species of larger mammal, and 238 species of bird. Among the rarer of its feathered residents are the endangered blue crane, longcrested eagle, crowned eagle and black eagle.

Large herds of impala, blue wildebeest, zebra and blesbok roam the Shonalanga and Phumalanga plains, while the riverine bush and reedbeds provide a valuable habitat for nyala, kudu and giraffe. For many years Mlilwane supported the only protected populations of hippo, sable and eland, but the main focus of these relocation programmes has since shifted to the superior lowveld habitat offered at the sister park, Mkhaya.

Other regularly seen species include klipspringer, waterbuck, common and mountain reedbuck, red duiker, serval and antbear. Mlilwane has also been responsible for bringing Swaziland's population of warthogs back from the brink of extinction (there were just 14 in Mlilwane originally), and has successfully exported warthogs to Hlane, Mkhaya and Malolotja game reserves.

Among the reptiles are crocodiles, pythons and garter-snakes.

Local fish, amphibian, and invertebrate communities have also been restored and augmented in a recreation of Swaziland's fauna as they were before the advent of humankind.

Mlilwane also serves as an orphanage for injured and abandoned animals, which are often hand-reared before being returned to the wild.

Where to stay Mlilwane's Rustic Rest Camp is unique for the numbers of tame animals that walk among the huts and tents day and night. Every day at 15:00 hippos, warthogs and birds congregate at the camp's hippo pool for 'feeding time', competing for scraps of food scattered almost at the feet of visitors.

Main Camp has a comfortable choice of accommodation, which includes a fully equipped, self-contained cottage ('Shonalonga'), two five-bed huts, four two-bed huts and two two-bed beehive huts. All the huts at Main Camp have new *en suite* shower and toilet facilities. The Beehive Village offers two three-bed beehive huts, five two-bed beehive huts and six 'dormitories', each with two double bunks, and a communal lounge, kitchen and diningroom. There's also an attractive camping and caravan site with communal washing and ablution facilities.

With the exception of Shonalonga, the rest camp is for self-catering visitors, and cutlery, crockery and cooking equipment are not provided. However, the Hippo Haunt Restaurant provides meals from breakfast through to dinner. This is the ideal place to relax in comfort and watch game come down to drink at the lake below.

Thunderous roar of the hippo

One of the night sounds commonly heard at Mlilwane is the hippo's bellow — usually a long, roaring grunt followed by four or five shorter ones.

The animals emerge — males first — from the water at night for supper, wandering as far as 30 km in their quest for food: mainly grass, which they crop with the tough edges of their enormous lips, but also leaves, shoots, bulbs and tubers, as well as domestic crops on which they can wreak havoc.

In one night an adult hippo can cram more than 100 kg of grass and other food into its multi-chambered, 200-litre stomach.

At dawn, the hippos return to their watery home, leaving a very well-defined double track of footprints in the sand, grass or mud. Often these hippo tracks serve to connect watercourses that have been separated by a receding waterline.

Fires are lit at braai places throughout the camp for the use of visitors (grids supplied), and special Hog-on-the-spit parties with Sibhaca dancing may be arranged guaranteeing an unforgettable evening.

Reilly's Rock Hilltop Lodge is the only retreat of its kind in Swaziland. It is situated on Mlilwane Hill and has stunning views of the valleys around it. The lodge is a favourite among families and businesses looking for an 'Out of Africa' experience in comfortable surroundings.

Other attractions at the rest camp are a river pool and a regular pool.

Game drives and trails Gamewatching trails are available by road, on foot or on horseback. More than 100 km of gravel roads provide exceptional game-viewing opportunities for motorists, who may take a guide with them at a modest fee. Guided game-viewing trips in open 4x4s are offered during the day and assisted by spotlight at night.

The Macobane Mountain Trail offers spectacular views and an easy gradient, while the newly completed Mhlambanyatsi and Hippo trails offer good birdwatching opportunities.

Mlilwane Wildlife Sanctuary at a glance

Locality:	Central Swaziland, about 24 km from Mbabane.
Climate:	Summer: hot, temperatures in high 40s. Winter: warm days, cold nights.
Number of camps:	One.
Game drives:	100 km of gravel roads.
Hides and waterholes:	An elevated hide at Main Camp, Hippo Dam and at strategic viewsites at other dams.
Trails:	Macobane Trail as well as several ranger-led walks and horseback trails.
Other attractions:	Tame animals in camp; animal feeding at the Hippo Pool, two pools.
Amenities:	Hippo Haunt Restaurant, shop selling curios, basic provisions and drinks.
Accommodation:	**Main Camp:** Self-contained cottage, two five-bed huts, four two-bed huts and two two-bed beehive huts. **Beehive Village** offers two three-bed beehive huts, five two-bed beehive huts and six 'dormitories'. Reilly's Rock Hilltop Lodge provides accommodation for families and also serves as a conference centre.
Booking address:	Central Reservations, PO Box 234, Mbabane, tel (09268) 4-4541 or 6-1591 after hours. All visits must be booked in advance.
When to go:	All year round.
What to take with you:	Own provisions, cutlery, crockery and cooking equipment (with exception of self-contained cottage).
How to get there:	Mlilwane is 378 km from Johannesburg and 547 km from Durban. From Johannesburg enter Swaziland through the Oshoek-Ngwenya border post to Mbabane, then drive south for 24 km. The main gate is on the right. From Durban enter Swaziland at Golela, head north for Big Bend, then westward to Manzini. Mlilwane Rest Camp is 26 km west of Manzini.
Nearest doctor:	Mbabane, 24 km away.
Nearest petrol:	In the rest camp.
Open:	Main gate: dawn to dusk; night gate (in the south): dusk to dawn.
Special precautions:	Antimalaria precautions should be taken before your trip.

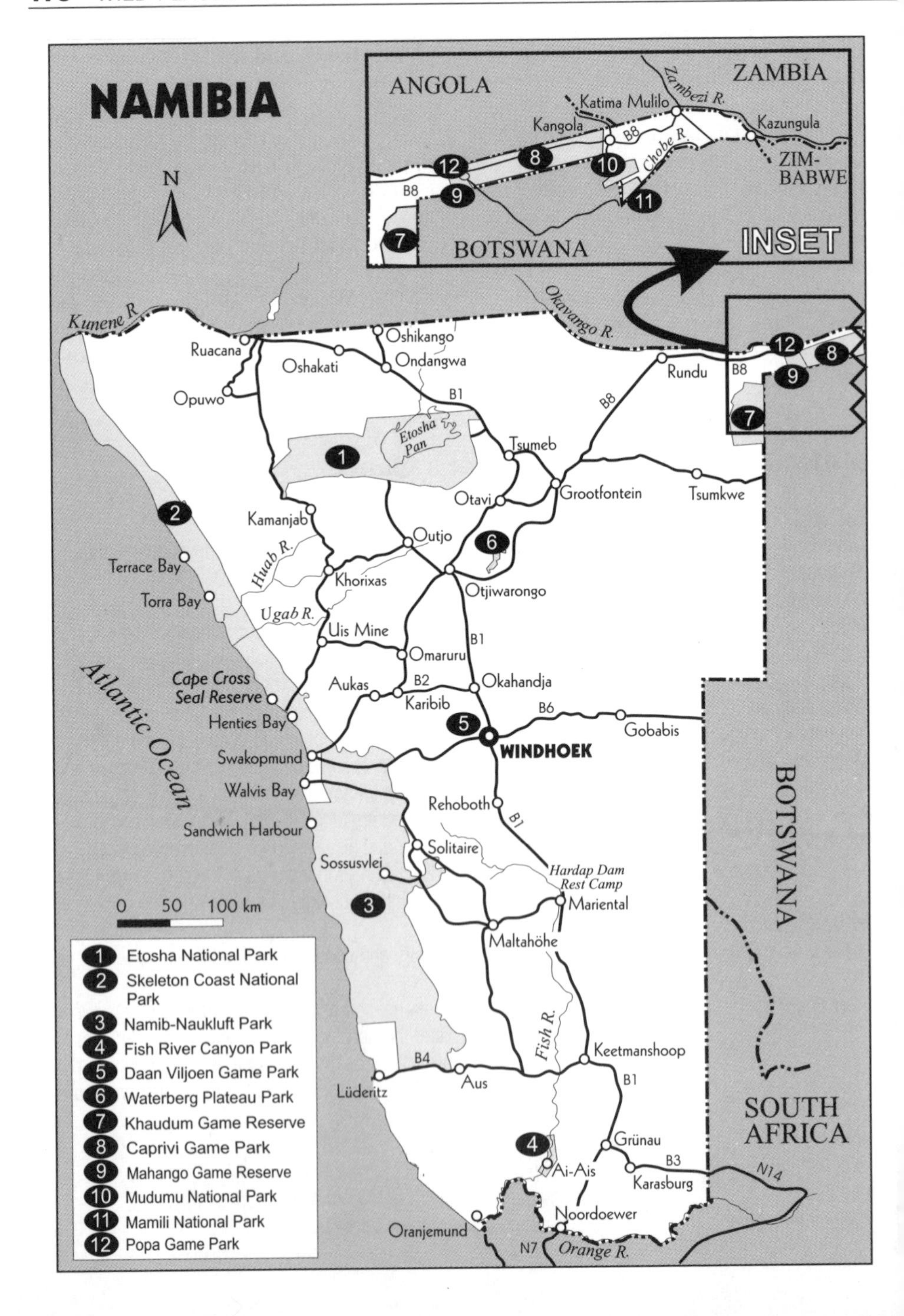
NAMIBIA
N
ANGOLA
ZAMBIA
Katima Mulilo
Zambezi R.
Kangola
Kazungula
B8
Chobe R.
ZIM-
BABWE
B8
BOTSWANA
INSET
Kunene R.
Okavango R.
Ruacana
Oshikango
Oshakati
Ondangwa
Opuwo
B1
Rundu
B8
Etosha Pan
Tsumeb
Grootfontein
Tsumkwe
Otavi
Kamanjab
Outjo
Terrace Bay
Huab R.
Khorixas
Otjiwarongo
Torra Bay
Ugab R.
Uis Mine
B1
Omaruru
Atlantic Ocean
Cape Cross
Seal Reserve
Aukas
B2
Okahandja
Karibib
B6
Henties Bay
Gobabis
Swakopmund
WINDHOEK
Walvis Bay
Rehoboth
B1
BOTSWANA
Sandwich Harbour
Solitaire
Sossusvlei
Hardap Dam
Rest Camp
0 50 100 km
Mariental
Maltahöhe
Fish R.
Keetmanshoop
B4
Lüderitz
Aus
B1
SOUTH
AFRICA
Grünau
B3
Ai-Ais
Karasburg
N14
Noordoewer
Oranjemund
N7
Orange R.
1 Etosha National Park
2 Skeleton Coast National Park
3 Namib-Naukluft Park
4 Fish River Canyon Park
5 Daan Viljoen Game Park
6 Waterberg Plateau Park
7 Khaudum Game Reserve
8 Caprivi Game Park
9 Mahango Game Reserve
10 Mudumu National Park
11 Mamili National Park
12 Popa Game Park

NAMIBIA

Larger than Texas and about four times the size of the United Kingdom, Namibia covers 824 268 km^2 along the western seaboard of Southern Africa. It shares common boundaries with Botswana and Zimbabwe in the east, South Africa in the south and Angola in the north. It is remarkable for having won its independence in 1990 after 106 years of foreign rule.

To visitors approaching from the south it is seen as a wild frontier — a gateway to endless dune seas, a ghostly coastline and an untamed interior of gravel plains, grasslands and wooded parkland where animals roam free in large numbers.

The country has one of the smallest populations in the world — one person per 1,7 km^2, or 1,4 million inhabitants nationwide. For the game-watcher this means unpopulated, wide-open spaces, distant reserves where you may drive for a day without seeing another soul, and a pristine wilderness, unlittered, unfenced and ecologically sound.

Wherever you travel in Namibia, there's a feeling of timelessness, where three-toed dinosaur footprints embedded in shale 200 million years ago could well have been left there yesterday; where you expect San to walk out of caves they inhabited in the Stone Age, and where fossilised trees and petrified forests stand as silent witnesses to 240 million summers.

The land

The Namib Desert forms a coastal plain which runs 140 km from north to south along the Atlantic seaboard, and extends 50 km inland. The desolate western fringes of this plain are known as the Skeleton Coast — graveyard of ships and men, and one of the most inhospitable places on earth.

Inland the Namib's corrugated dunes ascend gently to a central plateau — a rugged gravel plain cleaved by sandy valleys and ridged with ancient mountains. To the north lie the enormous salt pans and bush-covered plains of one of the world's great wildlife sanctuaries, the Etosha National Park, and, further east the woodland savannah of Kavango and Eastern Caprivi.

Wildlife

Like other Southern African countries, there's no shortage of game: 136 species of mammal, including the Big Five (elephant, rhinoceros, buffalo, hippopotamus and lion), giraffe, Hartmann's mountain zebra, Burchell's zebra and relatively rare species such as the honey badger and antbear.

The country is home to 20 species of antelope, from the tiny Damara dik-dik to plains animals such as tsessebe, roan antelope, eland, springbok and wildebeest. Such an abundance of prey attracts a variety of predators: spotted hyenas, wild dogs and blackbacked and sidestriped jackals.

Namibia also has the world's largest population of wild cheetah — between 2 000 and 3 000. It is also one of few African countries whose population of black rhino is growing.

Namibia is a birder's paradise: more than 620 of the 887 species listed in Southern Africa are found here. At least 500 of them nest here, including the fish eagle and sociable weaver, the latter in massive communal nests up to 100 years old.

The wild places

There are 20 game reserves and recreational areas, which together cover about 15 per cent of Namibia's land surface.

The most sought-after wildlife destination is the Etosha National Park, which covers 22 270 km^2 in the northern part of the country. The other major sanctuaries are the Namib-Naukluft Park, the Skeleton Coast Park, Khaudum Game Reserve, the Caprivi Game Park, the Waterberg Plateau Park, the Fish River Canyon Park in the south, and smaller conservancies such as Mahango Game Reserve and Mamili National Park.

Etosha National Park

A visit to Etosha is quite unforgettable. Among the memories you're likely to bring back are elephants crossing the road, wildebeest trekking across the endless horizons of the salt pans or lionesses stalking a kill at the Okaukuejo waterhole. The huge animal populations — 20 000 springbok, 300 lions and 1 500 elephants — guarantee good gamewatching.

Namib-Naukluft Park

This park is the largest in Africa, and the fourth-largest wildlife destination in the world. Its attractions are dealt with in detail in the individual entries, but some of its more memorable attributes are the stunning dune formations at Sossusvlei, the amazing community of animals that survive in the shifting sand-dunes of the Namib Desert and the wonderful, tranquil camping sites where you can lie under the stars and see the heavens as you'll see them nowhere else on earth.

Skeleton Coast Park

Travellers may visit the southern section of this park, which covers 1,5 million ha of one of the world's most treacherous coastlines. Solitude, silence, an amazing world of desert-adapted flora and fauna (including the prehistoric plant, *Welwitschia mirabilis*) and excellent angling are just a few of the attractions that lure visitors here.

Waterberg Plateau Park

This is one of the most underrated parks in the country, but a stay at this park's Bernabé de la Bat Rest Camp will bring you back for more. Hiking and bush trails take you into big-game country (the reserve also hosts rare and endangered species), and the views from the ramparts of Etjo sandstone are quite magnificent.

The park lies just east of the B1 highway southeast of Etosha, and a stop here could be included on your way to or from the pan.

Caprivi Region

The Caprivi Game Park, Popa Falls, the floodplains of the Kavango and Kwando rivers, Mahango Game Park, Mamili National Park and the Khaudum Game Park could all be part of your itinerary in the Caprivi area. Take a good field guide

▲ **58**

▲ **59**

▲ **60**

▲ **61**

58 Beautiful beaches such as this one lure travellers to the sultry shores of the Maputaland coast.
59 The interior of one of the rooms at Rocktail Bay Lodge, one of Wilderness Safaris' exceptional destinations.
60 Milkwood trees, palms and other indigenous vegetation form an idyllic setting for the cosy chalets at Rocktail Bay Lodge.
61 The Maputaland coast is special for its unspoilt, uncrowded beaches.

62 ▼

▲ 63

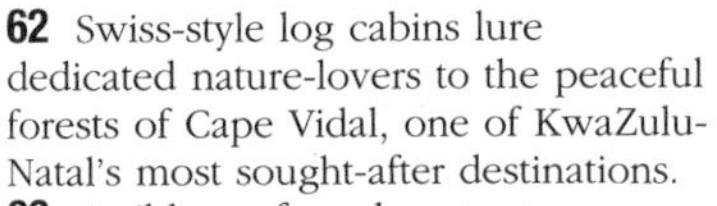

62 Swiss-style log cabins lure dedicated nature-lovers to the peaceful forests of Cape Vidal, one of KwaZulu-Natal's most sought-after destinations.
63 A ribbon of sand contrasts beautifully with the turquoise, white-crested sea of the Maputaland coast near Cape Vidal.
64 Sinuous lines of sand-dunes near Cape Vidal capture the sensuous magic of a place unmarked by the footprints of man.
65 The sands between Kosi Bay and Rocktail Bay are among the most important breeding grounds for leatherback turtles in the world.
66 Cosy interior view of a chalet lounge at Singita Game Reserve in Mpumalanga.

64 ▼

65 ▼

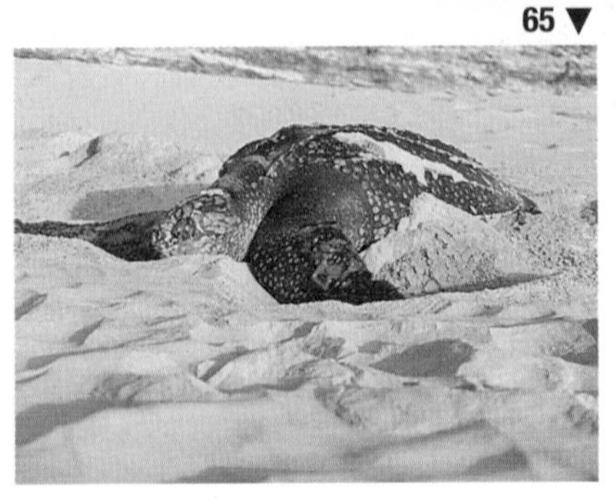

66 ▼

67 The magnificent sweep of the Amphitheatre forms a stunning backdrop to Tendele Rest Camp in the Royal Natal National Park.
68 Devil's Tooth, viewed from Tugela Gorge in the Royal Natal National Park.
69 Trees shelter the chalets at Notten's Bush Camp just inside the gate of Sabi Sand Game Reserve.

▲ 67

▲ 69

68 ▼

▲ 70

▲ 72

▲ 71

▲ 73

▲ 74

▲ 75

70 A crackling fire and good company are all that's needed at the end of a day at Djuma Bush Lodge in Sabi Sand Game Reserve.
71 Hunter's Lodge, run by Exeter Safaris, is a colonial-style camp with a beautiful swimming pool.
72 Long Lee Manor at Shamwari Game Reserve accommodates guests in de luxe, period-style bedrooms.
73 Five spacious double bungalows such as these accommodate guests at Leadwood Lodge.
74 Exeter Lodge in Sabi Sand Game Reserve lies under shade trees on the banks of the Sand River.
75 Albino bontebok are a rarity, but you'll see them at Shamwari Game Reserve.

▲ 76

77 ▼

78 ▼

76 The Tsitsikamma Hiking Trail offers hikers superb views of distant mountains, forest and sea.
77 An overnight cabin overlooks a steep gorge along the Tsitsikamma Hiking Trail.
78 Rugged, bush-covered mountains plummet to the sea in the Tsitsikamma National Park.

79 ▼

79 Dawn breaks with gentle serenity along the fringes of the beautiful coastline near Tsitsikamma National Park.
80 Indian Ocean breakers crash against the rocky shoreline of Tsitsikamma National Park.
81 Huge, creeper-clad trees are typical of the Tsitsikamma forest.

81 ▲

▼ 80

▲ 82

▲ 83

▲ 84

▲ 85

82 An umdoni tree stands as a lone sentinel above the lowlands of Umfolozi Game Reserve.
83 Gqoyeni Bush Camp in Umfolozi Game Reserve, which is world-renowned for its rhinos and ranger-led bush trails.
84 Rustic huts at Umfolozi's Mpila Camp, where you can see animals wandering among the green terraces on moonlit nights.
85 South Africa's long coastline offers hikers unsurpassed sunsets and the company of seabirds, seals and whales.

▲ 86

87 ▼

▲ 88

▲ 89

86 The change of seasons turns the barren coastline of the West Coast National Park into a colourful display of spring flowers.
87 The rich reds and pinks of *Protea compacta* bring colour to the interior of the West Coast National Park.
88 Peaceful coves and placid waters impart a spirit of serenity to the shores of Langebaan Lagoon in the West Coast National Park.
89 The moon gives a ghostly sheen to the Atlantic off the West Coast National Park.

▲ 90

▲ 91

90 A hippo hurtles through the water at Mahlindza waterhole in Swaziland's Hlane Royal National Park.

91 Gamewatchers on horseback in the long grass of Mlilwane Wildlife Sanctuary, Swaziland.

▼ 92

93 ▼

94 ▼

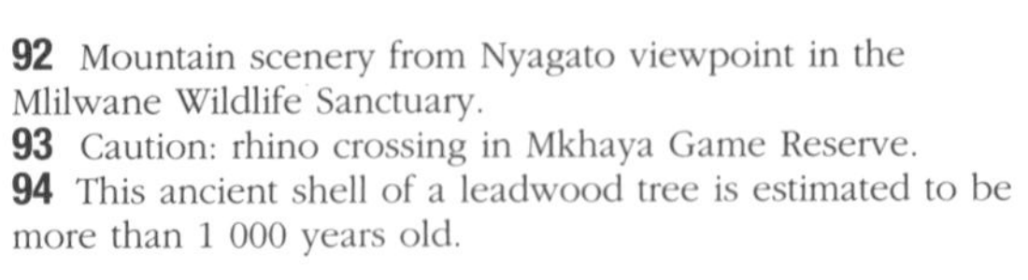

92 Mountain scenery from Nyagato viewpoint in the Mlilwane Wildlife Sanctuary.
93 Caution: rhino crossing in Mkhaya Game Reserve.
94 This ancient shell of a leadwood tree is estimated to be more than 1 000 years old.

95 ▼

96 ▼

97 ▼

▲ 98

95 Silent submarines at sunset – hippo at Mahlindza waterhole, Hlane National Park.
96 A formidable regiment of white rhino at Mkhaya.
97 A crocodile slithers towards water at Mkhaya Game Reserve.
98 A female giraffe and her calf at Mkhaya Game Reserve.

99 The enchanting sand-dunes of Sossusvlei in Namibia offer visitors an unequalled experience of the wilderness in one of the most remote destinations in the world.
100 Dwarfed by dunes, four springbok pause in a dry riverbed near Sossusvlei.
101 The amazing sandscapes of the Namib have been sculpted over aeons by the wind.

▲ **99**

▲ **100**

▲ **101**

▼ 104

105 ▲

102 A typical 'participation' safari tent, such as those used by Afro Ventures on trans-African safaris.
103 The Skeleton Coast is littered with the bones of wrecked ships, among them this one at Pelican Point.
104 Two elephants lumber through the golden grasslands of northern Namibia.
105 Gamewatchers in Namibia pause to watch a lioness pad by.

▲ 106

107 ▼

106 Canoeists ease along the Orange River in Namibia.
107 Cheetah at Okonjima Guest Farm, a stopover for travellers on safari from Etosha National Park.
108 Twyfelfontein in Namibia has one of the subcontinent's richest stores of San rock art.

▼ 108

▲ 109

110 ▼

109 A simple track through the veld leads gamewatchers deep into the heart of Namibia's wild country.

110 These quiver trees are especially adapted to withstand the arid, hot conditions so typical of southern Namibia.

▲ 111

112 ▼

111 The remote Saruza's Camp in the desolate reaches of the Skeleton Coast National Park.
112 It's safety in numbers for this family of giraffes at a waterhole in the Etosha National Park.

to birds, because the birding is excellent here (339 species in the Caprivi Game Park alone). Be sure to stop off at Lianshulu or Namushasha lodges — they're among the best in the country.

Where to stay

Accommodation varies from luxury hotels to game lodges, guest farms, rest camps, caravan sites and tented camps.

The Ministry of Environment and Tourism runs 15 rest camps in the game reserves. These accommodate visitors in bungalows, tents and luxury chalets. The camping and caravan facilities are clean and spacious, and usually include access to a braai area and an ablution block.

The rest camps do not supply cooking utensils, crockery and cutlery, but most of them have shops which supply basic provisions — fresh meat, bread, dairy products, beer and wine.

Luxury lodges are as good as any you'll find on the continent.

Ongava Lodge, which won the best guest farm award for 1993/1994, offers 10 double chalets with panoramic views over a waterhole and superb gamewatching opportunities on the slopes of the Ondundozonananandana range on the southwestern border of Etosha National Park. Other excellent lodges are Mokuti Lodge, Etosha Aoba Lodge and Hobatere Lodge.

Although the national parks, game reserves and private lodges attract the lion's share of visitors to Namibia, tourists are now savouring the delights of a very new attraction — the country guest farm. There are no less than 67 of these throughout Namibia, many of which offer gamewatching drives, hikes and a wonderful atmosphere of farm life in relaxing surroundings.

Among these are Phillip's Guest Farm, on the road to Karibib, Ameib Ranch near the famous Phillip's Cave, Immenhof Guest Farm near Omaruru and Schonfeld Guest Farm, also near Omaruru.

For more details on lodges and guest farms write to Namibia Tourism, Private Bag 13346, Windhoek 9000, or tel (09264-61) 284-2178. You can also contact them in Johannesburg at 11 Alice Lane, 3rd Floor, East Wing, Standard Bank Building, PO Box 78946, Sandton City 2196, tel (011) 784-8024/5 or in Cape Town at Ground Floor, Main Tower, Standard Bank Centre, Adderley Street, PO Box 739, Cape Town 8000, tel (021) 419-3190.

Climate

If you're looking for a place in the sun, Namibia's your destination. About 300 sunshine days a year guarantee a winter tan and warmth most of the year. Between October and February daytime temperatures soar to between 35 °C and 42 °C, while nights are warm to hot with temperatures often around 25 °C.

The winter days are sunny and clear, although frost may occur occasionally at night. The rainy season begins in October and extends through to April. While drenching thunderstorms do occur, some seasons pass with very little rain, and winter rain is almost unheard of.

When to go

Because of the heat in summer, winter (May–September) is usually preferred for visiting Etosha and the game reserves of the interior. The best time for birding, however, is between December and April when large numbers of migrants are here, particularly in the Etosha Pan and Mahango Game Reserve in the Caprivi Region.

Book your trip to Namibia well in advance — game reserves and recreational areas are in huge demand during the school holidays.

How to get there

By air Namibia's main concourse is Windhoek International Airport. International airlines landing here include South African Airways, Air Botswana, Air Zimbabwe, Air France, Lufthansa, TAAG and LTU. There are flights from Johannesburg to Windhoek daily, and flights from Cape Town to Windhoek every Friday and Sunday. Air Namibia flies regularly to London and Frankfurt, and offers regional flights to Harare, Victoria Falls, Livingstone, Johannesburg and Cape Town.

By road Two major highways have just been built — the Trans-Caprivi Highway, which links Namibia to Botswana, Zambia and Zimbabwe; and the Trans-Kalahari Highway, which links Windhoek, Gaborone and Johannesburg, and cuts 400 km off the old route.

The traditional north-south route from Cape Town is along the N7, an excellent highway which becomes the B1 as it enters Namibia at Noordoewer.

From Johannesburg, the best way to Windhoek is via Vryburg, Kuruman and Upington, and then along the B3 to Karasburg, which joins the B1 to Windhoek at Grunau.

By coach Intercape Mainliner runs comfortable coach trips from Windhoek to Johannesburg, and from Windhoek to Cape Town four times a week, while Ekono Liner operates a similar service to Cape Town once a week.

There are 30 border posts in Namibia. The main ones are: Namibia and South Africa — Noordoewer, Oranjemund, Ariamsvlei, Velloorsdrift and Hohlweg; Namibia and Botswana — Buitepos, Mohembo and Ngoma; Namibia and Zambia — Katima Mulilo; Namibia and Angola — Rundu, Oshikango, Omahenene and Ruacana.

Tips for travellers

- In 1994 Namibia introduced winter daylight saving from 21 March to 21 September. During this time the country is one hour ahead of South Africa.
- Permits to enter parks are paid for when checking in to the rest camp. To drive through the Skeleton Coast National Park or the Namib section of the Namib-Naukluft Park, you'll need a permit, which is available at the Central Reservations Office in Windhoek.
- Animals crossing the road at night, particularly kudu, are a common danger to motorists. Drive slowly and carefully.
- Check road conditions wherever you go in Namibia. Some roads, particularly in the far north, are sandy, have potholes and turn slippery in rainy weather.
- Although walking is allowed in many wilderness areas, watch out for dangerous animals, particularly in Khaudum, Mahango, Mudumu and Mamili parks.

Entry requirements

Foreign visitors need a valid passport to enter Namibia, as well as a visa. Nationals of some countries, including South Africa, don't need a visa. Holidaymakers may stay up to three months.

Getting around

By air Internal flights link up with such destinations as Mokuti Lodge near Etosha, Etosha National Park, Ondwanga, Tsumeb, Katima Mulilo, Lüderitz, Keetmanshoop, Walvis Bay, Oranjemund and Oshakati.

You can get to most of the parks and reserves by luxury coach, self-drive cars, fly-in safaris or regular air charter. There are more than 200 registered airfields, most of which are accessible from Windhoek International Airport. For details of fly-in safaris, see 'Safari Tours in Southern Africa' on p. 351.

By road There are about 4 400 km of tarred roads, 37 000 km of gravel roads and 22 000 km of farm roads in Namibia.

Most of the roads are navigable in two-wheel-drive saloon cars, but some of the reserves, notably Khaudum Game Park and parts of the Namib-Naukluft National Park, Damaraland and the Kaokoveld, require four-wheel-drive vehicles.

Remember that the distances between towns are great, and you should be equipped for possible breakdowns in remote places far from the nearest town. Take water and food along if you're driving in isolated areas.

Health precautions

Visitors to the northern parts must take antimalaria precautions. Be sure to take an insect repellent and sleep under mosquito netting or in an insect-proof tent.

Travel information

Namibia Central Reservations, Ministry of Environment and Tourism, Private Bag 13267, Windhoek, tel (09264-61) 23-6975/6/7 or Private Bag 13346, Windhoek 9000, tel (09264-61) 284-2178.

South Africa Namibia Tourism, 11 Alice Lane, 3rd Floor, East Wing, Standard Bank Building, Sandton City 2196, tel (011) 784-8024/5 or PO Box 739, Cape Town 8000, tel (021) 419-3190; Lodges and Guest Farm Reservations: PO Box 21783, Windhoek, tel (09264-61) 22-6979.

CAPRIVI RESERVES

The Caprivi stretches like an arm across northeastern Namibia, opening up into a hand-shaped, fertile wilderness of riverine forests, swamps and woodland in Eastern Caprivi. The east–west corridor and its adjacent wetlands are becoming increasingly popular among visitors seeking a distant retreat with large numbers of animals and birds (70 per cent of Namibia's bird species are found in Caprivi).

Star attractions of this region are the Caprivi Game Park, Mamili National Park, which was proclaimed in Eastern Caprivi in 1990, and the Mahango Game Park. Mudumu National Park, which also lies in Eastern Caprivi, is featured as a separate entry on p. 203.

Caprivi Game Park

Two great rivers form the eastern and western boundaries of the 600 000-ha Caprivi Game Park — a corridor of mopane, acacia and combretum woodland that runs for nearly 180 km between Angola and Botswana, in northeastern Namibia. In the west the waters of the Kavango River cascade over rapids at Popa Falls on their journey across the 32-km Caprivi area, heading southwards towards Botswana. In the east the Kwando River spills her precious cargo of water on to the surrounding floodplains, filling up papyrus-lined waterways and circling palm-studded islands.

These two rivers are linked to each other by a gravel and sand road known as the Trans-Caprivi Highway (the B8), which runs more or less in a straight line from Rundu in the west to Kongola in the east, and then on to Katima Mulilo. For more than 20 years, between the mid 1960s and the late 1980s, the Trans-Caprivi Highway served as a carriageway for military vehicles heading east or west during the bush war.

Public access was limited, the war put the brakes on the development of the area as a wildlife sanctuary, and many animals were lost to poachers or left the area because of the military presence.

Today all that has changed, and the Namibian Ministry of Wildlife, Conservation and Tourism is determined to improve existing facilities. The ministry has earmarked two vital conservation areas for future development — the Kavango Conservation Area, covering 50 000 ha east of the Kavango River, and the 90 000 ha Kwando Conservation Area west of the Kwando River.

Where to see game Although there are 35 mammal species inhabiting the park, the density of the woodlands fringing the Trans-Caprivi Highway makes it difficult to see game along this route. But you are likely to see any number of mammal species near the Kwando River, particularly along the sandy tracks between Kongola and Chisu Bush Camp, and Kongola and Nambwe Bush Camp in the south.

POPA FALLS AND KAVANGO FLOODPLAIN If you are entering the Caprivi Game Park from the west, spend a day or two at Popa Falls or at any one of several camps in the vicinity (see 'Where to stay' below). This will give you the chance to visit Mahango Game Reserve (see p. 185), with its dense riverine forests, woodlands and papyrus-fringed channels. The park is an important habitat for roan and sable antelope.

Mahango and the Kavango floodplain within the Caprivi Game Park are also home to red lechwe, reedbuck and the rare sitatunga, and you'll have a good chance of seeing them in the early mornings or late afternoons.

Various organised game drives and fishing safaris in the area are available (see 'Safaris, game drives and trails' opposite).

KWANDO RIVER AND FLOODPLAIN After travelling eastwards from Popa Falls for about 170 km, the mopane and teak forests of the Caprivi Game Park give way to the fringes of the Kwando floodplains. In the rainy season, seasonal flooding brings a resurgence of life to the pastures of the floodplain, and animals leave the teak forests to feast on this rich harvest.

Here water-loving antelope — red lechwe, sitatunga, reedbuck and waterbuck — head for the waterways and marshlands, accompanied by elephants, buffaloes, Burchell's zebras, Chobe bushbuck and giraffes. These animals bring with them a retinue of carnivores: wild dogs, lions, leopards, cheetahs and spotted hyenas. Hippos and crocodiles bask on the sandbanks or cruise along the deeper channels.

Birdlife No less than 339 species of bird have been identified in the park, including 88 wetland species, such as wattled crane, saddlebilled and woollynecked stork, swamp boubou and African skimmer. Woodland species include Pel's fishing owl, Narina trogon and brown firefinch. Raptors are also well represented, and your drive may reveal kori bustards, yellowbilled kites, gabar goshawks and ground hornbills.

Where to stay Camps and lodges in the Caprivi Game Park and on either side of it on the Kavango and Kwando rivers provide reasonable access to other national parks, and offer comfortable — and, in some cases, world-class — accommodation.

A great self-catering lodge is the Kavango River Lodge, set on the banks of the Okavango in Rundu. In 1996/7 it was voted best rest camp in Namibia.

There are 10 chalets with *en suite* facilities, air-conditioning, a restaurant and TV.

Another cosy place to stay opposite the Caprivi Game Park, close to Popa Falls, is Ndhovu Safari Lodge. The lodge is 2 km from Mahango Game Reserve and offers luxury tented accommodation, with *en suite* bathrooms, showers and buffet meals. There are also two wooden chalets. Contact the lodge at PO Box 559, Swakopmund, tel (09264-64) 40-3141.

Until a year or two ago, there were no places to camp within the Caprivi Game Park, and travellers were not allowed to leave the Trans-Caprivi Highway.

This has changed with the establishment of two camping sites along the western banks of the Kwando River — Chisu Bush Camp, about 12 km north of Kongola, and Nambwe Bush Camp, 12 km south of Kongola, an idyllic, rustic retreat which has six campsites set on a wooded island.

Permits to stay at these camps may be obtained from the Wildlife Conservation Offices at Susuwe Station or Katima Mulilo. Susuwe is just off the Trans-Caprivi Highway (follow the signposted sandy track 3 km west of Kongola).

If you're travelling west to east through the park, a recommended stopover is the Skimmer Camp, 5 km from Popa Falls. Alternatively you may stay at the Kaisosi Safari Lodge, 8 km east of Rundu (campsite and bungalows) or the Popa Falls Rest Camp (bungalows, campsites and well-stocked shop). Another place to stay is Suclabo Lodge, a few kilometres down from Popa Falls, which has bungalows, a swimming pool, restaurant and bar.

Rundu itself has a municipal camp in the centre of town. Sitwe Camp on the banks of the Kwando River has five twin-bedded chalets, and a campsite for 10 people.

If you're looking for luxury, head for the Kwando River's eastern banks (outside the Caprivi Game Park) where you'll find two extraordinarily good lodges: Lianshulu (see below and entry on Mudumu National Park, p. 203) and Namushasha (see separate entry, p. 186).

LIANSHULU LODGE in the Mudumu National Park offers 12 rustic A-frame chalets (with *en suite* facilities) on the banks of the Kwando River. The main lodge building has a large lounge, dining area, curio shop and bar under thatch. Regarded by many as one of the most rustic lodges in Southern Africa, Lianshulu has a rare tranquillity that visitors savour for the rest of their lives. The lodge offers day- and night-time nature drives in open 4x4 vehicles, guided walks in the Mudumu National Park, and fishing trips on its boat *Jacana.*

The cuisine is good, the scenery excellent, and there's plenty of game to keep your camera busy (for more information on Lianshulu, see the separate entry on Mudumu National Park, p. 203). Contact Lianshulu at PO Box 90392, Klein Windhoek, tel (09264-61) 21-4744.

Safaris, game drives and trails Suclabo Lodge near Popa Falls organises safaris into Khaudum Game Reserve and Mahango Game Park (see separate entries).

MAHANGO GAME RESERVE

This smallish reserve lies about 20 km south of the Caprivi Game Park (15 km southeast of the Popa Falls) on Namibia's border with Botswana.

The reserve consists of dry woodlands of Zambezi teak and wild syringa, with floodplains leading to a lush riverine fringe of wild date palms, Kalahari appleleaf and jackalberry trees.

Wildlife The abundance of vegetation attracts more than 400 species of bird and a variety of large, itinerant game, including elephants, packs of wild dogs and lions, which cross over from the Caprivi Game Park.

The abundance of water on the floodplains attracts water-loving antelope such as lechwe and reedbuck. If you're lucky you may spot a sitatunga plunging through the swamps. Dry woodland antelope species common to Mahango are roan and sable, as well as tsessebe, blue wildebeest, impala, buffalo and gemsbok. Smaller mammals include warthogs, chacma baboons and steenbok.

Crocodiles and hippos are part of the landscape of the Kavango River as they are elsewhwere along Botswana and Namibia's permanent waterways.

Birdwatchers will have a field day with sightings ranging from squacco and rufousbellied herons and longtoed plovers to western banded snake eagles, lesser blue-eared starlings and Dickinson's kestrels. The best time for birdwatching is from November to March.

Accommodation There's no accommodation in the park, but you may overnight at Popa Falls Rest Camp or Suclabo Lodge (see 'Where to stay' on p. 185), and drive though the park by day.

Game drives Two-wheel-drive saloon cars should bear left 1 km from the entrance to the reserve (on the Popa Falls side) for a safe excursion along a reasonable road along the edge of the Kavango floodplain, and a scenic stop under giant baobabs.

Four-wheel-drive vehicles may safely take the longer, 19-km circular route that heads westwards from the Popa–Shakawe main road and then loops backwards.

Namushasha Lodge

Floating down the Kwando River bordering the West Caprivi Game Park in a swamp boat at night is an experience you're not likely to forget. The eyes of hundreds of crocodiles light up in the spotlight, and when your guide suddenly plunges his hands into the reeds alongside and brings a metre-long baby croc aboard, you know you're in the heart of Africa. If you're brave enough you can even give it a try, but you'll need lightning reflexes because the croc will come up snapping and even the smallest can deliver a nasty bite.

This is just one of the adventures you're likely to experience at Namushasha Lodge, owned by Namibia Country Lodges. The lodge lies in Namibia's subtropical region of the Caprivi, close to the Botswana border. The Caprivi used to be the stamping ground of the South African Defence Force but the military are long gone and one of Africa's most unspoilt regions is once again open to tourism.

Tips for travellers

- Although two-wheel-drive saloon cars can negotiate the road between Rundu and Katima Mulilo, a 4x4 is recommended if you wish to explore the surrounding areas.
- The Trans-Caprivi Highway between Rundu and Kongola is riddled with potholes and should be treated with great respect. Many cars are written off annually on this road, so take your time if you're travelling through Caprivi Game Park — especially during the rainy season (December–March).
- If you are travelling along the Trans-Caprivi Highway from Popa Falls or Rundu, there are a few secondary sandy roads branching off, but check with the Wildlife Conservation Office at Susuwe or Katima Mulilo before you venture on to them.

Namushasha, 140 km from Katima Mulilo and 380 km from Victoria Falls, is a truly African experience. Just three minutes down the Kwando River by boat is the West Caprivi Game Park, where large herds of animals roam freely through subtropical bush and grassland.

Mudumu and Mamili national parks are 12 km and 70 km away by road respectively, while nearby Lizauli Village gives visitors a taste of traditional life in this unspoilt part of Africa.

The Kwando River is alive with fish, including tigerfish. The lodge has swamp boats and fishing tackle available for keen anglers. A guide accompanies guests on the river to point out favourite fishing spots and to ensure you don't get lost. The song of the bell frogs at night is one you'll never forget.

Wildlife The abundance of water and grazing, combined with the fact that there is no fencing, attracts a huge variety of game to the area. Elephant, hippo and giraffe are plentiful and when the buffalo and zebra herds pass through lions are everywhere. The world's largest antelope, the eland, occurs in herds of up to 40 and even the rare sable is sometimes seen.

Namushasha is a birdwatcher's paradise, with some 420 species, including woodpeckers, nightjars, owls, vultures, coucals, louries, bee-eaters, African jacanas, pygmy geese and waxbills. Many of these birds can be seen from the viewing deck at Namushasha in the early mornings and evenings.

Where to stay Namushasha accommodates 32 people in 15 tidy bungalows, all

Namushasha Lodge at a glance

Locality:	Central southern Caprivi on the Kwando River near the Botswana border.
Climate:	Fine throughout most of the year.
Game drives:	Daily through West Caprivi Game Park.
Fishing:	Many freshwater species, including bream and tigerfish.
Other attractions:	Birdwatching, neighbouring game parks and Lizauli Village where traditional handicrafts can be bought.
Amenities:	Pool, bar and viewing deck overlooking the Kwando River and West Caprivi Game Park.
Accommodation:	15 comfortable bungalows under magnificent trees.
Booking address:	Namibia Country Lodges, PO Box 6597, Ausspamplatz, Windhoek, tel (09264-61) 24-0375.
When to go:	All year round.
What to take with you:	Windbreakers, shorts and sneakers for the day; jeans and long-sleeved shirts at night when mosquitos are active. Insect repellent and sun cream.
How to get there:	The lodge's own landing strip is three hours by air from Windhoek in a Cessna 210. The distance by road (all tar except for the last 20 km) from Windhoek is 1 400 km. The lodge is 380 km from Victoria Falls.
Nearest doctor:	Katima Mulilo, 140 km away.
Nearest petrol:	At the lodge.
Special precautions:	The area lies in a malaria belt and all usual precautions must be taken.

with their own showers and toilets. The beds, covered with mosquito nets, are comfortable and bedding is provided. Kitchen staff prepare scrumptious breakfasts, lunches and dinners.

Guests can entertain themselves at the fully stocked bar and swimming pool when they've had enough of tigerfishing and game drives.

Game drives Every afternoon visitors are taken up the Kwando by boat to the West Caprivi Game Park for a two-hour game drive. The bush is dense and the grass long in the wet season, but you're still likely to see hippo and several antelope at close quarters. It's not unusual to come face to face with elephant, giraffe, buffalo and lion. Leopards are also occasionally seen, while baboons, monkeys and hyenas are plentiful.

Eastern Caprivi

Two highly recommended destinations in eastern Caprivi — east of the Caprivi Game Park, not far from Namibia's borders with Zambia and Botswana — are the Kalizo Fishing Lodge and Impalila Island Lodge.

Kalizo Fishing Lodge This lodge for anglers and lovers of wild places lies 40 km east of Katima Mulilo on the banks of the Zambezi River.

Here eight wood-and-thatch chalets, each accommodating four people, offer beautiful views at the river's edge, a walk away from the Mekoro Restaurant and Tuggers Nook Bar, also on the river.

There are separate showers, baths and flush toilets, and electricity is available from a generator, which is turned off late at night.

The camp has five St Lucia and Firefly boats, powered by 60-hp and 40-hp out-

The amazing aardwolf

In the darkness of a bushveld night the aardwolf, with its high, muscular forequarters and sloping back, could easily be mistaken for a hyena. But there are important differences.

While hyenas hunt and scavenge large and small mammals, the aardwolf does not eat meat at all. It spends much of its life thrusting its tongue into sand for its favourite food — termites.

It does have a carnivore's incisors and canines, but these are very small — quite incapable of capturing or killing large prey. The molars and premolars too are small — unable to crush bones or chew meat.

So it survives on termites, gobbling up to 300 000 in one night. Two species of harvester termite form nearly 100 per cent of the aardwolf's diet.

Nature has made the aardwolf immune to the sticky, painful repellent squirted out by these termites, so that it can feed for hours without ill effect.

boards. These are manned by a skilled driver who takes two or three anglers per boat to the hot fishing spots. Here, rich catches of tigerfish, bream, barbel, river pike and eels are caught. Tigerfish of up to 12 kg have been boated here, and the average fish caught weighs in at 6 kg.

The best fishing months are from June through February. Towards January drenching rains bring the water levels so high that the camp is eventually surrounded by the Zambezi's floodplains, and guests have to be boated into the camp.

The camp offers guided photographic and birdwatching safaris in the Caprivi Game Park and in the Mudumu and Mamili national parks. For more details, contact the lodge at PO Box 1854, Ngweze, Katima Mulilo, tel (09264-677) 2802 or (09264-61) 22-6160.

Impalila Island Lodge This superb lodge has been built at the confluence of the Zambezi and Chobe rivers at a site known as Kamavozu — 'the place of the baobabs' — and overlooks the Mambova Rapids.

The stunning architecture has made optimum use of the beautiful, wild surroundings by integrating eight double wood-and-thatch chalets into a riverine forest. These have elevated views over the surging waters of the Zambezi.

The main complex has been fashioned around two ancient baobab trees, and consists of a diningroom, bar, deck and lounge. There's also a sparkling pool, recreation area and curio shop.

Impalila offers excellent fishing opportunities — including fly-fishing for 'tiger' in the rapids just beyond the lodge. Visitors are asked to bring their own tackle because this is in short supply at the lodge.

Impalila specialises in birding safaris, on foot or by boat along the waterways. River safaris also yield sightings of the larger mammals, such as elephant, hippo, giraffe and kudu, as well as rarer species such as puku or Chobe bushbuck. If you want to see more game, a land safari into Chobe National Park is also available.

The best route to Impalila by road would be through Botswana — via Francistown on to Nata and then Kasane. The lodge will pick you up at Kasane by boat. From Zimbabwe travel by tar via Beit Bridge to Bulawayo, Victoria Falls and then on to Kasane.

For more details contact Impalila Island Lodge, PO Box 70378, Bryanston 2021, tel (011) 706-7207.

Mamili National Park

This park, covering 32 000 ha, lies in the southwestern corner of eastern Caprivi, just south of Mudumu National Park. Because of its wild state, and the fact that there's no permanent accommodation, it is recommended only for the hardiest (and bravest) gamewatchers.

For those who like the challenge of fluctuating floodplains, bad roads, an abundance of wild — and dangerous — game, and really beautiful and remote surroundings, Mamili is an ideal destination.

Visitors will have to travel in convoy of at least two 4x4s and head there between September and April (seasonal floods make much of the area impassable between May and August). There are no facilities and visitors must be completely self-sufficient.

You could consider Mamili as an extension of your visit to Mudumu National Park (see p. 203), if only for its extraordinarily rich birdlife.

Wildlife The reserve consists of swamps, islands, woodlands and thickets, floodplains and a maze of waterways that are home to the ever-present crocodiles and hippos.

Although you may see elephants, lions, buffaloes and giraffes, Mamili's other, sought-after mammals on the gamewatcher's list are waterbuck, lechwe and sitatunga, puku and spottednecked otters.

Birdlife As with the rest of eastern Caprivi, Mamili offers excellent birdwatch-

Caprivi game reserves at a glance

Locality:	Northeastern Namibia, between Angola and Botswana.
Climate:	Summers extremely hot, winters mild to cool. Annual rainfall 530 mm, most of which falls in summer (December–March).
Number of camps:	Two camps in Caprivi Game Park: Chisu and Nambwe bush camps; two campsites in Mamili National Park: Nzalu and Lyadura.
Game drives:	Drives available at Mahango, Mudumu and Mamili national parks.
Trails:	Nkwazi Africa Fishing and Photographic Tours operate guided photographic, birdwatching and boating safaris in the area. Contact Central Reservations, PO Box 195, Wilgeheuwel 1736, tel (011) 764-4606.
Other attractions:	Mekoro and boat trips on the Kwando River; angling.
Accommodation:	**Caprivi Game Park:** Chisu and Nambwe bush camps offer rustic campsites. Recommended places to stay outside the park are: **Kavango River Lodge** 10 luxury chalets; **Ndhovu Safari Lodge** tents and two chalets; **Lianshulu Lodge** — eight rustic A-frame chalets; **Namushasha Lodge** — six twin-bedded bungalows; **Popa Falls Rest Camp, Sitwe Camp, Skimmer Camp, Suclabo Lodge** and **Kaisosi Safari Lodge** near Popa Falls. **Mamili National Park:** Nzalu and Lyadura campsites have no facilities. **Kalizo Fishing Lodge:** Eight wood-and-thatch chalets; **Impalila Island Lodge:** six double wood-and-thatch chalets.
Booking address:	Campsites: Namibia Wildlife Resorts, PO Box 13267, Windhoek, tel (09264-61) 23-6975; Lianshulu Lodge: Wilderness Safaris, PO Box 78573, Sandton 2146, tel (011) 883-0745. Namushasha Lodge: PO Box 21182, Windhoek, tel (09264-61) 24-0375. Kalizo Fishing Lodge, PO Box 1854, Ngweze, Katima Mulilo, tel (09264-677) 2802; Impalila Island Lodge: PO Box 70378, Bryanston 2021, tel (011) 706-7207.
When to go:	June to October is best for gamewatching; November to March is best for birdwatching.
What to take with you:	Two spare tyres; tent, camping equipment and all provisions for camping within the park; torch; fresh water.
How to get there:	Drive east from Rundu for 200 km until you reach Bagani Bridge. Drive 190 km through the park to the exit point at Kongola Bridge. Katima Mulilo is 120 km further east.
Nearest doctor:	Katima Mulilo, 120 km from Kongola Bridge.
Nearest petrol:	About 7 km east of Kongola border post.
Open:	Throughout the year.
Special precautions:	Take antimalaria precautions when visiting the Caprivi.

ing and the local population ranges from the tinkling cisticolas and greater blue-eared starlings of the woodlands and thickets, to weavers and warblers of the reedbeds and the various geese and ducks of the swamps and islands.

Where to stay There are two campsites: Nzalu in the northeast and Lyadura in the east, both of which have no facilities at all. Campers should be cautious of wild animals wandering through the campsite at night, and be particularly wary of crocodiles and hippos.

How to get there The park can be reached via Malengalenga or Sangwali and permits are available from the Ministry of Environment and Tourism's office in Katima Mulilo.

Etosha National Park

Cumulonimbus clouds advance like grey galleons above the lion-coloured grasslands of northern Etosha. To the south, across the calcrete wasteland of Etosha Pan, cracked mud blisters and peels beneath the onslaught of relentless sun. It's so achingly hot that rivulets of dry air create dark, distorted images across the pan's endless surface.

The tension of heat and dryness is broken by a large, wet missile hurtling to the ground in the form of a huge raindrop; then another, and another. Suddenly, with a roar of thunder, the grey canvas of cloud above opens up and releases a maelstrom of wind and water.

One of nature's enduring spectacles — the summer rainy season in Etosha — has begun, signalling the start of one of Africa's great animal migrations.

Tens of thousands of zebras, wildebeest, giraffes, springbok and a dozen other different species of antelope abandon their winter feeding grounds on the Andoni Plains and head for the mopane woodlands, waterholes and sweet grasslands of Okaukuejo in the west.

It's a spectacle that knows no parallel on earth. The American trader Gerald McKiernan described the event in 1876 as 'the Africa I had read in books of travel ... all the menageries in the world turned loose would not compare to the sight I saw that day.'

Lake of a mother's tears In the early days indigenous tribes christened the Etosha area — 'the place of dry water' — a reference to the white salt pan at its heart. Legend has it that in the days when the nomadic Heikum San lived in the area, a raiding party killed all the menfolk of their small community. The mother of one of those killed was so distraught that her tears created a huge lake. When it dried, all that was left was salt.

The legend of the lake has some semblance of truth, for the pan, 130 km long, 50 km wide and covering 6 000 km^2, is

Tips for travellers

- Animals have the right of way in Etosha. If a group of elephants happens to be standing or lying down in the road, keep a respectful distance away, turn your engine off and wait.
- Do not get out of your car to photograph any animals.
- Although the water in Etosha is purified, many visitors prefer to take their own, or to buy water from the shops.

believed to have been part of the largest lake in the world. Known as the Etosha Basin, this lake included the Okavango Delta, and other smaller pans and lakes in Botswana.

Since the lake dried up millions of years ago, the pan has shrunk to a relic of its former size, but every summer, fed by the swollen Ekuma and Oshigambo rivers in the north, the pan fills with water, and the 'place of dry water' becomes the land of plenty. The shoots of new grasses spring from the ground in a frenzy of growth and the leaves of the mopane and acacia woodlands acquire a lushness almost impossible in a region of such dryness and heat, as the animals surge towards the fringes of the shimmering lake.

At least 15 species of antelope close ranks, and are joined by giraffes, rhinos, zebras and the inevitable retinue of predators, hungry for the easy pickings. Blackmaned lions, blackbacked jackals, cheetahs, leopards, spotted hyenas, wild dogs and an assortment of smaller predators, track the great herds.

Across the pan the sky is filled with divisions of flying ducks, airborne flotillas of waterbirds — greater and lesser flamingoes, pelicans, kingfishers and Egyptian geese, followed inevitably by migratory species and birds of prey.

Working together for survival

One of the most endearing sights of the African wild is a group of suricates standing bolt upright outside their warrens watching the world go by.

Using their tails as support, and baring their stomachs and chests to the warming rays of the sun, these whiskered little animals stand side by side in the early morning before they scurry off to forage for the day.

In the harsh environment of northern Namibia they have little chance of surviving on their own. Their chances of success depend largely on the size of the colony and the ability of its members to work unselfishly in the interests of the group as a whole.

A typical family numbers 14 or 15, but varies from two to as many as 30 individuals. One breeding pair — a dominant female and her male partner — heads this closely knit social group.

Suricates establish a network of individual warrens throughout the area, using each as a temporary apartment from which they can forage.

These 'boarding houses' also provide safe refuge in case of sudden attack. Because suricates move from apartment to apartment, they seldom seriously deplete food supplies in any one place, and therefore have enough to satisfy their needs in times of scarcity.

The pan also becomes the focal point for thousands of nature-lovers from around the world visiting the Etosha National Park — one of the great game parks of the world.

The park Etosha National Park is huge, covering no less than 22 275 km^2, and extending more than 350 km from Von Lindequist Gate in the east to its western boundary in Kaokoland. It lies in northern Namibia, a day's drive away from the Angolan border and the entrance to western Caprivi and Botswana.

The park was proclaimed in 1907 by Governor Frederick von Lindequist, and at one time covered 99 526 km^2, making it the largest natural park in the world. However, in 1967 it was reduced to its present size and officially christened Etosha National Park.

Wildlife Don't be disheartened if somebody tells you there is only one troop of baboons, and no impala, black wildebeest, white rhinos, monkeys, crocodiles, hippo or buffaloes in the Etosha National Park. The superabundance of other species makes this absence almost unnoticeable. Among the 114 mammal species that roam the park are 1 500 elephants, 15 000–20 000 springbok, 4 000–6 000 gemsbok, some 300 lions, 5 000–6 000 Burchell's zebras, 2 000 giraffes and about 300 black rhinoceros.

Etosha is also a sanctuary for several rarer species of mammal: the demure suni antelope that lives in the thick bush near Namutoni, the rare Hartmann's mountain zebra, blackfaced impala, tsessebe, roan antelope, eland, blackmaned lion, spotted hyena, cheetah and wild dog.

In addition, there are 110 reptile species, 16 amphibian and one fish species in the park.

Birdlife Etosha attracts about 340 bird species and is Southern Africa's most important breeding ground for greater and lesser flamingoes. These congregate in large numbers at Fischer's Pan and the Ekuma River mouth, and in times of flood may number upwards of a million birds. Other birds of the waterways are waders such as sanderlings, marsh sandpipers and Caspian plovers.

The grasslands of Etosha are home to such species as Namaqua sandgrouse, doublebanded plover and black korhaan, while the mopane woodlands attract the blackfaced and pied babbler, Swainson's francolin and blue waxbill.

The frequency of kills, the large number of small mammals and reptiles, and the abundance of carrion, attract no less than 35 species of raptor, including six vulture species. Among the rarer raptors seen at Etosha are the Egyptian vulture and the sooty falcon.

Where to stay There are three very attractive rest camps for visitors to Etosha: Okaukuejo, Halali and Namutoni. Okaukuejo and Halali offer luxury rondavels, bungalows, chalets and huts, while Namutoni offers rooms in the fort and mobile homes. Each rest camp has camping sites, with communal ablution blocks and kitchens, an attractive swimming pool, restaurant, kiosk, shop and petrol station. Okaukuejo also has a comprehensive Information Centre.

Bed-linen and bath towels are supplied at the camps, but you must bring your own cutlery and crockery. All rondavels, bungalows and mobile homes have fridges, hot plates and electric kettles (except the one-room bungalows at Halali).

OKAUKUEJO The name Okaukuejo means 'the place of women', although from the tourists' point of view it may well be called the place of elephants, lions, springbok, impala, rhinoceros, giraffe, kudu or just about any other mammal you can think of. For Okaukuejo Rest Camp has been built cheek by jowl with what is regarded as one of the finest waterholes in Africa. An added attraction is that the waterhole is floodlit throughout the night, and it is not unusual to witness a lion kill during the hours of darkness.

A low stone wall separates Okaukuejo Rest Camp's rondavels from an incredible variety of animals that come to drink. The elephants are so close that you can hear the rumbling of their stomachs as they pad around the waterhole; and you can see the whiskers of the lions as they walk down to the water.

A German tourist who slept on one of the stone benches overlooking the waterhole at Okaukuejo one night was killed by a lion. On another occasion visitors saw a lion pursue a kudu bull into the camp, then feast on the carcass outside their bungalows.

HALALI About 80 km east of Okaukuejo is Etosha's smallest camp, Halali, a peaceful settlement of huts under mopane and leadwood trees, which offers a lovely swimming pool, and its own new waterhole, a short walk away from the camp.

The Halali waterhole, built in 1992 at the foot of Tsumasa Koppie, offers great viewing of lions, elephants and black rhino. Use this camp as a base to explore the Rietfontein, Goas and Salvadora waterholes. Rietfontein is the largest and most-visited of the park's waterholes, and features most of the species found in the park, but particularly lion, blackfaced impala, zebra and wildebeest.

NAMUTONI A white, Beau Geste-style fort, with observation posts, interior courtyard (parade ground) and an unmistakeable aura of the days of German colonialism in Namibia, greet you as you drive into this easternmost of Etosha's camps, some 90 km east of Halali. Just 11 km from the Von Lindequist Gate, Namutoni offers accommodation in the fort's rooms or in huts just outside the fort. There's a well-stocked shop and kiosk here, a swimming pool and a restaurant.

Getting around Most of the roads and game drives in the Etosha National Park are located around the southern and eastern fringes of Etosha Pan, and the major concourses of these drives are the three rest camps: Okaukuejo, Halali and Namutoni. The gravel roads are mostly in very good condition.

The popular entry point to Etosha is via the Andersson Gate, and then up to Okaukuejo. From here several day drives are available, the most popular of which are the circuits and loops towards Halali Rest Camp, and the 100-km round trip to the Moringa Forest ('Sprokieswoud') and Okondeka. The administration office at Okaukuejo will supply detailed maps of the drives available throughout the park, as well as opening and closing times of the gates.

If you're staying at Halali, the central camp, you may elect to drive west (towards Okaukuejo) or east (towards Namutoni Rest Camp).

These routes bypass dozens of waterholes where game is abundant and varied. Namutoni also offers some spectacular drives, particularly the 100-km round trip to the Andoni waterhole in the north, and to the Klein Namutoni waterhole in the south. On your way to Andoni it's worth making a detour to Tsumcor waterhole on the way.

Another rewarding excursion from Namutoni is the Dik-dik Drive, a 5,3-km circuit that affords splendid views of this tiny antelope.

Those who would like to try something completely different — and even more on the wild side — may book an excursion through the restricted western part of Etosha, which has a number of exceptional waterholes, among them Renostervlei, Jakkalswater and Ozonjuitji M'Bari, and an abundance of game. This may only be done in the company of a registered tour operator, and should be organised from a base outside the park.

Private lodges of Etosha Several private game lodges in and around the Etosha National Park offer guests top-class accommodation and a chance to capture the real spirit of Africa in beautiful surroundings. Among the more popular of these lodges are Ongava Safari Lodge in the Ongava Game Reserve, Hobatere Lodge and Kavita Lion Lodge.

ONGAVA SAFARI LODGE Situated in the 35 000-ha Ongava Private Game Reserve on Etosha's southern boundary, Ongava accommodates 20 guests in 10 rock and thatch chalets, each of which has *en suite* bathrooms, with bath, flush toilets and shower. A small tented camp caters for those wanting a more rustic bush experience. The thatched main lounge, pub and diningroom are on a hill overlooking the rolling plains below. There is also a sparkling swimming pool.

Activities include game drives to Etosha, walks around Ongava, game viewing and birdwatching. Ongava has white rhinos, a variety of smaller mammals and plenty of raptors. Birding specials include Meyer's parrot, short-toed rock thrush, Hartlaub's francolin and freckled nightjar.

Contact the lodge at PO Box 6850, Windhoek, tel (09264-61) 22-5178.

HOBATERE LODGE Lying 65 km north of Kamanjab on the western border of Etosha National Park, the lodge is situated in a 32 000-ha concession area which is home to a wide variety of game, including elephant, giraffe, eland, and Hartmann's mountain zebra.

The lodge offers six attractive, two-bed chalets under thatch as well as six double rooms under thatch. There's a sparkling pool, restaurant, bar and lounge.

There is also a delightful tree house overlooking a waterhole, where you can watch elephants and other game come down to drink. Day and night game drives will provide sightings of aardvark, Cape and bat-eared fox, aardwolf, genet and other small mammals.

To get to the lodge drive 65 km north of Kamanjab towards Opuwo. Exactly 1 km past the Otjovasandu entrance to Etosha National Park turn left. From there follow the dirt road for 16 km. The lodge also has its own airstrip.

Contact the lodge at PO Box 40538, Windhoek, tel (09264-61) 25-3992/7.

KAVITA LION LODGE This homely lodge is situated on the border of Etosha National Park, Damaraland and Kaokoveld and offers six spacious *en suite* bedrooms and a pool. Farm-style meals are served outdoors.

The lodge is also the home of the Afrileo Foundation, a non-profit organisation dedicated to the protection and conservation of the Namibian lion. Game drives, guided bush walks and birding trails are offered and there's a fascinating trail to the Ohorongo village, where you can experience life amongst the Himba people first-hand. Three-day safaris to Epupa Falls on the Kunene River and various Himba villages are available to guests who stay longer than four days.

Etosha National Park at a glance

Locality:	Northern Namibia.
Climate:	Winter days are mild to warm, with cold nights; summers are hot to very hot (average annual maximum at Okaukuejo is 31 °C). Thunderstorms between December and April (358 mm average annual rainfall at Okaukuejo).
Number of camps:	Three: Okaukuejo, Halali and Namutoni. Halali camp is closed between 1 November and the second week in March.
Game drives:	There are hundreds of kilometres of game drives in Etosha, most of them around the pan in eastern Etosha.
Hides and waterholes:	There are about 40 waterholes commonly visited by gamewatchers in Etosha. Among the most rewarding for seeing and photographing game are Rietfontein, Okaukuejo, Goas, Halali, Klein Namutoni and Chudob.
Trails:	There is a trail at Halali (Tsumasa Trail) and walks at Hobatere Lodge.
Other attractions:	Birdwatching, braaiing under the stars.
Amenities:	All the camps have a pool, restaurant, shop, and post office.
Accommodation:	Self-catering accommodation in the three camps comprises rondavels, chalets and rooms (Namutoni). **Mokuti Lodge** is an upmarket, private game lodge outside the Von Lindequist Gate at Namutoni, and provides excellent accommodation in lovely surroundings. Other private lodge accommodation includes **Ongava Safari Lodge**, **Kavita Lion Lodge** and **Hobatere Lodge**.
Booking address:	Central Reservations, Ministry of Environment and Tourism, Private Bag 13267, Windhoek, tel (09264-61) 23-6975; Mokuti Lodge: Resorts International, PO Box 2862, Windhoek, tel (09264-61) 23-4512 or PO Box 403, Tsumeb, tel (09264-67) 22-9084/5; Hobatere Lodge: PO Box 90538, Windhoek, tel (09264-61) 25-3992/7.
When to go:	Throughout the year, although game-viewing around the waterholes is better in the dry season, between May and September; birdwatching around the pan is more rewarding in the rainy season (December–April).
What to take with you:	Although there are shops, stock up with food and cutlery and crockery. Don't forget sunglasses, sunhat, camera, binoculars, field guides.
How to get there:	The Andersson Gate (11 km from Okaukuejo) is about 450 km north of Windhoek, and is the preferred route of entry to the park. Drive north from Windhoek on the B1 to Otjiwarongo, then take the C38 to Outjo and Andersson Gate. To reach Namutoni, continue on the B1 through Otavi and Tsumeb, then turn on to the C38 to Von Lindequist Gate (550 km from Windhoek). All the camps have their own landing strip, and fly-in packages are organised by various tour operators. See 'Safari Operators', p. 363.
Nearest doctor:	There may be a doctor in the park, but don't count on it. In the event of an emergency, contact Mokuti Lodge outside the Von Lindequist Gate, which has a clinic staffed by a qualified nursing sister.
Nearest petrol:	Okaukuejo, Halali and Namutoni have petrol. Okaukuejo has a mechanic.
Open:	Sunrise to sunset.
Special precautions:	Take antimalaria precautions before entering the park.

The rustic Otjombungu ('place of the hyaena') bush camp under mopane trees has five thatched A-framed chalets, each accommodating two sleeping bags.

There's a flush toilet, hot and cold shower and firewood.

Contact the lodge at PO Box 118, Kumanjab, tel (09264-61) 33-0224.

Fish River Canyon

From the air, the second largest canyon on earth seems like a jagged wound, knifed recklessly through the rugged, lunar landscape of Namibia's southern frontier.

To the ancient San the canyon represented the trail of a giant serpent named Kouteign Kooru, which carved its way deep into the earth's crust to evade pursuing hunters. The Nama people who arrived after the San, likened the canyon to a furnace and called its southern section Ais-Ais, which means 'very hot'.

Today it is regarded as a geological wonder whose barrenness and haunting beauty attract geologists, nature-lovers, hikers and photographers from all corners of the globe.

Some 160 km long, 500 m deep, 27 km wide in places and rugged almost beyond description, the canyon is a natural museum of ancient history where the conflicts of sun, wind, water and stone throughout millennia have dwarfed the feeble faction fights and machinations of man.

Brooding sandstone ramparts surge majestically above the floor of the canyon, their oxide-tinged faces coloured orange, red and pink by the western sun. These sunburnt, weatherbeaten flanks reveal the various stages of momentous geological upheavals that started 1 800 million years ago. Massive buttresses, separated from the mainland of solid rock, fall sheer to the valley floor, their foundations all but washed away by the river.

Euphorbias and quiver trees cling to the rocky slopes, while along the river's banks are scattered camelthorn, wild tamarisk, ebony, ringwood and buffalo-thorn trees. There are even a few date palms, believed to have been planted by some Germans during World War II.

Here and there, dense stands of reeds and rushes rise from the river bed, camouflaging such birds as purple gallinules and African marsh warblers.

The canyon actually consists of an upper and a lower level. The upper level was formed by major fractures in the earth's crust about 500 million years ago. The huge cleavage which started as the Fish River Canyon was deepened 200 million years later by southward-moving glaciers.

Since then, the lower level of the canyon has been formed by the waters of the Fish River eroding the underlying sediments. The river continues to edge deeper into the earth's surface every year. Today, 56 km of this meandering river is the site of one of Southern Africa's most popular trails — the Fish River Canyon Backpacking Trail.

For those who don't have the time or inclination to go boulderhopping along the canyon floor for four or five days, several one-day hikes — and spectacular views — are available from the main viewpoint in the north, and from the Sulphur Springs viewpoint to the south. Leave as early as possible after sunrise to take full advantage of the cool morning air and take plenty of water and sun protection.

Wildlife The krantzes and kloofs are home to troops of baboons, their barks bouncing eerily off the canyon walls. Smaller mammals include rock dassies and ground squirrels. Although Hartmann's mountain zebras, kudu and klipspringers occupy the canyon's lower reaches, they are shy and seldom seen. The canyon floor is better suited to the variety of snakes and scorpions found there. If you're walking the canyon trail, keep a sharp lookout for puffadders, horned adders and Egyptian cobras. Another sometimes-seen reptile is the water monitor, which sets up home in the vicinity of the watercourses.

Five species of fish have been recorded in the canyon's pools.

Birdlife At least 60 species of bird inhabit the canyon, and range from water-loving species such as purple gallinule, African marsh warbler, Egyptian goose and hamerkop to Cape robin, dusky sunbird, bokmakierie, mountain chat and palewinged starling. Raptors include black eagles, rock kestrels and lanner falcons.

Relics of the past The Fish River Canyon harbours innumerable relics of previous civilisations which lived within its walls. In 1981 archaeologists uncovered 27 Stone-Age sites dating back more than 50 000 years. Another 18 sites dating back to the Later Stone Age were also uncovered.

Fish River Canyon Backpacking Trail Although the canyon is 160 km long, the trail itself covers 90 km along the course of the river, and takes four or five days to complete. Because of the scorching summer temperatures and the possible hazard of flash floods, the trail is only open from 1 May to 31 August.

Groups are limited to a maximum of 40 and a minimum of three (children must be over the age of 12, and must be accompanied by at least one adult).

The trail starts in the north with a 500-m descent to the canyon floor, a steep route made tricky by loose gravel and stones. Chains have been secured to stabilise hikers on the hour-long descent. The first 16-km leg is the most spectacular, and one of the toughest parts of the hike, because of its scattered boulders and sandy stretches.

There are two emergency exit routes (for sudden evacuations) at Palm Springs and Von Trotha's grave.

The most rugged section of the canyon is just north of Ais-Ais, where a giant rock has fractured into four parts, called the Four Sisters.

Where to stay If you would like to sample the scenery and atmosphere of the canyon without doing the backpacking

Tips for hikers

- A high degree of physical fitness is required, and a medical clearance certificate must be sent with your reservation advice.
- If it is excessively hot — the temperatures on the canyon floor range from 45 °C during the day to around 35 °C at night — take adequate precautions against the sun.
- Restrict your backpacking times to the periods between sunrise and 11:00 and between 15:00 and sunset. Try not to set up camp later than 18:00.
- Written reservations may be made 18 months in advance and are confirmed 11 months before the trail date.
- Everything that goes with you into the canyon must come out again.

trail, the place to stay is Ais-Ais, where you'll find some invigorating hot springs, and fascinating walks among the barren rocks and hillsides above Ais-Ais. Available here are campsites, flats and bungalows, as well as a shop and restaurant.

CAÑON LODGE This stunning lodge is situated in the privately owned, 520-km^2 Gondwana Cañon Park and offers cosy bungalows with natural rock walls, thatched roofs and *en suite* facilities. Each of the 26 bungalows nestles cryptically among the beautiful granite boulders which are so characteristic of the Fish River Canyon.

The park's original farmhouse, which was built in 1910, has been restored and

Fish River Canyon at a glance

Locality:	Southern Namibia.
Climate:	Daytime winter (May–August) temperatures average between 20–25°C, but can reach 40 °C. Night-time temperatures can fall to 5 °C or lower. Annual rainfall varies between 50–100 mm a year.
Number of camps:	Two.
Viewsites:	Main viewpoint, near Hobas, Sulphur Springs.
Trails:	Fish River Canyon Backpacking Trail (90 km). Walks at Ais-Ais.
Other attractions:	Angling, photography, Stone-Age and Iron-Age sites.
Amenities:	Swimming pools at Ais-Ais and Hobas. Licensed restaurant, shop at Ais-Ais.
Accommodation:	**Fish River Lodge:** Double and family rooms, dormitory accommodation. Other private lodges are **Cañon Lodge**, (26 bungalows) and **Auob Lodge** (22 luxury rooms). **Hobas:** 12 campsites, ablution facilities, shop and pool. **Ais-Ais:** bungalows, camping/caravan sites, flats and luxury flats.
Booking address:	Ministry of Wildlife, Conservation and Tourism, Private Bag 13267, Windhoek 9000, tel (09264-61) 23-6975/6/7. Fish River Lodge: Namibia Tourism, Private Bag 13346, Windhoek, tel (09264-61) 284-2111. Cañon Lodge: PO Box 80205, Windhoek, tel (09264-61) 23-0066.
When to go:	1 May to 31 August.
What to take with you:	Campers must be fully equipped with provisions and gear to last five days, including backpacking stove, torch and full medical kit. Light raincoat (thundershowers are possible in winter), full waterbottle.
How to get there:	From Keetmanshoop take the B4 southwest to Seeheim, then travel along the C12 for 77 km and turn right at the Fish River Canyon signpost (the D601). Shortly afterwards you will reach the main viewpoint. Access from South Africa is via Noordoewer along the B1, turning left to Ais-Ais on the D316.
Nearest doctor:	Ais-Ais.
Nearest petrol:	Ais-Ais.
Open:	The hiking trail is open from 1 May to 31 August. The Ais-Ais resort is closed between 1 November and the second Friday of March.
Special precautions:	Full medical kit and medication for tired or strained muscles. Take special protection against the sun, avoid walking in the midday heat and don't walk the trail unless you are 100 per cent fit.

now serves as the lodge's restaurant, with panoramic views over the canyon.

This park is a hiker's paradise and offers easy access to the canyon. To book contact the lodge at PO Box 80205, Windhoek, tel (09264-61) 23-0066.

FISH RIVER LODGE For hikers and backpackers or for visitors just passing through southern Namibia, Fish River Lodge is a comfortable, affordable stop-over which affords beautiful vistas and access to the Fish River Canyon.

The Main Lodge offers double and family rooms and a cosy restaurant and bar.

There's dormitory accommodation for hikers and backpackers at the Stable, an old stone building with beds and mattresses. Guests at the Stable must bring their own sleeping bags or bed linen.

Koelkrans is a delightful self-catering camp down in the canyon offering six wooden huts accommodating 12 people - it is ideal as a base camp for day trips through the canyon.

For more information contact Namibia Tourism, Private Bag 13346, Windhoek, tel (09264-61) 284-2111.

At Hobas, 12 km from the start of the trail there are 12 campsites, ablution facilities, a small shop and a swimming pool.

AUOB LODGE The lodge lies in the western Kalahari, not far from the small town of Gochas, and is the ideal stop-over on the long road between Keetmanshoop and Windhoek. Late-afternoon game drives take you deep into the red dunes and grasslands where you're assured of seeing zebra, gemsbok, springbok and giraffe. Jackals abound and you can admire the ingenuity of the sociable weaver nests, glass of champagne in hand, as the sun goes down.

The lodge can accommodate 48 people in 22 rooms, each with their own immaculate bathroom. No cost has been spared to ensure the comfort of guests and the jovial staff are always on hand to make sure you want for nothing. A fully appointed bar adjoins a magnificent swimming pool and thatched braai area, where master braaier and lodge manager Jan van Wyk delivers up some serious food.

Points of interest in the area are German war memorials and the kokerboom forest. The peace and tranquillity of Auob will linger in the memory long after you have left — and the stars at night deep in the Kalahari defy description.

Bookings for Auob can be made through Namibia Country Lodges, PO Box 6597, Ausspamplatz, Windhoek, tel (09264-61) 24-0375.

Khaudum Game Park

Elephants, lions, spotted hyenas and black-backed jackals are just some of the nocturnal visitors you may see in your camp at Khaudum Game Park in far northeastern Namibia.

Stretching across 384 000 ha of thick woodland savannah north of Bushmanland, this reserve is one of the wildest, remotest parts of Africa. Here large numbers of game, drawn by an abundance of waterholes in the baking Kalahari sandveld, thrive in a wilderness of rugged beauty and solitude.

For true nature-lovers Khaudum's attractions are tantalising: it is one of the few Namibian reserves hosting Africa's 'painted wolves' — the wild dogs; it is never crowded with human visitors; the distances to and from civilisation are vast; and access to the reserve is limited to 4x4s. Note that visitors entering the reserve must do so in a convoy of at least two 4x4 vehicles.

Most of the reserve consists of rolling Kalahari sand-dunes covered by Rhodesian teak, false mopane, kiaat and red syringa trees; thick savannah woodland; dry river beds; and flat, clay pans cloaked by camelthorn, umbrella-thorn and leadwood trees. It is the only Kalahari sandveld in Namibia that is protected.

Wildlife Khaudum does not have Etosha's huge numbers of game, but it is a sanctuary for some rare species of antelope such as roan, tsessebe and reedbuck. Elephants are plentiful (herds of up to 80 are known to come down to the waterholes in the dry season), and there are healthy populations of giraffes, wildebeest, lions, gemsbok, hyenas, kudu and eland. Less commonly seen are the wild dogs and cheetahs (the author and naturalist Austin J Stevens and his companion were woken one night by a pack of six wild dogs running over their sleeping bags while pursuing a steenbok).

Birdlife About 320 species of bird inhabit Khaudum Game Park, among them such rare ones as copperytailed coucal, blackfaced babbler and rufousbellied tit. There are plenty of raptors, including bateleur eagle, western banded snake eagle, whitebacked and whiteheaded vulture and Wahlberg's eagle. Other species include Meyer's and Cape parrot, Bradfield's hornbill, sharptailed starling, Dickinson's kestrel and African hobby.

Tips for travellers

- There is no fuel within the reserve. The nearest petrol is at Tsumkwe in the south, Bagani in the north and Rundu in the west.
- Before visiting Khaudum, try and get a detailed map of the area from the Surveyor General's office in Windhoek (ask for Map Number 1820 — Mukwe).
- Each 4x4 will need about 120 litres of fuel to get through the park from Katerere to Mukwe. Visitors to Khaudum must travel in parties of at least two 4x4s — a provision laid down to guarantee the safety of those in the reserve.
- No caravans are allowed and no night driving.
- Be prepared to get bogged down in mud in the rainy season.
- If you're towing a trailer, it must have the same track width as your 4x4.

Deadly queen of the hunt

Although the male lion is the battle-scarred warrior of his pride, the female is huntress supreme. She takes charge of the kill, doing so with such ruthless power and ferocity that, with her sisters, she can bring down a galloping adult giraffe at 60 km/h.

Her hunting success depends largely on the element of surprise, and the speed of her charge. Because she can only maintain her speed for one or two hundred metres, it's essential that she gets as close as possible to her quarry without being seen. Then she must bring it down in the very first charge.

A charging lioness mounts her fleeing victim with a flying leap from behind, and with one mighty swipe of her paw bowls the animal over. On the ground she sinks her fangs into the victim's throat, applying enough pressure to sever the oesophagus and strangle the unfortunate creature.

Game drives The tracks in the reserve cross the dunes and follow the course of dry river beds known as 'omurambas'. The three major omurambas are Khaudum and Cwiba in the north, and Nhoma in the south. Visitors usually follow these omurambas for the best game-viewing.

During Khaudum's dry season the floodwaters of the Okavango Delta in the north raise the water table of Khaudum's omurambas, providing a plentiful supply of drinking water at a dozen or so waterholes. These include the Khaudum, Bureka, Elandvlakte, Oussi, Tsau, Leeupan, Tari Kora, Kremetart, Soncana, Baikiaea and Tsoane waterholes.

Where to stay Two rustic rest camps, Khaudum Camp on the northern banks of the Khaudum Omuramba in the north of the reserve and Sikereti Camp in the south, offer basic facilities. Khaudum Camp has three wooden huts and a couple of campsites; Sikereti has three camp-

Khaudum Game Park at a glance

Locality:	Northeastern Nambia on the Botswana border.
Climate:	Hot to very hot summers, with most of the rain (550–600 mm) falling between December and March. Winters warm to mild, but cold at night.
Number of camps:	Two.
Game drives:	A 300-km network of deep sand tracks crisscross the reserve, providing access to all the major waterholes across the length and breadth of the reserve.
Hides and waterholes:	11 major waterholes: Khaudum, Bureka, Elandvlakte, Oussi, Tsau, Leeupan, Tari Kora, Kremetart, Soncana, Baikiaea and Tsoane.
Other attractions:	Star-gazing, recording night sounds.
Accommodation:	Two rest camps: **Khaudum** (three huts and campsites) and **Sikereti** (three huts and campsites).
Booking address:	Ministry of Environment and Tourism, Private Bag 13267, Windhoek, tel (09264-61) 23-6975/6. For an organised trip to Khaudum contact Namib Wilderness Safaris, PO Box 6850, Windhoek, tel (09264-61) 22-0947.
When to go:	Game-viewing is best in the dry season (June–October); birdwatching is best between November and March.
What to take with you:	All provisions (including food, water and plenty of fuel), bedding, cutlery and crockery, firewood, binoculars, camera.
How to get there:	From Bushmanland in the south travel via Grootfontein, Tsumkwe and Klein Dobe. From Rundu in the north, travel eastwards on the B8 for 115 km towards Katerere. Head south from Katerere for 75 km to Khaudum (allow two hours for this leg).
Nearest petrol:	Tsumkwe in Bushmanland; Mukwe or Rundu (be sure to have at least 120 litres of petrol when you leave Tsumkwe to get you through to Mukwe).
Open:	Sunrise to sunset throughout the year.
Special precautions:	Khaudum lies within a malaria area, so take precautions prior to departure. Be aware of dangerous animals walking through the camps at night.

sites and three thatched timber huts. The huts in each camp are equipped with a table and chairs, and four beds (mattresses only). Each camp has showers (heated by a wood-burning boiler), toilets and an open-air cooking area. No bedding, cutlery or crockery are provided, but firewood is available.

The rest camps are unfenced, and a variety of animals, including elephants, wander through them at night.

Where to see game If you're considering a trip to Khaudum, go in the dry season (May–November) when game populations are at their peak. Much of the game disperses in the wet season (December–April), and the elephants often leave the reserve. Game-viewing is best along the omurambas and close to the waterholes. Driving along the omurambas is slow-going, so be prepared to take your time, and take plenty of provisions and water.

You may leave your vehicle, but the Namibian Ministry of Wildlife, Conservation and Tourism will not accept responsibility for any injury or damage to property which may result from a visitor's encounter with a wild animal.

Mudumu National Park

A reed-walled, double-decker pontoon drifts down the lazy waters of the Kwando River, carefully avoiding pods of hippos half-submerged midstream. On the banks, rustic thatched chalets melt into the foliage of dense riverine bush and trees, casting welcome shade upon the grassed terraces.

It's another languid afternoon at Lianshulu Lodge in the Eastern Caprivi's Mudumu National Park, and the only sound to break the siesta is that of elephants crashing through trees in the mopane woodlands.

Mudumu National Park covers 850 km^2 of mopane, savannah and acacia woodlands east of the Kwando River, as it empties into the Linyanti Swamp. Here and there ancient baobabs, marulas, wild fig and leadwood trees tower over the vast floodplains.

The eight cosy A-frame chalets of Lianshulu (with *en suite* facilities) lie flush against the banks of the Kwando, on the western edge of Mudumu, close enough for you to hear the wind shuffling through the reedbeds. Looking on to the river is the splendid main lodge building with its lounge, diningroom, curio shop and bar. Here you'll be served excellent cuisine accompanied by some of the finest wines in Africa.

Wildlife The abundance of water, and the lush riverine vegetation of Kwando River attract a variety of game to Mudumu's precincts. Although the river is just 50 m wide, it serves as a perfect

Tips for travellers

- **Before you go, get a map of the area from the Chief Conservation Officer at Katima Mulilo.**
- **If you're visiting the area by road, you are advised to drive a 4x4 vehicle. To visit Mudumu National Park, you must first report to Nakatwa Station.**
- **You need a permit to fish in the Kwando River (available at Popa Falls Rest Camp or the Chief Conservation Officer at Katima Mulilo).**

retreat for hippos basking in its shallows, or for crocodiles lazing on its banks.

The hinterland of the Kwando provides rich feeding grounds for 500 elephants and water-loving mammals such as red lechwe, sitatunga and Cape clawless otters. The surrounding woodlands host bushbuck, buffaloes, impala, lions and spotted hyenas. If you're lucky, you may spot a pack of wild dogs — one of Africa's threatened species.

Birdlife There are at least 400 species of bird in the Caprivi area, and many of these are found in the Mudumu National Park. Species include western banded snake eagle, bateleur, fish eagle, pygmy goose, lesser jacana, purplebanded sunbird and African golden oriole.

Getting around If you'd like to try a boat ride on Lianshulu's pontoon *Jacana*, take along a camera, binoculars and a fish-

Mudumu National Park at a glance

Locality:	Eastern bank of the Kwando River (Eastern Caprivi), 150 km west of Katima Mulilo.
Climate:	Hot, wet summers (October–April); mild, dry winters.
Number of camps:	Nakatwa Hut on the banks of the Kwando accommodates eight people.
Game drives:	Various game drives are offered through the park.
Hides and waterholes:	Birdwatching hide at Lianshulu.
Trails:	Ranger-led trails take you along the river and inland.
Other attractions:	Swimming, visiting nearby Mamili National Park.
Amenities:	Bar, diningroom, swimming pool.
Accommodation:	**Lianshulu Lodge:** Eight two-bedded, A-frame chalets, with *en suite* facilities. **Mvubu Lodge:** Two-bedded luxury tents. Three campsites and one hut (eight people) at Nakatwa. **Namushasha Lodge:** six twin-bedded bungalows, each with *en suite* bathroom.
Booking address:	Nakatwa Campsite: The Chief Conservation Officer, Katima Mulilo, tel (067352) 27. Lianshulu Lodge: Wilderness Safaris, PO Box 78573, Sandton 2146, tel (011) 883-0747. Mvubu: Nkwazi Africa Fishing and Photographic Tours, PO Box 195, Wilgeheuwel 1736, tel (011) 764-4606. Permits: Wildlife Conservation and Tourism, P/Bag 1020 Katima Mulilo, tel (067352) 27. Namushasha: PO Box 21182, Windhoek, tel (09264-61) 24-0375.
When to go:	Game-viewing is best from May to September; birdwatching is best from November to March.
What to take with you:	Light, khaki-coloured clothing; your own provisions if you intend camping.
How to get there:	Turn off the B8 on to the D3511, east of the Kongola Bridge. The Lianshulu Lodge turn-off is 40 km further on; Nakatwa a little further. Lianshulu has its own airstrip near the lodge; and Air Namibia services the M'Pacha international airport near Katima Mulilo. Good gravel roads to Victoria Falls and Chobe.
Open:	Sunrise to sunset throughout the year.
Special precautions:	Basic medical aid. Take antimalaria precautions before you go. Beware of crocodiles and hippos in the Kwando River.

ing rod. Tigerfishing is one of the attractions of boat rides here, but keep a look-out for hippos basking in the shallows.

Lianshulu Lodge also offers its guests day- and night-time nature drives in open 4x4 vehicles; guided walks in the Mudumu National Park, and a visit to the Lizauli Traditional Village where you can witness the unique culture and traditions of the local people. Experienced guides are on hand to inform and entertain visitors.

If you'd like to explore further afield, there are several safari operators offering trips to the Linyanti Swamp and Mamili National Park further south. Contact the Namibian Ministry of Tourism, tel (09264-61) 23-6975.

Where to stay Apart from Lianshulu Lodge, the park offers accommodation at the well-appointed Mvubu and Namushasha lodges and at Nakatwa Campsite, just north of Nakatwa Island on the banks of the Kwando River.

NAKATWA The camp offers one hut accommodating eight people, and three campsites. The hut has crockery and cutlery, but you must bring your own bedding and provisions.

MVUBU LODGE Two-person luxury tents, a restaurant, superb bar and outdoor dining area form the nucleus of this delightful lodge, which lies a short distance from an oxbow in the Kwando River as it veers westwards and then turns sharply to the east.

The oxbow and accompanying floodplain alongside Nakatwa Island attract a variety of game, including elephants, buffaloes, kudu, roan and impala.

Mvubu, like Lianshulu Lodge, lays on game drives, fishing and mokoro expeditions daily.

NAMUSHASHA LODGE A fairly new lodge in the Caprivi, Namushasha is on the east bank of the Kwando River, just 12 km from the Mudumu National Park — and just across the river from the West Caprivi Game Reserve.

The lodge has six twin-bedded bungalows, each with *en suite* bathroom, and offers guests boat rides down the Kwando, guided game drives in open 4x4s, fishing and birdwatching trips.

Namushasha Lodge has its own airstrip (three hours from Windhoek), and is just 20 km by road from Kongola (See also main entry on p. 186.)

Namib-Naukluft Park

The apricot-coloured contours of the Namib's dune sea rise magnificently from the pallid grasslands and gravel plains of western Nambia — nature's own masterpiece in wind and sand.

Nearby the ice-blue waters of the Atlantic form a stunning contrast with the white sheets of the Skeleton Coast and a soothing mantle of grey fog.

In the distance, black islands of rock rise from the ground, their turrets blurred by heatwaves streaming from the desert floor.

This is the heart of Namib-Naukluft Park — for lovers of isolation and tranquillity, one of Southern Africa's treasured destinations. To fully appreciate this wonderful desert environment, you have to journey to the highest sand-dunes in the world at Sossusvlei, climb to their graceful summits and soak in the interminable, desolate beauty.

The Nama called it 'Namib' — which means 'a vast, seemingly endless plain'. And they always referred to this desert as a female, because only a devoted mother could sustain her offspring in such an inhospitable environment, where even the rain evaporates before it hits the ground.

The Namib-Naukluft Park, comprising 4,9 million ha, is the fourth largest national park in the world, and accounts for more than one-tenth of the surface area of Namibia. It's 400 km long — from Lüderitz in the south to Swakopmund in the north — and 150 km wide.

Because of its immensity, the park contains a great diversity of landforms, ranging from dune seas to open plains, gorges and high cliffs.

The giant dunes have been blown into parallel ridges and valleys running from north to south. The sand covers a vast plain, bisected by fossil rivers — the dusty, skeletal remains of watercourses that surged to the sea millions of years ago. Peppered across this plain are the weathered turrets of granite hills, desolate and devoid of life.

From the tourist's point of view, the park can be divided into five main areas: the Southern Section; the Middle Namib, incorporating Sesriem and Sossusvlei; Naukluft or the pre-Namib; the Northern Section, between the Kuiseb and Swakop rivers; and the Western Section, including Welwitschia Drive and Sandwich Harbour.

The Southern Section If you travel from South Africa, a good way to start your tour of the park is to stop off at Ais-Ais and Africa's largest canyon, the Fish River Canyon, for a day or two, then head northwards for Sesriem, stopping off on the way at Duwisib Castle.

The Middle Namib This part of the Namib-Naukluft Park is known as Gobaba — 'the endless plains of the dune country' — and it represents the heart of a desert born about 80 million years ago, between the Oligocene and Pleistocene times. For many visitors this section of the park is the most awesome, with such highlights as visits to Sesriem and Sossusvlei.

SESRIEM The camp at Sesriem lies at the western edge of the Namib-Naukluft Park, where the Tsauchab River enters the great dune sea. This is an ideal base for visitors to explore the area and the only point from which you can reach Sossusvlei, 65 km to the west.

About 4 km from Sesriem is the Sesriem Canyon, named after the six thongs (rieme) early Dutch settlers tied together to draw water from the canyon. A flight of steps takes you down to the refreshingly cool water, where you may swim. Another attraction near Sesriem is the huge Elim Dune, about 5 km west of the camp. Set aside an hour for a climb to the summit,

Tips for travellers

- **When you book for the park, you will receive a detailed map, showing the camps and the distances between them. Always bear in mind, though, that there is no water or firewood at the camps and that only basic toilets are provided. A golden rule of the park is: never leave the demarcated tracks in your own vehicle, because this can cause untold damage to the surrounding countryside.**
- **If you intend overnighting in the park, you'll need a permit — available at Hardap Dam, Sesriem, as well as the tourist offices in Lüderitz and Swakopmund. On weekends you can get a permit in Walvis Bay at Suidwes and CWB service stations, and in Swakopmund at Hans Kriess Motors.**

which gives you superb views of the surrounding desert and gravel plains.

There are 10 old camping sites and nine new ones (with ablution blocks) at Sesriem, where the only amenities are wood, fuel and cold drinks.

SOSSUSVLEI Some of the world's highest sand-dunes rear up like abstract, pastel-toned sculptures 300 m above the desert sea at Sossusvlei. Below them, on the fossil remains of the dry Tsauchab River bed, twisted camelthorns form canopies of green — incongruous against the shifts and turns of the ochre dunes.

Take your camera along and set aside a full day at Sossusvlei, so that you can trek to the highest dunes and later rest with a cool drink at the base of these giants.

The road from Sesriem to Sossusvlei is 63 km long and tracks the valley of the Tsauchab, a broad river bed highway (known as the Corridor), ending where the river does — at a flat, white pan, fringed with trees.

You can drive to within 4 km of Sossusvlei in a two-wheel-drive vehicle, but you'll have to walk the rest of the way. You may not stay overnight at Sossusvlei, but the park's authorities have extended the opening and closing times, so that you may arrive there before sunrise and leave after sunset — the best times to see the dunes. If you have your camera, places to visit are the Main Vlei, Dune 45, the Hidden Vlei and the Dead Vlei.

About 4 km beyond the parking area at Sossusvlei is a series of white pans, flanked by dunes of the Namib. It would be well worth your while to walk this distance for the beautiful landscapes, and the abundance of camelthorn and nara bushes here.

About 200 species of animal survive in the sweltering sands of the dune sea, thanks to wind-borne nutrients from the northeast, and wind-borne moisture from the west. Tiny silverfish feed on the wind-borne detritus that gathers in the slipfaces of the sand-dunes; and they, in turn, form the staple diet of larger creatures, such as scorpions, lizards, geckos, crickets, spiders and wasps.

These again sustain other species, such as the golden mole, the side-winding adder and a variety of beetles. The animals get their moisture from cooling fogs that creep in nightly over the desert sands.

NAMIBRAND NATURE RESERVE Some 50 km south of Sesriem lies one of Southern

How dune beetles stop the fog

The endless dune seas of the Namib-Naukluft Park are home to a variety of amazing insects. Among these is the black onymacris beetle which has devised an ingenious way of getting the water it needs to survive.

During the night, when cool coastal fogs roll inland from the Atlantic Ocean over the dune seas of the Namib Desert, the onymacris beetle positions itself on top of a dune ridge, its head down and its back pointed at an angle towards the approaching fog.

The fog condenses on the animal's back into tiny particles of water, which then form a single droplet. The droplet then rolls down the beetle's back to its mouth.

Another desert beetle collects its moisture by digging a trench on the seaward slope of a sand-dune. The fog collects in droplets on the ridges of the trench, and the beetle sucks in its required moisture.

Africa's largest private game reserve — the Namibrand Nature Reserve (110 000 ha). The reserve is stocked with such diverse game as leopards, hyenas, blackbacked jackals, bateared foxes, red hartebeest, aardwolves, Burchell's zebras and gemsbok. These animals find food and shelter among the dunes, the green-gold grasslands and the granite-capped outcrops peppered with euphorbias, African moringas and quiver trees.

Birds you are likely to see at Namibrand include the pale chanting goshawk, Rüppell's korhaan, Ludwig's bustard, barn owl and short-toed lark.

At the heart of Namibrand Nature Reserve is Wolwedans Dune Camp, which consists of six domed-shaped tents and a communal lapa — all constructed on elevated wooden platforms. The tents are equipped with beds, bedside tables and a book shelf and all lead onto a verandah with beautiful views of the surrounding desert landscape. A sundowner deck is used for stargazing.

Wolwedans Dune Lodge is similar to the camp, but the units are more permanent and slightly more luxurious, with the central lapa area consisting of a spacious bar/lounge, an open-plan kitchen and a stargazing deck. The lodge is also elevated on wooden platforms and the front of each chalet can be opened to allow for a 180 degree view. For booking and details write to PO Box 5048, Windhoek or tel (09264-61) 23-0616.

SOSSUSVLEI WILDERNESS CAMP This luxurious lodge some 30 km from Sesriem lies on 7 000 ha of privately owned land between scenic desert plains and rugged mountains. There are nine *en suite* rock, timber and thatch chalets, each with a wooden deck and a plunge pool. Elevated boardwalks connect the chalets with the main lodge which comprises a bar/lounge and dining area.

Highlight of a visit to this lodge is an early morning drive to a nearby vlei for breakfast under the camelthorn trees. Hot-air ballooning is an optional extra. For more details contact the lodge at PO Box 6850, Windhoek, tel (09264-61) 22-5178.

MÖVENPICK SOSSUSVLEI LODGE Situated on the eastern edge of the Namib-Naukluft Park some 84 km from Solitaire and a five-hour drive from Windhoek, this lodge, set on a private concession of 44 000 ha, offers visitors to Sesriem and Sossusvlei top-class accommodation in pristine surroundings.

Here the canvas of Bedouin tents blends in with the Arab-styled sloping adobe walls of apartments that are simply but tastefully furnished.

Most stunning of all are the burnt sienna and terracotta colours of the lodge which resemble those of the burnished dunes and grasslands.

Attractions include hot-air balloon rides over the endless plains of the Namib (superb for taking photographs) and 4x4 excursions in the concession and to the dunes at Sossusvlei.

For details contact Mövenpick Hotel Central Reservations, PO Box 87534, Houghton 2041, tel (011) 484-1641.

Naukluft This part of the park — Naukluft means 'narrow gorge' — lies 120 km northwest of Sesriem, and contrasts dramatically with the scorching dune sea. Here high cliffs, home of baboons and kudu, tumble down to deep pools fringed by trees and bushes.

There are four campsites with ablution facilities, each accommodating eight.

More than 50 species of mammal (13 of which are carnivores) have been identified in this area. They include springbok, klipspringer, steenbok, leopard, blackfooted cat, caracal, bateared fox, Cape fox, smallspotted genet and aardwolf.

The Naukluft complex is a birdwatcher's paradise. More than 193 species have been identified on the plains and surrounding mountains, while at the campsite itself more than 90 different species have been spotted.

Black eagles, augur buzzards, lanner falcons and Bradfield's swifts soar high above Naukluft's kloofs, while in the vicinity of the perennial streams you'll find hamerkops, crimsonbreasted shrikes, pied barbets and woodpeckers.

Three hiking trails radiate from the camp: two are less than one day, and the Naukluft Hiking Trail is an eight-day adventure that starts at the Naukluft Hut and covers 119 km of the beautiful countryside of the pre-Namib. On the way you'll see Hartmann's mountain zebra, kudu and many of the mammals mentioned above. Another remarkable sight is the nests of the sociable weavers.

The Northern Section This area between the Kuiseb and Swakop rivers does not have the majesty of the dune country, but the open plains, punctuated here and there by granite islands (inselbergs), narrow, deep canyons and dry river beds are worth seeing. The river beds and plains host a diverse community of mammals: gemsbok, spotted hyenas, blackbacked jackals and zebras. Birds include lappetfaced and whitebacked vultures and the rare dune lark.

There are nine campsites, some set at the base of inselbergs, others on dry river beds, which affords you the perfect opportunity to explore the surrounding countryside on foot. The sites are Vogelfederberg (nearest to the coast, where you will see *Aloe asperifolia*), Swakop River, Ganab (herds of gemsbok and springbok), Blutkoppe (inselberg), Mirabib, Kuiseb Bridge, Kriess-se-rus, Homeb and Groot Tinkas.

The Western Section The lichen-coloured plains of the western Namib-Naukluft Park have been described as one of the wonders of the world. You can see these, and the ancient, prehistoric plant, *Welwitschia mirabilis*, on the 100-km, circular Welwitschia Route (head south from Swakopmund on the main road). Some 72 km into the route, you'll come across a giant specimen of welwitschia, probably more than 1 000 years old.

Walvis Bay, and Sandwich Harbour south of Swakopmund, are a must for anyone with even a vague interest in birdlife. The salt pans and lagoon at Walvis Bay host flamingoes, pelicans, cormorants and terns. Sandwich Harbour, 40 km south of Walvis Bay, is one of the most important wetlands in Africa, offering food and shelter to more than 200 000 waders. You will need a permit (available from the Ministry of Environment and Tourism, Private Bag 13267, Windhoek 9000) to enter Sandwich Harbour. The avian population is protected within a sanctuary (accessible only on foot) where reed- fringed pools are alive with terns, pelicans, flamingoes, dabchicks, moorhens, sandpipers and shelducks.

If you continue past the sanctuary, you'll come to Sandwich Harbour, once an anchorage for 18th-century whalers and, years later, headquarters of a guano-harvesting plant that eventually went bankrupt.

Climb to the summit of the dunes here, and you'll be able to photograph a magical panorama of sea, sand, wetlands and birdlife seldom seen in such abundance anywhere on earth.

Namib-Naukluft Park at a glance

Locality:	Central Namib Desert.
Climate:	Coastal temperatures are warm to mild in summer, but inland the mercury goes well into the thirties. Winters are mild to cool, with cold nights. Along the coast rain seldom exceeds 10 mm a year. Inland rainfall varies between 80 and 500 mm per annum in the north. Coastal fog is common between April and August.
Number of camps:	Several small campsites have been established.
Viewsites:	Sand-dunes are the most spectacular, particularly at Sossusvlei.
Other attractions:	Prehistoric plants, animals of the desert.
Amenities:	Fireplaces, refuse bins, toilets.
Accommodation:	Lodge accommodation is available at **Mövenpick Sossusvlei Lodge**, **Namibrand Nature Reserve** and **Sossusvlei Wilderness Camp**. Camping sites are available at **Sesriem** (caravan and camping site); the **Naukluft** (you must book in advance); **Kriess-se-rus** and **Homeb** (in the Kuiseb River, near Gobabeb); **Ganab** (good gamewatching camp); and **Welwitschiavlakte.**
Booking address:	Ministry of Environment and Tourism, Private Bag 13267, Windhoek 9000, tel (09264-61) 23-6975/6/7; Charly's Desert Tours or Hans Kreiss Service Station in Swakopmund.
When to go:	Throughout the year.
What to take:	Sunhat, waterbottles, hiking shoes, firewood, basic spares in the event of breakdown.
How to get there:	To get to the southern dune area of Sesriem and Sossusvlei from Windhoek, travel via Solitaire (249 km from Windhoek), then head south for Sesriem. There is petrol and a shop at Solitaire, so before you go further take enough food for a week and plenty of water. The northern part of the park is accessible via Swakopmund.
Nearest petrol:	Naukluft section: Bullsport Farm, from sunrise to sunset.
Open:	Sunrise to sunset throughout the year. Gates to Sossusvlei open an hour before sunrise.
Special precautions:	In the Naukluft section stow food away if you're leaving camp — baboons frequently raid food supplies.

Skeleton Coast National Park

If there's one place on earth that evokes the primeval terror of a lonely death, it is Namibia's Skeleton Coast — a dramatic wasteland of sand-blasted shores, shimmering mirages and the crumpled wrecks of ships fringing an icy sea between the Ugab and Kunene rivers.

Early Portuguese navigators, creeping southwards in their flimsy caravels towards the southern point of Africa, called this wilderness of white sand the 'coast of hell'. And the Swedish explorer, Charles John Andersson, described it as a place of frightful desolation.

The aura of death still remains — a larger-than-life skull and crossbones mark the entrance gate at Ugab, the southern boundary of the Skeleton Coast National Park — a warning to visitors that the Skeleton Coast is not for the faint-hearted.

However, in spite of the dozens of ships and lives this treacherous coast has claimed over the centuries, it exists today as an extraordinary oasis of tranquil beauty, just about as far as you can get from the madding crowd.

The northern border of the park is the Hoanib River. But beyond that is the Skeleton Coast Wilderness Area, one of the country's remotest regions, which is accessible only to those who join a fly-in safari. If you have the time, this is a trip that should not be missed.

Ugab Gate is one of two check-in points to the park. The other is at Springbokwasser, which you reach via Khorixas in the east. To reach Ugab, head north from Swakopmund along the coast to Mile 108. Whatever your chosen route, be sure to reach Ugab or Springbokwasser before 15:00. This will give you enough time to get to Terrace Bay.

Getting around After you've checked in at the gate, stop for a while at the Ugab River bed. Here, where wind-blown acacias and stands of wild tobacco plants cling to the parched surface of the river bed, you may be lucky enough to see gemsbok, springbok, and maybe even lions and brown hyenas.

The Ugab is one of the major rivers in Namibia and, on the rare occasions that it carries water, serves as a lifegiving artery to the animals and plants of the desert.

Continuing on your journey northward, the road runs parallel to the icy coast, bisecting the lichen-covered gravel plains which sweep away to the interior.

The plains, and the clumps of dunes among them, may appear desolate and devoid of life, but they serve as home to five different species of lichen and a variety of small desert animals and birds. The

Scavenging nomad of the desert

The shaggy brown coat, sloping back and slavering grin of the brown hyena's massive head as it trots through the dusk of the Skeleton Coast, are enough to send a shiver down the back of any casual observer.

Its Afrikaans name, Strandjut, which literally means beach tramp, seems particularly well applied. For the brown hyena is an opportunistic and relentless scavenger that will eat almost any carrion, from dead seals to gemsbok.

It is the rarest large scavenger in Africa, having been pushed out of its habitat by residential development, and ruthlessly shot down by farmers.

The hyena's powerful forequarters help the jaws and teeth to twist and break bones.

Today it survives unhindered in the Kalahari Gemsbok National Park, and there are healthy numbers of brown hyenas in parts of Botswana and the Namib Desert.

Several studies of brown hyenas have shown that many of them are nomadic, wandering great distances across the arid areas of Southern Africa. Professor John Skinner of the Mammal Research Institute in Pretoria found that one hyena had wandered a staggering 550 km in four months; another had moved some 650 km from its home range.

Damara tern lays her mottled eggs here, and they hatch virtually unnoticed in their perfect camouflage among the lichen-covered rocks and sand. Other common birds are Gray's lark, the Namaqua sand-grouse, the cumbersome-looking kori bustard and the blackbellied korhaan. Snakes on the gravel plains include two species of whip snake, and the Namib sand snake, which feed mainly on lizards.

If you get close to the ground you'll see the black and white tenebrionid beetles of the Namib, and other beetles and fish-moths that survive on the sand. Among the wind-blown detritus of the sand-dunes, you may even spot such dune predators as lizards, snakes, spiders, crickets and chameleons.

The Huab Driving north of Ugab, you'll reach the Huab, a glacial river whose inland roots — as little as 10 km away — supply water to elephants, black rhinos, gemsbok and other smaller mammals. The northern banks also mark the beginning of whale-shaped sand-dunes known as barchan dunes. Driven by the wind through the years, these dunes actually 'march', carrying with them their precious cargo of lizards, rodents and insects.

Tips for travellers

- On entering the park you will be required to produce receipts showing your reservation number.
- Petrol and water are only available at Terrace Bay, so bring your own supplies if you intend camping at Torra Bay. The nearest towns are Khorixas in the east and Henties Bay in the south.
- The roads are suitable for saloon cars, but take along extra water and basic spares just in case.

Further north, towards Kiochab, the rusting hulk of the schooner *Atlantic Pride* wallows in the sand, keeping company with the brown hyenas and blackbacked jackals that prey on the pups of the local seal colonies. Further on you may spot gemsbok, ostrich or springbok.

Torra Bay Just south of the Uniab River is Torra Bay, a favourite fishing spot, and the only place in the park where you may camp. There are basic toilet facilities here, but that's just about all, although a refreshment kiosk is brought in by the park's authorities during December.

The bay marks the beginning of the huge dunefields of the Namib, and their associated wealth of dune life. Be on the lookout for the white onymacris or 'fog-basking' beetles that scurry along the sand here, collecting moisture from the ephemeral mists that roll in during the night.

Beyond Torra Bay you come to the reed-fringed pools of the Uniab River Delta — a birdwatcher's delight. Here one arm of the delta offers a covered hide from which you may see lions, porcupines (towards evening) or blackbacked jackals.

An elevated parking area at the fifth delta looks down on five pools swarming with flamingoes, plovers, moorhens, Egyptian geese, dabchicks and avocets.

Damaraland Camp If you want to see Namibia's elusive desert elephants, then this camp is the place to be. Positioned on the southern slopes of the Haub River, 90 km from Torra Bay on the Skeleton Coast, Damaraland Camp was awarded second prize in the prestigious British Travel Writers 'Silver Otter' awards for the best ecotourism project in the world. The camp was established with the assistance of the 'Riemvasmaker' people of the area and is a shining example of the benefits to the local community of such tourism projects.

Eight large, *en suite* Meru tents flank a lapa with a bar and diningroom and offer a breathtaking desert ambience, where silence and peace reign supreme under a star-studded sky. Activities centre on walks and drives in search of the desert elephants and other mammals like black rhino, gemsbok, kudu and springbok. Some 2 400 San paintings and engravings on the cave walls at Twyfelfontein are another drawcard.

Dinner is usually served outside around an open fire. A small curio shop displays local handicrafts.

For more details and booking write to Damaraland Camp, PO Box 6850, Windhoek, tel (09264-61) 22-5178.

Skeleton Coast National Park at a glance

Location:	West coast of Namibia, between the Ugab and Hoanib rivers.
Climate:	Along the coast: generally cool and windy, with foggy mornings and evenings. Inland: summers hot, with searing winds from the east. Average annual rainfall 16 mm.
Game drives:	Coastal salt road from Ugab to Terrace Bay, and the road from the coast eastwards to Springbokwasser.
Trails:	Two: the three-day Ugab River Guided Wilderness Trail and a shorter 6-km trail starting at the Uniab River delta.
Other attractions:	Fishing, birdwatching.
Amenities:	At Terrace Bay restaurant, bar, shop, petrol.
Accommodation:	Two- and three-bedded cottages at **Terrace Bay**. Campsite at **Torra Bay**. Luxury safari tents at **Damaraland Camp**.
Booking address:	Namibia Tourism, Private Bag 13346, Windhoek 9000, tel (09264-61) 284-2178. Skeleton Coast Safaris organises fly-in safaris. Write to them at PO Box 2195, Windhoek, tel (09264-61) 22-4248.
When to go:	Throughout the year. Torra Bay only open in December and January.
What to take with you:	Water, food, bedding, warm clothing (in winter), camera, binoculars, walking shoes. Spares for your car, fishing equipment. Your reservation receipts. Hikers: sleeping bags and trail food.
How to get there:	205 km by road from Swakopmund to the Ugab Gate; 238 km from Khorixas to Torra Bay. Skeleton Coast Wilderness Area: Skeleton Coast Fly-in Safaris offer five and 10-day trips. Contact: PO Box 2195, Windhoek or tel (09264-61) 22-4248.
Nearest doctor:	At Swakopmund.
Nearest garage:	At Terrace Bay. Torra Bay has fuel only during the December/January school holidays.
Open:	All year round. Arrive at Ugab no later than 15:00; at Springbokwasser one hour before sunset.
Special precautions:	Be prepared for extreme heat on the plains. Do not venture from demarcated roads.

Terrace Bay Your final destination in the Skeleton Coast National Park is Terrace Bay, which has a pleasant rest camp with two-bedded cottages. There's a restaurant with good food, a cosy bar, a shop, petrol, water and basic repair facilities — a welcome contrast to the desert and plains around you. Terrace Bay also has an airstrip.

On your way eastwards out of the park through the grey, lichen-capped hills to Springbokwasser and Khorixas, you'll probably get your first glimpse of the *Welwitschia mirabilis*. More than 1 000 years old, this plant has a long taproot, and its leaves are up to three metres long.

Hiking trails There are two hiking trails in the park. The main trail is the three-day Ugab River Guided Wilderness Trail, on which hikers follow a route adapted to the prevailing climatic conditions and the group's preferences.

Take your own food, bedding and water, and be prepared to sleep under the stars at overnight camping sites. On the last day of the trail, hikers are shown the remains of a whalebone hut settlement more than 200 years old.

The night before you start the trail can be spent at Mile 108 campsite, 40 km south of the Ugab River Gate. Book through the central reservations office in Windhoek (see 'At a glance' box). The other trail (6 km) starts at the Uniab River delta, and follows a narrow canyon towards the sea where you may catch a glimpse of the Skeleton Coast's rare Heaviside's dolphin frolicking in the waves.

Skeleton Coast Wilderness Area This part of the Skeleton Coast lies between the Hoarusib and Kunene rivers, the latter forming Namibia's northern border with Angola.

Desolate and remote, the long, wreck-strewn beaches are sandwiched between the endless dunes and gravel plains of the hinterland and the Atlantic.

Skeleton Coast Fly-in Safaris — the only tour group allowed to operate in the area — flies visitors in for five and 10-day safaris. This unforgettable trip introduces you to the amazing life forms of this desert pavement, the huge colony of Cape fur seals at Cape Frio, the remains of San rock shelters and the roaring sand-dunes of the Namib. The trip also usually includes a visit to a Himba village. To book a trip contact Skeleton Coast Fly-in Safaris, PO Box 2195, Windhoek, tel (09264-61) 22-4248.

WATERBERG PLATEAU PARK

Tinged orange and red by the rays of the late afternoon sun, the sandstone ramparts of the Waterberg Plateau tower above the scorched plains of northern Namibia. From the top a panorama unfolds of thornbush savannah stretching southwards towards distant horizons, and of the twin peaks of the stately Omatako Mountain emerging through the haze.

This is the scenery of the Waterberg Plateau Park, one of Namibia's most important sanctuaries for rare and endangered species of game, and also a delightful retreat for nature-lovers seeking tranquillity in the wild.

Some 91 km west of Otjiwarongo, the Waterberg Plateau is the remnant of a much wider terrace of compacted Etjo sandstone that has worn away over 200 million years. Just 250 m high and about 40 000 ha in extent, the plateau supports a variety of habitats. The foothills and slopes are crowned with lush bush, acacia and evergreen trees; the plateau is largely savannah grassland, dotted with wild syringa, laurel fig and Namib coral trees. In addition, there are about 140 lichen species around the sandstone pillars, domes and cliffs.

Wildlife This environment, with its abundance of water, was seen as the perfect refuge for rare and endangered species, particularly white rhinos, roan and sable antelope and tsessebe.

A massive game relocation programme started after 1972 when the park was proclaimed: sable and tsessebe were brought in from Caprivi, white rhinos and impala came in from the KwaZulu-Natal parks, black rhino were imported from Etosha, and Cape buffaloes were brought up from the Addo Elephant National Park.

Other residents include leopards, cheetahs, brown hyenas, giraffes, red hartebeest, eland, klipspringers and a variety of other large and small mammals.

All the animals brought in were first placed in a quarantine camp and then an acclimatisation camp before they were released into the reserve where, today, they are quite at home.

Birdlife Apart from the abundance of game, the birdlife is also prolific. Among the 200 species, persistent birdwatchers are likely to see Monteiro's hornbill, short-toed rock thrush, redbilled francolin and rockrunner. Raptors include black eagles and the only breeding colony of Cape vultures in Namibia. A vulture restaurant offers carcasses to the vultures every Wednesday morning.

Where to stay In June 1989 the Bernabé de la Bat Rest Camp, an attractive complex overlooking the escarpment, opened its doors to the public. This attractive camp offers three- and four-bedded bungalows, grassed camping sites (each site accommodates eight people) and a swimming pool. There are also a communal kitchen and ablution facilities, a restaurant and a shop.

Game drives and hiking trails Three options exist for getting around in the park: walking one of the several self-guided trails, taking an escorted walk, or hiring a 4x4 (with a driver) for escorted drives around the plateau. The most popular of these are the half-day driving safaris which take in several hides and waterholes.

The rest camp features nine short walks: among these are the Mountain View Walk, which leads to the top of the plateau; the Aloe Circle, which meanders through a wild grove of aloes; and the Kambazembi Walk, which tracks the base of sheer cliffs, where you may see dassies and baboons.

Apart from the shorter walks around the camp, two major hikes attract backpackers from all over Southern Africa. They are the four-day Waterberg Unguided Trail in the south, and the three-day guided trail in the west of the park. The guided trail (maximum eight

Tips for hikers

- **No children under 12 are allowed on the Waterberg Unguided Trail.**
- **No fires are allowed on the trail, so you must take a camping stove.**
- **You have to sign an indemnity form before setting out on the unguided trail.**
- **All refuse must be carried out of the trail.**
- **Walk quietly, and always be aware of the presence of large and potentially dangerous mammals.**

people) starts at 16:00 on a Thursday, and continues through to Sunday afternoon. The trails are offered on the last three weekends of every month. To secure a place on either of these trails, be sure to book well in advance.

Waterberg Unguided Trail This 42-km-long trail starts on top of the plateau near the Bernabé de la Bat Rest Camp (on Wednesdays only), and offers excellent vantage points of the plateau and surrounding countryside. Before you embark on it, however, be aware that you will be walking in the company of potentially dangerous white and black rhinos, Cape buffaloes and other mammals.

The walk is a real adventure for true naturalists, and highlights the extraordinary effect erosion has had on the sand-

Waterberg Plateau Park at a glance

Locality:	Northern Namibia, about 91 km east of Otjiwarongo.
Climate:	Winter days are moderately warm (25 °C); nights are extremely cold. Summers scorchingly hot with little rain.
Number of camps:	One.
Game drives:	Escorted game drives and half-day safaris available.
Hides and waterholes:	Several hides and waterholes.
Trails:	Two major trails: the Waterberg Unguided Trail and the Waterberg Guided Trail. Nine shorter trails around camp.
Other attractions:	Panoramic views; outstanding rock formations.
Amenities:	Restaurant, bar, swimming pool, information centre.
Accommodation:	Twenty three-bedded bungalows and fifteen five-bedded bungalows in the **Bernabé de la Bat Rest Camp;** 34 tourisettes (for bus-tour groups); 20 grassed tent sites accommodating a maximum of eight, and 20 caravan sites, with access to a field kitchen and ablution facilities. Restaurant and shop. **Waterberg Trail:** Two overnight stone shelters with water and toilet facilities.
Booking address:	Ministry of Environment and Tourism, Private Bag 13267, Windhoek, tel (09264-61) 23-6975.
When to go:	1 April to 30 November.
What to take with you:	Trailists should take all basic provisions, camping stove, inflatable mattress (if possible), warm clothing, hiking boots, binoculars.
How to get there:	From Windhoek drive north on the B1 through Okahandja towards Otjiwarongo. About 29 km south of Otjiwarongo turn right on the C22 and drive for 41 km, before turning left on the D2512. The park, which is signposted from the B1, is 17 km further on.
Nearest doctor:	Otjiwarongo.
Nearest petrol:	At the park.
Open:	08:00–sunset (closed 13:00–14:00). Because of the extreme summer temperatures, the trail is only open from 1 April to 30 November.
Special precautions:	If you're hiking, be aware that white rhinos and buffaloes in the park are potentially dangerous, and you may need to take sudden evasive action.

stone ramparts. Pillars, domes and massive craters have been carved out of the sandstone by wind and rain. The hollows, filled with water in the rainy season, bring sustenance to the park's animal populations in the dry season.

The first day's hike (13 km) includes a stop at the Omatako Viewpoint, from which you may see the twin peaks of the Omatako Mountain rearing 2 286 m above sea level, and the Omatako Canal, a 203-km-long irrigation canal.

After crossing the Ongorowe River you arrive at the Otjozongombe Shelter, a basic overnight stop with waist-high walls of natural rock covered by a corrugated iron roof. There's a central dining area and four sleeping rooms (you sleep on the sand). From here you may walk to the edge of the plateau for panoramic views of the Otjozongombe Valley.

The second leg (7 km, from Otjozongombe to Otjomapenda) close to the plateau edge, meanders past fascinating rock formations, including Mushroom Rock, down through Klipspringer and Kudu kloofs to Otjomapenda Shelter, a snug overnight stop with two sleeping 'rooms' and a central eating area, built against a sandstone cliff-face.

On the return leg of the trail (Otjomapenda to Otjozongombe) the path winds through open bushveld and grass, dominated by wild syringa trees. This is white rhino territory, so keep a sharp lookout for potential trees to climb.

The final leg from Otjozongombe to the Bernabé de la Bat Rest Camp takes you across the Ongorowe River and the Burkea Plain (the name comes from its wild syringa trees). The last stage takes about four-and-a-half hours.

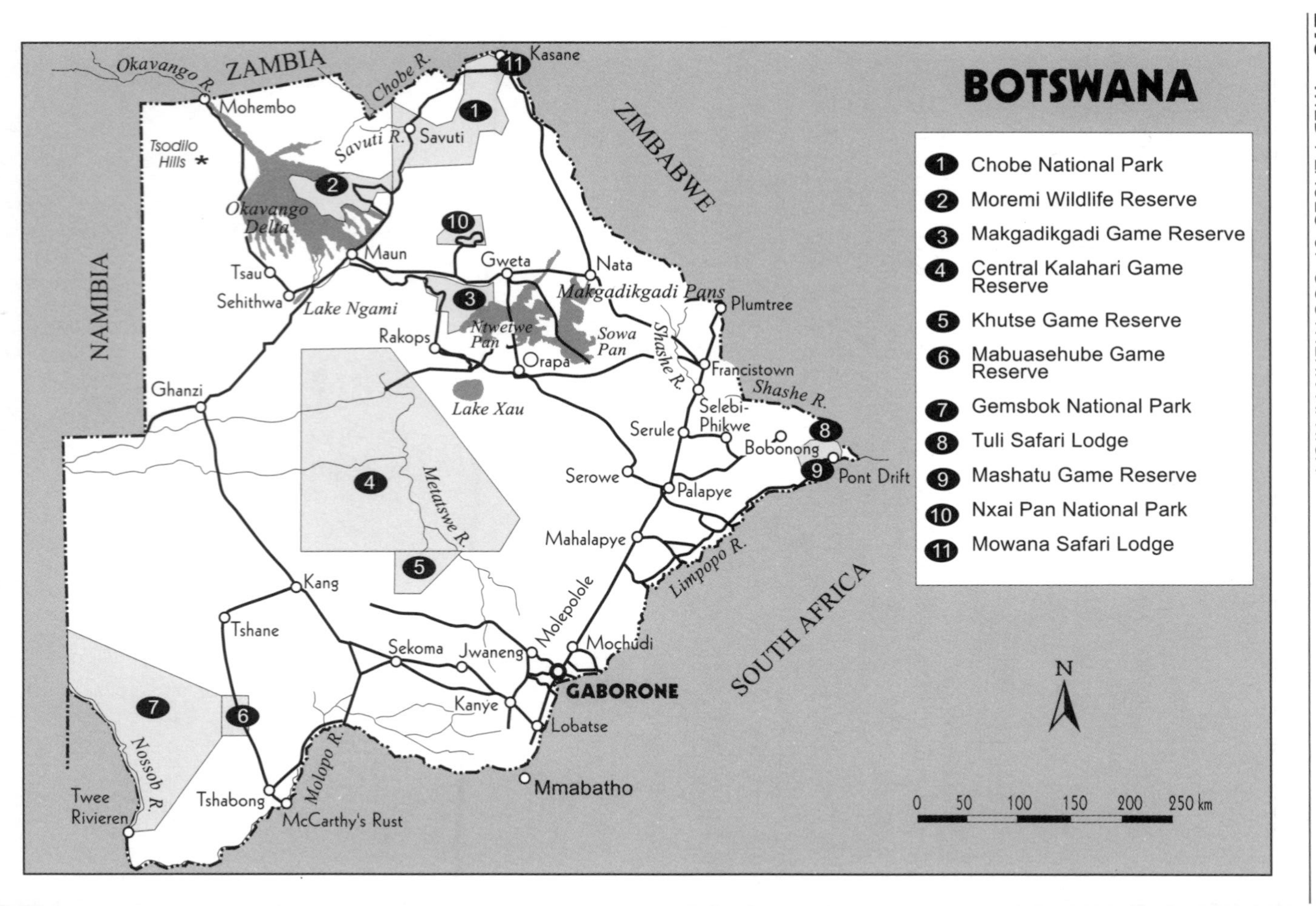
BOTSWANA
1 Chobe National Park
2 Moremi Wildlife Reserve
3 Makgadikgadi Game Reserve
4 Central Kalahari Game Reserve
5 Khutse Game Reserve
6 Mabuasehube Game Reserve
7 Gemsbok National Park
8 Tuli Safari Lodge
9 Mashatu Game Reserve
10 Nxai Pan National Park
11 Mowana Safari Lodge
N
0 50 100 150 200 250 km
ZAMBIA
ZIMBABWE
NAMIBIA
SOUTH AFRICA
Okavango R.
Mohembo
Tsodilo Hills
Okavango Delta
Chobe R.
Savuti R.
Savuti
Kasane
Maun
Tsau
Sehithwa
Lake Ngami
Ghanzi
Rakops
Gweta
Nata
Ntwetwe Pan
Sowa Pan
Makgadikgadi Pans
Lake Xau
Orapa
Metatswe R.
Shashe R.
Francistown
Plumtree
Selebi-Phikwe
Bobonong
Pont Drift
Serule
Serowe
Palapye
Mahalapye
Limpopo R.
Mochudi
GABORONE
Molepolole
Lobatse
Mmabatho
Jwaneng
Kanye
Sekoma
Kang
Tshane
Molopo R.
McCarthy's Rust
Tshabong
Nossob R.
Twee Rivieren

BOTSWANA

Nowhere in Africa is the cycle of life and death, birth and renewal, survival and decline more apparent than in the great sun-scorched spaces of Botswana. Here desert and delta survive as seemingly impossible neighbours in one of the great wildernesses of the world — the Kalahari.

Larger than Spain and nearly the size of Texas, Botswana is a land of baking sand wedged between Namibia in the west, the Caprivi in the north, Zimbabwe in the east and South Africa in the south.

About 85 per cent of its surface area consists of Kalahari sand, an ochre to light-brown mantle that carries the footprints, skeletons and fossils of 160 species of animal and an extraordinary community of hardy hunter-gatherers known as the San.

The scorching sun, the inhospitable terrain and the generally featureless landscape would hardly seem to hold many attractions for visitors arriving here for the first time.

But the very remoteness of Botswana, the amazing ability of its animals and humans to survive in such wild surroundings, and the pristine beauty of its untouched spaces are the very ingredients that lure adventurers into its rugged heart.

Anyone who doubts the attractions only has to join a 4x4 safari to the primeval fringes of Kubu Island in the Makgadikgadi Pans and watch a bateared fox at sunset coax her youngsters to sniff out termites in the gathering gloom. Or lie under the stars at the Mgobe wa Takhu waterhole, and listen to the sound of hyenas and hyphaenae palms shivering in the wind.

Wildlife

From the calcrete floors and ancient baobabs of the Makgadikgadi Pans to the savannah grasslands of Chobe National Park and the mopane woodland of the Tuli Block, there's an enormous variety of wildlife in Botswana.

But it is in the Okavango Delta and Moremi Game Reserve that visitors will find unforgettable beauty.

In the lush indigenous forests of the delta and its islands, and along the floodplains spawned by this great marriage of water and sand, more than 400 species of bird flourish.

On the mainland and among the islands lions, elephants, hyenas, wild dogs, rhinos, hippos and crocodiles congregate with a teeming variety of antelope and other smaller mammals— warthogs, mongooses, spotted genets, monkeys, bushbabies and tree squirrels.

Chobe National Park itself has 450 species of bird and most of the large mammals, as do the safari lodges and reserves of the Tuli Block. The central Kalahari, too, will impress even the most seasoned gamewatchers.

The wild places

Botswana's commitment to conservation is considerable: national parks and game reserves cover 17 per cent of the country's surface, while wildlife management areas cover a further 20 per cent. There are eight national parks and game reserves.

Okavango Delta and Moremi Game Reserve

Towards the northwestern corner, the burning sands of the Kalahari suddenly surrender to an amazing flood of water that charges through a long panhandle, then spills out across the Kalahari in an amazing labyrinth of waterways that covers more than 22 000 km^2 of Botswana.

This is the Okavango Delta, one of the world's great wetlands and undoubtedly one of Africa's favourite wild places.

Fed by the Kunene River in the north, the waterways of the delta annually transport more than 10 billion tons of water across the scorched plains of Botswana.

As the crystal-clear waters of the delta's tributaries seep and ooze through carriageways of reeds and waterlilies, the air is filled with the call of the fish eagle, the loping splash of a sitatunga darting through the shallows, or the roar of hippos surfacing from the deep.

This is the setting for a large variety of some of Africa's best bush camps, and the destination for visitors from around the world.

Chobe National Park

Lying in the northwestern part of Botswana, Chobe is Botswana's third largest wildlife sanctuary, covering 11 700 km^2 of dusty plains, mopane woodland, desert-adapted grassland and, to the north, a forested floodplain fed by the Chobe River.

It is famous mostly for its large herds of elephants, buffaloes, lions and hyenas, the last two of which are commonly seen in and around the Savuti area. It is also popular for its abundant birdlife. But many visitors choose Chobe because it's close to the Victoria Falls (90 km from its northern extremity).

Apart from its public campsites, Chobe has some of the finest safari lodges in Africa. These offer superb game-viewing, excellent cuisine and sumptuous service.

Makgadikgadi Pans

These pans, the remnants of a great lake that once covered most of Botswana, are the largest of their kind in the world. Nearly three times the size of Etosha Pan, they sprawl across 12 000 km^2 of central Botswana, and incorporate the Makgadikgadi and Nxai Pans National Park.

Seasoned travellers searching for the remotest corners of the globe have described the Makgadikgadi as a destination unparallelled for its serenity and peace — a place where man is dwarfed by the sheer size and silence of the open spaces.

There are several safari companies offering tours of the Makgadikgadi, and full details of these are available on p. 356 of the chapter 'Safari Tours in Southern Africa'. The names of tour operators are also listed in the section on the Makadikgadi on p. 236.

Central Kalahari

The Central Kalahari Game Reserve, one of the world's largest reserves and probably

Southern Africa's most remote, is the final refuge for the subcontinent's San population. Only the most intrepid travellers venture into this and the other remote Kalahari reserves — Mabuasehube to the southwest and Khutse Game Reserve to the south.

Most visitors head for the northern section of the Central Kalahari Reserve, seeking out the interminable spaces and haunting silence, and the migratory herds that head for the waterholes of Deception Pan, Sundays Pan and Piper's Pan in the north.

Khutse and Mabuasehube have special attractions — lions, wild dogs, cheetah and the semi-desert-adapted species such as bateared fox, brown hyena, honey badger and gemsbok.

Gemsbok National Park

Abutting South Africa's Kalahari Gemsbok National Park and having recently been linked to it to create a 3,2 million-ha wilderness sanctuary, this park is typical sandy Kalahari, with seas of apricot-coloured dunes, fossil riverbeds and vast herds of springbok, zebra, gemsbok and wildebeest. There's no formal accommodation here, and travellers wishing to visit it will have to use South Africa's Kalahari Gemsbok National Park as their base.

Tuli Block

Two reserves deserve special mention in this region in southeastern Botswana — Mashatu Game Reserve, one of the largest privately owned game reserves in Southern Africa, and Tuli Safari Lodge — both upmarket destinations offering luxury accommodation, pampered personal service and superior game-viewing.

Where to stay

Accommodation ranges from international-standard hotels in the major cities to thatched bush chalets, safari tents and tree-houses — A-frame units solidly built in the branches of indigenous trees — in the national parks and game reserves.

Most of the camps in Botswana are quite small — accommodating between eight and 24 guests at a time.

Many lodges and camps offer pools, scenic riverside restaurants and bars, regular game-viewing trips in four-wheel-drive vehicles, mekoro, and power boats, and walking trails through the bush.

Climate

During summer (late October to March) most of Botswana is extremely hot, with temperatures reaching 44 °C in some places. The rainy season starts in November, peaks in January and ends in March, and rainfall ranges from 650 mm in the northeast to 250 mm in the southeast.

Winters are sunny and mild to warm, although night-time temperatures sometimes plummet to zero.

When to go

The autumn, winter and spring months between May and November, when large numbers of animals migrate towards the waterways of the Okavango Delta, are the best time to go.

November and December — the calving months — are an excellent time to witness nature's own timetable of regeneration. The rainy season, from January to March, sees the migration of large numbers of game into the summer grazing areas, while the delta comes alive with sounds of hundreds of bird species.

In March and April thousands of zebras and other animals migrate towards the Savuti area of Chobe Game Reserve.

How to get there

By air Two international airports service Botswana, a new one at Kasane which provides easy access to the northern regions, and Seretse Khama International Airport in Gaborone.

British Airways flies to Gaborone twice a week via Johannesburg from Gatwick Airport. There are regular flights from Windhoek in Namibia to Maun.

Other airlines servicing the country are Kenya Airways, Zambian Airways, Lesotho Airways, Air Tanzania, Air Zimbabwe, Royal Swazi Air, South African Airways and Air France. Air Botswana regularly flies to Lusaka, Victoria Falls, Harare, Maputo, Manzini, Maseru and Johannesburg.

No regular taxi or combi service is available to and from Seretse Khama International Airport, but there is a regular bus service.

By road Botswana's main tarred highway runs from the South African border in the southeast through Gaborone, Francistown, Kazungula and on to Kasane where the borders of Botswana, Zimbabwe, Zambia and Namibia converge.

The main road from Maun to Nata in the Okavango Delta is tarred. Botswana is also easily accessible from Victoria Falls, Bulawayo (Zimbabwe) or Lusaka (Zambia).

There are some 20 different border posts on Botswana's borders, the main ones being: Kazungula (Zambia Zimbabwe), Ngoma (Namibia), Pont Drift Pioneer Gate (South Africa).

By rail Botswana Rail links Lobatse Gaborone and Francistown, while a daily service operates between Mafikeng in South Africa and Bulawayo in Zimbabwe. A twice-daily train shuttle operates between Gaborone and Francistown.

Tip for travellers

The distances between towns in Botswana are usually vast, and many of the game reserves are remote, with no basic provisions, petrol, medical facilities or even accommodation.

Before you leave establish the state of the roads and the distances to nearest petrol stations, food and water supplies and medical services.

This applies particularly to the reserves of the central, southern and southeastern Kalahari, where 4x4 vehicles are the only way to travel.

Where to go

The Okavango Delta is Botswana's prime destination, but the great game reserves — among them Chobe, Mashatu and Tul Lodge — offer excellent gamewatching prospects. The other destinations, Central Kalahari Game Reserve, Mabuasehube Kutse and the Makgadikgadi Pans usually require a four-wheel-drive vehicle, and are best visited in a convoy of 4x4s or with a registered safari company.

Entry requirements

All visitors require valid passports, but many countries are exempt from visas including South Africa. For details contact the Chief Immigration Officer, PO Box 942, Gaborone, tel (09267) 361-1300, or telephone the Botswana Consulate in Johannesburg at (011) 403-3748, or Cape Town at (021) 421-1046.

Getting around

The most popular ways of exploring the wild places of Botswana are by mokoro (dugout canoe), along the maze of waterways of the Okavango Delta; on foot, in the company of a professional game ranger; or overland in a 4x4 vehicle.

Several excellent tours and safari packages by air, road and waterway are avail able throughout the year to the Okavango Delta, Makgadikgadi Pans, Chobe Game Reserve, the Central Kalahari Game Reserve and the Gemsbok National Park. The most attractive safari packages are featured in detail in the chapter 'Safari Tours in Southern Africa' (p. 351).

Health precautions

Visitors from infected areas must have valid yellow-fever vaccination certificates. Malaria is endemic in some areas, so be sure to take a course of antimalaria tablets.

Travel information

Contact any travel agent or the Director of Tourism, Private Bag 0047, Gaborone, tel (09267) 35-3024, or the Department of Wildlife and National Parks Reservations Office, PO Box 20364, Maun, tel (09267) 66-1265.

CENTRAL KALAHARI RESERVES

Three major sanctuaries form the heart of the central Kalahari, and together they cover a staggering 56 372 km². The largest of these by far is the Central Kalahari Game Reserve, followed by Khutse Game Reserve which adjoins it in the south and Mabuasehube Game Reserve in the southwest. West of Mabuasehube is the Gemsbok National Park. This huge park and South Africa's Kalahari Gemsbok Park have been linked to form one massive wilderness area, where there is a free flow of game between the two reserves, and opportunities for visitors to the region to stay in both parks. Although the Gemsbok Park has no lodge accommodation there are a few pleasant campsites.

The Two Rivers Camping Ground near the park's entrance have three undeveloped campsites, while the Rooiputs Camping Ground, 25 km up the Nossob River Valley, has six campsites without facilities.

The Poletsaw Camping Ground in the northern section of the Nossob River Valley has three campsites.

Full lodge accommodation and camping sites with all amenities are available at South Africa's Kalahari Gemsbok Park (see entry on p. 59).

Central Kalahari Game Reserve

An endless sea of shimmering pans and golden grasslands stretches from one horizon to the other in the Central Kalahari Game Reserve. Across this sea of singing grass and sand, mopane, camelthorn, Kalahari apple and silver cluster-leaf trees stand in grand isolation.

Believed to be the second largest reserve in the world, it covers 51 800 km² in the Kalahari Basin, one of the largest uninterrupted areas of sand known to man (1,2 million km²). It is also one of the world's most uninhabited regions, with less than 1 000 people living there — half of whom are San.

Four fossil rivers flow through the reserve, among them the dusty carriageway of a watercourse that meandered through the northern Kalahari 16 000 years ago, and which today is known as Deception Valley — a prime gamewatching and camping area.

Although the south and southwestern Kalahari are often associated with large plains of ochre sand and linear dunes, much of the Central Kalahari Game Reserve — especially the northern part — is covered by a variety of grasses, acacia thorn trees, tough, drought-resistant shrubs and a number of flowering plants.

Scattered along the shallow valleys are tsamma melons and gemsbok cucumbers, the major source of water for gemsbok, hartebeest, and San during the dry season.

The reserve was established in 1961 as a sanctuary for the San — a wilderness where they could live in peace in their own natural home. Today they occupy the southern parts of the reserve.

Wildlife The cycle of life and death, birth and renewal revolves around the meagre rain that falls in the Central Kalahari Game Reserve. But even without it, a remarkable array of mammals manage to survive.

The Kalahari is home to 300 000 hartebeest, some 300 000 wildebeest and more than 100 000 springbok, which invariably attract a retinue of predators, such as lions, jackals, wild dogs and hyenas.

These, and other mammals adapted to the harsh, dry environment, such as gemsbok, honey badgers, impala, caracals, mongooses, suricates and ground squirrels, manage to eke out nourishment and survival on the plains and around the several hundred pans of the central Kalahari. The same is true of a variety of snakes.

Birdlife Semi-desert-adapted species such as kori bustard, korhaan, secretarybird and ostrich are fairly common in the region, as are raptors such as pale chanting goshawks, blackshouldered kites and blackbreasted snake eagles.

Among the smaller birds are the colourful lilacbreasted rollers with their beautiful turquoise and blue plumage, Marico flycatchers, pied barbets, Namaqua sandgrouse and Kalahari robins.

Where to stay There's no formal accommodation in the reserve, but camping is allowed at Deception Valley, one of the prime destinations of the Central Kalahari Game Reserve. You can camp just about anywhere at Deception Valley, but most travellers head for Owens Camp or choose the shade of acacia trees in the valley. Other popular camping areas are Piper's Pan and Sundays Pan.

Game drives If you're based at Deception Valley you may drive north to Sundays Pan, Passage Pan and the Khuke fence, or head south to Letiahau waterhole and Piper's Pan.

Piper's Pan, 70 km southwest of Deception Valley, has a waterhole lit by solar power, which attracts a variety of game.

Alternatively, drive 20 km north of Deception Valley to Sundays Pan, which offers shady campsites some distance from the waterhole.

KHUTSE GAME RESERVE

Established to conserve the pans of the central Kalahari, Khutse covers 2 600 km^2, and is the southern extension of the Central Kalahari Game Reserve.

It is the most accessible of the central Kalahari reserves, lying 250 km northwest of Gaborone, and the Khutse Gate can be reached via Molepolole and Letlhakeng.

From the west, it's a two-day drive on a rough gravel and sand road from Hukuntsi via Kang, Dutlwe, Letlhakeng and Kungwane.

Tips for travellers

- **Don't travel in the central Kalahari without a 4x4, and then preferably in a convoy of at least two vehicles. Always take sufficient petrol to cover the return journey to your final destination.**
- **On your journey be sure to stop every couple of hours to remove grass seeds from the radiator.**

Wildlife The reserve consists of short grass- and shrublands, interspersed with shallow dune valleys and about 60 clay pans. These attract the ever-present herds of wildebeest, springbok and hartebeest, and rarer species such as cheetah and wild dog. Smaller mammals include caracals, porcupines, bateared foxes, pangolins, meerkats and mongooses.

In the rainy season large herds of springbok, gemsbok, hartebeest, lions, giraffes and brown hyenas usually congregate around Moreswa Pan.

Birds In times of good rains you'll see a good number of the 150 bird species in the vicinity of the pans, among them whitebacked vulture, greater kestrel, kori bustard and lark.

Game drives A circular 135-km game drive starts and ends at the Galabodimo Game Scouts' Camp at the reserve's entrance. It heads southwest to Moraye Pan and then north to Molose Borehole, Mahurushele Pan and Khutse Pan, where you can be assured of seeing an abundance of game.

For something completely different, take the two-day, 190-km drive from Khutse to the San village of Molape and stop on the way at the San community at Metsamanong.

About 100 km north of Molape is Deception Pan (see p. 228).

Where to stay Apart from the Galabodimo Pan Game Scouts Camp at the gate, there are half a dozen campsites in Khutse Game Reserve, the largest of which is Khutse Campground, between Khutse 1 and Khutse 2 pans.

The other campsites are Mahurushele Pan (one site at the edge of the pan), Sekushuwe Pan (one site under a camelthorn tree), Khakhe Pan (four campsites on the dune overlooking the pan), Molose Waterhole (three campsites) and Moreswe Pan (four campsites and a small saline waterhole).

MABUASEHUBE GAME RESERVE

This park covers 1 972 km^2 east of Botswana's Gemsbok National Park, and its name is taken from the Kgalagadi word for 'place of red earth' — a reference to the ochre sands so characteristic of the southwestern Kalahari.

Remote and desolate, the reserve is covered with vast, grassy plains, peppered with distinctive bastard umbrella-thorns

Armoured tank of the Kalahari

One of the seldom-seen nocturnal creatures of the Central Kalahari is the pangolin, an animal so secretive and solitary that it is known by some tribespeople in Africa as 'the son of shyness'.

Shuffling half-erect across the moonlit sands of the Kalahari it casts an eerie shadow, leaving behind it a tell-tale trail of clawmarks and dragging tail.

Of four species of pangolin on the continent, just one — the ground pangolin — lives in Southern Africa. The creature reaches a mass of 15 kg and grows up to one metre long.

The light-brown horny scales which cover its body are actually compressed hair-like filaments once prized throughout rural Africa as charms, or as a vital component of a witchdoctor's brew. These scales are so strong that, according to wildlife author Charles Astlet Maberley, they can deflect the bullet of a high-powered rifle fired 100 m away.

and camelthorns, and sinuous rows of ochre dunes with massive pans sprawled among them.

In the first 60 years of this century herds of springbok numbering tens of thousands roamed these vast plains and were hunted down with relish by large prides of lions. Today, just a remnant of these vast herds still exists.

Wildlife Large herds of springbok and hartebeest congregate around the pans in the rainy season, followed by the larger carnivores — lions, hyenas and black-backed jackals.

Smaller predators include caracals, African wild cats and Cape foxes, while the insect-eating bateared foxes are often seen scurrying along the dusty highways of sand, with noses or ears to the ground.

Subsurface water in this part of the Kalahari is not far down, and gemsbok may be seen using their hooves to dig the sand out when their traditional menu of tsamma melons and gemsbok cucumbers is in short supply.

Birdlife About 170 species of bird congregate along the edges of the pans and in the grasslands, among them the secretary-

The savage bride of dawn

For sheer savagery and feline grace, there is little in the Southern African wild that matches the caracal or lynx. The San of the Kalahari call the female caracal 'the bride of dawn' — their name for the Morning Star. The ancient Egyptians honoured it by setting its image in the tombs of the Pharaohs. Its power, agility and grace are legendary. Some reports claim that a caracal can kill several birds in an airborne jump in a few seconds. Asian royals, who kept caracals as domestic hunting pets, claimed they could kill up to 10 pigeons in one jump.

Caracal means 'black-eared' in Turkish, a reference to the dark markings behind the ears. These and other dark marks on the face, and the animal's reddish-brown coat, camouflage it exceptionally well against the tan colours of its home range.

The large triangular ears serve as amplifiers that can pick up the faintest sounds in the bush: a springhare hopping across the sands of the Kalahari; a Damara dik-dik brushing its flanks against stems of grass or a striped mouse scuttling from its burrow.

Central Kalahari reserves at a glance

Locality:	Central Botswana.
Climate:	The summers are hot to very hot, with temperatures sometimes up in the forties. Winter days are warm (average 25 °C); the nights cold with frost.
Number of camps:	The major camping spots in the region are: **Central Kalahari Game Reserve:** Deception Valley, Sundays Pan, Piper's Pan; **Khutse Game Reserve:** Galabodimo Pan Game Scouts' Camp, Khutse campground, Mahurushele Pan, Sekushuwe Pan, Khakhe Pan, Molose Waterhole, Moreswe Pan; **Mabuasehube Game Reserve:** one campsite at the Game Scouts' Camp.
Game drives:	The region has hundreds of options for game drives.
Hides and waterholes:	There are no formal hides here, but the waterholes and pans are excellent for watching game.
Trails:	Penduka Safaris, PO Box 55413, Northlands 2116, tel (011) 883-4310/15.
Other attractions:	San villages.
Amenities:	Water is not available at the campsites in the reserves, with the exception of the Matswere Game Scouts' Camp (Central Kalahari Game Reserve) and the Galabodimo Pan Game Scouts' Camp (Khutse Game Reserve).
Accommodation:	No formal accommodation, but there are camping sites in the reserves (see camps above).
Booking address:	Department of Wildlife and National Parks, PO Box 20364, Maun, tel (09267) 66-1265, Gaborone, tel (09267) 37-1405 or the Department of Tourism, The Mall, Gaborone, Botswana, tel (09267) 35-3024.
When to go:	March to April, after summer rains, when new vegetation attracts game.
What to take with you:	Detailed maps, compass, all provisions, including plenty of water, camping equipment, spares (at least two spare tyres), complete first-aid kit, firewood, light clothing (anoraks and warm clothes for winter nights), torches.
How to get there:	Central Kalahari Game Reserve: From Maun head eastwards for Nata. After 50 km turn right on the tar to Makalamabedi village. When you get there turn right on the western side of the fence and drive south for 108 km until you reach the Matswere entrance to the reserve. Head west for 10 km to the Matswere Game Scouts' camp. Permits and water are available here. From Rakops head south-west for 55 km towards Matswere Game Scouts' Camp. From Ghanzi you'll have to hire a guide to direct you to Xade. Khutse Game Reserve: Drive north-west from Gaborone to Molepolole and then to Letlhakeng. Mabuasehube Game Reserve: From South Africa travel from Kuruman to McCarthy's Rest border post, then drive 120 km north to Tshabong. Continue northwest to the reserve. From the north travel to Tshane. The northern entrance is 125 km further on.
Nearest doctor:	Maun, Francistown.
Nearest petrol:	Rakops, Mopipi and Hukuntsi.
Open:	Central Kalahari Game Reserve, Khutse and Mabuasehube: April to September: 06:00–18:00; October to March: 05:30–19:00.
Special precautions:	Breakdowns are your biggest concern in the Kalahari. Take adequate spares and plenty of water. Avoid heat exhaustion and sunstroke.

bird, kori bustard, black korhaan and a variety of smaller species.

Game drives The main road through the reserve is the south-north Tshabong–Tshane road which bypasses three huge pans. Another three pans can be reached by arterial routes branching east and west of the main road.

Bosobogolo and Mpathlutwa pans in the south, Mpathlutwa Pan in the central area and Mabuasehebe Pan in the north are good vantage points for viewing game and birds.

Beyond the reserve Petrol and supplies are available at Hukuntsi, about a day's drive north of Mabuasehube, and if you'd like to travel to Khutse Game Reserve from Hukuntsi, it's another two days' drive (be sure to take plenty of water and food). From there you may head north into the Central Kalahari Game Reserve towards Deception Pan.

Another rewarding drive is the one northwest of Mabuasehube to Masethleng Pan which, when the summer rains come, is covered by a carpet of short green grass, attracting herds of springbok, impala, wildebeest and red hartebeest.

Where to stay There are some attractive undeveloped campsites within Mabuasehube Game Reserve, all superbly located for watching game.

A popular camping area is that at Mabuasehube Pan where there are four sites with pit latrines and a small waterhole. Mpaathutlwa Pan offers two campsites with pit latrines and a small waterhole, while Khiding Pan has the same facilities. Lesholoaga Pan has two sites — one with a toilet and another without. This campsite also overlooks a small waterhole.

Chobe National Park

More than 30 000 elephants — the largest concentration in any national park in the world — roam the vast open spaces of Chobe National Park, a wild country of floodplain, baobab, mopane and acacia woodland, stretching across the endless face of Africa.

In this land of lumbering giants on the edge of the mighty Chobe River, visitors find rich rewards in the ever-changing panorama of animals.

The park is huge, covering 11 700 km^2 in northeastern Botswana. Flowing along its northern boundaries are the Linyanti and Chobe rivers, while in the south the Savuti Channel brings its precious cargo of water into the Mababe Depression.

Spurred northwards by the aching dryness of the Kalahari, massive herds congregate along the sumptuous and cooling floodplains of these rivers. In the north, legions of elephants wallow in the marshlands of the Chobe, joining squadrons of multicoloured birds that hover around the islands. Streams of buffaloes, pods of hippos and rarer species such as suni, puku and red lechwe, occupy the river banks.

In the southern part of the park, blue wildebeest, zebras, buffaloes and a variety of antelope form massive chains of animals on the endless plains of the Savuti and in the Mababe Depression. Among the plains animals are the lions, leopards, spotted hyenas and wild dogs.

Northeast of Savuti are the Ngwezumba Pans which, filled by water during the rainy season, become a major meeting point for thirsty animals, including the oribi antelope and a retinue of other species.

These wonderful natural spectacles are within the reach of tourists in Chobe National Park with a selection of superior accommodation, ranging from basic safari-tented camps to luxury lodges.

Northern Chobe There are three superb lodges in the northern part of the park.

CHOBE GAME LODGE Chobe Game Lodge, in the northern extremity of Chobe National Park, is one of Southern Africa's most exclusive safari resorts. Situated just 90 km west of the Victoria Falls, the lodge offers 45 luxury *en suite* bedrooms with full glass windows overlooking the river, as well as four private suites with their own swimming pools and private patios.

Facilities include the Linyanti Bar — acknowledged as the best in Botswana — a lounge area, a wildlife reference library and a curio shop.

Motswana game rangers take guests on early morning and late afternoon game drives in open 4x4s right into the midst of buffalo and elephant herds. Other all-day safaris (with a packed lunch) take guests into the wilderness areas of Nogatsha and Ngwezumba pools, 80 km south of the lodge. The lodge also offers tigerfishing expeditions on the Chobe River (boats and fishing tackle are supplied).

Guests may choose between a sunset cruise down the Chobe River on the *Mosi-Oa-Tunya*, a river barge that once plied the waters of the Zambezi, or a cruise in a simple dugout.

CHOBE SAFARI LODGE A popular venue for tigerfish anglers, this lodge lies just west of Kasane, on the edge of the Chobe River. Accommodation is in 22 thatched rondavels, with access to a restaurant, cocktail bar and a lovely old riverboat — the *Fish Eagle*. Sunset cruises, safaris, bird-watching trips and transfers to other camps in the park are the main attractions here.

CHOBE CHILWERO A lovely thatched diningroom with an observation platform upstairs overlooks the Chobe River as it snakes through the bushland of the Chobe National Park at this attractive camp in the northeastern section of the park.

Chobe Chilwero — which means 'the beholden view' — accommodates 16 guests in tidy A-frame thatched bungalows, equipped with gas lamps and ethnic wall hangings.

The bungalows have *en suite* showers and toilet facilities. Other attractions are a fireside bar and professional rangers who are at your service 24 hours a day.

Southern Chobe The southern Chobe offers wonderful camping and spectacular lodges.

ALLAN'S CAMP AND SOUTH CAMP Two delightful Gametracker camps, Allan's Camp and South Camp, have been established along the banks of the Savuti Channel in the wilder southern section of

Tips for travellers

- **Kasane Village, on the park's northeastern border, is a major junction for visitors entering the park, or travelling to the Caprivi region, Zimbabwe or Zambia. It serves as the park's headquarters, and its facilities include an international airstrip, bakery, hotel, service station and off-sales.**
- **When driving in the park, keep a respectful distance from the elephants. Many of the pachyderms are mothers with calves, and getting too close may spark off a charge.**

Chobe Game Reserve known as Savuti South. Both camps offer game drives twice daily, with boating and fishing as optional extras.

Allan's Camp is a 16-bed safari camp consisting of reed-panelled A-frame chalets with *en suite* shower, toilet and washbasin. Light is supplied by paraffin lamp and candles, and there's hot and cold running water.

South Camp accommodates guests in eight safari tents, with access to an ablution block with showers and flush toilets.

Each camp has a well-stocked bar, lounge and diningroom.

LLOYD'S CAMP For the best guides in Botswana, there's no place to beat Lloyd's Camp, an exclusive bush retreat catering for 12 people. Game drives start with the rising sun, and the guides follow animal spoor until they find the animals. Afternoon drives end with a fireside meal under the stars, and bushveld banter over drinks.

CAMPING SITES There are five public campsites: Serondela, Tjinga, Nogatsaa, Linyanti and Savuti, all of which have water toilets and showers, except Tjinga, which has no toilet facilities. Serondela, at the northernmost part of the reserve, is the only camp you can reach with a two-wheel-drive vehicle. Keep your provisions well stowed at Serondela — baboons consistently poach from campers here.

Savuti campsite, deep in the bush off the western road from Kasane, bears the nocturnal tracks of predators and other big game on its sandy surface. Spotted hyenas, elephants and lions are among the animals roaming around the camp here. Park authorities warn visitors not to bring citrus fruits into this area, because elephants here have broken into cars in search of oranges.

Linyanti Private Game Reserve This 125 000-ha sanctuary is bordered in the north by the Linyanti River and in the east by the Chobe National Park, an area that includes a large section of the Savuti Channel as well as vast savannah grasslands. The combination of wetlands and dry plains supports a huge variety of animals, ranging from water-adapted species such as lechwe, waterbuck, hippo and crocodile to lion, hyena, elephant, wildebeest, impala, roan and sable antelope, giraffe, baboons and monkeys.

In this paradise of mopane and acacia trees, of river and lagoon, are three very special camps, isolated and on the doorstep of vast herds of animals. These camps are Duma Tau, King's Pool and Linyanti Tented Camp.

DUMA TAU This recent addition to Wilderness Safaris' Okavango stable is built in the shade of large mangosteen trees overlooking the shimmering waters of a large lagoon, east of the source of the Savuti Channel. The luxury thatched, elevated suites are a few paces from the water's edge — perfect for watching lion, wild dog and cheetah come down to drink, or to see the blazing eyes of nocturnal species such as aardwolf, genet, pangolin, springhare and bushbaby.

The suites accommodate 16 people and are all *en suite*, with hot and cold running water, flush toilets and shower. There is also a well-appointed diningroom, cosy pub and plunge pool to cool off in after a day in the bush.

You'll see plenty of hippos and lions at Duma Tau and the birdlife along the waterways is prolific. Boats and four-wheel-drive vehicles are available for gamewatching trips, and the camp has some wonderful hides to take you close to the big game.

For more information or to book contact Wilderness Safaris, PO Box 78573, Sandton 2146, tel (011) 883-0747.

KING'S POOL CAMP Hippos snort and splash metres from the 10 luxurious tented rooms at King's Camp, which lies on the banks of the Linyanti River near the source of the Savuti Channel. Like Duma Tau, King's has access to all the big game of the Okavango, including large numbers of elephant, giraffe, buffalo, zebra, wild dog, cheetah and hyena. The waterways and reedbeds are home to a huge variety of birds, such as herons, fish eagles, stilts, plovers and storks.

The rooms have been built on raised teak decks with superb views of the lagoon and surrounding bush and as you stroll out to the water's edge you can almost smell the lions, elephant and buffalo that move up from the Savuti Channel. Each room has *en suite*, tiled bathrooms with showers, toilets and hand basins. There's a central lounge, diningroom and pub under thatch, as well as

How zebras outwit the enemy

Gamewatchers in Chobe National Park will invariably see large herds of Burchell's zebras mixing freely with blue wildebeest and other antelope. This gregarious behaviour is not accidental — different groups of animals mix with each other to give the group increased vigilance, a strategy that greatly enhances their chances of survival.

When Burchell's zebras are on the move, the young bachelors guard the rear and flanks. If the herd is pursued by a predator, such as a lion, it runs at half speed — a ploy which actually helps their chances of survival.

The slower the zebras run, the more compact the group; and the more compact it is, the less chance predators have of singling out individuals. The tactic only fails when an individual breaks rank or is left behind.

This is especially true of hot pursuits by hyenas and wild dogs, which tend to single out an individual that lags behind the rest of the herd.

The flailing hooves of fleeing zebras are particularly lethal to pursuing predators, and spotted hyenas, wild dogs and even lions have been floored or killed by the zebra's devastating kick.

an open-air 'kgotla' for meals under the stars. A sparkling swimming pool is built into the elevated deck.

Each tent has an *en suite* bathroom with shower, toilet and washbasin, built at right angles to the tent and overlooking King's Pool lagoon.

A teak-floored main lounge, bar and diningroom also overlook the lagoon and as you stroll out to the water's edge you can sense the presence of lions, elephants and buffaloes that move up from the Savuti grasslands in winter.

The Chobe-Linyanti area guarantees excellent elephant viewing, but the real perks are night drives where you'll see leopards, cheetahs, servals and other carnivores, and game-viewing cruises on the Linyanti River on a double-decker boat.

For details and reservations contact Wilderness Safaris in South Africa, PO Box 78573, Sandton 2146, tel (011) 883-0747.

Linyati Tented Camp This camp, east of King's Pool, near the western boundary of Chobe National Park, lies on the edge of a complex of lagoons, flowing waterways and woodlands which merge with dry plains further away from the Linyanti River. The area is popular for its large herds of elephant which head for the Linyanti River at the beginning of winter and migrate back to the plains during the onset of the rainy season.

The five luxury tents are set amongst game trails of sable, roan antelope, sitatunga, red lechwe and buffalo. In and around the surrounding forests and thickets you will also see kudu, zebra, waterbuck and impala which attract lion, leopard and wild dog.

Birdlife is abundant and outdoor pursuits include game and birding walks, day and night drives in an open 4x4 and exploring the waterways in Canadian canoes.

Access to the camp is by charter flight from Maun to Kasane.

To book contact Wilderness Safaris, PO Box 78573, Sandton 2146, tel (011) 883-0747.

Savuti Trails Camp Another addition to the Wilderness Safaris stable is this small (eight-bed) camp within the Savuti Channel.

The Meru-style tents, tucked into the bush, also lie within the Linyanti Private Game Reserve, where good concentrations of roan, sable, bushbuck and wild dogs mix with lions, leopards, cheetahs and elephants.

The camp's waterhole is one of the best in the Chobe-Linyanti region, and game-viewing there is supplemented by the usual day and night drives.

For more information contact Wilderness Safaris (see address above).

Getting around In the north a dirt road tracks the Chobe River along the park's boundary for 35 km until it reaches Ngoma, offering a number of secondary roads from which you may explore the adjacent mopane forest.

Keep a lookout here for buffaloes, elephants, white rhinos, wildebeest, zebras, impala and the rare fawn-coloured Chobe bushbuck.

For a great game-viewing trip, continue southwest from Ngoma through Kavimba and Kachikau until you reach Savuti. This will entail leaving the park and re-entering it north of the Goha Hills.

Fly-in safaris and trails The Desert and Delta Trail is a fly-in safari from Windhoek and Johannesburg that takes guests to Chobe and Etosha national parks.

The Ngamiland Trail is for those who wish to explore such wild places as the Okavango Delta, Moremi Wildlife Reserve and Chobe National Park.

Chobe National Park at a glance

Locality:	Northern Botswana, south of the Chobe River.
Climate:	Hot summers with thunderstorms between December and March. Mild to warm winters (nights can be cold).
Number of camps:	Numerous camps, ranging from luxury safari tents to basic stands with minimal facilities (see Accommodation).
Game drives:	All the game lodges and upmarket camps offer game drives.
Hides and waterholes:	Waterholes and pans are scattered throughout the park. Excellent places to watch game are along the 35-km road tracking the Chobe; at Ngwezumba Pans; at Savuti and in the Mababe Depression.
Trails:	Walking through the park is not allowed, but the five-day Fish Eagle Trail includes a two-day stopover in the park.
Other attractions:	Fly-in safaris to the Okavango Delta; river cruises; tigerfishing on the Chobe River. Get your camera out for the bush sunsets of winter.
Amenities:	The safari lodges are equipped with restaurants, bars, swimming pools, curio shops and river boats.
Accommodation:	**Chobe Game Lodge:** 45 luxury *en suite* rooms and four private suites; **Chobe Chilwero:** 16 guests in tidy A-frame thatched bungalows; **Chobe Safari Lodge:** 22 thatched rondavels and camping site; **Linyanti Camp** has eight twin-bedded luxury safari tents; **Allan's Camp:** eight A-frame chalets; **South Camp:** eight two-bedded safari tents. In addition there are five public campsites: **Serondela**, **Tjinga**, **Nogatsaa**, **Linyanti** and **Savuti**. **Linyanti Private Game Reserve:** King's Pool Camp and Savuti Trails Camp.
Booking address:	Chobe National Park: Department of Wildlife and National Parks, PO Box 20364, Maun, tel (09267) 66-1265; Linyanti, Chilwero, Allan's Camp, South Camp: Gametrackers: 31 Harley Street, Randburg 2194, tel (011) 781-0137, or Gametrackers Botswana, PO Box 100, Maun, tel (09267) 66-0302; Chobe Game Lodge, PO Box 32, Kasane, tel (09267) 65-0340; Chobe Safari Lodge, PO Box 10, Kasane, tel (09267) 65-0336; Safari operators: Afro Ventures, PO Box 1200, Paulshof 2056, tel (011) 807-3720; Drifters Adventure Tours, PO Box 48434, Roosevelt Park 2129, tel (011) 888-1160.
When to go:	The dry winter months, between April and October, are the best for viewing game at Chobe and Savuti.
What to take with you:	Light safari wear in summer, warm jacket in winter, sturdy walking boots, camera, lots of film, binoculars, field guides.
How to get there:	From South Africa Air Botswana will fly you to Maun; or Air Zimbabwe will fly you to Victoria Falls. From there most safari companies offer charter flights to Kasane.
Nearest doctor:	Kasane, just beyond the park's border.
Nearest petrol:	Kasane.
Open:	Chobe National Park: open all year round, but Mababe Depression and Savuti Channel area closed during rainy season (1 December–31 March).
Special precautions:	Take a course of antimalaria tablets before your departure.

The five-day Fish Eagle Trail, which starts in the Okavango Swamps, includes a two-day stopover in the park, either at Savuti or nearby Linyanti where you may fish for tigerfish, bream or barbel, or explore the waterways in a mokoro (dugout canoe).

Contact Okavango Tours and Safaris, PO Box 3666, Rivonia 2128, tel (011) 803-4464.

Mashatu Game Reserve

This beautiful sanctuary, one of the largest privately owned game reserves in Southern Africa, is home to seven of Africa's giant phenomena — the Limpopo River, the African elephant, the baobab tree, the eland, the ostrich, the kori bustard and the endless African sky.

Lying in a wild enclave of land in eastern Botswana between the Shashe and Limpopo rivers known as the Tuli Block, Mashatu covers 46 000 ha of savannah plains, riverine forests, open marshland and rugged outcrops of sandstone. The name comes from the Mashatu or nyala trees — round-topped leafy giants which cover the huge open spaces of this wilderness.

As prominent as the Mashatu trees of this reserve is its population of elephants, the largest group of pachyderms on private land in the world.

Wildlife The elephants of Mashatu are known as the relic herds of Shashe, which once roamed the Limpopo Valley in vast numbers. The elephants disappeared for about 60 years, but after 1947 they started slowly returning to the Tuli Block. Today there are more than 700 at Mashatu.

Visitors may drive into the midst of these mighty herds and marvel at how their numbers have been restored by conservationist Mike Rattray and his exceptional field officers. Elephants are not all you'll see on the game drives. A ranger and tracker at the helm in open four-wheel-drive Land Cruisers, linked by two-way radios, will follow the spoor of lions, leopards, elephants, giraffes, spotted hyenas, bateared foxes, aardwolves, cheetahs, kudu, Burchell's zebras, bushbuck and baboons. Spotlight-assisted night drives may reveal porcupines, aardvarks, spotted genets and civets, in addition to the larger carnivores. Other antelopes are eland, impala and steenbok.

Tip for travellers

Mashatu is one of Southern Africa's more upmarket reserves and, although it's costly, the reserve's management spares no effort in pampering its guests. The tariff is fully inclusive and includes all meals, snacks, accommodation, safaris and transfers from the airstrip or Pont Drift border post. Bar service and curios are charged separately.

Where to stay There are two camps at Mashatu — Mashatu Main Camp and Tent Camp, each providing a different style of accommodation.

MAIN CAMP The camp offers seven thatched rondavels and eight luxurious double bedrooms with private verandahs, air-conditioning and insect-proofed screen doors. Thirty people can be accommodated.

Attractive features of the chalets are the 'his' and 'her' bathrooms, and French doors which open out on to a private verandah with superb views of the bush.

The Gin Trap, an elevated fully licensed bar, overlooks a large waterhole at Main Camp. Guests may watch the animals come down to drink as they sip sundowners. Drinks are also served at the poolside nearby.

Buffet lunches are served in a thatched, open-sided building which also commands first-rate views of the waterhole. Elegant wines, mouthwatering venison dishes and a view of animals coming down to the spotlit waterhole at night lie in store for guests at the ilala palm boma, where dinner is served every night.

In winter a blazing fire burns in the centre of the boma as guests wine and dine to the sounds of Africa, and listen to yarns of the wild.

TENT CAMP The camp lies in the remote northern section of the reserve, and is just the place for those who don't mind sleeping within metres of lions or elephants padding by. There are seven luxury safari tents with *en suite* shower and toilet. Lion kills (of animals) have been reported in this camp before.

The tents are spotlessly clean and have comfortable single beds. A plunge pool in the camp offers cooling relief after a sweaty day in the bush, and guests may recline at the poolside with a drink before dinner is served in the boma.

Breakfast and lunch are served on an open-sided thatched deck.

Mashatu Game Reserve at a glance

Locality:	In the Tuli Block region of northeastern Botswana, five-and-a-half hours' drive from Johannesburg.
Number of camps:	Two.
Game drives:	Dawn and dusk drives daily.
Hides and waterholes:	Main waterhole in front of Main Camp.
Other attractions:	Drive to the Motloutse ruins; visiting historic sites.
Amenities:	Curio shop and swimming pool.
Accommodation:	Chalet accommodation at **Mashatu Main Camp;** two-person accommodation in seven twin-bedded safari tents at **Tent Camp.**
Booking address:	Mala Mala and Mashatu Game Reserves, PO Box 2575, Randburg 2125, tel (011) 789-2677 or tel Air Botswana on (09267) 975-3901.
When to go:	Year-round, but winter is cooler, and better for game-viewing.
What to take with you:	During winter (May–September) take very warm clothes with you.
How to get there:	From Johannesburg take the N1 to Pietersburg. Turn left at the Dendron turn-off, and continue along the R521 through Dendron, Vivo and Alldays to Pont Drift. Complete your customs clearance in South Africa, and park your vehicle. A Mashatu representative will collect you and accompany you through Botswana immigration. Collection times are between 12:00 and 14:00. The border closes at 16:00. Rattray Reserves offers chartered flights direct from Johannesburg, Maun, Gaborone or Kasane to the Tuli airstrip.
Nearest doctor:	Alldays, 58 km away.
Nearest petrol:	Alldays, 58 km away.
Open:	Throughout the year. The border post is open between 08:00 and 16:00.
Special precautions:	Large, potentially dangerous animals are likely to be encountered on game walks: exercise caution. Take antimalaria precautions before your visit.

Makgadikgadi and Nxai Pans

A committee of old baobabs, their ghostly arms and fingered branches creating eerie shadows around them, tower majestically above granite boulders on the edge of Kubu Island.

Around them on all sides a sea of salt-encrusted sand stretches off to distant horizons, distorted by rivulets of heat rising from the ground.

This is the central Makgadikgadi, the burial place of an ancient lake that once covered most of central Botswana, and which today represents the largest system of pans in the world.

To some travellers venturing into the shimmering wasteland of the Makgadikgadi — 'go kgala' means to 'dry up' — it seems as if they have arrived on some distant planet where nature has all but forgotten her design for living things. The scorching heat, the endless vistas of white, the merciless sky devoid of birdsong and flight, and the incessant dust-devils scuttling across the surface, combine to create an atmosphere of complete desolation.

But look a little closer, and the signs of life begin to appear. In the changing textures of the pan's vast surface are the imprints of a diverse, silent community of mammals: the spoor of hyenas and wildebeest, blackbacked jackals and gemsbok. In the distance, a column of dust betrays the duel of horn-locked springbok rams; and a dark outline on the horizon assumes the shape of an elephant.

The canvas of open blue sky seems to have no end to its depth and serenity. As the glare and heat of the day evaporate into the night, millions of stars appear, pinpoints of light against a black background of darkness stretching from one horizon to the other.

Around the campfire the desert chill intrudes from the blackness beyond, and you wonder how the animals adapt to such extremes of heat and cold.

Tips for travellers

- You don't have to reserve campsites in advance.
- Wherever you are in the Makgadikgadi you must travel in a 4x4, and don't venture on to the pans in your vehicle. The danger of getting bogged down on the pans is very real. Keep your vehicle on the designated tracks at the fringes of the pans.
- The possibility of getting lost is real. Take good maps and a compass with you.

The main pans There are two main pans in the Makgadikgadi — the Ntwetwe and Sowa — separated by a broad terrace of grassland that seems to go on forever.

Although these pans, and a number of smaller ones around and between them, are mostly dry, after heavy rains in the north the Nata River disgorges a deluge of water into Sowa Pan (Sowa means 'salt'), and an enchanting transformation occurs. Hundreds of thousands of flamingoes, drawn by aquatic shrimps and algae, form great skeins of pink on the horizon. They are joined by other birds: pelicans, avocets, blackwinged plovers, stilts and ducks. The transformation is brief, but so spectacular that this area has been declared a sanctuary (the Nata Sanctuary).

Apart from the grasslands and baobabs that fringe the great pans, you will see such hardy trees as the African star chestnut and the Transvaal sesame bush.

Getting around Several reliable operators offer safaris to the Makgadikgadi, with specified routes through Ntwetwe and

Sowa pans, which together cover about 12 000 km^2 south of the Nata–Maun Road. These trips usually include a visit to the Makgadikgadi Game Reserve.

Safaris are run from Gweta Rest Camp, and range from one day to 11 days. The five- to 11-day safaris include transport, tented accommodation, all meals and drinks, and a visit to the Makgadikgadi Game Reserve and Nxai Pan National Park. Visitors can be picked up from Francistown or Maun.

Nata Lodge has a five-day safari that includes Kubu Island, Makgadikgadi Pan Game Reserve, Nxai Pan National Park, Baines' Baobabs and the Nata River. Safaris depart from Nata Lodge every Monday at noon.

Self-drive routes If you're taking your own vehicle, here are some travelling options:

THE CIRCULAR ROUTE FROM NATA This is probably the best route to see both pans, and includes a visit to the Makgadikgadi Game Reserve and Nxai National Park at the same time.

Head south from Nata Lodge towards Mosu (the Setswana word for 'umbrella-thorn'), skirting the eastern edge of Sowa Pan, past Kukonje Island. At the southern end of the pan, near Kukonje, drive to the summit of the calcrete escarpment that flanks the pan. This is an excellent vantage point to pitch a tent, and marvel at the immensity of the pan and the strange outcrop of Kukonje at your feet.

KUBU ISLAND The next stop is Kubu Island, possibly one of the strangest places on earth and an important stopover point for safari operators exploring the Makgadikgadi from Maun or Nata.

Kubu, which means 'hippo' in Tswana, is a small island, dominated by outcrops of granite and ancient baobabs which rise 20 m above the expanse of Sowa Pan. The island is littered with artefacts from other ages: Stone-Age cutting tools, shards of pottery at least 2 000 years old, and the remains of a low, circular wall. These, and the presence of round pebbles washed smooth by the action of waves, indicate that Kubu was once an ancient resort on the edge of an immense lake. And it is not

Brazen hunters of the wild

The spotted hyena, the second largest carnivore in the Kalahari, is probably the most misunderstood creature in the animal kingdom.

Recent research into the life and ways of spotted hyenas has shown that far from being lone scavengers, hyenas are intelligent, sophisticated and disciplined pack hunters that get 50 per cent of their meat from their own kills. And they certainly cannot be called cowards — they will brazenly challenge lions and other carnivores at the site of a kill, sometimes even putting them to flight.

Spotted hyenas live in clans numbering from 30 to 80 individuals. The females head a distinct hierarchy and, together with their pups, are the centre of all clan activity.

The females' superiority entitles them to first choice of meat at a kill. This ensures that nursing mothers are nutritionally capable of looking after their young. Female pups inherit their mothers' social rank and dominate the males.

difficult to imagine that Kubu would have been a resting place for hippos when the lake was filled so many years ago.

From Kubu, you may head west to the Makgadikgadi Game Reserve (4 200 km^2), flanked in the west by the Boteti River. Last stop before heading east back to Nata is an island group of baobabs known as Baines' Baobabs — the Seven Sisters — on Kudiakam Pan. This island was portrayed on canvas by the artist and hunter Thomas Baines, and is a fine place to stop over and pitch your tent.

THE SOUTH-NORTH TRACK This track, linking Orapa with Gweta, takes you through Ntwetwe Pan, at the northern end of which you will come to Green's Tree. Here, the brothers Charles and Frederick Green carved their names into the bark on a pioneering expedition to the Chobe River in 1852. Southeast of Green's Tree is Chapman's Baobab, a giant tree that served as a beacon to men such as David Livingstone on their routes of exploration through Africa.

To the west of the south–north track is the Land of a Thousand Islands — a reference to legions of sand-dunes that have been dumped on the fossil-lake's bed.

Further north, past a waterhole known as Mgobe wa Takhu, a column of stately hyphaenae palms shiver in the dry wind. Here the gentle rustling of the palm fronds creates the illusion that you are on the edge of a gentle sea.

The final leg back to Nata offers the prospect of spending a few pleasant days at Nata Lodge in comfortable A-frame bungalows nestling between marula, monkeythorn and palm trees.

Makgadikgadi Game Reserve In the summer rainy season massive herds of zebra and wildebeest trek to the rolling grasslands and bush country that make up the Makgadikgadi Game Reserve, just south of the main Francistown–Maun road (east of the Boteti River). In their wake come lions and cheetahs, herds of gemsbok and springbok, and smaller carnivores such as hyenas and blackbacked jackals.

The amenities in this 3 900 km^2 reserve are fairly spartan: there are no fences, and the reserve is served by a series of unsignposted tracks.

However, two camping sites are well worth visiting — Njuca Hills, and Xhumaga on the Boteti River. Njuca, which is set among shady acacias, has a basic toilet; while Xhumaga offers a cold shower and one flush toilet.

Be sure to take all your own provisions, camping equipment, cooking utensils and firewood to these campsites. A four-wheel-drive would be ideal here, but is not essential.

Nxai Pan National Park This delightful park, 36 km north of the Francistown–Maun road, on the northern fringe of the Makgadikgadi Basin, is centred on the Nxai Pan. During the rainy season (December–April), large herds of game (wildebeest, zebra, gemsbok, springbok and eland) converge on the area, and gamewatching can be exceptionally rewarding. Giraffes are also found here, as well as an occasional elephant, venturing down from further north. Birds include kori bustards, korhaans and rednecked falcons. The park has been extended to include the Kudiakam Pan and Baines' Baobabs.

Three camping areas have been designated for visitors to Nxai Pan National Park: South Camp, which is set in a well-treed area near the entrance gate, has four campsites with an ablution block containing showers and flush toilets. There is water on tap plus a braai area for each campsite. Two elevated viewing platforms have been set up at South Camp.

North Camp offers three campsites with ablution block, showers, hand basins and flush toilets.

The area around Baines' Baobabs has three informal, undeveloped campsites, each of which can accommodate a maximum of 12 people and three vehicles.

A 4x4 is essential for travelling within the park.

Makgadikgadi and Nxai pans at a glance

Location: Northeastern Botswana.

Climate: Summer days are scorchingly hot; nights cool to cold; rain falls between January and April. Winters are cool to very cold at night.

Number of camps: Two each in Makgadikgadi Game Reserve and Nxai Pan National Park. Various natural sites throughout the pans, where you may stop and pitch your tent.

Hides: Eastern shore of Sowa Pan in the Nata Bird Sanctuary.

Accommodation: No formal accommodation in Makgadikgadi Game Reserve or Nxai Pan National Park, but basic camping sites have been established. **Nata Lodge** offers A-frame bungalows with access to à la carte restaurant, swimming pool and shop.

Booking address: Department of Wildlife and National Parks, PO Box 20364, Maun, tel (09267) 66-1265.

When to go: Makgadikgadi pans — April to July when game concentrates in the vicinity of the Boteti River. Nxai Pan — December and April.

What to take with you: All your basic provisions; compass, extra fuel; repair and tool kit; full first-aid kit; bedding, firewood, water, torches, gas lamps, eating utensils, binoculars.

How to get there: Makgadikgadi and Nxai pans are accessible from Maun in the west, or from Francistown in the east, via Nata and Gweta. There's a good tarred road between Gaborone and Nata. You can hire a 4x4 from Avis Car Rental, PO Box 222, Francistown, tel (09267) 21-5901.

Opening times: Reserves open throughout the year.

Safari operators: Go Wild Safaris, PO Box 056, Kasane, Botswana, tel (09267) 65-0468; Penduka Safaris, PO Box 55413, Northlands 2116, tel (011) 883-4310.

Special precautions: Do not deviate from designated tracks. Take plenty of precautions against sunburn. Take warm clothing for cold nights under the stars.

Mowana Safari Lodge

Like a broad ribbon of gold in a sea of shadows, the Chobe River drifts across the northeastern corner of Botswana towards the setting sun. Along the banks, towering above emerald canopies of indigenous trees, are the thatched turrets of Mowana Safari Lodge, undoubtedly one of the most luxurious lodges in the wildernesses of Southern Africa.

High up on an open deck overlooking the landscape of river and plain, guests enjoy sundowners while a lone mokoro slides across the surface of the river, losing itself in the gathering gloom and the silhouettes of hippos grunting in midstream.

Mowana is the Setswana word for 'Place of the Baobab' and, indeed, the name is justly earned, because the lodge has been built around the trunk of a baobab with a girth of more than 4 m and a height of 9 m. The baobab's presence here enables Mowana to retain a spirit of 'wild Africa', in spite of its more luxurious components.

The design and building of the lodge was undertaken with extreme care: the central block was built above the ground to protect the roots of the baobab; the main wood-and-thatch buildings blend in so well with the natural vegetation that they're almost camouflaged from the river, and all the surrounding trees have been preserved intact, so that they still serve as a sanctuary for a large variety of birds.

Accommodation The lodge has been built on different levels, each served by staircases, while slatted boardwalks and balconies make optimum use of the superb views. Soapstone carvings on the tables, African murals and a mokoro (dugout) exhibited inside with fishing baskets, create a very distinctive atmosphere at Mowana.

There are 104 luxury *en suite* bedrooms and four suites, fronted with gardens of indigenous shrubs and bushes, and each with a view of the Chobe River and surrounding bush. The tastefully decorated bedrooms are air-conditioned, have overhead fans, mosquito nets and direct-dialling telephones.

The rooms are redolent of the ambience of Africa, with wall-to-wall carpets of woven grass; ethnic designs on curtains, scatter rugs and upholstery, and comfortable furniture of wood and cane. Wildlife prints on the walls and small items of pottery complement the effect. The bathrooms, with their earthy tiles and ceramic basins, are modern and well appointed.

Breakfast, lunch and dinner are served in the Serondella Restaurant on the ground floor, while one floor up is the

Mowana Safari Lodge at a glance

Locality:	Northeastern Botswana, 3 km from Kasane Village and 77 km from Victoria Falls.
Climate:	Summers hot to very hot, with thunderstorms between December and March. Winters mild to warm (nights can be cold).
Game drives:	Daily drive to Chobe Game Reserve.
Other attractions:	River cruises on the *Mmadikwena.*
Accommodation:	104 *en suite* bedrooms and four suites overlooking the Chobe River.
Booking address:	Mowana Safari Lodge, PO Box 266, Kasane, tel (09267) 65-0300.
When to go:	Throughout the year.
What to take with you:	Camera, binoculars; field guides, light clothing for game drives; jersey for river-boat cruises.
How to get there:	Mowana is 3 km from Kasane and 77 km from Victoria Falls.
Nearest doctor:	Kasane.
Nearest petrol:	Kasane.
Open:	24 hours a day.
Special precautions:	Antimalaria precautions should be taken.

Savuti Cocktail Bar and residents' lounge. The restaurant's menu is highly adventurous and features, among other exotic dishes, warthog cutlets, ostrich fillets and eland ragout.

If this all sounds like a five-star hotel, it is nothing compared to the five-star adventures that beckon outside.

River cruises One of the most popular pastimes at Mowana is a cruise on the *Mmadikwena*, a riverboat owned by the lodge. The cruiser leaves Mowana in mid-afternoon, and soon reveals the real wealth of Chobe's wildlife community: elephants and hippos cavorting on the river's banks, herds of Cape buffalo marching along the plains, as well as baboons, warthogs, red lechwe, impala and waterbuck.

The islands in the Chobe River are a haven for a variety of waterbirds: African jacanas, spurwing geese, flocks of Egyptian geese, lilacbreasted rollers, malachite and pied kingfishers, squacco herons and, of course, the beautiful fish eagles with their haunting cry of Africa. The *Mmadikwena* passes many of these islands, providing superb birdwatching opportunities.

Game drives and trails More than 30 000 elephants and a huge variety of other game find sanctuary in Chobe Game Reserve, just 8 km from Mowana Lodge. Daily game drives starting at 06:00 in an open 4x4 take guests into the reserve where sightings of lions, Burchell's zebras, giraffes, buffaloes and a variety of antelope are common. Take your camera and binoculars along — this could be the game-viewing opportunity of a lifetime.

You'll be accompanied by an experienced tracker, and may end up following animal tracks to the site of a kill.

Included among the birds are hornbills, francolins, paradise whydahs, kori bustards, marabou storks, hamerkops and pearlspotted owls.

The lodge is just 3 km from Kasane Village, 5 km from the new international airport, and 77 km from Victoria Falls.

OKAVANGO DELTA AND MOREMI WILDLIFE RESERVE

In the sun-scorched reaches of northern Botswana the Okavango River knifes its way southwards through the ochre sands of the Kalahari, breaking out near Shakawe to form a panhandle 16 km wide.

About 80 km further on, at Seronga, the wrist of the panhandle opens out into a massive alluvial floodplain — a fan-shaped wilderness of waterways, swamps, islands and reedbeds that are known as the Okavango Delta.

During the rainy season and through the dry months which follow, more than 10 billion tons of water pulse through the panhandle into the burning sands of the Kalahari.

In its fantastic 260-km journey from the Angolan Highlands to the southern end of the delta, the Okavango River survives by the sheer weight of its volume. Spurred on by the runoff of huge subtropical storms in Angola, the Okavango writhes through the panhandle like some bloated serpent, and then fragments into dozens of smaller tributaries.

The waters ooze across the floodplain, circling islands of sycamore fig, kigelia and leadwood trees, breaching ramparts of papyrus and palms and bringing sustenance and survival to myriad living creatures.

The ebb and flow of the Okavango's waters through the delta, the very remote-

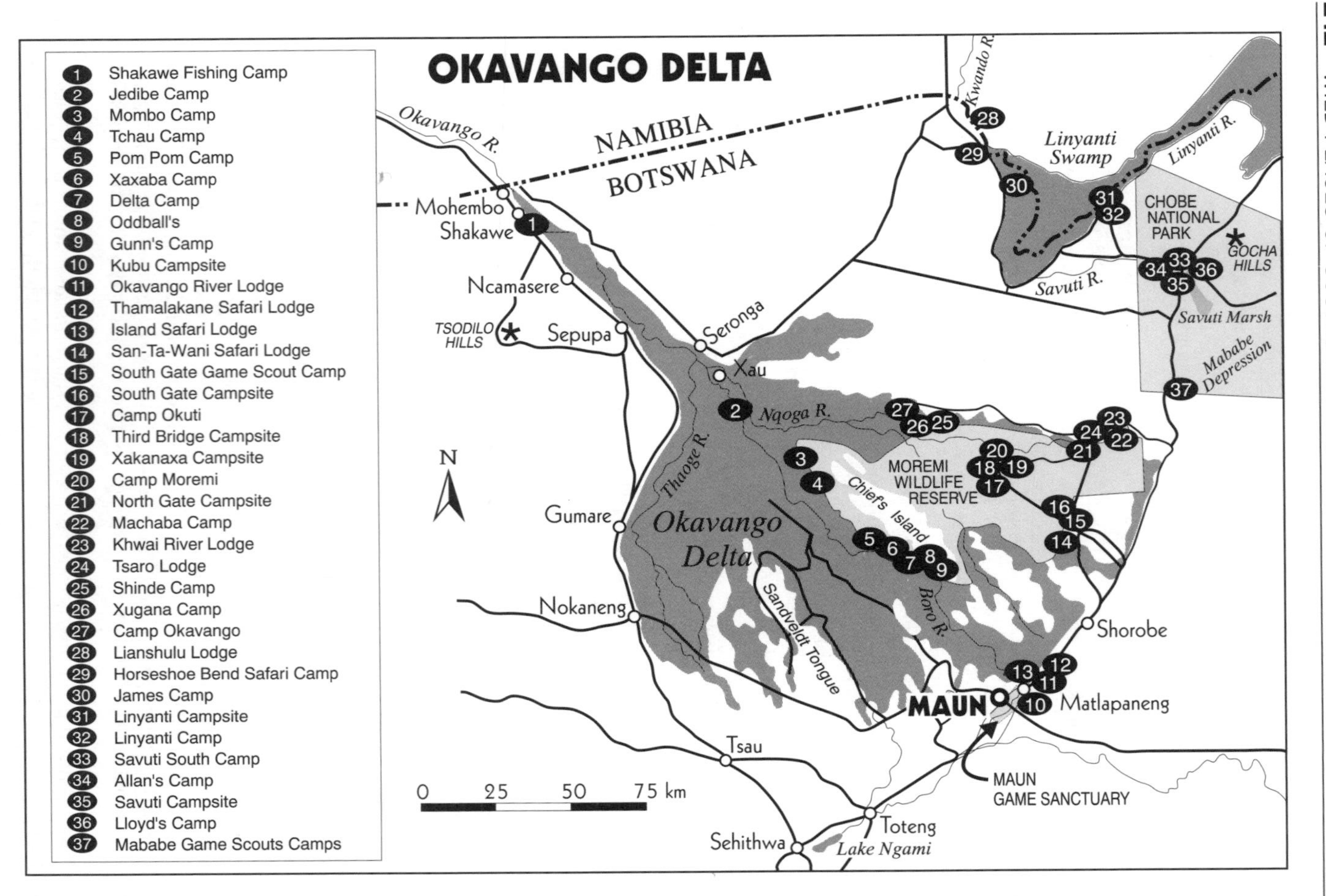
OKAVANGO DELTA
1 Shakawe Fishing Camp
2 Jedibe Camp
3 Mombo Camp
4 Tchau Camp
5 Pom Pom Camp
6 Xaxaba Camp
7 Delta Camp
8 Oddball's
9 Gunn's Camp
10 Kubu Campsite
11 Okavango River Lodge
12 Thamalakane Safari Lodge
13 Island Safari Lodge
14 San-Ta-Wani Safari Lodge
15 South Gate Game Scout Camp
16 South Gate Campsite
17 Camp Okuti
18 Third Bridge Campsite
19 Xakanaxa Campsite
20 Camp Moremi
21 North Gate Campsite
22 Machaba Camp
23 Khwai River Lodge
24 Tsaro Lodge
25 Shinde Camp
26 Xugana Camp
27 Camp Okavango
28 Lianshulu Lodge
29 Horseshoe Bend Safari Camp
30 James Camp
31 Linyanti Campsite
32 Linyanti Camp
33 Savuti South Camp
34 Allan's Camp
35 Savuti Campsite
36 Lloyd's Camp
37 Mababe Game Scouts Camps
NAMIBIA
BOTSWANA
Okavango R.
Mohembo
Shakawe
Ncamasere
Sepupa
TSODILO HILLS
Seronga
Xau
Nqoga R.
Thaoge R.
Okavango Delta
Gumare
Nokaneng
Tsau
Sehithwa
Lake Ngami
Toteng
Sandveldt Tongue
Chief's Island
Boro R.
MOREMI WILDLIFE RESERVE
MAUN
MAUN GAME SANCTUARY
Matlapaneng
Shorobe
Linyanti Swamp
Kwando R.
Linyanti R.
Savuti R.
CHOBE NATIONAL PARK
GOCHA HILLS
Savuti Marsh
Mababe Depression
N
0 25 50 75 km

ness of its position in the Kalahari, the abundance of natural vegetation and the huge quantities of game combine to make this one of the most attractive wild places in the world — a place described by Swedish explorer Charles Andersson as one of 'indescribable beauty'.

Showpiece of the Okavango Delta and focal point of many travellers' itineraries through Southern Africa is Moremi Wildlife Reserve, a huge network of waterways surrounding two major islands — Chief's Island in the west and Mopane Tongue in the east — and hundreds of smaller islands.

The reserve, established in 1963 by the Batswana people, became the first wildlife sanctuary on the subcontinent to be proclaimed by an African community on their own land. Today it is administered by Botswana's Department of Wildlife and National Parks.

Lovers of the wild prefer it to others because of its gentle, waterside ambience, huge numbers of game, and romantic and rustic camps perched on the edge of vast and beautiful carriageways of water.

Getting around The ebb and flow of the Okavango Delta's waters, and the immensity of its 12 000-km^2 floodplain dictate the nature of travel for visitors. You may get to some parts of the delta by road, but many of the camps are accessible only by air or water.

Safari operators (mostly based in Maun) offer packages that fly you in and out of the delta, accommodate you in luxury lodges, private reserves, or rustic bush camps of your choice, and then fly you out again.

These packages include transport by air or water to your chosen destination, mokoro (dugout) and fishing trips, game drives, accommodation, food and drink. Visits to two or more camps may be arranged, with transport between the camps (often by mokoro) included in the package price.

Because of the remoteness of many of the private camps, their tariffs aren't cheap, but the rewards are exceptional: abundant game, extraordinary birdlife and complete tranquillity.

Mokoro safaris A cheaper option than staying at the private camps is to hire a mokoro and paddle through the reserve yourself, spending the nights camping on islands along the way. To hire a mokoro, contact Maun's Island Safari Lodge at PO Box 116, Maun, tel (09627) 66-0300; or Crocodile Camp, PO Box 46, Maun, tel (09627) 66-1005.

Wilderness Safaris offers a mokoro safari through the delta called Boro River Adventures. If you enjoy sleeping under the stars in the company of lions, hippos, wild dogs and other animals, this four-night mokoro trail is for you. All provisions are carried on your mokoro, and you camp out on remote islands.

For more details, contact Wilderness Safaris, PO Box 78573, Sandton 2146, tel (011) 883-0747,

Wildlife The abundance of water and the variety of habitats on the islands of the Okavango Delta attract a colourful variety of land-based mammals, amphibians and reptiles. Chief's Island and the Mopane Tongue are home to elephants, lions, buffaloes, wildebeest, reedbuck, impala, roan and sable antelope, wild dogs, leopards, cheetahs, giraffes, zebras, warthogs and baboons; while the rivers and channels teem with hippos, crocodiles and 80 species of fish. The reed- and papyrus-fringed banks of the waterways host such water-loving antelope as suni, red lechwe and sitatunga.

Individual camps have their own unique wildlife attractions. Mombo Camp, for instance, is renowned for its wild dogs — the 'painted wolves' of Africa — lions and leopards, while Jedibe Island Camp has a variety of water-adapted species of antelope such as red lechwe and sitatunga, as well as hippos, crocodiles and clawless otters.

Abu's Camp is internationally known for its elephant-back safaris, while Tsaro Safari Lodge, with its tree-house hide, will inevitably reward gamewatchers with views of vervet monkeys and baboons.

The abundance of game and the density of the mopane woodlands and riverine forests pose a threat to visitors walking carelessly about. Always be alert to possible danger in the Okavango, particularly from lions and crocodiles — several fatal attacks have been recorded here.

Birdlife The Okavango Delta is one of the subcontinent's premier birdwatching paradises — the more than 400 species include a dazzling array of waterbirds, such as breeding colonies of wattled cranes and unique, rarely seen species such as the blackfaced babbler and Cape parrot. Other specials are Heuglin's robins, arrowmarked babblers, Scops owls and Pel's fishing owls.

Many of the islands are fringed by thick clusters of water figs, or gamoti figs, whose branches not only shade crocodiles and hippos, but provide luxuriant nesting quarters for marabou, yellow- and openbilled storks and several species of heron and egret, especially the slaty egret. In winter the islands become the centre of frenetic activity as the birds prepare their nests for the breeding season in spring.

Where to see game The Mopane Tongue is an excellent place for four-wheel-drive tours of Moremi Wildlife Reserve, particularly during the dry season (April–October), because it combines vast numbers of game with some excellent camps (see below).

The two access points to the reserve here are North Gate (from Chobe) and South Gate (from Maun). Chief's Island also offers vast numbers of game, but is usually surrounded by water, so that access is by mokoro (dugouts).

Where to stay There are four public campsites: North Gate, just inside the reserve, flanking the Khwai River; South Gate, just outside the reserve, which is really only used as an overnight spot for travellers who arrive after the gate has closed; Third Bridge, near Xakanaxa, probably the busiest camp in Moremi; and Xakanaxa, also a popular camp, which can be crowded in the high season.

The Okavango Delta is increasingly being recognised as one of the world's premier wildlife destinations. To cater for the huge upsurge of visitors an excellent variety of private camps is on offer, including some that are still under construction.

XAKANAXA CAMP Some 90 km by road from Maun, Xakanaxa nestles in the shade of huge kigelia (sausage) and mopane trees, a stone's throw from the edge of Xakanaxa Lagoon.

The camp offers six walk-in safari tents near the water, each set on a concrete base, and furnished with two beds, a table and chairs. There's a reed-walled diningroom and bar, hot- and cold-water showers and flush toilets. Light is supplied by hurricane lamps.

Game-viewing drives in open 4x4s offer you the chance to see lions, wild dogs, leopards and honey badgers, in addition to the conventional game found in the Moremi Reserve.

Other attractions are boating, fishing for tigerfish and bream, walks on the islands, and visiting the heronries of Xakanaxa, Godikwe and Xobega lagoons.

Swimming is not safe at Xakanaxa — a woman has been taken by a crocodile here — and there are no mokoro trips.

For booking information contact Okavango Tours and Safaris, PO Box 3666, Rivonia 2128, tel (011) 803-4464.

CAMP OKUTI Shaded by towering indigenous trees, this small camp lies on the edge of Xakanaxa Lagoon at the western edge of the Mopane Tongue.

Seven thatched and whitewashed chalets offer comfortable accommodation to visitors who come to see the wildlife of Moremi and marvel at the prolific birdlife. More than 40 endangered species of bird are found in the vicinity of Camp Okuti and the heronries of Gadikwe and Kobega Lagoon are unique to this region. On offer are game drives in open 4x4s, boating and birdwatching trips.

For bookings contact Okavango Explorations, PO Box 69859, Bryanston 2021, tel (011) 708-1893.

CAMP MOREMI Giant ebony trees tower above the 11 Meru-style tents at this camp, which lies on the edge of Xakanaxa Lagoon at the eastern extremity of the Okavango Delta, within the Moremi Wildlife Reserve. Sister camp to nearby Camp Okavango, Camp Moremi is regarded as one of the finest safari lodges in Botswana. The camp has a magnificent thatched central complex known as Moremi Tree Lodge, which consists of a main lounge, stylish cocktail bar, diningroom and wildlife reference library. Here guests may sit on the sundeck and gaze across the lovely vistas of Xakanaxa Lagoon.

There's also a curio shop, swimming pool, covered boma and an elevated observation platform guaranteeing excellent game-viewing.

The safari tents are furnished with Rhodesian teak wardrobes, dressing tables, directors' chairs and ethnic woven rugs.

For wildlife connoisseurs who like to be pampered, the Chief Moremi III suite offers its occupants private game-viewing trips.

Camp Moremi keeps guests busy with regular gamewatching drives, boat trips on the river to visit the heronries on Gadikwe and Xakanaxa lagoons, and angling excursions.

Access to Camp Moremi is by air from Maun or Kasane (there's an airstrip at Xakanaxa), by boat from Camp Okavango (three hours) or by 4x4 vehicle.

For bookings contact Central Reservations, Desert and Delta Safaris, PO Box 1200, Paulshof 2056, tel (011) 807-3720.

CAMP OKAVANGO This lovely camp lies on the remote Nxaragha Island in the heart of the delta — a luxury hideout with 11 East African safari tents furnished with Rhodesian teak wardrobes, designer linen and ethnic woven rugs.

The elegant thatch and lethaka main complex houses a cocktail bar, lounge and diningroom, while *al fresco* meals are served on the open-air patio.

There's a special honeymoon suite, as well as the luxury Jessie's Suite, which lays on private game-viewing excursions.

A superb sundeck, shaded hammocks, reading benches and a plunge pool provide undisturbed relaxation during the scorching middays.

Professional guides conduct game-viewing expeditions by canoe or on foot among the delta's magical islands.

Here guests may expect to see such rare mammals as sitatunga and red lechwe, and birding specials such as Pel's fishing owl.

Angling excursions offer guests the chance to catch tigerfish, bream and pike.

Access is by charter aircraft or helicopter from Maun and Kasane (served by daily road transfers from Victoria Falls) to the Camp Okavango airstrip. Alternatively, you may get there by boat from Camp Moremi.

For more details and booking contact Central Reservations, Desert and Delta Safaris, PO Box 1200, Paulshof 2056, tel (011) 807-3720.

DUBA PLAINS Located in the northern reaches of the Okavango, Duba Plains is one of the region's remotest camps, lying on an island under the shade of large ebony, fig and garcinia trees and surrounded by expansive floodplains.

Duba caters for just eight people, and its remoteness guarantees a private, personalised adventure where visitors share an environment teeming with lions, elephants, buffaloes and lechwe.

Walking trails, mokoro trips and night drives right off the beaten track ensure excellent game-viewing. And after a long, hot day, you may retire to the comfort of an exquisite pub and diningroom under large riverine trees.

For bookings and enquiries, contact Wilderness Safaris, PO Box 78573, Sandton 2146, tel (011) 883-0747.

MOMBO CAMP The shriek of a terrified impala in the night; the ponderous thud of an elephant's foot outside your tent; the eerie scuffling in bushes fringing the river — these are just some of the experiences that await you at Mombo Island in western Moremi.

Mombo Camp is one of Africa's best and most private game-viewing sanctuaries, lying on the fringe of a floodplain that attracts a huge variety of animals and birds. The camp's island is joined to Chief's Island in the Moremi Reserve by an isthmus of land often submerged by the delta's waters.

Its very remoteness, proximity to the water's edge and the rustic atmosphere of its 10 Meru-tented rooms are unforgettable.

Mombo Island lies at the northwestern tip of Chief's Island, where the waters of the Boro River ooze through beds of

Tips for travellers

- All passport and visa requirements must be seen to by visitors or their travel agents.
- Many visitors regard the entrance and camping fees in Botswana as excessive. Be prepared to fork out for bringing in your vehicle into the Moremi Reserve, using a boat and camping.
- At some of the lodges the electricity is turned off at 23:00, so a torch is indispensable for any trip to the delta.
- Although accommodation in most of the lodges and camps is geared to two or more people, single accommodation can be arranged at additional cost.
- Children under 12 years old are not allowed in Camp Moremi and Camp Okavango.
- Most camps have a curio shop stocking a limited range of handicrafts, safari accessories and wildlife books.
- Jedibe, Mombo and Boba camps all belong to Wilderness Safaris, who will be quite happy to arrange a safari package that includes two or all three of these camps. See *Booking address*, 'At a glance' box.

papyrus and phoenix palms. During Angola's rainy season the Boro River, fed by floodwaters pouring into the Okavango Delta, spills over the grassy floodplain surrounding Mombo Island. When these waters recede, the floodplain's lush, sweet grasses are exposed, and thousands of animals move in from the acacia and savannah woodlands of the arid interior to feast at nature's banquet table.

Migratory visitors to Mombo include buffaloes, zebras, gemsbok, kudu, red lechwe, impala, lions, leopards, cheetahs and spotted hyenas. Permanent residents include elephants, warthogs, honey badgers, civets, aardvarks and aardwolves.

The real VIPs at Mombo are its 40 or so wild dogs, which are holding their own in spite of Africa's shrinking wilderness.

Mombo's proximity to water makes it ideal for a variety of waterfowl, and waders, particularly, are very common. Other species seen on the floodplain, or among the baobabs, umbrella-thorn, acacia, leadwood or jackalberry trees, include wattled crane, hooded vulture, malachite kingfisher, fish eagle, Dickinson's kestrel, pinkthroated longclaw, black coucal and Meyer's parrot.

You can get within metres of Mombo's renowned wild dogs, catch a leopard in the arc of a spotlight, or see warthogs in their burrows on one of Mombo Camp's organised game drives.

Gamewatching expeditions are available at sunrise or in the late afternoon in three open 4x4s through the game-rich grasses of the savannah and floodplains.

The 'breakfast run' is followed by a brunch, while the afternoon drive is a scene-setter for a relaxing evening around the campfire. Here you may hear Joseph Tekanyetso, an Okavango tracker, recount the story of his life-and-death struggle with a lion.

Night-time drives bring visitors close to leopards, lions, spotted hyenas, honey badgers and genets. Walking safaris are conducted by an experienced ranger who is conversant with the habitats and habits of the area's prolific wildlife.

Mombo Main Camp nestles beneath huge trees on the fringe of the floodplain. The 10 large Meru-tented rooms accommodate 20 guests and are equipped with a private *en suite* toilet and shower as well as solar-powered lights.

A separate dining area and the lounge-bar have sweeping views of the floodplain and its sprinkling of wild date and ilala palms. A plunge pool has been built into the teak deck below the bar, and there's a pond and feeding table for birds nearby.

The camp is unfenced, and it is quite common for animals to wander among the tents at night. Don't be surprised if you hear hippos or elephants outside your tent, or the deep, throaty grunt of a lioness padding through the thickets on the fringes of the camp.

Evenings around the campfire are interrupted by the tremulous winnowing of Natal nightjars, and the eerie squeaks of fruit bats whistling close above your head. Hurricane lamps are provided to illuminate a path to your tent at night.

Mombo Trails Camp, on an island near the main camp, offers dome-tents with groundsheets and mosquito netting (beds and duvets are supplied), and may be booked exclusively by one group. Meals are served under a giant fig tree.

Mombo has its own airstrip. Most visitors fly in from Maun as part of a package trip. Options include a five-day safari from Maun, staying at Mombo and Jedibe.

For booking contact Wilderness Safaris, PO Box 78573, Sandton 2146, tel (011) 883-0747.

VUMBURA AND LITTLE VUMBURA These two delightful camps, situated in a private concession area 25 km north of Mombo, lie near the fringes of the Okavango's open savannah, and apart from wetland species such as hippo, crocodile, red lechwe and waterbuck, you will also find plains animals like sable, kudu, wildebeest, tsessebe and impala. Elephant and lion are seen regularly as well as wild dog, cheetah and leopard. Birders will also find an exciting mix of wetland-, acacia- and mopane-loving species.

Eight luxury tented rooms accommodate a maximum of 16 guests and nestle in the shade of indigenous trees with excellent views of the surrounding waterways. There's a cosy lounge and pub area, a plunge pool and a feeling of remoteness about the camp.

Less than a kilometre away is the five-roomed Little Vimbura Camp, also situated on the edge of a waterway.

Activities include mokoro trips, walking, boating and game drives in the company of an experienced guide. For more information and reservations contact Wilderness Safaris, PO Box 78573, Sandton 2146, tel (011) 883-0747.

JAO CAMP One of Wilderness Safaris' newest camps, Jao is situated west of Mombo on a wooded island bordering Moremi Game Reserve, and gives guests exposure to some of the most diverse wildlife populations in the country.

Sixteen guests can be accommodated in the luxury rooms which overlook vast stretches of savannah inhabited by Botswana's largest population of lion. The rooms have a contemporary African flavour, and are constructed of split bamboo and thatch, with canvas walls. *En suite* facilities include a shower, flush toilet and basin, and there is also an outdoor shower.

Game includes leopard, wildebeest, tsessebe, hippo and crocodile. Game drives and walks, mokoro excursions and night drives are available daily to guests.

Chase of the painted wolves

Wild dogs — the painted wolves of the Okavango Delta — are known universally as bloodthirsty killers that can pursue fleeing prey for up to 5 km before bringing it to ground.

The chase is led by the dominant male of the pack, who carefully selects the victim and then homes in with such determination that he may even overrun other fleeing animals.

The hungry pack, numbering between 10 and 15 individuals, will tear apart a duiker or steenbok in a matter of seconds. But a larger animal, such as a wildebeest or a zebra, may be disembowelled where it stands in an orgy of slashing teeth and jaws that may last up to 15 minutes.

In spite of their grisly killing methods, wild dogs have a highly evolved family spirit in which they show great unselfishness, devotion, tenderness and sacrifice on behalf of other members of the pack.

When a litter of pups is born, the pack devotes itself to the care and welfare of the youngsters for three months. After a kill, the hunters return to the den and regurgitate their hard-earned meat for the whining, hungry pups and the suckling bitch.

Access to the camp is by charter plane from Maun or Kasane.

For more details contact Wilderness Safaris, PO Box 78573, Sandton 2146, tel (011) 883-0747.

JEDIBE ISLAND CAMP Lazy lagoons cloaked in waterlilies, fast-flowing channels bearing a startling variety of fish, palm-fringed islands alive with the sound of birds — such are the attractions of Jedibe Island Camp, one of the Okavango Delta's more rewarding safari destinations.

Nestling in the shade of giant jackalberries on the edge of a tranquil lagoon just 145 km northwest of Maun, Jedibe is special for its wealth of waterways, the abundance of its natural vegetation and its rich, land-based and aquatic life.

Here ilala palms, wild date palms, sycamore fig, knobthorn, marula and African mangosteen trees provide food and shelter for a wonderful variety of birds. The melodious calls of Heuglin's robins, whitefronted bee-eaters, longcrested eagles, marsh harriers and swamp boubous bring early-morning symphonies of sound to guests stirring from their beds.

Jedibe Camp's thatched lounge, diningroom and bar complex lies at the water's edge, within whistling distance of hippos and crocodiles and a stone's throw away from a jetty shaded by a generous jackalberry tree.

Just a few hundred metres from the camp the Boro River flows southward to form the western boundary of the Moremi Wildlife Reserve. A channel drifting past the camp gives access to the Boro, with its singing reeds, quiet tributaries and islands rich in animal life.

Jedibe Camp's rustic appeal is enhanced by the fact that there are no motor vehicles; travel around Jedibe is by foot, mokoro or motorboat.

Sunset cruises are offered daily in the camps's new double-decker houseboat, *The Crake*. Powered by two Mariner 40-h/p engines, *The Crake* accommodates 16 guests, and the elevation of the upper deck provides excellent views across the reed-fringed waterways. Other attractions of a houseboat trip are fishing for bream, pike or tigerfish, or swimming (keep an eye open for crocodiles).

Some visitors swim in a channel near the camp, but crocodiles are always a danger.

Jedibe accommodates 16 guests in eight spacious walk-in, twin-bedded safari tents, each with an *en suite*, reed-and-thatch bathroom equipped with shower, flush toilet and washbasin. The tents are set under palm trees to ensure maximum privacy. Solar-powered lighting is complemented by hurricane lamps.

A walkway leads from the main camp across a lagoon to the moorings of *The Crake*.

Access to the camp is by light aircraft from Maun to the Jao Village airstrip and from there it is a 10-minute powerboat ride to Jedibe Camp.

For more details contact Wilderness Safaris, PO Box 78573, Sandton 2146, tel (011) 883-0747.

DELTA CAMP This exclusive lodge is built on a small island just across the river from Chief's Island in the southern part of the Moremi Wildlife Reserve. The eight beautifully rustic chalets have been built from natural materials — reeds, poles and thatch, and some even incorporate the indigenous trees in their structures. There's a cosy, thoroughly African ambience to the chalets and to the diningroom overlooking the Boro River, where mekoro have ousted powerboats as the sole form of water transport.

Main attractions are mokoro trips down the delta's waterways and guided walks on Chief's Island.

For booking details contact Wilderness Safaris, PO Box 78573, Sandton 2146, tel (011) 883-0747.

KWETSANI CAMP This charming eight-bedded camp, which opened in 1999, consists of four spacious tree-house chalets under thatch on Kwetsani Island — an elongated strip of land surrounded by waterways and vast plains. The chalets nestle in the shade of giant mangosteen and fig trees and afford superb views of the floodplains. Each chalet has a shower, flush toilet and outside shower.

Kwetsani is a gamewatcher's paradise, and apart from regular sightings of lion, wild dog, tsessebe and lechwe, there are also plenty of nocturnal species such as aardwolf, serval, genet and bushbaby.

Regular game walks are available and mokoro trips take guests right among the crocs, hippos and a fascinating array of birds along the waterways.

Contact Wilderness Safaris, PO Box 78573, Sandton 2146, tel (011) 883-0747.

XAXABA CAMP This small camp — Xaxaba means 'island of tall trees' — is regarded as one of the most beautiful in the world. Unspoilt and remote, it lies on the banks of the Boro Channel just south of Chief's Island. Attractions are geared towards exploring the area's scenic and natural wonders: photographic safaris, river trips in mekoro or powerboats, bird-watching, fishing and game drives are available on a daily basis.

Guests are accommodated in 12 thatched chalets, comfortably furnished with ethnic themes, with *en suite* bathroom facilities, electricity and waterborne sanitation. There's a lovely, elevated bar with superb views over the lazy waters of the delta, and a sparkling swimming pool.

For more details contact Gametrackers, 31 Harley Street, Randburg 2194, tel (011) 781-0137.

XIGERA CAMP Lying within Moremi Wildlife Reserve in the central-western part of the delta, Xigera consists of eight comfortably furnished walk-in tented rooms on a large island which adjoins a river.

Each tent has a traditional bucket shower and chemical toilet, and there's an attractive dining area under canvas.

Mokoro trips, walking trails and game drives reveal a stunning variety of birdlife, including Pel's fishing owls, slaty egrets and wattled cranes.

For more details contact Wilderness Safaris, PO Box 78573, Sandton 2146, tel (011) 883-0747.

SANDIBE SAFARI LODGE Nestling under a canopy of wild palms and lush indigenous forest, this lodge is one of the the latest in the Conservation Corporation's stable of eco-friendly safari lodges in Southern Africa. And true to the Conservation Corporation's high standards, Sandibe is a top-class lodge situated along the permanent channels which flank Chief's Island in Moremi Wildlife Reserve.

The eight twin-bedded chalets have been designed to blend in with their forest milieu and the private verandahs and wooden decks merge inobtrusively with the vegetation surrounding them. Each chalet has an *en suite* dressing room and an open-air shower.

There is a central lounge and dining area in the heart of the camp, with hammocked decks affording beautiful views across the waterways and grasslands.

African cuisine, candle-lit tables and fine wines make this camp a worthy stopover for those with means and the desire to explore the best the Okavango has to offer.

For more details and booking contact the Conservation Corporation, Private Bag X27, Benmore 2010, tel (011) 784-6832.

ABU'S CAMP Elephant-back safaris are the prime attraction of this remote camp on the banks of the Xhenega River in the southwestern Okavango Delta — just one hour's drive from Pom Pom Camp (see entry on p. 253).

The safaris are part of an upmarket package organised by international tour operators Ker and Downey, and are supervised by elephant expert Randall Moore.

Guests fly in from Maun (30 minutes) and spend the first day at Abu's Camp getting to know Abu, Kathy, Bennie and some younger elephants.

The next day guests mount their elephants and trundle off for an unforgettable gamewatching experience in the delta. The elevated positions afford views of lions, leopards, other elephants and plains mammals such as lechwe, impala, buffaloes, giraffes, zebras and tsessebe.

Guests lunch on one of the remote islands and return to camp for sundowners around the camp fire.

Apart from elephant rides visitors can fish in the Matsibe River on the western side of Ngabega Island, walk along the river or go for evening game drives.

Accommodation at Abu's is in five twin-bedded safari tents, with sewn-in floors and windows, and a private safari-style bucket shower and toilet.

There's a dining tent and bar with a tantalising array of cocktails or more basic drinks. The bush cuisine, cooked by a safari chef, is of the highest standard, and served with freshly baked bread.

The typical safari to Abu's Camp is six days, but guests may tailor their trip to take in one of Ker and Downey's standard fly-in safaris or private custom safaris under canvas.

The fly-in safaris take in one or more of Ker and Downey's other three camps — Machaba, Shinde Island and Pom Pom.

For more details contact Ker and Downey Safaris, PO Box 27, Maun, tel (09267) 66-0375.

ODDBALLS Just to the west of Chief's Island, Oddballs is used mainly by campers as a start and stop point for mokoro trails of the delta, and guests will stay there at least two nights. Bring your own tent and mosquito netting or, if you would like to try something completely different, reserve the tree-house 'bridal suite' for rustic comfort 5 m above the ground.

Oddballs hires out mekoro at a daily rate, and offers such luxuries as a small shop (Molly's Pantry), the reed-walled Skull Bar and a pleasant diningroom.

You may hire camping equipment and utensils at the camp. Access to Oddballs is by air, and all factors considered, it is probably one of the cheaper options for exploring the waterways of the delta.

For booking contact Okavango Tours and Safaris, PO Box 3666, Rivonia 2128, tel (011) 803-4464.

TSARO SAFARI LODGE Shaded by groves of sycamore fig, knobthorn and leadwood trees, Tsaro Lodge lies on the banks of the Khwai River on the northern border of the Moremi Wildlife Reserve, 160 km by road from Maun.

The lodge overlooks the Moremi floodplains, where hippos wallow in the deeper waters and red lechwe graze on the riverside grasses. This is an ideal departure point for explorations down the waterways of the Okavango, or game drives across the Moremi Reserve.

Six thatched rondavels, with *en suite* facilities (hot and cold running water and flush toilets) accommodate up to 12 people.

Game drives are held in the early morning and late afternoon in open 4x4s, and local species include giraffe, lion, buffalo, wild dog, sable, roan, spotted hyena, tsessebe, hippos, red lechwe, wildebeest, impala, baboon, vervet monkey and zebra. A tree-house hide is an excellent vantage point for gamewatching.

The hotter parts of the day are usually spent around the swimming pool, from which you may spot any of the 100 species of bird that occur here.

For further information and booking contact Okavango Explorations, PO Box 69859, Bryanston 2021, tel (011) 708-1893.

XUGANA CAMP Hidden under a canopy of wild ebony and garcinia trees on the edge of Xugana Lagoon, this lodge in the northern reaches of the Okavango Delta is remote and restful.

The San name Xugana means 'kneel down to drink', and it was here, at the lagoon's edge, that the San hunters used to rest and quench their thirst.

Just 110 km from Maun, the lodge is open throughout the year, and offers an attractive schedule of things to do: walks, boating, mokoro trips, nature drives and angling (bream and tigerfish). The game drives take place in a 'puddle-jumper' — a vehicle specially adapted to cross fairly deep channels. Among the rarer birds here are pinkthroated longclaws, pratincoles, bat hawks and slaty egrets.

Accommodation is in eight spacious twin-bedded safari tents, with built-in ground sheets and mosquito nets. Each tent is mounted on a plinth, and has electricity as well as its own bathroom.

There's a sparkling pool, and a diningroom, lounge and fully stocked bar under thatch nearby.

African elephants under threat

While African elephants in Southern Africa are on the increase, numbers are dwindling at an alarming rate elsewhere in Africa — from about 1,3 million in 1981 to 625 000 today.

Between 1979 and 1989 herds in South Africa grew from 7 800 to 8 200, in Namibia from 2 700 to 5 000, in Zimbabwe from 30 000 to 43 000 and in Botswana from 20 000 to 51 000.

In spite of this conservationists are very concerned at the decline in numbers in other African countries.

Elephants have often been blamed for destroying large tracts of natural forest by breaking down trees, but there is increasing evidence that the destruction of certain types of woodland actually benefits some animals.

In South Africa's Hluhluwe Game Reserve, for instance, an absence of elephants for almost a century has resulted in an overgrowth of woody shrubs which has led to the decline and disappearance of wildebeest and other antelope through a lack of grazing.

If you come close to elephants feeding, you may hear a deep rumbling noise issuing from their bodies. The sound is produced by the pachyderm's vocal chords, and is one of the many remarkable ways in which they communicate.

KHWAI RIVER LODGE Cradled on the curves of the Khwai River — Moremi's northern border — this lovely old lodge offers visitors glorious views of elephants, hippos and other game cavorting at the riverside in front of their verandahs.

The lodge nestles in the shade of huge sycamore fig and acacia trees, not far from the Moremi's North Gate, and is an excellent place to start an extended tour of the delta. At night you may hear the wail of hyenas or the grunting of lions, or you may wake to the sound of red lechwe splashing through the water.

Accommodation is in 12 thatched, twin-bedded brick bungalows with *en suite* flush toilets and showers. There's a large diningroom offering sumptuous meals.

Half-day and full-day game drives into the Moremi Game Reserve are offered, after which you may cool off in the swimming pool or have a drink in the well-stocked bar. The drives may go as far as the Xakanaxa Lagoon.

Bush walks accompanied by a game scout are another option.

Khwai River Lodge is 140 km (four hours' drive) from Maun.

For bookings and enquiries contact Gametrackers, 31 Harley Street, Randburg 2194, tel (011) 781-0137.

SAN-TA-WANI SAFARI LODGE This lodge just south of Moremi's South Gate, 74 km from Maun, is within a stroll of elephants, lions, wildebeest, wild dogs, kudu, zebras, hyenas and buffaloes. The lodge, beautifully positioned near a lagoon under indigenous trees, gets its name from a mythical fox which, legend has it, leaves purple footprints in the dew of the Okavango's grassy banks. There are eight thatched African-style bungalows which have access to a well-stocked bar, swimming pool and a reed-enclosed boma, a lovely venue for candle-lit fireside meals under a brilliant canopy of stars. Game drives, birdwatching and boating trips are available.

For bookings contact Gametrackers, 31 Harley Street, Randburg 2194, tel (011) 781-0137.

MACHABA CAMP This beautiful camp on the edge of the Moremi Game Reserve is among Botswana's best, lying in its own game reserve. Here elephants trudge past the camp seeking out acacia pods on their way to the Khwai River, the natural boundary between Machaba and Moremi.

In the evenings you may watch sandgrouse come down to the river to drink or listen to the hippos grunting in midstream, or prepare for a game drive that may reveal spotted hyenas, leopards, jackals, genets and bushbabies.

Day drives take you into the heart of populations of big game that include lions, buffaloes, giraffes and wildebeest.

Luxury tents with *en suite* ablution facilities offer access to a reed-panelled diningroom, a tree-house that serves as an observation platform, and a boma where the very best bush cuisine is served.

For bookings and enquiries contact Ker and Downey Safaris, PO Box 27, Maun, tel (09267) 66-0375.

POM POM CAMP The splash of hippos in surrounding waterways, the rush of birdsong in the reeds, the chance of sudden encounters with big game in the bush — these are just a few of the attractions that await visitors to this luxurious camp, remotely situated to the west of the Moremi Reserve.

Pom Pom lies at the edge of a tranquil lagoon in the heart of the Okavango Delta, and each of the seven luxury tents, with *en suite*, reed-walled shower and flush toilet, has a jacana's-eye view over the channels. The tents are scattered around an open thatched diningroom, lounge and bar complex.

Attractions are mokoro trips, day and night 4x4 game drives and walks. This camp is expensive, but guests are pampered with excellent cuisine, five-star se vice and professional rangers who operat first-class wildlife excursions.

For bookings and enquiries contact Ke and Downey Safaris, PO Box 27, Maun, te (09267) 66-0375.

Okavango Delta at a glance

Locality:	Northwestern Botswana.
Climate:	Subtropical climate: hot summers (40 °C maximum), with summer thunderstorms. Winter days mild (25 °C), but nights cold.
Number of camps:	There are at least 24 excellent camps in the delta region, ranging from rustic to luxurious.
Game drives:	Most of the camps on the Mopane Tongue and Chief's Island offer game drives. A circular drive (4x4s only) skirts the edge of the delta, offering outstanding opportunities for game and birdwatching.
Trails:	Most of the camps offer walking and mokoro trails. Some offer game drives in open 4x4s. Wilderness Safaris offers four-night mokoro trails, during which you overnight on islands under the stars.
Other attractions:	Fishing, photography, birdwatching.
Amenities:	Some camps have swimming pools, most camps have small shops, diningrooms and fully stocked bars.
Accommodation:	Most camps offer rustic accommodation in twin-bedded safari tents, brick-and-thatch bungalows or bandas — huts raised on stilts.
Booking address:	Government rest camps: Department of Wildlife and National Parks, PO Box 20364, Maun, tel (09267) 66-1265. Private camps: see individual entries, or contact any one of the following safari operators: Wilderness Safaris, PO Box 78573, Sandton 2146, tel (011) 883-0747; Gametrackers, 31 Harley Street, Randburg 2194, tel (011) 781-0137.
When to go:	In the dry season (May–November), when game-viewing is at its best.
What to take with you:	Casual, lightweight clothing; jersey and anorak for cold evenings; hat, sunglasses, binoculars, torch, camera.
How to get there:	Safari operators will fly you into your delta camp from Johannesburg, Maun or Victoria Falls. There are two flights from Johannesburg to Maun every week.
Nearest doctor:	There are doctors in Maun. A flying doctor insurance scheme is available that covers the cost of flying you out to the nearest doctor (usually in Maun) in an emergency.
Nearest petrol:	Maun.
Open:	Most camps are open throughout the year.
Special precautions:	Beware of bilharzia, crocodiles, lions and hippos. Take antimalaria precautions before and during your trip.

Tuli Safari Lodge

In the extraordinary wilderness of Botswana's Tuli Block you will come closer to the hot breath of Africa than in any other game reserve on the subcontinent. And, say the Tswana people who live there, once the dust of Tuli has touched your heels, its magic remains in your heart forever.

An astonishing variety of animals, more than 350 species of bird, and a safari lodge that's really quite exceptional, are the ingredients that make this magic.

The animal populations are always changing here, because there are no fences to stop them moving in from the Tuli Circle that extends into southwestern Zimbabwe.

Tuli Safari Lodge is located in the heart of a 7 500-ha private game reserve, just five hours' drive from Johannesburg, along the western bank of the Limpopo River. Across the riverbed, which is dry for most of the year, is South Africa. To the east lies Zimbabwe.

The lodge itself is a lush oasis in the baking wilderness of southern Botswana — its flower-laden garden bursting with the colours of myriad blooms, including cascades of bougainvillea.

This oasis is the daily departure point for game drives or walks (see p. 256) that introduce you to Tuli's untamed wilderness, taking you along rough river banks, through mopane forest, thornveld and singing grassland to the secret hideouts of the birds and animals.

Accommodation Guests are accommodated in 10 thatched chalets, with ethnic African furnishings, *en suite* bathrooms

Tips for travellers

- **Lodge staff meet you on the South African side of the border at Pont Drift and ferry you to the lodge in their own safari vehicles.**
- **The Tuli Lodge Airstrip is an official entry point for Botswana, so all immigration formalities are tended to on site, making the procedure very easy for visitors.**

Lone ranger of the woodlands

One of Botswana's lesser-seen inhabitants is the civet, a doglike relative of mongooses and genets, with its distinctive black 'face-mask', white muzzle and long body ending in a thick, bushy tail with 20 dark rings.

Twice as long as a genet and five times its weight, the civet is a quiet, shy creature of the night whose simple tastes for a variety of foods enable it to survive all over Southern africa.

It forages on the ground at night, following established paths through the grass. Moving slowly, with its head down, it sniffs for potential prey.

Victims include reptiles, gerbils, springhares, rodents and large birds such as francolins and guineafowl. Often unable to kill its larger prey with a single bite, a civet may resort to shaking it vigorously – in much the same way that a dog shakes a towel — and then throwing it, a strategy which protects it from counterbites.

Other items on the civet's menu are millipedes, beetles, grasshoppers and fruit, in particular the sweet, yellow fruits of the mokutshumo (African ebony) trees which grow on the island woodlands of the Okavango. Although they will clamber along low branches of fig trees to get at fruit, they prefer to be on the ground.

(hot and cold running water) and wall-to-wall carpeting. Each chalet is equipped with mosquito netting, overhead fans and guide books. The chalets are a stroll away from a sparkling pool and the lodge's sprawling gardens. Here you may encounter Botswana's unique yellow-backed squirrels, or watch the resident vervet monkeys parachuting between the branches of the shady trees. Antelope, dassies and various mongooses also scurry across the garden's lovely lawns.

Nearby, set under the shady canopy of a 600-year-old mashatu tree, is an enticing bar called the 'Watering Hole'. Here you may sip exotic frosted cocktails at sunset, before enjoying cuisine that is unashamedly African in the reed-enclosed boma. Kudu steaks, roast leg of warthog, guineafow casseroles, fillet of impala and venison ar typical of the meals, served by friendly attractive Tswana waitresses. Afterward tribal dancers perform the mystical dance of Africa to the beat of Tswana drums.

For more economical accommodation you can try Nkolodi Tented Camp which nestles in a riverine forest under a clif face, and comprises four units with toile and shower.

Game drives and walks Game drive led by professional guides and gam trackers in open 4x4 safari vehicles take you wherever you want to go. The drive skirt towering cliffs, dense bush and the fossils of trees that died hundreds of thou

Tuli Safari Lodge at a glance

Locality:	Northeastern Tuli Block, 520 km from Johannesburg, 410 km from Gaborone.
Climate:	Warm to hot; occasional thundershowers in summer. Winters mild to cool.
Number of camps:	One tented camp.
Game drives:	Two daily throughout Tuli Block, plus a foot safari.
Hides and waterholes:	Three reed-walled hides.
Trails:	Born to be Free trails are the major draw-card. Others range from one-hour to three-day hikes.
Other attractions:	Tribal dancing, swimming, examining fossilised trees, San paintings.
Amenities:	Swimming pool, fully licensed bar.
Accommodation:	14 thatched chalets, with *en suite* bathrooms; tented safari camp, guest-house.
Booking address:	Tuli Safari Lodge, PO Box 32533, Braamfontein 2017, tel (011) 726-6894.
When to go:	The best time to see game is between April and December.
What to take with you:	Binoculars, light clothing, camera. In winter take warm clothing.
How to get there:	From Johannesburg take the N1 to Pietersburg, turn left on to the R521 and drive 210 km to the border post at Pontdrift. By air (1,5 hours) from Gaborone, Harare or Johannesburg — Tuli Lodge has its own airstrip.
Nearest doctor:	Messina. Travelling medical clinic at Alldays.
Nearest petrol:	Selibe Pikwe.
Open:	Throughout the year.
Special precautions:	Take antimalaria precautions before your visit. Be aware that there are large, potentially dangerous animals may be encountered on game walks.

sands of years ago. Track a lion on foot through the long grass; pause to watch a leopard draped across the branches of a tree; or stand back and watch as a herd of 300 elephants come crashing through the bush. The guard carries a 458 Magnum just in case things go awry.

Spotlight-assisted night drives reveal seldom-seen creatures of the dark: spotted genets scurrying through the scrubland, the piercing, luminous eyes of a black-footed cat, the rattling armoury of a porcupine, springhares, civets and aardvarks. A highlight of the night drives is a waterhole stop where you may see spotted hyenas coming down to drink.

During the dry season, when water is scarce, large groups of animals converge on Tuli's waterholes, creating excellent gamewatching and photographic opportunities. There are three discreet hides with reed screens from which you may watch the wildlife pageant for hours. Among other animals you're likely to see are cheetahs, Burchell's zebras, giraffes, eland, impala, steenbok, kudu, bushbuck, baboons and blackbacked jackals.

Foot safaris These range from a short, leisurely stroll along the river bank (the Limpopo is just a short walk away from the lodge) to a hard day's hike through the bush. On the way you may track bushbuck through thick riverine forest or catch a glimpse of the majestic spiralling horns of a male kudu.

For a complete bush adventure visitors may overnight in the bush under the stars, listening to the sounds of the wild around a crackling fire before dining on deep-fried mopane worms and antelope steaks cooked on the coals. Alternatively, guests may overnight in one of the spotlit hides, watching game (or sleeping) until daybreak.

Born to be Free A highlight of any trip to Tuli is a chance to take part in the Born to be Free Experience, a three-day programme that includes special wildlife expeditions, game drives, wilderness walks and educational talks. Born to be Free is run by the head ranger of Tuli, Hugh Jenkins, and Gareth Patterson, the natural successor to the late George Adamson as the Lion Man of Africa.

Patterson relocated Adamson's lions from the Kora Reserve to Tuli, where one of them, Rafiki, gave birth to cubs. Patterson has written three books: *Cry for the Lions, Where the Lion Walked* and *Golden Lost Souls.*

Other attractions Tuli Lodge organises drives to the nearest Tswana village, where guests may witness the ritual of the 'kgotla' or people's court, where tribal law is administered by the chief and headmen.

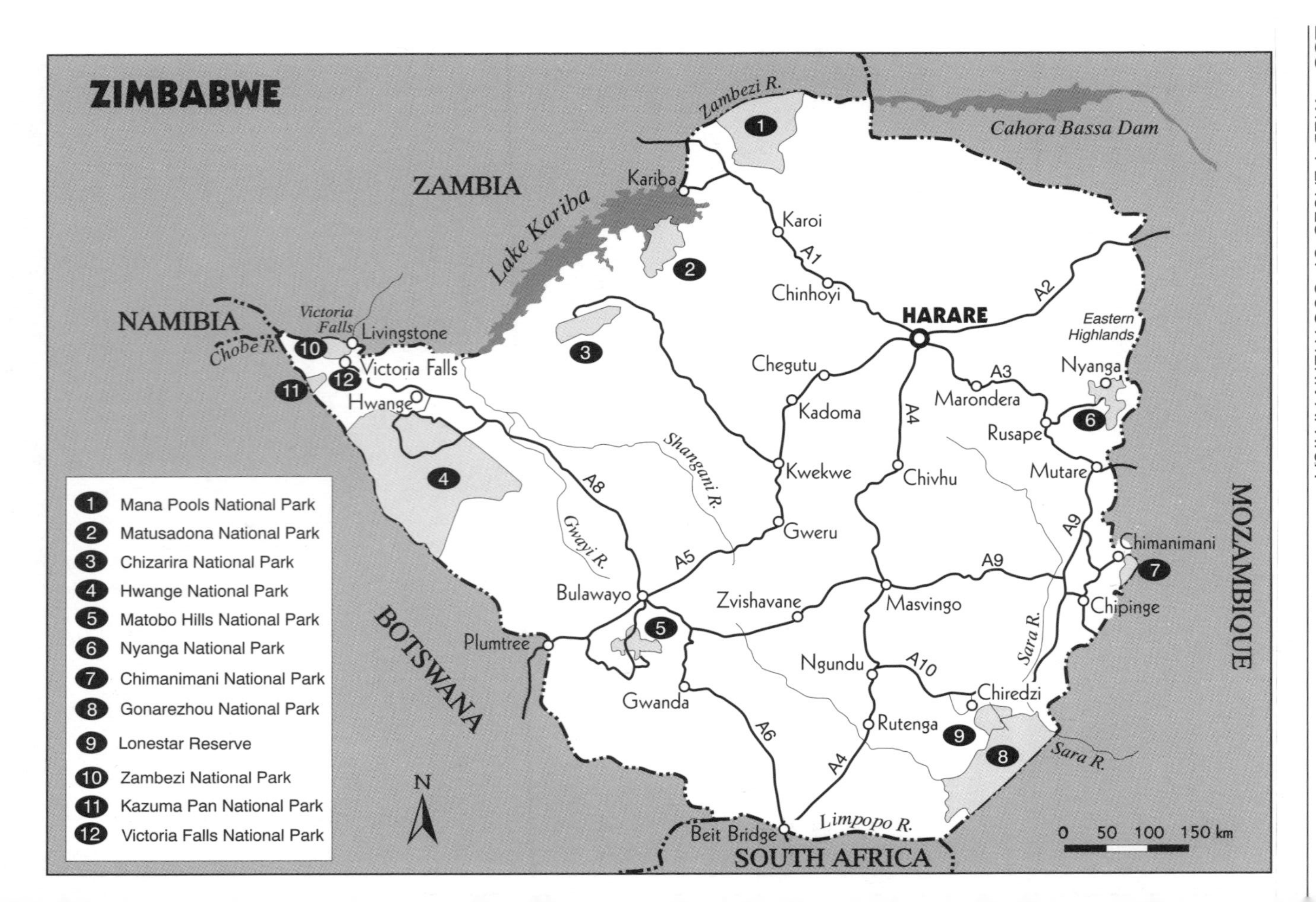
ZIMBABWE
ZAMBIA
NAMIBIA
BOTSWANA
MOZAMBIQUE
SOUTH AFRICA
Cahora Bassa Dam
Zambezi R.
Lake Kariba
Chobe R.
Victoria Falls
Shangani R.
Gwayi R.
Sara R.
Limpopo R.
Eastern Highlands
HARARE
Kariba
Karoi
Chinhoyi
Chegutu
Kadoma
Kwekwe
Gweru
Livingstone
Victoria Falls
Hwange
Bulawayo
Plumtree
Gwanda
Zvishavane
Masvingo
Ngundu
Rutenga
Chiredzi
Beit Bridge
Chivhu
Marondera
Rusape
Nyanga
Mutare
Chimanimani
Chipinge
A1
A2
A3
A4
A5
A6
A8
A9
A10
N
0 50 100 150 km
1 Mana Pools National Park
2 Matusadona National Park
3 Chizarira National Park
4 Hwange National Park
5 Matobo Hills National Park
6 Nyanga National Park
7 Chimanimani National Park
8 Gonarezhou National Park
9 Lonestar Reserve
10 Zambezi National Park
11 Kazuma Pan National Park
12 Victoria Falls National Park

ZIMBABWE

Next to South Africa, Zimbabwe is fast becoming the major wildlife destination of the subcontinent. Roughly the size of California (390 000 km^2), and landlocked by Botswana, Mozambique, Zambia and South Africa, more than 12 per cent of its land surface has been set aside for use as natural sanctuaries for animals, birds and plants.

Dominating these sanctuaries are the country's 11 national parks, ranging from the 14 561 km^2 Hwange National Park to the 23 km^2 Victoria Falls National Park. These are essentially the wild places of Zimbabwe, places that remind visitors of their primal past — when men were hunted by lions, and security was a roaring fire at the entrance of a cave.

Today Zimbabwe brings you back to the savannah — right into the company of elephants and lions, wild dogs, rhinos and crocodiles. But this time you have a choice of experienced game rangers, exceptional bush accommodation, and a safari network that will get you wherever you want to go in comfort and style.

The wild places

All the wild places of Zimbabwe have their own unique character and particular attractions, so first-time visitors should consider visiting two or more wildlife destinations during their stay (for details of wildlife packages refer to the section 'Safari Tours: Zimbabwe', p. 358). The most attractive of these are listed below.

Lake Kariba

Occupying centre stage in Zimbabwe's theatre of the wild is Kariba — the lake of burnished gold. Stretching nearly 300 km from southwest to northeast and more than 40 km along its north-south axis, it is the third largest man-made dam in the world.

This is the setting for several top-class game lodges which provide superb accommodation and the chance to explore the length and breadth of the lake on houseboats or smaller craft.

Lake Kariba lodges offer angling safaris (for tigerfish and bream) or overnight visits to the beautiful islands that are strung out like pearls across the vast expanse of shimmering water (see 'Lake Kariba lodges', p. 276).

Hwange National Park

One of the largest national parks in Africa, Hwange straddles an unspoilt wilderness of 14 000 km^2 in northwestern Zimbabwe, ranging from Kalahari sandveld to vast forests and open grassland. Its very remoteness, wildness and large numbers of animals (105 species of mammal and more than 400 of bird) have attracted a profusion of beautiful and luxurious game lodges to its borders.

Visitors may choose between luxurious chalets, idyllic tree-houses with spectacular views or more basic tented accommodation on the ground.

Because it captures the spirit of old Africa, Hwange is becoming more and more popular among South Africans and visitors from abroad looking for a wildlife holiday beyond their own borders.

As with the other major parks in Africa, it offers game drives, bush-trail adventures and tours to the Victoria Falls and Lake Kariba.

Victoria Falls

Just north of Hwange National Park the Victoria Falls — known to local tribespeople as 'Mosi-oa-Tunya' — the Smoke that Thunders — plunges ferociously into a chasm of rock 1 700 m wide.

For visitors drenched in its swirling mists the falls are probably the highlight of their trip to Zimbabwe. The falls and their surrounding rainforest form the heart of the Victoria Falls National Park, a World Heritage site of fern-clad creepers and forest giants. Some 6 km upstream from the falls is the Zambezi National Park, a 56 000-ha game sanctuary popular for its abundant game and superb rustic lodges.

Moving northeastwards from Victoria Falls visitors will encounter the Chizarira, Matusadona and Mana Pools national parks which, together with Hwange, attract the majority of tourists to Zimbabwe's wild places.

Chizarira National Park

This park lies 90 km south of Lake Kariba — a wild and untamed country that sprawls 192 000 ha across the Zambezi Escarpment. Here you may sample the rugged vistas of Zimbabwe's mopane plains from the luxurious comfort of the Chizarira Wilderness Safari Lodge which is perched on the edge of a vast sandstone plateau.

Matusadona National Park

Matusadona is probably the finest game conservation area lining the shore of Lake Kariba. Elephants, buffaloes, rhinos and hordes of other animals flock to this mystical shoreline, with its beautiful sunsets and graceful hides. Just across the lake from Kariba village, Matusadona invites visitors to sample the tranquillity of three exclusive bush camps.

Mana Pools National Park

If there's one reserve that could be rated higher than Hwange, Chizarira or Matusadona national parks with their extraordinary wildlife and natural attractions, that park is Mana Pools. Covering 250 000 km^2 in northern Zimbabwe, Mana Pools is the continent's fourth largest game park.

Wild, beautiful and unforgettable for its scenic waterside ambience, it is one of the world's four World Heritage sites.

The numbers of game here, attracted by the seasonal flooding of the Zambezi River, are legendary, and are fully described in the entry on p. 279.

Gonarezhou National Park

This park, which lies in the southeastern corner of Zimbabwe bordering Mozambique, has been ravaged by a crippling drought in recent years, but its vastness (50 000 km^2) and abundance of game (elephants, particularly) justifiably make it one of Zimbabwe's most remarkable wilderness areas.

Here visitors may choose accommodation ranging from luxury thatched Shangaan lodges to rustic bush camps.

When to go

The best time for game-viewing in Zimbabwe's national parks is during the dry season from May to October, when the animals tend to congregate around waterholes and other perennial sources of water. Bear in mind, however, that it is very hot in Zimbabwe from October through to January, and that winter, by contrast, is mild and pleasant.

During May the water plunging over the Victoria Falls is at peak volume, and the level of Lake Kariba is at its highest.

The first rains usually fall in late October, signalling the start of the flowering season and the calving of several species of antelope such as impala.

How to get there

By air At least 16 international airlines (including South African Airways) service Harare's international airport, while Air Zimbabwe runs daily flights to the country's other major centres. These include Victoria Falls and Bulawayo whose airports, in turn, service dozens of private air charter companies ferrying visitors to and from the game reserves and back.

By road There are 10 entry points from neighbouring countries, of which the busiest is Beit Bridge at the Limpopo River — the point of entry between Zimbabwe and South Africa. The other entry points are: from Zambia (Victoria Falls, Chirundu, Kariba); Botswana (Plumtree, Mpandamatenga); Mozambique (Mutare, Mount Selinda and Nyamapanda); Namibia (Kazungula).

Getting around

Most of the game parks are easily accessible by road (there are 5 000 km of national highways, and about 45 000 km of secondary roads), and many of them by air. But bear in mind that in the more remote areas you may need a four-wheel-drive vehicle. Where access by road is a problem because of seasonal flooding (as in the Mana Pools National Park), visitors have the option of getting there by air, or by boat. For details of self-drive and safari options available in Zimbabwe, refer to the section 'Safari Tours in Southern Africa', p. 351.

Where to stay

Zimbabwe has an excellent tourist infrastructure which caters to the accommodation needs of a wide spectrum of people. A good example of this is Hwange National Park which has no less than seven public rest camps, 14 private bush camps or safari lodges, and five hotels in and around it.

All 12 national parks offer excellent, clean accommodation in their public rest camps. Visitors may choose between serviced chalets, lodges, cottages, tented camps, and camping and caravan sites. Campers and caravanners usually have access to outdoor ablution blocks and braaiing facilities, and in the less remote reserves, to shops, restaurants and swimming pools.

Not all the parks — or camps — provide cutlery and crockery, and not all chalets have self-contained ablution facilities, so it would be wise to enquire whether the units are equipped with these essentials, and whether or not they are self-catering.

Zimbabwe's private bush camps and safari lodges rank among the best in the world and, although they are more expensive than the national parks' public camps, they provide just about everything a guest could want on a safari holiday. This includes superior accommodation, game drives, wilderness trails, swimming pools, African cuisine and superb gamewatching opportunities (see *Accommodation* in the individual entries). Some lodges have their own waterholes within the camp, so guests may watch animals come and go from the comfort of their chalet porch.

Travel information

Game reserves and national parks: Department of National Parks and Wildlife Management, PO Box CY826, Causeway, Harare, tel (09263-4) 70-6077. For tourist enquiries in South Africa, contact the Zimbabwe Tourist Office, 2nd Floor, Finance House, Ernest Oppenheimer Drive, Bruma Lake 2026, tel (011) 622-5741.

Road travel information and maps: Automobile Association of Zimbabwe, Ground Floor, Fanum House, Samora Machel Avenue, PO Box 585, Harare, tel (09263-4) 70-7021.

Safari tours and touring: Zimbabwe Association of Tour and Safari Operators, PO Box A483, Avondale, Harare; or contact the Zimbabwe Tourism Development Corporation, PO Box 8052, Harare, tel (09623-4) 70-6511.

After-hours tour hotline service: Tel Harare (09623-4) 887-5524.

Chizarira National Park

The primal pulse of Batonka drums floats across the dark corridors of the Zambezi Valley, eerily ascending the ramparts of a massive sandstone barrier known as Chizarira. At the edge of this escarpment, from a chalet that seems to hang above the void, you gaze northwards across the Zambezi Valley's mopane plains to the distant shores of Lake Kariba.

The air is warm in the afterglow of sunset; the view quite spectacular; and the promise of an unsurpassed adventure in the wild brings a shiver of anticipation to first-time visitors. For here, on the edge of Chizarira National Park, you're just about as far removed from civilisation as you're likely to get anywhere in Southern Africa. More significantly, the heart of this wilderness, with its teeming populations of birds and animals (including the Big Five), is just a few hours' hike away.

Chizarira National Park, 50 km south of the Binga tribal area of Lake Kariba, is Zimbabwe's third-largest park, covering 192 000 ha of pure African wilderness, across the highest point of the Zambezi Escarpment. The ridge of the escarpment runs from the southwest to the northeast for 30 km along the park's northern boundary, rising to 1 434 m at Tundazi Peak, reputed to be the lair of a giant serpent.

From the air, the escarpment reveals deep cracks in its rugged folds — these are a series of ravines whose almost sheer sides are cloaked in woodland and dense bush. In the north a deep gorge in the Lwizilukulu River reveals secret groves of sycamore fig and jackalberry trees.

To the south mopane and msasa scrublands, punctuated by old baobabs, applering thorn trees and large-leaved strangler figs along the watercourses, roll off to distant horizons.

These plains and the escarpment became the refuge of thousands of animals, including 12 000 elephants, displaced when the Zambezi River was dammed to create Lake Kariba.

Tips for travellers

- You can get to the park in a saloon car, but a 4x4 is essential in the park.
- Only one party may book a bush camp at a time.
- Be aware that the nearest petrol is at Binga 90 km away.

Wildlife In the copper-toned bush country of the south the elephants, lions, leopards, buffaloes and baboons congregate in the company of a mixed bag of antelope such as tsessebe, waterbuck, duiker, roan antelope, impala, kudu and klipspringer.

In the north the dwindling remnants of a once-great population of black rhinos occupy the high ground. This section of the park was once regarded as one of Zimbabwe's best areas for seeing black rhino, but poaching has taken a dreadful toll: since 1989 numbers have dwindled from 300 to about 20 individuals.

Birdlife Some 406 of Zimbabwe's 580 bird species have been sighted in the park. Birds include black, martial and crowned eagles, augur buzzards, peregrine, lanner and the seldom-seen Taita falcons. Other birds include Böhm's spinetails, Livingstone's flycatchers, scarletchested sunbirds, orangebreasted bush shrikes, rattling cisticolas, threestreaked tchagras, whitebacked vultures, giant, pied and malachite kingfishers, Pel's fishing owls, pearlspotted owls and bat hawks.

Where to stay There are three camps in Chizarira National Park. The most popular is Kasiswi Bush Camp on the Lwizilukulu River, 6 km from the park's headquarters at Manzituba. Here three-walled thatched units raised on stilts are open to the bush. During the night you may hear the roars of warring lion prides drifting in from the amphitheatre of darkness outside. Mabolo Bush Camp, on the Mucheni River 6 km from Manzituba, is a more primitive camp,

Caring matriarchs of the wild

Game trails in Chizarira National Park will certainly bring you into the company of large groups of elephants — and provide an intimate view of elephant society.

Females tend to dominate this society, forming matriarchal herds led by older, experienced cows. Although they wield the power, these cows are caring, generous and gentle with their own calves and the offspring of other females, and will often adopt a youngster that has lost its mother. When a cow approaches full term of a pregnancy, the other cows will rally around her, providing support and comfort.

Cows reach sexual maturity when they are about 12 years old and produce calves until a fairly ripe old age: one 60-year-old cow here produced 11 calves during her life. On average, cows produce one calf every four-and-a-half years.

The calves are born in summer after a gestation period of about 22 months. They suckle from their mothers for three or four years, and remain with their parents until they reach sexual maturity at 12 or 14 years old. They keep in close contact with their mothers, walking under her stomach or grasping her tail with their trunks.

but like Kasiswi it has a raised sleeping and dining area. Bring your own tent to Mabolo. Busi Bush Camp is 35 km away on the Busi River. On the southwestern corner of the park's boundary is Jedson's Camp for walking safaris. The camp is situated 100 metres up on the lip of a sandstone escarpment. All the camps offer hot and cold water, cooking facilities and flush toilets (but be sure to bring your own toilet paper).

CHIZARIRA WILDERNESS LODGE Perched on the edge of the escarpment just outside the park, this beautiful lodge offers eight thatched, stone chalets, each named after an animal or bird and decorated with African furnishings. Each chalet has an *en suite* shower, toilet and a private verandah overlooking the Tyetyebwende Spring, 160 m below,

There is a large open-plan dining and bar area and a swimming pool built into

Chizarira National Park at a glance

Locality:	Northwest Zimbabwe, 313 km southeast of Victoria Falls and 500 km west of Harare.
Climate:	Mild winters; hot to very hot summers, with occasional thundershowers.
Number of camps:	Three camps: Kasiswi Bush Camp, Mabolo Bush Camp, Busi Bush Camp.
Game drives:	Getting around is confined mainly to trails.
Trails:	Variety on offer, main ones are the three-day Nyagangara and Machininga trails and the five-day Wilderness Safaris Trail.
Other attractions:	Panoramic views from edge of escarpment.
Amenities:	Swimming pool, bar and dining area at Chizarira Wilderness Safari Lodge.
Accommodation:	Three bush camps offer camping facilities on elevated platforms. **Chizarira Wilderness Safari Lodge** offers eight *en suite* stone-and-thatch chalets.
Booking address:	Central Booking Office, Department of National Parks and Wildlife Management, PO Box CY826, Causeway, Harare, tel (09263-4) 70-6077. Trails: Wilderness Safaris, PO Box 78573, Sandton 2146, tel (011) 883-0747.
When to go:	Winters are mild and more suited to camping and hiking than the very hot summers.
What to take with you:	Trailists: tour operators will provide all camping equipment and food. Take along camera, torch, warm and cool clothing, good hiking boots and running shoes and a water bottle.
How to get there:	You may fly or drive from Harare (there's a small airstrip at Manzituba, the park's headquarters). From Harare drive via Karoi along the Hostess Nicolle Drive. From Victoria Falls it's a six- to eight-hour drive down the Zambezi Valley escarpment, and up through the Chizarira Hills.
Nearest doctor:	Binga, 90 km away.
Nearest petrol:	Binga, 90 km away.
Open:	Sunrise to sunset throughout the year.
Special precautions:	The game trails and safaris take you into the company of predatory and dangerous animals. Although the professional guides are highly experienced, you should be prepared for any eventuality in the bush. Before you go, see your doctor about an antimalaria course.

the rock with breathtaking views over the valley. The honeymoon suite has a queen-size bed and a private plunge pool.

Activities at the lodge include game drives in two Land Rovers, bush safaris with Steve Alexander and visits to Batonka villages in the Zambezi Valley.

The lodge has a small shop equipped with local crafts, T-shirts and other odds and ends.

The lodge is 530 km from Harare and you can get there via Binga (90 km away) and Gokwa, which is 3 km from the Chizarira National Park entrance.

Fly-in charters can be arranged from any major city in Zimbabwe. Children under 12 are accepted by special arrangement only.

To book contact Afro Ventures, PO Box 1200, Paulshof 2056, tel (011) 807-3720.

Trails and game drives The park offers various escorted hiking trials during the dry season, varying from a few to 10 days. These include the Nyagangara Trail, a three-day hike which covers the beautiful countryside between Kasikili and Nyangangara springs. The Machininga Trail starts and ends at Machininga Spring, one-and-a-half hours' drive from the camp's headquarters. Bring your own tents for this hike.

A popular hike is the five-day wilderness trail organised by Wilderness Safaris. The tour price includes transport from Victoria Falls, park fees, food and drink, cost of a professional guide and accommodation at the Chizarira Wilderness Safari Lodge. The lodge also offers daily game walks and drives, accompanied by professional rangers.

For information and reservations contact Wilderness Safaris at PO Box 78573, Sandton 2146, or at tel (011) 883-0747.

GONAREZHOU NATIONAL PARK

The soaring turrets of the Chilojo Cliffs stand like ancient warriors above the plains of Gonarezhou National Park. To the north, the sandy highway of the Runde River meanders through a landscape of baobab, mopane and acacia woodlands.

This is the heart of Gonarezhou, which means 'horn (tusk) of the elephant' — one of Zimbabwe's greatest and driest wilderness areas, bordered in the south by Mozambique.

The sun-scorched plains merge in the southeast with a beautiful wetland area caused (in years of good rain) by the convergence of the Save and Runde rivers before they enter Mozambique. An 8-km floodplain between the rivers, known as the Tamboharta Pan, attracts a large variety of game, as well as some 230 species of bird.

Wildlife Covering about 50 000 km^2, Gonarezhou hosts most of the large species of game — elephant, rhino, hippo, giraffe, lion and crocodile — but drought and poaching from Mozambique during the eighties and early nineties exacted a savage toll on the park's animal populations.

In the summer of 1992 the carcasses of elephants, hippos, Lichtenstein's hartebeest and other animals lined the dusty bed of the Runde River. Conservationists battled to rescue the survivors — picking up baby elephants that had been left behind by fatigued herds searching for water, and rounding up emaciated individuals of other species for relocation to private game farms.

Subsequent rains have brought relief to Gonarezhou, and the game populations are slowly being restored to their former numbers, thanks in part to the owners of private game farms such as Lonestar Reserve, which borders the park.

Getting around For first-time visitors to Gonarezhou, it's important to know that the park is divided into two distinct regions: the Chipinda Pools area in the north and the Mabalauta area in the south, each having its own road network. Although no road crosses the central wilderness area between Chipinda and Mabalauta, there are ample opportunities for gamewatching and some excellent walking trails.

How to get there To reach Chipinda Pools from Bulawayo and Harare travel via Ngundu Halt and Chiredzi. Access to Mabalauta is via Ngundu Halt and Rutenga. From South Africa you may reach Mabalauta via Rutenga or Chipinda Pools via Chiredzi.

Where to stay Accommodation in Gonarezhou ranges from rustic bush camps with the barest facilities to luxury safari lodges with all the mod cons. Whichever option you choose, the rewards are an abundance of game, a feeling of the 'real' Africa and exquisitely peaceful surroundings.

Tips for travellers

- **New arrivals must report to the tourist offices either at Chipinda Pools or Mabalauta.**
- **Saloon cars will reach Swimuwini and Chipinda Pools, but you'll need a 4x4 for getting around the park.**
- **Gonarezhou is one of the hottest areas of Zimbabwe. Be prepared for temperatures exceeding 40 °C (temperatures above 50 °C have been recorded).**

The northern camps include Chipinda Pools, a delightful fishing spot which has chalets and basic camping facilities, ablutions and water, and Chivilila Camp which lies in a beautiful setting at Chivilila Rapids, where the Runde River cascades down a series of steep waterfalls.

Each camp has a thatched communal dining area and ablution facilities.

Two other 'Out of Africa' camps in the north are Chinguli and Massasanya camps — both with minimal facilities.

Apart from these camps, there are at least 10 other bush camps with the barest facilities — long-drop toilets and a braai area. One of the best of these, but without any facilities at all, is Fishans Camp, a beautiful spot on the Runde River under a canopy of nyalaberry and jackalberry trees. Here you may relax at sunset and watch the moon rise above the sun-tinged sandstone peaks of the majestic Chilojo Cliffs. These cliffs, their lower reaches garlanded with baobabs and acacia woodland, track the course of the Runde River for 32 km.

Animals here include elephants, eland, lions, giraffes, buffaloes, Lichtenstein's hartebeest and nyala. In years of good rain Chipinda is an excellent fishing area.

There are about 200 km of game drives in the Chipinda area, including a drive along the Runde River as far as the reed- and waterlily-covered Mchininwa Pan near the Mozambique border.

In the south of Gonarezhou is the delightful Mabalauta Camp, which offers two tidy chalets and a camping and caravan site. This is elephant country — many animals arriving here after the long trek north from the Kruger National Park. Another place where you are bound to see elephants is Swimuwini Rest Camp, with its five attractive chalets set on the banks of the Mwenezi River. The chalets each have a verandah and nestle in the shade of large baobabs — hence the name Shimuwini, which means 'place of baobabs'.

During the day a variety of game, including waterbuck, nyala and blackbacked jackal roam the perimeters of the camp, and at night you can hear the roar of lions nearby.

The chalets are equipped with gas fridges, beds and linen, but bring your own cutlery and crockery. Lighting is solar powered. Swimuwini also offers five caravan and camping sites.

There are some lovely picnic sites and hides in the vicinity. One of these — a thatched shelter — overlooks the Mwatombo crocodile pool.

LONESTAR RESERVE This reserve — an idyllic retreat for nature lovers — lies in the Malilangwe Conservation Trust Area, a 40 000-ha wilderness adjoining Gonarezhou in the Chipinda Pools area.

Lonestar is currently being upgraded into one of Africa's leading wildlife sanctuaries under the guidance of the Malilangwe Conservation Trust. The primary aim of the trust is to create a role model at Lonestar which will serve as an example and inspiration to other reserves throughout Africa. Money generated by tourism will be channelled back into the reserve and the local communities.

Lonestar has been substantially restocked with the indigenous game which, in the past, had been seriously depleted by drought and today Malilangwe features most of the large mammals such as lion, hippo, white rhino, elephant, leopard, buffalo and giraffe.

Star attraction at Malilangwe is Wilderness Safari's Induna Sandstone Lodge, one of the finest lodges in Zimbabwe, which opened in 1995. Here six luxurious stone-and-thatch cottages, set under shady trees on the edge of a gorge overlooking a sparkling lake, accommodate guests in tranquil and beautifully terraced surroundings.

Each twin-bedded chalet has an *en suite* bathroom and access to a communal bar and lounge area, as well as a swimming pool.

Induna Lodge offers day drives into Gonarezhou, as well as hikes and game drives through the reserve.

You can fly from Harare to Buffalo Range, a five-minute air transfer to the reserve, or there's an excellent tarred road connecting the reserve with Chiredzi, Buffalo Range, Birchenough Bridge and Mutare.

Not far off, near the Malilangwe Dam, is Kwali Camp which accommodates 22 people (the camp is geared for self-drive guests). Induna and Kwali offer easy access to the large game populations of Lonestar and to the scenic and wildlife attractions of neighbouring Gonarezhou National Park. Other attractions are birdwatching and river trips, drives to the Chilojo Cliffs, and visits to caves exhibiting San art.

For booking details contact Wilderness Safaris at PO Box 78573, Sandton 2146, tel (011) 883-0747.

CHILO GORGE SAFARI LODGE This attractive lodge on the edge of Gonarezhou National Park offers 14 twin-bedded thatched chalets with stunning views of the Save River Valley. The chalets are decorated in ethnic Shangaan style and have all the mod cons, including *en suite* bathroom with shower, bath, toilet, telephone and immediate access to a sparkling pool near a central bar/lounge complex.

On offer are bush walks and game drives into Gonarezhou National Park. The drive takes in a stop-over at a birdwatching platform at Tambahata Pan where you can see an astonishing variety of birds, from a pied barbet and a sabota lark to a lemonbreasted canary and a narina trogon. Trips are also offered to Mahenye Village to see how the local Shangaan people live. Full- or half-day excursions can be arranged to the Chilojo Cliffs, 70 km away.

For more details and booking, contact Afro Ventures, PO Box 1200, Paulshof 2056, tel (011) 807-3720.

MAHENYE SAFARI LODGE Situated on the eastern edge of Gonarezhou, this lodge offers eight delightful twin-bedded Shangaan thatched lodges set under the shade of huge indigenous trees on an island in the dry bed of the Save River. The units have ethnic African furnishings, *en suite* shower and toilet, balcony and access a large reed-walled lounge-diningroom area. Game drives, birdwatching trips — to nearby Tambahata Pan — and walks are among the many attractions of Mahenye. The lodge has its own runway.

For more details contact Zimbabwe Sun Hotels, 271 Oak Avenue, Ferndale, PO Box 1617, Randburg 2125, tel (011) 886-2130; or tel Harare (09263-4) 73-6644.

Gonarezhou National Park at a glance

Locality:	Southeastern Zimbabwe.
Climate:	Winters mild (sometimes cold at night); searingly hot summer days with thundershowers.
Number of camps:	Fourteen camps, some with chalet accommodation.
Game drives:	More than 200 km of game drives, including one along the Runde River to Mozambique.
Hides and waterholes:	Hides at Swimuwini and Manyanda Pan; waterholes throughout the park.
Trails:	Four: Mabalauta, Pombadzi and Sibonja trails (four days) and the Runde Trail (five days).
Other attractions:	Birdwatching, photography.
Amenities:	Nearest shop is at Chiredzi.
Accommodation:	**Chipinda Pools:** chalets and campsites; **Chivilila Camp**: camping sites, caravan park; **Chinguli** and **Massasanya Camp:** camping sites; **Mabalauta Camp:** chalets, campsites; **Swimuwini Rest Camp:** chalets, campsites.
Booking address:	Central Booking Office, Department of National Parks and Wildlife Management, PO Box CY826, Causeway, Harare, tel (09263-4) 70-6077.
When to go:	The winter months (May–October) are cooler.
What to take with you:	All your own provisions (available at Chiredzi). For the bush camps, all the necessary camping equipment; spare wheels, light clothes, sunhat, plenty of fresh water, spade, binoculars, compass and camera.
How to get there:	Chipinda Pools: from Bulawayo and Harare travel via Ngundu Halt and Chiredzi; from South Africa via Beit Bridge and Chiredzi. Mabalauta: from Bulawayo and Harare travel via Ngundu Halt and Rutenga; from South Africa via Rutenga.
Nearest petrol:	Chiredzi, 60 km north of Chipinda Pools.
Open:	The park is only open between 1 May and 31 October.
Special precautions:	Antimalaria precautions must be taken. Beware of bilharzia in the rivers. Exercise caution while walking anywhere in the park.

Game drives and trails You'll need a four-wheel-drive vehicle to get around Gonarezhou, especially to the bush camps. All game drives are escorted, and permits are required from the Department of National Parks and Wildlife Management in Harare (see *Booking address*, 'At a glance' box). The drives take you through mixed mopane woodland and some of the most magnificent baobab trees in Africa.

Four wilderness walking trails have been laid out: the Mabalauta, Pombadzi and Sibonja trails (four days) and the Runde Trail (five days). The last three trails cover the Chipinda Pools area around the Runde River, while the adventurous Mabalauta Trail explores the periphery of pools, riverine woodland, gorges and mopane woodland around the Mwenezi, Mawange and Machisamba rivers in the Mabalauta region. The trails offer rewarding game-viewing.

All the trails require a reasonably high standard of physical fitness.

Hwange National Park

The primal heartbeat of wild Africa beats strongly in this beautiful park — a 14 651-km^2 wilderness that serves as a sanctuary to one of the most diverse and largest concentrations of game in the world.

Lying in the northwestern part of Zimbabwe, the park is bordered by the Zambezi River and its watershed to the north, and by the vast spaces of Botswana in the west. Here the gently undulating countryside is bisected by fossil river beds that drain southwestwards towards the vast Makgadikgadi Pans in Botswana.

Hwange has become a mecca for gamewatchers and travellers in recent years. South Africans, in particular, are finding that Hwange has just as much to offer — if not more — than many of South Africa's wildlife sanctuaries — very often on more economical terms.

Because it lies in the transition zone between the burnt sands of the Kalahari to the west, and the friendlier savannah woodlands and teak forests of Zimbabwe, the park accommodates animal species adapted to totally different habitats.

The game populations are truly staggering: there are at least 100 mammal species, including between 15 000 and 22 000 elephants that wander through the flat Kalahari scrubland with its stunted woodlands of teak and umtshibi trees. These are complemented by some 15 000 buffaloes, 3 000 zebras, an equal number of giraffes, and no less than 16 species of antelope, notably impala, kudu, hartebeest, tsessebe and sable.

All the large carnivores are well represented — lions, cheetahs, leopards, spotted hyenas, wild dogs and a variety of other cats, and the list of smaller animals, such as reptiles, amphibians and invertebrates, is endless. Add to this a bird population of more than 400 species, and you have the ingredients for a wildlife paradise of magnificent proportions.

Formerly the hunting-ground of the great chief Mzilikazi, Hwange was named after Hwange Rosumbani, a Rosvi warrior who lived in the area in the 19th century. It was proclaimed a reserve in 1928, when animal populations had virtually been exterminated by the hunter's bullet.

Fewer than 1 000 elephants remained and white and black rhinos — prized by poachers for their horns — had been wiped out completely.

Severe and prolonged droughts further threatened the future of the once-massive game populations. Rescue came in the form of Ted Davidson, the founding warden, who drilled dozens of boreholes and established 60 new pans throughout the park. Slowly the animals started returning to the area, and in 1949, together with the adjacent Robins Game Sanctuary, it was declared a national park.

Another major reason for Hwange's success is the fact that most of the huge southern section is virtually untouched by roads, railways or human construction, allowing the animals to live as they did before the advent of humankind.

Getting around The main Victoria Falls–Bulawayo road runs almost parallel to Hwange National Park from northwest to southeast for about 250 km. Travelling from Bulawayo, the turn-off for Main Camp (and Dete) is about 17 km past Gwaai River. Further north, just east of the town of Hwange, is the turn-off that takes you to the other major public rest camps (see below). For details of game drives, see 'Where to see wildlife' on p. 276.

Where to stay There are no less than seven public rest camps, 14 private bush camps or safari lodges, and five hotels in and around Hwange National Park, most of them in the central, northern and northwestern sector.

The public rest camps are: Main Camp, Sinamatella, Lukosi, Bumbusi, Robins, Nantwich and Deka exclusive camps. All offer accommodation in serviced lodges or chalets, tented camps and caravan sites.

MAIN CAMP Known for its accessibility to some excellent game drives, Main Camp offers tidy chalets (no crockery or cutlery), lodges and cottages, with *en suite* bathrooms and verandahs. There are also camping and caravan sites. Communal cooking facilities are provided here, and there's an open-sided thatched dining area (with fridges), a fully licensed bar and a restaurant.

SINAMATELLA CAMP Perched on a plateau above the Sinamatella Valley, this camp lies west of Main Camp between the Deka and Lukosi rivers, a region famed for its leopards. Chalets and cottages similar to those at Main Camp have access to a shop, fine restaurant and bar, and there are also camping and caravan sites. A popular game drive is that along the Lukosi River loop.

LUKOSI CAMP Situated on the western bank of the Lukosi River, this camp accommodates 12 guests from November through to April in comfortable thatched cottages.

BUMBUSI EXCLUSIVE CAMP This camp is usually chosen by small groups (no more than 10) looking for an intimate holiday in rugged surroundings. Accommodation is in two-bedded A-frame huts and one two-bedded cottage. Communal cooking and ablution facilities are provided. Access during the rainy season is by four-wheel-drive vehicle only.

ROBINS, NANTWICH AND DEKA CAMPS These three camps are situated on the western side of Hwange National Park close to each other and the Deka River. Robins Camp is rustic and wild, with its thatched chalets camouflaged under a canopy of trees deep in lion territory. Major attractions here are the crocodile pools on the Deka River close by. The camp is named after Herbert Robins, a reclusive bachelor who bequeathed the land to the nation in 1939. There are outdoor cooking facilities (bring your own cutlery and crockery), communal ablutions, a small shop and petrol.

Nantwich Camp, just 11 km from Robins, has three self-contained cottages, and lovely views across a stretch of water.

Deka Camp, 25 km west of Robins, is relatively tiny — offering guests remote comfort in two six-bedded family units with *en suite* bathroom and toilet. The camp is accessible by four-wheel-drive vehicle only, and is sometimes closed completely during the rainy season.

Private safari lodges The private bush camps or safari lodges in and around Hwange National Park offer different degrees of luxury in tents, tree-houses, bungalows and chalets, as close to the animals as you can get. The more popular of these lodges are:

GIRAFFE SPRINGS Elephants literally walk up to your tent looking for water in the dry season at Giraffe Springs, a small, well-appointed camp in a private concession near Shapi Pan, southwest of Main Camp within Hwange National Park.

And when the waterhole in front of the camp is full, you can expect a feast of other mammals trekking in to slake their thirst. From the deck of your elevated tented room you're likely to see roan and sable antelope, buffalo, lion, leopard and the occasional hyena and jackal.

There are 10 large canvas bedrooms with hexagonal floors, carved doors and a distinct East African ambience. The honeymoon suite must be one of the most original in Southern Africa. Its bathroom has been constructed on a viewing deck outside, partially enclosed by a wall of reeds, with a superb view over the waterhole. The rooms and the main lodge have been lavishly decorated with fabrics and carpets that could have come from Persia or Zanzibar.

Game drives in 4x4s and walks with an armed guard are on offer daily and there is a selection of unobtrusive hides which will guarantee excellent game-viewing. The camp has a plunge pool.

Access to Giraffe Springs is by air from Hwange and all accommodation, meals,

How animals cheat the cheetah

Most people know the cheetah is one of the fastest animals on earth — capable of reaching 72 km/h in two seconds flat and 112 km/h at full tilt. But how successful is a cheetah on the hunt?

In spite of their speed, hunting cheetahs such as those found in Hwange National Park more often than not fail to bring down their prey. A local study on cheetah hunting rituals in Southern Africa found that of 97 hunting attempts on impala, only nine were successful; while five out of 12 pursuits on giraffe resulted in kills.

There is one recorded case in the Nairobi National Park of a cheetah making no less than 15 futile attacks in two days.

One reason why cheetahs often fail miserably in the hunt is that they lack an antelope's ability to zigzag, so while their superior speed may enable them to overhaul their chosen quarry this advantage is often neutralised by the victim breaking off suddenly to the left or right.

Cheetahs mostly hunt between dawn and midday, because during this time lions and hyenas sleep and are less likely to plunder their hard-earned meals.

game drives, walks and drinks are included in the tariff.

To book contact Wilderness Safaris, PO Box 78573, Sandton 2146, tel (011) 883-0747.

DETEMA SAFARI LODGE This lovely lodge lies perched on a hill overlooking the plains and forests on the border of Hwange National Park. Accommodation is in seven thatched one-bedded units, four two-bedded chalets and two luxury tree-lodges. A first-rate restaurant, swimming pool and game-viewing platform are attractions within the camp, while game drives and foot safaris bring you into the company of the big game. For more information contact Afro Ventures, PO Box 1200, Paulshof 2056, tel (011) 807-3720.

IVORY SAFARI LODGE Lying on the northern fringes of Hwange National Park, this lodge has been described as one of the best safari camps in Southern Africa. Here 10 thatched, teak tree-houses offer total serenity, verandah views over a waterhole and easy access to a lovely observation platform where you may view the passing parade of game in silence. There's also a shaded swimming pool and a delightful bar nearby.

At night guests may dine by the light of kerosene lamps in a central thatched diningroom, or listen to the whirring symphony of cicadas and frogs around the boma's fire.

JABULISA The Ndebele word Jabulisa means 'Place of happiness and delight', and that's what guests invariably find at this lodge built on a high ridge overlooking the Gwaai River valley and Sikumi Vlei. There's a solid 'Out of Africa' ambience to the lodge, whose original farmhouse was built in 1922, and which was more recently restored with an ethnic African theme.

The lodge lies on an 80 000-acre estate near Hwange National Park, and among its attractions are drives through big-game country on the estate and into Hwange Game Reserve, as well as horseback trails. Other highlights are visits to a nearby crocodile farm and a traditional African village. Seven thatched chalets (including a honeymoon suite), equipped with three-quarter beds, verandahs and *en suite* facilities, offer guests comfortable accommodation in scenic surroundings. The lodge is 40 km from Hwange Airport.

JIJIMA SAFARI CAMP Built by rancher Ron White on the eastern boundary of Hwange National Park, Jijima Safari Camp offers luxury tents under thatch (all the tents face eastward towards the rising sun), a swimming pool and a pan which attracts large concentrations of game. Day and spotlight-assisted night drives and walks are provided at Jijima and within Hwange National Park, and visitors may expect to see an abundance of game (including the Big Five).

Jijima is a family business providing top-class game scouts, scrumptious home-cooked meals and fireside tales from Ron, who has been in the bush for 30 years. For more information contact Wild Horizons, PO Box 159, Victoria Falls, tel (09263-13) 2001 or Afro Ventures, PO Box 1200, Paulshof 2056, tel (011) 807-3720.

KANONDO TREE CAMP This small camp in the heart of elephant country offers six romantic twin-bedded tree-houses and three cottages with bathroom, set in a private game reserve bordering Hwange National Park.

Each exquisite tree-house has two comfortable single beds, bedside tables, *en suite* facilities and its own panoramic view of the waterhole.

Just 30 minutes' drive from Hwange Airport, Kanondo has been built in a teak forest which is a favourite haunt of elephant, leopard and a herd of roan antelope which has taken up residence in the area.

Meals are served in the central boma, which encloses another, larger game-viewing platform over the permanent waterhole.

Kanondo is well known for its unique Underground Hide close to the water's edge, which provides breathtaking close-up encounters with animals on the ground. These include the 'Presidential' herd of elephants, specially protected by Zimbabwe's president.

For more information and bookings contact Afro Ventures, PO Box 1200, Paulshof 2056, tel (011) 807-3720.

CHOKAMELLA LODGE Situated on its own private estate adjoining Hwange National Park, Chokamella has a breathtaking setting on sand cliffs overlooking the Chokamella River and the distant floodplains.

Nine thatched bungalows and a honeymoon suite offer privacy and exceptional views of the floodplains. The thatched main complex overlooks the seasonal river and permanent waterhole, a magnet for the rich birdlife of the area.

Night drives on the lodge's estate, game walks or visits to Hwange National Park are standard fare.

There's a swimming pool and open-air boma for sundowners and meals.

Children under 12 are allowed only on request.

For more details contact Afro Ventures, PO Box 1200, Paulshof 2056, tel (011) 807-3720.

KHATSHANA TREE LODGE This lodge, completed in late 1995, lies on the edge of Dete Vlei, and offers six luxury tree-houses with French doors and thatched verandahs overlooking a waterhole. The camp's theme is African village life, and is richly portrayed in ochre walls, ethnic rugs and fabrics adorning the tree-houses and central complex. A swimming pool is available nearby.

The thatched lounge/bar is surrounded by a grove of msasa trees which provide welcome shade for meals outside in the heat of the day.

Katshana lies in a prolific game area, with three waterholes within a kilometre of the camp. Game drives take guests into the midst of elephants, buffaloes, lions and other animals.

MAKOLOLO PLAINS & LITTLE MAKOLOLO Makololo Plains camp, which opened in 1997, was built on the site of the old Touch the Wild Camp in the southeastern corner of Hwange National Park. Set among mopane and acacia woodland, palm-fringed plains and grasslands, this camp and its smaller satellite camp, Little Makololo, offer an excellent variety of wildlife from these diverse habitats.

The nine luxury safari tents are built on elevated teak decks on the edge of Samavundha Pan, a meeting point for herds of elephant which can number more than 100. The tents are linked to a communal diningroom and bar by a series of boardwalks, which often intersect the paths of elephants. It is quite common for guests to encounter these large pachyderms on their way to dinner.

Little Makololo has just eight beds in four safari tents on the ground — an ideal venue for a family wishing to hire the whole camp. The camp has a cosy hide under jackalberry trees and a sparkling plunge pool to cool off in after a bush walk or game drive.

Apart from regular sightings of sable and roan antelope, buffaloes, giraffe, wildebeest, impala, lions, leopards, wild dogs and cheetahs, Makololo has a huge array of birds, from miombo species to birds typical of the Kalahari sandveld.

Access to the camps is by air from Hwange — a 15-minute flight. To book contact Wilderness Safaris, PO Box 78573, Sandton 2146, tel (011) 883-0747.

SABLE VALLEY LODGE This double-storey hexagonal lodge on the edge of Dete Vlei is one of Zimbabwe's most luxurious small safari lodges, and in 1991 hosted Queen Elizabeth II and Prince Philip during their official visit to the country.

The main lodge, a soaring Matabele-style structure built of thatch, Gwaai River stone, pink slate and tough tropical hardwoods, is situated in its own exclusive forestry reserve on the border of Hwange National Park.

Within this architectural delight a spiral staircase leads up to a bar and overhead platform from which guests may drink cocktails and watch elephants, sable antelope, lions, leopards, wild dogs and cheetahs come down to the waterhole below.

The three luxury double-bedded lodges and eight twin-bedded lodges have *en suite* bathrooms and solar-powered electric lights, and are spaced well away from one another to ensure maximum privacy. The lodge is a 20-minute drive from Hwange Airport, and is ideal for game-watchers seeking an intimate safari experience in comfortable surroundings. For more information contact Touch the Wild Central Reservations, Private Bag 6, PO Hillside, Bulawayo, tel (09263-9) 7-4589.

SIKUMI TREE LODGE Eleven tree-houses, tucked into the branches of massive mangwe trees, beckon visitors to Sikumi, a very special camp next to Hwange, 3 km off the Bulawayo–Victoria Falls road. Each thatched, carpeted tree-house is beautifully constructed of Zimbabwe teak, and accommodates guests in safari-style luxury with *en suite* showers and flush toilets. Two of the units are double-storeyed family units which can sleep four.

A central thatched dining complex, lounge and bar overlook the Dete Vlei, in the middle of which is a waterhole illuminated by floodlights at night. A sparkling swimming pool is set between the wood thickets and lawns. The lodge offers day and night game drives around the 100 km² estate, and into Hwange Game Reserve, as well as ranger-led bush walks. Sikumi is the site of Zimbabwe's famous 'Presidential Elephants'. For more information contact Touch the Wild Central Reservations, Private Bag 6, PO Hillside, Bulawayo, tel (09263-9) 7-4589.

SIMBA LODGE Six sandstone-and-thatch bungalows nestle in the shade of msasa trees at the edge of a dense forest at Simba, a photographic safari camp which opened in 1994.

Situated in a wild 800-ha concession in the Gwaai Forest Lands east of Hwange National Park, Simba Lodge is a spectacular retreat in pristine surroundings.

A communal dining boma overlooks a natural waterhole, and there are observation platforms above other waterholes in the area, where guests may see elephants, lions, buffaloes, kudu, gemsbok and more than 200 species of bird.

Hwange National Park is some 40 minutes' drive away, and guests may elect to spend a day in the park, after which sundowners are served at Simba. Day and night drives are available at the lodge, as well as walking safaris.

Access is by road from Victoria Falls or Bulawayo, but a four-wheel-drive vehicle is necessary. Alternatively guests may fly into Hwange Airport, where staff will meet them for the 90-minute drive to Simba. For more information contact Simba Lodge, PO Box 5615, Harare, tel (09263-4) 70-7438/9/0.

Hwange National Park at a glance

Locality:	Northwestern Zimbabwe, south of the Zambezi River.
Climate:	The summers are very hot (sometimes exceeding 50 °C); winters mild to cold (especially at night). Rainy season: November–March.
Number of camps:	Seven public rest camps, 14 private bush camps.
Game drives:	482 km of game drives, of which the 'Ten Mile Drive' is the most popular for gamewatching.
Hides and waterholes:	Dozens throughout the park and in the private safari lodges. Kanondo's 'Underground Hide' is unique and Hwange Safari Lodge's large observation platform is popular.
Trails:	Most of the safari camps and public camps offer walking trails through the bush (see 'Safari Operators in Southern Africa' on p. 364).
Other attractions:	Photography, birdwatching.
Amenities:	The larger camps have shops and restaurants.
Accommodation:	Chalets, cottages and camping sites at the public campsites. Safari tents, tree-houses, bungalows at the private lodges (see individual entries).
Booking address:	Central Booking Office, Department of National Parks and Wildlife Management, PO Box CY826, Causeway, Harare, tel (09263-4) 70-6077. Sikumi Tree Lodge, Kanondo Tree Camp: Touch the Wild, Private Bag 6, PO Hillside, Bulawayo, tel (09263-9) 7-4589.
When to go:	The winter months (May–September) are the best game-viewing months.
What to take with you:	Warm clothes in winter, light clothes in summer, camera, lots of film, binoculars.
How to get there:	Main Camp from Bulawayo: drive north to Gwaai River (247 km); continue for 17 km then turn left onto the tarred road that leads to the camp (23 km). Main Camp from Victoria Falls: drive south through Hwange for 157 km and take the Dete turn-off before Gwaai River. Sinamatella and Lukosi camps: 3 km south of Hwange turn on to the gravel road towards Lukosi and Sinametella. Robins, Nantwich and Bumbusi camps: drive north from Bulawayo for 391 km and turn left to reach the camps via Matetsi.
Nearest petrol:	Main Camp and Robins Camp.
Open:	Main Camp and Sinamatella, Lukosi and Bumbusi camps are open throughout the year from 07:00–18:00; Robins and Nantwich camps are open 1 May–31 October.
Special precautions:	Bilharzia and malaria are present in Zimbabwe. Swimming, wading, fishing and drinking unboiled water should be avoided. Antimalaria precautions should be taken.

THE HIDE SAFARI LODGE As its name suggests, The Hide has been designed to give visitors superior game-viewing opportunities from their own doorstep.

The Hide lies on the eastern edge of Hwange National Park, and offers specially constructed observation huts near the waterholes, where visitors may view such species as black rhino, bateared fox, wild dog and honey badger. A diffused orange light is used at night to illuminate leopards, lions and spotted hyenas coming down to drink. Guests stay in East African safari tents, each of which has an *en suite* shower and toilet and a large front verandah from which visitors may view game. For more information contact Afro Ventures, PO Box 261, Victoria Falls, tel (09263-13) 5822.

HWANGE SAFARI LODGE The reputation of this three-star hotel is built on its magnificent setting among the teak forest and bush just outside the park near Main Camp. A large game-viewing platform attached to the bar offers guests elevated views of animals coming down to drink at the waterhole below.

Where to see wildlife Three safari circuits covering 482 km link the main camps in central, northern and northwestern Hwange. Main Camp itself offers nine game drives, varying in distance from 9 km to 120 km. One of the most popular of these is the 'Ten Mile Drive' between Nyamandlovu Pan and Main Camp, which is likely to yield as many animals as you hope to see. Safari operators in Hwange, Harare, Bulawayo and Victoria Falls offer detailed tours featuring stops at luxury lodges and camps throughout the area. For names, addresses and telephone numbers, see 'Safari Operators in Southern Africa', p. 364.

Other drives take visitors to the fossil rivers at the Kennedy Pans and Linkwasha Vlei, and Zimbabwe's teak forests in the northeastern sector of the park.

In view of the variety of mammals and birds in Hwange, a good field guide for these is essential.

LAKE KARIBA LODGES

Lake Kariba is the gem of Zimbabwe's wild places: backdropped by the magnificent Matusadona Mountains, it is mystic, beautiful and seductive, embodying the timeless spirit of Africa in its wild shores and full-blooded, spiritual sunsets.

This is the setting for some of Zimbabwe's finest lodges and private game reserves — and the favoured destination for visitors in Africa. For those embarking on a trip to the magical shores of Lake Kariba, here are some of the best destinations.

HOUSEBOAT SAFARIS You may board a houseboat in Kariba and cruise from one end of the lake to the other. Along the way you'll see the ghostly remnants of drowned mopane and teak forests on the shoreline, and huge populations of game — ranging from elephants and wildebeest to waterbuck, hippos and crocodiles.

The gentle lapping of water against the bow, the haunting cry of a fish eagle, the impatient snorts of hippos, elephants in silhouette on the lake shore — these are some of the highlights of a unique safari concept known as Water Wilderness. It is run by Zimbabwe Sun Hotels and offers four houseboats situated on a tributary of the Ume River in Lake Kariba for a superb wildlife holiday with a difference.

▲ 113

113 A mokoro glides across the waters of the Okavango Delta.
114 Dome tents and the communal dining area under a giant fig tree at Mombo Trails Camp.
115 A spotted hyena skulks past gamewatchers near Mombo Camp in the Okavango Delta.

▲ 114

▲ 115

▲ 116

117 ▲

116 Mombo Main Camp lies on the edge of a floodplain beneath huge indigenous trees.
117 Jedibe Island Camp's cosy twin-bedded safari tents each have an *en suite*, reed-and-thatch bathroom.
118 A houseboat on the Okavango offers cooldrinks and long, lazy hours of fishing.
119 Wilderness Safaris' Jedibe Island Camp is special for its lagoonside setting among jackalberry trees, ilala palms and sycamore figs.

▲ 118

119 ▼

▼ 120

120 Lions pad through the short, golden grasslands of Moremi Wildlife Reserve.
121 A Karibu Safari vehicle, loaded to the hilt, makes a routine stop in Botswana's Makgadikgadi Pan.
122 Tidy thatched rondavels and the beautiful surroundings of the Okavango's Tsaro Elephant Lodge.
123 The Okavango Delta's Xugana Island Lodge offers eight spacious, twin-bedded safari units under indigenous trees.

▼ 121

▼ 122

▼ 123

▼ 124

▼ 125

▼ 126

124 Gamewatchers near Tuli Safari Lodge pause to revel in the mellow radiance of the sunset.
125 A reed-panelled lounge and attractive bar bask in the rays of the late afternoon sun at Tchau Camp on the western edge of Moremi Wildlife Reserve.
126 Camp Moremi on the edge of Xakanaxa Lagoon is one of the finest safari lodges in Botswana.

▲ **127**

127 The soft textures of dusk provide a romantic setting for gamewatchers easing along the delta's waters in a mokoro.
128 Honeymooners revel in the remote surroundings of Camp Okavango on Nxaragha Island in the heart of the delta.
129 Gametrackers' new Savuti Camp features eight luxury tents, each built on a deck of indigenous teak.

▲ **128**

▲ **129**

▲ 130

131 ▼

132 ▼

130 Khwai River Lodge, on the northern border of Moremi Reserve, is a natural paradise of tall trees and abundant wildlife.
131 Kings Pool Camp in Linyanti Private Game Reserve near Chobe is one of southern Africa's newest lodges.
132 Xigera Camp, within Moremi Wildlife Reserve, is one of Wilderness Safaris' newest camps in the Okavango Delta.

▲ 133

134 ▼

133 Savute Camp, another of Wilderness Safaris' new camps, caters for small groups in wild surroundings.
134 Moremi Game Reserve's abundant birdlife includes the stately saddlebilled stork.
135 These queens of the jungle rule supreme in the rich savannah of the Savute in Botswana's Chobe Game Reserve.

▼ 135

▲ 136

137 ▼

138 ▼

136 Sunset over the Okavango Delta reflects the magic and haunting beauty of Botswana's wild places.
137 A Penduka Safaris odyssey through the Kalahari gives travellers superb gamewatching opportunities.
138 A San woman prepares a meal in a remote village in the Central Kalahari.

▲ 139

▲ 140

▲ 141

139 Mahenye Safari Lodge's thatched Shangaan cottages nestle in the shade of huge indigenous trees.
140 Classic ethnic furnishings are an attractive feature of Mahenye's cosy interiors.
141 Houseboats offer gamewatchers the chance to see the abundant wildlife of Kariba's lakeshore in undisturbed surroundings.
142 Elephants browse on the grasslands below hillside chalets of the magnificent Bumi Hills Safari Lodge.

142 ▼

143 ▼

▲ 144

145 ▼

143 The lounge of Bumi Hills Safari Lodge, a comfortable and elegant meeting place for gamewatchers at the end of the day.
144 Sanyati Lodge's cosy, stone-and-thatch chalets offer excellent views of Lake Kariba.
145 Canoeing down the Zambezi is a popular adventure option with Karibu Safaris.
146 Induna Sandstone Lodge – one of Zimbabwe's newest lodges and one of the country's finest.

146 ▼

▲ 147

▼ 148

▲ 149

147 The cottages at Gache Gache Lodge overlook the Gache Gache Estuary.
148 Comfortably furnished tents, mounted on teak platforms under thatch, afford sweeping views of the surrounding bush at Masuwe Lodge near Victoria Falls.
149 Cosy beds are a colourful complement to the thatch and pole interiors of Landela Safaris' Gache Gache Lodge on Lake Kariba.
150 The thatched main complex at Chokamella Lodge, adjoining Hwange National Park, overlooks a waterhole which attracts a profusion of birds and animals.

150 ▼

▼ 151

151 The newly opened Tulani Camp is a major drawcard at the Zambezi National Park.
152 A magnificent view of the Victoria Falls from Mosi-oa-Tunya National Park in Zambia.

152 ▼

▲ 153

▼ 154

153 Lake Itezhi-tezhi in Zambia's Kafue National Park.
154 A sundowner cruise sets out from Lufupa Lodge in Kafue National Park.

155 The attractive rondavels at Wasa Camp are situated on the edge of a lake in Zambia's Kasanka National Park.
156 Visitors to the South Luangwa National Park encounter hyena pups on a game drive.
157 One of Zambia's best-loved parks, South Luangwa National Park, is situated in the Luangwa River valley.

▼ 155

▲ 156

157 ▼

▲ 158

158 Tongabezi Lodge, situated on the banks of the Zambezi, upstream from Victoria Falls, is one of the finest lodges in Zambia.

159 Mvuu Wilderness Lodge, in the Liwonde National Park, is one of Malawi's most popular wildlife destinations.

159 ▼

▲ **160**

▲ **161**

▲ **162**

▲ **163**

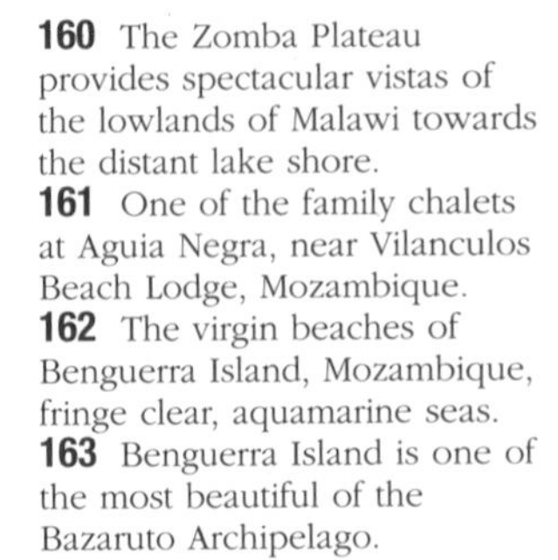

160 The Zomba Plateau provides spectacular vistas of the lowlands of Malawi towards the distant lake shore.
161 One of the family chalets at Aguia Negra, near Vilanculos Beach Lodge, Mozambique.
162 The virgin beaches of Benguerra Island, Mozambique, fringe clear, aquamarine seas.
163 Benguerra Island is one of the most beautiful of the Bazaruto Archipelago.

Guests are flown to their houseboats from the Zimbabwe Sun Hotel lodge of their choice and step aboard for a few days of gamewatching, canoeing, tiger-fishing, birdwatching and relaxing along the Ume River estuary and Lake Kariba.

Each houseboat has solar power, hot and cold water, a shower, chemical toilet and comfortable bedding. Meals are taken on a 'mother craft' nearby, and excursions — by canoe or on foot — are led by an experienced game scout.

The houseboats are tethered to half-submerged trees, and there's nothing but the sounds of nature to disturb your tranquillity under the vastness of the African sky.

For more details contact Zimbabwe Sun Hotels, 271 Oak Avenue, Ferndale, PO Box 1617, Randburg 2125, tel (011) 886-2130; or tel Harare (09263-4) 73-6644.

BUMI HILLS SAFARI LODGE Hotel staff usually have to chase elephants and buffaloes off the runway before guests land at the airstrip of this magnificent Kariba lodge on the southwestern banks of the Ume River just west of Matusadona National Park (see p. 287).

The lodge is just 55 km southwest of Kariba town, and offers a variety of activities, from game walks with professional guides to fishing trips down Lake Kariba.

With its 20 twin-bedded chalets strung across the hillside overlooking Lake Kariba and its floodplain, Bumi Hills affords some of the best game-viewing in Zimbabwe in cool, air-conditioned comfort.

Each chalet is built of stone and has its own *en suite* bathroom and private balcony — the ideal venue for sundowners as herds of buffalo graze on the torpedo grass below, and elephants join hippos and crocodiles at the waterside. You can also watch these animals from a thatched tree-top observation deck mounted on stilts.

At night the grey shapes of buffalo and bushbuck move across the terraces around the swimming pool — so close that special narrow archways have been built to prevent them from wandering into the sleeping quarters.

High on the list of attractions are game drives along the lake shore and walks in the Matusadona National Park.

For more details and reservations, contact Zimbabwe Sun Hotels, 271 Oak Avenue, Ferndale, PO Box 1617, Randburg 2125, tel (011) 886-2130; or tel Harare (09263-4) 73-6644.

FOTHERGILL ISLAND Backdropped by the magnificent Matusadona Mountains, Fothergill Island invites visitors to soak in breathtaking scenic beauty, a procession of large animals and an avian world that thrives in the combination of lake shore and mopane woodland and grassland.

Here elephants, lions and buffaloes compete with goliath herons, fish eagles and malachite kingfishers for a share of the visitor's attention.

The island was named after conservationist Rupert Fothergill, who rescued 5 000 animals from the rising waters of Lake Kariba after the new dam was built in the 1950s.

In recent years Fothergill has become more of an extension of the mainland than the island it once was.

Fothergill Safari Lodge offers 14 thatched, A-frame lodges with *en suite* facilities accommodating 28 people in luxurious style — four-poster beds, mosquito nets and overhead fans.

Perhaps the pride of Fothergill is its double-storey dining lodge under thatch, which has an elevated bar/lounge and magnificent views of the lake shore. There's also a sumptuous pool in the shade of indigenous trees.

Activities at Fothergill include fishing and game-viewing excursions by boat, boat trips to Sanyati Gorge, three- to five-day backpacking trips into the Matusadona Mountains, and 4x4 safaris through Matusadona National Park.

Fothergill has its own airstrip, and guests fly in from Harare and Victoria Falls to Kariba Breezes Marina in Kariba village. They are then transported in a 12-m boat to Fothergill (50 minutes).

For more information and reservations contact Zimbabwe Sun Hotels, 271 Oak Avenue, Ferndale, PO Box 1617, Randburg 2125, tel (011) 886-2130; or tel Harare (09263-4) 73-6644. Alternatively, write to Afro Ventures, PO Box 1200, Paulshof 2056, tel (011) 807-3720.

SPURWING ISLAND A two-storeyed thatched pub flanked by date palms overlooks an open dining area and the Lake Kariba shoreline at Spurwing Island, alongside Sanyati Gorge.

Buffaloes, elephants, hippos and most of the animals you can see at Matusadona are on parade here, including about 150 species of bird.

Accommodation is in rustic chalets, cabins and tents under thatch. For more details and bookings contact Afro Ventures, PO Box 1200, Paulshof 2056, tel (011) 807-3720.

SANYATI LODGE This remote and rustic lodge, just 300 m from the precipitous edges of Sanyati Gorge, offers cosy stone-and-thatch chalets with exceptional views of the lake. The six twin- and two double-bedded chalets have *en suite* bathrooms, and lighting is gas- and solar-powered. There is also a double-storey honeymoon chalet with its own private plunge pool, and a cottage with one double- and one twin-bedded room.

The diningroom, bar, lounge and plunge pool have panoramic views of the lake.

The lodge offers a comprehensive range of fishing, game-viewing and birding trips, on the water, in 4x4 vehicles or on foot through Matusadona National Park.

For more information contact Afro Ventures, PO Box 1200, Paulshof 2056, tel (011) 807-3720.

TIGER BAY SAFARI RESORT Twelve beautiful chalets on the lakeshore, a sparkling pool and a gracious, thatched restaurant beckon visitors to indulge themselves at this lovely resort on the Ume River, south of Bumi Hills. Just an hour-and-a-half by boat from Kariba, Tiger Bay offers game-viewing trips by boat and 4x4 vehicles along the lakeshore, fishing trips and bush walks (including a four-day trail). For further information contact Tiger Bay Safari Resort, PO Box 102, Kariba, tel (09263-61) 2569.

MUSANGO SAFARI CAMP Lying on a small island between Tashinga and Bumi Hills, this resort, with attractive twin-bedded safari tents under thatch and outdoor diningroom, offers cruises and canoe trips along Lake Kariba's shoreline, as well as game-viewing drives and walks in Matusadona National Park.

For more details contact Musango Safari Camp, PO Box UA306, Union Avenue, Harare, tel (09263-4) 79-6821.

GACHE GACHE LODGE This modern thatched complex, run by Landela Safaris, overlooks the Gache Gache Estuary on Lake Kariba and is favoured for its view of Kariba's magical sunsets, rich birdlife and abundant game.

Accommodation is in eight twin-bedded, thatched terracotta cottages and two special honeymoon cottages. Each cottage has *en suite* facilities and a private verandah that overlooks the estuary.

Forty-five minutes by boat from Kariba, Gache Gache offers day and night game drives in 4x4s, walking safaris and game-viewing by boat.

Children under 12 are allowed at Gache Gache only on request. For more details contact Afro Ventures, PO Box 1200, Paulshof 2056, tel (011) 807-3720.

KATETE SAFARI LODGE This exclusive thatched safari lodge, 5 km west of Bumi Hills, has 16 twin beds and one suite.

The lodge is built of local timber and adorned with period furniute. Superb cuisine and plenty of game guarantee a great holiday. Contact Zimbabwe Sun Hotels, PO Box 1617, Randburg 2125, tel (011) 886-2130; or Afro Ventures, PO Box 1200, Paulshof 2056, tel (011) 807-3720.

MANA POOLS NATIONAL PARK

The pristine beauty, wildness and huge numbers of game in Mana Pools National Park combine to make it perhaps the finest wildlife sanctuary in Africa.

Indeed, if the Zambezi Valley is the amphitheatre of the wild, then Mana Pools must occupy centre stage. Covering an area of nearly a quarter of a million square kilometres in northern Zimbabwe, Mana Pools National Park is the fourth largest game park on the continent, and one of Zimbabwe's World Heritage sites.

The Zambezi River, which flanks Mana Pools for 70 km, is largely responsible for the park's great importance as a game sanctuary. Over the centuries, the river's 2 700-km journey to the Indian Ocean in Mozambique has shifted northwards, leaving behind the hollow remnants of its former course.

In the rainy season these hollows, fed by the coursing arteries of the great river, fill up and spill over into the surrounding plains.

Nature celebrates the event with an explosion of life along the borders of these sparkling pools. Riverine terraces of lush, sweet grasses cover the floodplain, as animals descend in their thousands to revel in the coolness of these waters and feast on the nutritious grasses and the protein-rich pods and foliage of Natal mahogany, apple-ring thorn trees and the sausage trees that tower above the tangled bush.

For those who haven't seen the great herds of Africa, the event is truly unforgettable: buffaloes, in herds numbering 2 000 and more, thunder through the acacia and mopane woodland; the rallying whinny of zebras mingles with the grunting and bawling of scores of wildebeest on the run. Down on the riverine terraces, stately columns of elephants march towards the Zambezi, displacing legions of birds. And in the long grass, the lions and leopards wait for unwary antelope.

Against this background, nature-lovers keep to the fringes in silence, for here there are no fences, no protective barriers and no guarantees of personal safety — the rules are for the protection of the animals, not for their human observers.

Tips for travellers

- **Before going, check on the condition of the roads — heavy rains often make them impassable.**
- **You may only camp in the park between May and October.**
- **Only 50 vehicles are allowed in the park at any one time.**

Wildlife A recent census at Mana Pools revealed that there were no less than 12 000 elephants, 3 000 hippos, 16 000 buffaloes — often seen in herds of 2 000 and more — an unspecified number of crocodiles, and thousands of antelope, ranging from impala, kudu and eland, to waterbuck, lechwe and nyala. Other species you will certainly see are lion, leopard, hyena, wild dog and troops of baboons numbering up to 100 individuals.

Life in the river includes tigerfish, tilapia, vundu, lungfish, Cornish Jack and chessa.

Birdlife The floodplains and flanking bush host one of the greatest varieties of birds in the world — more than 380 species of woodland and waterbirds, including kingfisher, stilt, plover, goliath and greenbacked heron, hornbill, bee-eater, Egyptian and spurwing geese, whitebacked vulture, fish eagle, pratincole and Livingstone's flycatcher.

Where to watch game Although you can see game just about anywhere at Mana Pools (including elephants, buffaloes, lions, jackals and hyenas outside your hut or tent in the camps), there are some particularly good areas.

Long Pool (lions, cheetahs and possibly leopards) and Chine Pool both offer rewarding game-viewing, but the former poses some degree of risk because of thick bush surrounding it.

A good gamewatching walk is that along the Zambezi, between Nyamepi and New Kupe. Mbera River is also an excellent place to take a picnic and watch the game come down to drink. Other recommended walks are from Chine Pool to New Kupe, and between Vundu Camp and the Rukomechi River, but be sure to watch out for lions, rhinos and buffaloes along the way.

Wilderness trails Three major trails are available at Mana Pools — one circular four-day trail, and two wilderness trails one in the north, starting at Nyamepi Camp and traversing the floodplain of the Zambezi. The southern trail starts at Nyakasikana Gate, where trailists meet their ranger at 12:00 on the first day of the

Thunder on the plains

The solitary African buffalo bull stands erect on the Mana Pools floodplain, sturdy on its massive hooves as a Sumo wrestler, its huge head and broad, moist muzzle held high, sniffing for signs of danger.

Suddenly, with flared nostrils and ears held at right angles to the body, it sweeps its head sideways, thrashing at the air with sickle-shaped horns.

Massive, menacing and unquestionably majestic, the buffalo is reputed to be one of the most dangerous animals in Southern and East Africa.

Hikers at Mana Pools should be wary of buffaloes — 16 000 of them live in the park, and some have killed humans.

A herd of buffaloes may range from 30 to 40. Herds of several hundred are not uncommon.

A dominant bull asserts its authority over another with aggressive body language: it stands sideways to emphasise its size, shakes its head, tosses its horns and paws the ground. If none of these postures induces the other bull to lower its head submissively, a fight is almost guaranteed.

trail. For more details on wilderness trails contact Wild Frontiers, PO Box 844, Halfway House 1685, tel (011) 468-1218.

River safari Another way of seeing game is to take a safari down the Zambezi on a floating observation deck, mounted across three canoes which have been lashed together.

Here you'll drift past Chikwenya Island, and down the edge of the Zambian side of the Zambezi, where you'll see elephants and buffaloes, waterbuck, impalas and zebras moving slowly along the shoreline.

Where to stay Visitors to Mana Pools have a choice of upmarket lodge accommodation or more rustic tented accommodation at small camps.

RUCKOMECHI CAMP Voted the best safari camp in Zimbabwe for three consecutive years, Ruckomechi lies on the western side of Mana Pools, 40 km from Chirundu. It is a real home-from-home, with 10 cosy thatched twin-bedded chalets and a delightful bar, lounge and open-air diningroom under acacia trees.

Morning and afternoon game drives in an open Land Rover, and ranger-led walks through the bush will take you into the company of lion, wild dog, hyena, leopard, elephant, buffalo, kudu, zebra, impala and waterbuck. Or, if the idea of walking sounds too strenuous, you can lie back in your bush bath, which is open on one side, and watch game coming down to the Zambezi to drink. There is also a 'loo with a view' next door.

Ruckomechi is fully equipped for conferences, and activities at the camp include tigerfishing, pontoon cruises and a three-night canoe safari. Ask the lodge manager about Chimombo Tented Camp, a superb destination for canoeists on the Zambezi.

Clients of the camp are brought to Ruckomechi by boat from Chirundu (after being transferred from Kariba).

To book contact The Zambezi Safari & Travel Co, Suite 3, The Heights Centre, PO Box 158, Kariba, tel (09263-61) 2532.

CHIKWENYA CAMP The newest camp at Mana Pools, Chikwenya opened in mid-1999, a joint venture between Zimbabwe Sun hotels and Wilderness Safaris.

The camp has eight comfortable twin-bedded tents with *en suite* facilities raised off the ground, as well as a natural bath under the stars. There is a separate lounge, dining area and an outdoor diningroom beneath mahogany trees.

The camp is shrouded in the brooding atmosphere of the Zambezi and its floodplains, and guests are guaranteed the wildlife experience of a lifetime, with a good chance to spot elephant, buffalo, hippo, eland and a variety of antelope along the fringes of the Zambezi.

A variety of trails in 4x4s, on foot or by motorised canoe are on offer daily, and some excellent hides bring you within touching distance of the big game. This is a photographer's paradise with stunning backdrops of the albida-studded floodplain and spectacular Rift Valley.

Access is by charter aircraft to the camp's airfield.

To book, contact Wilderness Safaris, PO Box 78573, Sandton 2146, tel (011) 883-0747.

CHIMOMBE TENTED CAMP This secluded canoe camp on the banks of the Zambezi River offers a real taste of the wild, with large, twin-bedded tents fronting the river and spectacular views of the game which comes down to drink — lion, wild dog, elephant, buffalo, zebra and an incredible array of antelope.

The canoes arrive at the camp towards sunset, and dinner is a sumptuous three-course affair, served in a boma on the banks of the Zambezi.

There are morning game drives after breakfast or bush walks in the company of a game ranger. After lunch an escorted canoe trip down the Zambezi will take you amongst hippos and crocodiles, and you will see elephants, buffaloes and a variety of antelope on the river bank.

NYAMEPI CAMP The 4-ha Nyamepi Camp, 42 km beyond the gate to the park, has two lodges accommodating six to eight people as well as 29 camping and caravan sites, with four ablution blocks, and hot and cold running water. A maximum of six people and one vehicle is allowed per site (take your own gas stove and firewood).

Upstream are two serviced riverside lodges: Musangu and Muchichiri, each have two lodges accommodating six to eight people, equipped with gas stove, fridge/freezer, bedding, cutlery and crockery, and mosquito nets.

There are also four so-called remote camps: Gwaya (Old Tree Lodge) accommodates 12 people and has a cold water shower and flush toilet. Mucheni, Nkupe and Ndungu have a total of seven campsites with just a toilet and a braai facility.

Vundu Camp, 17 km upstream from Nyamepi, has two sleeping huts (maximum 12 people), and a basic communal hut for relaxing in, a kitchen and ablution facilities.

At Chikwenya, 25 km from the park's headquarters, there's a luxury Batonka-style safari camp, with mud-walled, lime-plastered huts, perched on a terrace above the dry Sapi River. The shower and toilet are open to the stars.

You should book any park accommodation at least two months ahead.

If your taste is for something more luxurious, you can book a tour of Mana Pools through a safari operator. Amongst the more reputable are: Chikwenya Safaris, Private Bag 2081, Kariba, tel (09263-4) 70-5144; Goliath Safaris, PO Box CH294, Chisipite, Harare, tel (09263-4) 3-0623; Natureways, PO Box 5826, Harare, tel (09263-4) 79-5202. To book at Ruckomechi Camp contact Zimbabwe Safari and Travel Co, Suite 3. The Heights Centre, PO Box 158, Kariba, tel (09263-61) 2532.

How to visit the park The best way to go to Mana Pools is fully equipped, in your own saloon car or 4x4, with your own tent or caravan. If you choose this option you will need a passport, prior antimalarial course, food, plenty of water (boil the Zambezi's water before drinking it, because of bilharzia), enough petrol to get there and back from Makuti, two torches with batteries, candles, gas stove, compass, binoculars, camera, plenty of film, puncture kit and car spares, insect repellent and a basic first-aid kit, which includes a sun-screen.

Rules of the park Specific rules apply in the park and should be closely observed:

- Driving in the park is allowed only between half an hour before sunrise and half an hour after sunset.
- You may leave the road only on foot.
- Don't walk in long grass or thick bush.
- Do not approach lions, buffaloes or black rhinos.
- Don't feed the animals.
- Don't take fruit into the park.
- When walking in the bush know where you're going and how to get there.
- Much of Mana Pools is forest, a breeding ground for tsetse fly and malaria-carrying mosquitoes.

Mana Pools National Park at a glance

Locality:	Far northern Zimbabwe.
Climate:	Summers hot to very hot with thundershowers; winters mild to cool with very cold nights.
Number of camps:	Six.
Game drives:	Numerous game drives crisscross the reserve.
Hides and waterholes:	The abundance of water makes waterholes almost redundant but there is no shortage of these throughout the reserve.
Trails:	One circular three-day trail; two wilderness trails, one in the north, starting at Nyamepi Camp, the other in the south, starting at Nyakasikana Gate; one four-day guided circular trail.
Other attractions:	Boating and fishing.
Amenities:	Nearest shop at Makuti, 100 km away.
Accommodation:	**Ruckomechi Camp:** 10 twin-bedded chalets; **Chikwenya Camp:** eight luxury twin-bedded tents, **Chimombe Tented Camp:** twin-bedded riverside tents; **Musangu** and **Muchichiri**: two lodges accommodating six to eight people, both serviced, with gas stove, fridge and mosquito nets; **Nyamepi Camp:** two lodges, accommodating six to eight people, plus 29 camping and caravan sites with ablution blocks and hot and cold water; four remote camps: **Gwaya Camp:** (12 people) has cold water shower and flush toilet; **Mucheni, Nkupe** and **Ndungu:** seven campsites with toilet and braai. **Vundu Camp:** two sleeping huts (maximum 12 people) with kitchen and ablution facilities.
Booking address:	Central Booking Office, National Parks and Wildlife Management, PO Box CY826, Causeway, Harare, tel (09263-4) 70-6077/8, or 72-6089.
When to go:	The best time to go is between October and November, when the herds of game congregate around the watercourses (although you'll see more crocodiles between May and August when they tend to bask more frequently to raise their body temperature).
What to take with you:	Refuse bags for removing your own refuse in the bush camps; these can be discarded at Nyamepi.
How to get there:	From Kariba it's a 45-minute charter flight. Airstrip at the park's headquarters and at Chikwenya.
Nearest doctor:	Kariba village.
Nearest petrol:	Makuti, 100 km away.
Open:	For campers, from 1 May to 31 October after a six-month closure. The lodges are open throughout the year.
Special precautions:	Antimalaria precautions must be taken. Avoid contact with water in the river, as bilharzia is present. Boil all drinking water. Your tent must have mosquito-proof gauze.

Matobo Hills National Park

The granite domes of the Matobos huddle on the ancient hillsides of southwestern Zimbabwe like a congregation of wise old men. In the dying light of day there's an eerie magnificence that radiates from this boulderland — the remnants of a landscape that was born more than 3 300 million years ago. The Matobos were named after the Ndebele warlord Mzilikazi, who likened the circular, smooth surfaces of the granite domes to the bald heads (amaTobo) of his senior indunas (advisers).

As you stand on the granite terraces of the Matobos and look down across the tumbling woodlands, high cliffs and balancing rocks below, it's easy to understand why Cecil John Rhodes chose this as his final resting place.

The 'chaotic grandeur' Rhodes spoke about is overwhelming in the debris of the volcanic eruptions that rocked the earth so very long ago. At the time, molten masses of granite reared up through the earth's crust, then solidified — some on top of each other — like huge bubbles blown across the supporting pavement of lava by some careless giant.

Nature's extraordinary architecture here has filled people with awe since time immemorial. The Matabele regarded the Matobos as their spiritual home, paying homage to Umlimo — an ancestral spirit that even intimidated Mzilikazi.

Two thousand years ago, the San lived in caves among the remoter parts of the Matobos, leaving priceless galleries of rock art on the walls.

These paintings are one of the main attractions in the 43 200-ha Matobo Hills National Park. The park is 54 km south of Bulawayo, and the first stop is Maleme Dam, an ideal base for exploring the Matobos and its wildlife and San paintings. From Maleme you can take guided or self-guided trips on foot or horseback around the dam, or into the Malelame central and northern wilderness areas.

You may also fish in the dam (angling permits are available in the park), or take a boat on to the water (for which permission must be obtained).

Wildlife The wooded valleys, kloofs and tumbling rockscapes of the Matobos are home to the largest rhino and leopard populations in Southern Africa, as well as a variety of other animals and birds. Gamewatching drives or hikes through the major wilderness areas bring you into the company of black and white rhinos, giraffes, zebras, impala, warthogs, blue wildebeest, monkeys, baboons, porcupines, and many smaller mammals.

Although leopards inhabit the area, it's unlikely you'll see one. But there are plenty of dassies, and you may hear the shrill call of a klipspringer, and see it bounding off through the rocks.

No less than 39 species of snake flourish here, including the lethal black mamba, so watch your step while walking, and your hands while climbing.

Birdlife For bird-lovers the Matobos is a very special place. It is the natural home of the world's largest concentration of black eagles, lured to the area by the great number of dassies, which account for 98 per cent of their diet. A 20-year census counted 20 pairs of black eagles in an area of 620 km^2.

The huge variety of other species includes 32 species of birds of prey, such as African hawk eagles, crowned eagles, snake eagles, augur buzzards, Verreaux's eagles, Wahlberg's eagles, tawny eagles and Peregrine falcons. Other notable species are Mackinder's eagle owls, freckled nightjars, boulder chats, purplecrested louries, lilacbreasted rollers, black whydahs, sunbirds and starlings.

Where to stay Visitors have a choice of staying in the park or at one of various superb lodges on the park's perimeter. Highly recommended lodges are Big Cave Camp, Matobo Lodge and Camp Amalinda.

PARK ACCOMMODATION Maleme Rest Camp offers rustic thatched chalets and communal ablution facilities. Perched high among the rocks, Fish Eagle and Black Eagle lodges (five beds each) offer panoramic views of the surrounding countryside. There is also park accommodation and camping sites along the dam.

BIG CAVE CAMP This lovely lodge, built on a huge whaleback of granite overlooking the Matobos National Park and backdropped by giant boulders, has been fashioned with such natural lines it could be part of the mountain. The hill behind Big Cave has dozens of secret passages and caves where the San etched their masterpieces in ochre paint on the rock walls.

Big Cave lies in a private reserve of some 2 000 acres, and the six thatched A-frame chalets are a perfect base from which to explore the grandeur of the Matobos, and its rich animal and birdlife. The chalets are *en suite* and each has a private balcony overlooking the vast panorama of the Matobos below.

Nearby, the Leopard's Lair diningroom and bar offers superb cuisine and relaxation after a day out in the wilds. The private wilderness at Big Cave is home to more than 140 bird species, among which are a large number of raptors. Here you can spot black eagles, African hawks and Cape eagle owls, as well as most of the species of mammal found in the park. Organised game walks and drives are offered daily.

To get there take the Matobo road out of Bulawayo. After 20 km you will pass the turn-off to Maleme Dam/Matobo National Park. Continue on the Kesi Road until you reach the Big Cave sign at the 46 km peg. Turn left and continue for 4 km until you reach Big Cave Camp.

For more information or to book contact Afro Ventures, PO Box 1200, Paulshof 2056, tel (011) 807-3720.

MATOBO LODGE Situated in a private reserve next to the Matobo Hills National Park, this lodge has been landscaped into the granite rocks on a ridge overlooking the Maleme Valley and Mount Ififi, 50 km from Bulawayo.

The lodge has 17 thatched Matabele-style chalets which are joined by raised walkways to shady gardens and a swimming pool built into a natural rock cleft. There is a cosy bar and lounge, and meals are taken in the thatched diningroom or open-air gazebo.

Day drives take in the reserve's wildlife, the fascinating galleries of San paintings and the sites where Matabele armies fought to the death with white settlers in 1896. Cultural trips include visits to Matabele and Kalanga villages for a glimpse into their community life and traditions. Trails on foot or horseback are also available.

Contact Touch the Wild, Private Bag 6, Hillside, Bulawayo, tel (09263-9) 7-4589 or 4-4566/7/9 or 4-4572 or 4-4529.

Tip for travellers

If you're carrying photographic equipment into Zimbabwe from outside the country, write down all the serial numbers of your cameras, as Customs will require them.

CAMP AMALINDA The architectural ingenuity of this lodge sets it apart from other lodges in Southern Africa. The 10 inconspicuous granite chalets have been carved into huge boulders and the lounge and recreation area have been landscaped into an old San shelter, with superb views of the Matobo Hills. Even the wine cellar has been built in a natural cave, and you can order some of Zimbabwe's finest wines while dining at a huge teak table in the open-sided diningroom.

A natural rock swimming pool overlooks a waterhole and is the perfect place to relax after a game drive or bush walk. Camp Amalinda goes the extra mile to entertain its guests and you can choose to go on an elephant-back trail, visit the grave of Cecil John Rhodes or the mission at Cyrene, explore San rock art sites or spend the night in an Ndebele village.

Camp Amalinda is 45 km southwest of Bulawayo on a tarred road with only 1 km of dirt road.

To book contact The Zambezi Safari & Travel Co, PO Box 158, Kariba, tel (09263-61) 2532.

Rock art One of the more impressive caves adorned with San paintings is Nswatugi Cave, an easy 7-km hike west of Malelame. The walls of this 14-m-deep cave depict port-coloured giraffes, kudu and human beings.

Silozwane Cave, south of the Maleme Wilderness area, which was used for rain-making ceremonies, is a gallery for a stunning frieze of wild animals. They include giraffes, lions, kudu, tsessebe, impala, fishes, birds, a flying ant (with veined wings), and a 2-m-long snake.

Gulubahwe Cave, 19 km past the Matobos Mission on the old Gwanda Road, features a 4,5-m snake, carrying on its back 14 humans, seven baboons, three antelope, and a baboon with an antelope's head.

Pomongwe Cave, a short climb up the hill behind Malelame Dam, is the former home of Stone-Age dwellers who left thousands of artefacts, later discovered by modern man.

World's View A 10-km hike north of the Malelame Dam lodges leads you to World's View — the site of Cecil John Rhodes' grave — which reveals the full awe-inspiring majesty of the Matobos' bald hills.

It's easy to picture how Rhodes' remains were brought up here in a gun carriage drawn by 12 black oxen on 10 April 1902. On the summit, in a tomb hewn out of solid granite, Rhodes' casket was laid to its final rest. Matabele warriors bade him farewell, with their royal salute, 'Bayete!' ringing through the hills.

World's View was known to the Ndebele as Malindidzimu, the 'Place of Benevolent Spirits', and as you stand on the wind-swept heights, there is an eerie, spiritual feel about the place. Nearby is a stone memorial to Major Allan Wilson and members of the Shangani patrol who were killed by Ndebele warriors while pursuing Chief Lobengula in 1893.

A less publicised spectacle at World's View is the feeding of the lizards — a ritual performed three times a day by an attendant who calls the multicoloured colony of lizards to eat sadza (mealie meal) for the benefit of visitors. The frenzied scramble for food by these reptiles is worth filming.

Two kilometres north of World's View is the White Rhino Shelter, whose San murals (in outline) of wildebeest, rhino, humans, a lion and other animals show an unusual appreciation and understanding of form.

Matobo Hills National Park at a glance

Locality:	Matobo Hills are 32 km southwest of Bulawayo on a tarred road. The park is 54 km from Bulawayo.
Climate:	Summers are hot to very hot, with rain between November and April. Winters are cold and dry.
Game drives:	There is a variety of game drives and picnic sites.
Viewsites:	World's View; other elevated points throughout the Matobos.
Trails:	A marked network of trails crisscrosses the park.
Other attractions:	Birdwatching, rock art, hiking, fishing in the dam.
Amenities:	Ablution facilities at Maleme.
Accommodation:	**Maleme Rest Camp** offers fully equipped one- and two-bedded lodges, with their own kitchen and bathroom; and one- and two-bedded chalets with outside cooking facilities. **Fish Eagle** and **Black Eagle lodges** are more luxurious. There are caravan and camping sites at Maleme and Mtshelele dams and at the Arboretum. Other places to stay (outside the park) are: **Big Cave Camp,** six thatched 'A'-frame chalets; **Camp Amalinda,** which offers 10 rustic thatched bungalows and has a lounge and bar built into a natural rock shelter; **Matobo Hills Lodge,** a secluded, comfortable lodge offering chalet accommodation for 36 people; **Malalangwe Lodge** (on the road to Plumtree), with seven secluded stone, timber and thatch chalets, is highly recommended.
Booking address:	Department of National Parks and Wildlife Management, PO Box CY826, Causeway, Harare, tel (09263-4) 70-6077; Bulawayo Booking Agency, PO Box 2283, Bulawayo, tel (09263-9) 6-3646.
When to go:	Any time of the year, but winter, with its milder climate, would be preferred.
What to take with you:	Own cutlery and crockery at some camps; campers should be self-sufficient, although there is a store with basic foodstuffs in the park; binoculars; camera.
How to get there:	From central Bulawayo take Grey Street into Matobo Road and drive 54 km to the Rest Camp at Maleme Dam.
Nearest doctor:	Bulawayo, 54 km away.
Nearest petrol:	Bulawayo, 54 km away.
Open:	Sunrise to sunset throughout the year.
Special precautions:	The dams are infested with bilharzia. Boil all drinking water in the Matobos. The Matobos lie within a malaria area, so take precautions prior to departure. When hiking, watch out for snakes.

Matusadona National Park

The skeletons of drowned mopane trees rise eerily from the fringes of Lake Kariba as the western sun turns the lake into a sea of molten lava. Down at the water's edge, the shadows of buffaloes and elephants move slowly across the crimson, orange and russet-brown colours of the lake's surface.

Fifty metres offshore, in the branches of a huge dead tree, a thatched hide overlooks the panorama of sunset and drowsy lake, offering its guests one of the finest gamewatching vistas in the whole of Africa.

This is Matusadona National Park, a ruggedly beautiful wilderness covering 1 407 km² in northwestern Zimbabwe. Remote, almost inaccessible by car and impossibly beautiful, Matusadona is bordered in the north by Lake Kariba and in the west by the Ume River.

To the east waterfalls roar down the granite face of Sanyati Gorge, which forms a 12-km tongue of deep water.

A 40-km boat ride across the lake from Kariba village, Matusadona's shores reveal an enchanting string of secret coves, bays and magical inlets, each one a stage for an extraordinary array of animals.

Behind them, undulating hills give way to thickets of commiphora and bushwillow leading up to the brachystegia woodland of the Zambezi Escarpment. Here the peaks of the Matuzaviadohna Hills rise above the ancient landscape and the floodplain of Lake Kariba.

Wildlife The outstretched plains of Matusadona and the escarpment are home to more than 1 000 elephants, thousands of buffaloes and at least 400 black rhinos. Lions, leopards and spotted hyenas prey on the large variety of antelope, which includes eland, bushbuck, sable and roan antelope, impala, waterbuck and greater kudu. Buffalo and antelope are drawn to the water's edge by the rich fringes of torpedo grass, so named because when the lake's waters are high, the grass grows underwater — it only appears above the surface in times of drought when the waterline recedes, and when the animals need it most.

Matusadona also has the largest population of hippos of any game park in Zimbabwe, as well as a large contingent of crocodiles.

Birdlife The Matusadona waterfront and its hinterland serve as sanctuary to more than 240 bird species. Fish eagles find ample nesting sites in the branches of drowned mopane trees, while the nutrient-rich waters of the lake attract African jacanas, cormorants, storks, plovers and African darters.

Fishing Tigerfish, bream, Cornish Jack and catfish are among the 20 species of angling fish that live in Lake Kariba, and you'll find them generally around Matusadona, which is a mecca for anglers. The best fishing months are September and October, and the place to be is Sanyati Gorge, which teems with 'tiger'.

The amazing elephants of Kariba

Can elephants swim? The answer is a resounding 'yes'! In fact, the history books record what is possibly the longest distance ever swum non-stop by an elephant — 40 km. The feat was performed in 1982 by two elephants which swam from Matusadona, past Spurwing Island, across the lake to Kariba village in 30 hours.

The pair swam almost submerged, with their trunks serving as snorkels above the waterline, and arrived at Kariba village quite exhausted. Conservation officers believe the elephants were following an ancient migration route that had been blocked by the waters of Lake Kariba.

Elephants enter deep water at a trot, plunging into the stream in single file, so close to each other that they follow trunk to rump.

How to explore the park One reason why Matusadona retains its pristine charm is that only one third of the reserve is open to the public. Much of this is centred on the shoreline (see *Accommodation*, 'At a glance' box), and there are various options for exploring it, of which canoeing is one of the most popular.

The Department of National Parks and Wildlife Management will supply details of canoe trips available, and will recommend a guide. Contact them at PO Box 8151, Causeway, Harare, tel (09263-4) 70-6077.

Alternatively, the many lodges along the Kariba shoreline offer their own boat and canoe trips, as well as 4x4 gamewatching safaris into the park. Another option is to take one of the walking safaris (between one and five days) offered by Bumi Hills, Spurwing and Fothergill islands, Musango Safari Camp, Sanyati Lodge, Gache Gache Lodge or Tiger Bay Fishing camp (see 'Lake Kariba lodges', p. 276).

Where to stay Accommodation in the area ranges from luxury lodges to more rustic tented camps.

KIPLING'S LODGE This superb lodge was designed by architect Ivan Pantic to blend in with the natural surroundings and to provide direct access to the visual delights of Lake Kariba and the animals which graze along its shoreline.

The 10 two-bed chalets are colourfully decorated and have private decks overlooking the lake, Ume River and the Matusadona Mountains. The surrounding mopane bush grows right up to the chalets, which have eight-metre high sloping roofs. The honeymoon suite, with its bar fridge and intercom for room service, occupies prime position.

The main lodge has a diningroom, bar, splash pool and superb viewing decks encircling the building. Chess and backgammon are available in the library.

Activities at the lodge include game drives in the Matusadona National Park, game walks with an armed ranger and canoe trips along the shores of the Ume River. Angling expeditions for tigerfish and bream are available (tackle is supplied). There are also pontoon cruises and boat safaris for game-viewing. Flights over Lake Kariba and Matusadona National Park are optional at extra cost.

To book contact The Zambezi Safari & Travel Co., PO Box 158, Kariba, tel (09263-61) 2532.

SANYATI WEST CAMP This lovely camp, run by Sengwe Safaris, lies in the eastern section of Matusadona and offers visitors a real taste of the wild as they explore the shoreline of Lake Kariba. Also on offer are various canoeing combinations in Mana Pools National Park.

There are no permanent facilities at Sanyati West, which means there is very little disturbance to the huge populations of game that frequent this area. It is quite common for elephant and lion to venture into the camp.

The tents are equipped with fold-up camp beds, paraffin lamps, bedside tables and mosquito netting. There is a flush toilet and a bush-bucket shower.

Brunch and three-course dinners are laid on and there is a good selection of minerals, wine and beer. A professional armed guide accompanies guests on drives and game walks.

To book contact The Zambezi Safari & Travel Co., PO Box 158, Kariba, tel (09263-61) 2532.

KAINGWE SAFARI CAMP Situated on the shores of Lake Kariba within Matusadona National Park, Kaingwe is run by one of Zimbabwe's most experienced guides, Andy Webb. It is a small camp, with only six beds in *en suite* cottage tents on raised platforms. The tents afford superb views across the lake of the Matusadona Mountains.

Matusadona National Park at a glance

Locality:	Southern shore of Lake Kariba, 40 km from Kariba village.
Climate:	Summers are hot to very hot; winters mild to cold (especially at night). Rainy season November to March.
Number of camps:	Three bush camps; two camping sites.
Game drives:	Several game drives are offered by the lodges around the park.
Trails:	Most of the lodges offer trails ranging from short rambles to four- and five-day hikes through the park.
Other attractions:	Tigerfishing.
Amenities:	Swimming pools at bush camps; all amenities at the lodges, including swimming pools and fully licensed bars.
Accommodation:	In the park: three bush camps with thatched chalets at **Ume**, **Mbalala** and **Muuyu**. **Tashinga** and **Sanyati camps** offer camping sites with ablution facilities. Other accommodation: **Kipling's Lodge:** 10 two-bed chalets; **Sanyati West Camp:** tented safari camp; **Kaingwe Safari Camp:** six-bed tented camp; **Bumi Hills Safari Lodge, Fothergill Island, Spurwing Island, Tiger Bay Fishing Camp, Sanyati Lodge** and **Musango Safari Camp**. Camping facilities at **Tashinga**, the park's headquarters, and **Sanyati Camp**.
Booking address:	Central Booking Office, National Parks and Wildlife Management, PO Box CY826, Causeway, Harare, tel (09263-4) 70-6077/8, or 72-6089.
When to go:	Throughout the year, but it can be scorchingly hot in summer.
What to take with you:	If you are camping in the national park take all your own provisions (including tent and camping equipment). For the lodges or luxury camps take light clothing in summer, torch, camera and plenty of film, sunhat and a pair of strong hiking shoes or boots.
How to get there:	Access is usually by boat from Kariba (Tashinga, the park's headquarters, is 55 km from Kariba by boat). Getting there by road is difficult, and involves a bone-crunching 486-km ride from Harare via Karoi, or a similarly difficult drive from Victoria Falls via Binga. There are regular flights from Victoria Falls and Harare to Kariba village, and smaller charters fly visitors in from Kariba or take them across the lake in their own boats. If you're not part of a package group, consider using the Kariba Ferry to access Matusadona.
Nearest doctor:	Kariba village.
Nearest petrol:	Kariba village.
Open:	For access by boat: throughout the year, from sunrise to sunset; for access by car: May–October.
Special precautions:	Malaria and bilharzia are endemic to the area, so take precautions against both. Be alert to the presence of dangerous animals, particularly crocodiles, buffaloes and black rhinos.

Activities include walks, game drives in the park, lake cruises and trips to Sanyati Gorge. Tigerfishing is also available.

The lodge has a 10-metre boat on standby at Kariba for exclusive transfers across the lake to Kaingwe Camp.

Contact The Zambezi Safari & Travel Co., PO Box 158, Kariba, tel (09263-61) 2532.

BUSH CAMPS Guests may choose between three exclusive bush camps: Ume, Mbalala and Muuyu — each of which accommodates 12 people in rustic, thatched chalets. The family chalets are equipped with crockery and cutlery, and have their own linen, bath and toilet. They each have access to a communal living area, including a kitchen and diningroom.

Ume and Mbalala are about 55 km from Kariba village and offer beautiful vistas across the Ume River. Muuyu, 10 km further east, is 44 km from Kariba.

Tashinga Camp, the park's headquarters on the Ume River, and Sanyati Camp offer camping sites with ablution facilities (hot and cold running water, baths and toilets). Tents, camping equipment and firewood may be hired at these camps.

OTHER ACCOMMODATION There are no lodges or hotels within the park, but excellent lodge accommodation is available at Bumi Hills, Spurwing and Fothergill islands, Tiger Bay Safari Resort, Sanyati Lodge, Gache Gache Lodge (see 'Lake Kariba lodges', p. 276).

For a novel experience, visitors can stay at the new Matusadona Water Lodge, a floating safari camp run by Wilderness Safaris, just off the shoreline of the park.

A maximum of eight guests stay in four twin-bedded chalets, and commute by canoe or motorboat to a 'mother ship' which houses a central bar, lounge and diningroom. The chalets have their own verandah, complete with table and chairs, in a secluded bay.

In keeping with Wilderness Safaris' high standard of accommodation and facilities, this floating camp is memorable for its scenic beauty, escorted game trails and herds of elephants, antelope, buffaloes and predators on the shoreline.

To get to the water lodge guests fly to Kariba Airport where they transfer by charter to Tashinga Airstrip (20 minutes). From there a five-minute drive takes them to the water's edge for the final leg (15 minutes) by water to the camp. For details contact Wilderness Safaris, PO Box 78573, Sandton 2146, tel (011) 883-0747.

Another magnificent houseboat option near the Matusadona shoreline is Zimbabwe Sun's Water Wilderness, in a tributary of the Lake Kariba's Ume River. Accommodation comprises four twin-bedded houseboats tethered to half-submerged trees. Other attractions include fishing, birdwatching, canoeing and escorted game walks. There are daily flights to and from Bumi Hills Safari Lodge, and the photographic opportunities must rate amongst the best in Africa.

For more information write to Zimbabwe Sun Hotels, PO Box 1617, Randburg 2125, or tel (09263-4) 73-6644.

VICTORIA FALLS

The Victoria Falls announce themselves as a distant roar of thunder, muffled under fantastic plumes of mist and spray that soar 500 m into the African sky.

For visitors approaching the cascade for the first time the spectacle is truly astonishing. As the thunder grows to a furious roar, the falls come into view, revealing the widest sheet of falling water in the world. The earth seems to shake as the water plummets into the cauldron of battered spray below, releasing clouds of rainbowed mist over the surrounding rainforest.

Kololo tribespeople, too frightened to venture near this monstrous cascade, called it Mosi-oa-Tunya — 'the smoke that thunders'. And when the explorer David Livingstone crept to the edge of an island on the rim of the falls on 16 November 1855, he described them as: 'The most wonderful sight I had witnessed in Africa. Scenes so lovely must have been gazed upon by angels in their flight.'

As the Zambezi slides slowly eastward towards the rim of the falls, there's no hint of the drama to come. Then, suddenly, the entire river disappears into a void 1,5 km wide. In the rainy season, more than 500 million litres of water cascade over the rim each minute, a rush of water so vast and so overwhelming it leaves you breathless.

Twice the height of the Niagara Falls, the Victoria Falls lie midway along the 2 700-km course of the Zambezi River, near the northwestern corner of Zimbabwe. The falls actually comprise five separate cascades — the Devil's Cataract, Main Falls, Horseshoe Falls, Rainbow Falls and the Eastern Cataract. The lowest is 61 m, the highest 108 m.

Born about 150 million years ago, the falls are retreating all the time, wearing down the basalt rim at a rate of 1,6 km every 10 000 years, and leaving deeply incised ravines in their place.

The Victoria Falls, their adjacent village and the surrounding rainforest are all incorporated within the Victoria Falls National Park, and lie just 6 km from the Zambezi National Park to the west. Also in the area is Mosi-oa-Tunya National Park, on the Zambian side of the falls.

VICTORIA FALLS NATIONAL PARK

Gently soaked by the mists of Mosi-oa-Tunya, this beautiful park covers 2 340 ha of pristine forest around the falls, and remains just as it was when David Livingstone discovered the area. The park and its rainforest have been declared a World Heritage site, and for nature-lovers its attractions are exquisite. The huge creeper-draped trees shelter a world of luxuriant beauty. Among the sodden branches and leaves of ebony and strangler fig, false date palms and waterberry trees, you may see the metallic, blue-black plumage of a Livingstone's lourie (or turaco), or the long, trailing tail of a paradise flycatcher. Other specials that flit through the treetops include scarletbreasted sunbirds, Heuglin's robins, tawnyflanked prinias, blue waxbills, firefinches and tchagras.

On the ground, in an Eden-like atmosphere of ferns, orchids and creeping vines, you may spot the spoor of leopard, bushbuck, warthog or waterbuck.

How to see the falls For a panoramic, all-encompassing view of the falls, there's nothing to beat an aerial tour over the chasm called the 'flight of Angels'. Angel helicopter flights are available on a daily basis; or you can take a 30-minute charter trip with Southern Cross Aviation (PO Box 210, Victoria Falls, tel (09263-13) 4618), or United Air (PO Box 50, Victoria Falls, tel (09263-13) 4530). The Batoka Sky Company in Zambia offers four microlite flights a day over the falls and rainforest.

For hikers, paths leave from a statue of David Livingstone to spectacular viewpoints of Devil's Cataract, the Main Falls, the Boiling Pot, Cataract Island, Livingstone Island, and the Horseshoe, Rainbow and Armchair falls. Another option is a river cruise (see p. 295).

Where to stay There is superb lodge accommodation in the immediate vicinity of the Falls.

VICTORIA FALLS SAFARI LODGE About 3 km from the Victoria Falls, flanking the Zambezi National Park, is the state-of-the art Victoria Falls Safari Lodge, an architectural masterpiece of tiered residential suites designed to resemble an open-plan tree-house. The elevated position of the lodge on top of a natural plateau facing westwards, guarantees exceptional views of unforgettable sunsets and the surrounding Zimbabwe countryside.

The lodge, built to reflect the ethnic colours and textures of Africa, has 72 rooms of which six are split-level suites with lounge and balcony on one level and an *en suite* bedroom upstairs. The comfortable suites are elegantly furnished with local hardwoods and rustic finishes.

The lodge is famed for its two restaurants, The Boma, and the Makuwa-Kuwa restaurant. The Boma — 'the place of eating' — is an extraordinary culinary adventure. Here in the company of gyrating Ndebele dancers you can sample such authentic African specialities as mopane worm in peanut butter and taste the local village beer, while a witchdoctor throws his bones and tells you what the future holds.

After dinner guests are invited to listen to the enchanting tales of The Boma's own sangoma (storyteller), who will give an insight into local customs and traditions. You will need advance booking to get into The Boma. Dinner is served daily from 19:00 to 22:00.

For lodge bookings contact The Zambezi Safari & Travel Co, Suite 3, The Heights Centre, PO Box 158, Kariba, Zimbabwe, tel (09263-61) 2532.

LOKUTHULA LODGE The word Lokuthula means 'peace' in the local dialect, and that is exactly what you will find at this lodge, which is part of the same complex as Victoria Falls Safari Lodge. Thirty-seven thatched lodges overlook the Zambezi National Park and a waterhole which attracts a large variety of game.

The two- and three-bedroomed lodges are self-catering and accommodate six to eight guests each, making them ideal for families. Other amenities include a swimming pool, poolside bar and restaurant, and access to The Boma Restaurant.

The decor, service and comfort of Lokuthula has put it among the top five lodges of its kind in the world.

To book, contact The Zambezi Safari & Travel Co, Suite 3, The Heights Centre, PO Box 158, Kariba, Zimbabwe, tel (09263-61) 2532.

MASUWE LODGE Set in a 1 000-ha game reserve next to the Zambezi National Park, 7 km from Victoria Falls, Masuwe offers accommodation to 20 people in 10 tents under thatch. The tents are set on teak platforms with views of the surrounding countryside.

The thatched main building, which houses the bar, diningroom and lounge, overlooks a waterhole on one side and a rocky swimming pool on the other.

There are game drives available on the lodge's private estate and cruises down the Zambezi.

The so-called adrenaline sports — white-water rafting, riverboarding and bungee jumping — are just a short drive away.

To book at Masuwe contact Afro Ventures, PO Box 1200, Paulshof 2056, tel (011) 807-3720, or contact The Zambezi Safari & Travel Co, Suite 3, The Heights Centre, PO Box 158, Kariba, Zimbabwe, tel (09263-61) 2532.

Apart from the above lodges, Victoria Falls offers dozens of accommodation options, from the five-star Elephant Hills Hotel, with its 18-hole golf course and the largest water entertainment complex in Zimbabwe, to the A'Zambezi River Lodge upstream of the falls. This lodge, the largest thatched complex in Africa has 83 rooms and overlooks the Zambezi River.

Accommodation of another kind is offered in the double cabins of Westwood Safari Lodge, an hour's drive upstream from Victoria Falls.

The Zambezi National Park also offers lodge accommodation (see opposite), and Imbalala Safari Camp, set among the riverine forest, has comfortable, attractively furnished chalets.

Victoria Falls Craft Village Replicas of Batonka, Ndebele, Nyanga and Venda huts, an area depicting the lifestyle of the San, two witchdoctors and a variety of African arts and crafts are on display at the boma-enclosed Falls Craft Village.

Highlights here are Shangaan, Makishi and Nyau tribesmen performing ritual dances, including a fascinating performance on stilts. The masks and traditional wear are outrageously African, and the tribal dances are excellent.

Other attractions In the past few years the Victoria Falls and Zambezi River have become a mecca for adrenaline lovers seeking the thrill of white-water rafting, bungee jumping, riverboarding or shooting the rapids in a dinghy. All these options are available and invariably form a part of the itineraries of visitors to the Victoria Falls.

WHITE-WATER RAFTING The section of the Zambezi near Victoria Falls know as Batonka Gorge is regarded internationally as the finest white-water rafting trip in the world. Annually more than 50 000 people take to the water for the hair-raising, 24-km trip down the river over the Grade 5 to Grade 8 rapids.

Safari Par Excellence (at the Zambezi Safari Travel Co) and Shearwater Adventures offer a variety of rafting trips, ranging from one-day excursions throughout the year from both sides of the Zambezi to five-day trips.

Safari Par Excellence's trip includes a 15-minute 'Float of Angels' — to view the majesty of the falls from the river before you start your trip. Lunch is served on the river bank and at the end of the trip clients have to walk up a fairly steep path out of Batonka Gorge. Children under 15 may not participate in the trip.

Shearwater's five-day rafting trip is from Victoria Falls to the Matetsi River Mouth. Clients must report to the Shearwater office in Victoria Falls the day before the trip. For details contact The Zambezi Safari & Travel Co (see address opposite) or Shearwater (African Extreme) at Edward Building, First Street/Baker Avenue, PO Box 3961, Harare, Zimbabwe, or telephone them at Victoria Falls (09263) 475-7831.

CANOEING Safari Par Excellence (at the Zambezi Safari & Travel Co) operates canoe safaris on the upper Zambezi — the 70-km stretch between Katambora, 10 km south of the Botswana border, and Victoria Falls. The canoe safaris in Zambia are operated from Thorntree Lodge (see entry on p. 316).

Canoe safari options range from half day- to three-day, two-night safaris. Clients are picked up at their Victoria Falls Hotel and taken to the canoe launch site in the Zambezi National Park. Accommodation on the overnight trips are in tented riverside bush camps.

RIVERBOARDING This sport, imported from New Zealand, is catching on fast on the Zambezi, where enthusiasts hurtle down the river on riverboards, riding 'whirlies' and defying the rapids. A short training programme is given to enthusiasts before the trip, and they have to be reasonably fit, fearless and able to swim proficiently.

To participate in any of the above adrenaline sports contact The Zambezi Safari and Travel Company, Suite 3, The Heights Centre, PO Box 158, Kariba, Zimbabwe, tel (09263-61) 2532.

BUNGEE JUMPING The Victoria Falls Bridge has become one of the most sought-after bungee-jumping venues in the world. Spanning Batonka Gorge between Zimbabwe and Zambia, the bridge is 111 m above the ground and every year thousands of adventurers choose to dive into space off it, secured only by a bungee chord. If you want to jump just go through the border post and stroll onto the bridge.

For more details contact Africa Extreme (Shearwater), Edward Building, First Street/Baker Avenue, PO Box 3961, Harare, Zimbabwe, or telephone them at Victoria Falls (09263-13) 475-7831.

OTHER ATTRACTIONS Victoria Falls offer a host of other activities, including:
- Microlight trips over the falls (contact African Extreme).
- The daily Sundowner Cruise, which gives you superb, water-level views of the falls (enquire at any hotel).
- The Crocodile Ranch, home to more than 2 000 reptiles of all shapes and sizes.
- The Big Tree, a giant baobab believed to be between 1 000 and 1 500 years old. This remarkable tree has a 16-m circumference and is 20 m high.
- A visit to the Zambezi National Park, or a trip across the bridge to the Mosi-oa-Tunya National Park in Zambia, should be on your list of priorities.

Zambezi National Park

This 56 000-ha park, flanking the Zambezi 6 km upriver from the falls, offers some superb game-viewing and rustic lodges on the river bank.

Wildlife White rhinos, lions, elephants, cheetahs, leopards, spotted hyenas, buffaloes and giraffes may be seen in the company of zebras, eland, sable antelope, impala and waterbuck.

Among the birds you may see are malachite kingfishers, goliath herons, egrets, darters and fish eagles.

Where to stay Pride of the Zambezi National Park is Wilderness Safaris' Tulani Camp which opened in July 1996. The camp has 10 large, walk-in safari tents accommodating 20 guests. Tulani (meaning 'place of rest') is set under shady trees on the river bank and guests report sightings of elephants, lions, sable and otters.

An hour's drive or eight-minute flight from Victoria Falls, Tulani offers daily game drives and walks with a professional guide as well as canoeing and boating along the Zambezi (tigerfishing included).

Other accommodation includes fully equipped two-bedroomed lodges, but you must supply your own provisions. There are also three fishing camps — Kandahar, Mpala Jena and Sansimba. Kandahar and nearby Palm Island are not far from Kalai Island, where David Livingstone camped the night before he discovered the falls.

Four basic camping sites along the river bank will suit those who want to rough it, without the luxury of modern ablutions or

Victoria Falls at a glance

Locality:	Zambezi River, northwestern corner of Zimbabwe, on the border of Zambia.
Climate:	Summers hot, winters warm. Rainy season runs from November to March.
Number of camps:	There are no camps within Victoria Falls National Park, but there are several campsites. Zambezi National Park offers three fishing camps: Kandahar, Mpala Jena and Sansimba, and four basic campsites along the Zambezi. Wilderness Safaris run the 10-tent Tulani Camp.
Game drives:	Ask at any Victoria Falls hotel about game drives in Zambezi National Park (see main entry), at Masuwe Lodge, Mosi-oa-Tunya National Park (on the Zambian side) and at Hwange National Park.
Hides and waterholes:	Chamabonda platform in the Zambezi National Park is recommended.
Trails:	A safe network of paths through the rainforest affords excellent views of the falls from the bank opposite the main gorge.
Other attractions:	River-rafting downstream of the falls, angling along the Zambezi, sunset cruises, African crafts and curios, tribal dancing.
Amenities:	Victoria Falls village has all the amenities required for a perfect holiday.
Accommodation:	**Elephant Hills Hotel**, PO Box 300, Victoria Falls, tel (09263-13) 4793; **A' Zambezi River Lodge**, PO Box 130, Victoria Falls, tel (09263-13) 4561; **Masuwe Lodge**, c/o Landela Safari Adventures, PO Box 66293, Kopje, Harare, tel (09263-4) 70-2634; **Westwood Safari Lodge**, PO Box 132, Victoria Falls, tel (09263-13) 4614; Zambezi National Park, Department of National Parks and Wildlife Management, PO Box 8151, Causeway, Harare, tel (09263-4) 70-6077; **Imbalala Safari Camp**, PO Box 110, Victoria Falls, tel (09263-13) 4219. National Parks chalets, caravan and camping sites are also available.
Booking address:	Department of National Parks and Wildlife Management, PO Box CY826, Causeway, Harare, tel (09263-4) 70-6077.
When to go:	The falls are best viewed from June to September. The river is at its peak in April, but the volume of spray then makes photography difficult. The water volume is lowest in October.
What to take with you:	Light clothes, raincoat, sunscreen, hat, sunglasses, binoculars, camera.
How to get there:	There are regular scheduled flights to Victoria Falls from most major cities in Southern Africa, either direct or via Bulawayo or Harare. To get to the falls by road from South Africa, travel via Beit Bridge and Bulawayo (761 km). From Kasane in Botswana travel via the Kazangula border post to Victoria Falls. United Touring Company (UTC) runs a shuttle between Chobe Game Lodge and Victoria Falls village — a journey of just over an hour (contact Chobe Lodge at (09267) 65-0300).
Nearest doctor:	At Victoria Falls.
Nearest petrol:	At Victoria Falls.
Open:	Victoria Falls and Zambezi national parks are open from sunrise to sunset.
Special precautions:	Take antimalaria precautions when visiting Victoria Falls.

electricity. Also in the park is the Chamabonda platform, an excellent game-viewing post about 30 km from Victoria Falls, where you may overnight.

Game drives include a beautiful, 46-km drive along the Zambezi, from which you may see hippos, crocodiles and other game coming down to the river to drink. The Chamabonda Drive is another game-watching route (25 km) that covers the southern part of the park.

Overlooking the Zambezi National Park, just 11 km from Victoria Falls town off the Victoria Falls–Bulawayo road, is the beautiful Sekuti's Drift Lodge, offering direct access to the Zambezi and Chamabonda national parks. The lodge is set on a private game reserve and offers 10 twenties-style bedrooms (with wrought-iron beds), swimming pool and an open-plan diningroom, bar, lounge and verandah.

Included in the price are transfers to all the scenic delights the Victoria Falls and surrounding parts have to offer.

For more information contact the Central Booking Office, Department of National Parks and Wildlife Management, PO Box CY826, Causeway, Harare, tel (09263-4) 70-6077/8; or the Victoria Falls Publicity Association, PO Box 97, Victoria Falls, Zimbabwe, tel (09263-13) 4202.

MATETSI GAME LODGES Nestling on the banks of the Zambezi some 40 km above the Victoria Falls, these elegant lodges are part of a natural wilderness covering 50 000 ha. They offer visitors comfort, serenity and plenty of encounters with a variety of mammals, ranging from impala and cheetah to elephant, buffalo and lion.

The lodges have been built along 15 km of river frontage which belongs to the Conservation Corporation, and are the ideal vantage point to watch game and birdlife congregating at the water's edge.

There are two camps, Water Lodge and Safari Camp. Water Lodge occupies 500 m of Zambezi River frontage and offers morning and evening game cruises, canoeing, fishing and sumptuous dining at the river's edge.

Water Lodge consists of three individual camps of six air-conditioned suites, each with private plunge pool, river deck and *en suite* bathroom. The suites are built of teak, thatch and slate and nestle in the shade of giant mangosteen and waterberry trees.

Safari Camp is a 24-bedded camp, set at the water's edge where animals converge daily from the open savannah surrounding the lodge. There are sparkling swimming pools, tree-shaded decks and an old-world colonial charm reminiscent of Livingstone's Africa.

There are flights daily to and from Matetsi to Victoria Falls International Airport. For more details contact the Conservation Corporation, Private Bag X27, Benmore, 2010, tel (011) 784-6832.

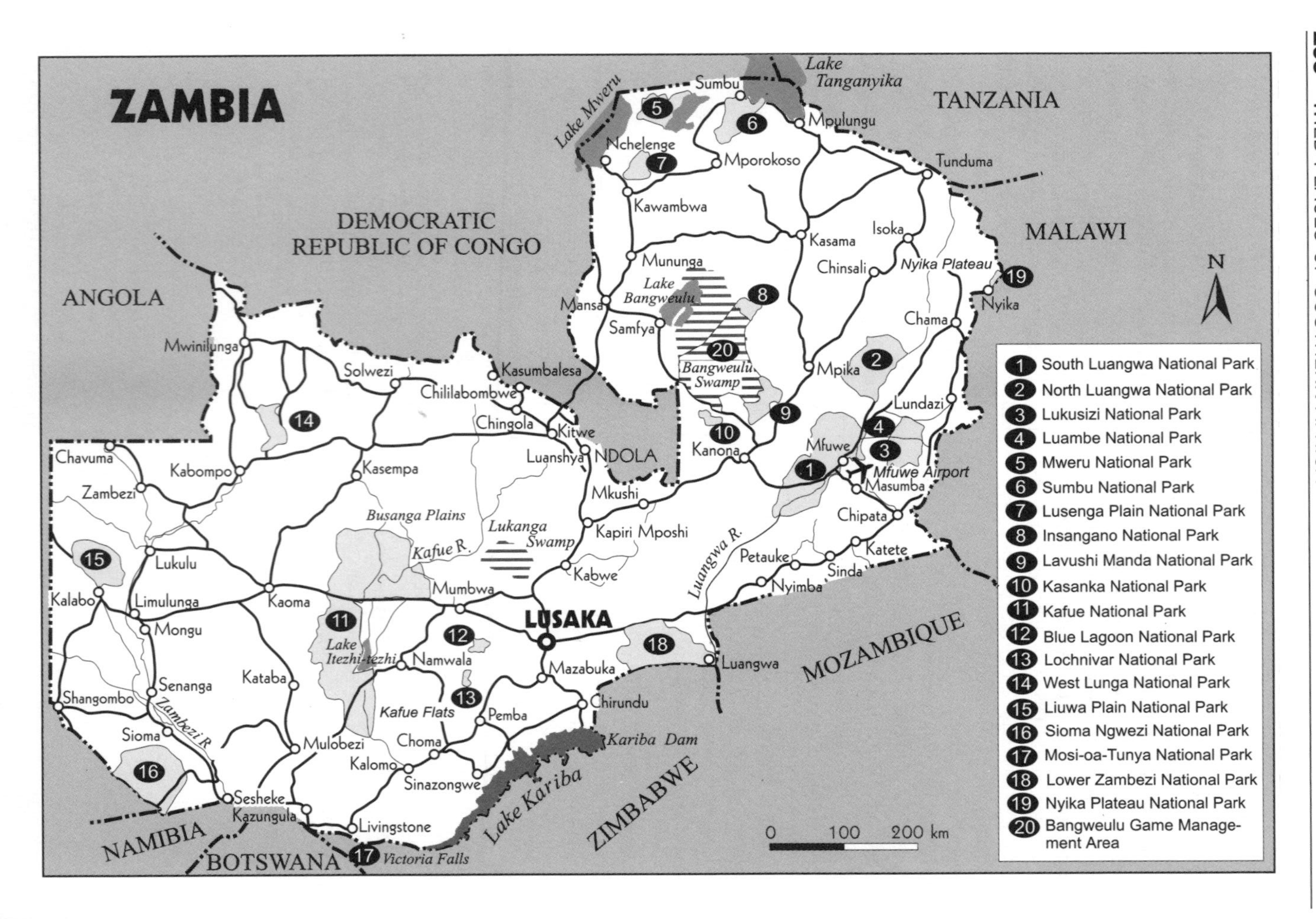
ZAMBIA
1 South Luangwa National Park
2 North Luangwa National Park
3 Lukusizi National Park
4 Luambe National Park
5 Mweru National Park
6 Sumbu National Park
7 Lusenga Plain National Park
8 Insangano National Park
9 Lavushi Manda National Park
10 Kasanka National Park
11 Kafue National Park
12 Blue Lagoon National Park
13 Lochnivar National Park
14 West Lunga National Park
15 Liuwa Plain National Park
16 Sioma Ngwezi National Park
17 Mosi-oa-Tunya National Park
18 Lower Zambezi National Park
19 Nyika Plateau National Park
20 Bangweulu Game Management Area
N
0 100 200 km
TANZANIA
MALAWI
MOZAMBIQUE
ZIMBABWE
BOTSWANA
NAMIBIA
ANGOLA
DEMOCRATIC REPUBLIC OF CONGO
Lake Tanganyika
Lake Mweru
Lake Bangweulu
Bangweulu Swamp
Lukanga Swamp
Busanga Plains
Kafue Flats
Lake Itezhi-tezhi
Lake Kariba
Kariba Dam
Victoria Falls
Nyika Plateau
Luangwa R.
Kafue R.
Zambezi R.
LUSAKA
NDOLA
Mfuwe Airport
Sumbu
Mpulungu
Tunduma
Nchelenge
Mporokoso
Kawambwa
Kasama
Isoka
Mununga
Chinsali
Nyika
Mansa
Samfya
Chama
Mwinilunga
Mpika
Solwezi
Kasumbalesa
Chililabombwe
Lundazi
Chingola
Kitwe
Mfuwe
Kanona
Luanshya
Chavuma
Kabompo
Kasempa
Masumba
Zambezi
Mkushi
Chipata
Kapiri Mposhi
Katete
Lukulu
Petauke
Kabwe
Sinda
Nyimba
Kalabo
Kaoma
Mumbwa
Limulunga
Mongu
Namwala
Luangwa
Kataba
Mazabuka
Senanga
Shangombo
Chirundu
Pemba
Siomа
Mulobezi
Choma
Kalomo
Sinazongwe
Sesheke
Kazungula
Livingstone

ZAMBIA

Larger than France, Austria, Switzerland and Hungary combined, Zambia sprawls across 750 000 km^2 in central Southern Africa. Completely landlocked by Zimbabwe, Malawi, Mozambique, Tanzania, Democratic Republic of Congo and Angola, the country consists mainly of a kidney-shaped plateau about 1 300 m above sea level that descends gently in the south towards the Zambezi River.

Here the cauldron of white water known as Mosi-oa-Tunya — 'the Smoke that Thunders' — tumbles over the Victoria Falls as the mighty Zambezi sloughs through the African bush on its way to Lake Kariba.

Nestling under giant indigenous trees on the northern banks of the Zambezi are a series of beautiful safari lodges — rustic, clean, comfortable and within easy reach of the Victoria Falls, Lake Kariba and the Kafue National Park.

Further north are South Luangwa and North Luangwa national parks, which stretch northeastwards towards the Nyika Plateau and the country's border with Malawi.

Dotted with vast, grassy plains, Zambia is also an extremely well-watered country. The Zambezi and Kafue rivers and their tributaries, Lake Kariba and Lake Tanganyika and the hundreds of other smaller rivers comprise about 45 per cent of all the water in Southern Africa.

In spite of its size, Zambia is fairly densely populated, with eight million inhabitants speaking 73 different dialects. English is the language most people use.

Wildlife

During the first 70 years of this century Zambia was the cradle of some of the world's largest game populations. Hundreds of thousands of elephants, great herds of antelope, zebras, wildebeest and buffaloes, thousands of black rhinos and an incalculable number of smaller mammals roamed the plains and valleys.

After 1970, however, the importation of firearms into Zambia, indiscriminate hunting, lack of government controls and poaching decimated the natural populations, reducing them to 20 per cent of their former numbers.

Black rhinos — prized for their horns — were completely wiped out, and you won't find one in Zambia today. Elephants, once numbering more than 100 000 in the Luangwa Valley alone, were reduced to about 25 000 in the whole country.

Recently, however, under the control of the National Parks and Wildlife Services of Zambia, these numbers have started increasing, and today there is considerable optimism that former numbers of many species will be seen again.

Zambia doesn't have nearly as many mammal species as South Africa, but its numbers are impressive. Among the more common species seen in the major national parks are elephant, leopard, lion, cheetah, zebra, wildebeest, spotted hyena, wild dog, warthog, water monitor, crocodile, hippo, mongoose and vervet monkey.

The variety of antelope is enormous and includes such species as Lichtenstein's hartebeest, eland, roan and sable antelope and impala.

The abundant floodplains and waterways also attract large numbers of such water-loving antelope as red lechwe, puku and sitatunga.

In addition, there are some mammals not seen in South Africa at all, such as Thornicroft's giraffe, Cookson's wildebeest and Defassa waterbuck.

More than 400 species of bird include some specials such as Chaplin's barbet, the rare taita falcon and Pel's fishing owl.

The wild places

About 30 per cent of Zambia consists of national parks or game management areas. There are 19 national parks, at least 10 of which have no overnight facilities. Some of the parks are difficult to reach, others are impassable, while the standard of facilities in a few of them does not match the national parks of South Africa, Zimbabwe, Namibia and Botswana.

The exceptions, however, are the South Luangwa and North Luangwa national parks, Kafue National Park, Kasanka National Park, the Lochinvar National Park and the Nyika National Park.

South Luangwa National Park This is Zambia's princess of parks. Its wildlife community includes one of the continent's most important elephant populations, buffaloes, giraffes, zebras and lions, and the largest number of crocodiles of any river in Africa. It also hosts a dozen or so of the country's finest lodges, run mainly by experienced safari operators.

North of South Luangwa, separated by a strip of land known as the Munyamadzi Corridor, is North Luangwa National Park, 4 700 km^2 of miombo woodland that has not really been developed for tourism, and which has no road network.

Kafue National Park Although this park is not as streamlined or as well geared to tourism as South Luangwa, it does, in fact, have a greater diversity of animals and birds — and some excellent lodges set in scenic surroundings on the banks of the Kafue River. The park is huge, covering 22 400 km^2 in central Zambia, and its habitats range from mopane woodland to grassy floodplain and riverine forest.

Among its attractions are the greatest variety of antelope of any African park, all the large predators, more than 400 species of bird and a huge lake in the southeastern corner (Lake Itezhi-tezhi) which offers fishing, cruising and various watersports.

Where to stay

Most of the safari lodges and bush camps of Zambia's national parks are of a very high standard, and offer comfortable accommodation in thatched chalets and tented camps (with and without *en suite* facilities).

In some parks old rest camps have been abandoned and are derelict, such as Nanzhila, Ntemwa and Moshi in Kafue (where some visitors still camp). However, the boom in Zambian tourism has seen moves recently to upgrade these places, and they're likely to see changes soon.

Because of the general lack of basic provisions and facilities in Zambia, it would be wise to stay in a well-established, fairly upmarket safari lodge, such as Tena Tena, Nkwali, Kapani Safari Lodge or Chibembe Safari Lodge in South Luangwa, or Musungwa Safari Lodge, Lunga Cabins or Lufupa Lodge in Kafue National Park. Here all facilities arê provided and game drives, safaris and cruises are the order of the day.

Alternatively the various upmarket lodges along the Zambezi provide excellent accommodation for visitors who want to see the falls (see 'Zambezi lodges' on p. 315).

For travellers in transit most Zambian towns have a rest house run by the local council, but the standard of some of these is questionable, so a hotel would probably be a better alternative.

In Lusaka the Hotel Intercontinental is a four-star establishment with a swimming pool, squash courts and casino. Another popular stopover is Lusaka's Pamodzi Hotel, which has a health centre, swimming pool, shopping arcade and superb restaurant.

Climate

Summers (October–April) are hot and dry, with temperatures ranging from 19 °C to 32 °C; winters (May–September) are cool with temperatures ranging from 10 °C to 25 °C. Rain, in the form of thunderstorms, falls between December and April.

When to go

The best time to visit is the dry season, between May and October, when the bush dries and game-viewing is optimal. Most of the parks are accessible at this time, but some are closed during the rainy season (December–April). In South Luangwa and Kafue national parks many camps close in November and reopen again in May.

How to get there

By air Lusaka International Airport services a large number of airlines, including South African Airways (twice a week from Johannesburg), British Airways, Aeroflot, Air France, Air Zimbabwe, Air Botswana, Air Namibia, Royal Swazi Air, Mozambique Airlines, and Air Tanzania.

Zambian Airways flies to Johannesburg three times a week, and to Bombay and London once a week.

Sun Air flies from Cape Town to Livingstone via Sun City on Wednesdays, Fridays and Sundays.

By road For a scenic route which takes in the panorama of the Victoria Falls, travel from Harare to Bulawayo and continue past Hwange Game Reserve, entering Zambia at the Victoria Falls. The most direct route from South Africa is via Beit Bridge and Harare, entering Zambia at Chirundu. The road is in good condition.

If you would like to travel through Botswana from South Africa and see the Chobe National Park, travel via Francistown and Nata to the Kazungula border post.

Visitors from Namibia should travel via Botswana to Kazungula, as the alternative route from Katima Mulilo to Livingstone is in very bad shape.

By coach The United Bus Service of Zambia travels from Lusaka to Harare via Chirundu and back six days a week. There's a regular coach service which operates between Johannesburg and Harare, with a connecting bus service to Bulawayo and Victoria Falls.

By rail The Tanzania–Zambia Railway, also known as the Tazara Express, travels between Kapiri Mposhi in Zambia and Dar es Salaam in Tanzania once a week. Rovos Rail in South Africa runs a spectacular steam-train adventure between Johannesburg and Dar es Salaam via Zimbabwe and Zambia. For details contact Rovos Rail, PO Box 2837, Pretoria 0001, tel (012) 323-6052.

Getting around

By air Zambian Airways flies daily between Lusaka and Ndola, and three times a week between Lusaka and Livingstone and Lusaka and Mfuwe. Once a week Zambian Airways flies from Lusaka to Mansa, Kasama and Kasaba Bay.

By road Travel by road in your own vehicle is the recommended way to see the country. Although the main camps of South Luangwa, Kafue, Lochinvar and Kasanka national parks are accessible by ordinary saloon car, a 4x4 is essential if you want to fully explore these parks and other wild places of Zambia. Many of the roads in and out of the parks are in a bad state and are impassable in the rainy season, even with a 4x4. And in some parks, two 4x4s are advisable in case of a breakdown. If you're unfamiliar with the road network, hire a game scout to show you around.

Western Zambia's sandy roads pose a particular problem to two-wheel-drive vehicles. Drive slowly in Zambia and be aware that there have been car hijackings in the vicinity of the Copperbelt.

Although fuel is in good supply, there are shortages from time to time, so travellers should take at least 100 litres of petrol or diesel along. Check on the fuel situation before your trip and take essential spares, including engine oil, hydraulic fluid and distilled water (for batteries).

On foot The concept of walking safaris was born in Zambia, and over the past 50 years thousands of visitors have experienced the thrill of walking through the untamed reaches of the Zambian national parks with some of the best safari guides in Africa.

The pioneers in this field were Robin Pope and Norman Carr, two dedicated conservationists who probably know the wild places of Zambia better than anyone.

Their safari companies offer two- to seven-day adventures, led by an armed scout, through lion, buffalo and elephant country, with stopovers in rustic, comfortable bush camps. These safaris, and those run by Busanga Trails, are detailed in the individual entries.

Tip for travellers

Compared to other Southern African parks, Zambian parks are costly. Permits are needed to enter all the national parks and a fee is levied according to the number of days spent in the park. There is also an entry fee for cars, and campers are charged an additional amount for each day they camp in the park.

Game drives

Private tour companies offer game-viewing drives in 4x4s through national parks and private reserves, where there are plenty of animals and birds to see. Spotlight-assisted night drives usually target lions, leopards, hyenas, civets, genets and porcupines.

Entry requirements

Visitors entering Zambia need a valid passport. Those from non-Commonwealth countries need a visa. Indian, Greek, Ghanaian, Nigerian and Pakistan passport-holders must apply for a visa at least one month before the visit. For further enquiries write to the Chief Immigration Officer, PO Box 50300, Lusaka, Zambia.

Health precautions

Malaria is rife in parts of Zambia, so prophylaxis is essential. You'll need to be inoculated against yellow fever and a tetanus vaccination is recommended.

Other possible illnesses in Zambia are sleeping sickness (caused by the bite of a tsetse fly, which resembles a horsefly) and tickbite fever. Both conditions are unpleasant and, although not life-threatening, should be avoided.

To minimise the chance of tsetse fly bites, use a gauze screen to cover open windows of vehicles and tents during your stay.

And after walking in the bush, check your clothes and body for the presence of any ticks.

Because of the remoteness of many of Zambia's parks be sure to take a comprehensive first-aid kit (see, 'Health risks' in the chapter 'On Safari in Southern Africa', p. 13). This should include anti-snakebite serum and a wide-spectrum antibiotic.

Travel information

Zambian National Tourist Board, PO Box 30017, Century House, Cairo Road, Lusaka, tel (09260-1) 22-9087/90; 1st Floor, Finance House, Ernest Oppenheimer Road, Bruma Lake Office Park, Bruma 2198, tel (011) 622-9206/7; Tourism Council of Zambia, PO Box 30093, Lusaka, tel (09260-1) 22-8682/3; Zambian Wildlife Society, Box 30255, Lusaka, tel (09260-1) 25-4226; National Parks and Wildlife Service of Zambia, Private Bag 1, Chilanga (18 km south of Lusaka).

Kafue National Park

Lying about 330 km west of Lusaka in central-western Zambia, the Kafue National Park, the second largest national park in the world, covers about 22 400 km² — an area roughly the size of Wales or the American state of Massachusetts. Although the South Luangwa National Park is regarded as the topmost Zambian reserve, Kafue, making amends for a neglected past, is challenging for a very close second place.

Tourism in Zambia is booming — old, derelict lodges in Kafue are being reconstructed, new lodges are being introduced and private safari operators are offering packages that compare very favourably with the best in Africa.

Kafue has an amazing diversity of habitats — from tall mopane forests to sweeping savannah grasslands dominated by baobab and euphorbia trees.

In the north are the Busanga Plains, a vast floodplain fed by the Lufupa River. In the dry season the shallow waters of the floodplain recede, exposing short grasslands that attract huge herds of antelope, zebras and wildebeest.

These dry plains — called 'dambos' — are peppered with massive termite mounds — islands that sustain groves of Phoenix palms and giant fig trees, home to a cosmopolitan community of birds. Here and there deep pools harbour pods of hippos and crocodiles awaiting the onset of the seasonal floods.

The Kafue River itself runs southwards through the park, flanked by a riverine fringe of palm trees, coconut ivory and wild pear. At its southeastern end it empties into the 370-km² expanse of Lake Itezhi-tezhi. The shoreline of this lake and the rich grasslands of the Nanzhila Plains are also prime wildlife areas in Kafue and attract large herds of antelope, zebras and buffaloes.

Wildlife Although Kafue is less developed than South Luangwa National Park, it has more wildlife species than Luangwa or any other reserve in the country. It is also one of Africa's great sanctuaries for antelope. Across the floodplains of the north and down to the Nanzhila Plains in the south, gamewatchers may see Lichtenstein's hartebeest, eland, roan and sable antelope and several other species of water-adapted antelope.

The fringes of the oxbows and lakelets of the floodplains attract a rare subspecies of waterbuck — the Defassa waterbuck — as well as red lechwe, puku and sitatunga, whose splayed hooves enable it to walk across floating carpets of reeds.

Across the Nanzhila Plains cheetahs send up clouds of dust and sand as they pursue impala and warthogs, while zebras and wildebeest fall prey to lions, spotted hyenas and packs of wild dogs.

Along the banks of the Kafue River, crocodiles laze in the sun or erupt from the surface to snatch unwary antelope at the waterside. They are joined by water monitors, hippos and smaller mammals such as mongooses and monkeys roaming the river banks in search of food.

Birdlife The abundance of water, combined with the diversity of habitats, attracts more than 400 species. The riverine vegetation flanking the Kafue and Lufupa rivers and their woodlands are home to Pel's fishing owls and carmine bee-eaters, while the Busanga Plains accommodate large flocks of pelicans, pratincoles and wattled cranes.

Tip for travellers

In the dry season you can get to Lufupa Lodge and Chunga Camp, but a four-wheel-drive is essential to get to the Busanga Plains in the north and the Nanzhila Plains in the south.

Where to stay There are a dozen or so private camps and lodges in Kafue. Busanga Trails, the major tour operator for Kafue National Park, runs three attractive, comfortable game lodges in the area — Lufupa Lodge, Shumba Camp and Kafwala Lodge. However, Lunga River Lodge, run by Ed and Rona Smythe of African Experience, is probably the most sought-after camp in the park.

LUNGA RIVER LODGE This lovely camp, sheltered under a canopy of indigenous trees on the west bank of the Lunga River, accommodates 12 guests in six luxury *en suite* thatched chalets. An elevated diningroom leads on to a cosy bar and sundeck suspended over the river. There's also a sparkling swimming pool and a steam bath.

The accent is on outdoor living and the open-air boma is the venue for fireside meals under the stars. A walkway leads down to a jetty and a boat, which takes guests upriver for birding and game-watching trips.

A special attraction is the Lupemba Bush Camp, which is accessible only by river. Here three tents under large trees on the river bank accommodate six guests. Meals are cooked on an open fire and served in the open-air diningroom.

Lunga Cabins offers walking safaris and game drives through Kafue National Park (see 'At a glance' box for address).

LUFUPA LODGE North of Kafwala, on a high bank at the confluence of the Kafue and Lufupa rivers, this is the most centrally situated of the lodges. Lufupa is an angler's paradise, offering catches in both rivers of pike, bream, silver barbel and catfish. There's also a lovely swimming pool.

The area is inhabited by numbers of lions and leopards, and you can see these on escorted game drives and bush walks. To book contact Busanga Trails, PO Box 31322, Lusaka, tel (09260-1) 25-4226.

SHUMBA CAMP This is the second of the Busanga Trails camps. Shumba means lion in the local dialect, and you're likely to see plenty of these in the vicinity of the camp on the Busanga Plains.

The lodge, the only one of its kind in Zambia, has been built on an elevated platform above the plains, so the views are exceptional.

KAFWALA LODGE Beautifully situated among woodlands above the Kafwala Rapids in North Kafue, this camp is open only to members of Zambia's Wildlife Conservation Society. To become a temporary member contact the society at PO Box 30255, Lusaka, tel (09260-1) 25-4226 or by booking a stay through Busanga Trails.

MUSUNGWA SAFARI LODGE This lodge lies on a hill overlooking the southern shore of Lake Itezhi-tezhi on the edge of the Kafue National Park, and is open throughout the year.

The 25 *en suite* chalets cater for 70 people, and each has its own private verandah, with beautiful views of the lake.

Amenities include a lovely swimming pool, and a reception area, bar and restaurant housed in three rondavels. The cuisine — served indoors or outdoors around a fire — is first class, and entertainment is provided by ila dancers. Other facilities include a sauna, squash and tennis courts,

Deadly armoury of the porcupine

The long-whiskered porcupine is smaller than a turkey, but it carries a murderous arsenal of flexible black spines on its back, sharp and deadly enough to kill a leopard or a lion.

Predators fooled by the timid, inoffensive gait of this animal as it waddles across the floodplain of Kafue National Park at night, have found to their cost that it is not a creature to be tangled with.

Lions, in particular, have paid dearly for regarding a porcupine as a potential meal — in South Africa's Kalahari Gemsbok National Park a study found that porcupines were responsible for more than 25 per cent of all lion deaths.

Surprised or alarmed, the porcupine's quills rattle like arrows in a quiver, a warning reinforced by much grunting, foot-stamping and the shaking of the hollow quills in its tail.

If the aggressor ignores these vital warnings, the porcupine charges backwards to impale the enemy on its raised and lethal spines.

Pursuing predators — including lions and wild dogs — sometimes impale themselves on the animal's quills when the latter stops suddenly in full flight.

The porcupine does not, as some scientists once believed, shoot its quills into its adversaries.

Kafue National Park at a glance

Locality:	South-central Zambia, north of the Zambezi River, 330 km west of Lusaka.
Climate:	Summers (October–November) are hot and dry (19 °C–32 °C); winters (May–September) are cool and dry (10 °C–25 °C). The rainy season is between December and April.
Number of camps:	Some lodges have their own bush camps. These include Lunga Cabins (Lupemba Bush Camp) and Musungwa Safari Lodge (Nanzhila Bush Camp and Puku Pan).
Game drives:	These range from two-hour excursions to three- and four-day safaris.
Hides and waterholes:	There are hundreds of natural waterholes created by the seasonal ebb and flow of the major rivers. Private lodges have their own hides.
Trails:	Busanga Trails do trails of northern Kafue, while Chundukwe Safaris cover the Nanzhila Plains (see *booking addresses* below).
Other attractions:	Cruising Lake Itezhi-tezhi on the *Zambezi Queen*; trips to Victoria Falls.
Amenities:	Most of the lodges are fully equipped and provide catering, accommodation, food, bedding, crockery and cutlery. Musungwa Safari Lodge and Lunga Cabins both have swimming pools.
Accommodation:	More than a dozen safari lodges in and around Kafue offer accommodation ranging from luxury wood-and-thatch chalets to tented camps.
Booking address:	**Lufupa Lodge**, **Shumba Camp** and **Kafwala Lodge**: Busanga Trails, PO Box 37538, Lusaka, tel (09260-1) 22-7739/40; **Lunga Cabins**: African Experience, PO Box 31051, Lusaka, tel (011) 462-2554; **Musungwa Safari Lodge**: Musungwa Safaris, PO Box 31808, Lusaka, tel (09260-1) 27-3492; **Chundukwa Adventures**, PO Box 61160, Livingstone, tel (09260-3) 32-4006.
When to go:	The dry season (June–October).
What to take with you:	Light, khaki clothing in summer; warmer gear in winter (include long-sleeved shirts and trousers at all times to prevent bites from tsetse flies); camera, binoculars, field guides, torch and fly-screen for your car windows.
How to get there:	Head west from Lusaka on the main road to Mumbwa. Some 66 km west of Mumbwa a road turns right to Lake Itezhi-tezhi and the lodges of southern Kafue, such as Musungwa Safari Lodge, New Kalala Camp and the Nanzhila Plains. This broken tar road is in very poor shape, so drive slowly. To get to the northern lodges (Hippo Camp, Lunga Cabins) you can turn north at Mumbwa. For the other northern lodges continue straight, cross the Kafue River, and then turn right for Kafwala and Lufupa lodges and the Busanga Plains. To get to Chunga Camp, head south after crossing the Kafue River — the road doubles back eastwards to the camp, just 17 km from the main road.
Nearest petrol:	Mumbwe and Musungwa Safari Lodge.
Open:	Most of Kafue's interior is inaccessible during the rainy season (November–May) but Musungwa Safari Lodge and the new Kalala Camp are open throughout the year.
Special precautions:	Malaria is endemic so a course of antimalaria tablets is essential.

a library, curio shop and access to windsurfing and waterskiing. Petrol is also available to guests.

The lodge offers gamewatching on foot, by boat or in open 4x4 vehicles. But the real highlights are a lake cruise on the *Zambezi Queen* or river cruises along the Kafue on the *Sea Truck*, a 24-seat cruiser. The *Zambezi Queen*, built in the 1950s as a pleasure cruiser on the Zambezi, has been retired to the quieter waters of Lake Itezhi-tezhi. Fishing trips are available to guests, and rods and tackle can be hired.

The lodge also invites guests to overnight at the rustic Nanzhila Bush Camp where they may tune in to the sounds of the wild (see 'At a glance' box for address). Another bush camp, completed in 1994, is Puku Pan.

CHUNGA CAMP Situated 17 km south of the main road which runs east to west through the park, this camp has six comfortable rondavels, camping facilities and reputable kitchen staff who will prepare all your meals.

HIPPO CAMP This is a well-appointed tented camp in northeastern Kafue, which offers an adventurous combination of game-viewing on foot, Land Cruiser or boat, as well as canoeing safaris down the Zambezi. Opportunities for photography and birdwatching are outstanding. For more details contact Bushwhackers, PO Box 32172, Ridgeway Hotel, Lusaka, tel (09260-1) 25-0310.

NEW KALALA CAMP This small camp, open throughout the year, accommodates eight guests in rondavels overlooking Lake Itezhi-tezhi. The camp is ideal for small groups seeking privacy and pampered attention. Birdwatching, fishing, boating, walking and game safaris (in the park and on islands in Lake Itezhi-tezhi) are available.

MUKAMBI SAFARI LODGE This lodge, a three-and-a-half hour drive from Lusaka, lies on the banks of the Kafue River. It has seven chalets, a swimming pool and offers game drives, walks and river cruises.

Kasanka National Park

Forest giants loom 30 m skyward above the swamps and wetlands of this national park, one of the country's smallest yet most attractive sanctuaries for animals and birds.

Situated about 50 km south of Zambia's Bangweulu Game Management Area, Kasanka covers just 420 km^2 on the edge of the vast wetlands of Lake Bangweulu. Its own wetlands incorporate eight lakes, large areas of papyrus swamps, huge swamp forests, floodplains and four rivers, the largest of which is the Luwombwa.

Wildlife Unique among Kasanka's many attractions are the huge colonies of fruit bats that descend on the reserve in the November and December rainy season. As the sun sets over the floodplains, more than a million of these small mammals take to the air, creating a breathtaking black cloud above the horizon.

Other rare species of animals include the blue monkey, yellowbacked duiker, Defassa waterbuck and the slendersnouted crocodile.

While elephants, jackals, hyenas and leopards may be spotted on game walks, it is the reserve's large population of sitatunga and puku that entice many nature-lovers to the area. Other antelope include bushbuck, reedbuck, Sharpe's grysbok, sable and common duiker.

The waterways are alive with pods of hippos, while crocodiles lie in serried ranks along the sandbanks. The forests are home to bushbuck, chacma baboons, warthogs, monkeys and civets.

Birdlife Not may birders have ticked off the shoebill stork, which with its bulbous bill and dodo-like appearance is a rare bird indeed. This and 350 other varieties, ranging from grassland species to birds of the swamps and forests are a major attraction at Kasanka, so be sure to take a comprehensive field guide and a good pair of binoculars along.

Where to stay Three attractive lodges offer comfortable accommodation with full board or self-catering.

Perched on the edge of a lake, Wasa Lodge offers four well-appointed, twin-bedded rondavels. Luwombwa Fishing Lodge accommodates 10 people in comfortable rondavels on the Luwombwa River; and Musande Tented Camp, also on the Luwombwa, can accommodate 12 in luxury safari tents. For a more rustic option, Kankonto Campsite offers basic cooking and washing facilities, but campers should provide their own tents, food and bedding.

Kasanka National Park at a glance

Locality:	Northern Zambia, 50 km south of the Bangweulu Swamps.
Climate:	Between May and August it is cool to mild; September and October are warm to hot; October to April is hot with thundershowers.
Number of camps:	Four.
Hides and waterholes:	A tree-hide for watching puku and sitatunga.
Trails:	Walking trails into the forests and across grassy plains.
Other attractions:	Drive to Bangweulu Game Management Area.
Amenities:	Full board is offered at Wasa and Luwombwa fishing lodges and at Musande Tented Camp. Cooking and washing facilities at Kankonto Campsite.
Accommodation:	**Wasa Lodge** — rondavels; **Luwombwa Fishing Lodge** — rondavels; **Musande Tented Camp**; **Kankonto Campsite**.
Booking address:	All reservations can be made through Intercontinental Travel, PO Box 320187, Lusaka, tel (09260-1) 26-3951 or 26-0705; or contact the Tour Operators Association of Zambia, PO Box 30263, Lusaka, tel (09260-1) 22-4248.
When to go:	The dry, winter season (May–September) is best for game, but birds are most visisble from October to March. The bats come out in November and December.
What to take with you:	Camera, binoculars, field guides, torch; light clothing in summer; warmer garments in winter.
How to get there:	Head north from Lusaka to Mkushi and Serenje; 39 km north of Serenje turn left on the Mansa road and travel about 55 km until you see the entrance to Kasanka.
Open:	Throughout the year from sunrise to sunset.
Special precautions:	Take antimalaria precautions; beware of crocodiles and hippos.

Game drives and trails Boating and fishing trips are available along the park's many waterways, and excursions are also laid on to the memorial marking the spot where explorer David Livingstone died.

Livingstone mistakenly believed that the vast waterways of the region represented the source of the Nile.

Special trips may be arranged to the Bangweulu Game Management Area (see below) — in particular to Shoebill Camp — and to the Kundalila Falls and Nsalu Cave.

Guided walks take hikers into the dim, green world of the 'mushito' forests where the canopy is 30 m high and envelops a wonderful world of animal and plant life. Other walks across the grassy plains take in a special hide built into a mululu tree for watching water-adapted antelope species.

Bangweulu Game Management Area Visitors to Kasanka should make a point of visiting Bangweulu Game Management Area — if not for the thousands of black lechwe that roam the floodplains, then for the magnificent wild vistas of the grassy plains interspersed with lakes, swamps and rivers.

The area is only passable between May and December but boat transfers to, and accommodation at, Shoebill Island Camp can be arranged by the authorities at Kasanka.

SOUTH LUANGWA NATIONAL PARK

Covering an area of 9 050 km^2 in the Luangwa Valley, the South Luangwa National Park is to Zambia what the Kruger National Park is to South Africa — a wildlife sanctuary of gigantic proportions. Here, along the banks of the lazy Luangwa River, a succession of idyllic game lodges offer guests a taste of real Africa in the middle of generous populations of game.

The 700-km-long Luangwa Valley is the southern extension of the Great Rift Valley that stretches from North Africa to the Zambezi River. The river and floodplain that created it is the umbilical cord that nourishes a startling variety of fauna and flora. Some 15 000 elephant and an equal number of hippo live in the valley.

In times of flood the river charges on to the low-lying plains around it, changing its course and spawning oxbow lakelets and lagoons.

The shallow expanses of water attract a great variety of waterbirds and mammals seeking relief from the searing summer temperatures.

Wildlife There are 50 mammal species (excluding bats) in South Luangwa, and although this is nowhere near the diversity of South Africa's Kruger National Park (147 mammals), the park does cater to visitors in search of large mammals and carnivores.

In times of flood, the surrounding plains come alive with herds of elephants — among the largest in Africa — as well as roan antelope, impala, waterbuck, zebra, greater kudu and eland.

In their wake come the predators — lions, hyenas, wild dogs and leopards.

Along the fringes of the floodplain you'll also see hippos, puku, warthogs and impala.

The riverine vegetation is breathtaking — giant mahogany, leadwood and baobab trees cast their long shadows across Cookson's wildebeest, Thornicroft's giraffes, black rhinos and buffaloes. There are also seven species of mongoose, including the bushytailed and whitetailed varieties.

At night porcupines, bushbuck, bushbabies, servals, aardvarks, honey badgers, longtoed elephant shrews and a large number of genets emerge from their daytime retreats to forage in the forest or through the long grass.

Birdlife More than 400 bird species are found in the Luangwa Valley, including woodpecker, parrot, kingfisher, roller, hornbill and hoopoe. Birds of prey are also plentiful and include Wahlberg's eagles, whitebacked vultures, western banded snake eagles and yellowbilled kites.

Near the water's edge you'll see chestnutbellied kingfishers, blackcrowned night herons and goliath herons.

Where to stay There are at least 12 private lodges in or around the South Luangwa National Park, most of them run by experienced safari operators who have been in the area for decades. Among the more popular of these are:

TENA TENA *The Times* of London describes Tena Tena — 'temporary home' in the local dialect — as one of the best safari camps in Africa.

Situated on the banks of the Luangwa River under a grove of mahogany trees within the park, the camp comprises six large, custom-made Manyara tents, with bathroom, shower and flush toilet.

Tips for travellers

- **During the rainy season only the central part of South Luangwa is accessible.**
- **South Africans who want details of tours to Zambia should contact Pulse Africa, PO Box 2417, Parklands 2121, tel (01)1 788-3916; or Thompsons Travel, PO Box 41032, Craighall 2024, tel (011) 788-0810.**

Tena Tena was built in 1986 by Robin Pope Safaris, a company which provides some of the best foot safaris in Zambia (see 'Walking safaris' on p. 314). Pope's specialised knowledge of the local wildlife and countryside makes a stay at any of his camps unforgettable.

Accommodating 12 guests, Tena Tena is private and personal, and offers superb service in dramatically beautiful surroundings.

The thatched diningroom and bar, set on a bend in the Luangwa River, provide excellent views of elephants and various species of antelope, and a hide behind the camp overlooks a waterhole.

The camp offers daily walks through the bush as well as all-day drives, morning drives or night drives. Guests may dine in the bush. Tena Tena is only open from 1 June to 31 October.

To book contact Robin Pope Safaris, PO Box 80, Mfuwe, Zambia, tel (09260-62) 4-5090.

NKWALI This private camp, which lies outside the park on Robin Pope's own land, is some 30 km south of Tena Tena. It was built in 1991 in an area of ebony woodland and open grass plains in superb game-viewing country.

The six chalets are made of woven bamboo and overlook the river. The *en suite* bathrooms are open to the sky and offer guests the chance to shower in the moonlight. At night you may waken to hear zebra or giraffe browsing outside your chalet.

The bar, built around a massive ebony tree, is an excellent vantage point for spectacular sunsets over the river, and herds of elephant wallowing in the twilight shallows. The diningroom, built around a mahogany tree, overlooks the lagoon — a magnet for animals during the day.

Day drives and walks include a stop at

Chinendi Hills from which you'll get panoramic views across the valley.

Nkwali is open from April to November.

To book contact Robin Pope Safaris, PO box 80, Mfuwe, Zambia, tel (09260-62) 4-5090.

KAPANI SAFARI LODGE Nestling on the fringes of a tranquil lagoon next to the Luangwa River, Kapani was built in 1986 by conservationist Norman Carr, and he lived there until his death in 1997.

The lodge caters for 16 people in eight twin-bedded chalets with *en suite* toilets and showers, stocked fridges and verandahs. The chalets have been designed for the hot climate and have high ceilings and overhead fans. The large windows are covered with protective gauze.

The rooms lead on to a thatched, open-plan bar and diningroom with five-star cuisine. A shaded viewing platform and two thatched, open lounges (chitenges) overlook the lagoon. There's also a secluded pool and a gift shop stocked with books and souvenirs.

Norman Carr was a man who knew the bush like the back of his hand, and his walking safaris are legendary. The walking safaris at Kapani include overnight stays at three bush camps: Kakuli, which accommodates six guests in walk-in, *en suite* safari tents at the confluence of the Luangwa and Luwi rivers, Nsolo Camp, which has four spacious grass and bamboo chalets, and Luwi Camp on the banks of the Luwi sand river.

Luwi, set under a grove of trees, is the most rustic of the bush camps, while Kakuli and Nsolo have access to a central bar-diningroom complex.

The trails are led by professional scouts who were trained by Norman Carr.

Day trips take guests to hides and waterholes in the bush for a picnic or sundowners, while further afield there is a crocodile farm and a traditional village to visit.

To book contact Kapani Safari Lodge, PO Box 100, Mfuwe, Zambia, tel (09260-62) 4-5015.

CHIBEMBE SAFARI LODGE This camp lies on the banks of the Luangwa River under a grove of Natal mahogany and winterthorn trees, just opposite the South Luangwa National Park, and offers sightings of big game such as crocodiles, hippos and elephants.

Wooden chalets with charming verandahs, four-bedded family rooms, and single and double rooms accommodate up to 40 people.

Morning and late afternoon game drives are tailored to guests' needs and, in-between, poolside cocktails are available from the riverside bar.

A few hours' drive north of the camp is the Mupamazdi River bush camp on the banks of the Mupamazdi River.

A special attraction at Chibembe is its day-flights to the Bangweulu Swamps, a haven for waterbirds and animals.

Chibembe is open between 1 July and 31 October.

NSEFU CAMP This is the oldest camp in Zambia, but it's been refurbished recently and the view from its open chitenge must rate among the most stunning in the Luangwa Valley.

Accommodation is in six twin-bedded thatched rondavels, each with *en suite* shower and toilet. A bar, built beside a huge termite mound, overlooks a waterhole.

Because only 12 can stay in the camp at any one time, game-viewing and meal times are flexible.

To book contact Robin Pope Safaris, PO Box 80, Mfuwe, Zambia, tel (09260-62) 4-5090.

KAINGO CAMP This camp — Kaingo means 'leopard' — nestles in the shade of beautiful mahogany and ebony trees on the banks of the Luangwa River. Accommodation is in five thatched chalets (maximum of eight people) with *en suite* bathrooms and views of the river. All windows are screened and mosquito nets are provided.

A large, open-sided diningroom/lounge or chitenge overlooks the river and affords excellent gamewatching opportunities.

Guests have access to a well-stocked bar, and solar power provides lighting.

Upstream from the camp is a lovely hide from which you may watch a large resident herd of hippo.

The camp is a one-and-a-half hour drive from Mfuwe Airport.

To book contact Shenton Safaris, PO Box 57, Mfuwe, Zambia, tel (09260-62) 4-5064, or (09260-53) 6-2188.

MWABA BUSH CAMP A few kilometres from Kaingo is Mwaba, a six-bed bush camp which opened in 1999. The camp is set under ebony trees on the bank of the Mwaba River and is within walking distance of Kaingo Camp. The camp consists of three reed-and-thatch chalets with *en suite* bathroom facilities. Meals are prepared outside and served under the stars with full bar facilities.

An experienced Zambia National Parks scout, Derek Shenton, conducts game walks from the lodge through a mopane forest populated by elephant down the river to Lion Plain.

To book contact Shenton Safaris, PO Box 57, Mfuwe, Zambia tel (09260-62) 4-5064 or (09260-53) 6-2188.

CHINZOMBO SAFARI LODGE Visitors sip cocktails in the chitenge and gaze across the Luangwa River as hippos, elephants and giraffes come down to drink at the water's edge. In fact the camp is so rustic that the animals often wander between the nine two-bedded thatched chalets that recline under mahogany and ebony trees. The lodge is owned by the Save the Rhino Trust, and has been rated

Furious fighter of the wild

One of the bravest fighters in the African bush is an 11-kg bundle of ferocious energy called the ratel. Also known as the honey badger, this smallish creature could deceive you into thinking it's quite harmless as it huffs and puffs its way along the ground like a docile, untrained jogger.

Nothing could be further from the truth. The ratel is notorious for its power, courage and frightening ability to inflict lethal wounds on almost any animal.

The fur-covered skin on its back is loose, tough and resilient — qualities that make it extremely difficult to penetrate with tooth and claw. This skin also enables it to turn easily upon any animal that takes it from behind.

Left alone ratels are mostly harmless. But if they feel threatened or cornered, they will not hesitate to attack. Stories are legion of ratels defending themselves viciously against packs of dogs. There is one instance of a ratel attacking a tractor.

Colonel Stevenson-Hamilton recorded cases in the Kruger National Park where ratels attacked and killed wildebeest, waterbuck and buffalo bulls by seizing them by the scrotum. The animals were not eaten, but bled to death as a result of their injuries. Ratels have been known to challenge lions, usually unsuccessfully.

South Luangwa National Park at a glance

Locality:	600 km northeast of Lusaka.
Climate:	Luangwa Valley has moderate winter climate: daytime temperatures range between 10 °C and 25 °C. Summer daytime temperatures can reach 40 °C.
Number of camps:	There are at least 12 lodges.
Game drives:	Most of the private lodges offer morning, afternoon and evening game drives.
Hides and waterholes:	There are dozens of hides throughout the park, with a particularly lovely hide and waterhole at Tena Tena.
Trails:	Robin Pope Safaris, Norman Carr Safaris, Chinzombo Safaris (see *booking addresses* below) offer a variety of trails through the park ranging from morning walks to seven-day overnight adventures.
Other attractions:	Birdwatching, visiting the Bangweulu Swamps.
Amenities:	Kapani Safari Lodge and Chibembe Safari Lodge have swimming pools.
Accommodation:	At least 12 private lodges: **Tena Tena** — six Manyara tents; **Nkwali** — six bamboo chalets; **Kapani Safari Lodge** — stone rooms cater for 16 people; **Chibembe Safari Lodge** — wooden chalets, family rooms, single and double rooms; **Nsefu Camp** — six twin-bedded thatched rondavels; **Kaingo Camp** — four thatched chalets (maximum of eight people); **Wildlife Camp** — family rooms, *en suite* chalets, campsites.
Booking address:	Tena Tena, Nkwali, Walking Safaris — Robin Pope Safaris, PO Box 320154, Lusaka, fax (09260-1) 24-5076; Wildlife Camp: The Wildlife Camp, PO Box 510190, Chipata, tel (09260-62) 2-1606; Kapani Safari Lodge: PO Box 100, Mfuwe, tel (09260-62) 4-5015; Chibembe Safari Lodge: PO Box 30970, Lusaka, tel (09260-1) 21-5946; Chinzombo Safari Lodge, PO Box 85, Mfuwe, tel (09260-62) 4-5053.
When to go:	The dry season (May–October) when game-viewing is at its best. Many camps close during the rainy season (December–April).
What to take with you:	Two or three neutral-coloured safari outfits; sweater or anorak for cooler months, light long trousers, walking shoes or boots, binoculars, hat, camera and film.
How to get there:	By air: there are regular scheduled flights from Lusaka, Harare, Lilongwe and Victoria Falls to Mfuwe Airport which has customs, immigration and refuelling facilities. From there you can transfer by road to the park nearby. By road: two-wheel-drive vehicles should head eastwards from Lusaka along the Great East Road to Chipata (via Petauke). From Chipata turn left towards Masumba and the main gate at Mfuwe. Four-wheel-drive vehicles may continue from Petauke northwards to the park (without going via Chipata).
Nearest doctor:	At Mfuwe.
Nearest petrol:	At Mfuwe.
Open:	Tena Tena: June–October; Nkwali: April–January; Kaingo Camp: June–October.
Special precautions:	Antimalaria protection is essential, so is a yellow fever vaccination certificate.

as one of Zambia's best, offering excellent cuisine and service.

A major attraction at Chinzombo is its seven-day tailor-made safaris which cater for ornithologists, photographers and even artists wishing to portray the surrounding wildlife on canvas. These safaris include stays at two special bush camps inside the South Luangwa National Park — Kuyenda, which accommodates six guests in reed-and-grass huts.

The bush camps are open from June to November, while the lodge itself is open from April to early January.

To book contact Chinzombo Safaris, PO Box 30106, Lusaka, Zambia, tel (09260-1) 21-1644.

WILDLIFE CAMP Run by the Wildlife Conservation Society of Zambia, this camp lies on the banks of the Luangwa River overlooking the national park.

The accommodation ranges from camping sites to family rooms and *en suite* chalets, and there's a lovely bar-restaurant where guests may have sundowners in the privacy of the bush.

Birdwatching here is excellent and the usual range of game drives and walking safaris in the company of an armed scout is offered. Catering and self-catering options are available.

For more information contact the Wildlife Camp, PO Box 510190, Chipata, tel (09260-62) 2-1606.

MFUWE LODGE Built between two tranquil lagoons, this lodge lies 3 km inside South Luangwa National Park's Mfuwe Gate — a sumptuous retreat with superb exposure to game.

There are 18 chalets with private balconies overlooking the lagoons and migrating herds of animals. Each chalet has an *en suite* bathroom, which can be opened completely so you can watch animals come down to the water as you bathe. The chalets, built in the shade of giant ebony trees, also have a shower and private bar.

The main complex consists of central lounge, diningroom and bar under thatch. This leads onto a timber deck and swimming pool overlooking the main lagoon. There is also well-stocked book and video library.

Mfuwe Lodge has two bush camps in the south of the park: Bilimungwe Bush Camp and YendaYenda Bush Camp, both of which are within walking distance of each other.

Bilumungwe, which means 'chameleon', nestles in the shade of Natal mahogany and winterthorn trees on the edge of a lagoon. The camp has four reed-and-thatch chalets accommodating eight people, mainly on walking safaris. Yenda-Yenda also accommodates eight people on the banks of a lagoon. The bush camps have a diningroom and lounge.

To book contact Mfuwe Lodge, Box 91, Mfuwe, Zambia, tel (09260-62) 4-5041.

Walking safaris Robin Pope is an honorary ranger with the Zambian Department of Wildlife and has led walking safaris through some of the remotest parts of the Luangwa Valley for about 20 years.

The trails traverse vast grassy plains, woodlands and hills, and bring you into the midst of mammals large and small, as well as an endless variety of birds.

Hikers assemble at Nkwali Camp and then take a five-hour drive to the safari's starting point. Escorted by Robin Pope or an armed scout, the group then walks for five days along the Mupamadzi River, covering about 10 km a day.

Each night an advance truck sets up a safari camp with walk-in tents, camp beds, mattresses, hot and cold shower and a long-drop toilet. The night camps are run by a caterer and a field staff of eight.

For more information contact Robin Pope Safaris, PO Box 320154, Lusaka, Zambia, fax (09260-1) 24-5076.

Norman Carr was the founder of walking safaris in Zambia. His safaris leave from Kapani Safari Lodge and range from three hours to overnight adventures which include stays at two lovely bush camps, Nsolo and Luwi. Both camps operate only from 1 June to 31 October.

Nsolo's four rooms are built of grass and have *en suite* shower, washbasin, flush toilet and a verandah. The rooms access a thatched chitenge with a bar and dining area. A nearby hide overlooks a waterhole.

Luwi offers four simple thatched bamboo rooms which lead on to an *al fresco* dining area. Close by is a large lagoon teeming with hippos and crocodiles.

For more information contact Kapani Safari Lodge, PO Box 100, Mfuwe, tel (09260-62) 4-5015.

Zambezi River Lodges

Although the Zambezi River and its spectacular Victoria Falls are shared by Zimbabwe and Zambia, it is Zimbabwe and its excellent safari lodges and hotels near the falls that have grabbed the lion's share of world interest and tourist support. But for those looking for a more rustic, but no less scenically spectacular location on the Zambezi, Zambia and its Zambezi River lodges are an adventure-lover's dream.

Tongabezi Possibly the finest lodge in Zambia, Tongabezi is a superb combination of rustic luxury and superb views of the Zambezi, with easy access to islands on the very edge of the Victoria Falls.

Just 17 km upstream of the falls, the lodge is a cosy Eden of thatched cottages nestling under a canopy of ebony and acacia trees. It flanks the swirling waters of the Zambezi and caters for 16 guests in five beautiful, twin-bedded tented cottages, and three luxury double-bedded units — the Honeymoon, Tree and Bird House.

The units have been built from local rocks, thatch and poles, and are designed to share the ambience of river, trees and birds. Ochre cement floors lead on to wooden balconies where you may peer across the Zambezi as it twists silently towards the Victoria Falls.

Each of the luxury units is built on three levels, of which the middle is the living area with a gracious double bed, protected by drapes of mosquito netting. From your bed you can see across the bush and river and share the views with monkeys and wood owls. Downstairs there's a bathroom and upstairs a toilet.

The tented cottages are spread across a gentle terrace, shaded by riverine trees, and at night hippos wander between the tents.

Among Tongabezi's many attractions are its two- to five-night canoe safaris along the upper and lower Zambezi, boat trips to nearby islands, microlight flying trips above the falls, white-water rafting on the Batonka Gorge rapids below the falls, and walking safaris in the Kafue National Park.

For the sports buffs there's a lovely golf course at the Elephant Hills Hotel on the Zimbabwean side of the Zambezi and lawn tennis courts at the lodge. An attractive feature at Tongabezi is the natural swimming pool built into a cliff.

Guests may take a boat ride to nearby Chundu Island for a stroll beneath the canopy of kigelia, jackalberry and mahogany trees which shelter bushbuck and a variety of birds, including trumpeter hornbills, scimitarbilled woodhoopoes, giant eagle owls and Ayre's hawk eagles.

The island is just 200–300 m long, but the trip is worth it.

Tongabezi has two other lodges — one on nearby Livingstone Island, and another small camp under trees at Sindabezi Island.

Thorntree Lodge Six Mara-style stone-and-thatch safari tents overlook the Zambezi, 15 km upstream from Victoria Falls, at this cosy little camp in the Mosi-oa-Tunya National Park. It is the ideal base from which to explore the Victoria Falls and the waterways of the Zambezi.

Each room has a private balcony overlooking the river, and the main lounge-diningroom area has a raised deck overlooking the river.

Among the services offered at the lodge are game drives within the park, river cruises, fishing and visits to ethnic villages in the area.

The wildlife at Mosi-oa-Tunya Park includes white rhino, wildebeest, buffalo, zebra, giraffe and impala.

Visitors can fly into Livingstone or Victoria Falls International Airport where they will be met and transferred to the lodge. The lodge is run by Safaris Par Excellence, one of Zimbabwe's leading operators of canoeing safaris.

To book contact The Zambezi Safari & Travel Co, Suite 3, The Heights Centre, PO Box 158, Kariba, Zimbabwe, tel (09263) 61-2532.

The River Club For a real taste of the old colonial Africa, a stay at the River Club, 18 km upstream from the Victoria

Shriek of terror in the night

For gamewatchers in Zambia no sound in the wild is more chilling than the hysterical, terror-driven shriek of a chacma baboon being savaged by a leopard.

The crashing in the bush, the savage roar, the melee of snarls and spits and the screams of a dying baboon are enough to make you pack up your tent and go home.

But it's all part of an age-old battle for survival between the two species. While leopards enjoy baboon meat enormously, baboons will do anything to ward off an attack.

Confronted by a leopard, baboons tend to show amazing courage. The adult males of the troop may advance threateningly, unleashing a barrage of hysterical shrieks, barks and anxious grunts. These may, or may not, send the predator slinking away.

Falls, should be on your itinerary. The lodge is adorned with sumptuous period furniture dating back to the 1850s and paintings of the Victorian era hang from the walls.

There are eight split-level, timber-and-thatch chalets and two honeymoon chalets, nestling in the treeline on the river bank opposite the Zambezi National Park. Guests can lie in the warm comfort of their ball-and-claw baths and watch a variety of game ambling along the river.

The main lodge, with its colonial-style tin roof consists of a lounge, diningroom, drawing room and library with superb views of the Zambezi and the croquet lawn which stretches down to the river.

Activities include a visit to museums in Livingstone, a walk along the Zambian side of the Victoria Falls and a visit to an island in the Zambezi for a picnic. There are also drives into Mosi-oa-Tunya Zoological Park and sunrise and sunset excursions on the river in a pontoon. You can also enjoy some fly-fishing, play croquet or bridge, have English high tea, or just relax at the swimming pool.

To book contact Namibia Tourism, Private Bag 133461, Windhoek, tel (09264-61) 284-2111.

Sindabezi Island Camp This island is barely 50 m long, but if you're looking for a tranquil retreat under the stars, with only the sound of the river and birds to disturb you, then you should stay here for a few days at least.

There's no electricity, but the four double-bedded, thatched chalets (all with flush toilets and bucket showers) are open to the river.

Guests are ferried to the island 4 km downstream from Tongabezi in motorised 'banana boats' or by canoe, and the hospitality is second to none.

Livingstone Island Camp Because this island is so close to the Victoria Falls, it is drenched in spray during the high-water season. This and the fact that bull elephants roam the area means that the camp is only a temporary one, and usually only inhabited between July and December (the low-water season).

Accommodation is in bow-style tents sheltered under indigenous trees, and they're so close to the falls that you could almost topple into the gorge.

Chundukwa River Camp Across the Zambezi from Tongabezi this camp — Chundu means bushbuck in the local dialect — consists of three timber, reed and thatch chalets built on stilts which are connected by wooden boardwalks above the river.

Chundukwa is popular for its horseriding expeditions through the teak forests, where you're likely to see elephants and other mammals. Guests choose between tented horse trails, where they overnight in the bush, half-day trails or full- and half-day canoe safaris.

The camp also organises 4x4 game-watching and walking safaris in the Kafue National Park and escorted trails in the Livingstone Zoological Park.

Royal Zambezi Lodge This lodge lies close to the entrance to the Lower Zambezi National Park not far from the confluence of the Zambezi and Chongwe rivers. Its royal title marks its association with Her Royal Highness Chieftainess Chiyabaya.

Six well-ventilated, mosquito-proof tents (with *en suite* facilities) accommodate 12 guests.

Centrepiece of the lodge is the remarkable outdoor Kigelia Bar, built around a giant sausage tree overhanging the

Zambezi River lodges at a glance

Locality:	On the banks and islands of the Zambezi River, upstream from the Victoria Falls on Zambia's border with Zimbabwe.
Climate:	Hot summers, warm to mild winters. Thunderstorms between November and March.
Game drives:	To Kafue National Park, Mosi-oa-tunya Zoological Park and Livingstone Zoological Park.
Trails:	Walks on Chundu Island, horseriding expeditions from Chundukwa River Camp and walking safaris in Kafue National Park.
Other attractions:	White-water rafting on the Zambezi, microlight flying above the falls, kayaking and canoeing upstream, bungee-jumping off Victoria Falls Bridge, birdwatching on the islands.
Amenities:	Swimming pool, tennis courts, golf course, hot and cold water, electricity (but not on Livingstone Island or Sindabezi Island Camp).
Accommodation:	**Tongabezi**: five twin-bedded, tented cottages, three luxury double-bedded units; **Sindabezi Island Camp**: four double-bedded, thatched chalets; **Livingstone Island Camp**: temporary bow-style tents; **Chundukwa River Camp**: three timber, reed and thatch chalets.
Booking address:	Tongabezi, Sindabezi Island Camp and Livingstone Island Camp: Private Bag 31, Livingstone, Zambia, tel (09260-3) 32-3232/32-3296 or Thompsons Travel, PO Box 41032, Craighall 2024, tel (011) 788-0810; Chundukwa River Camp: PO Box 61160, Livingstone, Zambia, tel (09260-3) 32-4006.
When to go:	The Zambezi is at its peak in April, and the falls are at their best from June to September but the huge amount of spray makes photography difficult. Tongabezi and the other lodges are best in the low-water season (July to December).
What to take with you:	Insect repellent, sun hat, light clothing (but long-sleeved shirts and trousers for mosquito protection at night), binoculars, field guides.
How to get there:	There are regular flights from most major cities in Southern Africa, either to Livingstone Airport (25 minutes by road to Tongabezi) or Victoria Falls (75 minutes by road to Tongabezi from the Zimbabwean side). To get to the falls by road from South Africa, travel via Beit Bridge and Bulawayo (761 km). Tongabezi is a two-hour drive from Kasane in Botswana.
Nearest doctor:	Victoria Falls.
Nearest petrol:	Victoria Falls.
Open:	Tongabezi and Chundukwa River Camp are open throughout the year; Livingstone Island is open July–December (low-water season).
Special precautions:	Malaria is rife in Zambia — visitors must take antimalaria precautions before leaving for Zambia. Tsetse flies are also common and if you're driving, it will help to tape a protective fly screen to open car windows.

Zambezi River. From here guests may sip cocktails and watch the wildlife on nearby islands.

Attractions include day and night game drives, walking safaris, motorboat or canoeing trips and tigerfishing in the Zambezi. Less energetic pursuits include lounging round the swimming pool or a crackling outdoor fire at night.

You can get to the lodge by boat from Kariba or Chirundu or by road (in a 4x4) from Lusaka.

For more information contact Royal Zambezi Lodge, PO Box 31455, Lusaka, tel (09260-1) 22-3504.

(For further details of what to see and do at Victoria Falls, see the entries on pp. 291–299.)

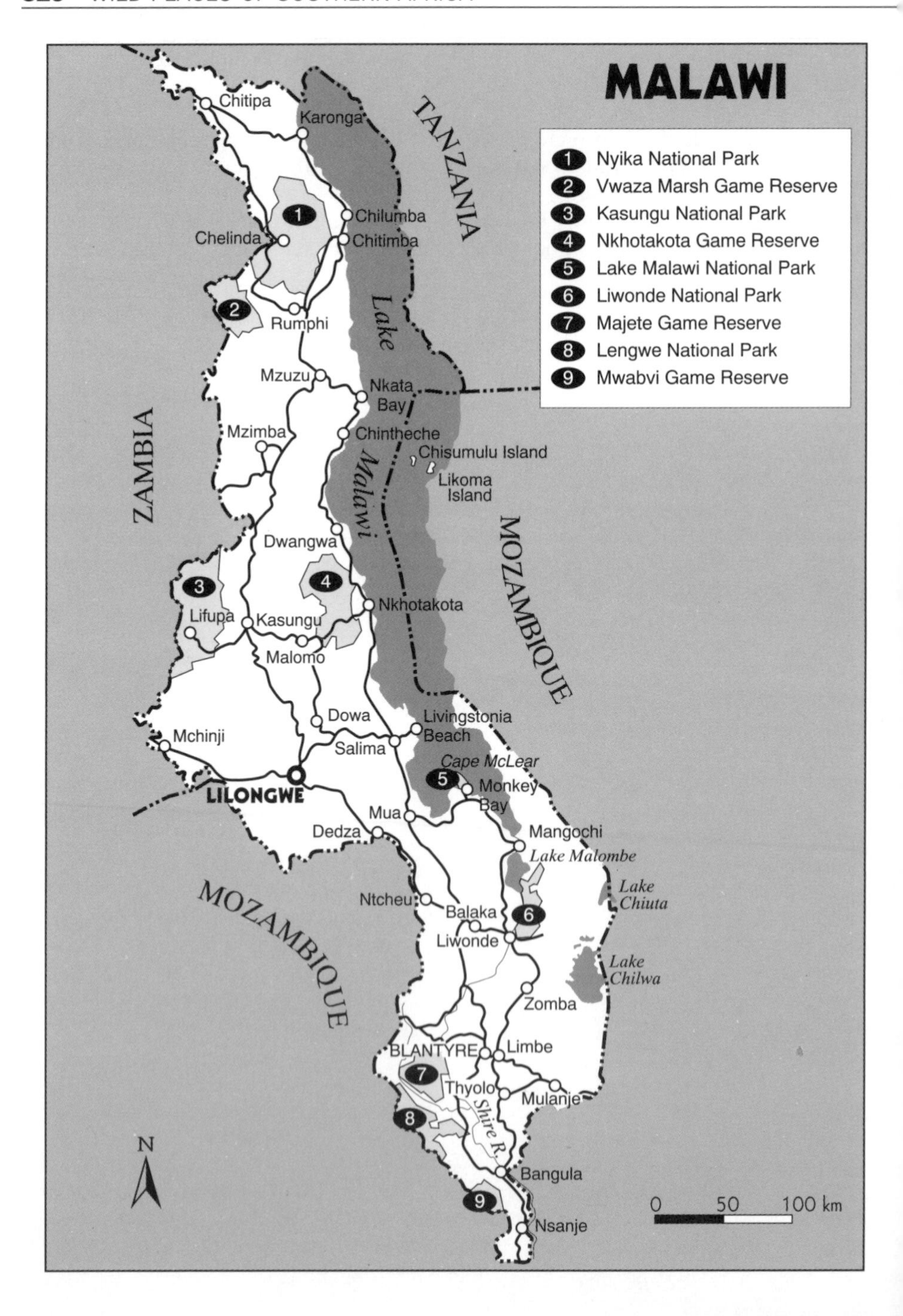
MALAWI
1 Nyika National Park
2 Vwaza Marsh Game Reserve
3 Kasungu National Park
4 Nkhotakota Game Reserve
5 Lake Malawi National Park
6 Liwonde National Park
7 Majete Game Reserve
8 Lengwe National Park
9 Mwabvi Game Reserve
TANZANIA
ZAMBIA
MOZAMBIQUE
MOZAMBIQUE
Lake Malawi
Chitipa
Karonga
Chilumba
Chitimba
Chelinda
Rumphi
Mzuzu
Nkata Bay
Mzimba
Chintheche
Chisumulu Island
Likoma Island
Dwangwa
Nkhotakota
Lifupa
Kasungu
Malomo
Dowa
Livingstonia Beach
Salima
Mchinji
LILONGWE
Cape McLear
Monkey Bay
Mua
Dedza
Mangochi
Lake Malombe
Lake Chiuta
Ntcheu
Balaka
Liwonde
Lake Chilwa
Zomba
BLANTYRE
Limbe
Thyolo
Mulanje
Shire R.
Bangula
Nsanje
N
0 50 100 km

MALAWI

Travellers to Malawi know it as the warm heart of Africa — a reference not only to its climate, but to the friendliness of its people and beauty of the land in general. By African standards, it is a smallish country, covering 118 000 km^2 — about one-tenth the size of South Africa. It is situated in south Central Africa at the southern end of Africa's Great Rift Valley and cradles Africa's third largest lake, Lake Malawi. It is bordered by Mozambique in the south, west and east, Zambia in the west and Tanzania in the north.

The eastern half of the country is dominated by Lake Malawi, the largest expanse of water in the Rift Valley. The lake is 575 km long and 85 km wide at its widest point and, together with the country's other waterways, covers a fifth of its surface area.

In the southeastern corner, Central Africa's highest mountain, Mount Mulanje, towers 3 002 m above the surrounding plains. Further north, Michiru, the rain mountain, and Ndirande, the sleeping man mountain, are etched against the skyline of Blantyre.

North of Blantyre the Zomba Plateau provides a stunning panorama from 2 133 m above the rest of the country. On the edge of this plateau the beautiful Kuchawe Inn hangs over space, sharing the thermals with raptors and crows.

Wildlife

Malawi is justly famous for the huge diversity of fish in its lake. Between 500 and 1 000 species of fish are believed to live here — more species than any other lake in the world. In Lake Malawi National Park alone there are 350 endemic species.

However, for visitors the real attractions are the herds of elephant and buffalo, the large carnivores — lions, leopards, spotted hyenas and cheetahs — and the variety of smaller mammals and antelope.

Each reserve has its particular attractions: Lengwe National Park is known for its herds of nyala, Livingstone's antelope and buffaloes; Liwonde for its magnificent birdlife (there are lions and elephants and hippos here, too); Nyika for the greatest numbers of leopards in the country and Kasungu for its variety of large mammals, including cheetah.

The smaller mammals include monkeys, baboons, warthogs, civets, jackals, honey badgers and porcupines.

Because Malawi is so narrow, you'll be able to see big game within an hour or two by road, no matter where you are.

The wild places

Malawi has five national parks — Liwonde, Nyika, Kasungu, Lake Malawi and Lengwe — and a number of less-developed wildlife sanctuaries and nature conservation areas, some with basic camping facilities but no formal accommodation. This network of wildlife sanctuaries conserves a variety of habitats, from the undulating grasslands to tropical, riverine forests.

The lakeshore itself is flanked by rolling hills and luxuriant subtropical vegetation. This makes a perfect setting for some superb resort hotels which offer boating, sailing, snorkelling, scuba-diving, windsurfing, swimming and organised trips to nearby game reserves.

Nyika National Park

This lovely mountain sanctuary in north-eastern Malawi is the largest of the national parks, and highly popular for its scenic attractions. Carpets of wild flowers, mountain streams, waterfalls, sweeping valleys and the chance to explore the 1 800-m Nyika plateau, attract visitors from all over Southern Africa.

This is the haunt of leopards and hyenas, zebras and such antelope as eland, roan, reedbuck, red duiker and klipspringer.

Kasungu National Park

Another favoured destination in Malawi, Kusungu is about two thirds the size of Nyika, covering some 2 000 km^2.

Just a few hours' drive from Lilongwe, the park lies on Malawi's western border with Zambia. Its rolling woodland, 'dambos' or grassy plains and reed-fringed rivers are a sanctuary for several large mammals — elephants, lions, leopards and several species of antelope.

Upmarket Lifupa Wildlife Lodge commands lovely views of the Lifupa Dam and offers suites, rondavels and a self-catering tented camp.

Liwonde National Park

Much smaller than Kasungu or Nyika national parks, Liwonde is, nevertheless, one of the most talked-about parks in the country. Flanking the eastern bank of the Shire River, about an hour's drive north of Zomba, Liwonde hosts the magnificent Mvuu Wilderness Lodge, whose luxury safari tents overlook the river and surrounding floodplain, home to elephant, hippo, crocodile, lion and leopard.

Game and forest reserves

Discerning travellers will find a fascinating array of smaller sanctuaries in Malawi, such as the Vwaza Marsh Game Reserve (for elephant, buffalo and hippo), which is situated on the floodplain of the South Rukuru River north of Rumphi.

Lions, leopards, elephants, buffaloes, hippos and hyenas are found in the Nkhotakota Game Reserve 30 km west of Nkhotakota.

The major attractions of Majete Game Reserve, a sanctuary on the west bank of the Shire River, are the spectacular Kapichira Falls and the wealth of birdlife.

The lakeshore

David Livingstone called Lake Malawi the lake of stars, and visitors, too, become starry-eyed at the natural beauty of this vast, sparkling expanse of water.

Surrounded by coastal plains rising to steep escarpments, the lake stretches from the southern resorts of Nkopola Lodge and Club Makokola northwards to Tanzania.

On the way visitors will find the attractive Livingstonia Beach Hotel on the lakeshore at Salima. For campers, Cape Maclear south of Monkey Bay is one of the most tranquil and scenically beautiful places in Malawi — and far from the madding crowd.

Climate

Malawi has a tropical continental climate, with three distinct seasons: hot and dry (September–November), hot and wet (November–April) and cool and dry (May–August).

Temperatures range from freezing point (on the Nyika Plateau in winter) to 40 °C. The lakeshore areas have little rain and a mild to warm climate ranging from 21 °C daily mean in July to 26 °C in January.

When to go

If you intend visiting game parks in a two-wheel-drive saloon car, the best time to go would be between May and October. The onset of rains between December and April renders many of the dirt roads impassable (especially in the national parks).

However, the lakeshore resorts are open throughout the year, and summer is the time to take full advantage of the lovely beaches and array of watersports.

Getting around

By air Kamuzu International Airport, 23 km from Lilongwe, is serviced by South African Airways, British Airways, Air France, Air Zimbabwe, Mozambique Airlines and Air Tanzania, among others.

Air connections can be made from Lilongwe to Blantyre and Club Makokola in the south, and Mzuzu in the north.

By road Malawi has a network of well-surfaced tar and gravel roads covering 12 000 km. Although most of these are untarred, the M1 — the major highway which runs from Blantyre in the south to Mzuzu in the north — is tarred and in good condition. Many of the arterial roads leading off the M1 are untarred, as are those within most of the game reserves and national parks.

Many of Malawi's country roads are just one lane wide, and call for some skilful driving in the face of fast-approaching traffic.

The rainy season between December and March makes a large number of gravel or sandy roads impassable to two-wheel-drive cars, so take a 4x4 if you intend bundu-bashing during this time. If you're driving to the Nyika National Park, the road beyond Rumphi is untarred and you'll certainly need a four-wheel-drive to get there in the rainy season.

If you intend hiring a car, reputable car-hire firms operate in Lilongwe, Blantyre, Zomba, Limbe and Mzuzu — among them Avis, Grand Prix, Luntha, Apex and Rainbow car hire.

By coach A luxury, air-conditioned coach service, known as the Coachline, operates three times daily between the capital, Lilongwe, and Blantyre, and three times a week between Lilongwe and Mzuzu (gateway to the Nyika National Park).

The Lilongwe–Blantyre coach leaves Lilongwe Bus Station in Old Town at 07:00 every day and arrives in Blantyre at 11:10. The Blantyre–Lilongwe Coach leaves Hall's Car Hire in Blantyre at 07:00 every day.

Coach travel to less accessible parts of Malawi is run by Express and Country lines which, because of the many stops along the way, is not the fastest way to travel. But it is colourful, with its complement of squawking chickens, bleating goats, piles of luggage tied to the roof and stops to retrieve an occasional bag of maize that comes adrift from the roof.

For further details and bookings on coaches in Malawi contact Stagecoach Limited, PO Box 176, Blantyre or tel (09265) 67-1388, or (09265) 74-0111 (Lilongwe).

By water One of the highlights of any visit to Malawi is a six-day cruise on the *Ilala II* from Monkey Bay in the south to Chilumba, via the beautiful Likoma Island where you can spend a few days.

The trip takes in the magnificence of the lakeshore on both the Malawian and Mozambique sides, as well as many of the smaller islands, set like jewels in the shimmering expanse of blue.

Contact Malawi Lake Services, PO Box 15, Monkey Bay, tel (09265) 58-7311.

On safari Safari companies offer probably the best way of getting around Malawi, on escorted game walks, in a minibus or a 4x4. Although this is the more expensive option, it's safe, reliable and comfortable.

Central African Wilderness Safaris, who have been operating in the country since 1987, offer some excellent packages taking in the new Mvuu camps in the Liwonde National Park, Nyika National Park and the shoreline of Lake Malawi. Their five-night safari package, which includes two nights at Club Makokola on the shore of Lake Malawi and three nights at the Mvuu Lodge in Liwonde National Park, is recommended. For this and other tour packages see 'Safari Tours in Southern Africa', p. 361.

On foot All the reserves offer walking trails or foot safaris. For details contact The Department of National Parks and Wildlife, PO Box 30131, Capital City, Lilongwe 3, tel (09265) 72-3505.

How to get there

By air Every Friday and Sunday Air Malawi flies from Johannesburg to Lilongwe. South African Airways offers return trips to Lilongwe on Mondays and Thursdays, and to Blantyre on Saturdays.

By road The most common entry point is from Zambia via the Chipata/Mchinji border post or from South Africa via Zimbabwe and Tete in Mozambique to the Mwanza border post. The latter route, however, is not advisable on account of isolated attacks on travellers during the civil war in that country.

By coach Stagecoach runs a trip from Harare in Zimbabwe to Lilongwe, via Lusaka in Zambia. This is a 24-hour journey covering 1 300 km (see address under 'Getting around').

Entry requirements

All visitors need a valid passport to enter Malawi, but 47 countries are exempt from having a visa. It would be advisable to check with your travel agent before you leave.

Health precautions

Take prophylactics against malaria. Bilharzia is not really a problem, but mosquitoes are abundant, so be sure that you have an insect repellent.

Travel information

Malawi Department of Tourism, PO Box 402, Blantyre, tel (09265) 62-0300; The Department of National Parks and Wildlife, PO Box 30131, Capital City, Lilongwe 3, tel (09265) 72-3505; Wildlife Society of Malawi, PO Box 1429, Blantyre, tel (09265) 64-3428.

Tip for travellers

Some hitchhikers and bus travellers have found getting around the country unreliable. If you intend doing it alone, consider hiring a car.

Kasungu National Park

This park is emerging as one of Malawi's most popular wildlife sanctuaries. Situated 158 km north of Lilongwe on the Zambian border, it covers about 2 000 km^2 of gently rolling miombo woodland, interspersed with rivers and sprawling grassy plains or 'dambos'.

The park has a superb variety of game and offers first-class accommodation at Lifupa Lodge.

Wildlife Elephants are the big drawcard at Kasungu, but there's no shortage of other mammals. The abundance of antelope ensures the presence of most of the large predators — lions, wild dogs, spotted hyenas, cheetahs and black-backed jackals. And if you follow the herds of buffalo, hartebeest and impala which graze in the dambos adjoining the park's rivers, chances are you'll see most of these carnivores.

Kasungu is bisected by several rivers, whose lush, grassy shores and floodplains attract such water-loving antelope as puku, waterbuck and reedbuck. Other less frequently seen antelope include kudu, sable and roan antelope, klipspringer and duiker.

The best time to see these animals is towards the end of the dry season (August–November) when water sources dry up, and the game heads for isolated waterholes.

Family ties of the clan-killers

A pack of wild dogs, such as those found at Kasungu, number between 10 and 15 animals — an affectionate, tightly knit clan that survives through teamwork and co-operation.

Adult wild dogs returning to their lair from the hunt, greet their youngsters with excited calls and body postures.

Their tubby, short-legged offspring bound out from the den with short, sharp squeals of delight to greet the returning hunters, who affectionately lick and nibble the mouths of their pups.

Then, in a spontaneous gesture that highlights the strong dependence of pups on their parents, the whining youngsters edge their muzzles between the teeth of their parents: a classic, uncomplicated request for food.

The adults comply, regurgitating raw meat from their stomachs for the pups to feed on. Afterwards, when the pups have eaten their fill, they may join their resting mother to suckle, or take part in energetic games outside the lair.

Unlike the offspring of lions, hungry wild dog pups will be allowed to feast on a kill even before the adults that were involved — yet another example of the astonishing family bonds that exist.

Birds There are more than 200 species, including an abundance of waterbirds such as the wattled crane and saddlebilled stork, at Lifupa Dam, while elsewhere, among the miombo woodland, eagles and vultures are plentiful.

Other species found in the park include yellowbilled hornbill, redwinged warbler and giant eagle owl.

Where to stay Set among 22 000 ha of pristine wilderness, Lifupa Lodge offers four luxury suites overlooking the Lifupa Dam, as well as 16 rondavels with *en suite* showers and toilets.

The lodge has a superb restaurant, lounge and a charming bar at which you may drink sundowners while watching hippos in the dam below.

There's also a lovely swimming pool. If you like, there is a car to hire, and petrol is also available.

Within walking distance of the lodge is a 24-bedded, self-catering tented camp. The tents are serviced by a central ablution block and kitchen, which may be used by residents staying in the rondavels.

If you don't wish to overnight at the Kasungu National Park, you may overnight at the Kasungu Inn Motel at Kasungu.

Kasungu National Park at a glance

Locality:	Central Malawi, 55 km west of Kasungu.
Climate:	Tropical continental climate, with warm to hot, humid summers and cool, dry winters. The rainy season is between December and March.
Game drives:	280-km network of game-viewing drives.
Hides and waterholes:	Lifupa Lodge Restaurant overlooks Lifupa Dam.
Trails:	Several trails, including 10-km guided bush hike.
Other attractions:	Iron-Age smelting kiln on banks of Dwangwa River, hippo-watching from restaurant.
Amenities:	Swimming pool at Lifupa Lodge, restaurant, cars for hire.
Accommodation:	**Lifupa Lodge**: 12 thatched rondavels; campsite with seven fully equipped two- and three-bedded tents.
Booking address:	The Department of Tourism, PO Box 402, Blantyre, tel (09265) 62-0300.
When to go:	Game-viewing is best in the dry season between July and November when large numbers of game congregate at waterholes.
What to take with you:	Summer: khaki shorts and shirts, sunhat, binoculars, torch, field guides, camera. Winter: jersey or long-sleeved shirts and trousers.
How to get there:	From Lilongwe drive 127 km north to Kasungu. From Kasungu take the D187 west to the park entrance, 38 km away. Lifupa Lodge is another 14 km on. There is a private airstrip at Kasungu, 4 km from the lodge.
Nearest doctor:	Kasungu.
Nearest petrol:	Lifupa Lodge, inside the park.
Open:	The park is closed between January and March.
Special precautions:	Antimalaria precautions must be taken. Don't leave your car during game drives through the park. Beware of hippos in the vicinity of the campsite alongside Lifupa Dam.

Game drives and trails A 280-km network of untarred roads in reasonable condition takes visitors to vantage points throughout the park, but some of these may be impassable to two-wheel-drive vehicles during the rainy season (November–April).

Lifupa Lodge offers escorted wilderness trails in 4x4 vehicles, as well as daytime game walks through the bush, visits to some fascinating archaeological sites and sundowner cruises. The warden will tell you about the 10-km walking trail and animals you may expect to see.

Liwonde National Park

The raucous grunts of hippos filter up from the languorous waters of the Shire River as they slide past the thatched hide of the Mvuu Wilderness Lodge. On either side of the river, amid the canopy of apple-ring thorn trees, red mahogany and palm trees, a choral symphony of bird-song rises to greet the day.

On the distant floodplain, elephants trundle in stately procession through the mud, trunks swaying and heads rocking. Their early morning walk displaces a flock of pygmy geese, and they rise, wings flapping above the waterline.

For visitors to the Liwonde National Park, south of Lake Malawi, witnessing the arrival of the new day from the comfort of a game-viewing hide is a very special experience.

The park lies 64 km north of Zomba and covers 580 000 ha of mopane woodland, papyrus-fringed river, open grassy floodplain and riverine forests punctuated by towering palm trees. It was established in 1973, 11 years after Malawi's independence, with the intention of restoring the large herds of animals (black rhino, buffalo, Burchell's zebra, Lichtenstein's hartebeest and roan antelope) that had all but been destroyed by the hunter's bullet in the vicinity of the Shire River.

Wildlife There's no shortage of game at Liwonde. On the floodplain or at any one of the park's waterholes you may watch elephants lumbering down for an early morning mudbath, or see lions reclining in the shade of mopane trees or long grass. Other cats include leopard and serval.

The elephants move to the pasture-rich floodplains of the Shire River during the dry season, and return to the evergreen forests of the Mangochi Hills in the wet season.

Other mammals range from kudu, sable, waterbuck, black rhinos and buffaloes to yellow baboons (an East African subspecies of the chacma), hippos, warthogs and impala.

After initial setbacks, the Malawi Parks Department worked together with the South African National Parks Board and the Kruger National Park at restructuring the park and restocking it with game.

Lions and other animals were brought in from the Kruger National Park, new boundaries for the park were defined, work began at two new camps and, during the 1980s, there was a dramatic increase in the game populations of the park — particularly among hippos, crocodiles, warthogs and impala.

Tip for travellers

The camp at Lifupa Dam is visited by an elephant called Charlie. Don't feed the elephant, and keep any fruit stowed away while at the campsite.

More recently, black rhinos have been reintroduced in the area. Today Liwonde is poised to become one of the premier African game parks.

Birds The birds of Liwonde, probably more than anything else, account for its growing popularity as one of the great game parks of Africa. Recently just over 400 of Malawi's 645 species were counted here, many of them rarely seen in other Southern African reserves.

From your lodge at the water's edge you may catch a glimpse of Lilian's lovebird or hear the noisy flight of Pel's fishing owl flushed from its daytime refuge in the trees.

Other birds you may see along the palm-fringed banks of the Shire are openbilled storks, longtoed plovers, pygmy geese, pelicans and herons, to name a few.

Tip for travellers

Access roads to the park are closed during the rainy season (late November–April), although you can get to the camps by boat from Liwonde Barrage.

Liwonde National Park at a glance

Locality:	On the eastern plain of the Upper Shire River Valley, north of Blantyre, Malawi.
Climate:	Hot to very hot summers, with rain between December and April; winters mild to cool, but not cold.
Number of camps:	Two. Mvuu Wilderness Lodge; Mvuu Camp.
Game drives:	There are 97 km of game drives.
Hides and waterholes:	Chisuse and Kalunga waterholes.
Trails:	Guided walks led by game scouts.
Other attractions:	Birdwatching, boating.
Amenities:	Bar, restaurant and self-catering facilities.
Accommodation:	**Mvuu Lodge**: Five luxury, twin-bedded tents. **Chiguni Guesthouse** near park entrance (5 double rooms, diningroom, kitchen, bar).
Booking address:	Wilderness Safaris, PO Box 78573, Sandton 2146, tel (011) 883-0747.
When to go:	August–October. Access roads are closed during the rainy season (late November–April).
What to take with you:	For Mvuu Camp bring your own cutlery, crockery and bedding; binoculars, camera.
How to get there:	Drive north from Blantyre for 120 km, turn right and drive another 6 km to the park's entrance.
Nearest doctor:	Liwonde, 10 km from park's southern entrance.
Nearest petrol:	Liwonde, 10 km from park's southern entrance.
Open:	Sunrise to sunset throughout the year.
Special precautions:	Take antimalaria precautions prior to departure. When hiking, keep an eye open for snakes and crocodiles. Avoid hippos in the Shire.

Birds of the evergreen forests include such species as Hildebrand's francolin, Whyte's barbet, Bertram's weaver, and bartailed trogon.

Where to stay All the creature comforts of a modern game park can be experienced at Mvuu Wilderness Lodge and Camp. Mvuu Lodge, 28 km north of Chiunguni, has been built on the eastern banks of the Shire, under a grove of baobabs, bird plums and umbrella-thorns.

The main complex consists of a lovely restaurant, bar and reception area. Nearby five luxury, twin-bedded tents overlook a tranquil lagoon. Each tented room has two queen-size beds, bathroom with flush toilets and solar-powered showers, and mosquito netting.

Game drives and trails There's a 97-km network of gravel roads through the park, giving you access to picnic sites and waterholes.

The camp and lodge offer morning, afternoon and evening game drives in open 4x4 vehicles; gamewatching trails (accompanied by an armed scout) are optional daily, and include visits to the Chisuse and Kalunga waterholes. There are some lovely nature walks along the banks of the Shire. You may also hire a 15-seater boat, which affords excellent game viewing and birdwatching opportunities.

Nyika National Park

Tucked into the northwestern corner of Malawi, Nyika is the largest of Malawi's national parks, covering 3 000 km² on the Nyika Plateau. This fairytale region of undulating grasslands, tinkling mountain streams and river valleys, fringed by beautiful forests, is a perfect combination of scenic beauty and teeming wildlife.

As you make the ascent to the rim of the plateau, 1 800 m above sea-level, the road twists and turns between great canopies of wild flowers and sentinels of rock that plummet to the valley floor. To the west, Nyika's peaks command a view of the plains of Zambia stretching endlessly to the horizon.

Because of the park's altitude — 90 per cent of its area is above 1 800 m, the air in winter is crisp and bracing and the views are probably better than anywhere else in Malawi.

Nyika means wilderness, but this is not the typical wilderness of Africa — in fact, there is a European flavour to the swathes of wild gladioli, satyrium and alpine flowers that carpet the countryside, and to the emerald hills that carry ribbons of white water to the valleys below. The uplands are peppered by flowering proteas, orchids and heathers, which are at their best between December and March.

Four large rivers plunge from their source on top of the plateau to the valley floor in a succession of cascades that provide year-round nourishment to the rich riverine vegetation.

Wildlife The largest population of leopards in the country stalks the mountains in the company of klipspringers and dassies (rock hyraxes), while the grasslands are home to herds of eland and hartebeest.

These antelope are best seen during the wet season, from November to May, grazing on the grasslands of the plateau.

Other species regularly spotted are red duiker, blue duiker, reedbuck, warthog and zebra. In the forests you'll find bushbuck, blue monkeys and porcupines.

As the sun sets over Nyika, night creatures emerge from their daytime lairs, among them spotted hyenas, aardvarks, honey badgers, civets, serval and jackals.

Birdlife The variety of habitats ensures an abundant birdlife in Nyika, ranging from grassland species such as redwinged francolin, Denham's bustard and wattled crane, to birds of the evergreen forest, such as Sharpe's akalat, bartailed trogon, cinnamon dove, and oliveflanked and starred robin.

The proteas and orchids are alive with sunbirds — the greater doublecollared sunbird and the redtufted sunbird, in particular — while streaky seedeaters and churring cisticolas inhabit stands of bracken briar.

Walks and trails Nyika is ideally suited to long walks and drives: its elevation guarantees excellent viewing points, many of which are within walking or driving distance of the main camp, Chelinda.

Among these are Domwe Viewpoint on the western fringes of the plateau, which offers panoramic views across Zambia; Kasaramba Viewpoint, and the highest point in the park, Nganda Hill (2 607 m). Jalawe Hill, a 45-minute drive from Chelinda, is another outstanding point from which to photograph the valleys and mountains of Nyika.

West of Chelinda the North Rukuru River cascades over precipices and rocky valleys to reach the Chisanga Falls near the Zambian border. A hike to the falls (you may drive part of the way) from Chelinda is highly recommended.

More ambitious hikes — ranging from one to five days — are available, and give hikers the chance to soak up the natural beauty and sleep under the stars. Group trails are led by a game ranger and porters may be hired if required.

The park will take you to the beginning of the hike and fetch you from the end point, or arrange to bring your own vehicles to these points.

When hiking, it is essential that you get a comprehensive map of the park and study your route carefully before you set out, so that you can plan to arrive at your destination before dark. You will also need a compass and binoculars. The going in some places is tough, and may take longer than you expect.

Take your own camping gear, cooking utensils, gas stove and sleeping bag.

For more information on trails and reservations contact The Department of

Nature's clean-up crew

Oxpeckers and cattle egrets — the birds you'll invariably see riding piggy-back on black rhino and buffaloes as they browse or graze in the grasslands — have a unique relationship with their hosts.

Oxpeckers, in particular, spend most of their lives on the backs of their hosts in Liwonde National Park, gorging on the blood of bloated ticks and flies.

They are incredibly efficient cleaners, not only ridding their hosts of parasites, but also cleaning up abscesses or festering sores on the hide. They sleep on the buffalo or rhino's back, and, in the breeding season, even mate on it.

White egrets and oxpeckers perform another vital service for their mammalian hosts: they warn of impending danger, by flying up suddenly with flapping wings if they detect the presence of an intruder.

National Parks and Wildlife, PO Box 30131, Capital City, Lilongwe 3, tel (09265) 72-3505 or 72-3566.

Where to stay Chelinda Camp, 56 km north of the park's entrance, offers four self-contained chalets, each with two double bedrooms, bathrooms and kitchen. There is also a separate block of six double bedrooms which is serviced by a housekeeper, and a campsite.

A four-bedded cabin in the Juniper Forest offers overnight accommodation to hikers, but they must supply bedding, crockery and cutlery.

Bring your own provisions, although a small shop provides basic, non-perishable items, including paraffin and firewood.

Nyika National Park at a glance

Locality:	Northwestern Malawi, between the Zambian border and Lake Malawi.
Climate:	Mild summers, with temperatures rarely higher than 22 °C; winters cool to cold with frost. Rain falls between February and March.
Number of camps:	One, Chelinda.
Game drives:	Variety of drives to viewpoints and waterfalls.
Trails:	Vary from one hour to five days.
Other attractions:	Juniper Forest, wildflowers.
Accommodation:	**Chelinda Camp** has four self-contained chalets, six double bedrooms and a campsite; four-bedded cabin in the **Juniper Forest**.
Booking address:	The Department of Tourism, PO Box 402, Blantyre, tel (09265) 62-0300.
When to go:	The best time for game-viewing and walking through the park is between May and November; birding is at its best from November to January; spring and summer (November–January) witness an explosion of flowers and orchids.
What to take with you:	Dress warmly in winter, and take a jersey along in summer. Be well equipped with basic provisions (and sleeping bags, camping gear, cutlery and crockery, if you intend hiking). Binoculars, compass, torch, gas stove, field guides, medical kit.
How to get there:	There are two entrance gates: at Kaperekezi, close to the Zambian border and at Thazima, the main entrance in the south. Regular flights from Lilongwe land at Mzuzu, 135 km south of Thazima. Or you may drive north from Lilongwe to Thazima, via Kasungu, Mzuzu and Rumphi. Access to Kaperekezi is from Chipita in the northwest. Both gates close at 16:00, and once through them it's 90 minutes by road to Chelinda Camp.
Nearest doctor:	Mzuzu, 189 km south of Chelinda Camp.
Nearest petrol:	Rumphi, 121 km south of Chelinda Camp.
Open:	Throughout the year 08:00–14:00.
Special precautions:	Antimalaria precautions must be taken.

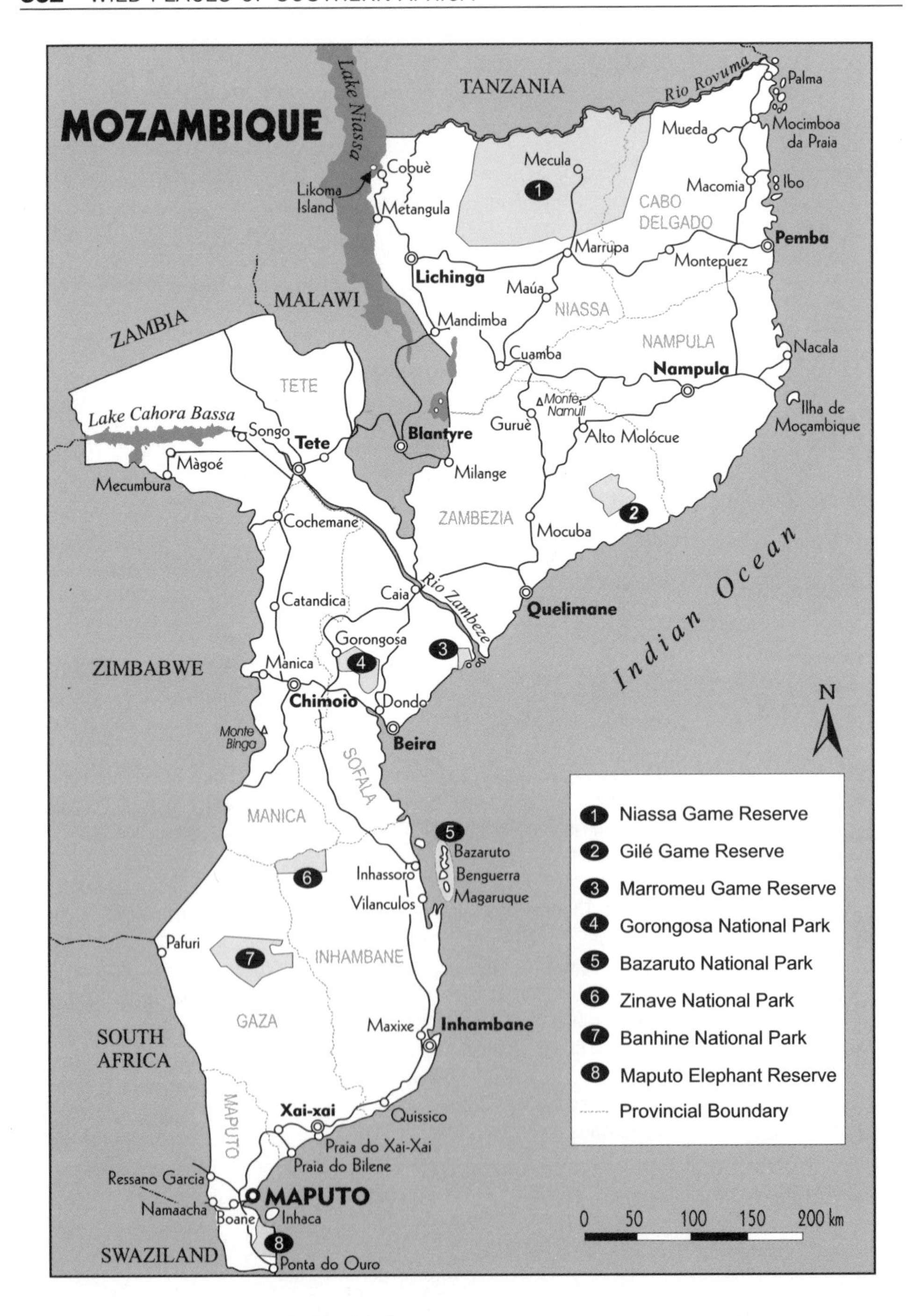

MOZAMBIQUE
TANZANIA
Lake Niassa
Rio Rovuma
Palma
Mocimboa da Praia
Mueda
Mecula
Cobuè
Likoma Island
Metangula
Macomia
Ibo
CABO DELGADO
Pemba
Marrupa
Montepuez
Lichinga
Maúa
NIASSA
MALAWI
ZAMBIA
Mandimba
NAMPULA
Nacala
Cuamba
Nampula
TETE
Monte Namuli
Ilha de Moçambique
Lake Cahora Bassa
Songo
Tete
Blantyre
Guruè
Alto Molócue
Màgoé
Mecumbura
Milange
ZAMBEZIA
Cochemane
Mocuba
Indian Ocean
Rio Zambeze
Caia
Catandica
Quelimane
Gorongosa
ZIMBABWE
Manica
Chimoio
Dondo
Beira
Monte Binga
N
SOFALA
MANICA
Bazaruto
Inhassoro
Benguerra
Vilanculos
Magaruque
Pafuri
INHAMBANE
GAZA
Maxixe
Inhambane
SOUTH AFRICA
MAPUTO
Xai-xai
Quissico
Praia do Xai-Xai
Praia do Bilene
Ressano Garcia
MAPUTO
Namaacha
Boane
Inhaca
SWAZILAND
Ponta do Ouro
1 Niassa Game Reserve
2 Gilé Game Reserve
3 Marromeu Game Reserve
4 Gorongosa National Park
5 Bazaruto National Park
6 Zinave National Park
7 Banhine National Park
8 Maputo Elephant Reserve
Provincial Boundary
0 50 100 150 200 km

MOZAMBIQUE

Mozambique, the thirty-third largest country in the world, is roughly two-thirds the size of South Africa — a sprawling land of forest, mountains, tidal estuaries and palm-fringed shores. The coastline stretches 24 700 km from its northern border with Tanzania to Ponta do Ouro in the south and, together with its islands, is the mainstay of the tourism industry. Anglers, divers, birders and families looking for an affordable, relaxing holiday at the sea find Mozambique's virgin beaches, aquamarine waters and long, unexplored stretches of coast irresistible.

The country is bordered by the Indian Ocean in the east, South Africa and Swaziland in the south, Tanzania in the north, Zimbabwe in the west and Malawi and Zambia in the northwest.

For 16 long years Mozambique's 10 provinces were ravaged by a devastating civil war that had a profound effect on wildlife and the environment and left the country's tourism industry in tatters. But since the cessation of hostilities in 1992, the government has slowly begun putting the pieces back together again, and there's no doubt Mozambique is rapidly emerging as a tantalising holiday destination. New lodges and hotels are springing up, especially in southern Mozambique, and many are on a par with other upmarket resorts in Southern Africa.

Wildlife

Like the other countries featured in this book Mozambique was once a crucible for vast populations of game — herds of elephant, buffalo, zebra, rhino and antelope of every imaginable species, as well as lion, cheetah, primates, crocodile and hippo. But during and immediately after the civil war wholesale poaching and slaughtering decimated the wildlife population. In Gorogonsa National Park, for instance, 90 per cent of the original wildlife is gone. Before the war there were 3 000 elephants; now there are fewer than 200 and the 6 000 hippos have dwindled to 200. However, the government, assisted by the World Conservation Union, is trying to rehabilitate the park to its former resources.

In the south, the South African Endangered Wildlife Trust is assisting the Mozambique Government to halt poaching in the Maputo Elephant Reserve and restock it, after it, too, lost most of its wildlife to poachers. Today there are some 150 elephants in the reserve.

Although the animal populations have suffered huge losses, birdlife — both marine and terrestrial species — has withstood the ravages of the war, and birders will be rewarded with a rich diversity in all parts of the country. The variety of habitats, ranging from grassland and forest to riverine bush, estuaries, marshland, mountain and mangrove swamp, protect a diverse and colourful avian population, including such rare species as bluethroated sunbirds, Mozambique batis, chestnut-fronted helmetshrike, whitebreasted alethe and Böhm's bee-eater.

For those interested in diving and snorkelling, Mozambique's marine treasures compensate for its lack of terrestrial mammals. Coral reefs along this coastline of clear, warm water are among the richest in the world, and are home to a colourful array of tropical fish. In the channels and other deeper waters gamefish abound — from blackstriped and blue marlin to sailfish, kingfish, yellowfin tunny, bonita, barracuda, dorado and king mackerel. In these seas of plenty cruise a large variety of sharks, from the huge, gentle whale shark to voracious species such as Zambezi, tiger and hammerhead sharks.

Marine mammals also ply these fish-rich waters, including families of the rare dugong, at least five species of dolphin and humpback whales.

Such marine delights as loggerhead and leatherback turtles, moray eels, manta rays and giant potato bass consistently delight divers exploring the coral gardens.

In an attempt to protect the plundering of marine species and their habitats, most lodges apply a tag-and-release principle to gamefish caught, and strict laws are in force to protect the fragile coral reefs.

The wild places

The wild places of Mozambique in this book have been confined to the coastal region, largely because they're more accessible than the inland regions, are generally landmine-free and offer accommodation and amenities on a par with some of the best lodges elsewhere in Southern Africa. These places are accessible by road from South Africa and Zimbabwe — most by two-wheel-drive — but are suitably off the beaten track to guarantee a 'wild' ambience in a delightful coastal environment.

There are four national parks in Mozambique — Gorongosa in Sofala, Zinave in Inhambane, the Bazaruto Archipelago, and Banhine in Gaza. Gorongosa has basic accommodation facilities and there are half a dozen or so private lodges in the Bazaruto Archipelago National Park. Mozambique has four nature reserves: the Maputo Elephant Reserve, which has one bush camp for overnight visitors, Marromeu in Sofala, Niassa in Niassa Province and Gill in Zambezia.

Where to stay

The destinations featured in this chapter all offer comfortable accommodation, access to beautiful beaches and amenities that will ensure a relaxing and memorable stay. They are fairly easily accessible from South Africa. They include: Ponta do Oro, its neighbour, Ponta Malongane, Barra Lodge, Vilanculos Beach Lodge, Marlin Lodge, Bazaruto Island Lodge, Benguerrua Island Lodge, Morrungulo Lodge, Indigo Bay Lodge, Zongoene Lodge on the Limpopo River and Inhaca Island.

If you're in transit from South Africa to one of the lodges along the coast, consider stopping over for the night in Maputo. Two top hotels are the Polana (five star) and the Cardoso (four star), both of which have all the amenities of top-class international hotels. Contact the Polana at Avenida Julius Nyere 1380, Maputo, tel (09258-1) 49-1001; or the Cardoso at Avenida

Maritires De Mueda 707, Maputo, tel (09258-1) 49-1071. Alternatively try the Hotel Terminus, which is five minutes away from the city centre. This is a clean three-star hotel with two bars, restaurant, air-conditioning and swimming pool. The hotel is at Rua Orlando Francisco Magumbue 587, tel (09258-1) 49-1333.

A cheaper option is to spend the night at Marracuene Camping Park 39 km north of Maputo, just 4 km from Marracuene village, which offers chalets accommodating seven people. The two-bedroomed chalets also have a diningroom, kitchenette and bathroom. There are also camping sites here.

Climate

Mozambique has a tropical to subtropical climate, with hot, wet summers and warm, drier winters. Although the country averages 1 000 mm a year, rainfall in the summer can be unpredictable, and flash floods are not uncommon between November and March. In 1999, more than 1 000 mm of rain fell in parts of the Bazaruto Archipelago in one week. Heavy rain may affect the accessibility of some of the lodges, and it would be wise to check with your chosen destination whether the road is navigable with a two-wheel-drive car if you're travelling in one.

When to go

The winter months between April and September are the best time to visit Mozambique. The summer months between November and March are very hot, rainy at times and tend to have more mosquitos.

How to get there

By road From South Africa you can get to Maputo quite easily from Johannesburg via Nelspruit and Komatipoort. The tar road between Komatipoort and Maputo is fairly narrow, but in reasonably good condition. If you want to get to Ponta do Ouro or Ponta Malongane from Durban, take the N2 to Mkuze. A tar road north of Mkuze leads to KwaNgwanase. From there a dirt road leads to the border 18 km to the north (the border closes at 17:00). About 4 km further on take a right turn at the airstrip and travel 9 km until you reach an intersection with signs indicating Ponta do Ouro and Ponta Malongane.

By train Spoornet has three trains leaving Johannesburg for Maputo on Tuesdays, Thursdays and Sundays at 16:45. There is also a service between Durban and Maputo departing on Tuesdays and Thursdays.

By air South African Airways, LAM (Linhas Aeras de Moçambique) and Air Portugal run direct flights to Maputo. Metavia runs charters to Vilankulo Airport and some of the private lodges have their own charters.

Getting around

Mozambique's principal highway is the north-south EN1 from Maputo to Beira, a narrow tarred road in fairly good condition, which will give you access to all the coastal lodges and resorts.

There is a regular bus service between Maputo and Beira run by Transportes Virginia and Transportes Oliveiras. Several smaller bus companies operate between coastal towns and resorts.

In Maputo you can hire a car, but for getting around town or to the airport it is probably best to use a taxi — the road system can be confusing.

Landmines

Visitors should be aware that there are more than 400 000 undetonated landmines in Mozambique, and although most of the roads and all the resort areas have been cleared, it is strongly recommended you do not wander into the bush anywhere, unless you know it is a 'safe' area.

Entry requirements

All foreigners visiting Mozambique need a visa which should be applied for a week before your trip. You can pay a little more and get an emergency visa in one day. Visas can be arranged through the Mozambique Consul at the following addresses: Cape Town: 45 Castle Street, Cape Town 8001, tel (021) 26-2944; Durban: 5th Floor, 320 West Street, Durban 4001, tel (031) 304-0200; Johannesburg: 13th Floor, Bosman Building, 99 Eloff Street, Johannesburg 2001, tel (011) 336-1819; Pretoria: 199 Beckett Street, Arcadia 0083, tel (012) 343-0957. If you want to spare yourself the hassle of standing in queues, contact Mozambique Connection Visa Services in Johannesburg, tel (011) 626-2650, to organise your visa for you.

Health precautions

Malaria is rife in Mozambique, particularly chloroquine and pyrimethamine-resitant strains, so vistors must take the necessary precautions. Take as many bottles of mineral water as you can, and don't drink from public water points. Be sure to take a comprehensive first-aid kit (see p. 13).

Travel tips

It is vital to take along your vehicle registration papers if you intend driving in Mozambique. You will also need third-party insurance, which is compulsory there. You can take out third-party insurance at the border posts. It is essential to stick to the speed limit, and to slow down to 50 km/h and sometimes 30 km/h in the villages — there are radar speed traps in the least expected places. Be sure to have the driving licence of the country where you reside — you can be jailed if you are caught driving without it. If you need to stop alongside the road to spend a penny, don't walk off the road into the bush. There are still many undetonated landmines off the main roads.

Border post hours vary according to the time of the year. Usually they are open between 07:00 and 17:00 daily. Consult your closest Mozambican Consulate for more information.

Exchange rates and currency

The metical is the standard unit of currency and its value fluctuates with the strength of the US dollar, as does the rand. Acceptable currencies in Mozambique are South African rands, US dollars and British pounds. These are accepted in cash and travellers' cheques. Visa and Mastercard are also accepted.

Petrol and diesel

Petrol and diesel are available in most towns and engine oil is available at most fuel stations. The price increases as one travels further north of Maputo.

Barra Lodge

A sandy track through a grove of ilala palms brings you to this charmingly secluded lodge on the tip of the Inhambane Peninsula, 485 km north of Maputo. The lodge is about 30 minutes' drive from the town of Inhambane, the capital of Inhambane Province. Known by locals as the 'jewel of the coast' Inhambane is one of the oldest settlements in Africa, and lies in a region that is regarded as one of the most scenic and peaceful in Mozambique.

At Barra Lodge tidy, thatched, two-bed casitas open onto sand and the crashing surf. There's a homely, snug atmosphere about the lodge with its beach bar metres from the sea and its restaurant, lounge and other pub nestling under the coconut trees nearby.

The chalets have *en suite* showers, toilets and mosquito nets. In addition, there are luxury self-catering cottages, each with six comfortable single beds, showers with hot and cold water, a fridge, two-plate stove, bed-linen, cutlery and crockery. The cottages each have their own lounge, diningroom and patio. The cottages and casitas are serviced daily.

The beach bar is the place for sipping cocktails as the sun goes down, listening to fishermen's yarns or playing pub games.

Angling The lodge has its own angling centre and offers skiboat charters daily, weather permitting. Deep-sea angling yields a rich harvest — kingfish, barracuda, eastern little tuna, bonita, dorado and a variety of sailfish. Fishing from the

Barra Lodge at a glance

Locality:	In Inhambane Province, 485 km north of Maputo.
Climate:	Mozambique has a subtropical climate, with hot wet summers and warm dry winters.
Trails:	Walking trails track the adjoining mangrove swamps, and there is a lovely walk to the lighthouse west of Barra Lodge.
Other attractions:	Diving, angling, visits to Inhambane, quad-bike rides and dhow trips.
Amenities:	Restaurant, two bars.
Accommodation:	Two-bed casitas, luxury six-bed self-catering cottages, campsite.
Booking address:	Barra Lodge Bookings, PO Box 6921, Halfway House 1685, tel (011) 314-3355.
When to go:	Throughout the year, but October to March can be hot, humid and very wet.
What to take with you:	Light clothing, such as shorts and T-shirts, mask, snorkel, flippers, anti-mosquito sprays and ointments, bottled water, torch, walking shoes, sunscreen, camera, film, binoculars and fishing gear (can also be hired).
How to get there:	Take the EN1 north of Maputo for 485 km. Turn right at the signpost for Inhambane town which is 33 km away. In Inhambane turn right into the Avenida Independencia and follow the road until you come to a half-circle. Turn right here and follow the road until you see a signpost indicating Tofo, Coconut Bay and Ponta Barra. Barra Lodge is 25 km from this point. The last 7 km are very sandy and if you drive a two-wheel-drive vehicle there is a parking area where you can leave your car. The lodge will pick you up from this parking area.
Nearest petrol:	Inhambane.
Nearest doctor:	Inhambane.
Open:	Throughout the year.
Special precautions:	Antimalaria precautions must be taken — consult a doctor prior to your visit to the area.

shore, especially in front of the lighthouse, west of Barra Lodge, is excellent.

Diving The lodge has its own dive shop which offers beginner's resort, open water 1 and advanced courses in diving, followed by trips to some beautiful coral reefs, ranging in depth from 12 to 30 metres. A popular dive site in about 12 metres of water is Mike's Cupboard. Many of the reefs are accessible from the shore and you can swim out to them if you're moderately fit. Manta rays, turtles, whale sharks and an enormous variety of reef fish are often seen, and if you're lucky you may spot a family of dugongs gliding through the depths.

Other attractions Barra is geared to accommodate a variety of sea-related activities. A 12-metre, live-aboard catamaran offers day trips and snorkelling adventures along the coral reefs and a picnic at a secluded beach. Other activities include dhow trips across Inhambane Bay and excursions to the market, museums, cathedrals and colonial houses of Inhambane. Special trails around the mangrove swamps will introduce you to a huge array of crustaceans, flocks of flamingoes, local fish traps and beautiful sunsets.

To book contact Barra Lodge Bookings, PO Box 6921, Halfway House 1685, tel (011) 314-3355.

Zavora Lodge This lovely lodge lies 80 km south of Inhambane, on the edge of a secluded bay which promises excellent diving and fishing. If you're driving from Maputo, turn right at the signpost Praia da Zavora, 196 km north of Xai-Xai. A half-hour drive will take you to the rustic lodge which offers six- and eight-bed beach houses, four- and six-bed bungalows and attractive camping sites.

There is hot and cold water, flush toilets and, for campers, 220v power points for deep freezers and ice. The bungalows and beach houses are fully equipped and serviced and meals are served at the bar under ilala palms. The snorkelling and fishing are great all year round. To book contact (013) 706-4926 and ask for Thalia.

Barra Reef This is another idyllic spot at the water's edge, 20 km from Inhambane, which offers safe swimming, snorkelling and wreck dives. There are two- and four-bed lodges and a camping site. To book contact (011) 803-3356.

BAZARUTO ARCHIPELAGO

The Bazaruto Archipelago, a necklace of five stunningly beautiful islands and peninsulas of sand off the mainland in southern Mozambique, about 750 km north of Maputo, is probably one of the finest seaside holiday destinations in Southern Africa.

Comparable to Australia's Great Barrier Reef, it offers virgin beaches, azure seas, palm-fringed shores and a peace and tranquillity you'll never forget. Here, the pansy-shelled sand is so clean it squeaks under your feet, and the air so clear you can see for miles.

The reefs, virtually unexplored for the duration of the civil war, are home to plate, branching, soft and hard corals. Around these corals and in the deeper channels cruise more than 600 species of fish and marine mammal. Among these are scores of species of gamefish, humpback whales, dolphins, leatherback, loggerhead, green and hawksbill turtles, moray eels and dugongs.

The archipelago was declared a national park in 1971 and its principal islands are Bazaruto, Margaruque, Benguerra and Santa Carolina (Paradise Island).

Although there are not many animals on the islands, there are more than 170 species of bird, many of them waterbirds such as herons, storks, petrels and whimbrels attracted to the nutrient-rich shores of the islands. Thousands of Palaearctic and inter-African migrants visit the archipelago every year, among which are sandwich, roseate and lesser-crested terns, flamingoes, sandpipers, crab plovers, swallows, shrikes, cuckoos, robins and flycatchers.

There is also a host of endemic butterflies and crocodiles in the freshwater lakes of the islands. Mammals seen occasionally include red duiker, suni, samango monkeys and red squirrels.

Bazaruto Island

Bazaruto, the largest island in the archipelago, is 35 km long and 7 km wide and offers accommodation at the delightful Bazaruto Lodge.

Bazaruto Lodge Rustic A-frame chalets accommodating 32 people nestle among forested dunes at the northern tip of Bazaruto Island, a tranquil and soothing retreat for those who need a break from the rat-race. The main lodge, with its spacious thatched lounge and colonial-Portuguese atmosphere, overlooks a shimmering lagoon and the ochre cliffs of mainland Mozambique in the distance. There is a swimming pool, cosy bar and plenty to do on the island, from angling and diving to snorkelling and sunbathing.

Wildlife Apart from suni, red duiker and samango moneys, there aren't many mammals on Bazaruto Island, but the 170 species of bird, ranging from kingfishers and cormorants to Narina trogons and bee-eaters, provide excellent birdwatching opportunities. Because the Bazaruto Archipelago is a national park, efforts are made to conserve the existing populations of fish by following a policy of tag-and-release. Great care is also taken to protect the fragile coral gardens of the archipelago.

Angling The lodge is an angler's paradise and fishermen have four new 6,8-metre-long Cobra Cat ski-boats available for deep-sea angling trips. The archipelago's waters are renowned for catches of blue, black and striped marlin — averaging 350 kg — and for record strikes of sailfish and tropical species such as giant kingfish, wahoo, king mackerel, bonito and dorado. Among the superb fishing spots are Sailfish Bay and Mush's Hole.

Saltwater fly-fishing off the island is also very popular and attracts many overseas enthusiasts. October to March are the best months for marlin, with June to September being the best for sailfish. Shore angling from Bazaruto Island is superb, with frequent catches of ignoblis kingfish, king mackerel, queenfish, jobfish and bonito.

Diving A resident diving instructor will kit you out with tanks and gear and take you for dives ranging between 12 metres and 30 metres. There are some 37 km of coral reefs around Bazaruto. One of the most popular diving spots is Lighthouse Point, a dive in 8 to 12 metres of water, where you will see barracuda, king mackerel, jobfish, rainbow runner and about five species of kingfish. You can also spot turtles and blacktipped or blacktailed reef sharks. Other dive spots are Greek Temple, 1 km out to sea, known for its giant brindle bass and beautiful corals, 12 Mile Reef, Whale Rock, Gengarema Point,

Manta Reef, Rainbow Runner Dive and Two Mile Reef off Benguerra Island.

Walking trails Mangrove swamps, stretches of bone-bleached sand, turtle nesting sites and freshwater lakes are at your beck and call on Bazaruto's magical walking trails. If you stroll along the beach take a mask and snorkel along — you'll find coral gardens and schools of tropical fish within swimming distance of the shore. Include the 100-year-old Bazaruto Island Lighthouse (*Farol do Bazaruto*) on your walking itinerary.

To book or enquire about Bazaruto Lodge, contact Mozambique Island Tours in Johannesburg, tel (011) 447-3528.

Benguerra Island

This attractive island 14 km off the mainland at Vilanculos is 11 km long and 5 km wide, and hosts two upmarket lodges, Marlin Lodge and Benguerra Island Lodge. There are no shops, tarred roads, blaring hooters and bustling crowds on Benguerra Island — instead there is a feeling of gentle serendipity that surrounds you, from the moment the sun peeps over the eastern horizon until the canvas of stars spreads across the cloudless skies at night.

Marlin Lodge Built in September 1997, this attractive lodge set on the doorstep of ivory beaches and rustling palms is an architectural delight. Twenty chalets constructed of reed, thatch and hardwood, and joined by a 1,5-km-long boardwalk, are positioned so that each one has a private, unobstructed view of palms, beach and sea.

Here the aquamarine waters of the Mozambique Channel dance at your feet, while above, squadrons of gulls and terns wheel and dip above a sea bristling with fish and playful schools of dolphins.

Benguerra Island was originally named 'Santa Antonio' by Portuguese explorers and was later named 'Benguera' after a local tribal chief. The lodge faces the tidal channel and sand flats that separate it from the mainland 14 km away and is ideally placed for skiboats heading out to sea through the gap between Benguerra and Margaruque to the south or through the gap that separates the southern tip of Bazaruto from the northern tip of Benguerra.

WILDLIFE Benguerra Island is home to a number of crocodiles in the freshwater lakes, but there aren't many mammals. Occasionally you may see a suni or duiker and there are plenty of red squirrels cavorting in the bush around the lodge. Birders, however, will have a field day, with more than 160 species of bird. These include purplebanded and black sunbirds, lilacbreasted rollers, olive bee-eaters, mannikins, paradise flycatchers, flamingoes, starlings and various waders such as curlews, bartailed godwits, whimbrels and crab plovers.

Dugongs feast in family groups of about five, grazing on grass meadows in the sheltered bays. There are five species of dolphin in the archipelago and humpback whales cruise the deeper waters.

ANGLING Like the other islands of the archipelago, Marlin Lodge offers quick access to the deep channels and drop-offs which are the haunts of marlin, sailfish and roving game fish such as kingfish, barracuda, bonita and king mackerel. Four deep-sea fishing boats are available for catching marlin, sailfish and smaller gamefish. The lodge's Invader skiboats, powered by 90 hp Honda engines will accommodate between three and six people per outing. While king mackerel, queenfish and bonito can be caught throughout the year, the best time for marlin is mid-September to the end of December.

DIVING The lodge management at Marlin are very flexible and will take you diving just about anywhere you want to go, but a favourite snorkelling and scuba area is Two Mile Reef.

OTHER ATTRACTIONS For those less interested in fishing, there are plenty of other things to do. The boathouse on the beach offers sea-kayaks, paddle-skis, hobie-cats and sailboards on which you can ply the tidal waters between the lodge and the mainland. Drives around the island by Land Rover, sunset dhow cruises and picnics on the beach are other options. Many guests prefer to sun themselves at the pool in front of the main lodge.

The Bazaruto Archipelago is a shell collector's haven and Marlin runs trips to Pansy Island, home of the beautiful pansy shell, and numerous surrounding sandbanks, including the infamous Death Island, a sandspit halfway between Benguerra Island and the mainland. Locals say that during the civil war many prisoners of war were left on the island at low tide to drown when the tide came in.

Marlin Lodge has employed the services of some of the best *cordon bleu* chefs in Southern Africa, and there is a mouthwatering array of culinary delights to choose from — ranging from crab and calamari to crayfish, yellowtail and tiger prawns. The lodge pampers its guests with braais on the beach under the stars.

Marlin Lodge draws its electricity from solar power, and the hot and cold running water is supplied from a well about 1 km from the lodge. The water is purified through a filter system and is safe to drink.

To book contact Marlin Lodge at PO Box 15013, Sinoville, Pretoria 0129, tel (012) 543-2134.

Benguerra Lodge This lodge, facing the mainland on the northern fringes of Benguerra Island, wakens to the sound of the sea and the call of gulls, sanderlings and plovers that wheel and squawk around the fish-rich waters of the Mozambique Channel. There is a rustic and peaceful ambience about the place and, because the island is so small, there is a lazy, unhurried atmosphere.

In fact it is so quiet on this beautiful island that the only sounds you hear at night, or when the sun peeps over the eastern horizon in the mornings, is the rustling of the ilala palms along the ribbon of sand around the island.

There are 13 delightfully rustic chalets in an indigenous forest of milkwood and Natal mahogany 20 metres from the sea. The chalets have woven reed walls overlooking the sea and are built on stilts, with wooden floors, thatched roofs and open walls which merge inconspicuously with the surrounding bush.

The twin-roomed chalets are spaced 10 to 15 metres apart and, because of the open walls, windows and doors are redundant. All the chalets have an *en suite* bathroom and shower, and lead onto a private balcony.

Cuisine at the lodge is invariably marine and features crayfish, crab, calamari and a variety of fish fresh from the sea. Evening braais are held on the beach and *al fresco* meals are served under the palms.

WILDLIFE Red squirrels play on the terraces overlooking the sea in front of the lodge's thatched lounge, diningroom and bar complex, and the bush and trees around the lodge host more than 100 species of bird. The island is home to crocodiles and the occasional suni, but apart from that there are very few mammals.

ANGLING Fishing is the main attraction at Benguerra, and the lodge runs trips into the deeper waters south of the island on four 6,6-metre Acecats, which are equipped with outriggers, rods and bait. Saltwater fly-fishing has taken off on the archipelago and the lodge caters for fly-fishermen wishing to test their skill against such local species as green-spotted or brassy kingfish and kawa kawa (also known as eastern little tuna).

DIVING The lodge has a fully equipped dive school with a qualified dive master, and the many reefs around the island offer unsurpassed opportunities for snorkelling and scuba-diving. Night and wreck dives can be organised on request.

OTHER ATTRACTIONS There are several other options for relaxation and recreation. You can stroll the 42 km around the island in a day, wander through the forest for some birdwatching, take the lodge's Land Rover for a picnic on the beach or climb the dunes to see if you can spot some of the island's crocodiles in the

Bazaruto Archipelago at a glance

Locality:	740 km north of Maputo off mainland Mozambique in Inhambane Province.
Climate:	The summers between October and March are hot, humid and wet with wind, while April through to September are drier and less humid.
Trails:	Walking trails cross most of the islands of the Archipelago.
Other attractions:	Angling, diving, swimming, boardsailing, kayacking, picnicking, dhow cruises, visiting other islands of the Archipelago.
Amenities:	Swimming pools, Land Rovers (for beach drives), electricity, restaurants, bars.
Accommodation:	**Bazaruto Island Lodge:** A-frame chalets; **Marlin Lodge:** reed, thatch and hardwood chalets; **Benguerra Lodge:** thatched reed chalets.
Booking addresses:	Bazaruto Lodge, contact Mozambique Island Tours in Johannesburg, tel (011) 447-3528; Marlin Lodge, PO Box 15013, Sinoville, Pretoria 0129, tel (012) 543-2134; Benguerra Lodge, PO Box 87146, Houghton 2041, tel (011) 483-2734.
When to go:	October to March is best for marlin fishing, while June to September is preferred for sailfish. December to March are hot and windy months.
What to take with you:	Shorts, T-shirts, mask, snorkel, flippers, anti-mosquito sprays and ointments, bottled water, torch, walking shoes, sunscreen, camera, film, binoculars and fishing gear (can also be hired).
How to get there:	Take the N4 from Gauteng to Komatipoort via Nelspruit. From Komatipoort it is 50 km to Maputo and 750 km to Vilanculos, which is on the doorstep of the Bazaruto Archipelago.
Nearest doctor:	Vilanculos on the mainland.
Nearest petrol:	Most of the lodges have diesel and petrol for skiboats.
Open:	Throughout the year.
Special precautions:	Antimalaria precautions must be taken — consult a doctor prior to your visit.

lakes. The lodge also lays on trips to the mainland where you can visit Vilanculos, pop into the old Donna Anna Hotel or do some grassroots shopping in the market. The sea in front of the lodge is ideal for windsurfing and hobie-cat sailing and there's a dhow for sunset cruises.

To enquire or book contact Benguerra Lodge, PO Box 87146, Houghton 2041, tel (011) 483-2734.

Margaruque

Smaller than the other islands of the Bazaruto Archipelago, Margaruque offers superb snorkelling and diving on a reef just in front of the island and access by boat to all the marine treasures of the archipelago. A hotel on the island is currently being refurbished, but visitors to Benguerra and Bazaruto islands will have the chance to visit Margaruque on day excursions.

Santa Carolina Island

Many South Africans will remember idyllic holidays spent on Paradise Island before the civil war in Mozambique. Today the island, the smallest in the Bazaruto Archipelago, is called Santa Carolina. The island, once referred to as the Pearl of the Indian Oceans is 3 km long and 500 metres wide. There is no accommodation there today, but if you're staying on Bazaruto or Benguerra Island, the lodges will be happy to take you to Santa Carolina Island for a day's swimming or snorkelling on its beautiful coral reefs.

Inhaca Island

Serious fishermen get restless when they hear the name Inhaca. Lying just 35 km off Maputo, this once-neglected holiday paradise is staking a claim as one of Mozambique's most sought-after fishing spots. Shoals of gamefish, attracted to the prawn-rich waters of Maputo Bay cruise the depths around the perimeter of the island. Anglers rarely return from a day's outing without a haul of species such as tuna, kingfish, sailfish, queenfish, dorado, wahoo, and king and queen mackerel. And in the deep, just 12 km off the island, you have a good chance of hooking a marlin.

Inhaca Island Lodge The Portuguese hotel group, Pestana, has recently revamped and refurbished the old Inhaca Island Hotel and called it Inhaca Island Lodge, a beautiful complex of chalets fronting 600 metres of white beaches.

The chalets are set amongst ilala palms overlooking the sea, and offer double or twin beds and family rooms, all of which have *en suite* bathrooms and an extra bunk bed which can accommodate two children.

Fresh seafood is served daily in the restaurant-bar complex and the menu includes calamari, tiger prawns, various species of gamefish and crayfish. Seafood braais, accompanied by live music by a local band, are held on the beach in the evenings.

If you'd like to try some authentic Mozambiquan cuisine, there is a charming place called Lucas Restaurant in the village, a 10-minute walk away.

For enquiries or to book at Inhaca Island Lodge, contact Pestana Hotels, tel (09258-1) 42-9277.

Angling This is the major pastime on Inhaca. There is a new diving-angling operation on the island which runs fishing charters in a a seven-metre OrionCat powered by twin 90s. The boat, skippered by a South African, has the latest fishing gear, outriggers and fighting chair. Saltwater fly-fishing is also very popular off Inhaca, whose waters are home to the world's largest bonefish.

Diving The many coral reefs around Inhaca make it a paradise for scuba-divers and snorkellers. Santa Maria, at the northern tip of Inhaca Island opposite the Maputo Elephant Reserve on the mainland, is a popular snorkelling and scuba-diving venue, with excellent beaches and superb angling. You can get there by dhow from the hotel (a two-hour journey) or by skiboat. Another great snorkelling spot is Coral Gardens.

Portugeuse Island Inhabited by a lone conservation officer, Portuguese Island is a short cruise or walk (at low tide) from Inhaca and a wonderfully isolated and tranquil spot for a picnic.

Other attractions Inhaca Island Lodge offers a variety of watersports, including canoes to explore the bay and paddle across to Mozambique Island. If you're not relaxing at the lodge's salt-water swimming pool, playing tennis or table-tennis you can join one of the regular trips to the lighthouse, Maritime Museum or Marine Biology Station by tractor. If you do take a ride or walk to the lighthouse, take along a mask and flippers. If you're fairly fit you can swim out to a wreck southeast of the lighthouse.

How to get there The easiest way to get to Inhaca is by light plane from Maputo Airport. It is an eight-minute flight at a reasonable price — probably a better option than taking the bumpy government ferry which departs from the jetty at 10 De Outubro in Maputo. If you'd rather go by speedboat, telephone Nkomati Safaris in Maputo at (09258-1) 49-8139.

If you do go to Inhaca by boat bear in mind that there are no mooring facilities, so passengers will have to wade ashore with their baggage.

Morrungulo Lodge

A meandering, sandy road through groves of coconut trees and indigenous bush brings you to the edge of a hill overlooking a sweeping bay 520 km north of Maputo. This is Morrungulo Beach Resort, also known as Nelson's Bay, one of Mozambique's more remote lodges. The activities here centre around diving on the fantastic coral reefs and fishing for the shoals of gamefish that patrol the warm waters of the Mozambique Channel.

To get there take the EN1 north of Maputo. Some 20 km north from Massinga turn right at the Morrungulo turn-off. It's 13 km to the resort along a dirt road. A 4x4 is recommended, particularly in the rainy season, but generally two-wheel-drive vehicles can get there. The nearest petrol is at Massinga.

Where to stay Morrungulo is geared to accommodate families and medium-sized groups in four-bed, self-catering chalets and communal living areas called casitas or baraccas. These are double- and single-story thatched units with concrete floors and electric light and plug points. Up to 15 guests can be accommodated in tents around the baraccas, a stone's throw away from a fully equipped diving centre, terraced lawns and the sound of the waves.

The self-catering chalets each have two twin-bedded rooms with *en suite* bathrooms equipped with shower and toilet, and a fully equipped kitchen with enough cutlery and crockery for six people. An additional two guests can be accommodated in the lounge at extra cost. Each chalet has a private garden extending onto the beach, and all of them are within earshot of the breaking waves.

Nestling under palms on the northern side of Morrungulo are two-bedded dive centre bungalows and one eight-bedded dive centre bungalow. Constructed of reed, thatch and local indigenous wood, these bungalows have *en suite* bathrooms with showers and toilets. There's a communal kitchen about 25 metres away. Electricity is supplied by generator which is operated mornings and evenings.

The camp has an attractive bar and there's a local market and bakery nearby, but the nearest restaurant is at Massinga, so guests must take all their own provisions.

Attractions The 16-year-long civil war in Mozambique has left the reefs of Mozambique in pristine condition, and Morrungulo's coral reefs are among the best in the world.

A qualified dive instructor runs daily charters to some delightful sites, including Sylvia Shoal, one of Mozambique's best diving spots. Qualifying diving courses are also available and while scuba gear is supplied, the lodge owners prefer divers to bring along their own wetsuits, demand valves and BCs.

Barracuda, kingfish, queen mackerel and various billfish are caught on a daily basis and fishing charters on rubber ducks are available.

Morrungulo, popular with holidaymakers who like the ambience of a remote, uncluttered beach resort, is recommended for those who prefer to cater for themselves and is an ideal stop-over for those heading further north to Vilanculos Beach Lodge or the lodges of the Bazaruto Archipelago.

Ponta do Ouro

Cosy bungalows and chalets nestle among indigenous bush in the gentle curve of the secluded bay at Ponta do Ouro, a popular destination for sun-seekers from Southern Africa looking for a holiday off the beaten track. Since the end of the civil war in 1992 Ponta do Ouro and Ponta Malongane have attracted hundreds of divers to their aquamarine seas and coral reefs — some of the best offshore diving spots in Southern Africa.

Ponta do Ouro means 'place of gold', a reference to its stunning sunsets, but the name could equally apply to its pristine beaches and crystalline waters.

Where to stay The Motel do Mar has been renovated completely recently and offers 64 fully serviced, four-bedded self-catering cabanas, as well as a small shop, recreation room and cosy restaurant and bar. It is the ideal family destination with swimming, angling and diving opportunities. From your cabana you look out onto the gentle sweep of the bay backdropped by bush-covered dunes.

Alternatively you can stay at the Ponta do Ouro Holiday Resort which offers two- and four-bed chalets and an economical camping site where you can pitch a tent and sleep under the stars. The camping site has hot water and toilet and washing facilities. The chalets are fully equipped, with cutlery, crockery, bed-linen and a two-plate gas cooker. There is also a restaurant. Skiboats launch from the beach and divers can access the inshore coral reefs within minutes.

For more information contact Maputo at tel (09258-1) 42-2120 or Johannesburg at (011) 849-5184.

Wildlife Vervet monkeys are part of the furniture in and around Ponta do Ouro, and there are about 140 species of bird. Elephants are the main attraction at Maputo Elephant Reserve, a short drive to the north.

A large variety of fish — from emperor angelfish and parrotfish to butterflyfish and kingfish — is drawn to the coral reefs and deeper waters off Ponta do Ouro. The area is renowned for its shark population and divers regularly see hammerheads, Zambezi sharks and occasionally tiger sharks. There are also huge potato bass, whale sharks and ribbon-tail rays.

Diving Three diving companies operate from the Motel do Mar and provide diving gear, tuition and some of the best dive sites along the Mozambique coast. There are about 15 dive sites, ranging from 14 to 20 metres, offering coral reefs which were virtually undived for the entire duration of the civil war. For more experienced divers there are walls and pinnacles which drop off to 40 metres and more.

To enquire about diving and reservations contact the Motel do Mar at Central Bookings, 101 The Works, 258 Brooklyn Road, Menlo Park 0102, tel (012) 362-1355.

Angling Skiboats launch from the beach at Ponta do Ouro and guests can be assured of excellent catches of gamefish which are prolific along this stretch of coastline.

Other attractions Motel do Mar lays on a variety of activities for its guests, ranging from a short sightseeing trip through the village to romantic sundowners on the beach. If you drive to the southern edge of the village a steep footpath takes you down to the beach and the lighthouse, which affords breathtaking 360° views of the Kosi Bay lakes in the south, Lake Zitundu and Ponta Malongane.

The motel lays on a three-hour trip to Lake Zitundu, home of crocodile and hippo, as well as a drive to the turtle breeding grounds at Ponta Mamoli south of the Maputo Elephant Reserve. You can spend the day snorkelling in the pools of this lovely bay.

Two other drives take guests to Ponta Malongane and Lake Sugi, whose once-threatened population of birds is returning to the area. These include various water-birds, crowned hornbills, African jacanas and purplecrested louries.

PONTA MALONGANE

Vervet monkeys leap from branch to branch among the trees of this little resort, which lies 10 km north of Ponta do Ouro. Metres from the beach, nestling in the lush dune forest, is a tidy camp of 10 chalets, 22 rondavels and 45 caravan and camping sites.

This is Parque de Malongane, a lovely resort which has become a mecca for scuba-divers, snorkellers and South Africans looking for a quieter alternative to the hustle and bustle of Sodwana Bay and Kosi Bay. In fact it is just 14 km from the Kosi Bay border post.

There are plenty of facilities here for ensuring a great holiday. Accommodation comprises four-, five- and six-bed chalets and two- and four-bed rondavels, all with self-catering kitchens and bathrooms. The resort also features an attractive bar and restaurant, a store stocked with essentials, a swimming pool, beach bar and 17 'trataruga tendas' (safari tents).

A fully equipped dive camp, with four experienced skippers and qualified diving instructors, features 60 two-man tents, all of which are on raised platforms. There are two kitchens at the dive camp — one self-catering, and the other catered. An entertainment centre with a bar has been built and there is an air station for divers.

The bay around Ponta Malongane offers safe swimming and snorkelling and easy entry by skiboat for diving and angling expeditions.

Angling The sea off Ponta Malongane is marlin country, and in one three-month period recently 21 marlin were caught, tagged and released. In addition, the area hosts most of the gamefish species found along the Mozambique coast — kingfish, eastern little tuna, queen mackerel, bonita, barracuda and sailfish.

Wildlife There are not many mammals in the area, but you will see samango monkeys and, if you are lucky, bushbabies. More than 150 species of bird live in and around the resort, with an additional 250 species in the surrounding areas. Inland there are freshwater lakes, home to hippo and crocodile.

The pristine coral reefs off Ponta Malongane lie close to the shore, while further in the channels are home in summer to cruising whale sharks, humpbacked whales and dolphins. In summer loggerhead turtles hitch themselves across the sand near Ponta Malongane to lay their eggs on the beach.

Diving The coral reefs, pinnacles, steep drop-offs and an abundance of fish make Ponta Malongane easily one of the best scuba-diving areas in Mozambique. Some of the dive sites, such as Bass City, are

Spotted hunters of the night

The largespotted — or rustyspotted — genet is a cat-like carnivore whose elongated spots and stripes camouflage it perfectly in its chosen habitat, which was severely threatened during the long civil war in Mozambique.

It has a varied diet which may include locusts, beetles, spiders, ground birds, mice, rats and wild fruit.

Its hunting technique is cat-like: the genet stalks its quarry slowly, pauses, then springs on to it with claws outstretched. While cats despatch their prey with a fatal bite to the neck, genets usually hold their prey with all four limbs and eat it while it is still alive.

A largespotted genet walks with its head held low, stopping now and then to sit down and look around. It does this with its paws up, balancing on its outstretched tail.

Threatened, it will bound for a tree, jumping from branch to branch and disappearing in the foliage. The little animal is so agile it can clear 4 m in a jump from one branch to another.

famous, not only for their abundance of sharks, but also for their legends. One is Bert, a 70-kg potato bass, who is reputed to have swallowed a camera, a buoy, a diver's watch and innumerable hooks.

Bass City is a popular diving site in 22 metres of water and consists of six small rock islands. These waters are inhabited by devil firefish, moray eels, octopus, electric rays and banded cleaner shrimps.

Ponta do Ouro and Ponta Malongane at a glance

Locality:	Ponta do Ouro and Ponta Malongane lie 10 km north of Mozambique's border with South Africa and 117 km south of Maputo.
Climate:	Mozambique has a subtropical climate, with hot, wet summers and warm, dry winters.
Trails:	Walking trails along the beach afford stunning views.
Other attractions:	Diving, angling, visits to Maputo Elephant Reserve and lakes in the vicinity.
Amenities:	Shops, restaurants, swimming pools and bars.
Accommodation:	**Ponta do Ouro:** Motel do Mar has 64 fully serviced, four-bed self-catering cabanas; Centro Turìstico da Ponta do Ouro has two- and four-bed chalets and a camping site; **Ponta Malongane:** Parque de Malongane: four-, five- and six-bed chalets with self-catering kitchens and bathrooms; two-bed and four-bed rondavels with self-catering kitchens and bathrooms; there are 60 two-bed tents at the dive camp and an additional 17 safari tents.
Booking address:	**Ponta do Ouro:** Central Bookings, 101 The Works, 258 Brooklyn Road, Menlo Park 0102, tel (012) 362-1355; **Ponta Malongane**: contact Polana Tours in Maputo at tel (09258-1) 493-533/4.
When to go:	October to March is best for marlin fishing, while the months of June to September are preferred for sailfish. December to March are hot and windy months.
What to take with you:	Light clothing, such as shorts and T-shirts, mask, snorkel, flippers, anti-mosquito sprays and ointments, bottled water, torch, walking shoes, sunscreen, camera, film, binoculars and fishing gear (can also be hired).
How to get there:	From Durban take the N2 to Mkuze. Just past Mkuze a tar road leads to KwaNgwanase, where you can fill up with petrol, let down your tyres and head for the border 18 km away. From Johannesburg: Travel to Maputo via Komatipoort. In Maputo take the hourly ferry from Avenue 10 de Novembro to Catembe. From there it is about 117 km or a three-hour drive to Ponta. You will need a 4x4, especially over the last 25 km where the track degenerates into thick sand. Don't stray off the established tracks here, which hive off into occasional detours. There are a few unmarked turnoffs to the Maputo Elephant Reserve along the way. The border post is open seven days a week from 08:00–17:00. It is vital that you bring your vehicle registration papers with you.
Nearest petrol:	Ponta do Ouro.
Open:	Throughout the year.
Special precautions:	Antimalaria precautions must be taken — consult a doctor prior to your visit.

The Pinnacles is one of the best shark dives off Mozambique. The summit of the pinnacle lies at 32 metres, then shears off to 55 metres. Here divers regularly encounter hammerhead, tiger, Zambezi and blacktip sharks as well as black marlin. If you are lucky you might see a whale shark or a bullnosed shark.

Other reefs to look for are Texas — a big reef with caves and holes — Shallow Malongane, Anchor, Three Sister, Paradise Ledge and Kevs Ledge.

There is a local charter, Malongane Dive Charters, which is based at the campsite. To book contact Empresa Nacional de Turismo in Mozambique, tel (09258-1) 4-2179.

Apart from diving or angling there is a host of other recreational activities. Overnight trails have been set out through the bush, or you could go for long walks along the beach to collect shells or explore secret coves.

Maputo Elephant Reserve For something out of the ordinary, visitors to Ponta Malongane can drive to the Maputo Elephant Reserve 120 km south of Maputo. The reserve's wildlife was decimated by the civil war and various conservation organisations are working hard to restock the reserve. The elephant population, which was 8 000 before the war, now stands at 150.

Msala Bush Camp is one of the few reserve camps in the country that offers overnight accommodation – in this case a two-person dome tent situated on a lake, just metres from the ocean.

About 450 species of bird have been recorded in the reserve and you can see many of these on game drives or birding expeditions. Other attractions are snorkeling among the nearby coral reefs or visiting turtle egg-laying sites.

To book contact Polana Tours in Maputo at tel (09258-1) 493-533/4.

Vilanculos Beach Lodge

If you want to sample the delights of all the islands of the Bazaruto Archipelago and stay in a lodge that is affordable, homely and provides excellent accommodation and friendly service, Vilanculos Beach Lodge is the place to be. It is the perfect springboard to Bazaruto, Benguerra, Margaruque and Santa Carolina islands and will also put you in touch with the attractions of the mainland.

Ten rustic thatched chalets raised on ironwood stilts peer out over the bushes and sea, a short walk from the main lodge complex. There are five two-bedroomed family chalets, each with a lounge and verandah and five one-bedroomed, two-bed chalets connected by a boardwalk to a plunge pool, private bar and the beach. A cosy restaurant offers superb cuisine.

Attractions The coastline north of Vilanculos Beach Lodge is strewn with conch and pansy shells and reveals a succession of secluded bays with virgin beaches and beautiful diving spots. If you do walk along the coastline take a diving mask and snorkel with you.

Vilanculos Lodge does not specifically cater for scuba-diving expeditions, but they will organise diving packages through some of the island lodges which will enable you to explore the coral reefs of the Bazaruto archipelago.

The lodge also offers day cruises in a 10-metre catamaran, which will provide ample opportunities for snorkelling as well as various fishing options.

The sea in front of the lodge is calm, shallow and ideal for swimming, sailing and paddling. A laser sail boat, windsurfer, surf-ski canoes and paddle skis are available to guests free of charge.

How to get there From Maputo drive north on the EN1 for 700 km before turning right to Vilanculos. When you reach the town follow the signposts to the lodge 5 km away. If you're driving from South Africa to Vilanculos and want to overnight on the way, consider Casa Lisa 48,5 km north of Maputo on the road to Vilanculos. Casa Lisa offers accommodation for small groups in chalets and a cottage. The accommodation is safe and comfortable and the restaurant serves tasty meals. There is also a cosy bar. To book contact Paul/Lisa Hellowes on (013) 744-9102 ask for 433.

Metavia offers twice weekly flights into Vilanculos from Durban, tel (031) 469-3400; Johannesburg, tel (011) 394-3780; and Nelspruit, tel (013) 741-3141.

For booking and more information contact the lodge at PO Box 23821, Claremont 7730, tel (021) 683-5337.

Zongoene Lodge

Nestling on the beach between dunes and indigenous trees at the mouth of the Limpopo River, 247 km north of Maputo, this lodge is one of Mozambique's newest — tailor-made for family and fishing holidays, and for conference groups.

The elegant, double-storey four-bed chalets or two-bed pool chalets have *en suite* bathrooms and sliding doors opening out onto wooden balconies.

Zongoene also has a fully equipped conference centre catering for 60 people, a swimming pool, bar with satellite TV, and a cosy restaurant.

What to do Birdwatching around Zongoene is excellent. The lodge offers three-hour conducted trails through the indigenous forests to the beach where giant sand-dunes tower above the sea.

A more leisurely option is to paddle along the Limpopo River in a canoe and soak in the tranquillity of your surroundings. The lodge also ferries guests across the Limpopo for a day at a private beach.

Saltwater fly-fishing is becoming more and more popular in Mozambique, and Zongoene caters for enthusiasts. The lodge has a skiboat for deep-sea angling, scuba-diving and snorkelling expeditions. There are some pristine coral reefs within striking distance of the lodge, and fishing in the deeper waters is exceptional, with regular catches of kingfish, dorado, bonita, barracuda and sailfish.

Diving instruction is available at the lodge and scuba equipment is provided.

Guided quad-bike trails are offered through the Limpopo's floodplains and the surrounding forests, or if that sounds too energetic you can take a sundowner cruise off the beach or stroll to the lighthouse near Zongoene Lodge.

Getting there The turn-off to Zongoene Lodge is 247 km north of Maputo on the EN1. A sand road here leads 34 km through the Limpopo floodplains to the lodge. You can get there in a two-wheel-drive vehicle, but a 4x4 is necessary in the wet season. Alternatively, you can fly from Gauteng, via Nelspruit and Maputo to Xai-Xai airport. From there it is a 45-minute road transfer to Zongoene.

To book contact Zongoene Lodge at PO Box 35555, Menlo Park, 0102, tel (012) 346-1286, or Nelspruit, tel (013) 755-4883 or Maputo, tel (09258-1) 40-0979.

SAFARI TOURS IN SOUTHERN AFRICA

The past few years have witnessed a huge growth in wildlife tours throughout Southern Africa. In line with a greater urgency to preserve and protect our dwindling game populations, more and more game parks, nature reserves and private lodges are springing up in the wild places of the subcontinent.

At the same time, the international and local demand to visit these unique sanctuaries has spawned a new generation of safari operators in a very competitive market.

Visitors may choose from a range of options, including one-man operators leading dugout (mokoro) safaris through the Okavango to multinational corporations that will pick you up, fly you to five-star game lodges in the bush, escort you on 4x4 game trails and walking safaris, feed you sumptuously and bring you home again. Or gamewatchers may choose an overland camping safari in which they rough it with the rangers, help to strike and pitch camp, prepare meals and clean up.

These safaris usually range from a couple of days to three weeks, and have one common purpose — to bring travellers into the extraordinarily beautiful habitats of Southern Africa's wild, and introduce them to the animals and birds.

Since the cost of the various packages fluctuates from day to day and from season to season, tariffs have not been included, but are readily available by phoning the contact numbers below.

The operators listed here are all experienced in the ways of the wild and have been organising tours for some years. They know the subcontinent, the animals and the travelling conditions throughout the year, and are worth the extra expense if you want a trouble-free holiday in the wild secure in the knowledge that you are in good hands.

The safari packages which follow have been carefully selected for their mix of scenic attractions, abundance of wildlife and general popularity. All they require from their participants is an open mind, a spirit of adventure and a love of the outdoors.

SOUTH AFRICA

SAFARI	START	DURATION	DESTINATIONS	HIGHLIGHTS	SAFARI OPERATOR
Tamboti Safari	Kruger National Park	10 days	Kruger NP, Timbavati, Phophonyane and Malolotja (Swaziland), Rocktail Bay, Ndumo GR, Phinda Resource Reserve (KwaZulu-Natal)	Africa's best game viewing in Kruger NP, overnight at Phophonyane Lodge, beach walks at Rocktail Bay, rock chalets at Phinda	Wilderness Safaris, PO Box 78573, Sandton 2146, tel (011) 883-0747 Rhino Safari
Durban	5 days	Zululand,	Swaziland, Kruger NP, Blyde River Canyon (alternative option to Sabi Sabi GR)	Zulu villages, Swazi crafts, Big Five, scenic beauty of the Blyde River Canyon	Springbok Atlas Tours, 179 Albert Road, Woodstock, Cape Town 8000, tel (021) 460-4700; 48 Tulbagh Rd, Pomona, Kempton Park, 1619, tel (011) 396-1053
Karibu Overland Safari	Johannesburg	21 days	Kalahari Gemsbok Park, Mukurob (Finger of God), Windhoek, Etosha NP, Twyfelfontein Petrified Forest, Cape Cross seal colony, Moon Valley (Namib Desert), Kuiseb Canyon and Sesriem (Namib Desert), Lüderitz, Kolmanskop (ghost town), Fish River Canyon, Augrabies Falls NP	Animals of Kalahari Gemsbok Park, dunes of the Namib, Augrabies Falls	Karibu Safari, 50 Acutt Avenue, Rosehill, Durban, tel (031) 83-9774; or (011) 462-6414
Panorama Tour	Johannesburg	13 days	Mpumalanga, Kruger NP, Swaziland, Zululand, Durban, Port Elizabeth, Wilderness, Garden Route, Oudtshoorn, Cape Town	Scenic beauty of the Drakensberg, animals of Kruger, Swazi crafts, beaches of Durban and east coast, lakes of the Wilderness area, forests of the Garden Route	Springbok Atlas Tours, 179 Albert Road, Woodstock, Cape Town 8000, tel (021) 460-4700; 48 Tulbagh Rd, Pomona Kempton Park, 1619, tel (011) 396-1053

SOUTH AFRICA

SAFARI	START	DURATION	DESTINATIONS	HIGHLIGHTS	SAFARI OPERATOR
Karibu Camping Tour of South Africa	Johannesburg	20 days	Kimberley, Karoo NP, Paarl Wine Estates, Cape Town, Cango Caves, Tsitsikamma NP, Mountain Zebra NP, Aliwal North Springs, Golden Gate Highlands NP, Durban, Mkuzi GR, Swaziland, Kruger NP	Fossils of Karoo NP, walks in Mountain Zebra NP, geological wonders of Golden Gate Highlands NP, white rhinos in Mkuzi GR	Karibu Safari, 50 Acutt Avenue, Rosehill, Durban, tel (031) 83-9774; or (011) 462-6414
Africa Alive	Johannesburg	6 days	Blyde River Canyon, Kruger NP, Swaziland, Lebombo Mountains, Hluhluwe GR, Shaka-land, Durban	Scenic splendour of Blyde River Canyon, animals of Kruger NP, rhino of Hluhluwe GR	Connex Travel, 6 Sandown Valley Crescent, Sandown, Sandton, PO Box 1111, Johannesburg 2000, tel (011) 884-3007
Kruger National Park	Johannesburg	3 days	Skukuza Rest Camp	Game drives through the park	Afro Ventures, PO Box 1200, Paulshof 2056, tel (011) 807-3720
Rovos Rail Train Safari	Pretoria	4 days	Bulawayo, Victoria Falls	Victoria Falls, Southern African landscapes from the window of your compartment	African Sun Safaris International, PO Box 55370, Northlands 2116, Johannesburg, tel (011) 327-0467
South African Highlights Tour	Cape Town	13 days	Garden Route, Tsitsikamma Forest, Durban, Zululand, Swaziland, Kruger NP, Blyde River Canyon, Johannesburg	Forest giants in the Tsitsikamma NP, hills of Zululand, animals of Kruger NP, scenic vistas of the Blyde River Canyon	Springbok Atlas Tours, 179 Albert Road, Woodstock, Cape Town 8000, tel (021) 460-4700; Tulbagh Rd, Pomona, Kempton Park, 1619, tel (011) 396-1053

SWAZILAND

SAFARI	START	DURATION	DESTINATIONS	HIGHLIGHTS	SAFARI OPERATOR
Swaziland Tour	Mbabane	7 days	Mountain Inn, Forester's Arms Hotel, Mkhaya GR, Mlilwane Wildlife Sanctuary	Game of Mkhaya and Mlilwane	Umhlanga Tours, PO Box 2197, Mbabane, tel (09268) 4-6416 or 6-2180
Lugogo–Mlilwane Tour	Mbabane	4 days	Lugogo Sun, Piggs Peak, Mlilwane Wildlife Sanctuary	Animals of Mlilwane, views from Piggs Peak	Umhlanga Tours, PO Box 2197, Mbabane, tel (09268) 4-6416 or 6-2180

NAMIBIA

SAFARI	START	DURATION	DESTINATIONS	HIGHLIGHTS	SAFARI OPERATOR
Wings over Namibia	Windhoek	6 days	Etosha NP, Mokuti Lodge, Mudumu NP (Caprivi)	Game migrations at Etosha, river cruise at Mudumu	Wilderness Safaris, PO Box 78573, Sandton 2146, tel (011) 883-0747
Namibia Adventure	Windhoek	12 days	Keetmanshoop, Fish River Canyon, Lüderitz, Sossusvlei, Sesriem, Etosha, Mokuti Lodge	Geology of Fish River Canyon, sand-dunes of the Namib, gamewatching in Etosha	Oryx Tours, PO Box 2058, Windhoek, tel (09264-61) 21-7454
Skeleton Coast Fly-in Safari	Windhoek	5 days	Swakopmund, Khumib River, Skeleton Coast	Exploring canyons, castles, roaring sand-dunes and shipwreck sites of Skeleton Coast	Wilderness Safaris, PO Box 78573, Sandton 2146, tel (011) 883-0747
Desert and Waterways Safari	Windhoek	13 days	Etosha, Caprivi, Victoria Falls, Okavango Delta (Jedibe Island Camp, Tchau Camp and Mombo Camp)	Game drives in Etosha, Victoria Falls, wild dogs of Mombo	Wilderness Safaris, PO Box 78573, Sandton 2146, tel (011) 883-0747

NAMIBIA (continued)

SAFARI	START	DURATION	DESTINATIONS	HIGHLIGHTS	SAFARI OPERATOR
Namibia Classic Safari	Windhoek	15 days	Hardap Dam, Hobas Campsite (Fish River Canyon), Swakopmund, Aba-Huab Campsite (Damaraland), Okaukuejo Rest Camp (Etosha NP), Namutoni Rest Camp (Etosha), Gross Barmen Hot Springs	Geological wonders of Fish River Canyon, elephants of Etosha, soothing springs at Gross Barmen	Afro Ventures, PO Box 1772, Swakopmund, tel (09264-64)) 46-3812
Namibian Sky Safari	Windhoek	15 days	Okonjima Lodge (Waterberg), Caprivi Strip (Lianshulu Lodge), Etosha NP, Ongava Lodge, Epupa Falls, Damaraland, Swakopmund, Namib Naukluft Park	Balloon flight over Namib Desert, igloo-style tents at Epupa Falls	Wilderness Safaris, PO Box 78573, Sandton 2146, tel (011) 883-0747
Namibian Safari	Windhoek	16 days	Sossusvlei, west coast, Swakopmund, Damaraland, Ovahimba and Epupa falls, Etosha NP	Breathtaking views of Namibian Plains, 80 000 seals at Cape Cross seal colony, largest collection of San rock art ever discovered, desert elephants, unique baobab trees	Penduka Safaris, PO Box 55413, Northlands 2116, tel (011) 883-4303
Namibia/Etosha Safari	Windhoek	15 days	Waterberg Plateau Park, Etosha NP, Damaraland, Twyfelfontein Petrified Forest, Cape Cross Seal Colony, Moon Valley (Namib Desert), Sesriem (Namib Desert), Namib-Naukluft Park	Bush walks among rhino in the Waterberg Plateu Park, the most beautiful sand-dunes in the world at Sossusvlei, ancient welwitschia plant of the Namib	Karibu Safari, 50 Acutt Avenue, Rosehill, Durban, tel (031) 83-9774; Karibu Safari PO Box 80674, Windhoek, tel (09264-61) 25-1661

NAMIBIA (continued)

SAFARI	START	DURATION	DESTINATIONS	HIGHLIGHTS	SAFARI OPERATOR
Chameleon Safari	Windhoek	19 days	Namib Desert, Swakopmund, Cape Cross Seal Colony, Damaraland, Hobatere, Etosha, Okavango River, Mahango GR, Mudumu NP, Chobe NP, Victoria Falls	The world's highest sand-dunes at Sossusvlei, seals at Cape Cross, birdwatching on the Okavango River	Wilderness Safaris, PO Box 78573, Sandton 2146, tel (011) 883-0747
Namibia/ Botswana Safari	Windhoek	21 days	Namibia: Sossusvlei, west coast, Swakopmund, Damaraland, Etosha NP, Shakawe, Okavango Delta, game parks of Botswana and Victoria Falls	Highest dunes in the world at Sossusvlei, animals of Etosha, Victoria Falls	Penduka Safaris, PO Box 55413, Northlands 2116, tel (011) 883-4303

BOTSWANA

SAFARI	START	DURATION	DESTINATIONS	HIGHLIGHTS	SAFARI OPERATOR
Bushman Safari–Central Kalahari	Johannesburg/ Gaborone	15 days	Kubu Island, Deception Pan, Nxai Pan NP, Moremi Wildlife Reserve, Okavango Delta	San communities, Baines' Baobabs, huge pans of Central Kalahari	Penduka Safaris, PO Box 55413, Northlands 2116, tel (011) 883-4303
Elephant-back Safaris	Maun	6 days	Abu's Camp, Okavango Delta	Gamewatching from elephant-back	Ker and Downey, PO Box 27, Maun, tel (09267-6) 6-0375
Botswana Par Excellence	Harare	13 days	Pazimunda Safari Lodge, Victoria Falls, Chobe NP, Okavango Delta, Zambezi River	Exploring the Okavango in a mokoro (dugout), game-viewing in Chobe, white-water rafting below Victoria Falls (optional)	Run Wild, 1st Floor, Wetherby House, 55 Baker Avenue, Harare, tel (09263-4) 79-2333

BOTSWANA (continued)

SAFARI	START	DURATION	DESTINATIONS	HIGHLIGHTS	SAFARI OPERATOR
Camper's Delight	Maun	8 days	Oddball's Camp, Okavango Delta, islands of the delta	Cruising the waterways in a mokoro, animals and birds of the delta	Okavango Tours and Safaris, PO Box 39, Maun , tel (09267-6) 6-0220
Botswana à la Hemingway	Maun	13 days	Central Kalahari GR, Okavango Delta, Mombo Island Camp, Chobe NP (Savuti, Serondela), Victoria Falls	Game drives through Central Kalahari GR, heronries at Xakanaxa Lagoon (Okavango Delta), big game of Moremi, Chobe River and Zambezi River cruises	Afro Ventures, PO Box 323, Kasane, tel (09267-6) 5-0119
Western Kalahari	Johannesburg	10 days	Salt pans of western Botswana, western Kalahari, Mabuasehube GR	Nama San, sunset over the Kalahari from your tent, game drives through Mabuasehube GR	Penduka Safaris, PO Box 55413, Northlands 2116, tel (011) 883-4303
The Lion and Elephant Safari	Maun	10 days	Okavango Delta, Moremi Wildlife Reserve, Chobe NP, Victoria Falls	Mokoro trips on the delta, gamewatching in Moremi, the falls	Wilderness Safaris, PO Box 78573, Sandton 2146, tel (011) 883-0747
Luxury Okavango Safari — fly-in safaris to luxury lodges	Maun	9 days	Mombo Island Camp (Camp Moremi, Tsaro Lodge), Chobe NP (Savuti Lodge, Chobe Game Lodge), Victoria Falls (Victoria Falls Hotel)	Cruising waterways of Okavango Delta, watching elephants in Chobe NP, tribal dancing at Victoria Falls	Afro Ventures, PO Box 323, Kasane, tel (09267-6) 5-0119
Parks of Botswana	Maun	15 days	Central Kalahari GR, Maun, Okavango Delta, Mombo Island Camp, Chobe NP, Victoria Falls	Camping in Deception Valley (Central Kalahari GR), camaraderie around the campfire, exploring floodplains of Okavango Delta	Afro Ventures, PO Box 323, Kasane, tel (09267-6) 5-0119

BOTSWANA (continued)

SAFARI	START	DURATION	DESTINATIONS	HIGHLIGHTS	SAFARI OPERATOR
Game Parks of Botswana	Maun	15 days	Etosha, Shakawe and Tsodilo Hills, Namibia's Caprivi Strip, Victoria Falls, game parks of Botswana	Rugged beauty of the Kalahari, Victoria Falls, vast game populations of Botswana	Penduka Safaris, PO Box 55413, Northlands 2116, tel (011) 883-4303
Botswana Explorer	Maun	10 days	Okavango Delta, Mombo Island Camp, Chobe NP, Victoria Falls	Game-viewing walks on Okavango Delta islands, camping under the stars along the Chobe River, rubbing shoulders with rhinos	Afro Ventures, PO Box 323, Kasane, tel (09267-6) 5-0119
Karibu Camping Safari	Johannesburg	15 days	Serowe, Makgadikgadi Pans, Maun, Okavango Delta, Moremi Wildlife Reserve, Chobe NP	Bush camp in the pans, waterways of the delta, game-viewing in Chobe	Karibu Safari, 50 Acutt Avenue, Rosehill, Durban, tel (031) 83-9774 or (011) 462-6414

ZIMBABWE

SAFARI	START	DURATION	DESTINATIONS	HIGHLIGHTS	SAFARI OPERATOR
Victoria Falls Adventures	Harare	5 days	Victoria Falls, Chobe NP	The falls, game drives across Chobe's flood-plains	Wilderness Safaris, PO Box 78573, Sandton 2146, tel (011) 883-0747
Canoeing Safari	Lake Kariba	3 days	From Lake Kariba to Kanyemba on the Mozambique border (250 km)	Superb game-viewing, magical sunsets, excellent photography	Abercrombie and Kent, PO Box 782607, Sandton 2146, tel (011) 781-0740

ZIMBABWE (continued)

SAFARI	START	DURATION	DESTINATIONS	HIGHLIGHTS	SAFARI OPERATOR
Zimbabwe Explorer	Harare/Victoria Falls	12 days	Hwange, Chizarira and Matusadona national parks, Zambezi Valley, Zambezi River, Lake Kariba, Victoria Falls	Black rhino in Chizarira, camping in Zambezi Valley, elephants in Matusadona, drifting in canoes through the Mana Pools NP floodplains	Afro Ventures, PO Box 261, Victoria Falls, tel (09263-13) 5822
Run Wild Lake Adventure Safari	Harare	10 days	Lake Kariba, Victoria Falls, Zambezi NP	Cruising the expanse of Lake Kariba for five days	Run Wild, 1st Floor Wetherby House, 55 Baker Avenue, Harare, tel (09263-4) 79-2333
Zimbabwe Classic Safari	Victoria Falls/Harare	15 days	Hwange NP, Matobos, Great Zimbabwe, Vumba, Nyanga NP, Harare, Lake Kariba, Victoria Falls	Rock paintings of Matobos, game-viewing in Hwange NP, game-viewing on Lake Kariba	Afro Ventures, PO Box 261, Victoria Falls, tel (09263-13) 5822
Zambezi White-Water Spectacular	Harare	10 days	Victoria Falls, Zambezi River, Zambezi NP	Canoeing and rafting down the Zambezi, game drives in Zambezi NP	Run Wild, 1st Floor Wetherby House, 55 Baker Avenue, Harare, tel (09263-4) 79-2333
Flying Safari from Harare	Harare	3 days	Kariba, Mana Pools NP, Hwange NP	Boat cruises along Mana Pools shoreline, game drives in Hwange NP	Abercrombie and Kent, PO Box 782607, Sandton 2146, tel (011) 781-0740
Msasa Safari	Harare	13 days	Eastern Highlands, Chimanimani NP, Induna Lodge, Matobo NP, Hwange NP, Victoria Falls	Mtarazi Falls, silvery cheeked hornbills in the Vumba mountains, wildlife at Gonarezhou	Wilderness Safaris, PO Box 78573, Sandton 2146, tel (011) 883-0747
Rhino Safari	Harare/Victoria Falls	13 days	Victoria Falls, Hwange NP, Chizarira NP, Matusadona NP and Lake Kariba, Lower Zambezi NP, Zambia	The falls, watching wild dogs, leopards and lions in Hwange	Wilderness Safaris, PO Box 78573, Sandton 2146, tel (011) 883-0747

ZAMBIA

SAFARI	START	DURATION	DESTINATIONS	HIGHLIGHTS	SAFARI OPERATOR
Shoebill Safari	Lilongwe, Malawi	15 days	Lilongwe, South Luangwa, North Luangwa, Kapishya Hot Springs, Bangweulu Swamps, Kasanka	Watching shoebills on Shoebill Island Camp; elephants and buffaloes of Luangwa	Wilderness Safaris, PO Box 78573, Sandton 2146, tel (011) 883-0747
South Luangwa Safari	Lusaka	5 days	Mfuwe, Chinzombo or Tena Tena camps	Game-viewing drives in open safari vehicle	Abercrombie and Kent, PO Box 782607, Sandton 2146, tel (011) 781-0740
Tongabezi Camp	Livingstone Airport or Victoria Falls	3 days	Tongabezi Camp, Livingstone Island	Walking along Zambezi, game drives, canoeing	Abercrombie and Kent, PO Box 782607, Sandton 2146, tel (011) 781-0740
Busanga Trail	London/Lusaka	9 days	Lufupa Camp, Kafue NP	Day and evening game drives, night trip to Shumba Camp	Lawson International, 113–119 High Street, Hampton Hill, Middlesex TW121PS, tel (0944-081) 941-7300

MALAWI

SAFARI	START	DURATION	DESTINATIONS	HIGHLIGHTS	SAFARI OPERATOR
Rift Valley Safari	Lilongwe	8 or 15 days	Mulanje Mountains, Shire River, Liwonde NP, Lake Malawi, Vwasa Marsh, Nyika Plateau, Viphya Plateau	Exploring foothills of Mount Mulanje, snorkelling in Lake Malawi, watching elephants at Mvuu Lodge	Wilderness Safaris, PO Box 78573, Sandton, 2146 tel (011) 883-0747
Palm Tree Safari	Lilongwe	8 days	Lake Malawi, Club Makokola, Liwonde NP	Watersport on Lake Malawi, Mvuu Lodge, game drives	Wilderness Safaris, PO Box 78573, Sandton 2146, tel (011) 883-0747
Baobab Safari	Blantyre	8 days	Zomba Plateau (Kuchawe Inn), Liwonde NP, Lake Malawi	Stunning views of Malawi plains from Zomba Plateau, beauty of Mvuu Lodge, luxury of lakeshore hotels	Wilderness Safaris, PO Box 78573, Sandton 2146, tel (011) 883-0747
Malawi Explorer	Johannesburg/ Lilongwe	8 days	Nkopola Lodge, Lake Malawi, Mvuu Wilderness Camp, Zomba Plateau, Mount Soche	Watersport in Lake Malawi, gamewatching in Liwonde NP, views from Zomba Plateau	African Sun Safaris International, PO Box 55370, Northlands 2116, Johannesburg, tel (011) 327-0467
Leopard Safari	Lilongwe	15 days	Lilongwe, Luangwa (Zambia), Viphya Plateau (Malawi), Nyika Plateau (Malawi), Lake Malawi, Livingstonia Beach Hotel	Two of the best leopard-viewing spots in Southern Africa (Luangwa Valley and Nyika Plateau)	Wilderness Safaris, PO Box 78573, Sandton 2146, tel (011) 883-0747

SAFARI OPERATORS IN SOUTHERN AFRICA

South Africa

- Abercrombie and Kent, PO Box 782607, Sandton 2146, tel (011) 781-0740.
- Adventure Runners, PO Box 31117, Braamfontein 2017, tel (011) 839-4105.
- Africa Travel Centre, Military Road, Cape Town 8001, tel (021) 423-4530.
- African Adventures Unlimited, PO Box 1557, Northcliff 2115, tel (011) 678-5490.
- African Sun Safaris, PO Box 55370, Northlands 2116, tel (011) 327-0467.
- Afro Ventures, PO Box 1200, Paulshof 2056, tel (011) 807-3720.
- Bill Harrop's Balloon Safaris, PO Box 67, Randburg 2125, tel (011) 705-3201.
- Bonaventure Tour Operators, PO Box 785620, Sandton 2146, tel (011) 783-5248.
- Call of Africa Safaris, PO Box 125, Constantia 7848, tel (021) 794-2284.
- Connex Travel, PO Box 1111, Johannesburg 2000, tel (011) 884-3007.
- Conservation Corporation, Private Bag X27, Benmore 2010, tel (011) 784-6832.
- Country Escapes, PO Box 11068, Hatfield 0028, tel (012) 362-1375.
- Destinations Africa, PO Box 786432, Sandton 2146, tel (011) 884-2504.
- Drifters Adventure Tours, PO Box 48434, Roosevelt Park 2129, tel (011) 888-1160.
- Exeter Safaris, PO Box 988, Umhlanga Rocks 4320, tel (031) 562-8112.
- Felix Unite Tourism Group, PO Box 96, Kenilworth 7745, tel (021) 683-6433.
- Gametrackers, 31 Harley Street, Randburg 2146, tel (011) 781-0137.
- Jambo Safari,, PO Box 319, Strand 7140, tel (021) 854-8897.
- Karibu Safari, PO Box 35196, Northway 4065, tel (031) 83-9774.
- Ker and Downey, PO Box 411288, Craighall 2024, tel (011) 327-0161.
- Moremi Safaris and Tours, PO Box 2757, Cramerview 2060, tel (011) 465-3842.
- Okavango Explorations, PO Box 69859, Bryanston 2021, tel (011) 708-1893.
- Okavango Tours and Safaris, PO Box 3666, Rivonia 2128, tel (011) 803-4464.
- Penduka Safaris, PO Box 55413, Northlands 2116, tel (011) 883-4303.
- Rovos Rail, PO Box 2837, Pretoria 0001, tel (012) 323-6052.
- Safaris Par Excellence, PO Box 1395, Randburg 2125, tel (011) 787-9756.
- Safariplan, PO Box 4245, Randburg 2125, tel Johannesburg 886-1810;
- Shearwater Adventures, PO Box 76270, Wendywood 2944, tel (011) 804-6539.
- Thompsons International, PO Box 41032, Craighall 2024, tel (011) 788-0810.
- Timbavati Trails, PO Box 577, Bedfordview 2008, tel (011) 453-7645/6/7.
- Welcome Tours and Safaris, PO Box 2191, Parklands 2121, tel (011) 442-8905.
- Which Way Adventures, PO Box 2600, Somerset West 7129, tel (024) 845-7400.
- Wild Frontiers, PO Box 844, Halfway House 1685, tel (011) 315-4838.
- Wilderness Safaris, PO Box 78573, Sandton 2146, tel (011) 883-0747.

Swaziland

- Big Game Parks of Swaziland, PO Box 234, Mbabane, tel (09268) 4-4541 or 6-1591.
- Connex Travel, PO Box 1111, Johannesburg 2000, South Africa, tel (011) 884-3007.
- Drifters Adventure Tours, PO Box 48434, Roosevelt Park 2129, South africa, tel (011) 888-1160.
- Umhlanga Tours, PO Box 2197, Mbabane, Swaziland, tel (09268) 6-2180 or 4-6416.

Namibia

- Africa Adventure Safaris, PO Box 20274, Windhoek, tel (09264-61) 2-3002.

- African Extravaganza, PO Box 22028, Windhoek, tel (09264-61) 26-3088.
- Afro Ventures, PO Box 1772, Swakopmund, tel (09264-64) 46-3812.
- Charly's Desert Tours, PO Box 1400, Swakopmund, tel (09264-64) 40-4341.
- Cheetah Tours and Safaris, PO Box 23075, Windhoek, tel (09264-61) 23-0287.
- Desert Adventure Safaris, PO Box 1428, Swakopmund, tel (09264-64) 4072.
- Drifters Adventure Tours, PO Box 48434, Roosevelt Park 2129, South Africa, tel (011) 888-1160.
- Etosha Fly-in Safaris, PO Box 1830, Tsumeb, tel (09264-71) 2-0574.
- Karibu Safari, PO Box 80674, Windhoek, tel (09264-61) 25-1661.
- Namib Air Fly-in Safaris, PO Box 731, Windhoek, tel (09264-61) 22-6770.
- Namib Travel and Tours, PO Box 24064, Windhoek, tel (09264-61) 22-9162.
- Oryx Tours, PO Box 2058, Windhoek, tel (09264-61) 21-7454.
- Penduka Safaris, PO Box 55413, Northlands 2116, South Africa, tel (011) 883-4303.
- Resorts International;. PO Box 2862, Windhoek, tel (09264-61) 23-4512.
- Skeleton Coast Fly-in Safaris, PO Box 2195, Windhoek, tel (09264-61) 22-4248.
- Springbok Atlas Tours, PO Box 11165, Klein Windhoek, tel (09264-61) 23-0534.
- Trans Namibia Tours, PO Box 20028, Windhoek, tel (09264-61) 221549.

Botswana

- Afro Ventures, PO Box 323, Kasane, tel (09267-6) 5-0119.
- Avis Safari Hire, PO Box 130, Maun, tel (09267-6) 6-0258.
- Bushdrifters, Private Bag 035, Maun, tel (09267-6) 6-0351.
- Desert and Delta Safaris, Privat Bag 198, Maun, tel (09267-6) 6-1791.
- Destination Africa, PO Box 78823, Sandton 2146, South Africa, tel (011) 884-2504.
- Drifters Adventure Tours, PO Box 48434, Roosevelt Park 2129, South Africa, tel (011) 888-1160.
- Gametrackers, Botswana, PO Box 100, Maun, tel (09267-6) 6-0302.
- Go Wild Safaris, PO Box 056, Kasane, tel (09267-6) 5-0468.
- Karibu Safari, PO Box 35196, Northway 4065, South Africa, tel (011) 462-6414.
- Ker and Downey Safaris, PO Box 27, Maun, tel (09267-6) 6-0375.
- Linyanti Explorations, PO Box 22, Kasane, tel (09267-6) 5-0352.
- Moremi Safaris, PO Box 2757, Cramerview 2060, South Africa, tel (011) 465-3842.
- Okavango Explorations, Private Bag 48, Maun, tel (09267-6) 6-0528.
- Okavango Tours and Safaris, PO Box 39, Maun, tel (09267-6) 6-0220.
- Okuti Safaris (Pty) Ltd, Private Bag 47, Maun, tel (09267-6) 6-0570.
- Penduka Safaris, PO Box 55413, Northlands 2116, South Africa, tel (011) 883-4303.
- Photo Africa Safaris, PO Box 11, Kasane, tel (09267-6) 5-0385.
- Safari Par Excellence, PO Box 1395, Randburg 2125, South Africa, tel (011) 888-3500.
- Wilderness Safaris, PO Box 78573, Sandton 2146, South Africa, tel (011) 883-0747.
- Wild Frontiers, PO Box 844, Halfway House 1685, South Africa, tel (011) 315-4838.

Zimbabwe

- Abercrombie and Kent, PO Box 782607, Sandton 2146, South Africa, tel (011) 781-0740.
- Afro Ventures, PO Box 261, Victoria Falls, tel (09263-13) 5822.
- Call of Africa Safaris, PO Box 125, Constantia, 7848, South Africa, tel (021) 761-5892.
- Gemsbok Safaris, PO Box FM 525, Famona, Bulawayo, tel (09263-9) 6-3906.

- Frontiers White Water Rafting, PO Box 26350, Arcadia 0007, South Africa, tel (012) 329-3765.
- Kariba Ferries, PO Box 578, Harare, tel (09263-4) 61-4162.
- Karibu Safari, PO Box 900, Greendale, tel (09263-4) 48-1182.
- Run Wild, 55 Baker Avenue, Harare, tel (09263-4) 79-2333.
- Safari Par Excellence, PO Box 1395, Randburg 2125, South Africa, tel (011) 888-3500.
- Safari Tours and Travel, PO Box 1161, Kloof 3640, tel (031) 764-3151.
- Shearwater Adventures, PO Box 3961, Harare, tel (09263-4) 75-7831.
- The Travel Company, PO Box CY2203, Causeway, Harare, tel (09263-4) 79-1610.
- Time for Africa, PO Box HG 940, Highlands, Harare, tel (09263-4) 70-3633.
- Touch the Wild, Private Bag 6, Hillside, Bulawayo, tel (09263-9) 7-4589.
- Wilderness Safaris, PO Box 78573, Sandton 2146, South Africa, tel (011) 883-0747.
- Zambezi Safari and Travel Company, PO Box 158, Kariba tel (09263-61) 2532.
- Zim Tours, PO BOX 8052, Causeway, Harare, tel (09263-4) 70-6511.

Zambia

- Africa Tour Designers, PO Box 31802, Lusaka, tel (09260-1) 22-4248.
- Big 5 Tours, PO Box 35317, Lusaka, tel (09260-1) 21-8310.
- Busanga Trails, PO Box 31322, Lusaka, tel (09260-1) 25-4226.
- Bushwackers, PO Box 32172, Ridgeway Hotel, Lusaka, tel (09260-1) 25-0310.
- Chinzombo Safaris, PO Box 30106, Lusaka, tel (09260-1) 21-1644.
- Chundukwa Safaris: PO Box 61160, Livingstone, tel (09260-3) 32-4006.
- Drifters Adventure Tours, PO Box 48434, Roosevelt Park 2129, South Africa, tel (011) 888-1160.
- Musungwa Safaris, PO Box 31808, Lusaka, tel (09260-1) 27-3493.
- Shenton Safaris, PO Box 57, Mfuwe, tel (09260-0) 536-2188.
- Thomsons Travel, PO Box 41032, Craighall 2024, South Africa, tel (011) 788-0810.
- Tukuluho Wildlife, 137A Jan Smuts Avenue, Parkwood 2193, South Africa, tel (011) 442-2942.
- Wilderness Safaris, PO Box 78573, Sandton 2146, South Africa, tel (011) 883-0747.
- Wild Frontiers, PO Box 844, Halfway House 1685, South Africa, tel (011) 315-4838.

Malawi

- Adventure Tours and Safaris, PO Box 31282, Lilongwe, tel (09265) 73-0405.
- Car-Hire Ltd, PO Box 51059, Limbe, Malawi, tel (09265) 67-1495.
- Kambuku Trails, PO Box 121, Kanengo, Lilongwe, tel (09265) 73-1141.
- Soche Tours and Travel, PO Box 2225, Blantyre, tel (09265) 62-0812.
- Wilderness Safaris, PO Box 78573, Sandton 2146, South Africa, tel (011) 883-0747.

Mozambique

- African Sunset Adventures, PO Box 650884, Benmore 2010, South Africa, tel (011) 784-6852.
- Barra Lodge Bookings, PO Box 6921, Halfway House 1685, South Africa, tel (011) 314-3355.
- Dee-Jean Travel Promotions, PO Box 1172, Wilgeheuwel 1376, South Africa, tel (011) 662-1478.
- Drifters Adventure Tours, PO Box 48434, Roosevelt Park 2129, South Africa, tel (011) 888-1160.
- Sundown Travel, 1st Floor Inter Franca Shopping Centre, Maputo, tel (09258-1) 42-5842.

PHOTO CREDITS

Afro-Ventures 99, 100, 101, 102, 103, 104, 105, 106, 107, 108, 109, 110,
Big Game Parks of Swaziland 90, 91, 92, 93, 94, 95, 96, 97, 98
Camp Moremi 126
Camp Okavango 128
Conservation Corporation 41, 43, 44, 52, 53, 54, 66
Cox, Daniel, APBL, front cover
De la Harpe, Roger, Natal Parks Board 8, 11, 12, 13, 14, 15, 16, 17, 18, 19, 20, 21, 45, 46, 47, 62, 63, 64, 67, 68, 82, 83, 84
Djuma Bush Lodge 70
Exeter Safaris 71, 73, 74
Gametrackers 127, 129, 130
Karibu Safari 120, 121, 145
Landela Safaris 144, 147, 148, 149, 150
Madikwe Game Reserve 42
National Parks Board 2, 4, 7, 22, 23, 24, 25, 27, 29, 30, 31, 34, 36, 37, 38, 39, 48, 55, 78, 87, 88, 89
National Parks Board, Eric Reisinger 3, 28, 56
National Parks Board, Lorna Stanton 1, 5, 6, 26, 32, 33, 35, 40, 86
Notten's Bush Camp 69
O'Hagan, Annalé 9
O'Hagan, Tim 10, 76, 77, 79, 80, 81, 85, 160, 161, 162, 163
Patzer, Marek 152, 153, 154, 155, 156, 157, 159
Penduka Safaris 112, 134, 135, 136, 137, 138
Shamwari Game Reserve 72, 75
Tsaro Elephant Lodge 122
Tuli Safari Lodge 124
Wilderness Safaris 49, 50, 51, 57, 58, 59, 60, 61, 65, 111, 113, 114, 115, 116, 117, 118, 119, 125, 131, 132, 133, 146, 151, 158
Xugana Island Lodge 123
Zimbabwe Sun Hotels 139, 140, 141, 142, 143

INDEX

Page references in bold refer to 'At a glance' boxes.

S